STEEL POT

A Vietnam Memoir

VOLUME I

CURT STOCKER

Olympus Story House

In memory of:

John Imbach III
Frank Marion Streamer
Ken Lawlor
Michael R. Shapard
Colonel Willie O. Lawton (USA, Ret'd)
Captain William D. Robinson Jr.
Thomas J. Roberts

Prologue

Steel Pot is a memoir. Obviously, nobody can remember everything, especially when the subject matter includes some events one would prefer to forget. The disclaimer you see in the front matter of many books, "This is a work of fiction. Any resemblance of characters to real people or events is entirely coincidental," is not in play here. This is a recollection of real people and real events. There is no fiction in this tale. I can affirm that I have made a sincere effort to ensure that this a true and accurate account of my Vietnam tour.

Within those bounds of accuracy, it sadly became true to me, with the passage of time, that there were some exact names I could not recall. In such cases, I have bestowed upon those individuals nicknames, but in all, there are no fictional characters in this book. The nicknames do represent real people involved in real events.

The only contrived portion of Steel Pot is the dialogue, which obviously I could not remember word for word. However, if I were to append each bit of dialogue with the caveat; "or words to that effect," it would be cumbersome.

Suffice it to say that the dialogue is accurate in terms of speaking to the events of each situation.

I found the names of some of the Vietnamese individuals mentioned herein to be even tougher to recall. Generally, I defaulted to the name Nguyen, Kahn, or Thanh. But in each case, these names represent real people who were involved in the actual situations being detailed. It is my hope that our interpreter, Corporal Ba and our counterpart, Ti Ui Troung, survived the war and that one day I might see them again.

Along with depicting the unavoidable violence of war, Steel Pot is a firsthand account of the GI marijuana subculture birthed by the Vietnam experience.

I began smoking pot in October of 1966, more than a year before I went to Vietnam, so I was not among the uninitiated upon my arrival. Considering how much pot I have smoked in my life, I understand why some people find it amazing that I am able to remember anything at all! Apart from the fact that I am a journalist who takes good notes, I can tell you for a fact that pot does not terribly damage a person's memory. Feel free to ask all the people whose butts I've kicked in Trivial Pursuit!

Vietnam exposed hundeds of thousands of young Americans to marijuana who otherwise would have never found it. Because of this, I firmly believe that the war may be the single most important factor in today's looming marijuana legalization.

The clash between the pot cultrure and the alcohol culture was epic; it went on 24/7, for all the years of the war. What made it an even match, was the fact it was fought out at a time when there was no medical test to prove if one smoked it or not. Thank God!

Chapter 1

Pulling the bathroom door shut, he locked the bolt and set his shaving kit down on the small counter to the left of the minuscule sink.

Twisting to his right, he bent down and lifted the toilet seat cover. After unbuckling his belt, then dropping his pants and green boxer shorts in one motion, he sat down on the commode. Staring at himself in the mirror, he was galled by his appearance: the short military buzz haircut made his head look way too round, and the gray-plastic-framed glasses made him look like a dork, not the ultimately cool and hip dude he had once been. *How did I come to be here?*

He took a leak, but what he really wanted to do was to take a shit. He had not been able to accomplish that feat anytime in the past thirty-six hours.

Constipation had never before been a problem in his life. He recalled the time back in Boulder, Colorado, at the Pi Kappa Alpha fraternity house when one of the brothers passed around a box of chocolate chip cookies "from his mom" that turned out to be laced with Ex-Lax. He had eaten three of them and crapped his brains out for two days. *One of those cookies would be real tasty right about now.*

Maybe he'd feel better if he were to wash his face and shave. Standing up in the cramped quarters, he hiked up his pants and buttoned them, unbuttoned his shirt, and contorted to remove the khaki garment. *Ha! This reminds me of a mime in a box!* Loosely folding his shirt, he tossed it on top of the commode lid and ran some water in the sink, which was about the size of an army helmet. He splashed water on his blondish stubble, then pulled out a can of Burma Shave from his kit and lathered up. Just as he began to pull the double-edged safety razor down the right side of his face, the big jetliner hit a pocket of turbulence. He cut himself with the Wilkinson Sword blade ever so slightly. *Damn.*

He completed the rest of the shave without incident. After rinsing the remains of his day-and-a-half-old growth out of the sink, he put away the razor and got out his toothbrush and a tube of Colgate. He applied a dab of the white paste to his brush and commenced to vigorously clean his teeth. After

1

about a minute, he spit the white foamy residue into the sink and rinsed out his mouth, swigging from the little paper Dixie cup so handily dispensed from the clear plastic tube located to the left of the mirror.

I do feel a little better. While brushing his teeth, he had noticed that the cut near the edge of his right-side chinbone was still bleeding, so he stopped and pulled a small piece of tissue paper off the roll and stuck it on the wound. The blood soaked up into the tissue, forming a crude outline of a heart. *May you be my only Purple Heart.*

Once finished, he did a quarter turn in the cramped chamber and picked up his class A khaki uniform shirt. When it was back on and tucked in, he sat down on the commode to unroll the bottom end of the Colgate tube, from which he extracted a plastic baggie. The marijuana inside it had been cleaned free of seeds and prepared for rolling before being hidden inside the toothpaste tube, so all he had to do now was take one of the loose Zig-Zag papers from the bag, put on a pinch of pot, and twist it up. As he licked and sealed the number, he noted that he was down to about his last five joints. *That's the least of my problems.*

Digging the Zippo lighter out of his right pants pocket, he flipped it open, cranked the wheel, and touched the fire to the end of the joint. He lit it by inhaling the initial hit.

The smoke curled off the end of the joint, snaking up between his face and the mirror, only about two and a half feet away. He exhaled the first hit off to the side and, leaning his nose over the rising column of smoke, inhaled it French style, straight through his nostrils and into his lungs. Holding the toke in, he continued to study himself in the mirror. *How did I fucking get to be here? Even after the wash and shave, I still feel like a refried shit sandwich. Too bad I can't take a shower. Wouldn't that be novel, a shower on an airplane?*

He took another hit, sucking on the joint, taking the smoke as deep as possible into his lungs and holding it for as long as he could, then exhaling it into his reflection in the mirror. His glasses were filthy. *God, they make these bathrooms small.* At least there were a lot of them, and he knew there wasn't a long line of people outside waiting to get in, so he could take all the time he wanted and nobody was going to care.

Reaching into the left breast pocket of his uniform, he took out Flo's picture and studied it as closely as he could. Just a little more than forty-eight hours ago, they had said a tearful goodbye at the San Diego airport. The picture, which he'd taken last winter with his Polaroid camera, showed her reclining on the beach at Oceanside, California. She was propped up on her left elbow with her long black hair nearly touching the sand. It was

2

unseasonably cool for California on that December day, so they had decided not to go swimming. Rather than a bathing suit, she had worn a brown, yellow, and orange pinstriped blouse with matching pants. Smiling, her brown eyes sparkled, and several locks of her black hair were frozen in a windy toss for eternity through the miracle of Polaroid film.

One more hit and he began to feel the grass. Its mellowing effect spread through his brain, and he could now see that the ultrasmall bathroom would be a great place to inhale the secondhand smoke for a few minutes when he was done. He was in no hurry to return to his seat. From as near as he could figure, the flight still had at least another six or seven hours before arriving at their destination.

The DC-8 was somewhere just over the International Date Line.

Soon, he was stoned enough that he let the joint go out. After first making sure it was cold, he returned it to the plastic bag. Carefully stuffing it back into the Colgate tube, he rerolled the end to make it look like any other slightly used tube of toothpaste. He had no fear of being caught from the smell because the only people in 1968 who really knew what marijuana smelled like were people who also smoked it. But he lit up a Kool and took a few puffs just for safety's sake.

Crushing the menthol cigarette into the pillbox-sized ashtray, he zipped up his shaving kit, unbolted the lock on the door, and stepped back into the cabin of the DC-8 jetliner. Another expressionless private moved forward to take his place in the john, also carrying a shaving kit. There were only three guys waiting for an opening, and with six johns in the back of the plane, nobody was keeping track of how long anybody stayed inside one of the closet-sized toilets.

Standing in the rear of the jet and looking forward, he thought that the aircraft was like a tube that ran for infinity. *Parallel lines really do meet,* he mused as he slowly started forward. The whole plane was a haze of smoke. There wasn't much else to do on a flight of this length, and the atmosphere was also beginning to reek with the odor of unwashed men, so he did not for a second worry about anybody analyzing the odor emanating from him.

Four female flight attendants were milling around the aft galley, in the midst of preparing breakfast. *Or is it lunch?* He had lost track of time since boarding the massive jet near midnight at Travis Air Force Base outside Oakland, from which the majority of all troop flights departed for Vietnam. He had never even heard of Capitol Airlines until he emerged from the terminal and saw the giant DC-8 sitting on the runway bathed in floodlights.

The flight attendants on this flight weren't as stereotypically cute as the ones on the PSA flight he had taken from San Diego up to Oakland. Their uniforms were accented by ruffled petti pants that suggestively peeked out from beneath their skirts. The uniforms worn by the flight attendants of Capitol Airlines were more like Catholic schoolgirl uniforms. All the flight attendants he had seen on the few flights he had previously taken in his life before this one were really young, energetic, and attractive. This crew seemed to be a little more about work and less about cute than their domestic counterparts, and in general, they looked older and more seasoned—or kind of burnt out; he couldn't decide which.

From the very back of the craft, he noted that the sheer size of the ultralong cylinder was made possible by the fact that on this flight there was no first-class section. He could see clearly up to the tiny postage stamp of a cockpit door. As he maneuvered up the aisle, he found it somehow strange to be on a plane where every single passenger on board was male and dressed in the same way: class A khaki uniform with a short-sleeve shirt. *Uniformity—that's what the military is all about.*

His seat was near the middle, about five rows behind the wing on the left side. As he made his way forward, the plane encountered some more turbulence, but not enough to make the pilot hit the Fasten Seat Belt sign. He liked walking the aisles in turbulence because it kind of reminded him of skiing. *And, of course, there won't be any of that for a year.*

As he passed the fiftieth row, Tom Davies, one of his classmates from the Defense Information School, looked up and smiled at him. "Hey, Kid," he said.

"Hey, Tom," the Kid said, returning the salutation.

"Don't you think you should take the tissue paper off your face? It makes you look far more stupid than you really are."

"Oh yeah. I hope the bleeding has stopped. It was either this or a tourniquet."

"So, Kid, I was thinking about washing up and shaving myself. Is there much of a line back there?"

"No, not really."

"Uh, I'm out of toothpaste." Tom smiled. "Do you think it would be possible that you would loan me some?"

The Kid smiled back. "Sure, Tom. Your breath really does reek. I can smell it from here." He turned to his seatmates. "How can you guys sit next to him?" He returned his attention to Tom. "And I don't suppose I have to

4

tell you to bring it back to me and not to lend it to anybody else," he said, unzipping his shaving kit and handed Tom the Colgate.

"Thanks, Curt."

"No brushing them twice." The Kid knowingly wagged his finger before pushing on to his row, where both his seatmates got up and let him ease in next to the window.

"Feel better?" the GI sitting next to him inquired. His name tag informed anybody who might glance at it that his last was name was Harrington, and the rank insignia on his sleeve went on to tell the world that he was a PFC, private first class.

"Yes, I do. Much better," replied the Kid, who was also a PFC.

Although quite thoroughly stoned, he really didn't feel all that much better. How much better could he feel? He was one of two-hundred-odd soldiers on a jet plane, and their destination was Vietnam. As he reclined back in his window seat, the first thing he did was light up another Kool. There was literally nothing else to do on this flight. As he had been walking back from the john, it occurred to him that just about every swinging dick on the plane was smoking a cigarette. *I mean, if the smoke were any thicker on this plane, we'd have to ditch at sea. Yeah, that's what I'll say in the book!*

Speaking of the sea, he turned his gaze toward the vast emptiness. It was a fishbowl view of the world, created when endless sea came together with endless sky, broken occasionally by sailing galleons of clouds a few thousand feet below the airplane.

Ha, I'm trapped inside one of those shaky snow globes, and my world has truly been turned upside down. The Kid was twenty years old. Let's see, he thought, it's May, and if I live another three and a half months, I'll be twenty-one. For the slightest instant, he wondered if he'd make it. *How did I come to be here?*

Casting a disparagingly sad eye toward the sea, he imagined what it must have been like in World War II when the guys had to fly out from the aircraft carrier to look for the Japanese fleet, hidden somewhere down there among the cloud banks. *Well, I'll be damned, there's a ship!* The ant-sized black speck sat at the front of a white wake line as the craft plowed across the Pacific.

Amelia Earhart is down there somewhere. No wonder they never found her ass; this place is way beyond huge!

Leaning back, he closed his eyes and let his mind float above the monotonous din of the jet engines right outside the window. *How did I end up here? Let's see, he pondered, one year ago, I was a disc jockey in Nashville*

5

and I had the world by the ass. I was enrolled at the University of Tennessee and had a student deferment for the draft, or so I thought, until Dad called at the beginning of June and said my draft notice had just arrived at the house in Boulder and he would send it to me in Tennessee.

"But Dad, I'm *in school!*" the Kid had exclaimed into the black phone receiver.

"Well, fine," his father had replied. "However, when you left the University of Colorado [CU], you apparently dropped out and did not formally withdraw, so they drafted you before you enrolled at the University of Tennessee. Wouldn't hurt to appeal …"

His head lolled from side to side as the plane hit some more turbulence. *But I didn't appeal because Gil, my neighbor, my friend—Captain Gil, who just happens to be the head of army recruiting in Nashville—said, "Hey, I can get you into Armed Forces Radio! You're already a real big-time announcer, and you can take the test to qualify before you sign the papers. I'll get you delayed enlistment for three months, and you'll have the whole summer here in Nashville. And the best part of all is, when you come back, WKDA has to give you your job back. It's the law."*

"Really?" the Kid had asked.

"Really!"

"Well, OK, sign me up!"

I should have not have left CU. OK, I should have left, but I should have first taken the time to fill out the fucking paperwork. But if I'd have stayed at CU and not gone to Tennessee just because I wanted to see Donna, I never would have gotten the job at WKDA. And if I hadn't gone to Tennessee to see Donna, I never would have met Flo. How fucking ironic!

OK, nine months ago I was in basic training with the assurance that, because I had taken an extra year of enlistment to be guaranteed a spot in Armed Forces Radio and Television, I would never be in combat. And if I did get sent to Vietnam, I would be at a radio station, of the well-fortified variety, in Saigon and would never see a Vietcong, a rice paddy, or a foxhole. Then the only thing I'd have to worry about would be a terrorist attack, like when they blow up a restaurant or an embassy.

It was on the occasion when their class assembled for picture day at the Defense Information School, at Fort Benjamin Harrison in Indianapolis, that everybody got their orders. "Where you going?" "Where you going?" "Vietnam." "Vietnam." "And what does *psyops* mean?"

Psyops, it turned out, was army speak for psychological operations.

"Wait a minute, I got a contract. Armed Forces Radio. My next-door neighbor Gil got me a contract for Armed Forces Radio."

"No, Private, your contract is for the school. And we gave you the school, so now the army can do anything with you it wants." Fucking army logic! But it doesn't make any sense to spend thousands of dollars training somebody to do a job and then not let them do it. "Oh no, you're qualified and trained for the job you're going to be doing. You're going to be a foreign-language announcer—that's an FLA, which has the same MOS [military occupational specialty] as a radio announcer."

"Gee, how can I be a foreign-language announcer if I don't speak Vietnamese? You'll just have to get me another assignment."

"Not a problem, because you won't really be making the announcements; you're just going to be advising the South Vietnamese soldier who makes the actual announcements."

"OK. What announcements are we talking about? Cut to the chase and tell me: what are the fucking announcements?"

"You'll be going into the field with a South Vietnamese army unit. Then, when you get the Vietcong pinned down in a tree line or somewhere, you get as close as you can get and, with a bullhorn, you broadcast appeals for them to surrender or die. This position has the same MOS as disc jockey; the slot calls for a 71R20, a radio announcer, and you are one."

Case closed. Don't that beat all?

"Curt." A voice interrupted the Kid's fitfully wandering thought pattern. "Here's your toothpaste back, unless you want to give it to me." Tom Davies was standing in the aisle, extending his hand with the Colgate over the Kid's two row mates.

"Oh, thanks." The Kid reached up and took the tube. "I suppose they're squeaky clean now."

"I don't think they're squeaking, but yes, they are clean." He smiled. "Can't thank you enough. Wouldn't it be nice if they had some way to listen to music on this plane?"

"Yeah, wouldn't that be cool? Imagine if somebody invented something like a little tape recorder and you could sit there with headphones on and listen to music. Hey, someday it could happen," the Kid speculated.

"Probably not in our lifetime," Tom answered, "especially if we get our asses shot off in the rice paddies next week." Tom was also earmarked to join a psyops unit.

The jet took a big drop in a pocket of turbulence, and the Fasten Seat Belt sign dinged on. Tom grabbed the headrests of two aisle seats to keep from falling. "Ooh, that felt kind of cool! I'd better go sit down. Catch you later. And thanks!"

"OK, no problem." Pulling out his shaving kit, the Kid cached his stash and hit the recline button on his seat so he could lean back to try to get some more sleep.

As he closed his eyes, he thought about what Tom said. *It would really be nice to have some music right now.* One of the best things about being stoned was that it enhanced the experience of listening to music. If he could just put on some headphones, like those he worked with as a disc jockey, and listen to some Beatles tunes, it would be so bitchin'. Sometimes when he thought about a song, he could actually hear it in his inner ear, so realistically that he felt as if he were hearing the record play, which was at times almost as good as the real thing. As if by cue, a song popped into his head: "I'm a loser, and I'm not what I appear to be."

But, yes, he was a loser at the biggest game of chance every draft-age boy in the United States was playing, and here he was on the all-expenses-paid loser's flight to Vietnam, where he'd be for the next year. If he lived that long.

A year before I'll see Flo again. A year before we can make love again.

He escaped into a memory, back to the motel room in Oceanside where they'd gone four days earlier. It was the only solace on that flight he could find to salve his feelings about his fate. Flo's parents, they had been sure, would believe their cover story that they would be spending the day at Disneyland, the Magic Kingdom. But after being there for about three hours, so they would have entrance tickets and souvenirs to back up their deception, the Kids said, "Let's go get the room now."

"OK," he could still hear Flo's soft voice saying. "OK, let's go."

He drove his green 1965 VW Bug back down Interstate 5 about ninety miles an hour, which was as fast as it was capable of going, and got off at the first Oceanside exit. Her family lived in Vista, about eight miles away, so this should work. Pulling in to the Traveler's Motel, he parked in front of the office. He wanted to run, but he walked in, cool and deliberate. "How much for a room?"

"Ten bucks," the fat, balding, and bespectacled manager said. Fine. The Kid didn't care what the room was like as long as it had a bed. He was finally going to consummate the relationship with the love of his life, before he went off to war.

He and Flo unlocked the door and entered into a beige-painted room. It held nothing but a double bed in the middle flanked by a nightstand and a battered wooden dresser on one side, and by an open closet opposite, with about a dozen slightly twisted and bent wire coat hangers dangling from the bar. Light streamed in through a crack in the dingy yellow curtains covering the lone window next to the closet, casting a shaft of illumination on the bed like a spotlight. *It's showtime!*

Although they had smoked pot on the way to, on the way from, and while on the Skyliner ride at Disneyland, Flo looked anything but relaxed. Clearly, she was nervous. What seventeen-year-old virgin wouldn't be slightly apprehensive at the sight of the bed where she was about to give up her most precious cherry? He took her, looked deep into her brown eyes and kissed her on the lips. Locked in her embrace, he thrust his hand down the back of her pants and fondled the cheeks of her exquisitely tight little ass. *Oh God.* How he had anticipated this moment since the time he'd met her back in Nashville. He broke the embrace and pulled her T-shirt out of her jeans. Lifting it up over her head, he pulled it off and tossed it on the dresser. Unbuttoning her jeans, he worked them down past the white cotton panties that covered her shapely hips. As they fell to the floor, she stepped out of them, then kicked off her loafers and turned to get into the bed, quickly crawling under the covers with her bra and panties still on. He unbuttoned his shirt, dropped his pants to the floor, and with his huge throbbing boner scarcely concealed by his boxers, climbed under the covers with her.

Taking her in his arms, he kissed her long and deep, their tongues dueling as their hands ran up and down each other's backs. In a move that he had developed while making out in countless dark back seats of parked cars, he undid her bra hooks with one hand and slipped the garment off, exposing her beautiful young breasts and pert little nipples. Throwing back the covers all the way to the end of the bed, he propped himself up on one arm and looked at her lying there next to him, clad only in panties with one leg slightly bent at the knee. This was as naked as he'd ever seen her up to this stage of their relationship. It was hard to score when he was in Indianapolis and she was in California, but now, at last, the time had come. Softly, he caressed her right breast with the back of his hand before he kissed her nipple. Taking it into his mouth, he gently sucked it, feeling it grow immediately hard against the tip of his tongue. Then he got up on his knees beside her and, putting a hand on the elastic band of her panties on each shapely hip, began tugging on the white cotton briefs. Lifting her hips up off the bed, she facilitated their removal, then there she was in all her natural glory.

"Ready for a little lunch?" The Kid was reeled back to reality by the flight attendant plopping trays of airline food in front of his seatmates. "How about

9

you?" She looked at him, kind of pointing at his tray holder, with the plate in her hand.

"Sure, why not?" He flipped the catch and let the seat-back tray drop open, watching the plate arrive in front of him. *Oh, how nice. A roast beef sandwich and a bag of chips. What a surprise.*

"God, I could have sworn it was breakfast time." His seatmate had turned and spoken as he ripped open his little packet of mayo and doctored his sandwich. "What the fuck difference does it make?" Harrington lamented after swallowing a mouthful. "I'm a dead man anyway."

He had earlier poured out his life story to the Kid, of how he came to be where they were; he had washed out of MP school.

"Military police school. For Christ's sake, how do you wash out of that?"

"I wasn't badass enough," Harrington said, showing his gentler side. "I just couldn't bring myself to get with the program, namely that it was OK to beat the shit out of prisoners." He described to the Kid the situation that had gotten him scrubbed. "It was at Fort Leonard Wood. I was assigned to the stockade, and it got a lot of basic trainees who thought they could just take off and, you know, like, just quit the army. Desert, or go AWOL at least. And the MPs used to say, 'We're going to beat you up *real good,* so the last thing you're ever going to want to do is come back here.' And then they would do it. I couldn't do it; I wasn't into beating people up. Now I'm fucked. Infantry, 11B10. I'll probably end up in I Corps or the Central Highlands."

Tell it to the chaplain, the Kid thought. *We've all got our problems.* But all he said was, "That's too bad."

"And what about you? What's your MOS?" Harrington asked.

"I'm 71R2W and 71Q20, radio announcer and journalist."

"Wow, cool. You might get to meet that 'Good morning, Vietnam,' guy. What's his name?"

"You mean Adrian Cronauer. They used to play us some of his tapes at DINFOS. He sucks, really."

"So, you were a DJ?"

"Yep. Nashville. Doing midnight to six o'clock on WKDA. I was one of the Good Guys. I should be ready to crank up my show on Armed Forces Radio, but no go. When I got drafted, *Sgt. Pepper's* had just come out. So I put together a show idea package for Armed Forces Radio, with promos and everything. I called it 'Sgt. Pepper's Family Band and Hit Parade Show.' But I somehow acquired this qualifier W rating, meaning they could assign me to psyops."

While being jostled down the aisle from a forward seat, the Kid spotted one of his DINFOS schoolmates making his way to the back. It was Al Viator. When his name had been put up on the door of his room, it said "A. Viator." A. Viator soon became "Flyboy."

"Hey, Kid." Al stopped and smiled down, his very oval facial structure heavily accented by his buzz cut. "What's cookin'?"

"Not much, Flyboy. Just working on my book, you know the one, the quintessential Vietnam novel, the *Catch-22* of our generation. Right now I've decided to make it a memoir. Like, from the viewpoint of the Kid. That way, all I have to do is remember what happens and write it down. Other than that, I'm just hanging out and brushing my teeth."

"Imbach and Smith are cutting cards for a dime a cut." Al chuckled. "Imbach is up almost three dollars, and he can't lose. It's pretty fucking funny!"

"Hmm, no doubt I'd die if I had to sit next to Imbach and listen to the Boy Scouts shtick the whole way," the Kid said.

"Aw, Baby Huey's not such a bad guy, Kid. Just because he doesn't like the Beatles doesn't make him a bad person."

"Hey, I never said he was a bad person, but if somebody doesn't like the Beatles, it is a reason for suspicion. Bob Dylan, I can understand. That is an acquired taste, like drinking beer or eating pussy. But not liking the Beatles? Unthinkable."

Imbach was the straightest guy in the world. The Kid had to wonder how somebody from California could be as straight as Imbach was. To his credit, he was also one of the nicest guys in the world. His main ambition in life was to be a small-town journalist there in Carpentaria and be the leader of the local Boy Scout troop. There was just no talking to the guy about the stuff that mattered— radio, music, women, and of course, heaven forbid, pot. He was innocent to the point of being childlike. But the reason the Kid had given Imbach the nickname "Baby Huey" was that he kind of looked like the big baby duck in the comics: small upper body, huge ass and huge legs, and a rounded angelic face with light red hair and hardly any beard growth at all. Always smiling.

"Well, Price and the boys should be getting in right about now." Al was referring to one of the Kid's roommates and some of the other members of their class who had flown in on a jet in front of them. Twelve of the class had gotten orders for 'Nam. Some of them were even lucky enough not to have orders for psyops. And although these soldiers all had as much chance of becoming public information specialists in a combat unit as the Kid had, they each maintained a glimmer of hope to be assigned to AFRN—Armed Forces Radio Network—in Saigon.

"My teeth are floatin'. Gotta go!" Al departed for the rear of the aircraft.

Finishing up his meal, the Kid lit another cigarette and leaned back to let out a long exhalation of smoke. He noticed that he'd almost filled up the little ashtray that was affixed to the armrest of his seat. His gaze went back to the unending panorama of sea and sky outside his small porthole of a window. He watched the wingtip buck up and down a little as the aluminum tube sped on its way to deliver its mixed load of trained killers and cannon fodder to the destiny that awaited each. A certain percentage would die; a certain percentage would get wounded; a certain percentage would make it home; and certainly a percentage would catch a case of the clap.

Soon after the Kid crushed out the butt and sank back into a fitful sleep, his mind took off again on a roller-coaster ride through the wild blue yonder, thinking most bizarre thoughts. He fixated on his brother, Scott. Almost two years older than the Kid, Scott was the second of the two to go into the army. He got drafted out of the Peace Corps. What a shocker. He didn't think that could happen, but it did.

One week, Scott was going to Kenya, and the next week, he was in the army. Worse yet, he was headed for medic school at Fort Lewis in Washington State, which really meant he was headed for some deep shit in the combat zone. *But, of course, should I get killed, according to the "Sullivan rule," Scott wouldn't have to go to Vietnam because he'd be the sole surviving son. What a bonus chance to miss the war. Talk about your good news / bad news.* The Sullivan rule was created when the five Sullivan brothers all went down on the same ship in World War II. Nowadays, brothers could avoid being in a combat zone at the same time.

But then it's only right, the Kid thought. *I was the one the army got first, so I should be the one to go to 'Nam first.* The brothers agreed on one thing: if they both lived, their parents would spend the next two years with a son in the war zone, and it would be hardest on their mom.

Readjusting his position and once again propping his head up against the window, the Kid continued to seek sleep with his eyes closed. He heard a woman's voice.

"Pillow?" The woman said, "Do you want a pillow?"

Somebody hit the Kid in the arm. "She's talking to you," Harrington said, grinning at him as the flight attendant stood in the aisle with an armful of those microscopically small airline pillows.

"You might as well take one," she said, smiling brightly. "It's a lot easier to really get some sleep with one, or even two if you want?"

"Yes, thank you, I will take one." *My, what lengths they will go to, to ensure our comfort.* Placing the white micropillow between the window and his left ear, the Kid closed his eyes and again attempted to drift off on the cloud of illusion that was fueled by his recent romantically fulfilling encounter. But no. That illusion was trumped by the fact that he was a GI on his way to Vietnam in May of 1968. The great Tet Offensive had happened in February, three months earlier, and now GIs were getting killed at a rate of about two hundred fifty or more a week. That was a thousand deaths a month. He'd read an article in Time magazine's most recent issue about a whole platoon of fifty guys getting wiped out in a big fight in Dong Fong Province or somewhere else to hell and gone.

The Kid had only been in the army since September of 1967 and had gone from boot camp to troop plane in a mere nine months! The previous year at this time, he had been a disc jockey, doing midnight to six in Nashville— Music City— hanging out with Roy Orbison, Billy Swan, and John "Bucky" Wilkin, the last of whom was actually Ronnie of Ronnie and the Daytonas fame.

"Hey, Kid," Harrington said in a quizzical tone, "has there ever been a troop plane shot down flying into Vietnam?"

Harrington is calling me by my DJ nickname. Points in his favor. "Well, Harrington." The Kid looked at him. "If one ever had been shot down, it would have made all the papers, don't you think? Maybe even have been on Walter Cronkite. Did you ever hear of one?"

"No."

"Me neither. But then there's the other side of the coin: is our government telling us the truth? I mean, if a troop plane has gone down, if ever there was a story they'd want to hide, that might be it. I can tell you that at DINFOS, where they taught us how to be public information specialists, which is what the army calls a journalist, they were quite clear that freedom of information is at the discretion of the chain of command. So who the fuck knows? However, from a journalist's point of view, if it was a plane leaving Vietnam, one full of soldiers who had served their year and survived, that got shot down, then that story would make a far greater impact."

13

"No shit!" Harrington nodded agreement. "Now you'll have me thinking about that my whole tour!"

Harrington, having heard enough, left the Kid to his solace. Now the Kid's mind drifted back to the Defense Information School and journalism classes. He had signed a contract for radio. Plain and simple, Gil had told him, "I'll get you in to Armed Forces Radio." That's what the man had said. But when the Kid arrived at Fort Benjamin Harrison on the outskirts of Indianapolis, one of the first things he found out was that he had been assigned to a Basic Military Journalism class.

"Hey, wait a minute, I've got a contract for radio," the Kid had told the first sergeant.

"Yes, you do," he said, "but the way the army does it, nobody goes to broadcast school until they pass basic journalism. That's the prerequisite."

Damn, the Kid thought, I can barely spell prerequisite. Shit, that's why I got into radio, so I could say things and not have to write stuff down for any further punctuation or spelling examination for correctness. He asked, "And what happens if I flunk out of the journalism school?"

"Then it's off to the infantry for you. Or maybe the artillery, but something like that for sure." The first sergeant smirked at him. "If you've got a brain in your head, you can probably pass BMJ, which is what we call it, that is, if you can type the prerequisite fifty words a minute. You do know how to type, don't you?"

Did the Kid know how to type? This was the sixty-four-thousand-dollar question, the answer to which would determine whether or not the Kid would be in Armed Forces Radio or the infantry. Could the Kid type? *Hell yes! Thank God, the Kid can type fifty words a minute!* Being a forward-looking boy who liked girls more than most boys did, almost as soon as he found out that girls were "different," the Kid had signed up for typing class in the seventh grade at Base Line Junior High School, in Boulder, Colorado, because it was full of girls. There were only three other guys in the class, and one of them might as well have been a girl himself.

The term *gay* was not yet in widespread use to refer to homosexuals back in 1959.

"Hell yes, I can type! And I've written a lot of speeches and commercials for radio, but I've never written for newspapers."

"Well, because we believe that all journalism, print or electronic, is basic, you're going to Basic Military Journalism whether you like it or not. Then, if you graduate, you might—and I stress, you *might*—get to go on to broadcast communications school. Here's your room assignment." The first sergeant dismissed him.

The Kid's journalism teacher at DINFOS, Specialist Fourth Class John Knight, was a recent graduate of the University of Missouri School of Journalism, one of the finest in the country. The Kid thought back to Specialist 4 Knight, who had been one of them. When he graduated from Mizzou and gotten drafted, Knight took an extra year to get into DINFOS so he could become a military journalist, with the goal of being a combat photographer. Then when he finished at the top of his journalism class, the army made him an instructor. Because of this, he was royally pissed.

"Any journalist worth his salt should want to be in Vietnam right now!" Specialist 4 Knight had lectured. "That's where the story is—perhaps the greatest story of our generation! Especially if you don't agree with the Vietnam War, you should really want to be there to document the things that are most wrong about it. Think of the photo opportunities! The Pulitzer is there, my boys! Doesn't the name Ernie Pyle mean anything to you guys?" Knight invoked the holy name of the greatest war correspondent of World War II, great in no small part because he was a gifted writer, for sure, but also because of the tragic story of his not surviving.

So, the Kid thought, I'm going to get Specialist 4 Knight's wish. I'll have to get a better camera.

Back at the window, the Kid spied a large group of islands below. "Excuse me, stewardess, what islands are those?"

"Oh, those are the Philippines," the redhead answered, passing his row.

How exotic. That's where Magellan bought the farm. Corregidor and MacArthur, "I'll be back," the Battle of Manila Bay. Wow, imagine having to find your way through that maze of islands with no map for the first time, the Kid marveled. He took pen in hand, got out a sheet of his new stationery, and began a letter to Flo.

Dearest Parnelli [he called her this because she had gotten two speeding tickets],

You'll never guess where I am right now. Thirty thousand feet over the Philippine Islands! Another place I thought I would most likely never go. After being in the air since 2100 hours [9:00 p.m.] on the twenty-first and crossing the International Date Line, I don't know what day it is.

All I know is that I miss you so much already. I don't know how I'll ever be able to survive the year without you. You hear guys on the plane talking about getting the million-dollar wound, the one that will bring you home from 'Nam and get you out of the army but not affect your life. I'll take one of those—upon arrival, if you please. Will you still love me if I get paralyzed from the waist down and can't ride your bicycle anymore? I'd rather be dead. I can't think about anything but the TM [that was code for Traveler's Motel, used here in case Flo's mom, who really didn't like the Kid, because she knew what he wanted, ever sneaked a peek at any of his letters].

So, we had to stop in Guam! It is a B-52 base, and the runways were linned with big bombers. Oops, I wonder if this is going to be censored and the army will take that out? They say all our mail is censored from now on, for security reasons, and there're things we can't say or talk about. Oh well, tell me if my letters start turning up all blacked out.

Anyway, we are flying over the Philippines, and in just a couple of hours, we are going to land at Long Binh. From what I'm hearing now, Long Binh will not be where I'm staying, although that's what it says on my orders.

Everybody who goes to Vietnam has Long Binh on their orders because that's where they process us and then disperse us to our real units. I still don't know if I can swing the Armed Forces Radio change yet, or if it is such a done deal that I'm stuck in psyops no matter what. But I'll never give up trying.

I'm so strung out from this flight, the only way I know down from up is that the ceiling of the plane is up, and the ocean is down. Sleeping has been difficult, but I've had one really good dream of us together. It was right after I brushed my teeth. After all, you are my dream girl, and I know how you like fresh breath. I'm looking at your picture and seriously considering brushing my teeth one more time before this plane gets to 'Nam.

I'll see you later.

Love,

Curt

"I'll see you later" was their signature phrase. Every time the Kid wrote it, he thought about their first encounter. The radio station where he labored, WKDA AM, had a disc jockey, Bill Craig, the afternoon guy, who had won a part in a movie about country-and-western singer Leroy Van Dyke. The movie was called *The Auctioneer,* which was also the title of Leroy's biggest hit. Baby Bill Craig, as he like to be called, had been hired to play the part of somebody just like himself in the movie. Because the film was about, and partially filmed in, Music City, it was premiering in Nashville. And since WKDA was the home of the DJ in the movie, the station got to host and broadcast the premiere at the Paramount.

In addition to Leroy himself, other stars who were in *The Auctioneer* included Kristin Harmon, daughter of Heisman Trophy winner Tom Harmon and the wife of Ricky Nelson—she played Leroy's love interest in the movie; and Chad Everett and Shelby Grant, Chad's wife at the time, who were there because Shelby had a part in the movie as well. It was with them that the Kid made one of the worst broadcasting mistakes of his life. His job that night was to introduce Chad Everett and his wife, Shelby Grant. When the couple pulled up and got out of the limo, the Kid introduced them as "Mr. and Mrs. Shelby Grant." If Chad had had a gun, he likely would have shot the Kid dead.

After the movie, when everybody was leaving, there was a crush of people pushed together as the celebrities passed through the lobby. They were on one side of a rope, and the non-famous people were on the other. At one point, the Kid got pushed up against a woman with this incredible captivating face, dark shoulder-length hair, and brown eyes, wearing a yellow dress. *Altogether too cute.* They made eye contact. He said, "I'll see you later," and was immediately pushed on down the line with no chance of talking to her anymore.

That night after the premiere, the Kid still had to be on the air at midnight, and he was. About ten minutes after he had gotten settled in and started taking calls for requests and doing the other things typical of a Top 40 radio station DJ in 1967, he took a call from a young woman.

"Do you have 'California Girls' by the Beach Boys?" the alluring voice on the line asked.

"Yes, I do," the Kid said. "And for whom shall I play it?"

"Play it for that girl you spoke to tonight leaving the premiere."

The proverbial frog jumped up into his throat. He had thought about the black hair and brown eyes almost constantly since that second. "And if I spoke to you, what did I say?"

"'I'll see you later.'"

Yes, yes, yes, it's her! The kid immediately shut down the phone lines and ended up talking nearly all night to Flo, which was what her name turned out to be, short for Floretta. He had never before met a Floretta. The first thing he found out was slightly disturbing to him: she was from California and was out in Nashville on vacation with her twin sister, Loretta, visiting their grandparents. They were only going to be here another two weeks. Bummer. She was sixteen and was going to be a junior in high school in Vista, California. Well, hell, the Kid was only nineteen, and he dated high school girls all the time. The reason he had come to Nashville was for a high school girl, Donna Nadeau. But Donna was having trouble letting him past second base. And being a DJ, the Kid had lots and lots of dates, as many as he wanted, with young women who were not even strangers to home plate. But when he saw Flo, he was a certified goner. For some reason, from that point on, Flo was the only one he wanted.

Plus, barely three weeks before he met Flo, the Kid had been drafted. So, his life was in such a vortex that he really didn't know what his future held in store for him. He had already cut his deal for DINFOS and knew he was going to be inducted into the military on September 11, 1967, eight days after his twentieth birthday. After that, outside of the fact that he still fully expected to be assigned to Armed Forces Radio, because he was one of the hottest up-and-coming Top 40 DJs in the country, he'd have to spend three years in the military.

Once he was totally gone in love with Flo, he fantasized that upon his return Stateside, he could request to be stationed in California and the two of them could pursue their romance. Of course, when he got out of the army and they got married, she'd come back to Tennessee because he was going to get his job back and continue his meteoric rise to the top of the radio world there in Music City. Until then, letters were all they had. They'd managed to have about half a dozen dates in Tennessee before she had to go home, partially chaperoned by her twin sister, Lo, who was not identical.

Before long, the flight attendant came by and commented to the GI across the aisle from the Kid, "We're just about to the coast of Vietnam, in case you're interested."

Yes, we are all interested.

Suddenly, from the other side of the plane, out of a strange lull of silence, there came an excitedly breathy exclamation: Ooh! There it is! The Vietnamese coast!"

"Oh yeah! Wow!" It was as if they were seeing fireworks on the Fourth of July. On the Kid's side, nothing could be seen yet because of the angle; the land below was obscured by the aircraft's wing. Then, almost like pulling back the curtain on a play, the wing cleared the sight line, unveiling the white waves of the South China Sea beating against a narrow strip of red-colored sand separating a sea of green foliage from the contrasting sea of blue they were now leaving in their wake.

The Kid looked. Harrington kind of wanted to look and was trying to catch glimpses around him. "Here." The Kid pulled back. "Take a look!"

"Thanks!" Harrington smiled. "Oh yeah, there it is all right. Well, the country isn't very wide, so it shouldn't be long now till we're on the ground!" He leaned back into his seat.

"Want a look?" the Kid offered to the guy on the aisle.

"No, thanks. I'll be seeing it for a year, so I'm not that anxious to get started."

The Kid went back to the window. The jet was descending, but they were still plenty high. Now he was starting to pick up some details on the ground, which was green as far as the eye could see. Then there were patches of brown and strange rows of long circles lined up that seemingly shone back at him.

"See those circles?" He heard a soldier with an east coast accent sitting behind him speak, "Those are bomb craters, from where B-52's, like we saw in Guam, dropped their loads. The craters fill up with water and just make more places for mosquitoes to have sex."

The forest gave way to terrain that resembled farm fields. *Oh, those are rice paddies!* the Kid realized. Now he could see towns, small collections of white and light-colored structures with afternoon sun reflecting off their metal roofs. The flaps began cranking down out of the wings, the landing gear was lowering, and all of a sudden the jet began to drop sharply. *We must be getting close to landing. Couldn't imagine that a pilot would much be into long, low, smooth approaches in this place,* the Kid conjectured.

Suddenly, the noise level decreased considerably. It seemed as if the engines had ceased to thrust, because the Kid could feel so much slowing that he anxiously gripped the armrests of his seat. Then, appearing under the wing was ground devoid of fields, trees, or roads. Next came row upon row of barbed concertina wire, strung out like so many giant Slinkies, running off into the distance, piled and twisted together in an unbroken barrier. This was followed by another completely open area. The pilot extended more flaps before another barrier of concertina wire appeared, marking the perimeter of the airfield.

The end of the runway flashed under the wing. The Kid braced himself. The big, lumbering jet jockeyed a little and then flat plopped down amid the very loud squealing of tires as some rubber was burnt off, the tires having just

19

accelerated from zero to one hundred fifty miles per hour in a millisecond. *Oh my God! How in fucking hell did I end up here?* Stuff rattled around in the overhead compartments as the massive jet was slowed with the reverse thrusters.

The Kid was on the ground in Vietnam. The day was—why, hell, he didn't know! It could have been Sunday or Wednesday; he was totally jet-lagged and running on adrenaline as he gawked at the base rolling past his window. It had to be the twenty-third or the twenty-fourth of May. One of the two. The year was 1968; he knew that. Three years earlier at about this time, he was graduating from Boulder High School. Fifteen months ago, he had been the youngest full-time DJ in Nashville. Four days ago he had finally consummated a relationship with the love of his life, and now he was in the war zone. *How in the world did I let this happen?*

After a very short taxi roll, the DC-8 made a quick left turn and lurched to a stop. The tops of ladders appeared above the wing, rolling along, pushed by unseen ground crew personnel, preparing to unload the new arrivals. Like a cave full of bears just awakened from hibernation, the soldiers of Flight 1547 began to rise, stretching, from their seats and attempted to gather their belongings.

Then the doors popped open at both ends of the jet. A tide of hot air poured in and came to rest in the middle of the craft, right about where the Kid was standing. *Welcome to hell. We do hope you have a pleasant stay.*

"If they've lost my luggage, I'll be *really* pissed!" some nameless GI hollered, eliciting nervous laughter from those within earshot.

"And they're going to give me all the bullets I can shoot? Really?" Gallows humor abounded. Back at Travis Air Force Base, the Kid had gotten the gallows flash.

Ha. It's more like out of the frying pan and into the firing range.

The Kid looked back at Davies. After exchanging smiles and chokes, they moved toward the rear door. "I can see this is not quite like hitting the beach in Normandy." The Kid grinned, letting Tom go in front of him.

Reaching into his pocket as he neared the door, the Kid pulled out his prescription shades. He hated the fact that his eyesight sucked so bad. The thought of being without glasses in the middle of a war zone was paralyzing to him. Placing the regular specs into his shirt pocket, he gave the Canadian beaver nickel hanging from his neck a good-luck squeeze. *If I ever needed you, it's now!* he silently addressed it.

"This is it," he said to Tom, who had worked his way up to the flight attendants, who were standing by the door saying goodbye to the soldiers.

"Bye-bye. We're not supposed to say, 'Enjoy your stay.'"

"What we like to say is, 'See you next year, same time, same place!'"

"Yes, thank you. You guys were great. Good luck!"

"Well, *schweetheart,* we'll always have Oakland," the Kid said, trying to do Bogart as he passed the redhead. She was mildly amused.

And there it was! No longer was it a concept or a story on the nightly news, or a gory picture in the paper. The Kid was now in Vietnam. Standing on the top step of the jet ramp, he looked out and saw a huge tin-covered building that easily was the size of two football fields, with a sign across the top that said: "Welcome to Bien Hoa, RVN."

Two tanker trucks pulled up, the crews of Vietnamese men in each truck jumping out and hustling to get some fuel into the DC-8 wing tanks as if they were doing a pit stop at the Indy 500. Another truck was backed up to the cargo door, catching duffle bags that began literally flying off the jet.

"Hey, look at that!" Tom pointed. Beneath the shade of the tin roof, there was row upon row of soldiers, all cheering, whooping, hollering, and carrying on as if it were New Year's Eve!

"Freedom bird! My freedom bird!" They were yelling and dancing, raising all manner of a commotion. Their jet to hell was the one those men were going to get on board this very second and *fly home!*

As the newcomers to Vietnam walked down the steps and onto the tarmac, the grins on the faces of the men who eagerly waited, each with a white boarding pass clutched tightly in his hand, became more visible. The celebration cacophony rose above the noise of the engine turbines, which still whined, even in their recently shut-down state. Quite a few of these individuals were crying as they hugged one another and patted each other on the back. There were cigars aplenty stuck in their teeth, wagging like happy dogs' tails. These were men who had survived their year and apparently had all their arms and legs. *These lucky fucks are flying home on our jet!*

Chapter 2

"Through these doors pass the finest fighting men in the world." The Kid stared at the sign placed squarely above the door of the Long Binh in-processing unit. *I am not now, nor will I ever be, a fighting man,* he thought. *How the fuck did I end up here?* Then he heard a familiar laugh.

"Wah-ha! Would ya look at this gaggle of green-as-booger newbies!"

The Texas accent belonged to David Waterhouse, in the company of Pete Erio and Larry Titley, all together three classmates from DINFOS who had been on the jet about three hours in front of the Kid's. The trio had already changed from their class A uniforms into jungle fatigues.

"Price!" The Kid smiled, extending his hand with his palm up. "Give me some skin!"

Waterhouse slapped his palm. "Welcome to the Republic of South Vietnam, Kid. You too, Imbach," he drawled. "I hear there's lots of opportunity to go camping here. What Boy Scout doesn't love that?" He slapped Imbach on the back. "This shit doesn't take too long to get done," Waterhouse said. He removed his glasses and wiped some sweat off the lenses using the bottom of his jungle fatigue. "We're in barracks Delta Four. I imagine you guys will be right down in that neck of the woods too. Tell you what, we'll meet you at the exit door."

"OK! We'll see you there!" The Kid gave Waterhouse a thumbs-up.

As the newcomers were stepping out from the in-processing center, a staff sergeant gestured with a clipboard for them to enter. "All right, ladies, this way, please, and we'll take care of this red tape ASAP. Let's go! There's another jet behind you, and we don't want to be here all night! Move all the way to the far end of the building so we can get as many in as possible. Gentlemen, let's go! Move it, move it, move it!"

Entering the building, the troops were greeted by long wooden tables that ran down each side of the huge room. In the middle stood two more staff sergeants and four PFCs, along with boxes of stuff to issue and stacks of paperwork to be filled out and then collected.

22

"Just move on down to the end. Make room for the guys behind you to come in so we can get to as many of you as possible. Put your duffle bags on the floor immediately behind you, and listen up!"

The Kid, Davies, Viator, and Imbach moved down the table on the left side of the entry. As they reached their spots, they could see another bus pulling up. After a couple of minutes of shuffling, both sides of the room were packed full with new blood.

"All right, gentlemen, listen up!" the fair-skinned, sunburned, and buzz-cut E-6 roared in his best command voice. "The United States Army welcomes you to the Republic of South Vietnam. There are a few basic rules and regulations we are going to cover here as we check each of you in and make sure your names get put into the process so you can get your assignments, get the fuck out of Long Binh, and hook up with your new units ASAP! The first thing we want you to do is rip the top page off your orders and lay it on the table in front of you." As everybody complied, a pair of PFCs moved up the row of tables, one on each side, and collected the sheets.

"Now, we are going to change your money."

The older E-7, who was black and almost bald, took over.

"Get out any and all of the US currency you have in your possession. We are going to exchange it for military payment certificates. Be advised that the possession of US currency in the RVN is against army regulations and punishable under the UCMJ, the Uniform Code of Military Justice. The reason is that the army don't want any of it falling into enemy hands, because it is worth a lot more to them than their worthless paper."

The Kid looked in his wallet. All he had was forty-five dollars in bills and seventy cents in change. This time, a pair of PFCs began working their way up the tables on each side, one with a ledger and one with a cashbox. When they got to the Kid, the one with the ledger took his money and counted it.

"Forty-five dollars and seventy cents," he said, handing the money to his partner, then writing the sum down in the ledger. His partner took the US currency and put it on one side of the cashbox. From the other, he pulled a stack of oddly colored bills and counted out forty-five dollars in MPC: a blue twenty, two reddish tens, and a brown five. Then, in little bills about a third the size of the dollar certificates, he counted out the seventy cents in change: a blue fifty-cent note and two red ten-cent notes. *How interesting,* the Kid thought, *paper change! Help me, I'm being held prisoner in a Monopoly game!*

As the money exchange continued, he looked at his watch. It said the time was four o'clock in the afternoon, which was 1600 hours in military time. He couldn't remember what time zone his watch was set to, and then his mind wondered what time it was back in the States and if Flo was awake or asleep, in school or out of school, or dressed or naked. *Or in the shower—yes, naked and in the shower.* His mind shot back to the only time he'd ever been naked in the shower with her, after they made love in the Traveler's Motel.

"OK, men." The sunburned sergeant's voice pulled the Kid rudely from his California daydream and back to Southeast Asia. "Now we're going to pass out ration cards. You need this card to buy cigarettes, booze, appliances, perfume, and just about everything they have in the PX except candy bars. So don't lose this card, because it's next to fucking impossible to get another one!"

The PFC helpers began moving down the rows, dealing out ration cards like blackjack dealers dealing playing cards in Vegas.

"And pull out your military ID cards so we can check your age," the sarge bellowed. "If you're underage, we gotta black out your liquor ration."

A pitiful moan swept through the assembled crowd, made obviously by the younger set.

"I know it's a rotten thing, granted," the E-6 said, raising his hand for silence, "but it's regulations. Hell, that doesn't mean you guys can't get a drink. So, no sweat, GI!"

Behind the ration card distribution, another PFC moved up each row, checking IDs and, with a black marker, x-ing out the liquor rations on the cards of those soldiers who were not yet twenty-one. When the PFC got to the Kid, he looked at his ID, poised the marker over the booze ration box, and then just moved on without dropping the *X,* even though the Kid would not be twenty-one for another four months.

All right! the Kid thought. *Today, I'm a man!* "Thanks!" he called to the PFC, who by now was past Davies, Viator, and Imbach, who all happened to be twenty- one.

"OK, gentlemen, you'll be quartered in barracks Delta Six for your stay in Long Binh. The way you find it is, go out the door and take a left, where you'll stop and pick up your sheets and a pillow at the quartermaster supply right there, then proceed straight ahead, down the walk to Delta Row. Then it's six buildings to your right again. And, gentlemen, if you're smart, you'll keep your duffle bags padlocked when you're out of the barracks. Otherwise, you can kiss most of your crap goodbye!

"There is a mess hall here that is open twenty-four seven. It's over that way." He swung his left arm back behind his head. "Assignment formation

24

is at zero six hundred hours, and after that, anybody who is not shipped out is required to pull casual duties until twelve hundred hours. The rest of your time is your own.

There's an enlisted men's club, where you can all get a beer, to the right of this building and across the open quad. Good luck on your tour, gentlemen!

Dismissed!"

"I feel so guilty. So far, we haven't really earned any of our combat pay." Davies chortled as they moved toward the exit.

"Let's see, a hundred dollars per month for combat pay divided by thirty days average means we get about three dollars and thirty cents per day. Dividing that by twenty-four hours, because we get combat pay if we are awake or asleep, it comes to about thirteen cents per hour, which is less than a quarter of a cent for every minute we are here." The Kid figured the rate of pay.

"I feel like I'm earnin' mine." Imbach smiled. "And I'm going to save every quarter penny of it!"

"To buy your dad a goat for Christmas?" Viator went after the always vulnerable Imbach.

"No. My dad hates goats," Imbach informed us. "We had a goat that ate his long johns off the clothesline once. No lie." The corners of his mouth turned up in a half smile. "Maybe a pig. He likes bacon!"

Waterhouse was waiting outside the in-processing building, puffing a butt. "So, what barracks did you get?"

"Delta Six," Davies replied.

"Take the lower bunk. That way, if a mortar should slam into your barracks tonight, at least you'll have one mattress, and possibly Imbach above you, for protection!" Waterhouse gave the others the benefit of his extra two hours of in- country experience.

"Hey, roommate!" Imbach shot back. "You said yourself at DINFOS that I'm too fat for the upper bunk."

"Yes, that's true. But that's when the only danger any of us were facing was you falling on us!"

Because they were some of the first ones into the in-processing building, the line for sheets was short and sweet.

Although the sun had gone down about twenty minutes earlier, the air was not beginning to cool. The tropical clouds were towering columns of

25

humidity that were turning from white to pastel colors before their eyes as they lugged their sheets, pillows, and duffle bags toward their barracks.

"Listen!" Davies stopped. "I think I hear explosions off in the distance!" Everybody stopped.

Yes, a faint rumbling was audible.

"Maybe a thunderstorm," Waterhouse speculated.

"Doubt it," Viator challenged. "Could be artillery or air strikes, but whatever it is, it's a long ways from here."

"Check out the bunkers." Waterhouse pointed to a long, sandbag-covered house-looking structure. There was one about every three barracks. "I thought about sleeping in there, but when I went into one to check it out, the heat and the smell just about killed me. Oh, here's our barracks. Yours is the building after next."

"Thank you, but we can count to six." Davies scoffed.

Entering their barracks, the four men stopped and pondered where to settle.

"Seems to me," the Kid said, "that we should take the bunks as nearest to the door as possible so that if we do get attacked, we can get to the bunker as quickly as possible."

"Brilliant!" Viator nodded in agreement. "I see mine." He dragged his bedding and baggage to an unoccupied rack and flopped on the bottom bunk.

The barracks windows contained no glass. Their screened coverings served a twofold purpose. If a mortar round were to come in, there would be no exploding shards of glass to increase the deadliness of such an occurrence. And just nailing up a role of screen meant the barracks could be constructed much more quickly than if they all had windows to make them air-conditioning-friendly.

The only relief from the heat came from the artificial breeze created by the large circular fan that spun with a whirring vengeance at the far end of the barracks.

"A fan at both ends would be nice," Imbach said, sitting on a lower bunk across from where the Kid had tossed his pillow and sheets.

"God, Imbach, is that all you ever do, complain?" Waterhouse feigned displeasure with the Boy Scout. "I'm surprised you haven't whipped out your Junior Woodchuck book and made your own fucking fan!"

"I, for one, want to hit the mess hall before we start drinking beer," Viator said, proposing a plan of action.

"Well, I don't know," the Kid replied. "I've got like six airline meals stuck in my gut, and I don't know where they went. They never came out, that's for sure, so hungry I ain't. I'm goin' for the suds!"

"Me too," said Waterhouse. "They have a whole bunch of slot machines in the club and the Kid has to rub his nickel on one for me!"

"Ha, joke's on you." Davies smirked. "That's a Canadian nickel, and slot machines don't take slugs."

"No, fuckface, the joke's on you. This is Vietnam, and they only take slugs. Besides, I said rub it, not stick it in it."

"Isn't that what Tina said the night before you left?" Davies shot back.

"You've got it half right. She said first rub it, then stick it in! Let's go, Kid." Waterhouse started for the barracks door.

"See ya!" The Kid half waved as he set off after Price.

Outside, the pair plodded slowly in the tropical heat, walking at the pace of men who really have no place to go. Although the sun had now set and it was starting to become dark out, there was no change in the stifling furnace to which they had been sentenced. They both lit up.

"Fuck, man." The Kid exhaled. "It is really hard to believe, but here we are, Price, in god-awful fucking Vietnam! Can you believe it? I mean, we are el-fuck-a- renoed or what? Chapter and verse screwed up the ass."

"Now, Kid, don't take it so hard. It doesn't do any good to go all negative. Aren't you the one who always says you gotta play the hand you're dealt, Mr. Poker Face?"

"Yeah, but this is one hand I'd love to just fold!"

They passed other GIs, moving toward the barracks with duffle bags, sheets, and pillows in hand, all with the same befuddled kind of expression on their faces. As the Kid looked at their disheveled class A uniforms, which were stained with sweat and stinking to high heaven, he wished he'd taken a minute to change into fatigues like Waterhouse.

"Hey, I might go back and take a shower and change." The Kid stopped in his tracks.

"What the fuck for? Look at me. I changed, and already these are just about as sweaty as yours. Don't bother!"

"OK, you're right." The Kid continued to walk. The two had been inseparable at the Defense Information School as roommates and pals who, in spite of their both being quasi-engaged, had continued to chase women together. They both figured there'd be plenty of time for monogamy, that is, if they lived long enough to take the walk down the aisle with their respective fiancées.

As they approached the enlisted men's club, the music coming from inside became louder and louder. It was "Hang on Sloopy" by the McCoys. The mix of GIs coming and going were half still in class A's and half in fatigues. This was, without a doubt, where the action was at Long Binh for unwashed enlisted and drafted masses.

"I got the first round." Price pulled out his wallet as he and the Kid entered. Walking toward the bar, they saw that the club was a good size, with a bar made of plywood and two-by-fours running down one side for about sixty feet.

Overhead, two rows of ceiling fans did their damnedest to create a cooling effect by evaporating sweat. There were plenty of tables, most of them filled with soldiers smoking and drinking. Some faces were smiling and joking; others looked as forlorn as the Kid felt.

"Two beers," Price called out to one of the three the staff sergeants manning the bar. He plunked down a brown fiver.

Pulling a pair of Falstaffs out of a cooler, the staff sergeant popped the pull-ring tops and slid the cans over. "That'll be a buck."

"Got anything but Falstaff?" Waterhouse asked with disdain.

The sergeant threw a surprised glance back at him. "Look, I know you just got off the boat, so let me be the first to tell you: this is fucking Vietnam, man. We take what we can get, and the only beer in the house today is Falstaff, so like it or take it to the chaplain!"

Well, OK. They both shrugged. Price picked up his pink ones in change as he shoved one of the Falstaffs over to the Kid. "A toast. To the day we are once again civilians!"

"I will absolutely drink to that, with Falstaff or even commode water." The Kid clicked his can against Price's, and they both took a long, cold drink of suds. "Ah. God, I needed that!"

Turning from the bar, they spied an empty table and began working their way toward it. Pulling out their chairs, they sat down facing each other. The Kid took his Kools out of his pocket and, after pulling one out, set the pack on the table.

"You're not high, are you?" Waterhouse watched him light it up.

"Well, sorta disoriented, to say the least. I did blow a J in the airplane can, but that was like eight hours ago. Feels like it was yesterday. I wouldn't call it high as much as I'd call it far."

"So," Waterhouse said, "did your mom cry?"

"Oh, fuck yes. She was a regular three coins in the fountain!"

"Mine too. What a major-league bummer. She actually walked around the house whimpering for about the last three days I was home. And Tina." He brought up his fiancée. "When I left, she and my mom were like Niagara Falls! Fuck, I was glad to finally get on the plane to Fort Riley for that worthless POR."

POR was army jargon for "Possible Overseas Replacement Training," a little session that the army arranged for all those GIs on their way to Vietnam who did not have a combat MOS. Funny that it was called "Possible" Overseas Replacement Training, because you didn't get assigned to it until you were going to Vietnam for a certainty. The army got all the clerks, accountants, mechanics, and other soldiers with noncombat MOS's together at Fort Riley, Kansas, and gave them classes in the kind of stuff other GIs learned at AIT— Advanced Infantry Training. The Kid had gotten to take AIT on his way home from Indianapolis before going on leave because his leave was to be spent in Colorado and California, which were well west of Kansas. Waterhouse had been assigned to take his at the end of his leave because Texas was not far enough west of Kansas for him to get it there first.

"Ha, it was pretty funny that me and Erio ended up in the foxhole you and Hoogs put your message in!"

Waterhouse was recounting the little field exercise the army put the attendees through, where they pretended to be on a search and destroy mission with blank ammo out in the woods along the Kansas River. Other GIs, dressed in black pajamas, enacted the role of the Vietcong and staged an ambush. The GIs then shot at them with the blanks. Then, at the end of the day, the attendees were put into a defensive position in predug wood-sided foxholes for the night assault class. While waiting for the night assault, the Kid had taken out his pen and written a message on the wood for his classmates who he knew were taking POR after his group. It was words to the effect of "Hello, Waterhouse, Erio, Titley, Davies, and Smith: While you are reading this, I will be in California lying on the beach and wallowing in the hot steamy love juices of my woman!"

"Yes, that was pretty fucking funny! That we would get *that* foxhole— what are the odds?"

"Well, considering that there were only ten foxholes, one in ten! Oh, Flo and I went to a Cream concert in San Diego on our last night!"

"No way! How were they?"

"Not as good as what we saw at Butler." The Kid compared the California concert to the one he, Waterhouse, and about five other DINFOS students had been to in March at the Butler University Auditorium. "I think they must have been burnt out. Ginger Baker didn't do half the drum solo we saw, and Clapton was, by comparison, just average."

"Really? Just average, you say?"

"Yeah, I was actually disappointed." The Kid took a long drink.

As they drank, the whirr of the overhead fans mingled with the whirr of the turning tumblers from the banks of slot machines that took up nearly half the club, just beyond the tables. The din of conversation and Top 40 music was punctuated by heavy metal clunking as soldiers stuffed slugs in the one-armed bandits and pulled the handles.

"Gee, look at this! Gambling. I wonder how much the noncoms who run this club pull down a month with these machines?" The Kid twisted in his chair to check out the action. "My grandma had a theory when we all went to Las Vegas, when I was a junior in high school, that the machines near the door were set to pay off more than the ones in the back row."

"Is that so?" Price looked at him with a grin. "Tell you what, let's finish these beers and get a roll of quarter slugs and see what happens. I've already lost five dollars. That's why I need to put in a call to Mr. Lucky!"

"For some reason, I don't feel too lucky today, Price. Shit, look at us. We are stuck in Viet-fucking-nam for the next year! Did you ever stop to think about how much of life you choose and how much of your life is decided by things and events and people making decisions that you have no control over? I mean, either one of us could have gone to Canada and, who knows, gotten hit by a bus and be killed just as dead as if we got shot here."

"True. And think of all the hot women you see and meet that you want who don't want you. Tell it to the chaplain, Kid. Come on, let's gamble!"

Leaving their empties on the table, they walked over to the change cage and got in line behind the three GIs who were standing there transacting.

"Give me another five's worth." Waterhouse slapped down his brown money. "OK."

The sergeant counted out his slugs. "And how about you, PFC?"
"Likewise," the Kid said, plunking down his MPC.

Waterhouse and the Kid walked over to the slot machines and looked them over: five cents, ten cents, and twenty-five cents. "If you want to do this for fun, we should have gotten nickels, because then we could play five times as long!" the Kid said, having done his computations.

30

"If you're gonna go, go big, my daddy says," Waterhouse replied. "So, rub your famous nickel on this one right here!" He laid his hand on a chrome-plated twenty-five-cent Jackpot-brand machine that was in the middle of the row.

"OK." The Kid reached into his shirt and pulled on the chain that held his lucky Canadian beaver nickel. Bringing it out, he leaned forward and rubbed the nickel, beaver side down, on the handle of the slot machine.

Waterhouse dropped the slug into the slot and yanked down on the lever, setting the wheels into motion. *Click.* A lemon. *Click.* A cherry. *Click.* A bar. Nothing.

He put in another, and this time gave the arm a vicious yank. The wheels spun and spun. *Click.* A plum. *Click.* A lemon. *Click.* A cherry.

"Fruit salad," the Kid jived. "Hey, Grandma Barnes was no slouch when it came to gambling. Why, she used to live at the bingo hall, and she played ten cards at a time and won, so I'm gonna take the little old lady's advice!" The Kid walked over to the first machine in the row, dropped in his first slug, and pulled the handle. The wheels spun and spun. *Click.* A bar. *Click.* A bar. *Click.* A bar. Bells rang, lights flashed, and slugs started pouring into the tray at the bottom of the machine.

"Fuck me! Jackpot on the first coin! You lucky fuckin' *son of a bitch,* Kid!" Price slapped the shocked and disbelieving Kid on the back so hard that he almost knocked him down.

"Goddamn! How much did I win?" "Fifty bucks!"

"Ha! I doubled my fucking money!" he said, flushed with the adrenalin of the moment. "I'm cashing out!"

"No, Kid, you're *hot!* Keep playing!"

"No way, I'm keepin' it. My dad says that the main mistake most gamblers make is that they win money and then just give it back and then some. My first night in Vietnam and I hit a jackpot on the first pull. I'm keepin it, Price!"

As the Kid began raking the quarter slugs out of the tray and putting them into a paper cup, a sergeant from the club came over and took one of the Kid's slugs out of the tray. Dropping it into the slot and hitting the machine, he said, "You gotta take the jackpot off." *Click.* Cherries. *Click.* Cherries. *Click.* A lemon. Five more slugs were spit out into the tray. *Ka-ching-ching-ching-ching-ching!*

"Kid, Kid, Kid! You're hot!" Waterhouse was just about jumping up and down.

31

"No. No way I want to waste any of my luck doing this anymore, Price. I've got a feeling I'm going to need all the fucking luck I've got left to stay alive. I'm cashing out. I'll watch you and rub my nickel on anything you want—within reason—but I'm done gambling tonight!"

"You pussy fuckin' killjoy!"

"Hey, I'm not stopping you! Go ahead! Grandma says try that one!" The Kid pointed to the first machine in the next row.

And go ahead Waterhouse did, dropping slug after slug.

"I'll get this round. Just let me cash out!" The Kid headed for the change cage, where he passed over his cup of slugs and received in return more funny-colored MPCs. It didn't seem like real money, but still, he felt like a winner.

I hope it's a sign, he wished, putting the bills in his wallet.

It took Waterhouse about fifteen minutes to lose all his slugs. He hit a couple of three- and five-coin payouts, and even a sixteen-coin payout, but he put the money back into the machine as quickly as possible. After another beer, which the Kid again generously bought, they split.

Returning to their barracks, they ran into Pete Cuzzo, another DINFOS grad who had arrived on a jet behind theirs. He was with Titley, Ken Smith, and Davies.

"Ah, Kid, just the man I was looking for." Peter C. smiled. "I was thinking about you when we landed. Do you think you'll be able to achieve your number one goal?"

"My number one goal? Besides being back in the States? Oh! You mean my number one goal for my Tour de Vietnam? To stay stoned the whole year I'm here?"

"Yes, that goal."

"I'm already working on it."

Peter C. laughed. The Kid had a way of making people laugh.

"Hey, the fucking Kid hit a fifty-dollar jackpot on his first pull at the club! Can you believe this lucky cocksucker?" Price punched him lightly in the arm.

"No shit!" Davies exclaimed. *Punch.*

"Fuckin' A, Kid, how do you do it?" Peter C. bounced him with a shove, and now the four of them pinballed him.

"Hey!" The Kid half tripped as he ducked out of the space between Davies and Waterhouse. "Take it easy on the goods!"

"So, we're going for a brew," Davies said.

"You mean a Falstaff," Price corrected him. "This is 'Nam, and that's that!"

"What the fuck is he talking about?" Peter C. put out his butt in the butt can by the door of Waterhouse's barracks.

"Fuckin' newbies who don't know shit." Waterhouse feigned disgust as he grabbed Cuzzo by the back of the neck and put a hand on his upper arm. "Can't teach 'em anything. Go ahead, just walk down into that club without a point man." He shook some common sense into him and released him with a shove. "Ah, wait a minute, Kid, I think I need to go back with these greenhorns and show them how to find beer here in a war zone."

"OK, guys. I'm too beat. Catch you in the morning." "Later, Kid." The four turned for the club.

Slowly walking the two buildings' distance to Delta 6, the Kid got into a Devil's Island frame of mind: a jungle environment, sentenced to a year, a chance that he could easily killed or injured, and the French were involved! "Bastard French," he lamented under his breath.

As he entered the barracks, he found himself noting the location of the bunker. *Wouldn't that be something if we got hit the first night?* Peeling off his filthy, stinking, and sweat-soaked uniform shirt and laying it across his duffle bag, he noticed Imbach lying on the bunk next to his, writing a letter.

"Hey, Kid."

"Hey, John," the Kid said. He unfolded his sheets and made up his bunk. Taking his wallet, which was fairly bursting with his newly won funds, from his back pants pocket, he stuffed it deep into his pillowcase. Then, removing his pants, he lay down on his bunk, clad only in the green boxers. *My God, it feels good to stretch out for the first time in two days*. He was exhausted. Closing his eyes, he drifted into a swirling mishmash of thoughts and impulses, attempting to ignore the low-level conversations that permeated the barracks by GIs who were not yet ready to retire.

The first thing the Kid noticed was the sweat that oozed from the pores of his body, drawn out by the osmosis-like effect of the tropical heat. The two thousand rotations per minute of the barracks fan created no evaporative effect anywhere within the immediate vicinity of his particular bunk.

Fuck me. How did I get here? Flo, Flo, Flo. Will I ever see her again? Will I ever hold her in my arms and taste her sweet kisses, or is my fate a trip home in a metal box?

The Kid's bunkmate Erio walked into the barracks with a towel wrapped around his bare shoulders. He was carrying his shaving kit, returning from the latrine. "Hi, Kid," he greeted him.

"Hey, Erio, how are the showers?"

"Refreshing. There's no hot water. Doesn't matter. You should take one," he said. He stepped onto the frame of the Kid's rack, then pulled himself up and rolled onto the top mattress, shaking the metal frame.

"Yeah, but I'm just too fuckin' tired. Good night, you guys." "Night," Imbach murmured in a low voice.

"No beating your meat, Kid." Erio snickered as he settled in. "This thing is pretty flimsy." He rocked the bunk for effect.

Drawing a deep breath and attempting to relax his mind, the Kid held the breath as the bed stilled its movements. Being a budding Buddhist who was just getting into meditation, he released the breath and attempted to focus on what he recognized as the point of light that was his third eye. *Om.* He flashed on his parents: little Irma and Dwain. He could see his mom crying as he prepared to get in his car and drive to California to spend a week and a half with Flo before he had to report to Oakland. He hugged her and consoled her. "It'll be OK, Mom. You know how lucky I am. I'll make it back, I promise!" His dad clearly fought to hold back his own tears as they embraced. Next, the Kid was able to conjure up Flo's face. She smiled at him. Then, she was gone and he was waiting for something, but he didn't know what it was or exactly where he was. *This is so confusing. Am I dreaming, or is this real?*

Suddenly feeling a gurgling motion deep inside his gut, he knew that the Paul Bunyan–sized logjam was just about ready to break up there on the Colon River. *Well, hallelujah, I finally gotta take a shit! Like right now!* He rose up from his bunk so quickly that it sent a shock wave up to Erio. Jamming on his flip-flops, the Kid hoped he could make it in time to the latrine.

Chapter 3

The light that came on in the barracks accented the fact it was still dark outside. Then came the voice, the command voice of somebody the rank of E-5 or above: "All right, gentlemen, fall out if you want chow before the zero-six-hundred formation. Be advised, if you don't eat now and don't get pulled out for assignment to your unit, this will be your only chance to eat before lunch, because all unassigned personnel will pull morning casual duty! Do I make myself clear?"

"Yes, Drill Sergeant! *Zzzz*," came the sweetly sarcastic, anonymously mocking retort from somewhere deep within the bunk bed jungle.

The Kid rolled out and sat on the edge of his bunk, his bare feet on the floor.

Ooh, the floor is nice and cool. I think I'll sleep on it tonight.

Many of Vietnam's newest residents were opting for the extra sleep, so there wasn't that much traffic heading down to the latrine. Clad only in boxers, they found the morning air cool by comparison to that of the past evening, but it was hot enough to let them know that as soon as the sun came up, things would be cookin'.

"A shower is what I want!" Davies spied the facility where a half dozen GIs were already standing under spigots, in various stages of soaping up and rinsing off.

"Good idea," the Kid agreed, flipping his half-smoked cigarette into the sand-filled receptacle that stood by the door.

A soldier in front of them had just hung up his towel and turned on a showerhead.

"Whoa, that's cold!" he said, his body reacting.

"Ain't no fucking hot water in this whole country, is what I hear tell," an already wet and soapy GI informed them. "Some guy told me if you shower right after sundown, the water in the tank is still kinda warmer than luke."

"Well, I don't care." The Kid dropped his boxers and hung them with his towel on a peg above the long, narrow wooden bench opposite the showerheads where everybody set their shaving kits. "I am looking forward to this in a big way!"

"Yeah, what the fuck!" Davies agreed, pulling out the plastic soap container that held his bar of Dial. "Bring it on!"

"Hey, it's not *that* cold," the Kid remarked, having discovered the temperature as he began to lather up.

"Enjoy it now," a faceless voice echoed. "There ain't no showers in the foxhole you'll soon be sitting in out in the boonies!"

As they walked back to Delta 6, it was getting lighter out. More soldiers were beginning to move around. The humid air felt thick in his lungs as the Kid recalled how dry the climate was in Colorado, also remembering that he had not been at all pleased with the humidity levels in Tennessee. This was easily twice as bad. He hadn't been in Vietnam for even a day, and already he hated the air. Not that he wanted to quit breathing it; that would be a bad thing. But the reality of having his whole year yet still in front of him was a total morale crusher.

The Kid, Viator, Davies, Erio, and Imbach were more than halfway through breakfast when Waterhouse and Titley finally showed up and set their trays down on table.

"Gentlemen!" Waterhouse intoned in his Texas drawl. "I have it on good authority that there is in all likelihood no way any of us will get out of here until tomorrow."

"What authority is that?" Imbach questioned.

"On the authority of some guys in Charlie Three. They said nobody gets out of here in less than a day, and in some cases, you can be here for a week or more."

"Is this a bad thing?" Viator asked.

"Could be. They said there's some gnarly casual duty that you can get stuck with."

"Like what?" Davies had finished his breakfast and was lighting up.

"Burning shit." "What?"

"Burning shit. They say that about forty guys a day get stuck on shit-burning detail because there aren't any sewers in this place."

"I don't even want to *think* about it." The Kid gasped.

"Hey, Price, did you find out where to mail letters yet?" Davies asked.

"Yeah, over at the PX, which is just behind this here mess hall."

"I got a letter to send to Flo that I wrote on the plane. I wonder how long it'll be before we have an address where we can get some mail back."

"Who the fuck could possibly know?" Waterhouse said between bites. "All I know is, after flying across the Pacific, I'd rather be here than sitting on Johnson Island, like Wilson!"

"You really think so?" Davies questioned. "I'd take the island. Bored to death as opposed to shot to death. Now wouldn't that be some kind of deal for Monty Hall to have behind door number three?"

"Hey, I saw this really great flick before I left Colorado!" the Kid cut in, changing the subject. "It's called *2001: A Space Odyssey,* by Stanley Kubrick."

"Oh yeah, I saw some ads for it," Imbach commented.

"It starts out with these monkeys seeing this black blocky kind of monolith thing, and they figure out how to make a club out of some animal's leg bone. Then one monkey kills another monkey and throws the bone up into the air, and it turns into a spaceship! It's just fuckin' cool beyond anything you could ever see! Then they take a spaceship to Jupiter, and a computer named Hal kicks them out of the spaceship! It's just plain major-league bitchin'."

"Did any of you see *Bonnie and Clyde?*" Viator asked the table.

"Oh yes, Nick, John, and I saw it in Manhattan while we were at Fort Riley! Was that wild or what?" the Kid said. "Gee, I wonder how Nick is doing? That was pretty strange what happened."

What happened was, when they had all checked in at the Oakland Army Terminal, Nicolas Hoogs, who happened to live in Oakland, told his DINFOS classmates that he was going to refuse to get on the plane to Vietnam. Nick had picked the Kid up at the San Francisco airport when he flew in from San Diego and took him over to his family's house before they were due to check in later that day. On the way out to the house, Nick had started telling the Kid that he'd been thinking about the war and how right or not right it was. He also said that he was seriously thinking about going CO, conscientious objector. None of them thought he'd really do it. Going CO before being in the army was one thing, but after going through basic and advanced training and turning CO only when you got orders to 'Nam was another. Hard to imagine what the army would do with him for refusing orders.

Nick had graduated number one in their class, and because of this, he'd been promoted to the rank of specialist E-5 out of DINFOS.

"He's probably in the stockade," Waterhouse mused as he shoved back his tray and lit up. "Bet you money he's not an E-5 anymore."

"I wonder if we'll ever find out." Viator sipped his coffee.

37

They all rose in unison and took their trays to the return window. Scraping their garbage into a can, they threw their silverware into the soaking tub and walked out the door, where they found themselves facing the quad where the formation was to take place in about five minutes. They all lit up except Imbach.

"Jeez, you guys, don't you know how bad for your health that is? I keep trying to tell you, but does anybody listen? No."

"Imbach, for Christ's sake, stop it," Davies said. "We are at war. Why not smoke?"

"Yeah, why not?" The Kid picked up the refrain. "Especially if we can find a little of the right stuff!"

"I do not plan on shortening my life span be doing something so obviously stupid. Stupid, stupid, stupid! Not to mention, you guys are going to smoke yourselves right into the stockade!" *Pope* Imbach had spoken.

"Doubt it." The Kid was cocky.

"Hey, it's the Long Binh Jail. LBJ, right? So it must be somewhere around here." Erio started looking around as if he was going to see it.

"LBJ should fucking go to LBJ," Titley remarked.

"Ooh, that's the commander in chief you're talking about," Price cautioned.

"Not for long," Davies said, reminding everyone that LBJ had stated he would not seek or accept his party's nomination for another term.

"Who do you think we'll get? Bobby Kennedy is killing them in the primaries now," Tom mused. "If he wins in California next week, he'll get the nomination for sure!"

"Hubert Horatio Humphrey. Bet on it." Waterhouse was resolute. "Who are you voting for, Imbach, Harold Stassen?"

"Harold Stassen would be OK. But not better than Nixon." Imbach was such a Republican.

"If RFK gets it, Nixon can lose to another Kennedy." Erio chuckled.

As the DINFOS men were standing there in the humid morning air, the odor of a foreign land hung heavy in their nostrils as they watched the first sergeant emerge from a staff building, march resolutely to the platform, and in crisp military fashion, climb the five steps to the microphone. Once he clicked the microphone on, the loudspeakers on posts at the front corners of the quad screeched with feedback and made popping noises.

"Ten-hut! Fall in! Dress down the rows on the men up front and then to the right! Come on, ladies, we are fighting a war here, and we do not have all fucking day!"

"Undress … right … day … fucking," the Kid joked in a military tone of voice, drawing smirks from his buddies, who had come to expect it.

"Parade ressstttt. OK, men, if I call out your name and serial number, you fall out and report to the orderly room. Line up and we'll give you your orders to your new units, tell you when your ride is coming to get you, and tell you where to sign out. OK, the following men are assigned to the Twenty-Fourth Light Infantry Brigade."

Then, with the sun approaching the eastern horizon, the sergeant commenced to read names, followed by serial numbers. "Hampton, Charles J., US 234-65-419. Ossenbacher, Dale P., US 445-67-873 …"

Moans rose from the men whose names were called. When they fell out, they walked ploddingly forward toward the orderly room with the resignation of British sailors on their way to a flogging. Infantry. The Twenty-Fourth. Tropic Lightning was their nickname, taken from the unit insignia, a lightning bolt on a red leaf. This was not necessarily a death sentence, but it was close. The proceedings reminded the Kid of that short story by Willa Cather "The Lottery," where this town in the Midwest had a lottery every year to pick somebody to kill for some vague reason. *Couldn't have been any more like this,* he thought. *Only a lot more than one of the people standing here will be killed. For sure.*

After about thirty names had been called for Tropic Lightning, there was a pause. "OK. Now the next names to be called are assigned to the Seventh Air Cavalry. Hodges, Harlen B., 756-94-216. Blair, Willie C., 454-98-098."

The Seventh Air Cavalry was George Custer's old unit sans air. These were the men riding choppers into hot LZs (short for landing zones) where the Cong were already shooting at them before they stepped out into the jungle. This was very close to a death sentence. Nearly fifty names were called.

"OK, men, the next group are assigned to the First Infantry Division, the Big Red One! You guys should be proud! Castenades, Manuel R., 357-98-735. White, Ronald G., 343-75-153. Yamamoto, Yamuri K …"

"What do you suppose the K stands for, *kamikaze?*" The kid joked out of the corner of his mouth, causing laughter in his vicinity, which unfortunately was near enough to the front of the formation that the sergeant picked up on it and shot them a nasty look.

When the sergeant finished with the Big Red One cannon fodder, he looked up and scanned the formation. "Orders have also been cut for the following individuals." He proceeded to read an additional fifty names, with no mention of what units they'd been assigned to. "That's all the orders we have for now. The rest of you stand by to get your casual-duty work assignments, and anybody not assigned to a detail is free until the thirteen-hundred-hours formation. First assignment, I want these four rows to my immediate right, from the front to ten back, to fall out and join Specialist Perkins over at those trucks." He gestured to four deuce-and-a-half trucks that had pulled up to the side of the parade grounds while assignments were being handed out. The forty men singled out for the trucks included all the DINFOS boys. "We'll see how much you guys are laughing at the afternoon formation." The sergeant grinned from ear to ear.

"Thanks a lot, Kid." Waterhouse scoffed. "I bet you've gotten us a punishment detail."

"Price, the whole fucking year is a punishment detail! What else can they possibly do to us? We are in *'Nam*, fuckhead."

As the group reached the trucks, they all found out what else their superiors could do to them.

"Good morning, gentlemen," Specialist 4 Perkins greeted them. "Climb on board. And no smoking. We've got gas cans in the trucks."

"Oh fuck!" Davies exclaimed. "Is this the shit-burning detail?"

"Yes it is! You gentlemen are the winners of today's prize plum, the PPP, the pyro pooh patrol!"

"You fucker, Kid, you did this to us!" Erio scoffed.

"Hey, you laughed. Who's to say this wouldn't have happened anyway?" The Kid defended himself as the men scrambled up the tailgate end of the deuce-and-a- halfs and found places to sit. As soon as they were settled, all four drivers took off in different directions.

The sun was now just peeking over the edge of their new world as their truck pulled up at the back of the first latrine on the day's schedule.

"Next to picking up butts, this is the easiest detail on the post." Perkins sat in his driver's seat, but he was half turned to address his workmen. "All you do is go over to the trapdoor, pull out the shit barrels, and slide them up here. A couple of you stay in the truck to move them to the back as we load."

Along the back of the latrine there were little trapdoors with handles spaced out identically to the shitters inside—about a ten-seater.

"When I saw the handles on these things last night, I got the worst fucking feeling. And now I know why." Davies moaned as he pulled the cut barrel drum from its porthole, where the Kid grabbed the other handle. They tried not to look at it, but it was unavoidable. The variety of the colors of shit was incredible, as were the consistencies. The only constant was the gas chamber lethal smell they got when the drum came up past their faces as they lifted it and pushed it onto the bed of the truck.

"This blows fucking chunks!" Cuzzo raged as he pulled the barrel toward the front of the truck. "I move blanket party for the Kid!"

"Second the motion!" Davies legislated.

"Yeah, yeah, ooh, ooh, ooh, blan-ket, blan-ket!" His DINFOS buddies got in the spirit, suggesting the time-honored military punishment for a member of an outfit whose actions had brought grief to the whole unit. The offender was beaten silly with bars of soap in socks while he was held beneath a blanket, which practice inflicted great pain but left no bruises.

"Oh yeah, I'm scared to fuckin' death. Like any of you even own a bar of soap!" the Kid shot back.

"Let's just push his *face* into one of these barrels," Waterhouse said, escalating the rhetoric.

Once they had removed all the half barrels of shit and urine from the latrine and pushed them onto the truck, the men climbed back on and looked for some way to sit that might grant them relief from the sight and odor of their cargo. They all ended up perched on the edge of the truck bed with a foot on either side of a shit container.

"Imagine if this truck got hit by a mortar. What a shitty way to go!" Price joked.

The ride to scene of the crappy crematorium took about five minute. Two of the other trucks were already there when the DINFOS boys pulled up to their unloading spot.

"OK, men, do your thing," Perkins said. He climbed down and walked far enough away from the gas and shit to comfortably light a cigarette. "Just pull 'em off, and dump 'em starting back there," he hollered, gesturing with his cigarette. "And some of you pour some gas on it. Soak it real good, and then stand back while one of you throws a match on it."

"This would be a perfect detail for fudge packers," a nameless GI from the next truck over loudly proclaimed.

The sun had now cleared the horizon, causing the tropical heat wave to commence. The men worked in pairs, pulling the barrels off the truck and walking them over to the dump point.

41

"Ew! Fuck me! Fuck me! Fuck me! It just splashed on my pants!" Titley screamed. "Oh my God! I'm hit! *Medic!*"

"Just stick your leg in there and burn it off when they torch the pile," the Kid suggested.

As the barrels were being dumped, Imbach and Davies each took a jerrican and dumped gas over the growing pile, making sure to get some on all of it. With the application of the last can of gasoline, Cuzzo jumped down off the truck and got out a book of matches.

"Step back, boys. Fire in the asshole!" In one motion, he struck the match and flicked it at the putrid pile, which ignited like a charcoal grill at a giant Jaycee Club picnic: Bouff! The two piles from the other truck were already in flames. The smell would remain, unfortunately, memorable for the rest of their lives.

They all stood back and lit up, except for Imbach.

The Kid appeared hypnotized by the fire. "If anybody ever says to me again,

'Let's go smoke some shit,' I will kill them!"

"Hurry up and finish those butts, men," Perkins hollered. "We've got another three latrines to cover before noon."

As the sun got higher, the sweat rolled off their bodies from pores they didn't know they had as they humped barrel after barrel, working their way through load after load at latrine after latrine.

"Man oh man!" exclaimed Imbach on the final load, where the barrels had proved to be much fuller than those from earlier latrines. "We're in some deep shit now!"

The group howled. It was so un-Imbach, who prided himself on not swearing, never using the *fuck* word, and never even saying *shit* when he was talking about shit. He normally used the word *poop*, as in "I gotta take a poop" or "I could have just pooped" and "We're in a world of poop." He once called the Kid a *poophead* in a fit of deep anger.

The Kid rode along, cursing the absence of his vaunted luck today. *How did I come to be here burning shit in the tropical fucking war zone? Flo, Flo, Flo, Flo.* He tried to concentrate on his lover as the truck bounced along the dirt road, causing the ultrafull barrels of shit and urine slop to undulate unpredictably and occasionally splash over the top.

"I'm gonna burn these fucking fatigues," Waterhouse exclaimed as the slop nailed his leg.

"No, let's mail them to somebody we hate, like Sergeant Major Blowhole back at DINFOS!" Davies brightly proposed a plan of action.

"Oh, great idea!" Titley enthusiastically agreed.

"Better yet, why don't we just mail him a bag of shit?" Cuzzo suggested. "Did any of you guys ever do the flaming bag of dog shit on somebody's porch before?"

"Yeah, I did once," Smith said, "but after today, I don't think I'll ever play with shit again in my whole life. I may not even wipe. If I could find a way not to shit anymore, I'd do it."

"Wasn't that your problem on the jet, Kid?" Waterhouse grinned.

"Yes. Was. But not anymore. My shit is on fire right now."

"Well, that's different. Usually, it's only your asshole that's on fire!" Davies cracked.

As the truck pulled up at the burning piles, columns of smoke hung in the highly humidified air. While they pulled the last of their cargo off the fecal express, a breeze was starting to pick up and dissipate the noxious fumes into the Long Binh complex. The sun was nearing its apex, and in the heat of Vietnam, this was exhausting work. All the men knew that this was just a preview of things to come.

"This is the last load, gents," Perkins called out. "Hurry up, so we aren't late for lunch."

"Fuck lunch. I'm back in the shower before I do anything!" Waterhouse exclaimed.

"Oh God, I hope we get our orders at the noon formation," Davies said, speaking the wish that was on everyone's mind. "If I have to do this again, I think I'll just shoot myself!"

"One thing I know, I ain't standing anywhere near the Kid at tomorrow morning's formation," Imbach said with a tone of certainty.

"Come on, guys," the Kid pleaded as they hopped off the end of the truck. "Tell you what, I'm feeling generous. I'll buy the first round, OK?"

"First three rounds," Waterhouse corrected him. "You won a jackpot, and you've got bucks. Fuck, it's only fifty cents a beer. You *owe* us, Kid!"

Removing his completely soaked baseball cap from his head and wiping his wet brow, the Kid said, "Two beers is my final offer. Take it or leave it."

"Fuck the brew, you owe me a joint." Davies changed the coin of the realm.

"And where do you suggest that we would smoke such a thing, assuming I had one?"

"Why, hell, you could smoke it here. I'll bet nobody hangs out here later in the day." Price wiped the sweat from his brow.

"I wouldn't come back here if Jane Fonda herself was parading around this fire buck fucking naked!" Erio declared.

"I would—with a gas mask," Cuzzo immediately shot back.

Perkins blew the horn. "Come on, gents, let's get the lead out. Chow time!"

They slid the last can back on the truck and clambered aboard. Perkins took off like a stock car racer at the drop of the green flag and was shortly back at the last latrine where they had to reinstall the barrels.

"Well, look at this," Price said as he lifted up one of the trapdoors. "Can you believe some dumbass took a shit without the barrel?"

Chapter 4

When the assignment formation was called to attention on their second day in- country, the DINFOS boys were strung out along the very back. Being a bunch of quick learners, they weren't going to make the same mistake twice.

"I'm warning you, Kid, keep your fuckin' mouth shut!" Waterhouse said out of the side of his mouth.

"Don't worry, Price, I don't think I could take two days of that shit!"

The sergeant began reading the day's orders. "OK, men, the following troops are assigned to the Ninth Infantry Division in My Tho: Parker, Charles J., 111-23-764. Jones, Willie M., 342-68-486. Joshkavoicks, or Hoskhafoviks, Votech P., 233-54- 979." He looked up. "Was I even close?"

"No, Sergeant," a voice boomed from the other side of the formation, "but you got the serial number right!"

The sergeant continued on for almost fifty names, and then it happened: "Waterhouse, David E., 233-45-987. Imbach, John III, 655-78-398. That's it for the Ninth."

"Infantry?" Price grimaced. "Not the fucking *infantry*!"

"And you get to go with Imbach!" The Kid laughed, but not too loud, as Waterhouse and Imbach broke formation. "You and Baby Huey. What a bonus!"

Price turned. "Fuck you, Kid. *Just plain fuck you!*" he hollered back at him. "At least we're outta here!"

After the big unit allocations, the sergeant again got into the list of names paired with different units. Just as the remaining DINFOS boys thought it was going to be another day of casual duty and another night at Long Binh, the sergeant said, "And last for this formation, the Fourth Psyop Group in Saigon: Davies, Thomas, 234-97-066; Titley, George C., 544-00-756; Erio, Peter B., 134-54-455; Viator, Albert, 227-64-288; and Stocker, Curtis L., 129-66-317. Gentlemen, that is all.

Company, ten-hut! Dismissed!"

The Kid's was the last name called. *A twinge of excitement!*

Back at the barracks, amid the hurried little bit of packing he had to do, the Kid sat down on his bunk and scribbled a quick note to Flo.

Dearest Parnelli,

It looks like the luck is holding! I just got orders for Saigon! We're driving down there this afternoon, and by tonight, I should have an address

where you can write to me. I can't wait to get a letter from you, since that's all I can have for right now. Saigon could be a really good deal. I can at least go by AFRN and see what it will take to get assigned there. Waterhouse is getting sent to the Ninth Infantry Division in a place called My Tho. And get this, Imbach is going with him! Ha-ha-ha! Davies, Erio, Titley, and Viator are going with me.

I'll write more tonight when we get there!

All my love,

Curt

PS: I'll see you later!

After stuffing the sheet into an envelope, the Kid sealed it, addressed it, and scooped up his gear. "Ready?" he called to his mates. Together, the four of them shouldered their bags and headed out the door to meet their transportation.

The sun was fully up when, after dropping Flo's letter off at the mail slot, the Kid arrived at the departure shed. Among the fifty-odd soldiers going to the Ninth, he found Waterhouse and Imbach still there, along with the rest of the DINFOS boys, even those who hadn't yet been assigned. It was kind of like a class reunion, but instead of the first time, it felt more like the last time.

"We're public information specialists with the Ninth." Waterhouse showed the psyops guys his orders. "Fuck me. Infantry. In the Mekong Delta."

"Maybe they have a unit newspaper and we'll at least get to write some stories." Imbach smiled, always one to look at the bright side.

"Most likely, we'll spend our time writing news releases about PFC Billy Joe Blow Job being a member of the Sixth Battalion," Waterhouse said, lamenting. "I can't believe I took an extra year for this!"

"Well, we got psyops all right, but the sergeant said we were all going to Saigon!" The Kid smiled.

"You're a lucky fuck, Kid, I'll give you that." Price lit a new cigarette. "But we're going to be first to ride in a chopper! The clerk said we'd be going down by chopper convoy."

"I can't wait!" Imbach seemed excited. "A chopper ride!"

Also there waiting with them were Peter Cuzzo and Ken Smith, both still unassigned. That meant they still had an outside chance that if, for some stupid reason, a slot at Armed Forces Radio opened up, their numbers could come up in the computer.

"Well," Cuzzo said to the Kid, "is your plan still to stay stoned the entire year?" "After giving it some additional thought, I'd say, yes, it still is."

"Are you stoned now, you rat?" Peter C. inquired.

"Only on life. But I tell you, the adrenalin rush of sitting here waiting for a truck to drive us into Saigon has definitely got my attention."

"Roger that attention thing." Waterhouse nervously lit up. "Nervous is just getting assigned to an infantry unit!"

"Come on, Dave, it won't be so bad." Imbach pal-punched him in the arm. "At least we'll be together!" The whole group fell down laughing. *Where did Imbach get this delivery all of a sudden?* "Weren't you just telling the Kid yesterday that I'd be a good shield against a mortar attack?"

"Yeah, Imbach," the Kid cut in, "I'm sure it'll be just like the field problem we did back at Fort Riley. Oh, by the way, you remember after the field problem, you wondered how I spotlessly cleaned my weapon so quick. You know where we went out and you had all that fun shooting off all that blank ammunition? And I said I'd tell you someday?"

"Yeah, I remember that. You even gave me some of your blanks to shoot!"

"Correction: I gave you all of mine and never fired a shot on that whole field problem, so there was nothing to clean. You know how dirty that blank ammo can make your piece!"

Imbach stared at him. "Kid, you're just too clever for your own good. You went and missed all that good training on how to clean your weapon. Now, what if the VC come rushing at your speaker team and your weapon is dirty and jams? Then what are you going to do?"

"Probably shit my fucking green boxer shorts, or, no, *poop* my boxers is how you say."

"I tell you one thing: I'd much rather be leaving on a chopper than driving down the highway to Saigon. Think about all the land mines and truck bombings they've shown on the news for the past three years." Flyboy was getting serious on them. "You can't flip a hand grenade into a chopper when it's up three thousand feet."

The gloomy group of soldiers sat there in the shade of the departure shed, feeling the heat of the day rising and sweat beads forming on their foreheads as they each silently contemplated their respective lots in life. They had been together in the same unit for most of seven months, and now some of them were leaving for what was certainly going to be dangerous duty. Not that it wasn't possible for a rocket to slam into the hut right where they sat that second, but the thought that this might be the last time some of them would see each other lay at the core of their muted feelings.

"Well. Fuck, you never know when you time is up," the Kid philosophized. "*But* we all just gotta think that a year from now, it'll be us crying and hugging and smoking big cigars when we get back on that jet to go home."

"Ah yes, the power of positive thinking." Waterhouse took the cigarette butt he was finishing and flipped it out into the quad. "At least I won't be the dumb fuck who picks that up tomorrow. That's what I'm thinkin' anyway."

"Hey, Kid," Cuzzo spoke up, "if you stay stoned for the whole year, you won't be able to *find* your way back here with a Seeing Eye dog."

"Bets. A year from now, I'm here and I'm goin' home. That's the only way I can think about it."

"Yeah, me too!" Titley said.

"Ditto," Erio responded.

"Your logic is screwed up, Kid," Imbach interjected. "You prefaced that remark with 'You never know when your time is up.'"

"Out of context!" the Kid shot back. He hadn't spent three years on the Boulder High School debate team for nothing. "You took it out of context. I said, you never know when your time is up, *but.* You left off the *but*, Imbach. Error. In fact, you flunk."

"The Lord knows when your time is up." Imbach went seriously pious.

As they sat there, a group of about a dozen GIs came by on police call. They spread out in a line and began picking up trash. One of them bent over and picked up Price's freshly tossed butt. It was still smoking. He held it up as he turned and shot a dirty glance at the group of soldiers from which it must have come.

"Go ahead, you can finish it." Waterhouse grinned.

The PFC shook his head, twisted out the ember, and went on with the group.

Small talk continued for another five minutes before a pair of deuce-and-a-halfs rolled to a stop by the hut.

"Ninth Division, let's get the lead out. Choppers are waiting!" the lead driver called.

As the new members of the Ninth picked up their gear and started loading up, the Kid and Price looked at each other through their sunglasses.

"Well, this is it. Good luck, Kid, not that you need it." They shook hands.

"We'll always have the Cream at Butler," the Kid said, reminding Price of the concert where they saw Eric Clapton and Cream in Indianapolis. "Here." The Kid reached into his shirt, pulled out the chain upon which his lucky Canadian beaver nickel resided, and rubbed it on Waterhouse's shoulder. "Luck for you. Imbach?" He gestured to indicate that he would rub some of the vaunted luck onto him as well.

"Kid." Imbach shrugged. "If you really want to do me a favor, why don't you just take my file and say you're me and get on the chopper with Waterhouse? I'll say I'm you and go to Saigon. It could work. Nobody where we're going has ever seen either one of us. Then you and Waterhouse can be together."

The Kid gave him a straight-faced look. "Imbach, there is not enough real or fake military money in the whole world to pay me to be you." He extended his hand. "But good luck, John."

"Thanks, Kid."

Once the trucks were loaded with their human cargo, the lead driver called out,

"Everybody set?" and gunned it. Off went Waterhouse and Imbach to the war.

The Kid checked his watch: 0730 hours. *The temperature must already be ninety-nine degrees.*

"I'm sure as fuck glad I'm not going to the Ninth Infantry Division," Cuzzo exclaimed. "I don't know where I am going yet, but I just get the feeling I'm glad it's not there."

49

Reddish dust from the departure of the trucks swirled around in the hot and humid morning air as silence again settled on the group now diminished in size. The GIs engaged in more cigarette smoking, like a bunch of guys waiting for the firing squad to show up. Different groups of GIs walked past the assignment shack, going this way and that. Then, the Kid looked out over the ground about fifteen feet away from the hut and spied a plastic bag lying in the dirt. Clearly, the bag hadn't been there when the police call came through. Walking over to it, he looked down and saw, much to his surprise, it was a sandwich baggie half full of marijuana! There it lay, partially open, an inviting little bundle of brownish resinous-looking buds that apparently had fallen from somebody's pocket as they passed by.

Slowly, the Kid walked back and sat down. "I don't fucking believe it. Look at that, a lid lying right in the middle of the quad."

"Where?" Cuzzo jumped up.

The Kid pointed and, with a condescending expression on his face, said, "It looks like a trap to me. As much as I'd love to pick it up and put it in my pocket, I'm sure that as I did so, some sergeant would be watching and waiting to bust the ass of the first GI who touched it."

"You think?" Peter C. asked. Then, trying to look casual, he walked over, kind of circling the pot and coming back. "Fuck, Kid, you could be right. It's so obvious, it could easily be a setup. But what if it's not? There's free Vietnamese grass, and we're leaving it on the street."

"Why don't you pick it up and walk toward the trash can? If they come to bust you, you can claim you were going to throw it away." Ken laid out his plan. "Then, if by the time you get to the trash can they haven't jumped out and busted you, you could slip it into your pocket."

"If that is such a good plan, why don't you do it, Smith?" the Kid suggested.

There was silence as Ken pondered the idea. Then he deliberately walked over to the pot, kind of kicked it with his boot, and started to bend and extend his hand, but then he straightened up, did an about-face, and returned to the hut without picking it up. "You're right, it must be a trap!"

They sat there and watched the bag resting on the ground, looking around to see if they could spot someone who might be keeping an eye on the bait, waiting to spring their trap.

A pair of GIs strolled by about five feet from the marijuana and paid it no attention. Another group of five walked by even closer, but they were engaged in conversation and didn't see it.

"Hmm, I think I'm going to try to get it," the Kid said. "What I need is a diversion. Anybody?"

As the DINFOS contingent exchanged glances, waiting for somebody to volunteer to become the Kid's coconspirator, another deuce-and-a-half pulled up, driving right over the baggie and stopping. There was a decal logo on the door of the truck: a flying bee carrying a bag and wearing a helmet and goggles, with L3 leaflets trailing behind with the written line, "Litterbugs."

"Yo! Which of you five guys are headed for the Fourth Psyop Group in Saigon?" the driver called out. His rank insignia showed he was a sergeant, E-5. Hatless and sleeveless under a flak jacket, he had black hair long enough to comb. Even from behind his sunglasses, he had an impatient air about him. "Come on, fuckers, let's get the lead out!"

"Moot point now." The Kid frowned. "Peter, use the truck as a diversion, then run out there and grab the baggie after we pull out!"

"Oh, sure, after you convince me it's a trap, right? Fat fucking chance!"

There was one GI already sitting in the back of truck, wearing a jungle hat with a white towel draped around his neck, a cigarette hanging from his lips, and a bandolier of M16 ammo slung over his left shoulder.

"Well, Pete, hope you get the AFVN thing we all missed, you dog." The Kid shook his hand. He was referring to the American Forces Vietnam Network.

"If I do, I'll play you something by the 1910 Fruitgum Company, you simple Simon." Pete turned to Davies. "Tom, your turn to watch the Kid, OK?"

"OK, I won't let him get any of us into any more trouble than we are already in." "Pete." Cuzzo turned to Erio. "Good luck. Stay low!"

"Yeah, thanks, Pete. You can bet your sweet ass I'll be the lowest mutha in the field!"

The five men waved to their comrades as the truck lurched into motion. The Kid, sitting at the end by the tailgate, looked down to see what condition the bag of pot was in as the truck cleared the spot where it had been. The driver ran right over it! The Kid dipped his arm and pretended that he was picking it up, then he pointed to Cuzzo, who was approaching it with his hands in his pockets, pretending to whistle. As the truck went around the corner and out of the quad, the Kid saw Peter pick up the baggie. He checked his watch: *Zero eight thirty hours, leaving for the front.*

He thought about his fellow DJ and friend from WKDA back in the States, Dave Allen. When Dave found out the Kid had been drafted, he said, "Oh, be sure to get a place up front, next to the cannons, so you can see what

51

the fuck is going on!" So every time the Kid wrote to Dave and his wife, Patsy, he always included a line about cannons: "closer to the cannon"; "flew over some cannons"; "got someone to polish my cannon." But now, he was absolutely on his way up next to the cannons.

"So." The Kid turned to the man with the M16 and the bandolier of ammo slung over his shoulder. He said over the mechanical noise of the deuce-and-a-half, "You riding shotgun?"

"Yeah, literally!" The specialist 4 chuckled.

"Then why aren't you sitting up in the passenger's seat?" The Kid thought for sure that his joke was funny, but the guy didn't laugh.

"Stocker, that your name?" he inquired.

"Yes."

"Stocker, if the truck hit a land mine, the front would blow up first. So, if you ride way in the back, you got the best chance of surviving that shit. Then, while I'm sitting here, I can best guard the back of the truck. If we are all looking forward, some gook kid can come up and flip a grenade in here, then we are all home in a box next week."

"OK. Glad I asked." The Kid shuddered as the true magnitude of what was going on around him began to sink in.

"Guys," the specialist 4, whose name tag said "Bennett," called out to the five newbies, "listen up. We shouldn't have any trouble between here and Saigon, but the fact of the matter is, anytime you are outside of the compound in this country, you're a candidate for a body bag. So, in the event of an attack, like by a sniper, I highly recommend you just lie flat in the bed of the truck. There's not much else you can do."

Now he had their undivided attention.

"If we should get disabled and the truck is stopped, we will get out of the truck and find the best cover that is available. If we are somehow involved, the truck could be the target of an RPG [rocket-propelled grenade], so I highly recommend you get away from it. And since Patrick and I have the only weapons, we will seek cover. You'd better fuckin' damn well be with us, got it?"

The GIs nodded and exchanged worried glances as the truck rolled past the road that led to the site of yesterday's flaming shit inferno. They rode past the road back to the air strip, and soon they passed the defensive berm line, arriving at the front gate to the Long Binh complex, which was flanked by big pillbox bunkers with machine guns sticking out the ports. There were a half dozen MPs eyeballing everything coming into the base, with a line of jeeps and small trucks backed up about six deep. On the going-out side, there were just two MPs, who waved the truck on through.

Reaching the end of the entrance drive, the truck took a right and gained speed as it traversed the area where there were no houses or Vietnamese businesses. After about two hundred meters, the road was suddenly lined with Vietnamese houses and shops.

Swarms of motor scooters flew by the truck in both directions, carrying Vietnamese to and fro, some of them in the uniform of the South Vietnamese army, and others dressed in civilian clothing. Stop-and-go herky-jerky driving was the rule since the driver couldn't get the vehicle out of second gear and lots of times had to drop down to first.

"Any one of those fucks could flip a grenade in here any second," Bennett, leaning over, hollered to the newbies while pointing to the driver of a Honda motor scooter with a passenger riding on the back. A motor scooter apparently passed for a family car in Vietnam. *There's one with a couple and their three kids,* the Kid noted. The dad had two kids on the gas tank in front of him, and a little girl was wedged between them.

The women walking on the slightly elevated sidewalks were mostly wearing white ankle-length dresses that were split up both sides, revealing black or white silky- looking pants underneath. *Hmm.*

"They call that kind of dress an *áo dài,*" Bennett called out, having noticed the Kid's eyes following an especially good-looking woman as the truck rolled past. "The women here are fucking dynamite! You can get an incredible piece of ass for ten dollars just about anywhere in Saigon!"

Yes, the Kid thought, *they are good-looking, and they've all got long black hair, like Flo!* He thought of how much he loved Flo, and in the next second, his twenty-year-old's hormones couldn't help but lead him to think how much fun it would be to do a really hot Vietnamese hooker. He'd never before paid for sex in his life. Yet. *This is a war zone,* he rationalized.

As they entered the city of Binh Hoa proper, the traffic got thicker. Now the streets were filled with all kinds of transportation, some larger trucks, both military and civilian, and jeeps loaded with GIs, both American and Vietnamese. The road was divided by a row of motor scooters parked down the center. Local transportation appeared to be in the form of buggies hooked to the backs of motor scooters, but some rigs that had a carrier in front and a man on a bicycle pedaling in the back were also making their way next to the motorized vehicles.

Then the Kid noticed some really small taxicabs, not all that much bigger than the cars found on the Autobahn ride at Disneyland, only these looked like little station wagons. *Fuck, you could get crushed in one of those,* the Kid pondered, glad he was up high in the deuce-and-a-half.

Wow! Look at that old black Mercedes-Benz full of Buddhist monks! That's something you don't see in Indianapolis.

The tropical sun beat down relentlessly on the passengers as the truck inched through Bien Hoa. Most of the buildings were two-story-tall storefronts, open to access from the front with steel grates rolled up above the entryways. Quite frequently the storefronts were accented by rows of bullet holes. In other places, sections of the sidewalk had apparently been blow up. Possibly at Tet.

The Kid spied a group of four policemen standing on the corner of an intersection, sporting sidearms and wearing white shirts and mirrored sunglasses like the boss man in the movie *Cool Hand Luke.*

"That's the White Mice." Bennett followed his gaze. "The national police. They'll shake your ass down quicker than salt and pepper will fall onto fried eggs, if they ever get a chance."

A noticeable number of men were walking on crutches, and there were amputees sitting on chairs in front of many of the shops and stores.

"As soon as you lose a limb, you don't have to be in the army anymore," Bennett commented. The truck had stopped momentarily in front of a collection of three men, each with a different length of stump. "Hard to believe they're some of the lucky ones!"

Another US military truck passed them in the opposite direction, pulling a 155- millimeter artillery piece behind it. *Look! Dave's cannon.* The Kid snapped a picture with his tiny Instamatic. The truck was followed by a jeep with a machine gun mounted on a tripod in the back, manned by a GI wearing a steel pot and smoking a butt as he braced himself against the handles of the black M60.

As the GIs' truck cleared the city proper, the buildings were now spaced farther apart, but traffic on the road to Saigon remained intensely heavy. More old black Mercedes-Benzes dotted the flow. *They must be another legacy of the French colonial occupation.* These Benzes were filled with Vietnamese men and women dressed in military and civilian clothes, along with a couple of shaved-headed Vietnamese Buddhist monks. *Must be a convention in town.*

Being a Buddhist himself, the Kid's eye was drawn to the monks. *Ho, there goes a monk in sunglasses on a Honda.* The Kid watched him pass, saffron robes flapping in the wind. *I wonder how it is a monk has a motor scooter?*

The truck passed by a very large-walled compound with a huge building in the center that towered up three stories. On the balcony in front of the second floor were about twenty more Buddhist monks, kind of standing against the rail, watching the flow of traffic go by.

"See that compound?" Bennett said to the Kid. "The army is sure that every single one of those monks is a VC, but the military can't go and burn down all the pagodas and monasteries in the country or the whole place would come unglued."

As the Kid pondered this new fact, one of the monks on the balcony waved at the truck. Impulsively, the Kid waved back.

Finally out in the countryside, the truck was able to pick up more speed, creating a little bit of a breeze for the passengers, but the road was still packed with traffic going both ways. There was also another lane of traffic—soldiers walking and pushing carts along the side of the road as jeeps, other trucks, and those black Mercedeses all jockeyed for position.

"Are we there yet?" the Kid asked Bennett after looking at his watch. It was 0930 hours. They had been on the road for an hour.

"Well, it's another twenty miles to the edge of Saigon, and then we gotta cross town and go almost clear to the other side, but at least it won't be at rush hour. Oh, wait a minute, every hour is rush hour in Saigon. So, say miles don't matter time-wise; we are like as much as two hours from HQ, an hour and a half if we get lucky. Hey, I brought you guys a canteen. You'd better drink some, all of you." He pulled the canteen out of his kit and handed it to the Kid. "You can get dehydrated here so quick that it'll kill ya!"

The Kid took a swig and passed the canteen to Erio. It was fucking scorching out. *Gotta be like this in hell. Wait a minute, I'm a Buddhist, so there is no hell except for the suffering here on earth.* And suffering he was. He was only four days into his tour, so it was still as good as a year that he had left. All the new smells and the sheer foreignness of the Vietnamese roadway were both certainly capturing his attention. Every so often, a daredevil motor scooter rider would come flying up the middle of the road, defying convention and logic, but going like a bat out of hell, splitting the difference between the northbound traffic and the southbound traffic.

A wall of palm trees sat back from the road about a hundred meters. Thick and inscrutable, the trees wavered in the optical illusion created by the heat as it rose in humid updrafts. *They could be loaded with VC ready to ambush us any second,* the Kid conjectured. Coming to an apparent bottleneck, the truck began to slow. It was a bridge over a river or a canal. The bridge itself was narrower than the road, so even though traffic was flowing both ways, it had slowed to about five miles per hour while crossing the slightly elevated span. Some trucks and buses were wide enough to require one-way traffic as they crossed. The GIs' deuce-and-a-half would be one of those.

As the roadway narrowed, the various trucks, jeeps, motor scooters, and little taxicabs began to merge and get in line to cross over the bridge. One of the old black Mercedeses was trying to push by the psyops truck on the left with not much more than half a foot of clearance.

To everybody's surprise, the driver whipped out his .45 pistol, cocked it, leaned down, literally stuck it in the passenger's window, and screamed, "Just a fuckin' minute, gooks! Ain't no fucking way you are gonna cross this bridge before me, so just back off, or I'll blow your fucking shit away! Do you stupid fucking bastards *bic?*"

The five DINFOS newbies all watch, their mouths agape, looking from each other to the mortified expression on the face of the old Vietnamese man in the passenger's seat, who was nearly cross-eyed as he focused on the barrel of the pistol. His wife or mother was cowering in the back seat as their truck inched forward ahead of the car. As it fell into line behind them, the Kid could clearly see the driver through the cracked windshield, who was wincing as an elderly passenger yelled and raged at him.

"Ain't no fuckin' gook gonna cut in line in front of me!" The driver scoffed, uncocking and holstering his .45.

"Could've just given him the finger." Bennett chuckled.

The truck eased past the sandbag blockhouse and up onto the bridge, giving the Kid a view up the canal. It was straight as an arrow, and the water was a very dark liquid that didn't appear to be flowing anywhere.

A local bus was next, sitting up on the other side of the bridge and waiting for the truck to pass, but a couple of motor scooters, refusing to wait, shot around it with scant clearance. As the truck came down on the far side, the newbies were eye to eye with all the Vietnamese who were riding on top of it, hanging onto plastic mesh bags, gunnysacks, and cardboard boxes wrapped together with twine. One skinny guy had a couple of ducks yoked together, with their feet tied to each end of a stick. He was riding in the Asian squat position. The top of the double-decker was looped by a skinny little metal rail, no more than a foot high, to keep the passengers from falling off when the thing was moving. Judging from the way the Vietnamese were sardine-packed into the bus, the top looked like a pretty good option.

The guard bunker on the south side of the canal seemed to be run by a more casual bunch of sentries than the one on the north. These dudes had hammocks set up under a lean-to they had attached to the side of their bunker.

Two guards were on duty, and two were stripped to their shorts, swinging away, catching some z's in the shade of a tin roof.

Motoring away from the bridge, the deuce-and-a-half could not have been doing more than forty-five miles per hour as the traffic thinned, but it felt like a hundred. The newbies relished the wind in their faces, although it still had a thick and humid heaviness to it.

The truck was out in the open countryside of Vietnam only for about ten minutes before, once again, buildings and businesses lined the roadsides.

"It's like this from here all the way into Saigon," Bennett said, waving his M16 barrel down the row of plaster storefronts. *Lots and lots of bullet holes in these! Looks like they were put there by automatic weapons.* Around one particular doorway, the bullet holes were extremely concentrated; it was hard not to wonder what had happened to invite that massive use of firepower.

There was a shoulder about fifteen feet wide on either side of the highway, jam- packed with scooters, microcabs, and jeeps. "A lot of black market stuff out here, because there aren't any White Mice outside the cities."

So much to learn, the Kid thought. Checking his watch, he saw it was still two hours until noon. Sweat rolled off his body from every pore. Whenever the truck slowed down enough, the newbies would all stick their baseball caps back on their heads for some relief from the sun. Now the Kid understood the functional viability of the conical hats worn by the general public of Vietnam, which were like little beach umbrellas, shading them from the tropical gamma rays.

The acrid smell of diesel fuel hung heavily in the air as the truck pulled ever closer to Saigon. Now, behind the row of buildings that fronted the road, the GIs could see more houses spreading out in a thick Southeast Asian urban sprawl.

When the truck slowed because it had encountered more traffic, the Kid lit up a butt.

"Gee, if we could only brush our teeth." Davies smiled from behind his sunglasses. He too pulled out a butt and lit it using the Kid's.

"Yeah, wouldn't that be nice? I bet they have facilities where we're going that might make it possible to brush our teeth. How much longer?" the Kid asked Bennett.

"God! You must've driven your fucking parents nuts!" he loudly exclaimed. "About another forty-five minutes to an hour. This is the edge of Saigon proper."

Wow! Here it is, Saigon. The frickin' Paris of the Orient! The capital of the rich Catholic Vietnamese who kissed the French's ass for hundreds of years. Going deeper into the city, they discovered streets lined with cement utility poles. In many stretches, there were tall, leafy trees rising up, offering the soldiers some shade.

Traffic steadily became thicker and more congested. Vietnamese civilians and military personnel strolled along the sidewalks. One of the White Mice stood directing traffic in the middle of an intersection, while another pair talked and smoked on the corner of the street. Honda scooters and bicycles buzzed every which direction.

At every other intersection, there was a pillbox bunker with a machine-gun barrel sticking out from a slot in the sandbag facade.

Soon, the streets were a canyon between higher-rising buildings, some as tall as a dozen stories. *Small wonder they call it the Paris of the Orient.* The Kid gazed at the decidedly French architecture, with little wrought iron balconies accenting the plaster walls. He'd never been to Paris, but he had seen pictures. *Hmm, kind of looks like Bourbon Street in New Orleans.* The ground floors of the buildings housed shop after shop, open across the front and from wall to wall, offering the latest in Japanese electronics, hardware, clothing, and bulk foodstuffs, as the great capitalist engine that was South Vietnam garishly displayed itself to the newbies.

A gigantic statue, a monument to the republic's soldiers, sat at the head of a long grassy parklike swath that led up to an official-looking structure at the end of the street. The soldiers depicted on the monument were crouching and apparently shooting off a mortar with determined looks on their faces.

"Looks like they're aiming that thing right at the Vietnamese congress building." Bennett snickered. A couple of blocks later, he said, "This is Tudo Street, the sin bin of Saigon. You can get anything you want here, and some things you don't want, like the clap."

Glancing down the street, the GIs saw signs in English announcing bars, women, music, and massages. The truck stopped for traffic. As it sat there, a throng of little Vietnamese boys and girls approached from the curb with their hands uplifted. Some had small white cards with English writing on them that they waved at the newbies as they panhandled. Mothers with kids hanging off their hips also put their hands up to get something from the Americans.

"They never fuckin' let up. You're an American, so they feel it's right for you to give them something. Anything! They'll dog you every step you take out on the street. They each have their own little sob story written on

58

those cards: 'My father and mother were beheaded by the VC'; 'Our home was accidently destroyed by American bombers'—anything to make you feel guilty and cough up the goods.

"See that building there behind the high fence? That's the US Embassy. Hard to believe that the VC actually held it for a day not more than three months ago!

Yep, things were different here in Saigon before Tet."

Yes, the newbies recalled Tet, having just received their orders for 'Nam a couple of days before it happened. The story about the fight for the embassy had been on Cronkite and Huntley–Brinkley, shot for shot. Bullet holes the Kid had only previously seen on TV rippled the plaster walls of the very modern-looking embassy. Marines attentively guarded their post by the gates, M16's front-slung with ammo clips in and ready.

Not far past the US Embassy, another rather modern-looking four-story building stretched out behind a high fence, sitting back from a meticulously well- manicured lawn, accented with tall, old, regal leafy shade trees. A Huey helicopter sat on the lawn with its crew lounging beside it.

"That's the Presidential Palace." Bennett pointed. "Thiệu is here today. See his helicopter?"

Guards were standing watch over the street on the roof and at the corners of the palace. Bunkers stood ready to repulse another Tet-like offensive, should one ever happen again—and nobody was betting against it.

A little bit farther down the road, Bennett used the barrel of his M16 as a pointer. "That there is the spot where the first Buddhist monk burned himself up in 1964 to protest the war. Bet you've seen that picture. This is the spot."

As they motored through the city, the section of high-rises gave way to a neighborhood that was markedly lower rent. They passed a canal, and looking up it, they observed a squalid line of shacks that stood on stilts, kind of hanging out over the filthy water. Stairs descended from some of the houses to little docks where skiffs were tied up. Talk about your projects.

"This is the beginning of Cholon, the Chinese section," Bennett informed them. "Right around the corner is the Cholon Fish Market, without a doubt the worst- smelling square mile on God's green earth!"

They were now parallel to a large river that was choked with a wide array of big oceangoing ships and smaller Vietnamese craft. The freighters were lined up waiting to use the dock facilities somewhere up ahead of them. And yes, something most foul drifted up to assault the GIs' nostrils. Then they were driving right past the source of the odor.

59

"I think you're right." Davies leaned over to Bennett. "I really don't think I've smelled anything more disgusting in my entire life!"

The Cholon Fish Market spread out before them, briskly engaged in the commerce of selling fish in the tropics. There was stand after stand of little workstations covered with dirty canvas tops trying to shield the bounty of the Lord's sea from the devil's sun. Vietnamese fishmongers were selling, or trying to sell, every kind of fish, octopus, or squid that they had spent all morning out on the water catching. Hacked, cleaned, and gutted on the spot, fish awaited their buyers in baskets, while their heads and entrails lay rotting and stinking on the grounds of the market.

I'm dying just driving by. What the hell would it be like to be out in the middle of that thing without a good excuse to leave?!

"This place is so French," Bennett said, "with no refrigeration to speak of. The poorer Vietnamese have to shop for the food for each meal right before they cook it, especially fish, although I can't imagine ever eating anything that comes out of this cesspool!"

Turning another corner, the truck drove parallel to multiple railroad tracks that ran away from the dock area into a warehouse section of town. The Kid checked his watch; it was just past high noon. *The temperature must be well over one hundred ten degrees,* he figured. It reminded him of the time when his family had vacationed in Las Vegas. There, clocks and temperature signs atop every hotel told even the most casually interested observer how hot it was outside. Here, one just had to guess. But judging from the sweat pouring from the Kid's body, he figured it had to be the humidity, not the heat, that was making the experience one of monumental unpleasantness.

As they pulled up parallel to an old high-roofed warehouse complex, Bennett began gathering his gear. "We're home," he said. The truck turned into a driveway and waited for a helmeted guard to open a gate.

Behind the guard, the GIs could see Quonset huts had been built under the high roof of the old warehouse building. Across the front of one was a sign: HEADQUARTERS, FOURTH PSYOP GROUP.

Pulling through the gate, the truck drove into the shade of the warehouse and parked.

"This is it, gentlemen." Bennett swung down from the back of the tailgate. "You'll all be bunking in hut four, the transit hut. Take your duffle bags down there, and then report in at HQ to sign the day log. The clerk will give you directions to the mess hall, where you can go and get some lunch. That's where I'm headed. See ya around!"

"Thanks, Bennett," they collectively mumbled. Erio, Titley, and Viator handed the bags down to Davies and the Kid.

Dragging their bags down to no. 4, the soldiers opened the door and were hit with a surprisingly cool breeze. *Ah, air-conditioning!* Six bunks were lined up on either side of an aisle. Five of them looked to be occupied, and seven were without bedding.

"I got mine." The Kid flopped down on the mattress nearest the air conditioner, which sounded as if it was working overtime, but who wouldn't trade a little noise for the pleasant relief it offered?

Davies took a bunk next to the Kid, and Erio and Viator picked a couple directly across from them.

"Look, an in-house latrine with a shower right here!" Erio exclaimed.

"Hmm." Davies appeared to be engrossed in thought. "I wonder why Bennett called this the transit hut?"

"Well, most likely because we won't be staying here in Saigon," Flyboy said, stating the obvious. "I mean, if we're gonna be doing foreign-language announcing crap, chances are it won't be in downtown Saigon."

"I wonder when we'll find out?" the Kid said.

"Hey, if we go sign in at HQ, I bet we can ask somebody who might know, like the company clerk. He's gotta know." Erio stood up and, grabbing his order pack, walked toward the door.

The five made their way back to the headquarters hut. Opening the door, they found it to be a typical orderly room, with a clerk pounding away at an ancient typewriter, working on a document that looked to be three sheets of carbon paper deep. A radio played in the background. "Sheila" by Tommy Roe was just ending. "And there you have it, sweet little 'Shelia,' by Tommy Roe from 1962. That's going out to all the gunners in the 167th Artillery, at an undisclosed firebase location."

"Wow, AFVN Saigon! Listen to that!" The Kid pointed at the radio.

"Hey, the newbies from DINFOS!" The specialist 4 stood and offered his hand. "I'm Stuart. Last name good as a first name, so you can call me Stu; everybody does. Welcome to the Fourth Psyop Group, men." He shook all their hands. "The daybook is right there. Just go ahead and sign on in."

"So, Stu." The Kid turned and addressed the clerk as Erio picked up the pen.

"What's in the works for us?"

"The plan is for you guys all to be out of here by tomorrow—or the next day at the latest. I'm working on your assignment orders right now. You're headed for the battalions, and we've got ten of 'em, spread out all over the country, from the Mekong Delta to the DMZ and everywhere in between."

"Gee, that's great!" Viator, intending sarcasm, slapped his left palm with his baseball cap. "So, we're all splitting up?"

"Yeah. The first sergeant wants to see you all one at a time as soon as he gets back from chow. That's where he is right now. He'll fill each one of you in on your specific assignments, and he has a little welcoming indoctrination spiel that he loves giving to all the newbies. In fact, you all ought to go on over and eat lunch yourselves if you're hungry. It's easy to get there—just down a block and over a block. You'll like it. We've got great chow here. Oh!" Stu stopped in midmotion. "That's right, none of you are staying!"

"Hey, where are the studios for AFVN?" The Kid followed him to the door. "Is there any way we could drop by over there today and check out their operation?"

"It's over by the embassy, but no, there's nobody who can take you over there today. And you'd never find it by yourself, not knowing anything about Saigon. I know what's on your mind: you want to get out of the psyop gig and be on the radio. The next Adrian Cronauer, right? Well, *cam bou ya.* That's Vietnamese for 'never gonna happen.' Don't even bother to ask!"

Chapter 5

Stu wasn't wrong. The Con Song Hotel mess hall was a place of culinary delights. Instead of the traditional army chow line, they had a buffet of both Vietnamese food and good ole American food, complete with a salad bar, incredible fresh fruit, and even homemade ice cream! *Un-fucking-real.*

Stu was ready for them when they got back. "Erio, you get to go in first." He pointed toward the first sergeant's door.

Pete gulped and pretended as if he were straightening his tie. Then he marched up and resolutely knocked on the door.

"Come in," came the somewhat gruff reply. Pete opened the door and went into the first sergeant's office, closing the door behind himself.

The Kid, Davies, Titley, and Viator lit up and found places to perch while awaiting their turns, the Kid seating himself at an empty desk across from Stu; Viator, on a filing cabinet abutting the empty desk; and Davies, on the right front corner of the army-issue metal box with drawers. They all shared an ashtray, located in the center.

"Top a pretty nice guy?" Tom inquired.

"No, he's a flaming fucking asshole with a bug so far up his butt that they'll have to embalm him with Black Flag before they bury him," Stu intoned in a mock whisper.

The song "Cherish," by the Association, came over the radio, playing softly in the background. *Insult to injury.* The Kid sat there in the chair, looking at the ash on his cigarette, thinking about the time he had hallucinated seeing soldiers in the jungle while marveling at the coals in a fireplace, the first time he'd ever tried acid, on New Year's Eve 1966, in Aspen. He was staying at the house of a friend who was actually from Aspen and skiing with even more mutual friends from the University of Colorado. He had gotten the sugar cubes of acid from an old high school buddy just before he hitchhiked his way up to Aspen.

Ha. He had to laugh, thinking back to what his best friend Larry Ryan had said when he told him about the hallucination. "Larry, I see soldiers standing in a jungle! A bunch of them, wearing steel pots, and they're looking at something, but I can't see what!"

"Well, if none of them is you or me, don't sweat it."

"What's he talking about?" Bob Munroe lifted his head up off a huge pillow from the spot where he lay across the living room.

"Soldiers in the jungle. Stocker's been watching too much Cronkite. All we have to do is stay in school, then we won't have to sweat Vietnam. Fuck, it'll surely be over in three or four years," Ryan said in a mellow tone. "God, I just wish we were twenty-one so we could have chased those incredible bitches into Little Annie's Bar!"

The door opened and Erio came out. Stu said, "Davies, Thomas A., you're next."

Tom snuffed out his cigarette, took a deep breath, knocked on the door, and awaited the summons.

"Yo! Enter!"

"So where you going, Pete?" Viator asked.

"Nah Trang?" he said more as a question, as if he wasn't sure if he had the name of the place right or, if he did, he didn't know anything about it anyway.

"Not bad duty. Near the coast. A little NVA action, but not a lot. Didn't get hit too badly at Tet." Stu gave a report-like synopsis of what Erio could expect from life in Nah Trang.

"Now that I have an address, I gotta go write home." Erio exited the room.

The Kid's thoughts returned to Larry Ryan. Larry had said, after the Kid was drafted and then enlisted, "There's no way the army will ever get me, not even with a cushy deal like Armed Forces Radio. At least you've got that going for you, Curt."

Larry didn't call Curt "the Kid," because that was Larry's nickname. In Boulder, Curt's nickname was "the Turc," which was Curt spelled backward. Curt had stolen "the Kid" from Larry when he went to Nashville. *What the hell, he is three states away.* Nobody in Nashville even knew Larry, let alone knew that *he* was the Kid. And Curt had always hated "the Turc." It was too easy to morph it into "turkey."

Sitting there in the Fourth Psyop Group headquarters orderly room, he recalled what he'd felt like sitting in the front offices of WKDA, the number one rocker in Music City, home of the Good Guys, the day he had applied for his job. He had applied first at another Nashville radio station, WMAK, where he'd heard that one of their DJs was leaving. He had an air check tape that he'd made during his first radio station gig, at KOLR in Sterling, Colorado. He'd gone there to get out of Boulder while waiting for his debate partner Larry to graduate from Boulder High so they could reunite as a team at CU.

The guy at WMAK listened to the air check and said, "Well, Kid, you've got some promise, but the spot I have open here is from four o'clock in the afternoon to eight in the evening, drive time. You'd have to go up against Dave Allen at WKDA, and you just wouldn't have a chance. I need somebody more experienced. But I tell you what: I know for a fact that over at WKDA, Dick Buckley, the program director, is leaving his air shift from nine until noon and they're moving the all-night guy, DJ Dan, into his spot. So they are hiring for midnight to six. But Kid, remember, you'll be walking into the number one station in Nashville, and they've been number one for ten years!" *Hmm, the guy called me Kid.* He inwardly laughed. He'd always envied Larry his nickname. *The Kid. I want to be the Kid.*

OK, he thought, *what have I got to lose? I will go over to WKDA and apply for that job.*

It was only two blocks from WMAK to WKDA, which was in downtown Nashville on the twelfth floor of the Stahlman Building at Third and Union. He went over and walked right in, wearing his best and only madras jacket with his hottest paisley tie. "Dick Buckley, please."

"Do you have an appointment? ... No? And you want to see him about?" "The midnight-to-six slot."

"Oh. Well, let me buzz him and see if he has a minute. ... Yes, he does. This way, please." The receptionist opened the massive mahogany wood door and ushered the Kid into the longest hallway he could imagine, with another huge wooden door at the far end with a big red light over it. "Y'all got a name?" she asked as they walked.

"Yes. Curt Stocker. ... No, I don't have a résumé."

They passed a room to the right with couches and vending machines. "Announcer's lounge," the receptionist said. They passed a glassed-in booth on the left side of the hallway. "That's production," she said. About halfway down, she stopped and dipped into a door on her right, and the Kid found himself standing eye level with a nameplate that read "Dick Buckley." She said, "Kirk Stockard here to see you, Dick."

As the Kid walked in, Dick rose up from his record- and magazine-cluttered desk and extended his hand. "Kirk? Pleased to meet you."

"And I am pleased to meet you, Dick." He had thought for just a second that he should call him Mr. Buckley, but "Dick" came out of his mouth kind of natural-like.

"So, you want to apply for the midnight-to-six slot, huh? You got any experience?"

"Yes, I worked for six months in Sterling, Colorado." "Got an air check?"

Since it had failed him the first time, and knowing that this was the number one station in town and the guy had better air checks on his desk, the Kid said, "No. It got sort of melted by a heater on the bus ride out here."

"Oh?" Dick didn't know where to go with that. "Well, your FCC third-class license with broadcast endorsement didn't get melted by the heater, did it?"

"No. I have one right here." He pulled it out and showed it to him. Dick nodded his approval.

"Oh, your name is Curt, not Kirk," he looked over the license. "Are you married? … No? That's good, because the guy we are replacing, we are moving into my slot because midnight to six has been too tough on his marriage."

The door to the first sergeant's office opened, returning the Kid to the present. Tom came out, looking somewhat distraught. "Pleiku, wherever that is," he said, informing the others of his assignment.

"Central Highlands. Thick jungle, lots of trees, beaucoup NVA and VC. The guy you're replacing got killed last week." Stu did not sugarcoat it.

"Oh well, *that's* a pleasant thing to know, thank you very much!" Tom looked plain disgusted. "I gotta write to Kate," he said, and left wearing a frown.

"Viator, you're next." Stu barely looked up from his typing.

Al was still digesting the "killed last week" line as he rapped his knuckles on the door.

"Enter!" Top bellowed.

The Kid lit up a new cigarette and returned the Zippo to his pocket. "Whose desk is this?" He wondered why somebody wasn't there working. After all, there was a war going on.

"Oh, that belongs to Win, our civilian secretary. She's off having a baby. One of our lieutenants knocked her up. Got his ass shipped to I Corps for it."

The radio behind Stu was now blaring "I'm a Man" by the Spencer Davis Group. Exhaling, the Kid returned his thoughts to his Music City days.

"So, why did you pick Nashville?" Dick Buckley inquired.

"I came here because of a girl who lives in Smyrna. I'm going to enroll in a college to keep my student deferment, so the midnight-to-six thing would work out OK for me. I mean, it wouldn't interfere with school."

"OK." Dick nodded. "Let me show you around." He took the Kid out of his office and led him down the hall to the big wooden door with the red light lit above it. As soon as the light went out, he opened the door and motioned for the Kid to go in. There, at a control board that looked about three times as complicated as the one the Kid had used when learning to DJ in Sterling, sat a black-haired, tan- skinned smiling announcer wearing a white shirt and a red tie.

"This is Baby Bill Craig," Buckley said, introducing him. "Bill, this is Curt, from

Colorado. He's here about midnight to six." "Hey, how are you?" They shook hands.

"This board was custom-built for this room," Dick proudly said. "We take all our forty-fives and put them on cart and play them on that bank of five cart machines. That way you don't have to cue any records unless you're playing an oldie."

Hmm, very nice. The Kid was inwardly salivating at a chance to get his hands on the two exquisite green-felted turntables that completed the announcing pit setup. You could see from the control room into the next room through a huge plate glass window. "That's the newsroom, and in the next room, that's where we have a fully automated FM station. Thanks, Bill," Dick said, motioning for the Kid to follow him. After going out the door and up the hall, Dick turned in to the production room. "This is where we make all our commercials. You do any production?" Yes, the Kid had produced some, but not many commercials, so it wasn't a lie. Dick pulled out a reel-to-reel tape and threaded it onto a waiting upright machine. "Go in the announce booth," he said to the Kid. "I'm going to roll the tape. Since you don't have an air check, I want to hear what you sound like. Just tell me a few things about yourself and why you think I should hire you."

"OK." The Kid was sweating bullets. "Now?" "Yes. Rolling."

"Hey, how ya doin'? I'm the Kid, from Colorado, and I've come here to Nashville because everybody knows this is a happening place and I want to be where the action is. You know, I spun that song 'Nashville Cats' by the Lovin' Spoonful every other hour on my show for three weeks, and I think it must have hypnotized me, because here I am! I mean, I've always loved cats, and now I think I'm gonna love Nashville too! And if I don't get this gig, I'm off to jolly ole England.

Yep, that's where I'm going, so I can get a job on that pirate radio station on the oil derrick in the middle of the North Sea and meet the Beatles!"

67

"OK! Thanks." Dick stopped the recorder and hit rewind. "I've heard enough. I'll call you."

"Well, gee, I don't have a phone number yet. I'm staying at the Savoy Hotel over by the bus station. I'm looking for a place. How about I check in with you every day or so till I get a place or you hire me?"

"Fine," Dick said with a laugh. Just then, another announcer walked into the production room. "This is Johnny Wailin," Dick said. "Johnny, this is Curt the Kid, from Colorado, applying for DJ Dan's spot."

"Yeah, so what?" Wailin frowned at him. "Care to get out of here? I've got to make some spots." *What a sour disposition.*

"He's eight to midnight," Dick said to the Kid. "That's who you'll relieve if you get the job."

Back in the present day, the door to Top's office opened, and Viator walked out. He closed the door behind him. "Danang," he said. "Where's the supply hut again?" he asked Stu.

"First Quonset hut to the right going out of here. Stocker, door number one." Stu typed on.

Taking a deep breath, the Kid knocked hard on the door. "Don't break it," Top's voice came from within.

Turning the knob, the Kid opened the door, then walked in and came to attention.

"PFC Stocker, Curtis L., reporting, First Sergeant!"

"At ease, PFC. Take a seat," the bald, somewhat tubby, bespectacled, and pudgy-faced top sergeant gestured with his left hand to the metal folding chair to the Kid's right.

"Thank you, First Sergeant."

"Welcome to the Fourth Psyop Group, PFC Stocker. Let me save you some time and cut to the chase: no, you cannot transfer to Armed Forces Radio. That is what you're were going to ask me, wasn't it?"

"Uh, well, I uh … yes."

"Right, there hasn't been an FLA who's ever been assigned to this unit who hasn't asked that question. There are very few AFVN spots, and I will tell you this: If you want to get to AFVN, first you pull your tour with the Fourth Psyop Group, then extend your time in Vietnam for a second tour. Then you can pick AFVN. Sound like a deal?"

"Another tour? I just want to live through this one, Sarge."

"And we *all* want you to live through this one. But we have a war to win, and sometimes people gotta make the supreme sacrifice. Now, I suppose you're wondering where you're going to be assigned?"

"Yes, First Sergeant."

"You're going to the Tenth Battalion, in Can Tho, which is the biggest city in the Mekong Delta. You'll be drawing your weapon, steel pot, and field gear today and shipping out of Ton Son Nhut Air Base tomorrow at zero eight hundred hours.

Your APO address is on this card, so you can write home and let your folks and girlfriend know where they can write to you. I know you'll be anxious to get some mail from home." He flicked an index card across the desk at him. "Can Tho's not a bad place." Top lit up a Marlboro. "There's a Vietnamese university down there. And they always said that Can Tho was the place where rich Vietnamese men would go to find a wife, as did the French while they were here. But don't you go looking for any wife material, PFC. I know that sometimes when a young guy is away from home for the first time, these Asian girls start looking pretty fuckin' good, and all of a sudden you want to marry one. We frown on that here and will try to discourage it any way we can."

"That's OK, Sarge, I'm engaged."

"Oh well, then, make sure you don't go off the deep end when you get your Dear John letter." Top didn't miss a beat. "More than half the guys who are engaged before they come here get the Dear John before they're halfway through their tour."

"Not me, Sarge." The Kid was somewhat offended that Top would even speculate on the viability of his relationship with Flo, whom he didn't even know. He whipped out her picture. "Here she is. And there ain't no way I'm losin' her!"

Top took the picture and looked at it for about five seconds. "Nice. Good luck," he said, and handed it back. "Between me and you, you're getting the best deal out of all the newbies. Can Tho, being in the Delta, is as far away from North Vietnam as you can get. Oh, there's some mean son-of-a-bitchin' VC down there, but almost never any North Vietnamese Army regulars. The real thing you gotta worry about is mosquitoes. They're so big down in the Delta that they fly in formation and check your dog tags to see what your blood type is before they bite you." A thin smile crept across his fat face.

The Kid smiled back.

"So, Stocker, you have any questions?" The Kid shook his head no. "Stu will help you with anything you need to get ready to go. Dismissed." He saluted.

The Kid rose, returned the salute, and doing an about-face, marched out of Top's office and into the orderly room.

"Can Tho," Stu said. "You're a lucky dog! University town at the far end of the Ho Chi Minh Trail, so you'll be up against the worst-supplied VC in the entire country!"

"Oh joy!" came his sarcastic reply.

"Get your weapon and ammo and field gear issued at the supply hut this afternoon. I'll have a man drive you to Ton Son Nhut in the morning. And then I'll never see you again, because I'm short; I've only got fourteen days left in- country!"

Well, rub it in, you little weasel of a fuckface, the Kid thought. "Thanks, Stu. You're a real pal."

Chapter 6

At 0700 hours on May 29, the Kid sat on his gear in front of the headquarters hut, waiting for the jeep that would take him to catch his flight out of Ton Son Nhut Air Base. It had taken a couple of days longer than originally planned for him to be shipped out, but the moment had finally arrived. His duffle bag was now augmented with an extra green laundry bag containing his field gear: steel pot, canteen, pistol belt and harness, rain poncho, bayonet, mess kit, and entrenching tool. A shiny, near-new, fully automatic M16 rifle was propped up against his left leg, and he had a pocket bandolier that held six clips of ammo. *I am so armed and dangerous!*

Tom Davies had gotten up to have breakfast with him and was now waiting to say goodbye. He was scheduled to fly out to Pleiku at noon.

The Kid and Davies smoked as they listened to the cacophony of morning city sounds building to a crescendo outside the Fourth Psyop compound.

"I left out the part about replacing a dead guy." Tom was telling the Kid about his letter to Kate. "I mean, why aggravate the situation?"

"Really," the Kid said, agreeing. "I wrote Flo that I was going to someplace that was marginally safe. I hope Stuball the Racehorse wasn't just jerking my chain, chain, chain," he said, imitating the refrain from the Aretha Franklin song.

"Yeah, wouldn't that be a bummer? I wonder how Waterhouse and Imbach are doing down at the Ninth Infantry Division?" Davies flipped his butt into the can of sand behind them by the door of the headquarters hut.

"No telling. I don't know what would be worse: being in the infantry or being stuck with Baby Huey as a roommate for the next year. I'm just happy as a pig in slop that *I'm* not going to any infantry unit!" The Kid finished his cigarette, but his shot was off the rim of the butt can, so he got up and retrieved it. Taking two steps away, he turned around and shot a fade, this time making it.

"Didn't that AFVN jock suck last night?" Davies grimaced.

"God, did he ever! We have a part-time high school kid in Nashville, Bill Langford, who's twenty times the jock that guy is. Fuckin' A, he needs some serious help, like a mercy killing."

"Didn't sound like a DINFOS grad, that's for sure—or even anybody who'd *ever* worked in radio! I'm gonna miss you, Kid. Thanks for leaving me that joint."

"No problem. I can't wait to hook up with some of this Vietnamese shit we've been hearing about all these months," the Kid said with a tone of anticipation. Just then, up rolled the jeep, with pistol-packing Sergeant Patrick at the wheel.

"Yo, who's the fare to Ton Son Nhut?"

"That'd be me." The Kid rose and began piling his duffle bag and gear into the back of the jeep. "Tom, good luck!" He pulled out the chain with his Canadian beaver nickel and rubbed it on Tom's shoulder.

"Why don't you just let me keep that?" Davies grinned. " I know, fat chance!"

They hugged and patted each other on the back, then the Kid climbed into the passenger's seat of the jeep and sat down, holding the M16 between his legs, barrel up. He and Tom exchanged flashes of the two-fingered Winston Churchill peace sign as the vehicle lurched forward.

The Vietnamese guard swung open the main gate, and off down the road Sergeant Patrick sped, causing the Kid to tighten his grip on the gun and his baseball cap. The unit chauffer seemed to be quite a bit more aggressive with this smaller, more maneuverable machine.

As they were driving through Saigon, the Kid marveled at the gushing rush of Asian life. A long line of a couple hundred young smiling, laughing boys, in the ten-to-twelve-year-old range, all dressed identically in dark blue shorts, white shirts, and red ties, carrying armloads of books, made their way to a school somewhere off the distance. An equally long line of adolescent girls, all clad in white *áo dàis,* made their way in the same direction, but on the other side of the street. The girls walked by a sleeping derelict, who lay on the sidewalk up next to the buildings. He was wearing only a pair of ragged filthy brown shorts over his grime-encrusted skin. Not one of the girls so much as glanced down at him. As he and the sergeant drove along, the Kid noticed there were lots of homeless, hungry, and destitute men and women living out their squalid existences on the streets of the South Vietnamese capital.

There was a cluster of the ubiquitous White Mice national police on just about every corner in downtown Saigon. *They must be very territorial,* the Kid observed.

Lots of Vietnamese, both men and women, were dressed in green Stateside-style US Army uniforms. These were our allies, the South Vietnamese, as distinguished from the North Vietnamese. *Surely,* the Kid thought, *some of these guys must be Vietcong spies.* "How do you tell whose on our side?" the Kid asked, attempting to engage Sergeant Patrick in conversation.

"The ones that are shooting at you are not on your side," he tersely replied.

Hmm, obviously not interested in being pleasant, the Kid realized from the Sergeant's acrid tone. The ride continued in silence, except for the clashing noises of Saigon's rush hour traffic. The Honda motorbikes were as thick as flies at the Cholon Fish Market, zipping in and out among the larger vehicles.

"We're turning right. Stick your hand out and signal like that guy in front of us," Patrick barked at the Kid. "This is international driving rules, and that's how you gotta signal. *Do it!*"

"OK!" The Kid, juggling to keep a good grip on his rifle, stuck out his arm as the sergeant whipped around the corner.

How'd I get to be in this place? the Kid's mind wondered as he marveled at the diversity of the Vietnamese population. They were small in a general sort of sense, he had to admit. The women wearing that split-sided dress thingy with the pantaloons underneath made the Kid realize something: *No checking out legs in this country.* He frowned. *But the ass isn't bad! And wow, really pretty faces.*

Off in the distance, the Kid saw an aircraft of some size lift off and slowly climb into the blue sky, which was slightly tinged with pollution and made yellow by the sun, which was rising steadily in the sky to their left. In the opposite direction, he could see another aircraft, a high-winged Caribou coming in from what must have been the west.

Soon, the road to the airport was bracketed by a chain-link fence with barbed wire on top. Traffic was slightly backed up as they came to the gate for the main terminal serving Saigon. Ton Son Nhut Air Base was, it was said, the busiest airport in the entire world during the peak years of the Vietnam War. And with this being late May of 1968, it was a peak year.

"There's a military and a civilian side," Sergeant Patrick said as they were waved through the gate by two American MPs, having obviously decided that he'd been quiet long enough. "This is the military side over here on the left." He wheeled the jeep toward a two-story green monster of a structure. Jeeps buzzed all over the place, what with the dropping off and picking up all being done at one location.

The sergeant nosed into a small opening, put the jeep in neutral, and set the brake with his foot. Jumping out, he took the Kid's bags out of the back and had them on the dirt before the Kid had collected his weapon and ammo.

"Just go in here and take a right over at the MACV [Military Assistance Command, Vietnam] manifest desk. You can't miss it. They've got this huge-ass sign. Show them your orders, and they'll take care of the rest. See ya!" Sergeant Patrick didn't look the Kid in the eye, shake his hand, or volunteer to help carry his stuff. In an instant, he was back in the jeep and to hell and gone in a cloud of dust.

Standing there with his baggage and his M16, the Kid realized that he was finally alone. He was in Vietnam walking around and didn't have somebody else with him or in charge of him. He was his own man. Exciting and scary at the same time. Still, he was essentially on a US base, but he was on his way out into the field.

Hefting up his duffle bag strap to his right shoulder, he slung his M16 over his left shoulder and kind of dragged the new gear bag on the ground as he entered the terminal, which was a beehive of activity. It was kind of strange to look around and see so many armed people. *This is what it must have been like in the Old West.* He chuckled to himself, seeking out the MACV manifest desk. *Yes, there it is, over there under the big red MACV shield.*

At the counter, dual lines led up to where two enlisted men were taking orders from troopers and writing stuff on clipboards. Arriving at the head of the line, the Kid showed his orders. "Morning," he said cheerfully.

"Morning!" the clerk answered back. "Looks like you're headed to Can Tho on the zero eight hundred and you're a priority two, so you'll get on the manifest for sure! OK, Stocker, you're all set. Go wait over there by door number four. I can see you're new in-country, so make sure you clear your weapon one last time before you go out to board the aircraft, OK?" He pointed to a barrel tilted up at a forty-five-degree angle that had a "Clear weapons here" sign above it.

"Roger that. Got it," the Kid responded.

Finding a seat on a long wooden bench, the Kid's gaze wandered. Beneath a sign that said "R & R" across the cavernous open terminal, he could see soldiers who were in a more happy frame of mind than the ones near him, who obviously weren't going on any R & R—that's rest and recuperation. *Or is it relaxation?*

Who cared?

There were a large number of Vietnamese military personnel in the terminal as well. The Kid lit up a butt and contemplated his situation. Thinking about Flo, he pulled out her picture from its handy place in the breast pocket of his jungle fatigues and gazed at it. *I wonder if she's pregnant.* The thought caused a shudder to run through him. He wanted to marry her and eventually have kids, but this was too early. Still, there was no way he was going to make love to her for what could conceivably be the only time in his life using a rubber. She wasn't on the pill. So far in life, he'd been lucky in that department. His first lover in high school, Karen, it seemed, was late every month, and they swore they'd never take a chance again, but as soon as she got her period, they were right back at it, like rabbits in heat.

The Kid watched the R & R guys all smiling and laughing, some off to Australia, others to Tokyo and Bangkok. The married guys all went to Hawaii to see their wives, but the Kid had heard that there would be no R & R for him until he'd been in-country for a minimum of six months. And to go to Australia, there was a waiting list that made it impossible for a soldier to go there before he had been in-country for almost nine months. If only the Kid could figure out some way to get Flo's parents to let her meet him in Hawaii. *Talk about your mission impossible!* Now that he had made love to her, the thoughts of not having her or of being eight thousand miles away from her for an entire year was a little slice of that hell-on-earth concept he accepted as a Buddhist. *I need a plan.*

A clicking and static popping electrical charge pierced his ears. "Now boarding the zero-eight-hundred-hours flight to Can Tho. If you're on the manifest for Can Tho, proceed through gate four for boarding. And remember, gentlemen, to clear your weapons."

One by one, the GIs got up. As they passed the door, they ejected clips, pull- cocked their weapons, and pulled the triggers, pointing the gun barrels into the sand-filled barrel by the door. As the Kid clicked his hammer, he wondered how often some doofus forgot and left a round in the chamber. *That must be something of a shock when that happens,* he mused, recalling the time he accidently shot out the basement window of his apartment when messing with his roommate's .22 while a freshman at Northeastern Junior College in Sterling.

Walking out into the tropical sunlight, the Kid looked at the high-winged twin- engine Caribou transport aircraft that was going to take him to Can Tho. The back ramp was dropped open, and an air force loadmaster stood at the top watching the soldiers file on board. The noise level at Ton Son Nhut was deafening. Waiting his turn to load, the Kid observed three fighter jets lift off from the military operations side of the airfield. Then he saw a commercial 707 take off from the civilian side as another approached to land in what was apparently a never-ending merry-go-round of arrivals and departures.

The Kid dragged his baggage up the ramp and nodded to the loadmaster. One of the crewmen took his duffle bag and gear, placed it on a pile near the ramp, and pointed him forward. Finding a place on the bench-like aluminum

75

tube and canvas seat row that was attached to left side of the fuselage, the Kid sat down and buckled up while the crew secured the baggage with broad yellow nylon straps. It appeared that in-flight military etiquette dictated that your weapon remain with you, held between your thighs, pointed at the ceiling. *So much to learn.*

The atmosphere in the aircraft was stifling. Looking back out the ramp end, the Kid watched the waves of heat rising off the rapidly warming tarmac as soldiers continued to file on board.

Soon, when all the passengers were seated and the baggage was belted down, a crewman walked down the aisle counting the troops. He confirmed the number with the clipboard-toting loadmaster, who, speaking into his headset with attached microphone, let the pilots know they were prepared for takeoff.

The twin engines revved up and the Caribou rolled forward. With the windows to the soldiers' backs, it was difficult to look out at Ton Son Nhut as they advanced into position for takeoff. Scanning the soldiers sitting opposite him, the Kid noted that nobody looked very happy. For the most part, all of them were wearing full- brimmed jungle hats, whereas he had on a standard-issue baseball hat, marking him as a newbie. *I gotta get me one of those cool jungle hats first thing,* he decided.

The Caribou turned onto the runway. Gunning the engines, the pilot had it airborne almost immediately. As the aircraft rose and circled to its proper heading to fly to Can Tho, the Kid twisted around in his seat to get a look at Saigon. There was the river with all the freighters. *Oh, there's the Cholon Fish Market!* He swore he could almost smell it from a thousand feet up! Remarkably, the air was now cool, and it was quickly getting cooler as they climbed to altitude for the flight. Not bad, the Kid thought. *Maybe I should have joined the air force!* That made him think of Donna, the young woman he'd gone to Nashville for, the one he'd dropped for Flo. Donna's dad, Dean, was a career air force man who was stationed at Stewart Air Force Base at Smyrna, outside Nashville, which was, ironically, a Caribou crew training center. The Kid had watched Caribous flying circles around Nashville for months, never thinking a thing about it. *Now I'm in one.*

After the craft had been in the air for about five minutes, a light over the cockpit door illuminated, and as it did so, nearly every person on the plane reached into his pocket, pulled out cigarette, and lit up. *The smoking lamp is on.* Following suit, the Kid marveled at how the fact that this was a war zone could lessen the worry of dying from cancer, to the point where everybody was a chain-smoker. When the surgeon general's first report on the dangers of smoking came out in 1964, the Kid's mother had gotten a copy and thrown it in his lap. He thought about his mom and what a worrywart she was about everything. *Me dying from smoking-related cancer is probably pretty far from her mind right about now.*

The Kid noticed that they were at a much lower altitude than they had been at on the jet when he arrived. A countryside of endless canals, trees, and rice paddies unfolded below, punctuated by towns and villages connected by roads that seemed strangely devoid of traffic. Smoke rose up in a couple of isolated and widely separated places. Combat action? Air strikes? Terrorist attacks? No way of telling.

About fifteen minutes later, the Kid spied an extremely wide river stretching out below. "That's the Mekong River," the sergeant sitting adjacent informed him, "and it's split up into about four major channels, which make up the actual Mekong River Delta."

The Kid spied a strange juxtaposition of one very large canal splitting into two at a forty-five-degree angle, only to be crossed by another canal a couple of miles downstream, which created a triangle-shaped island.

"See that down there?" the staff sergeant commented as the Kid looked intently.

"That's the Iron Triangle; it's a huge VC stronghold."

The Kid nodded. *Hope I never have to go in there,* he thought. What he really hoped was that he could just stay aboard this Caribou for his whole tour; at five thousand feet above the jungle, the air was perfectly cool and enjoyable!

"We're almost to Can Tho. Another ten minutes." The smoking lamp went off, and GIs proceeded to snuff their butts in the cans that were spaced out, attached to the row of seats by wires.

As the Caribou approached Can Tho Airfield, it made a radical drop in elevation and smoothed out smartly to make its landing. When it touched down, the landing gear made a strange kind of whirring noise the Kid had never heard before. When they had taxied to a stop and the rear ramp was dropped, the Kid could see why the craft had made that sound. The airfield at Can Tho wasn't concrete or tarmac, it was linked metal plates, perforated with round holes.

"Wow, that's a weird-looking runway," he commented to the sergeant as they stepped on the runway, where they waited for the crew to pass down their duffle bags.

"Yeah, out here they don't make concrete runways, because they're too hard to repair after a mortar attack. With this metal shit, they can just fill in the hole and link in a couple of new plates, and in a few minutes, they're good to operate again."

The Kid checked his watch: 0845 hours. Already, the heat was fierce as he looked around at his surroundings. Can Tho Airfield was a postage stamp compared to Ton Son Nhut. It was the difference between Chicago and North Platte, Nebraska. The terminal, sitting off to their left, was a modest two-story wooden structure that was much smaller than some of the private homes on Belle Meade Drive back in Nashville.

The Can Tho Airfield tower, barely taller than the terminal, sat to the terminal's north. In addition to the Caribou the soldiers had just flown in on, two others waited, spaced out on the metal runway with their back hatches open, receiving cargo in preparation for departure.

A shabbily painted civilian Air Vietnam DC-3 tail dragger also sat on the runway, with a small loading ladder pushed up to its rear door. Another type of airplane that the Kid had never seen before, a long needle-nosed silver and blue high- winged single-engine craft, sat to its right. It said "Air America" in small lettering on the fuselage. A pilot sporting tear-shaped aviator sunglasses, dressed in a white shirt and dark gray slacks and packing a .45 pistol on his hip, was giving it a preflight inspection.

"Air America *sem sem* CIA," the sergeant commented with a smile.

"Say what?" The Kid failed to understand.

"Air America. It's the CIA's private airline. And all the pilots are CIA agents."

"Oh. OK." The Kid, pondering what significance this could have for him, drew a blank.

"*Sem sem* is Vietnamese for 'the same,'" the sergeant continued. "It even sounds like it: *same same.* Get it? Let me tell you right now, it certainly won't hurt you to learn a little Vietnamese. They really like it when you try to speak their language!"

"Well, thanks for the tip!" *Sure, sure,* the Kid thought.

Two Vietnamese army guards with M16's paced somewhat aimlessly back and forth in front of the terminal. From inside, a line of predominantly civilian Vietnamese men, women, and children, and a few South Vietnamese military personnel, emerged. Carrying duffle bags, plastic woven shopping bags, cardboard boxes, and an occasional real suitcase, they made their way past the Kid on their way to board the DC-3.

Entering the Can Tho terminal, the Kid recalled Stu's instructions: find the comm desk—which was short for communications desk—and have the GI on duty phone out to the Tenth Psyop Battalion to send a jeep to pick him up.

Scanning the room, the Kid spied an American GI specialist 4 sitting at a counter with a phone in front of him. *Gotta be the comm desk. If not, that guy can tell me where it is.*

Crossing the dirty black and white checkered tile floor, the Kid dropped his bags in front of the counter. "Morning."

"Morning."

"This the comm desk?" the Kid inquired with an air of uncertainty.

"Well, yes it is." The blond soldier looked up from his writing. "And who y'all wantin' to communicate with, PFC?" he asked in a heavy southern accent.

"The Tenth Psyop Battalion. Somebody in Saigon said you could call them and they would come get me."

"Somebody tol' you that?" He looked startled. "OK, I admit, they're right." He grinned. "I reckon I kin call them. If the phone is still workin'." He dialed. "Hello, is this the Tenth? ... Good. This is the Can Tho Airfield comm desk, and there's a PFC Stocker here for you guys to pick up. Roger that. ... Right, roger that. ... In about fifteen minutes? Roger that. Out." He hung up the handset. "Says he'll be right out and that you're supposed to wait for him under the canopy to the right of the front door." He pointed with his pen to the exit directly behind the Kid.

"Thanks."

"Just gettin' in-country?"

"Yep, haven't been here a week yet. I must look like a newbie." The Kid shifted his M16 strap on his shoulder as he prepared to pick up his gear.

"That there baseball cap is a dead giveaway, for sure. Gotta get yourself a jungle hat. You'll see 'em cheap at stores all over downtown. Tell this guy who picks you up that you need to go shopping. Maybe he'll take you!"

"Yeah, maybe. Hey, does the PX here ... that is, does Can Tho have a PX, and if there is one, do they have things like transistor radios and batteries?"

"Yes, sure enough there's a PX, at Eakin Compound, the biggest American base in this province, where everybody in town eats chow. An', like, you'll find out where that is at lunch in about three hours. They got some shit like that, but you can likely find something betta downtown. Hey, it ain't Saigon, but Can Tho is the biggest city in the Delta. You can get jest about anythin' y'all might want here."

"Hey, thanks!" The Kid shot him a peace sign.

"You're welcome." He went back to his letter writing, no peace sign in return.

Walking out the door, the Kid saw two captains headed in, so he had to drop his gear bag to salute. They were followed by some uniformed South Vietnamese soldiers. Looking at their rank insignia, the Kid didn't know if they were officers or not or if he was required to salute them, so he did so. *What the hell, better safe than sorry.* They saluted back and smiled broadly, their eyes hidden behind the reflective mirrored sunglasses apparently preferred by the Vietnamese. Finally, the Kid dragged his baggage to the shady area of the cement pad that served as the waiting area right outside the terminal door. Sitting down on his duffle bag, he propped his M16 up against the wall and lit up a Kool. Exhaling, he realized that he was very thirsty. He certainly hadn't seen any Coke machines. *How would that work with no coinage?* he pondered.

Looking around, he spied the alternative: a Vietnamese woman minding a snack cart, apparently selling all kinds of strange and exotic-looking stuff. Rising, he started to walk over to see if he could buy a soft drink. After about three paces, realized he had just walked off and left his weapon unguarded with his baggage. *Oops.* So much to learn. He wasn't used to toting a gun around yet. *Better get used to it,* reality nagged him. He picked up his weapon and hung it over his shoulder by the strap.

Once standing next to the cart, he was amazed at the choices. The little dried squid that hung from a pole like strips of beef jerky were easy to pass on, as were the cake-like things that were sliced open to reveal fertilized yokes. The Kid could see the embryos of small chickens and ducks! *Yuck!* The stand also had a wide selection of Vietnamese and American cigarettes. The Marlboros were priced at nine hundred "p," whatever that was. There were two kinds of warm beer. One had a tiger on the bottle, with the name La Rue. The liquid inside appeared kind of cloudy. The other beer's label said its name was 33. The Kid didn't see any Cokes.

Off to the side, under a tan cloth awning, a pair of Vietnamese troops were sitting smoking cigarettes and drinking two of those beers with the tiger on the bottle. The Kid looked at his watch. *Zero nine thirty and they're drinking. No wonder we aren't winning this war. Om, hurry, guy from headquarters,* he silently chanted as he returned to sit on his duffle bag. He pulled out his picture of Flo, letting it wash his eyes and distract his consciousness. *Will I live to see you again? I wonder if you're pregnant.*

Jeeps came and went. Finally, one pulled up, and the Kid noticed it said "A CO 10BN" on the bumper. The driver was obviously looking for somebody.

"Yo, Tenth Psyop Battalion?" He raised his hand.

"Yeah, throw your stuff in here and let's get the fuck going!" the driver responded. Wearing a baseball hat and sunglasses, with sleeves rolled up showing really tanned arms, the driver wore a name tag that said "Wimbish."

The Kid loaded his gear and climbed into the shotgun seat. He had to laugh. *Not shotgun. It's riding "M16," not shotgun ever again.*

Checking over his left shoulder, the driver pulled away from the terminal and, gunning the jeep, slapped the stick shift into second gear. "Where ya from?" he asked.

"Well, when I got drafted, I was living in Nashville, but I grew up in Colorado. What about you?"

"I'm from Virginia Beach, Virginia. What's your MOS?" "I'm 71R20 and 71Q20."

"Oh, a DINFOS man, huh?"

"Yep, for all the good that it did me."

The jeep came to the edge of the Can Tho Airfield, where the driver stopped at the stop sign to let traffic pass. An old rusted tank sat just off the road, as if on guard, partially buried in the earth, with weeds growing up where the treads used to ride and a turret top that showed the damage from some sort of explosion.

Such a small tank! Not much bigger than a Volkswagen van.

"That's left over from the French," Wimbish commented, noting the Kid was closely examining the derelict piece of armor. "Somebody told me that's been there since 1953."

Taking a right turn, Wimbish punched it out onto the roadway and went through the gears. The Kid took off his hat and held it in his hand as the jeep flew by cyclos, bicycle carts, and a heavy volume of pedestrian traffic. The women of Can Tho were more into dressing in black pajama bottoms and separate white blousy-like tops. Most of the men were wearing loose-fitting shorts, and most of the Vietnamese civilians were wearing the traditional conical hat. In all, the residents were much more rural in appearance than the Vietnamese of Saigon. One guy was humping a huge load of live ducks that were suspended from either end of a pole, tied by their feet to hang upside down. The ducks strained and twisted their necks to satisfy their curiosity as to where they might be going. The Kid felt a little like one of the unlucky quackers, on his way to the butcher shop but really without the first clue as to what was in store for him.

There was considerable military traffic, but unlike that in Bien Hoa and Saigon, most of it was ARVN, the army of South Vietnam—the Army of the Republic of Vietnam—with virtually no US vehicles to be seen.

"Hey, what are the chances of taking a detour to a store where I can buy a jungle hat and a transistor radio?" the Kid yelled over the sound of the jeep engine and the wind produced from traveling at fifty miles per hour.

"Not now. We need to go straight back to battalion headquarters and check you in. But it's almost lunchtime, so you can hit the PX at Eakin."

The outskirts of Can Tho didn't look that much different from the roadside between Bien Hoa and Saigon: lots of shack-like structures, some of them businesses and some of them houses. Dirty children by the dozens were running and playing, chasing each other with sticks and pretending they had guns.

Turning a stick into a firearm is apparently a universal concept among the young.

Overhead, the Kid noticed a considerable amount of helicopter traffic. There were Hueys, Cobra gunships, and big double-rotary Chinooks buzzing everywhere. He wished he was up in one of them, sampling the cool breeze he had just experienced on his flight down here; the heat in prenoon Can Tho was already stifling, even in the convertible jeep with the wind blowing across his blond buzz-cut head.

Soon, they were in a more commercial-looking area. *Well, how about that! A Texaco station, just like home!* Wimbish slowed down as traffic became more congested. Just off the middle of an intersection that was formed by the convergence of two big streets was a towering blue sign with loudspeakers on top that must have been easily thirty feet tall.

"This is Bien Xi Moi, which means 'new bus stop' in English. That big sign is the bus schedule for buses leaving Can Tho. Signal me a right," Wimbish hollered. The Kid stuck out his hand. Wimbish made a right turn, then halfway down a row of buildings, he made another right down what appeared to be an alleyway. "This is our billet. We call it New Villa," he said as he pulled to a stop in front of an old French hotel. "We're going to drop your stuff here, so we don't have to worry about it getting stolen while you screw around at headquarters and we go to lunch."

The building was the last in line on the left side of the alley, but it butted up against the others in the row coming down from the street. A heavy-gauge screen enclosed the front of the three-story plaster and tile structure up to the third floor. The third-floor balcony was open, as if a Vietnamese person couldn't throw a grenade that high. A gaggle of about half a dozen dirty but smiling Vietnamese kids were playing some sort of game that must have been a form of tag, their voices rising to a high pitch as they raced up and down the alley.

A black American with short but extremely curly hair, dressed in red cutoffs with an olive-drab T-shirt and flip-flops, was standing in the doorway of the billet entrance, hollering up at a Vietnamese woman who was leaning over the balcony railing on the second floor of the building right across the alley.

"That's First Sergeant Ozelle Jones," Wimbish said as he began to help unload the Kid's gear. "He's on his second tour here in 'Nam. Not a man you want to get crosswise with. Yo, First Sergeant, this is the new guy for Company B. I'm taking him down to sign in but thought we'd drop off his duffle bag and park his M16. He won't be needin' it today, I don't reckon. Did you find a place for him tonight?"

"Oh yeah, we got a bunk in the transit room, right down the hall to the left, in the middle. That's all we got open right now," the first sergeant responded. "He won't be here long anyway. We've got field teams going out in a couple of days, and he's going to be on one of them."

Wimbish helped the Kid lug his gear through the gate and past the Vietnamese civilian guard who was smoking a butt as he sat on a barstool behind his sandbag post in a position to cover the front entrance. The orderly room was just off the front porch area. A somewhat round-faced GI with dark black hair and army-issue eyeglasses sat typing at one of the desks. *If Charlie Brown ever got drafted, this is what he would look like in a jungle fatigue uniform.* He didn't look up or say hi or boo or anything, just kept typing. Except he occasionally had to push his glasses back into place whenever they slipped down his sweaty nose.

"Leave your M16 here in the office, and me and Boujold will watch it. There isn't a locker in there you can use right now. There are only two right now, and the two other guys who just arrived two days ago are already using them."

All the while he was talking to the Kid, Ozelle kept getting closer to Boujold to see what it was he was typing. When the round-faced GI looked up, Ozelle's face was about two feet from his. Resolutely, Boujold pulled the piece of paper he had been typing from the machine and flipped it in his face.

"Here it is, my request for a transfer to a field unit!" he said, pushing back his chair and defiantly crossing his arms.

The Kid sensed that this was a fight that had been going on for some time.

"Aw, Jesus, Boujold." Ozelle wadded up the transfer request and pitched it into the wastebasket. "You're really giving me a case of the ass! If you don't cut out this wasting of your time shit and quit bawling like a baby about circumstances that you've got no control over, I will personally kick your fat fucking ass to the point where fubar will not describe it!" And then, in one of the most militarily threatening voices the Kid had ever heard, the scowling first sergeant slowly and deliberately added the closer: *"Do I make myself perfectly clear?"*

With that, Boujold's mouth suddenly hung open. He rose to his feet and sarcastically huffed, "Yes, Sergeant."

"Now, show our newbie to his room," the sarge said dismissively.

"You might want to pick up a lock at Eakin Compound iffen you don't have one," the sergeant advised. "You shouldn't leave anything unguarded in this whole fuckin' country—if you want to keep it, that is—but I'll watch your weapon for now." He sat down at his desk and proceeded to cool himself with an ornate paper Asian hand fan.

"This way." The Charlie Brownesque soldier beckoned for the Kid to follow him down the corridor to the left. "Here it is, transit room number two. I don't know if the two earlier guys have picked their bunks yet or not, but you can sort that out tonight."

"Thanks." Sweat rolled off the Kid's forehead as he dragged the laundry bag of gear into the dusty quarters and leaned it up against the foot of the bunk situated to the right of the door.

"I do know where there's an empty locker, and I'll get it moved in here for you by tonight," Boujold said as his right hand sought out the pack of Winstons in his left breast pocket.

When the Kid got back into the orderly room, he quickly saw that an impatient Wimbish was already out the door and waiting in the jeep. "Thanks, Top. See you tonight!" He casually waved on his way through the room.

As the Kid and Wimbish backed out of the alley, three Vietnamese women leered while hanging over the railing of the building across the street from the billet. The Kid gave them a friendly wave.

"Whores," Wimbish commented as he checked for traffic. "There's better ones to be had. But not any more convenient, just better-looking." He smiled.

"How do you say the name of this place again?" the Kid asked.

"Bien Xi Moi," Wimbish told him. "Sem sem. 'New bus stop.'"

Yes, indeed, there were a half dozen buses with Vietnamese loading and unloading over at one corner of the Texaco gas station's parking lot. The street to the airfield was paved, but the street coming out of Bien Xi Moi was just a dusty, dry-looking road that some farmer was driving a couple of water buffalo up, using a long willowy stick as a whip. The buildings that lined either side of Bien Xi Moi were all three stories tall and had the upper floors enclosed with screens. Signs in Vietnamese said all kinds of things about the shops of which the Kid had no idea.

A row of jeeps was pulled up and parked in front of the colorfully painted shops and stores. The Kid noticed armed Vietnamese soldiers walking back and forth on the sidewalks in front of them.

"Those guys are guarding the jeeps while their drivers are in doing something. If you don't watch it, a kid will come up and slip a grenade into the gas tank, with the pin pulled and the handle held down with electrical tape. Once they get it into the gas tank, the gas dissolves the tape, then the handle flips up. *Kabam!* The jeep and all its passengers are blown to fuck. The tape might take ten minutes or an hour to unravel, depending on how many times they wrap it around the grenade handle, but when it goes off, they just hope a lot of Americans are sitting in the vehicle."

Nice. The Kid looked at the children running pell-mell about the street, wondering which ones had the grenades.

"Is this place pretty quiet, war-wise?"

"Mostly. Can Tho is IV Corps headquarters for ARVN. We had some action here in town during Tet, but the majority of the time, the VC stay pretty much the hell out. Of course, we have our terrorist things that do happen. They will blow up a restaurant or throw a grenade from a motor scooter at a cluster of GIs from time to time. Or a sniper will take a potshot at some GI walking along the road. Here in

Bien Xi Moi, we've got the MP compound half a block down from us. They're always coming and going, so they're pretty high profile. And again, the VC stay pretty much out of here."

A half dozen blocks after Bien Xi Moi, the street began to look more like a real city than a rural town. Tall, majestic trees now lined the boulevard, offering shade to the guard shacks that sat in front of the wall that ran the length of the street on both sides, guarding the somewhat large-looking houses built along the main drag. Now the Kid was seeing more women wearing the *áo dàis* like the women of Saigon. The roadway rose up as it crossed a canal over a slightly elevated bridge.

"Villa Cruz, our leaflet printing facility, is down there." Wimbish pointed to the street that fronted the canal immediately on the far side of the bridge. "That's also where our officers' billet is, so you'd have to pull guard duty there if you were sticking around."

"If I was sticking around?"

"Yeah, you're only going to be here for a couple of days at the most before you get sent to the field."

The Kid digested Wimbish's comment in silence. He hadn't stayed in Long Binh, he hadn't stayed in Saigon, and now he wasn't going to be staying in Can Tho. He was falling farther and farther away from civilization as he knew it.

"Hey, I wrote my fiancée, and the first sergeant at Group said the Can Tho APO was my address. If I leave here, will I get any mail that comes here for me?"

"Oh yes, we're pretty good about forwarding mail to field teams, so this address is good for you."

What a relief. The Kid was used to getting a letter from Flo every day while he was in basic training and at DINFOS, and now, as he was nearing a week without one, the feeling of withdrawal from her letters' narcotic intoxicating essence of perfume was starting to set in.

"There's the USO." Wimbish pointed right to a gate in the long-running wall. "You can get cheeseburgers and stuff like that there, and you can see the only civilian American woman in all of Can Tho. She runs the place. But don't get your hopes up for a date. Everybody calls her 'Dog Lady,' but she has the men standing in line. And she only dates Special Forces, captains and above."

"That's OK, I'm engaged." The Kid dismissed the thought of Dog Lady from his mind.

The jeep came to a big, sweeping rounded curve in the road that ended in a ninety-degree turn to the right. As he cleared the curve, Wimbish slowed and said, "Signal me a right," then pulled up to a wrought iron gate in the wall. A uniformed Vietnamese guard ambled forth to open it, and the jeep drove through and into a shady courtyard, parking by the side of a two-story building.

"This is battalion headquarters," Wimbish said. "We have the top floor and half of the bottom floor. You know when Elvis Presley was in the army? And he met his wife, Priscilla, in Germany? Well, her dad, Lieutenant Colonel Beaulieu, is stationed here in Can Tho right now and works in the office right below our headquarters."

"Really? When I was a DJ in Nashville, I got an Easter card from Elvis. He used to send them to all the DJs. Of course they weren't signed; it just had his printed signature. I also got to go into the studio on Music Row at RCA where he records all his records. It's just a dinky little hole, but he stays there because it is good for him. And they say he's pretty superstitious."

"Is that so?" Wimbish responded with a quizzical look. He led the way through a screen door into a hallway and made an immediate turn into an open door to the right. A specialist 4, who sat typing at a desk beneath a slowly rotating ancient- looking black ceiling fan, looked up as they entered. "Hi, Lou," he greeted Wimbish.

"Hey, Paul, this is PFC Stocker, fresh off the jet from the world, and he's going to be assigned to B Company."

"Pleased to meet you." The blondish, slightly rotund soldier stood and extended his hand to the Kid. His name tag said "Coffman." "Welcome to the Tenth Battalion!"

Chapter 7

The abbreviation psyops, the Kid realized, was just a couple of letters off the word psycho, a reality that did not bode well given the Alfred Hitchcock thing. *I can only hope that Norman Bates is not my commanding officer.*

As the Kid was shaking hands with Coffman, a wiry-looking crew-cut captain with a 101st Airborne patch on the arm of his ultrastarched, sharply creased, and faded jungle fatigues, emerged from the office directly behind the clerk's desk.

"Captain Smith, this is PFC Stocker," Coffman announced. "I guess he's the new foreign-language announcer we've been waiting for."

The Kid came to attention and saluted. The captain returned the salute as he looked the Kid over from head to toe and back up again. "Welcome to the Tenth, Stocker." He extended his hand, and they firmly shook. "You need to go upstairs and sign the daily report. I was just leaving for lunch, which I imagine you'll be doing too, but when we get back, we'll get together and have a little chat about where you'll be going and what you'll be doing for the next year. At least we hope it's a year."

"Yes, sir. Thank you, sir." The Kid gave his best friendly smile.

Wimbish motioned for the Kid to follow him. They went outside and then entered an enclosed stairway that led up to the second floor. They emerged into a long, open room where a row of five desks ran down the interior wall, taking up the length of the building. A row of filing cabinets separated the desks from the front of the room, and the room was screened from floor to ceiling for its entire length. Three evenly spaced black ceiling fans cranked away on high, doing their best to create a breeze in the un-air-conditioned room. A number of geckos patrolled the screen on both sides; more of the little lizards waited patiently for bugs on the interior walls; and yet more hung suspended from the ceiling. They were fucking everywhere.

Wimbish, after giving salutations to the men who manned the first two desks, sat down at the third one in from the stairwell. He pulled a pack of Winstons out of his desk and lit one up. "Hey, Paul," he said, addressing the specialist 4 who was apparently engrossed in his work, sitting at the desk next to his, "this is Stocker, the new B Company guy. Stocker, this is Specialist Hoch, head clerk of the battalion."

"Welcome to the Tenth, Stocker." Hoch stood and extended his hand. The dark-haired, thin-faced company clerk smiled, revealing a chipped tooth. "Why don't you just sign in now?" He rotated the large daily report log and presented it to the Kid with a pen for his official signature, which would indicate the date and time he had arrived at the unit. The Kid, taking the black government-issue pen from Hoch's hand, complied. As he gave the pen back, a captain came walking into the room. He waltzed by Hoch's desk and stuck his head in the door behind him, over which a sign proclaimed, "LTC Jack N. Kimberly, Commanding Officer."

"That fucking goofball Boujold wasn't prepared to go on his guard shift at the New Villa again last night. Had to make a special run to take him over." The Kid watched Hoch and Wimbish exchange smirks. "I say send his lazy, miserable, worthless fat fucking ass to the field!" the captain further declared. "Too bad that's what he's trying to make us do."

"Maybe we should," an unseen voice said from within the room.

"Yeah, be careful what you wish for, because you might *get it!*" They shared a laugh, and then the captain continued down and into the next door, over which there was a sign reading, "Sergeant Major Lameroux."

"Boujold in the field!" Hoch looked at Wimbish. "Pardon me while I fucking die laughing! Can you imagine being stuck in a foxhole with Boujold?"

"No," Wimbish said flatly. "I can't imagine it, because if he was in it, there wouldn't be any room for anybody else!"

"And if he did happen to get shot, he'd bleed bullshit and fill the foxhole up!" Hock exclaimed. The two of them just roared.

"Then, we'd be living in Villa Boujold!" Wimbish was laughing so hard that his eyes teared up.

Since they were apparently talking about the guy who was back at Bien Xi Moi guarding his personal stuff, the Kid could only stand there with a half grin on his face.

"Hey, there's the chow truck! Let's show PFC Stocker Eakin Compound." Hoch stood up and reached for his baseball cap.

"Chow truck!" an unseen voice hollered from inside a room off the front. Almost as if on cue, men began emerging from the doors of the offices in the back. They appeared to be a cheerful lot. *How bad could this assignment be?* the Kid pondered.

Back down the stairs and out through the courtyard, the men clambered into the deuce-and-a-half that waited for them, idling and spewing exhaust out into the wickedly hot noon air. The Kid sort of stuck next to Wimbish and sat down by him in the truck. The rest of the men quickly noticed the new guy among them.

"Everybody," Wimbish said in a loud voice, "this is Stocker, a new guy for Company B."

Salutations were given. The Kid nodded back.

"So, you get to go to the field? You lucky fuck," a GI whose name tag the Kid couldn't read immediately commented.

"I guess. What's so good about the field?" the Kid asked.

"Well, stick around this shithole for about a week and you'll know. This is the high point of the day, lunch. This is one of the lamest fuckin' enclaves in all of IV Corps."

"Isn't the field where the fighting is?"

"Oh, well, yeah, some, but not so much that being out of this hole isn't a good deal. A Company has to pull guard duty both at New Villa and Villa Cruz, plus we have sandbag duty and all kinds of training bullshit to put up with that is just ridiculous beyond fuckin' belief!" All the guys nodded their agreement.

"And shakedowns and cleanin' shit that never ends." Another GI took up the case against Can Tho. "In the field, you might have to fly a leaflet drop like once a week, and then it's not an all-day deal."

"Leaflet drops?"

"Yeah, that's what psyops is mostly about, printing leaflets and dropping them on the Cong to get them to surrender. In fact," Hoch said, turning to him, "you're going to find out all about it. Because you aren't going out till Tuesday, you'll get to fly leaflet drops tomorrow!"

"If flying is involved, I'm there!" the Kid positively responded. "It was so cool being up there, flying here from Saigon. I'll fuckin' do anything to get out of the heat!"

"Sure, we all said that, until the planes we were in got shot at," Hoch said. "Luckily, we haven't lost any yet, but we came close last week. One of our C-47's got shot up pretty good."

Something more for the Kid to mull over.

90

"That place over there"—Wimbish pointed to a large military complex as the truck passed by—"is IV Corps headquarters, for both the Americans and the Vietnamese."

Vietnam was divided into four zones, or corps. I Corps was right up against the DMZ (demilitarized zone) in the northern part of South Vietnam. Corps II and III took up the middle of the country in the highlands, and IV Corps was the Mekong Delta.

"I don't know what you know, but IV Corps is a pretty good place to be, even out in the field, compared to I, II, and III Corps," Wimbish said. "We've got virtually no NVA down here, so it could be a hell of a lot worse than it is. That's not to say nobody ever gets killed, but all our field teams except one work with Vietnamese units, so even though you are a PFC, you'll get treated like an officer just because you're an American."

The truck arrived at a walled compound and passed through a well-armed gate, manned by Americans, not Vietnamese like most of the guard posts the Kid had noticed since leaving Bien Hoa.

Eakin Compound easily took up twenty acres. It was home to the mess hall, the PX, the library, the swimming pool, basketball courts, recreation rooms, and the administrative offices of the US IV Corps operation. Plus, there were rows of officers' billets there where men who were assigned to Vietnamese units came to stay when they weren't in the field.

Off to the side of the parking lot, which was full of trucks and was getting fuller by the minute for lunch, was an open field where an ambulance sat isolated, out by itself. Suddenly, *the pop, pop, pop* of a helicopter engine passed right over their heads, the bird setting down on a helipad by a truck marked with the Red Cross.

"Ooh, casualties," someone remarked. The men stood in the back of the truck as they watched the chopper touch down. A crew of two sprang from the back of the ambulance and met the chopper as it touched down. They immediately pulled a stretcher out of it. One man took an IV bag from a chopper crewman and held it over the stretcher as they hustled it over to the back of the ambulance. After the stretcher was slidden in, the man with the IV bag jumped in after it.

Simultaneously, the other man ran up to the passenger door. As soon as he was in, they were on the move. The ambulance passed right by the soldiers and went out the gate they'd just come in, its siren screaming.

"Just a Vietnamese guy," Sullivan commented. "If it was an American, they would have taken him to the Eakin medical facility."

There was a line at the mess hall. The soldiers of the Tenth Battalion made small talk as they shuffled through the door and into the dining facility. The Eakin Compound mess hall was a lot like the Long Binh mess hall, only smaller. The chow was OK, but not quite up to the level of the Saigon mess hall buffet, where the guys at Group got to eat.

"At least we don't have to pull KP," Wimbish said as they ate. "Vietnamese civilians do all the grunt work here. At least we've got that going for us."

"Hey," Hoch said excitedly, "I can't believe I forgot to tell you guys this! I heard this morning that New Villa came just a hair's breadth away from being named 'Villa Roberts'!"

"No shit!" one of the group exclaimed. "What happened?"

"Well, Lieutenant Kazmarskij said that their armor unit got into a hell of a fight yesterday and lost twenty KIA and twenty-two WIA and that Roberts got hit with shrapnel in the arm!"

"No fuckin' shit!" a GI who the Kid could see was named McCauley cut in. "I bet he's thinking twice about writing those articles now!"

The Kid was completely lost. "Who's Roberts?" he asked Wimbish.

"Tom Roberts was the head clerk at A Company until last month. He's a DINFOS grad, just like you, and he was writing articles from the front for his college newspaper at Lehigh University, back in Pennsylvania, until an ROTC major read them and told the Department of the Army, who sent an order here to stop him.

So, they sent him to the field as punishment." He turned to Hoch. "More details!"

"All I know is the ARVNs got into it and lost seven APCs! Really got their asses kicked. And Roberts got hit in the arm. Supposedly, it's only about an inch long, but he bled, so he's getting put in for a Purple Heart!"

"Wow!" went around the table as the men contemplated the significance of the event.

"Now let me get this straight," the Kid commented. "This Roberts guy gets sent out there for punishment, and I'm getting sent out there just for grins, and all you guys want to go there because you're bored?"

"Something like that." Hoch considered what the Kid was asking. "He had the MOS all along, just like you. But he was a kick-ass clerk and Ozelle loved his act until the antiwar article thing came out. Boujold had to take his place. Boy, was Ozelle pissed. Fat Boy has been trying to get into the field the whole time he's been here, and he thought he was going to get posted until they kicked Roberts's ass out of the A Company clerk's position. The captain told him it was obvious he had too much free time on his hands."

After chow, the Kid and Wimbish went shopping at the PX. The Kid bought some more stationery to write to Flo, his parents, and his friends back in Nashville, along with three cartons of Kool cigarettes and some more toothpaste. He also got the transistor radio and spare batteries he so badly wanted. At least he could listen to AFN (American Forces Network) and know how much better a DJ he was than anybody who was there.

Back at headquarters, the Kid was sent down to work with Coffman at B Company, where he filled out paperwork and read company policies that said what to do in case of an attack, not to fuck the whores without a condom, how "loose lips sink ships," and all that endless army crap that accompanied an assignment to any new unit in a combat zone. Then it was time to talk with Captain Ronnie J. Smith. The Kid marched into Smith's office, stood at attention, and saluted.

"PFC Stocker reporting, sir!"

Smith snapped off a return salute as he sat behind his gunmetal-gray army-issue office desk. A gold-framed picture of a pretty brown-haired wife and two kids, a boy and a girl, who appeared to be about four and possibly six, respectively, looked back at the Kid. "At ease, Stocker. Take a seat. I've been looking at your file. Gee, you don't meet many soldiers with a GT score of a hundred and thirty- eight." He looked at the Kid with a quizzical expression on his face, contemplating the fact that the Kid was, according to army testing, one smart mutha. "I like that in a soldier. Especially one who is going to be in the position you're slated for."

The Kid, burning with a desire to ask the captain his GT score, said nothing, half smiling at the perceived compliment.

Smith lit up a butt and exhaled. "I suppose a smart fellow like you knows all about foreign-language announcements."

"No, sir, I don't. We didn't do any psyops training at DINFOS, so basically I'm at square one on this FLA thing, sir. All I've ever heard is that since I don't speak Vietnamese, there will be some Vietnamese guys making the actual announcements."

"Well, yes. See? You do know! Anyway, that's about the size of it. You're going to the field with Lieutenant Hershel Wilson, an officer whom I was with at Fort Campbell, Kentucky, with the Hundred and First."

"Fort Campbell! That's where I did my basic training."

"Yeah, so I see." He flipped the pages of the Kid's file. "I think you'll find Lieutenant Wilson to be a very capable officer. Considering that most of the time it'll only be the two of you, or possibly three of you, operating with the Vietnamese, it's pretty important that you get along and that you give it 110 percent. The two of you will be leaving by chopper in a couple of days for Sa Dec, which is ARVN's Ninth Division headquarters, and from there, they'll decide where your team will be deployed."

"OK." *My God! I laughed at Waterhouse and Imbach when they got assigned to the American Ninth Division, and now I come to find out I'm being sent to the ARVN Ninth Division! Beyond ironic.*

"So, Stocker, tomorrow morning you're going to be flying leaflet drops with the rest of the guys out of Binh Thuy Air Base. You'll need to be up by 0530 hours for chow, and after chow, you'll truck out there with Lieutenant Reagan. And don't forget to bring you M16 and some ammo, in the unlikely event you get shot down." A thin smile broke across his lips. "Any questions?"

"Uh, no, sir."

"Good. Welcome to the unit, Stocker. I hope you have a successful tour. Dismissed."

The Kid rose to his feet and saluted. "Yes, sir. Thank you, sir!" He did a fairly decent about-face and exited the room.

Coffman grinned at him as he emerged. "Hey, if you want, I'll take you upstairs and show you around the unit and introduce you to some of the guys."

"OK!"

"Captain Smith, I'm going to take Stocker upstairs and show him around and fill him in on the unit's mission."

"Fine, just don't be gone too long. We've got those reports to get done." The captain's approval came from out of his office.

The pair walked upstairs and turned into the first open door off the main room of the headquarters office. A group of five desks filled the room. At one of them sat an American lieutenant, thin of build with red hair and a great many freckles. The other desks were occupied by four Vietnamese, a man and three women. The man, who was smoking a cigarette using the European grip, holding it between his thumb and index finger with the ember pointing up at a forty-five-degree angle, looked at the Kid and smiled. The women, who glanced at him out of the corners of their eyes, just kept working on whatever it was on their desks in front of them.

"This is our translation and interpretation room." Coffman gestured with a sweeping hand. "With Lieutenant Powell in charge. What happens here is, when we come up with a propaganda program, we take the verbiage from English and translate it into Vietnamese. Then we give it to another set of Vietnamese and have them translate it back into English to see if we've lost anything in the translation."

"I see," said the Kid.

"For example," Coffman continued, "we have this program called Chieu Hoi, which means 'open arms,' as in, 'We welcome you back with open arms.' When we first came up with it, we had it translated into Vietnamese, but when the Vietnamese translation came back in English, instead of 'open arms,' as in arms ready to give you a great big friendly hug, it was 'arms that are cut open'—not the image we were looking for!"

"Well, I guess not!"

Coffman led the way out of the office and past the desks of Wimbish and Hoch, who were feverishly working away on their typewriters. Stepping into the next room, the Kid noticed it looked very much like the first room: five desks, an American lieutenant, and three Vietnamese, two women and one man.

"This is the Propaganda Development Department, Lieutenant Turner in charge." Coffman nodded to Turner, and Turner nodded back to them, but he was too absorbed to speak. "This is where we come up with our new programs and try to fine-tune the ones we have in the field right now. They come up with the concepts for a lot of the leaflets we drop in here, like the B-52 piece." Coffman picked up a leaflet off one of the desks and handed it to the Kid. It was in Vietnamese, so the Kid did not understand a word of it. But the picture on it was easily worth ten thousand words: a B-52 in flight in profile with bombs streaming from its belly.

"This is one we drop right after a B-52 strike. And what this says," Coffman said, translating the concept, if not the exact words, "is what just hit you. And if you don't come over to the South Vietnamese side sooner or later, this bomber is going to kill you."

"Effective." The Kid dropped it back onto the desk from which Coffman had taken it.

"We've got lots of things going on and new stuff in development in addition to the leaflets, but leaflets are our main gig, along with the FLA stuff that you'll be doing—and the hamlet pacification programs that are really taking off."

Going out the door and walking down the room, past the CO's office and the XO's office, Coffman led the Kid into a hallway. They emerged in a spacious room with a high ceiling that took up the back of the building. Five

GIs were working away at drafting tables with racks of pens, pastel markers, X-Acto knives, and T-square bases that were hooked to guide wires on the sides of the tables. It was set up just like the publishing room at DINFOS, where the students had worked on their newspapers from journalism class. One GI hammered away at a typesetting machine stuck in a corner of the room. They were all stripped to their T-shirts in response to the oven-like heat of the room. Each drafting table had a small fan attached to a corner, as the one black ceiling fan that cranked away gave little or no relief.

"This is our art department. Once we come up with a concept for a leaflet, we send it in here, and these guys do the art, set the type, and prepare the plates for printing, which is done over at Villa Cruz. We've got a set of printing presses that run day and night kicking out leaflets. As you will see tomorrow, we dump thousands and thousands of them every day all over the country."

"And it is the main Vietcong source of toilet paper." One of the art workers scoffed at the Kid, eliciting laughter from all the others in the room.

"Yes." Coffman smiled. "We once had a lieutenant who came up with the idea that we should treat the paper with a chemical that would give their asses a rash when they wiped with it, but the idea was kiboshed because we figured we don't want to have the VC pissed off at us any more than they already are or stop them from wanting to pick up any leaflets at all!"

"We also put out the unit newspaper from this room, Dimension." Coffman handed the Kid a copy. "This is the editor, Specialist 4 Everett Regan." Reagan and the Kid shook hands. "Guys, this is PFC Stocker, one of the new FLAs, on his way to the field," he said to the rest of the room.

"Oh, then you're a DINFOS grad?" Specialist 4 Regan inquired.

"Yep, for all the good it did me."

"So am I. Well, hey, I'm always looking for stories from the field. You could be a stringer for me if you want. At least you'd be getting something into print."

"Sure, why not?" the Kid responded. He handed the paper back to Regan.

"Keep it. You can read this later back at New Villa. We put it out once a month as a morale booster and as a way of showcasing our unit activities for Group back in Saigon," the bespectacled and slightly bucktoothed editor explained.

Coffman turned to leave. The Kid followed. "Nice to meet y'all," he said, waving as he started up the hall behind the clerk.

"Well, that's pretty much it for HQ Company. It's pretty dull and boring around here. I, myself, like it that way, but lots of guys would give anything to get out of here and go to the field where you're headed."

"I'll swap with any of them. Dull and boring I think I can handle. This loudspeaker thing, I don't know."

"Well, now that you've seen the place, you can do whatever you want." He glanced at his watch. "It's fourteen thirty hours, so you can hang around here and wait for the chow truck for dinner or go back to the New Villa. It's pretty easy to hitch a ride. Just go out to the corner across from the gate and stick out your thumb. The first US jeep or truck to come by will give you a ride. You just have to remember where to get out—at Bien Xe Moi, the big blue sign by the Texaco station."

"OK. I think I'll hang out here and write some letters home now that I know what I'm gonna be doing."

"Well, you can probably sit at that empty desk in Propaganda Development. That would be pretty much out of the way, and I can't imagine that Lieutenant Turner would mind. If you need anything, just ask anybody. Or I'll be downstairs working on my reports."

"Thanks, Coffman."

The Kid walked into the Propaganda Development office to find that Lieutenant Turner had left. He looked at the Vietnamese man and asked, "Can I sit here?"

"Yeah, OK, you sit!" the sunken-cheeked man replied.

Rummaging through his sack of PX purchases, the Kid pulled out his new stationery and realized that he didn't have a pen. Using a made-up sign language, as if he were talking to the Plains Indians, the Kid made a writing motion with his hand.

"Oh, sure, I got beaucoup pens." The Vietnamese guy opened a drawer and held out a government-issue black medium point.

"Boocoo?" The Kid looked at him quizzically as he took the pen. He'd already heard that word a number of times.

"Ah, *beaucoup* is actually a French word," the man replied. "It means 'a lot of something' or 'plenty.' Many Vietnamese words are French. The French were here for many years."

"Thank you." The Kid nodded.

"In Vietnamese, you say, 'Thank you,' *'Cam on.'* Cam on u lam is 'Thank you very much.'"

"Cam on u lam!" the Kid repeated. Hey, *I'm goin' native,* he mused. The two Vietnamese women looked up and smiled broadly as he tried out his new vocabulary, nodding to each other approvingly.

As the Kid prepared to write Flo, he brought her picture out of his pocket and sat it on the desk in front of him. The women looked at him curiously, so he held it up for them to see. "Girlfriend," he said. One of them held out her hand, wanting to take a closer look, so he passed the Polaroid over to her. She and her partner looked at it, nodding their approval.

"Co dep hoa!" the first woman said, passing the picture back. "That means she is very pretty," the man translated for him. "Yes, she is." The Kid smiled back and began writing.

Dearest Parnelli,

Well, I figure, as of today, I've only got another 359 days to go! Hell, I've almost made it through a whole week! I have left Saigon, and now I'm in a city in the Mekong Delta called Can Tho. But, as I understand it, I'm not going to be here that long. I am destined to go to "the field." That is what they call it when you are outside a city and with a unit that goes into combat. I still don't know what these stupid foreign-language announcements are going to be like, and I hope I don't find out for a while. Right now, I'm at Tenth Psyop Battalion headquarters, sitting at someone's desk who is not here, writing you. A guy told me that Elvis Presley's wife's father is stationed next door to us! Haven't seen him yet. Everybody keeps saying that down here in the Delta, the VC are the weakest of anywhere in the country. I hope they are right! The captain who is in charge of the company I'm now in is from Kentucky and says the lieutenant who I will be teamed with in the field has spent some time in Nashville. Tom, George, Al, and Pete all went to units in other towns all over the country, so we are spread out across hell and gone and I am finally alone. There is not one person here I've known longer than a couple of hours. It's so strange to keep moving away from all that is familiar.

I know I'd like to be getting familiar with your lips about right now. TM is all I can think of. I bought a radio today, so now I can listen to Armed Forces Radio and hate these bastards even more than I already do for pulling this shit on me! Tomorrow, I am being sent on a leaflet-dropping mission, but don't worry: I'll be in a plane way high over the rice paddies, where the bullets can't reach, so I'll be safe. And it is hotter than blazes here! A regular miniature hell.

I know I tell you not to worry all the time, but you might as well not. What will happen, will happen, so why worry? It's so hard to believe now that we were ever together. For the time that we've been given to spend together up until now, I can't believe I love you as much as I do. But I do. Hey, look, I'm practicing my "I do"s. Do you know what I want to do? TM and more TM. Well, gotta write the folks and Dave and Patsy Allen.

All my love. ISYL—I'll see you later!

Curt

Sticking the letter into an envelope, the Kid addressed it and went on with his next one, to his parents, then the next one, to Dave and Patsy Allen, followed by one to Larry Ryan, all nearly carbon copies of the one he wrote to Flo, but without the mushy, gooey stuff. Before he knew it, somebody was yelling, "Chow truck!" *Is time going fast or slow?* he pondered as he gathered up his stuff. *Slow. Definitely slow.*

Chapter 8

When the chow truck dropped the soldiers off back at the New Villa, Boujold was waiting for the Kid in the doorway of the first sergeant's office.

"Hey, Stocker," he said. "I already took a locker to your room and locked up your gear and your M16. Did you get a lock?"

"Uh, I already have a couple of them."

"OK, I'll take mine off and you can put yours on." He stopped and faced the Kid, making sure he had his attention. "Never, *never* leave anything unlocked in this fucking country or the gooks will own it in a New York fucking minute!"

"I surely will take your advice," the Kid replied.

Entering the room, the Kid discovered that his bunkmates were in. One was a skinny kid with a narrow chin, thin lips, and rather plain-looking brown hair that was grown out just past the buzz-cut stage. His name tag said "Zewe." The other one was equally as slight of build, but his face was more round and he wore army-issue gray plastic glasses just like the Kid's. His name was McClain. A cigarette dangled from his mouth, and a Coke can loosely held in his left hand was serving as his ashtray.

"Gentlemen," the Kid offered in salutation as Boujold fumbled with his key to remove the lock from the newly installed locker. "How's it goin'?"

"OK, I guess. All things considered." Zewe stood up from the bunk upon which he was sitting. "I'm Rich."

"Nice to meet you." The Kid shook his hand. "I'm poor. And my name is Curt."

"And I'm Will, short for William, and not Bill." McClain also rose to shake the Kid's hand.

"Nice to meet you too, Will." The Kid smiled. "Uh, which of these bunks is open?"

"I'm on the bottom here, and Richard's got the top, so you can have either of those." Will pointed to the bunks on the right side of the room. "You just came down from Saigon today?" Will inquired as he watched the Kid pick the lower bunk.

"Yeah. I'll been in-country for a week tomorrow," he lamented.

"Well, we're in the same boat." Zewe nodded. "I'm just two days more than a week in-country myself. But McClain here, he's got almost two weeks!"

"OK." Boujold stuffed his padlock into his pocket. "There you go, Stocker." "Thanks."

"I'm going up to the Roof for a beer," Boujold said. "You two must have found the club by now." He looked at the Kid's two roomies.

"Yes we have, and we were also just heading up," Zewe said, turning to the Kid. "It's pretty nice, actually, because it's kind of open with a little breeze, not like this stifling toaster we have to call our room."

"Well then, let's go check it out!" the Kid said as he placed his own lock on the locker holding his stuff.

Out in the hall, the group moved toward the staircase, with Boujold in the lead. The Kid couldn't help but notice that beneath the stairs was a dark and foreboding kind of a grotto-looking deal that was full of water. "What's that?" the Kid asked.

"A cistern. Water used to collect on the roof and run into gutters and flow down here. It doesn't anymore since they put a roof on the club. Oh, it's unpotable. The maids use it to wash the floors, so now a tanker truck comes and fills it for them, just like the one that comes every day and pumps water to the holding tank on the roof so we can all shower every night." They started walking up the stairs. On the landing of the second floor, Boujold stopped and pointed to a line of men, all wearing nothing but towels and holding soap and shampoo bottles in their hands.

"Out that door on the balcony is where the showers are, right at the front of that line. There's two on each floor. I highly recommend you don't use the showers on the first floor. They've got a little bit of a snake problem."

"Snakes?" The Kid stopped in his tracks.

"Yeah, little poisonous ones called kraits. About the size of earthworms, but really deadly. They crawl up the drain from the swamp outside here." He pointed. "You gotta be really desperate to use the first-floor showers."

"Hmm," the Kid said, "on second thought, I think the beer can wait. I really want to take a shower in the worst way."

"OK, see ya," Boujold said. He and the pair of new roommates continued on up the stairs. The Kid returned to the room to get his shaving kit.

101

Sounds echoed through the building. The Kid could hear music, "Satisfaction" by the Rolling Stones. *Some guys must have some big tape recorders somewhere,* he thought.

The room was spartan in its furnishings. There was an old white porcelain sink attached to the wall beneath the one light bulb that illuminated the light green paint. Over the sink was stenciled the word *nonpotable,* which was army speak for "Don't drink the water." Other than the three wall lockers, there was a footlocker in the opposite corner of the room that was protected by a big old honking Master lock.

Opening his locker, the Kid pulled out the duffle bag and opened it to fish out his shaving kit. Unzipping the kit, he looked at the Colgate tube and wondered if there was anyplace in this godforsaken French hotel where he might be able to blow a joint. Couldn't be too careful, being the new kid in the unit; it might take a couple of days to find out whom he could trust, but apparently he wasn't going to have more than a couple of days here. The Kid was ready to bet any amount of money or extra days in 'Nam that Boujold was a pot smoker. He'd ask him later.

The Kid could see that the interior transit rooms on the bottom floor of the hotel were indeed low rent. Just how low became apparent when he stripped, put on his flip-flops, got his towel and shaving kit, and assumed his position at the end of the shower line on the balcony of the second floor. *Yes, rooms with windows and doors open to the air! Not half bad,* he thought, kind of looking into the one next to where he stood in line, about four guys back from the shower. Seeing a Janis Joplin and Big Brother and the Holding Company poster and a Jefferson Airplane poster, he thought, *These guys are obviously heads.*

"Hi," the red-haired GI standing in front of him in the line said.

"Hi." The Kid smiled.

"You're the new FLA, aren't you?" "Yep."

"I'm O'Hanrahan. Irish, if you can't tell." "I'm Stocker. Bohemian, if you give a shit."

Hearing some commotion coming up the stairwell, the Kid turned to see a soldier passing by with a big sack slung over his shoulder. Then the words rang out with a shout: "Mail call!"

A rush of GIs materialized out of thin air. Faces filled with anticipation hurried by on their way to see if anything in the bag was for them.

"Oh yeah, mail call is every night after chow on the roof," the Irishman intoned as one of the men in front of them got out of line to go see if he'd scored. "Hey, Simmons, get mine too!" he yelled after him.

The Kid knew that he, for sure, would be one of the guys not getting anything. Hell, with his having just sent word of his new address a day ago, it would realistically be another three weeks before he saw a letter from Flo—or anybody for that matter.

War's best ritual would have to wait. The only thing worse would be to go to mail call expecting something and come away empty-handed. It happened a lot.

As the Kid waited his turn, he gazed off the balcony through the mesh wire that protected them from somebody running up and pitching a grenade into their midst. Below was a murky-looking pond, about a third the size of a football field.

It started about three feet out from the wall and was about twenty yards wide and as long as the New Villa. A sidewalk on the opposite side passed in front of a row of Vietnamese houses in the neighborhood that stretched out for blocks beyond them. One of the grass-roofed houses to the left of the pond had a patio upon which some massively big earthenware jars sat. Just as the Kid was wondering what the jars might be for, two young Vietnamese children came out of the house, naked, then pulled a lid off one of the jars, which they started dipping into with a pan, pouring water over themselves in their bath ritual.

Beyond the house on the edge of the neighborhood to the left, there was open countryside for quite some distance, before it became thick with trees and bushes. It looked as if some of the area had been cleared, possibly to make it easier to see what was going on out there. Off in the far distance, the Kid watched three jet fighters taking off from an airfield. It seemed too far away to be Can Tho, so he figured it must have been the air base they would fly leaflet drops out of tomorrow.

As the Kid watched the children wash, their mother came out on the patio to see how they were doing. She stood there in the doorway with her arms crossed, first looking at her kids, then lifting her gaze to the Americans above her and staring with a quasi-contemptuous look on her face. She was distracted by a Vietnamese couple who had just walked up to her front door and began exchanging greetings. Pulling a pair of white towels off her outside clothesline, she handed them to her kids and invited the visitors in with a gesture.

O'Hanrahan stepped into the shower stall and closed the door, making the Kid next. There were now three other GIs behind him.

"Yeah, I think I'm gonna get the TEAC recorder, like Bob has. That's the best I've heard so far," a fair-skinned GI was saying as he twirled his soap on a rope like a long key chain. He was burned by the sun on his forearms, face, and neck, whereas the rest of him was as white as a sheet.

Turning to look at the speaker, the Kid asked, "Anybody here got a copy of *Sgt. Pepper's Lonely Hearts Club Band?*"

"Hmm, let me think. Yeah, Harvey has a copy. He's up on the third floor. Are you new?"

"Oh no, I've been here for six weeks. My job is to watch you. Haven't you noticed?" the Kid joked. Noticing the perplexed look on the man's face, he quickly corrected himself. "Yes, I'm the new guy. Just got in today from Group in Saigon."

"Welcome to the Tenth." The pale-chested guy grinned. "What's your job?"

"I'm a FLA, although I've never FLA'd, so I really don't know what the fuck is going on except that I'm flying leaflets tomorrow and shipping out to someplace called Sa Dec the day after."

"You lucky fuck! Going to the field! God, what I wouldn't give. But fuck me, they don't have any printing presses in the field, so I'm stuck here permanently."

"So, you're a printer, huh?"

"Yes. Joe. Nice to meet you." He extended his sunburned hand.

"Why is it that everybody thinks this place is so bad?" The Kid continued to wonder why it was that virtually everybody apparently wanted to abandon a safe haven.

"Well, when you step out of that shower, that will have been your high point of the day if you don't take one of the whores to your room. But hell, they've got whores everywhere, so that's no bonus."

"You can take whores to your room?" The Kid was more than mildly surprised.

"Sure. The ones from across the street are up in the club right now. Ozelle lets them in. We think he's getting a cut of the action."

"OK, whores, showers, club, music. What is it that's so bad about this place?"

"See my tan? After working all night at the printing presses, I have to pull sandbag duty, filling sandbags in the sun for at least three hours, before I can sack out. After you fill sandbags for a day in this heat, you'll know. That's my gripe du jour."

"And guard duty all night at Villa Cruz for the officers," the black GI standing behind Palmer said, getting into the conversation. "They've got more worthless time-wasting duty crap to pull around here than basic training! And you can't go out at night once the curfew goes into effect, so it's just like being locked up in a fuckin' jail."

The shower door opened. O'Hanrahan came out. The Kid's face lit up in a smile.

"If you gentlemen will excuse me!"

The Kid entered the two-square-foot enclosure and pulled the louvered door shut behind him. A pipe extended straight out of the wall above him, and a forty-five- degree bend placed the showerhead directly over his noggin. A hook protruded from the wall to the left of the door, and on the right was a little shelf where the bather could park his kit. There was only one knob for the water. *Cold will be more than fine,* he thought as he hung up his towel, parked his kit, and hit the slightly rusted handle.

Cold water poured out of the showerhead and cascaded down his skull. He put his face right in it and relished the cool, but not anything like cold, water as it ran off his shoulders and down his chest and belly. *Ah, the little pleasures.* Taking his shampoo, he lathered the short hair on his head and rinsed the shampoo out.

Then he cracked open his plastic soap dish and got out his bar of Dial.

As he soaped up, he thought of Flo and the shower they'd taken together at the Traveler's Motel. *I'd like to be soaping her up right about now,* he dreamed as he rubbed the yellowish bar in his pubic hair and lathered up his crotch to wash his dick and balls. Privacy was always a problem in the army. It would be a marvelous tension reliever if he could masturbate right now, but no, there was a time and a place for everything. He only wished he could find that time and place.

The floor of the shower was made of the same white tile that was in the halls of the hotel. The light green walls of the shower, like all the walls in the place, didn't extend the ceiling. A central light bulb hung suspended above where the plumbing came out of the wall of the Kid's shower and the one next to it. It was suddenly flipped on, supplying light to both cubicles as the sunlight was beginning to fade for the evening. As much as he could have spent another half an hour in the cold water, he wrapped it up and exited, knowing there was a line outside.

Back in his room, the Kid put on a fresh pair of boxers, some Bermuda shorts, and a clean army-issue jungle-green T-shirt. Grabbing his new transistor radio, his Kools, and his Zippo lighter, he locked up his gear and headed up to check out the club.

The club, he found, took up the whole roof. It had once been just a roof, until the unit got a hold of the place and put a wooden roof on top, easily twelve feet high, making the old roof of the hotel the floor of the club. A varnished plywood bar ran for a dozen feet down the side that overlooked the pond. About a dozen stools were lined up, eight of them occupied, as two Vietnamese women bartenders filled drink orders.

At least twenty square and slightly battered wooden tables were spread out around the room with some very colorful plastic woven butterfly chairs pulled up next to them. It was about 1900 hours, that is to say, seven o'clock in the evening, so more than half the chairs were occupied. A couple of poker games were in progress, along with a Monopoly game. And at another table, two soldiers were playing Stratego.

The edge of the building and three GIs clustered up stood out on the L-shaped walkway that lined two sides of the club. *Not a bad view from up here,* the Kid thought, gazing down at the minions of Bien Xe Moi below him. A very large and slightly elevated white movie screen took up the far wall of the club, and in front of the screen was a lectern. A sound system was playing "Cherish" by the Association, which could be heard in the background.

Walking up to the bar, the Kid ordered a beer. *Yuck, more Falstaff. But what the hell?* Here he was in Vietnam and it was a hardship tour, so he figured he'd better get used to it. Taking his can of beer in one hand and his radio in the other, he wandered among the tables, trying to figure out where to sit. *It's hard when you don't know anybody at all.*

Then, when he saw Boujold smoking a cigarette and talking to another GI out near the balcony rail, he moseyed on over and said, "Hey!"

"Hey," Boujold responded. "So, you got all showered up and everything, and I see you got a beer. How do you like your room?" he inquired with a wry grin.

"Well, I've already got what must be the bug around here, that is to say, I think I'm glad I'm headed to the field, because that room is a fucking Dachau oven!"

"Roger that! I was in that room for three weeks! Uh, Stocker, this is Manley. Manley, Stocker."

"Hey." Manley stuck out a huge hand that fittingly went with his gigantic frame and long lanky arms. "Glad to meet ya. So, you get to go to the field, huh?"

106

"Yeah, that's the word. What do you do here?"

"Motor pool mechanic, but I also do work on our printing presses. They're just diesel engines without wheels. Anyway, wheels that touch the ground and go anywhere. I guess they got lots of wheels when you stop and think about it."

"So, Stocker, finding everything you need?" Boujold flipped his butt off the balcony and into the pond below.

"Well, almost. I could use a joint of that Vietnamese pot I've been hearing about."

"Oh, really?" Boujold responded flatly as he turned his head and looked the Kid over from head to toe. Maybe the Kid had been too bold, approaching him on the first night, but from everything he'd seen and heard, he figured that Boujold must be a head.

"It appears that this young man is seeking a taste of the old vaporized libations. Ah yes," Boujold responded in the voice of W. C. Fields, which, the Kid had to admit, was pretty good! Boujold did slightly resemble W. C., especially in the face—only with a mustache. "Well," he said, switching back to his real voice, "I'm sorry I can't help you out right now. I'm sort of fucked up, and I'm on report for being unprepared for guard duty last night, so I've got to watch my ass right now. They're just looking for any way they can find to rack my balls." He paused and gave the Kid a serious look. "You're not here to rack my balls, are you?"

"Uh, no. No I'm not. Let's just say for the sake of argument that I don't need you to get me any, but—and once again, I express the hypothetical nature of this statement—*if I had some,* is there a place in this hotel where I could smoke it and reasonably expect not to get popped?"

"Come over here," Manley said, gesturing, as the big guy walked a few paces to his right, "and lean over this rail."

Following instructions, the Kid did exactly that. On the balcony a floor below him, as he leaned over, he saw the tops of the heads of three GIs standing there, their elbows on the railing, smoking. As the smoke drifted up, the unmistakable odor hit him! *Wow!*

"If you wanna smoke here, you just go out on the third-floor balcony and blow your J. If anybody you aren't sure of comes along, just drop it into the swamp and you're clean. As you can see, there's so many cigarette butts and stuff down there, they'd have to be standing right below you and catch it before it hit the ground to legally certify that it was yours." Manley smiled. "And of course, they're not standing down there. That whole pond is crawling

with those little poisonous krait snakes. And just look at the size of that rat!"
He pointed down.

Sure enough, right at the base of the hotel wall was a rat about the size of
a schnauzer, rooting through the accumulated trash.

"How about that!" The Kid took a long pull on his beer. "Thanks for the
info!"

"The guy's a DINFOS grad, like Roberts." Boujold gestured to the Kid as
he spoke to Manley. "So I imagine he's OK."

"In that case, Stocker, I was just headed down myself. Care to join me?"
"Sure!"

"I'll see y'all later," Boujold said as the pair walked off toward the
staircase.

"So, Stocker, where you from?" Manley asked in a deep voice that fit his
size.

"Well, right now, I'm from Nashville. But I grew up in Colorado and just
moved back there about a year and a half ago. And you?"

"I'm from California, up near Santa Barbara. Ever hear of Oxnard?"
"Yeah, I've even passed through. I'm engaged to a girl from Vista." "Really?
How'd you meet her?"

"She was visiting in Nashville with her grandparents, who live there, last
summer. It just sort of clicked, and here I am, an engaged man."

"That's nice," Manley said. They walked out on the third-floor balcony.
The three guys who were smoking looked up and, seeing it was Manley, just
continued to smoke.

"Men." Manley stopped next to them. "This is Stocker, a new guy, but a
DINFOS man like Roberts, so Boujold and I are pretty sure he's OK. And if
he's not, we'll just frag his ass!"

"Uh, that won't be necessary." The Kid smiled. "I mean, I got my own
shit, if you want me to prove I'm not a narc."

"Wow, that's heavy, a guy who brings grass to 'Nam! Talk about your
coals to Newcastle! Hey, we don't care." One of the three passed the Kid
a smallish dark brown pipe. "If you are a narc, you might well get your ass
fragged!"

"That's nice to know that the vigilantes are alive and kicking." He took
the nicely burning bowl and drew in his very first hit of Vietnamese weed.
Pungent, thick, exotic, and tasty! He held the hit, fighting the natural urge to
cough as he passed the pipe over to Manley.

When the bowl came around for the third time, the Kid was *off.* Way off. He'd never smoked anything that bulldozed him like this in just three hits. "Wow, talk about some killer shit!"

"That ain't no lie." Manley grinned from ear to ear. "Got to know that you have come to a place that has the best weed on fucking earth!"

As they stood there and toked, another GI walked out on the balcony. One of his hands was holding the hand of a young Vietnamese woman, and the other was holding a beer.

"Max, what's shakin'? A little boom-boom?" Manley gave him a sly look.

"Yep, me and Win are fixing to do a little short time!" he said as they eased by and walked around the corner.

The Kid checked Win out as they passed. Not his type. Sooner or later. He was glad that Flo had pretty much said she didn't expect him never to get laid in the war zone while he was away. "Just don't catch VD," she had said rather gallantly.

Another couple of hits and the Kid was devastated. "This shit is wicked! I hope I can find my room!" He laughed.

His smoking buddies kind of eyed him, amused, to say the least, watching his reaction to his first taste of 'Nam bud.

"This isn't even the best," one of them offered. "We got some one-hit crap that will knock you right off the balcony! But that'll be tomorrow night."

"What's the movie tonight?" Manley asked nobody in particular. The Kid didn't even know they had movies in Can Tho.

"Some Clint Eastwood thing. I think its called *High Plains Drifter*," one of the smokers replied. "I hear it startin' up there." He gestured to the roof with his thumb.

"I've seen it," the Kid cut in. "Not bad. Lots of shooting, if you go for that sort of thing and aren't getting enough around here."

"Let's go catch it!" With that, one of them knocked the filling out of the pipe and set it on a little ledge that ran near the bottom of the plaster railing. "That's where we keep it, in case you need to use it. Just put it back, OK?" he said to the Kid.

"Yeah, sure. Thanks!" the Kid exclaimed.

Up on the roof, the tables and chairs at the front near the screen had been turned to facilitate the watching of the movie. Out went most of the lights. When the movie projector began grinding away, the desert Southwest of the United States appeared on the silver screen. No fewer than a half a dozen geckos scurried around the far buttes and sagebrush, eating any bugs that had been attracted to the light.

At least three separate poker games continued at the rear of the club, where a setup of lowered lights didn't interfere with the viewing of the spaghetti western in the front of the club. A number of GIs sat at the bar talking and, of course, smoking—paying no attention to the movie whatsoever.

Sitting down on a folding chair in front of a remote table covered with almost- current magazines and paperback books, the Kid nursed his beer and fiddled with his new radio as, on the screen, Clint shot about a dozen guys. By transistor standards, this radio wasn't as small as the pocket-sized radio the Kid used to use for listening to the World Series during class in junior high, but at about ten inches long by three inches wide by six inches tall, it wasn't large by the new standards.

"You're listening to Armed Forces Radio Saigon." The DJ was working it. "And now, here's something new by the Box Tops!"

"Gimme a ticket for an airplane. Ain't got time to take a fast train. Lonely days are gone and I'm a-goin' home 'cause my baby done sent me a letter."

Lighting up a Kool, the Kid leaned back and listened to "The Letter," one of the his favorite songs, but hardly new to him. It had come out in the summer of 1967, before he got drafted, and for a while, because it was the "pick hit of the week," he had been required to play it every other hour on his shift. Now it was new in Vietnam, because Armed Forces Radio (AFR) had to wait for a song to be given approval and placed on a big 33 rpm disk along with twenty other popular songs, certifying it had been cleared for play to the troops. An example of a song that was once cleared for AFR but was no longer permitted to be heard in Vietnam was "We Gotta Get Out of This Place," by Eric Burdon and the Animals.

The lyrics of Alex Chilton came out clear, but low, since the Kid was keeping the sound down so as not to disturb anybody who was watching Clint bang away with his six-shooters. "Well, she sent me a letter, said she couldn't live without me no mo'. Listen, mister, can't you see I gotta get back to my baby once more? Anyway, yeahhhhhh!" The Kid looked at a GI who was sitting at an adjacent card table reading a letter from home. What the Kid wouldn't have given for a fresh letter from Flo right then and there, one dripping in her perfume, an aphrodisiac if ever there was one.

Closing his eyes and thinking about her high-cheekboned face and ever so beautifully chiseled nose and chin, he wanted to just cry out in despair. Life was so unfair. All he wanted to do was make love to her until the sun came up every day for the rest of time. Was that too much to ask? *How did I come to be in this fucking place?*

"And now, for all you soldiers on guard duty out on the perimeters tonight, we've got your theme song—by the Who!" Once the DJ introduced the next song, the electrical piercing chord of the opening to "I Can See for Miles" exploded from the little sound box. *God, am I ever high!* the Kid thought. The stuff in that joint he had hit fewer than half a dozen times on the balcony was kicking his cosmic ass. Closing his eyes, he floated with the music: "I know you deceived me, but here's a surprise. I know what you did because I've got magic in my eyes. I can see for miles and miles and miles, oh yeah."

After another couple of songs, the Kid got up and ordered a fresh beer, then went and stood at the edge of the club balcony. Below, he could see low light coming from some of the Vietnamese houses, glowing a kind of yellow, as if the light was coming from candles or kerosene lanterns and not by electric light bulbs. Staring out at the darkness now settled over the land, off in the distance, the Kid saw a yellow flare blossom and light up the sky, visibly rocking back and forth as it drifted by parachute toward the ground. Almost instantly, it was joined by three more flares; somebody apparently needed to light up a perimeter out there by the airfield.

Then a GI came running up the stairs and, bursting into the club, announced, "VC mortar attack on Binh Thuy Air Base!" Easily half the guys got up from the movie and came to the edge of the building where the Kid already stood.

"Spooky'll be here any second," the man who brought the message stated. "I heard them call for support on the TOC radio!"

Less than thirty seconds later, a stream of something red, like water out of a garden hose, poured from some unseen spot moving across the black sky as the tracer bullets from the Spooky gunship opened up on the VC who were attacking the airfield.

"Ooh, check this out!" As the real shooting war took the stage, the soldiers of the Tenth forgot about the movie, more and more of them coming to the railing to watch the war.

A Spooky gunship was equipped with three minicannons that, in unison, fired thousands of rounds a minute. Behind the Kid, Clint Eastwood was shooting up some little dirtbag town a round at a time—*bang, bang, bang*—and to the Kid's front, he could now hear the faint noise be carried on the air from the gunship off in the distance. First the tracers, then, like thunder from a distant bolt of lightning, the noise. The three minicannons made a soft, faint, almost purring sound: *Brrrrrrruuuuuuuppppp ... brrrrruuuuuuuppppp.* Thousands of tracers poured with an even flow from the sky. As they hit the ground, some bounced every which way, like upside-down Fourth of July fireworks. Then came the report.

"How far away is that?" the Kid inquired.

"About seven miles," the man next to him said.

"Wow, that sound really carries! How is that possible?"

"Well, there's no traffic noise from busy streets or anything else to compete with it," somebody theorized.

"Think we might get hit tonight?" The Kid was apprehensive as he watched the distant engagement unfolding.

"Doubt it," came an immediate reply from down the railing. "We never get it. Or at least we haven't gotten hit since Tet." On that note, most of the GIs went back to watch the movie.

The Kid stood glued to his spot, checking out his first real view of any live action. The Spooky continued shooting for another couple of minutes. More flares drifted down, but there wasn't any more ordnance being expended. Turning away, he walked up to the bar and ordered another beer. Boujold had suggested a couple of shots of Jack Daniel's as a sleeping aid, but the Kid hated bourbon.

Finding an empty chair at one of the tables, the Kid gave in and watched the rest of *High Plains Drifter.* As time passed slowly, he felt that the effects of the 'Nam weed were growing even stronger. At one point, he nodded out for a couple of minutes.

When the movie was over, he made his way back down to the first floor. After taking a leak, he went to his room. When he flipped on the light, he discovered that his roommates had not yet turned in. He stripped down to his boxers and climbed into his bunk. The hot, humid air hung heavy in the room, barely churned up by the laborious action of the ceiling fan, and made the Kid think that he was a loaf of bread climbing into an oven where he would bake all night.

He was very tired. How long had it been since he'd had a really good night's sleep? As he tucked in the mosquito netting, he counted up the different places he'd slept since he left Flo's parents' house. His first night was at the Oakland Army Terminal; he didn't sleep a wink. Then he spent one night on the jet, and thus far in 'Nam, he'd spent two nights at Bien Hoa and three nights in Saigon. Now this night in Can Tho made only six nights total. *Fuck! I have yet to even complete a week!*

112

Lying down and stretching out, the Kid could feel the sweat emerging from his pores, matting the hair on his chest. *Flo, Flo, Flo. How I love you, Flo!* Easily letting her image appear in his third eye, he thought about the first time they had kissed. It was at her grandparents' house in a suburb of Nashville. After she called him at the radio station, he'd arranged to meet her and her twin sister, Lo, for lunch at the Shoney's Big Boy in downtown Nashville, just a block from WKDA. There, she told him that if he was going to take her out while she was in town, he'd have to meet her grandparents so they could inspect him.

And so it was that he drove over to their house, where he and Flo; twin, Lo; the grandparents; and Gary, a fifteen-year-old cousin with a learning disorder, sat on the porch and drank lemonade and ate homemade chocolate chip cookies while making small talk. When it was time for the Kid to leave to go to work for his air shift, he said his goodbyes, then Flo walked him to his green VW Bug. Gary, it seemed, had circled around to the corner of the house, from where he not so subtly peeked out at them, hoping to see them kiss. Knowing he was there, Flo turned and said, "Gary, beat it or I'll tell Grandma that you're not being nice!" He pretended to leave, but as soon as Flo turned her attention back to the Kid, he could see over her shoulder that Gary was still peeking around the corner, watching them. As if the Kid cared! He put his hands on Flo's shoulders and looked into her brown eyes. It was eleven o'clock at night, but there was enough illumination from the corner streetlight to show him the tiny smile of anticipation she had on her pretty face as he drew her close and placed his lips ever so gently on hers. Almost at the same time, their lips parted and the tips of their tongues met in brief mutual wonder, before the Kid couldn't stand it any longer, at which point he went deep, to which Flo's tongue immediately responded. Right there, it was some serious tonsil hockey for about an eternity, that is to say, nearly thirty seconds. When they broke the kiss, they were both breathless.

"Do you think your grandparents will let you go to a movie tomorrow?"

"Well, they seemed to like you. I'll ask, then call you when you get on the air, OK?"

"OK." The Kid, it seemed, was not only going to be on the air; he was also *walking* on it!

Chapter 9

The Kid sat bolt upright in his bed. Looking at the illuminated face of the alarm clock, he saw that the time was half past eleven in the morning. *Holy fucking shit!* He must have slept right through the alarm. He was late for work. *My God, I've only had the job for three days, and now I'm late!* Jumping up, he threw on his clothes. *Jesus, do the buses in Nashville even run this late?* He didn't stop to wait for his usual bus. His workplace was a good two miles downtown from where he lived on the West End, so, being a half-miler and used to running, he just took off at a sprint. Halfway there, he spied a taxi and frantically waved it down. "Stalhman Building—and step on it!" he frantically screamed. The taxi driver took off like a shot.

Throwing the driver a five for a two-dollar fare, the Kid didn't wait for any change. Running into the lobby, he fumbled with his wallet, trying to find his after-hours pass to show the old elevator operator and night watchman who, it seemed, was waiting for him at the elevator door. "My God, I'm late!" he screamed.

"Yes, sir, you are! I thought y'all might come a-runnin' up here in a lather, which is why I'm a-waitin' here with the elevator." The doors closed, and the old Otis seemed to move in slow motion as it rose the twelve floors to the offices and studios of WKDA.

As the doors parted, the Kid broke from the chute. Running up and shoving his key into the door of the station, he opened it, then ran in through the reception area, opening the next door and sprinting down the eternally long hallway.

Bursting through the control room door, he found Johnny Wailin, the eight-to- midnight jock, sitting at the control board with the phone in his hand. "Oh, wait a minute, Dick, he just walked in." The Kid looked up at the clock. He was ten minutes late. "Dick wants to talk with you." Wailin handed him the phone and got up with the clipboard to read the meters and sign off on his shift.

"What happened?" Dick Buckley asked the Kid, who was breathlessly trying to organize his thoughts.

114

"Uh, well, I guess my travel alarm isn't loud enough. I swear it won't happen again, if you'll just give me another chance, just one more chance. One more chance …"

The Kid felt a shaking sensation, followed by intense heat. Then, when he gained consciousness, he realized that he wasn't in Nashville at all. He was in the bowels of the New Villa Hotel, and one of his roommates, Zewe, was shaking his bunk, rattling the whole frame.

"Yo, you awake?" Rich asked in a quiet voice.

"Ah, yeah," the Kid responded. "What time is it?"

"Zero five thirty hours. The maid was just here. You'd better get up if you want any breakfast. The chow truck is leaving for Eakin in fifteen minutes," Zewe informed the Kid as he pulled his shaving kit out of his locker, along with a towel. Then he walked out of the room.

Chow might not be a bad idea, the Kid thought as he untucked his mosquito netting and swung his feet onto the cool tile floor.

"Mornin', Stocker." McClain yawned from his top bunk.

"Morning," the Kid replied. Sitting there, he contemplated. *Am I still groggy from sleep, or am I still stoned on the weed I sampled last night?* No time to ponder. He grabbed his glasses and walked down the hall to the water closet to take a piss. Once he was dressed, he pulled his M16 and some ammo out of his locker, then relocked the locker and walked out and into the orderly room.

Fuck! He hadn't had time to shave. He wondered for a moment if anybody would hassle him about it.

A group of a half dozen GIs with M16's waited, all smoking their early morning cigarettes by the front gate, talking quietly among themselves. The Kid noticed that at least half of them also had bayonets strapped to their belts.

"Yo, newbie!" A GI whose name tag read "Zanzarella" greeted the Kid as he walked out onto the hotel porch. "Ready for some action?"

"No," the Kid replied as he, too, lit up and exhaled. "The only action I'm ready for involves my eyelids closing."

"You'll feel better after we get some coffee. Did you bring your canteen? You'll need to fill it at Eakin. It gets fucking hotter than Death Valley in the plane humping those boxes of leaflets."

The Kid wheeled around and ran back to the room, where he fetched his canteen, and was back just as the chow truck was arriving in the driveway. In a cloud of diesel fumes, the soldiers were off to Eakin in the almost cool morning

115

air—cool only in comparison to high noon. Local traffic was just starting to build on the roads, but it was still pretty light, so they quickly made it to Eakin.

As they sat down to eat, Zanzarella introduced the Kid around the table. "Guys, this is the new FLA, Stocker. And, Stocker, this is George McCauley, Eddy Reynolds, and Billy Smith. And this is another new guy, Richard Zewe. Then here's Sergeant Tucker and, of course, our driver, Moyssiadias."

"Hey." The Kid nodded as he dipped his toast into the bright yellow yolk of his over-easy eggs.

"So, Stocker," McCauley began, "what's the attitude in the States these days toward the war?"

"Same as it ever was. All the Hawks are saying we gotta hang in there and do whatever it takes to win it, and all the Doves are saying we gotta get out at the earliest possible moment. We had this instructor at DINFOS who thought we ought to use nuclear weapons on Hanoi! This guy, Major Thompson, we nicknamed him 'Nuke 'Em Thompson.'"

"And at the point of your arrival, where do you stand?" Smith looked at him with a serious expression. "Because you know how you feel about it now, whereas how you're going to feel about it in a couple of weeks could be different."

"Personally, I'm hoping that RFK gets the nomination, because he'll get us out of this fucking mess. He's doing pretty good, and if he wins in California next week, that should clinch it. We were all so happy when LBJ said he wasn't going to run again. If Bobby wins, he might find a way to get us the fuck out of here."

"So, you don't think that the peace talks in Paris are going to do any good?" McCauley inquired. "You know, we're so far out of the loop over here, we hear things days after they happen. *Stars and Stripes* is not a real newspaper, so we like to corner the newbies and pump them."

"Jesus H., McCauley!" Zanzarella's mouth dropped open in an expression of disbelief. "Do you have any idea how *queer* that sounded? You wanna corner the newbie and pump him?" Everybody roared.

"For information—*for information,* for chrissakes!"

"Sure." Zewe nodded. "Stocker, we'd better lock our door tonight—unless you wanna get pumped for information. I know I don't!"

As they walked out of the mess hall, every single one of the eight soldiers lit up. It was as if they were off to do the day's work just as if they had normal, everyday jobs back in the States, only in reality, they were all armed with M16's and were going off to participate directly in the war. Just how directly

116

would depend entirely on circumstances beyond their control. *What if the plane is shot down, or even more likely, what if it has engine problems and has to ditch in VC territory, which includes almost the entire country?* "What-if" hung like a dark little cloud over the Kid's head, like the one that followed the *Li'l Abner* cartoon character Joe Btfsplk.

Riding out to the Binh Thuy Air Base, the Kid looked at the Vietnamese who were moving about on the roadway. Some of them, without a doubt, were VC or VC sympathizers. *How they fuck can anybody tell them apart? Friend or foe? Ooh, I'd certainly like to be friends with* that, he thought as he spied a real cutie. What sweet torture it was becoming that so many of the young woman had long black hair that looked like Flo's.

Binh Thuy Air Base was a sprawling, built-from-the-ground up complex that was the center of air operations for IV Corps, for both the Vietnamese and the Americans. Fighter support missions, reconnaissance missions, helicopter gunships, and helicopter medevacs all flew out of Binh Thuy, which was also a takeoff point for aircraft doing leaflet drops.

"I wonder where they got hit last night?" Reynolds craned his neck to see if he could spot any damage as the truck made its way through the streets of the base, which were fairly crowded with US and South Vietnamese personnel making their way to work.

Soon, the truck arrived at a row of about a dozen CONEX boxes, which are quite large metal storage lockers measuring about ten feet square and eight feet high.

"This is where we keep the leaflets," Tucker informed the Kid, who must have had a quizzical look on his face as the truck stopped in front of the third one down in the row. Everybody hopped down to the ground except McCauley.

Sergeant Tucker, now equipped with a clipboard, climbed down from his shotgun seat in the deuce-and-a-half truck. "We're flying three missions today, men. B- 52's is what we need on this first load," he said as he studied the paperwork affixed beneath the chrome clip.

Throwing the handle up and swinging open the door, Smith walked into the CONEX and turned to say, "Yep, these are them! Line up, ladies!"

With that, five of them, excluding Tucker, who stood watching, and Moyssiadias, who sat passively in the driver's seat, formed a relay line and began passing boxes out of the CONEX and up to McCauley, who slid them back onto the truck. Each of the boxes, which must have easily weighed twenty-five or thirty pounds apiece, had a leaflet glued to the top, identifying its contents as copies of the B- 52 leaflet the Kid had seen at battalion headquarters the day before. After the tenth box, the Kid was sweating like Sea Biscuit at the end of a race.

"How many, Tuck?" Smith asked as he stood in the CONEX door, taking a breather.

"Thirty."

"Thirty? Fuckin' A, that's enough to do the whole goddam Ho Chi Minh Trail!" Smith exclaimed as he turned to keep the boxes coming.

Just as box no. 20 went up on to the truck, a pair of Vietnamese officer pilots came walking past the CONEX. Dressed in sleek, tight-fitting black one-piece flight suits with colorfully embroidered tiger heads on their sleeves, they both wore teardrop-shaped mirrored sunglasses and walked with a bit of a swagger.

"Rich muthafucking douchebag assholes!" Tucker spit out the epitaph like a man with Tourette's syndrome as the pair passed out of earshot.

"What?" The Kid stopped and looked at Tucker, wondering what it was that he was actually saying.

"I hate those fuckheads. They're all the sons of rich Catholic Saigon businessmen and politicians who had enough money to buy commissions in the South Vietnam Air Force to keep their sons out of the infantry. They fly their jets all over the fucking place in training but never take them into combat. The Vietnamese helicopter pilots won't fly into a contested area to pick up their wounded because they are too chickenshit to risk their precious necks to save any of their fellow soldiers."

"Tell us how you really feel, Sergeant," Zewe bugged him.

"What I want to know," the Kid asked, "is how you know they're Catholics?"

"All the rich South Vietnamese fucks are Catholics. It's the ones that worked for the French who work for us now. They might make up less than 20 percent of the population, but they control easily 90 percent of the money. They are the reason we will lose this war. They all wanna be rich, like Americans, but dying in the defense of their country would definitely hamper their ability to spend their dough. Come on, men, hump those boxes; we've got a schedule to keep!" Tucker said, spurring the line back into action.

Once loaded, the truck drove to a place just off one of the runways, where a DC-3, the old twin-engine workhorse of early American aviation, awaited them. In the military, the DC-3 is known as a C-47. The air force crew of three—pilot, copilot, and loadmaster—waited under the wing of the old tail dragger, which was painted olive drab. Back behind the rear door, the Kid noticed the opening of a square metal chute, roughly two feet wide, obviously where the leaflets got dumped out.

Moyssiadias backed the truck up to the rear door of the plane, close enough that the men, except for two, could step from its bed directly down into the fuselage. The line formed again, and the boxes of leaflets went quickly from the truck to the plane. Inside, the Kid was now sweating as if he were in a Turkish bath. The boxes of leaflets were stacked along the right side looking forward, creating an aisle down the left. Once the last box was off, Reynolds and McCauley jumped into the plane, and Moyssiadias moved the truck away.

The air force sergeant loadmaster appeared and, using some yellow nylon straps, secured the boxes. Leaning out the door, he hollered, "Load secured and ready for departure, sir!"

With that, the pilot and copilot climbed into the plane.

"Mornin', gentlemen," the captain said to the psyops crew. "All ready for another exciting day?" Mumbles and nods answered his question. "I just want to remind you, no smoking at anytime aboard this aircraft until after the drop."

"Yes, sir, we got it!" Sergeant Tucker answered for the group.

The loadmaster picked up a red mesh nylon net–looking affair and hooked it up one side and down the other, securing the door, but leaving it essentially open for ventilation. In the heat, some of the men began peeling off their fatigue shirts and throwing them into a pile up in front of the boxes. The Kid followed suit, feeling glad that he had left the picture of Flo he usually carried in his breast pocket back in his locker. The leafletiers all settled into place as the engines coughed, sputtered, and roared to life. The Kid was pleased that, after their rough start, things sounded to be running pretty smooth.

With a glance back to the loadmaster, the captain, upon receiving a thumbs-up, nodded and the C-47 began to taxi. The Kid noticed the other men had a grip on a nylon line that ran up the fuselage above their heads and that they had their feet braced against the boxes, so he did the same. On-the-job training, that's what it was. The engines were loud enough to prevent conversation as the soldiers bumped along the corrugated metal runway on their way to takeoff.

The Kid loved to fly. He'd never done enough of it, and he'd begun looking forward to being up in the air. From where he was sitting in the middle of the group, he could see into the cockpit, where the copilot sat. As the plane swung into position on the runway, the pilot locked the brakes and revved up the engines. Satisfied that all was running right and that his gauges read OK, he released the brakes, and the plane began its takeoff roll. The tail came up first, leveling out the interior floor, and then, quite quickly thereafter, the C-47 lifted into the air.

No longer was the Kid just a spectator of the Vietnam War; he was now a man on a mission. Surprisingly in the heat, a cold chill ran down his back. *How did I come to be in this place?* He flashed on what it must have felt like to be part of a bomber crew in World War II, lifting off, knowing that the Luftwaffe was waiting for them on their way to Berlin or Ploieşti. And flak—flak thick enough to walk on. Imagine taking off with a load of highly explosive ordnance, thinking that fighters were going to be shooting at you on your way to the target. Those guys almost always lost a few planes, and frequently more than half the planes on a mission. *And we are just one teeny-tiny little plane, dropping paper, not bombs. At least the VC don't have an air force!*

Almost immediately after lifting off, the C-47 banked to the right and came around on a course parallel to the wide brown river. "Looks like we're on our way to Cambodia," Tucker fairly hollered into the Kid's ear. "We turned upriver!"

The Kid just kind of nodded to this news, not knowing what going to Cambodia really meant or would entail.

"You can write home tonight and tell 'em all you've flew over the Ho Chi Minh Trail today in Cambodia!" Zanzarella caught the loadmaster's attention and made a jerking motion toward the door with his thumb, like an umpire calling someone out, to which the loadmaster nodded his head in the affirmative. "Come on!" He raised his voice while speaking into the Kid's ear, "We can go over to the door and take a look out!

"That's not the Mekong, you know. It's the Bossac, the south branch of the Mekong," Zanzarella said, with his hands cupped to protect his words against the air rushing past the door. Beyond the river, the countryside was a carpet of rice paddies that ran off into the infinite distance.

The reality became crystal clear: the Kid was now flying over enemy territory. Hidden in the tree lines that traced a border around the rice paddies were hundreds—no, *thousands*—of VC waiting for a chance to kill him and everybody on this plane. And they'd probably torture them all first.

After about ten minutes of flying, the Kid spied another river town, this one on the south bank of the Bossac.

"That's Long Xuyên." Zanzarella pointed down at it. "They say it's one of the safest towns in the Delta because the ethnic Cambodians who live there all hate the VC with a passion."

"How long to the drop zone?" the Kid asked, the equivalent of "Are we there yet?"

"Fuck, I don't know. It's generally not more than half an hour or forty-five minutes, though."

"How high are we?"

Zanzarella—"Z"—looked at the Kid, a trace of a smile crossing his lips. "I don't know about you, but I'm plenty fuckin' high!"

"No! Not that! How high is the plane above the ground?"

"About three thousand feet—high enough to be out of small-arms range, if that's what you're worried about," Z droned in his ear.

Yes, that was what the Kid was worried about. Some VC could just sit down there and wait for a low-flying plane to pass by and blast it out of the sky. But hell, nobody else seemed to be too worried, so the Kid's psyche calmed and he began to enjoy the ride. On the road to the northwest section of Long Xuyên, he picked out what appeared to be a column of APCs, armored personnel carriers, on the move. Pointing down, he said to Z, "Could be worse. We could be down there with them!"

"Ha! You *will* be in a couple of days, is what I hear." Z looked at him. "You'll like it. I've spent most of my time in the field with the Vietnamese, and I'm going back out after I take care of some admin shit at Group. I volunteer to fly these just to get some time in the cool air and fight the boredom."

One part of the comment had a devastating effect on the Kid's state of mind. If he'd had any idea that this might happen, that he was going to become a member of the South Vietnamese army, he might have given Canadian citizenship a little more serious consideration. He loved his country, but as he went from high school to college to draftee and had begun to sense that there was something inherently wrong with the Vietnam War, he had given some serious thought to the option of the frozen north.

The dilemma had been agony. Take Flo and go? Give up the possibility of being one of the WKDA Good Guys ever again? Or do his duty and, if called, serve— and if sent, go? If he made the wrong decision and got killed, well, that wouldn't bother him; he'd be dead. But to get wounded and be paralyzed from the waist or the neck down would make the rest of life a real hell on earth. Just like the Buddhists teach, the Kid mulled over one of the Four Noble Truths: *All suffering and all pain is felt here, on this physical level, where you have the physical body to suffer it with. Yes, on this plane.* He let his hand absorb the vibrations of the twin C-47 engines as they hauled their load of VC "TP" up the river. He stuck his hand out through the mesh to feel the intensity of the wind pressure. As he turned to look up the fuselage for a second, the loadmaster caught his eye and shook his finger at him in schoolmarm fashion as if to say, *No sticking your hand outside the moving aircraft. More on the job training.*

Instead of Canada, the Kid was on his way to Cambodia! *Way south.* He chuckled to himself as he looked out upon the flatness of the land of the river delta. The early morning sun was angling off the water that filled the rice paddies, creating a delicate quilt-like array of pastel squares, reflecting the colors off the clouds that caught its rays. Some of the paddies were empty and weren't reflecting the sun, which actually made them stand out even more.

The dikes of the rice paddies made it look as if somebody had thrown a net on a very large pond and the net hadn't ever sunk down beneath the water. In some places, the paddies were almost squares, and in others, their shapes were entirely random, some with curving sides, others being long and narrow.

The bright green tree lines that surrounded the extremely wide and expansive paddies were, in some places, very narrow and, in others, thick to the point of being wide enough to be called a forest.

The Kid signaled to Z to give him an ear, into which he joked, "It's a fucking jungle down there!"

"No shit! It's rare, but every once in a while, they do get a tiger down in this neck of the woods. Or that's what Ling Fook says."

"Who?"

"Ling Fook. Harold Ling Fook, our resident know-it-all. He's a photographer from New York, half black and half Chinese! I'll introduce you tonight." Z gave a thumbs-up gesture, indicating that he fully expected the Kid to like Ling Fook.

Suddenly, the Kid flashed on something: the tree lines reminded him very much of the hedgerows that the US Army soldiers had to fight their way through right after they got off the beaches in the D-Day invasion of France. The Kid had seen newsreel film of how the Germans had dug into the hedges and kicked the Americans' asses because they were out in the middle of the farmers' fields, trying to get into the hedges. *Ha. Glad I missed that one.* There must have been German youths, the Kid thought, who were nineteen and twenty and, like him, had ben forced into being soldiers against their will and didn't want to fight, but found themselves in the hedges, facing the Americans. Just like there had to be Vietnamese boys and young men down there trying to stay alive against the power and fury of the United States' B-52's, just like the Americans who were trying to stay alive against the wily, cunning VC. A few chords of "Where Have All the Flowers Gone?" by Pete Seeger played inside the Kid's head. "When will it ever end? When will it eevvvveerrr end …"

The Kid turned and looked at the B-52 pictured on the leaflet stuck to one of the boxes that sat about two feet behind him. As he understood the order of events, the B-52's were somewhere out in front of them right now, pulverizing expansive sections of jungle turf that may or may not have been in Cambodia. And right after they finished dropping their bombs, this very plane was going to swoop in and drop these threatening leaflets that promised death if the North Vietnamese did not desert their cause and cross over to the South Vietnamese / US side.

"See that?" Zanzarella caught the Kid's attention. "See where the rice paddies stop and the solid jungle starts? That's fuckin' Cambodia, man. Bet you never thought when you got up this morning that before lunch, you'd be going to Cambodia and back."

"You're right. I didn't!"

The pair held on to the doorframe of the C-47 as the aircraft made a banking turn to the right, at which time the loadmaster rose to his feet and signaled the crew that they were nearing the drop zone. At that, the men who had remained seated rose to their feet. Two of the men with bayonets strapped to their belts got out the boxes of leaflets and began slitting them open the boxes, starting with the ones near the end of the row next to the dump chute.

"All right, I'll take dump master!" Z yelled. "As soon as the loadmaster drops his arm, start passing me the boxes!"

With that, the Kid worked his way into position to fulfill his assigned duty. He didn't have to wait long because, almost immediately, the arm dropped and he passed an open box to Z, who took it and dumped it over the mouth of the chute. The flow of the wind by the fuselage virtually sucked all the leaflets out of the box much more quickly than the Kid could have imagined possible. "Come on, Stocker, another one. Move, move, move!"

So he picked up the pace. As they rapidly worked their way through the boxes, a new man would step into the lengthy line to continue rolling boxes back to Z at the chute. Not all the leaflets went out the chute. Some were sucked into the vortex of the wind inside the plane and blew all around the men.

When the empty boxes began to pile up, McCauley pulled the bayonet from his sheath and began slitting them and stacking them flat to get them out of the way. Between handling boxes, the Kid managed to sneak a look out of the mesh- covered door. Below them, he could see the black circles of

123

chewed-up earth that marked the path of the B-52's bombing run, which had just taken place before their arrival. How surreal, he marveled. *If a VC had been standing right where the bomb hit, he'd just be gone. Vaporized. There wouldn't be enough of him to put into a cigar box and bury.*

From the time the first box hit the chute to the time the last one did, about fifteen minutes had elapsed. That's how long it took for the psyops crew to deliver their load. Everybody went for their canteens and had a nice, long drink before sitting back down to catch their breath.

The Kid closed his eyes and tried to relax, taking full advantage of the coolness offered by the air at three thousand feet. This isn't so bad. He certainly hadn't known what to expect this morning, but apart from loading the plane in the tropical heat of the ground, this to him was pretty good duty.

All too soon, the C-47 arrived back at Binh Thuy Air Base and was on the ground. Immediately after it had come to a full stop, the psyops crew jumped out and, to a man, lit up. Then, they all hauled out their tallywhackers and, almost in unison, took long pisses right there by the plane. Looking at his watch, the Kid saw that it was 1000 hours. Over to the side, he spied the truck parked in the shade of a protective roof. He could see the soles of Moyssiadias's combat boots sticking out over the driver's-side doorsill as a column of smoke rose from behind the windshield.

"Hurry up and finish, men." Sergeant Tucker checked the clipboard. "We've got one more mission before lunch, safe conduct passes right back in the area we just covered," he hollered. The truck's engine came to life, followed by the sound of grinding gears.

Back into the truck and back over to the CONEX storage units, another relay line loaded another twenty boxes into the truck. Only these were safe conduct passes. They showed a smiling South Vietnamese soldier with his arm around the shoulder of a smiling North Vietnamese soldier as he pointed the way to safety. On the back, it had silhouette images of weapons and, across from each, the amount of the monetary reward the deserter would receive for bringing that weapon with him when he left the ranks of the VC. A machine gun was worth twenty-five thousand piastres; an AK-47 was good for ten thousand piastres; a pistol was good for five thousand piastres; and each hand grenade would net the deserter a tidy profit of two thousand piastres. Ah, the capitalist incentive used as a lever to pry the soldiers away from the communist army.

In forty minutes, the soldiers were all back in the C-47 and up in the air. On the second run, the air had become a little choppy, so the ride was not as smooth as the first run. *Looks like rain later today,* the Kid conjectured as he again spent the ride looking out the door.

When they got back from the second mission, it was lunchtime, so they trucked over to the Binh Thuy mess hall, which the kid found to be superior to that of Eakin Compound.

"These air force guys eat ten times better than we do," McCauley said with a full mouth. "I should've joined the fucking air force!"

The last mission of the day was not upriver but, rather, to the north of the Bossac and east of Binh Thuy Air Base. It was also a small drop; they loaded just ten boxes onto the C-47. The Kid recalled what *chu hoi* meant. Written in big red letters across the top was "Steel Pot audio 2."

Chapter 10

The Kid leaned upon the railing of the Roof Club, smoking a cigarette as he stared off to the west, watching aircraft land and depart from Can Tho Airfield and, farther off in the distance, Binh Thuy Air Base. *Now that I've actually been there, it doesn't seem to be too far off,* the Kid thought.

It was more interesting observing the movements of the civilian population below.

One woman in particular had caught his attention. She was dressed in a light green *áo dài* and had her graying black hair tied back in a bun. With a bundle of burning incense sticks clasped between the palms of her hands, she bowed to a statue of Buddha, perched on a tiny square wooden altar that was affixed to a post in the corner of her yard. She would bow to her right and left, three times to either side, and then to the statue. A shaft of sunlight struck the altar and lit the Buddha while the rest of her yard was still trapped in the early morning shade of the New Villa. After repeating the process another time, she took the smoldering bundle and stuck it into a holder in front of the Buddha. Then she bowed one last time and turned to go, most likely off to work somewhere in Can Tho, possibly for the Americans.

The events of the past three days played in the Kid's mind as he waited to be picked up by Lieutenant Wilson, with whom he and another GI would leave Can Tho today, headed for parts unknown. Once word had gotten out that the Kid would be going to the field with Lieutenant Wilson, a couple of the guys told him a thing or two about the man.

It turned out that the whole Tenth Psyop Battalion initially came over together on a boat. They called it the Packet. It had transported the whole battalion in one ship: men, trucks, jeeps, printing presses, paper, printing ink and supplies, office equipment, beds, bedding, weapons, and tons of extraneous gear. It took thirty-four days to cross the Pacific from San Francisco to Saigon, and it was a boat trip from hell. Then it took another three weeks to get everything down from Saigon to Can Tho. There was nothing to do on the boat but play poker and do PT, which to the uninitiated is physical training. The chow stank, the bunks stank, and the whole place smelled like puke, but there was this one officer, Lieutenant Wilson, who loved it. He said he'd been in the Merchant Marine and that all the seasickies were nothing but a bunch of land-lovin' pussies! He'd do stupid shit, such as do some extra PT by himself, and then he'd stand on the bow of the boat as far forward as he could get and just stare off into space for hours, as if he wanted to be the first one to see land or who knows what.

This was the man who had the Kid's future in his hands.

The Kid's traveling companion, one PFC Cleveland, had not yet arrived. The Kid had just met the black soldier the night before and quickly discovered he was from, not Cleveland or even Ohio, but Philadelphia.

The three days had been just enough time for the Kid to begin growing accustomed to Can Tho, the New Villa, and the giant Eakin Compound PX, all the while knowing he was predestined to keep moving farther and farther away from everything and everybody he'd ever known. The foreignness of Vietnam was engulfing him, drawing him into its mysterious aura, as entrancing as it was frightful. *Yeah, that's what I'll say in the book.*

A pair of maids sat on the floor just outside the Roof, at the end of the covered club. They were chatting in the melodic tones of their native tongue as they worked away, polishing a pile of combat jungle boots with their black leather bottoms, green canvas tops, and steel-plated punji stick-resistant soles. What a deal! All that residents of the New Villa had to do was leave their boots by their doors, and the maids would shine them up to regulation standards and return them to the proper rooms. Life here in Can Tho didn't appear to be that bad.

And the pot the Kid had been smoking on the balcony with Boujold and the boys was, indeed, one-hit shit, far superior to the stuff stuffed inside his Colgate tube.

The Kid lamented: Was he at the end of his famous luck? Was death waiting for him out in some rice paddy or jungle of the Mekong Delta? What was Lieutenant Wilson going to be like, a regular guy or really a major-league nutcase as advertised? Or maybe just a little eccentric?

The Kid's duffle bag, equipment sack, and M16 and ammunition were packed and ready to go, waiting in what had been his room on the first floor. Just as he finished his Kool and flicked the butt off the balcony and into the swamp, PFC Cleveland emerged from the stairwell and waved him a greeting. Cleveland was a tall, skinny drink of water with a clean-shaven oval face and a chin that was just the slightest bit pointy. As near as the Kid had been able to tell, Cleveland was in propaganda development—or was it deployment?

"Yo, how you doin' this morning?" He nodded to the Kid as he pulled a Winston from his left breast pocket and lit it with a Zippo that came out of his right pants pocket.

"Hey, Cleveland," the Kid said, remaining with his elbows on the railing, looking down at the trash below, where a local family pig had emerged from an enclosure and was rooting through the garbage right beneath him. What a scream this country was! Last night, he and the other guys had watched a pack of rats work over the same patch of garbage while they all got toasted. By *all,* the Kid realized that he didn't really know how many different guys from the unit had stopped by for a toke while he was there. But what did it matter, especially since he was traveling on to yet another place in what was, so far, an endless string of stops on the way to only God knows fucking where?

"I wonder how late this looie is going to be?" Cleveland said, blowing out a puff of smoke and checking his watch, discovering that it was 0820. As if on cue, an officer appeared out of the stairwell. The Kid and Cleveland both turned, came to attention, and saluted, Cleveland with the cigarette behind the back of his left leg. The lieutenant stopped in front of them and returned the salute.

"Good morning, sir," the Kid said in his most military voice.

"Good morning, PFC Stocker and … PFC Cleveland? I'm Lieutenant Herschel Wilson." Lowering his hand from the return salute, he extended his hand to shake both of theirs. "Nice to make your acquaintance. Are you both ready to move out?"

"Yes, sir," the Kid responded. "Our gear is waiting downstairs."

Lieutenant Wilson was dressed in lightly faded fatigues, and his sleeves were rolled up, revealing incredibly hairy forearms. A tattoo of an old-time sailing ship under full sail graced his right forearm, and the hint of another tattoo showed just below the sleeve of his left arm. But the Kid's eye was attracted to a gnarly gash of a scar on his left forearm. He wore a camouflage jungle hat with a gold second-lieutenant bar, its embroidered cloth faded, pinned to the front. Usually, officers in the combat zone did not wear their bright metallic insignia of rank as it greatly raised their viability and desirability as a target to the enemy.

"Good, let's get going. I've got a jeep downstairs to take us out to Can Tho field, where we're catching a chopper to Sa Dec," he said in a friendly voice and with possibly a hint of a smile hidden beneath his rather bushy handlebar mustache.

So, this is Lieutenant Wilson. Wow! Is that cookie duster regulation? The Kid looked him over as they headed for the stairwell. He was a tough-looking cuss, although he appeared to be a couple of inches shorter than the Kid, who stood at 5'10". And the Screaming Eagle patch of the 101st Airborne Division on the man's right shoulder spoke volumes in terms of where he stood on such issues as the war.

Down at the front of the New Villa, Moyssiadais waited in the jeep. The smallish New Yorker with the dark Greek features seemed to drive everything in town.

"Hi, Mike," the Kid said. He and Cleveland loaded their gear into the back of the jeep with Lieutenant Wilson's. "This looks like it's going to be a tight fit!" He smiled at Cleveland as the pair contemplated exactly how it was going to work.

"Lucky it isn't far out to Can Tho field," Moyzi replied in his normal bored-to-tears and I-don't-give-a-fuck-about-anything demeanor.

Speaking of fit, the Kid reached into the top of his laundry bag and pulled out a jungle hat he'd bought the day before at Taj, the tailor's shop that was just up where the alley and the street met. "Sir," he said, catching Wilson's attention, "since we're on our way to their field and you are wearing one, I was wondering if it'd be OK for me to wear this now."

Wilson stopped and pondered the request for a couple of seconds. "Yeah, I guess it'd be OK if you wear it now that we have officially left the unit."

"Thank you, sir!" The Kid quickly stuffed his baseball cap into the laundry bag and affixed his new jungle hat upon his head, with the drawstring hanging loosely under his chin. He smiled at Cleveland.

"Man, I gotta get me one of those today!" the Philly man immediately said, settling in on top of some of the gear for the ride.

Looking up, the Kid saw a couple of the neighborhood whores smiling down on them from their second floor. As the jeep took off, the women waved good-bye. When the jeep pulled out of the New Villa alley, the Kid noticed Taj was standing out in front of his shop, next to his sign, just as he was yesterday when they met. Seeing he was wearing the hat, Taj pointed to the Kid's head and flashed him a big thumbs-up and a white, toothy smile. Pulling his prescription shades out of his breast pocket, the Kid made the switch and slipped his gray-plastic-framed clear specs into their place. He actually felt a little on the cool side: jungle hat on his head, shades on his face, M16 in his hands. He'd have to have Cleveland or the lieutenant take his picture with his Polaroid camera to send to Flo.

On the drive out to Can Tho field, the Kid's mind wandered back to the States. *I wonder who's on the air at WKDA right now. Let's see, twelve hours' difference, so it must be about eight thirty at night in Nashville That would be Johnny Wailin's shift.* Wailin's real name was John Beaudoin, but his whole aura seemed to fit with his air name and to everybody, he was Johnny Wailin. Wailin was a really hot jock, but he was conceited and self-centered more so than the captain of any football team the Kid had ever known. The Kid remembered the second time he'd ever seen Wailin. He was downtown two days after he'd been in to apply for the job at WKDA, and being in need of a haircut, he decided he'd try the barbershop that he had spotted in the Stahlman Building. He went in and sat down to wait. Somebody said to him, "Hey, Kid, you still lookin' for a job in radio?" It was Wailin sitting in one of the four barber chairs, covered with a pinstriped white sheet, getting clipped.

"Oh, hi! Yeah, I'm still looking."

"Well, I heard Dick say to the secretary to give you a call earlier today. I guess you haven't been home since before noon or you'd have gotten the message."

"Really? You're not shitting me? Dick wants to hire me?" "Yeah, Kid, he does!"

Wow. He called me Kid! He decided the haircut could wait and went directly to the elevator, which he rode to the twelfth floor, then went into the WKDA reception area.

Donna, the secretary, was sitting at the desk. "Yo! I was trying to call you, but nobody was at your number. Dick wants to talk to y'all. Wait here and I'll go get him."

Could it be? Could the Kid actually be getting a job on the air in Nashville? Music City? Pinch my fuckin' ass!

Dick came out of the long hallway. "Hello, Curt. How are you?" "Good."

"I've decided to give you a week tryout, and if you do OK, the job's yours. How does ninety dollars a week to start sound?"

"OK, yes, I'll take it." Fuck. The Kid would have paid Buckley ninety dollars to be on the staff!

"Can you start tonight?"

Can I? Hell yes!

When the jeep arrived at Can Tho field, the Kid was still lost in the Nashville daydream as Wilson directed Moyzi to pull over to a spot to the far side of the control tower.

"This is good right here," Wilson said. He stepped out of the vehicle and stretched while Cleveland began unloading his bags.

The Kid unloaded his bags. Then he and Cleveland both grabbed the lieutenant's bags. The Kid tipped his hat to Moyzi, who backed the jeep up, turned it around, and left without so much as a goodbye.

There they were, the Kid, Cleveland, and Lieutenant Wilson, waiting for a chopper to go to someplace called Sa Dec. *How did I come to be here?*

"Captain Ronnie Smith and I are pretty good friends," Wilson spoke in his slow southern drawl. "He's got us a chopper over to Sa Dec. It's supposed to meet us at the helipad near the tower at zero nine hundred. I like to be a few minutes early," he said, pulling a pack of Winstons from his right breast pocket and a Zippo from his pants to fire it up. The Kid and Cleveland did exactly the same.

There was no shade on the field side of the tower in the mornings, and it was beginning to really heat up. The Kid sat down on his duffle bag and took a deep drag on his cigarette. Smartly, he had filled his canteen to the brim.

"So." Wilson turned to the Kid. "I understand you were a DJ in Nashville." "Yes, sir, I was. And I hope to be again after I get out."

"I've spent some time in Nashville," the lieutenant said. "In fact, I know some people there in the record business."

"Oh, really? Who?" "Snuff Garrett, for one."

"You know Snuff?" the Kid replied with a little bit of surprise. Snuff Garrett had a record label, if you could call it that. He didn't have anybody signed to a contract who could cut a record that would sell outside of Middle Tennessee, and his label was a caricature of him, big nose and all! He was considered by the Good Guy DJs of WKDA to be a typical music business wannabe flake. "How'd you meet him?"

"Oh well, I play guitar a little, and I went down to Nashville a couple of times while I was stationed up at Fort Campbell. A friend took me over to his studio."

"So, what radio station did you listen to in Nashville?"

"Mostly WENO," he answered, "and WSM. And the Grand Ole Opry." "Ever listen to WKDA?"

"A little, up at the fort during the day. Couldn't get it at night."

"That was going to be my next question, if you'd ever caught my show. I was midnight to six." The Kid smiled. The station had to power down at night.

"Nope, can't say that I did. We used to listen to Ralph Emery on WSM at night. The signal was so damn good, it was hard not to. And I like the country stuff a little, although my taste runs more to the traditional stuff."

Traditional stuff? What does he mean by that? the Kid wondered. *Oh well, at least he is into music.* That was a good sign, even if he did listen to Ralph Emery, against whom the Kid had been in direct competition.

"Do you like the Beatles?" The Kid went straight to the litmus test.

"You bet! I love the Beatles! And I love Bob Dylan too, but I hate the fucking candy-assed Byrds and what they did to his 'Mr. Tambourine Man'!"

"You hate the Byrds? I love the Byrds!" the Kid exclaimed. "The first time I heard Bob Dylan's 'Mr. Tambourine Man,' I thought it sucked, and then I found out he wrote it. Now, I appreciate them both for their unique presentations of the same material!"

During their exchange, Cleveland acted uninterested, staring off into space, smoking and most likely silently cataloguing his own musical likes and dislikes.

From a distance, and emerging amid the general din of large airplane engine noise, the rhythmic *thop-thop-thop* of a chopper grew louder. Looking up from their conversation, the Kid and Lieutenant Wilson watched a Huey easing its way over to a spot marked with the yellow *H* normally on a helipad.

"There's our ride! Right on time," Wilson exclaimed. They watched the chopper settle onto the pad as it kicked up dust and debris all over their gear. The Kid was especially upset that it was apparently getting crap down the barrel of his M16; he'd have to clean it again tonight.

As soon as the Huey was down, the gunner, a black GI who wasn't very big at all, jumped out and waved to them, indicating that, indeed, this was their ride to Sa Dec. He and Cleveland exchanged a strange kind of closed-fist greeting that the Kid had never seen before.

What a thrill the Kid felt as he anticipated his first helicopter ride ever in his life! They began ferrying their gear over to the Huey, which had a big knight chess piece painted on the front. The Kid would write to his dad about this one tonight!

His dad, Dwain, loved to fly and was a private pilot. He hadn't been drafted in World War II because he had polio, but he did work at the Omaha bomber manufacturing plant, out on the flight line where they tested their finished product. So, he missed his war. Yes, the Kid would write his pop a really exciting letter tonight describing the big black M60 machine gun that was mounted on a rack that hooked into the skid structure on the underside, putting it out where it had a greater field of fire. *Wait a minute, I don't want it to be too exciting.* The Kid's thought process immediately turned as he looked at the belt of shiny brassy cartridges that were loaded into the gun. *Real fucking bullets. We're not playing cowboys and Indians anymore, Batman.* He flashed on the potential for things to go wrong. Engine failure, getting shot down, pilot error.

While crouching low to make sure they avoided the Huey's whirling twin blades, the Kid, Cleveland, and Lieutenant Wilson passed their baggage to the door gunner, who shoved it on board and then jumped in to strap it down to rings on the floor. He wore a headset radio getup that he could unplug from the chopper's communications system.

The Kid was getting a lot of debris in his eyes and was relieved when they finally boarded. As he strapped himself into the door seat on the far side of the Huey, with Cleveland next to him, the door gunner pointed to the sets of headphones sitting on the seat next to them. After buckling up, the Kid carefully removed his new jungle hat and stuck it under his leg before picking up the headset and putting it on. Now he could hear every word of the conversation between the pilots and the door gunner. And wow, if he needed to say something, there was a mouthpiece.

"You boys all ready for Sa Dec?" the pilot's voice crackled over the earpieces in a southern drawl.

"Roger that!" Lieutenant Wilson responded with a thumbs-up, first to the pilot and then to his two charges, who smiled and returned the gesture.

Thumbs fucking up, right, the Kid thought. I hope not up my ass! After all, he had no way of knowing if Sa Dec was a good place or a bad place to be going. As if he had a choice of locations.

"Can Tho tower, chopper in front of you preparing to depart the airfield for Sa Dec. Over." *Click, snap, popple.*

"Roger, chopper, which I can see in my front yard, you are cleared to depart the airfield in the prescribed flight path. Have a nice trip. Tower, out!"

The blades of the chopper began to quickly increase in rotations per minute, and then the Huey popped up into the air, about six feet off the metal pad. After making a 180-degree pirouette, and with its nose dropped, it moved down the edge of Can Tho field, gaining forward momentum. Then the pilot abruptly climbed out to his left, leaving the Kid's stomach back on the ground, but the Kid was loving every second of it, sitting in the breeze next to the door.

The Bell-manufactured olive-green machine was headed north, traversing the land between the Bossac and the Mekong Rivers. The Kid, easily picking up the location of the New Villa and the street that ran through it, was surprised to see how quickly the land below gave way from city to rural countryside and the endless rice paddies.

Below, they observed a flock of white cranes winging across the man-made wetlands. Down among them, from the height at which they flew, they could pick out peasants tending the crop. One was plowing with a yoked buffalo in one square, and a row of a dozen others were working their way, bent at the waist, across another square, planting rice shoots in all likelihood.

The chopper had now climbed to the customary level of at least three thousand feet, the zone where pilots felt they were safe from ground fire. The Kid looked over at Lieutenant Wilson, who sat peering out the door on his side, a hand resting on his M16 lest a sudden pocket of turbulence should send it sliding out into space. As if feeling the gaze of the Kid on his back, Wilson abruptly turned and looked at him, immediately smiling and flashing another thumbs-up. The lieutenant was digging it to the max.

The door gunner occupied the seat behind the copilot, one hand also resting on the butt end of his automatic weapon as he surveyed the land below, looking through his shades. *I wonder how many times he's had to use his machine gun?* The Kid examined the sleek black instrument of death.

The pilot and the copilot were engaged in small talk about people and things of which the Kid had no idea, using aeronautical terms for navigation and flight or where they had to go after they dropped the psyops team off. Cleveland, it appeared, had decided to try to take a nap, his head bobbing and jerking from the mild turbulence.

The Kid drew in deep cool breaths of clean, fresh air—not like the air on the ground, which was superheated and full of humidity. The rhythmic *thropping* of the powerful rotator engine vibrated the craft as it cut like a massive prehistoric dragonfly through the air above the hostile land. The Kid recalled all the evening news footage he had seen of soldiers riding into combat aboard choppers exactly like this one. *Hmm, did I ever seen this one on TV? Only God, or the energy that was God, could know.*

Out of the mesh created by the rice paddies and the tree lines, the Kid could pick out occasional hamlets, collections of grass-roofed huts that were in close proximity to each other, with the smoke of cooking fires rising from some of them. *If only Flo could see me now,* he pleasantly thought, as if if she were in another helicopter flying along next to his and they could wave to each other. Then the reality hit him: this was nothing but another leg of a journey that he would have to repeat in reverse if he was ever going to be with her again. That is, if his journey did not take on a new form of conveyance, say, one of those flag-draped aluminum caskets that TV was forever showing being unloaded from cargo planes back in the States.

Soon, the chopper began to drop. Ahead of them, the Kid could see a sizable river and a town on either side of it. *That must be Sa Dec,* he thought.

There was a considerably denser amount of foliage and forest surrounding it than the town of Can Tho. He compared the two as the chopper arrived over the river and turned to fly down its center. Then he spied an island that had two bridges that extended to either side of the waterway. As the bird arrived over it, the Kid could see that it was fortified and acted as a military base. *This must be the headquarters of the ARVN Ninth Division,* to which he and Lieutenant Wilson were now attached. Slowing to a walk and almost stopping in midair, the pilot began to execute his landing. There were a total of four helipads below them, one occupied by another Huey. The chopper was set down on the one nearest a wooden shack that had a sign on its front: "Welcome to Sa Dec International Heliport."

The gunner hopped down and helped the soldiers pull their gear off the bird. He carried two of the bags to the international heliport as the Kid, Cleveland, and Wilson got the others. Once the crewman stepped back on board, the pilot gunned the engines and lifted the Huey off the ground, causing the trio to be sprayed with biting bits of debris as he maneuvered the aircraft back out over the water and began his run straight down the river. Then, as the Kid watched, the Huey popped up into the sky at an even more radical angle than the one that had taken them out of Can Tho.

"They like to get up and out of here quick," Lieutenant Wilson commented, watching the Huey grow small. "No telling who's waiting for them downriver. Well, you two, come on, let's go check in at headquarters!"

With each man lugging two bags and his M16, the pair made for what they thought must have been headquarters, a very colonial-looking set of buildings with a half dozen jeeps parked out in front of it and armed guards patrolling the immediate area. Dropping their gear on the cement porch that fronted the tan plaster buildings, the Kid pulled out a Kool. Cleveland went for a Winston. They both lit up.

"Wait here. I'll find out where we need to go and where we'll be billeted tonight," the lieutenant said, before turning and walking off.

Sitting down on his duffle bag, the Kid tilted back his new jungle hat, which had now been baptized with sweat. Taking a long pull on his canteen, he observed the guards observing him. He gave them a head nod of recognition and got smiles in return. Buckingham Palace quality they were not. He watched another chopper land and another take off as he waited for the lieutenant. Down the drive from headquarters, he saw an elongated older-looking building, one story tall, with a sign over the door: "The Lucky 9 Club." To either side of it were billets that had obviously been built on the grounds by the Army Corps of Engineers, from the same blueprints they had used to make the barracks at Long Binh.

From his seat, the Kid could see the front gate of the compound. Immediately outside it, there was a group of Vietnamese pedicabs, the ubiquitous rickshaw- like mode of transportation, and their drivers, waiting for fares who were going into the city proper.

Soon, Wilson emerged and said, "Stocker, you and Cleveland are gonna be in the air force billet, which is the second one back in the third row down toward the enlisted men's club." He pointed in the general direction. "I'm in the officers' billets right over there. Why don't you two go and stow your gear and meet me at the Lucky 9 Club, right there, in, say, about fifteen minutes. We've got a briefing to attend at ten thirty hours."

"Yes, sir." The Kid began picking up his gear. "How long do you think we'll be here?"

"Well, at least a day or two, but I imagine we'll find out exactly what they have planned for us at the briefing." Wilson began to pick up his own equipment.

Half carrying and half dragging their gear, the two PFCs made their way to the air force barracks. Upon entering the screened door, they found that it was set up more like a home than a barracks. In the front of the room, there was a pair of old sofas facing a cable spool that sat between them, serving as a coffee table.

There were personal areas that had been set apart by lockers and cloth dividers in which there were bunk beds with what looked to be deluxe mattresses.

A single GI sat on a brown sofa, his feet propped up on the spool table, reading the *Stars and Stripes* newspaper. "Oh, hello, can I help you?"

"Well, I don't know." The Kid dropped his stuff. "We just got in, and we'll be here for a day or two. We were told to bunk with the air force guys. Is this the right place?"

"Yes it is. This is the air force hooch. My name's Harvey Herrick," the tall, dark- complexioned man with black curly hair said, introducing himself. Because he was wearing only green boxer shorts and flip-flops, the Kid had no idea what rank he was.

"My name's Curt," the Kid said, "and this is Cleveland. I, he, and a lieutenant have just been attached to the ARVN Ninth to do psyops stuff."

"Nice to meet you both." Herrick dropped his paper and shook first the Kid's hand and then Cleveland's. "There's a couple of empty bunks that you psyops guys always seem to be in and out of over here." He walked a few steps behind the couch area and showed the Kid an enclosure that was behind a yellow cloth curtain set up on a rod that ran between two banks of metal lockers. "You can lock up whatever you need to lock up in one of these." He thumped the hollow metal chamber. "These bunks already have their netting up, and only one guy has slept on these bottom sheets for one night. Or, if you care, you can go over to supply and get some clean ones."

"Thanks." The Kid dragged his baggage into the enclosure. "Is this place pretty safe or what?"

"For the most part. But we do get hit with mortars occasionally, what with us being Ninth Division headquarters and all. In fact, whenever the local VC battalion graduates a mortar class, their final assignment is to mortar Sa Dec because Spooky always comes and the object of the class is how to avoid Spooky. Our bunker is right there." Herrick pointed through the screen window to a sandbagged structure that was located nearly adjacent. "In all the time I've been here, nobody has ever beat me into the bunker," he bragged to the Kid and Cleveland with a certain air of superiority.

While loading stuff into his locker, the Kid pulled out his transistor radio and turned it on. "Black is black. I want my baby back." Los Bravos was playing. "Gray, it's gray since she went away. Oh my, what will I do? 'Cause I, I, I, I, I'm feeling blue!" *How appropriate.* The Kid was blue and missing his baby as well.

"So," the Kid addressed Herrick, "what do you do?"

"I'm with tactical air ops. When you army guys get pinned down in the paddies and call for an air strike, I'm the guy who directs it in for you."

"How nice!" the Kid responded. "How long have you been in-country?" "I'm going on six months in a couple of weeks: halfway! And you?" "I'm in my second week, so don't get started with me."

"Wow, a real newbie. Jeez, you must still be getting sorta adjusted." "Yeah, right, as if you could ever adjust to this place."

"Well, today's June first, so the next time May comes up on the calendar, you'll be the short one." *Short* is what you call somebody whose tour of duty is almost at an end.

The Kid looked at Herrick and was trying to decide who it was that his face reminded him of. Ah, yes, sort of like Eddie Fisher, only with glasses.

"Where are you from?" Herrick asked the typical question.

"Nashville," the Kid replied, since after his conversation with Wilson, he was feeling more Nashville than Colorado. "And you?"

"Chicago. You a baseball fan?" "Yeah, I like the Yankees."

137

"Yankees? Yankees suck! In fact, the whole American League sucks!"

"I'm from Philly and I vote with you on that one!" Cleveland added his two cents' worth. "The American League is one team and a bunch of AAA players filling out all the other rosters."

"And the Cubs don't suck?" The Kid scoffed.

"Well, the Yankees have sucked since 1964, when they lost to the Cardinals in the Series."

"And the Cubs have sucked since, what is it, 1910 or thereabouts? And who can forget about the Black Sox!" the Kid smugly added.

"One of your battalion mates, Tom Roberts, who's with the Armored Cav, he's *really* a Yankee hater!"

There was that name Roberts again. Everybody was talking about Roberts.

"Haven't met Roberts yet." The Kid lit up a Kool and sat down on the red couch to catch a moment of relaxation. A floor fan whirred away, blowing out from its station in the corner of the common area. "He must be a pretty interesting guy, because people are always talking about him and things he's done or said."

"He's pretty fuckin' wild all right. When he first got sent down here, he was really pissed. Said it was the army's way of trying to kill him for the articles he wrote during Tet and stuff. He's from New York and is a Giants fan. We had a great time putting the Yankees down together!"

"Oops, look at the time. We gotta go and meet the Lieutenant." The Kid got up emphatically, rushing off. *Double whoops, forgot to lock up my gun—I mean my weapon! Wouldn't want the VC to steal it.* He returned to his bunk area, took the M16, and secured it. "We can talk more baseball tonight, fer sure. See ya!" He and Cleveland were out the door.

Walking up the gravel path from the barracks, the Kid appraised the Lucky 9 Club; it fit the trend he had noticed: they kept getting smaller. The club on the roof of New Villa had been about half the size of the club at Long Binh, and the Lucky 9 was like one-fifth the size of the one at New Villa.

Wilson was waiting for the Kid and Cleveland on the steps. Checking his watch, he confirmed that they were early.

"Afternoon, sir." The Kid and Cleveland saluted. Wilson returned the salute, but with a sour look on his face.

"Y'all can get in the habit of not saluting me." He partially smiled. "Out in the field, that's a good way to get an officer shot."

"OK, works for me! So, what's up, sir?"

138

"I was shocked to find out there is no separate officers' club here. Well, that's probably because there are fewer officers than enlisted men, don't you think?"

The Kid and Cleveland exchanged a knowing glance; neither of them could have cared less what Wilson thought! "Yeah, I guess," the Kid concurred.

The Kid was finding the lieutenant to be not unpleasant. He was still an officer, and the Kid was still an enlisted man, so in that respect, there were certain things the Kid could not discuss with the lieutenant. Such as, did he smoke pot? And seeing that he was a guitar player and from Texas, chances are he'd met up with "Mary Jane" at some point in his life.

"We're meeting with Lieutenant Colonel Atkins," Wilson spoke as they walked. "He's the XO for ARVN Ninth Division Adviser Operations. We're officially 'advisers' now. Sort of like being consultants."

"So, when do we start with the loudspeaker bullshit?" "That, PFC, is what we are about to find out."

Walking into the headquarters building, they witnessed a hub of activity. The reception area, in the old French plantation business offices, sat in front of five doors into other offices. The walls were a beautiful bright white and yellow tile pattern up to waist high, and the rest of the way leading to the open cinder block ventilation at the top, they were painted the same light tan as the exterior.

Vietnamese and US officers were coming and going in and out of offices, bustling around with arms full of papers and maps; it looked like something was really getting done!"

"We're here to meet with Lieutenant Colonel Atkins," Wilson explained to the Hispanic-looking clerk at the control desk.

"Yes, sir, he's right in there." He pointed over his shoulder. "You can just go on in."

The three new advisers walked into the office and found Atkins working at his desk. Looking up and seeing who it was, he continued to write, the pen looking to be lost within the huge black fingers of his right hand. Even though the hair on his head was cropped rather short, you could see the natural curliness of it, hugging tight to his head, above the double roll that made up his neck. Setting down his pen, he stood and extended his hand to the Kid. Atkins weighed three hundred pounds if he weighed an ounce. But with a height of easily 6'4" or 6'5", he didn't look that fat.

"PFC Stocker, pleased to have you aboard," he said as they shook hands. "PFC Cleveland, welcome to Sa Dec."

The Kid had expected his hand to be crushed in a viselike grip in the massive black paw, but was surprised to find a firm, but nonmacho, greeting. "Thank you, sir. I think I'm happy to be here. … Oh, maybe not!" He let the truth slip out at the end.

Atkins chuckled. "That's fair enough to say. I guess none of us are that happy to be here. Isn't that right?"

"You got that right." Cleveland smiled. "Definitely not happy to be here."

"No, sir, I volunteered to be here!" Wilson immediately shot back, practically beaming.

"That is admirable." Atkins sat back down. "I'm am a career man, but I can live without this shit! This is my third tour, and when I get back, I'll have done twenty years and my big black ass is out!" That got a big chortle out of Cleveland.

The Kid took an immediate liking to Lieutenant Colonel Atkins.

"Coffee?" the colonel asked. "Or something cold?"

"Yeah, something cold would be nice," Wilson responded.

"How about you two, Stocker and Cleveland?" "Yes, thank you. A Coke if you got it," said the Kid. "Ditto on the Coke," added Cleveland.

"Specialist Hernandez," Atkins hollered out the door, "would you please bring us three Cokes?"

"Yes, sir," came the reply. Amid the shuffling of his chair, Hernandez rose to comply with the request.

Maps on easels were spread out around the edges of Atkins's office, and upon them were squares with little numbers, some blue and some red. The Kid imagined the red ones must have been the commie positions. He actually recognized the area between Can Tho and Sa Dec, the land between the rivers, which ran all the way to the sea. Atkins took care of some last-minute stuff on his desk while waiting for Hernandez to bring the drinks. Once that task was done and they were sipping, Atkins cleared his throat and began.

"Gentlemen, here's the situation. The VC haven't really let up that much since Tet. In fact, we are now experiencing what they are calling their Spring Offensive, and we've been seeing quite a bit of action all through the sector. Your psyops field team has been assigned to the Fourteenth Regiment, which hasn't had a psyops team for quite a while. The ARVNs just put a new political warfare officer in Tra Vinh, and you will be working with him. His name is Troung—Ti Ui Troung. *Ti Ui* is Vietnamese for 'lieutenant.' Now, his loudspeaker equipment hasn't arrived yet, so you can't do any of that."

140

"In that case, I'll just go back to Saigon, since you don't need me here." The Kid got up, pretending as if he were going to leave. "See you guys. Take it easy. Call if you get any speakers."

Atkins laughed—the effect the Kid wanted. Wilson did not, instead giving the Kid something of a dirty look.

"Oh no, we still have things for you to do, PFC Stocker." Atkins was amused. "In fact, a couple of things. Lieutenant Wilson, since I don't know that much about psyops, I'll leave the choice up to you. Either you can start operating with Able Company or Baker Company, which are pulling search and destroy ops, or you can go to Charlie Company, which is currently in a fortified hamlet, here"—he pointed to a map—"northwest of Tra Vinh. We put Charlie Company out in the fortified hamlet because they got chewed up pretty bad in a recent operation and they needed to recover and train some new troops. The hamlet, Tan An, is in Cang Long Province, at the site of an old French Catholic cathedral, and it is completely surrounded. The only way in and out is by chopper. And in light of that, it's usually pretty quiet, but they got hit last night! Pretty damn hard, in fact, by at least a company of VC. They almost got overrun, but we sent out Spooky and were able to hold them off. They reported a body count of a hundred and twenty-five, but I'm willing to bet that is a little high."

The words and phrases that the Kid had zeroed in on were *surrounded, hit pretty hard, almost overrun,* and *body count.* He did not like the sound of any of them.

"During the day, Charlie Company's running operations out of Tan An into the surrounding countryside, trying to convince more Vietnamese to move into the fortified hamlet. The theory is, the more people who live in the fortified hamlet, the fewer people the VC will have to get food and help from. So far, they don't seem that anxious to move in."

Now what does that tell you? the Kid thought. *Either the people are VC themselves, or they're not and they distrust the government troops to defend them.* No more interruptions. This briefing had taken on a new level of seriousness.

"So, it's either that, or hook up with Able or Baker and run search and destroy missions."

Wilson looked to be deeply immersed in thought. Then he spoke, "On the search and destroy missions, are they getting a lot of action?"

"Well, more on some days than others. It's not unusual to run two or three operations and never even see the VC or have a shot fired at you. But you'll still take a few casualties on land mines and booby traps; they're everywhere!"

141

"In that case, I think I'd like to try the fortified hamlet with Charlie Company, sir."

It was a jaw-dropping decision. The Kid was aghast that Wilson had picked the surrounded fortified hamlet over the search and destroy missions that may or may not see action. *Maybe he is nuts! I'm fucked!* the Kid thought. *Fortified hamlet? I sign up for Armed Forces Radio and now my ass is getting shipped to a freaking fortified hamlet that is surrounded by the VC? As an adviser to the South Vietnamese army?* His right hand searched the neck of his uniform, where he found the chain that held his lucky Canadian beaver nickel. He subtly rubbed it between his thumb and forefinger, cursing the day he'd decided to take the extra year. Now he was apparently out of the frying pan and into the line of fire.

"Yep, we'll go to Tan An, at least until the loudspeaker equipment arrives." Wilson nodded his head in agreement with himself. "When can we leave, sir?"

"I think I can find you a chopper down to Tra Vinh in a couple of days, for sure. Three days, tops."

"And you." Atkins turned to Cleveland. "It is my understanding that you'll be assigned to be with Lieutenant Kazmarskij, who is currently working on a new way to field-deliver leaflets with mortars." Atkins smiled.

"OK," Cleveland said, as if there was anything else he could have said.

"We'll be ready, sir." Wilson rose and saluted, with the Kid and Cleveland following suit.

"Thank you, sir!"

Thank you? the Kid thought as they walked out of Atkins's office. *That's like Colonel Travis thanking Sam Houston for sending him to the Alamo!*

Oh, one more thang, Colonel Travis. Y'all'll be surrounded by a force twenty times the size of yours, and they'll all be trying to kill you at all hours of the day and night.

Chapter 11

After dinner, the Kid had scouted the Sa Dec compound and found a place where, as soon as the sun went down, he could smoke a joint. He did not recall seeing Cleveland on the third floor, so he did not ask him—or Herrick, or either of the other two hooch mates—if they wanted to join him or if they had some better stuff.

The spot he had found was down at the east end of the compound, where, from an old bench that sat on the path that circled the island, one could sit and look out at the Mekong River. *This could well have been the favorite spot of the French planters,* the Kid thought as he inhaled the reefer. Guard bunkers bracketed the place on either side of the island, and their fields of fire covered it, but the spot where the bench sat was isolated enough to offer a feeling of security for pot-smoking purposes. There was nothing in front of the Kid but river, so it wasn't as if there were a VC waiting out there in the dark to shoot anybody dumb enough to light up at night in the jungle in a combat zone.

Mentally and emotionally, the Kid was low. The speaker team bullshit had been too much, but now, having been volunteered to pull fortified hamlet duty, he was ready to swap with anybody at Can Tho who thought the field was a good deal.

As he puffed away, the Kid realized how weak his Mexican stuff was compared to the 'Nam weed he'd been smoking for the past three nights with the boys in Can Tho. *Gotta find me some 'Nam weed,* he resolutely declared to himself.

That's the new priority numba one! Oops, make that priority numba 2, right after staying alive.

As weak as it was, the Kid still managed to get a buzz going, and when the joint became a roach, he snuffed it and rose up to walk back to the hooch of his current residence. This not having a permanent place to be was starting to wear on him.

Taking out his pen, stationery, and transistor radio, he sat up in his bunk and began writing his customary daily letter to Flo, as soon as he had AFVN properly tuned. "I can't wait forever. No, I can't wait forever. Time won't let me. Time won't let me a-wait that long." The Outsiders were singing a medley of their only hit as the Kid began writing.

Dearest Flo,

Hope this finds you doing OK. Well, I'm no longer in Can Tho. Today I met up with the lieutenant who is in charge of our field team, and we flew in a chopper to a town called Sa Dec. That was pretty cool. I'd always wanted to fly in a helicopter! If you're following along on your map, you'll find Sa Dec right on the Mekong River, north of Can Tho. So now, I've been attached to the ARVN Ninth Division. I guess that's what I get for

laughing at Waterhouse and Imbach when they got sent to the American Ninth! As I understand it, they are only forty-five miles east of here. The lieutenant's name is Herschel Wilson, and he is from Texas. Dig this, he says he's a guitar player, and when he was stationed at Fort Campbell, he went to Nashville a couple of times to try to get a record contract. He's calling me his "main man from Nashville," and I think he thinks I'm going to help him get a recording contract when this is all over. Well, if I live, maybe I will. Who knows? All I know is that I love you, Flo, with all my heart. I think about you day and night, and I look at your picture and want you so bad that I can taste your kisses. TM. One of these days, I should be getting a letter from you. So far, I've been moving away so fast that no mail could catch up with me. Unfortunately, I think I've now found out where I'm going to be for a while.

The Kid stopped and pondered what, exactly, he should say about where they were going and what kind of a place it was. Not wanting to scare Flo or make her worry to excess, he decided to sugarcoat it.

The place is called Tan An, and it is what they call a fortified hamlet, so the defenses around it are real strong. They don't have any loudspeakers for us. Can you believe that? They make me a foreign-language announcer and don't have any loudspeakers. Typical army bullshit! What we are going to be doing, as near as I can understand, is going out and trying to talk some villagers into moving inside the hamlet. Seems easy enough! I've got my Polaroid and my Kodak, and when I get there, I'll take some pictures and send them to you. Tonight, I'm bunking with a bunch of air force guys who call in air strikes in this sector. They're OK. I kind of liked the guys in Can Tho I was telling you about. This Harold Ling-Fook, the half-black, half-Chinese photographer, had some incredible pictures of people and things. His eye for the shot was making me jealous. If he ever puts his stuff out in a book, I will buy it. Or maybe he'll give me a free one! Anyway, I've got to write the folks and Dave and Patsy in Nashville, so I'm signing off for now.

I'll see you later!

All my love,

C

When the Kid finally finished the last of the four letters he wanted to write that night, it was close to 2200 hours. He went down to the latrine and brushed his teeth, took a leak, and prepared for bed. As he tucked in the mosquito netting around his mattress, he was thankful that he wasn't spending another night in the bowels of hell, that is, the transit room of the New Villa. Perhaps tonight, with the fan going and with the air coming off the river and through the screens, he would get a decent night's sleep.

Closing his eyes, his visions and dreams started like turning on a switch. French. The fucking French were to blame for all of this. He tossed and turned, trying to find a comfort zone. Why did he hate the French so much? It occurred to him that he might well have been French in a previous life and got sent to Devil's Island or something like that. *Hey, this is an island,* he realized, before he slipped off into a Nashville dream:

It was his first night at WKDA. He had arrived for the midnight shift at about half past eleven, and Johnny Wailin was just finishing up his shift. Wailin, it turned out, was from Minnesota and had been a TV weatherman up there before going to radio DJ school at Brown's Academy of the Broadcast Arts and landing his job in Music City.

"So," Wailin said, "you got yourself a tryout! This control board is great. It was custom-made for this room." The Kid looked at the setup; there were two turntables on the announcer's left, but WKDA was rigged to play most of the pop records on five-cart machines that sat to the right, which up until now had only been used in the Kid's past to play commercials. But with the songs on cart, there was no cuing up—just slap it into the machine and hit a button. *That should make for a really tight show.*

The Kid watched Wailin work it. About midnight, Wailin said, "That fucker DJ Dan is always late by a few minutes. I won't miss his sorry butt relieving me at all.

You'd better not ever be late, Kid, or I'll kick your ass.

"Look," Wailin said, "I have to start his first record and he's still not here." Just then, the control room door flew open, and in rushed this tall, skinny, thin-faced man with a pasty-looking complexion and an Elvis Presley haircut. "Hey, Dan, you're late!" Wailin said. "This is Curt the Kid from Colorado, who is your replacement."

"Hello. Pleased to meet you. Let me get squared away, and we'll talk. You can just watch for now."

At about one o'clock in the morning, at the beginning of his second hour, DJ Dan said to the Kid, "Want to take it for a while and get your feet wet?"

"Sure," the Kid answered.

"Just put the song into the cart machine. The pods are numbered one to five here on the board. This is to cue this program, then hit the button!"

"Sounds easy enough."

The Kid took the chair for his Nashville radio debut. After the news feed ended and the jingle played, the Kid hit the button to begin his first song of his new job. For the honor, he had selected "Cherry, Cherry" by Neil Diamond, because it seemed entirely appropriate. He wondered if anyone else in addition to him would get the joke.

The first couple of guitar chords sounded, followed by an explosion.

An explosion?

"Incoming! Incoming!" he heard a voice scream as a siren was going off. "Mortar attack!" Then immediately the Kid was out of his dream. *Holy fuck! We are under attack!* He ripped the mosquito netting out of the mattress, hit the floor, and charged for the door. Another round slammed into the compound not far from their hooch. Bursting out the door, he made a left turn and then cut left again, heading for the bunker. Just as he arrived at the entrance to the sandbagged sanctuary, he ran into something and was knocked over backward, landing flat on his back!

"Ow!" Somebody groaned. It was Herrick! The two of them had collided right at the entrance to the bunker. As they lay there, the other men in the hooch rushed up and stumbled over them, turning it into a pile.

"What the fuck? Hurry! Move! Move! Get in!" a voice desperately yelled. The men all scrambled, their arms and legs flailing as they all tried to get inside the bunker, gasping for air. The Kid's head really hurt from bonking off Herrick's.

"Goddamn it!" Herrick moaned in the dark of the bunker. "Who the fuck was that?"

"Me!" the Kid exclaimed.

Another round came slamming in, close enough to make them know they were fortunate to be inside a decently enhanced bunker.

"You guys collided at the door? That's pretty fucking funny! Well, Herrick, there goes your little record of never being beaten into the bunker!" The person who'd said this laughed, then everybody laughed. The irony was not lost on the Kid: they were getting shelled on the outside but were laughing on the inside.

"Jesus Christ, this bunker reeks!" Cleveland screamed, followed by more explosions close by.

"That's because Sergeant White took a piss in here last week when the attack lasted more than an hour," Herrick said. "I hope to fuck this is a short one!"

A couple of explosions and a couple of minutes later, they heard a different kind of noise: *Brrrrrruuuup. Brrrrruuuuup.*

"Spooky's here! Let's watch!"

"You mean go outside?" the Kid questioned in an incredulous voice. "Is that smart?"

"Yeah, when Spooky gets here, the VC usually stop the mortars because they're too busy trying to hide. Have you seen Spooky up close yet?" Herrick said. "It's cool!"

Emerging from the bunker and looking up, they saw the red tracers streaming down out of the sky as Spooky circled overhead, pouring down death, or at least potential death. The first time the Kid had seen Spooky work, which was three nights ago, it had been seven miles off in the distance, but tonight, their seats were ringside!

Who could stand up to firepower like this? Now the Kid could really hear the reports of the miniguns: *Brrrrrruuuuuuupppp. Brrrrrruuuuuupppppp.*

It went on for more than ten minutes as Spooky flew circles around Sa Dec, trying to kill anything that moved outside the city proper. The Kid was in total awe of the weaponry as he could see tracers bouncing off the ground and back up into the air in little arcs, falling for a second time to the ground.

The men stood there in the dark, leaning on the bunker, watching. "Yeah," Herrick finally spoke, "I came out the front door, Stocker came out the back door, and right here we hit!" Everybody laughed some more. "You wouldn't be laughing if it was your head. Right, Stocker?"

"Yeah! Hey." The Kid had a thought. "If I'm bleeding, do I get a Purple Heart?"

Chapter 12

PFC Cleveland was picked up by Lieutenant Kazmarskij and taken off to his assignment the day after their arrival in Sa Dec, but Lieutenant Wilson and the Kid ended up waiting for four days before finally getting a chopper ride down to the town of Tra Vinh. The Kid was enjoying Sa Dec, the Lucky 9 Club, and the air force guys who were his hooch mates. In addition to Sergeant Herrick, there was Sergeant Redd and Sergeant White. It seemed that every enlisted man in the air force was at least a sergeant. When he had been introduced to them, the Kid made a crack: "Where is Sergeant Blue?" it turned out that there was indeed a Sergeant Blue! He was home on emergency leave, so the Kid hadn't met him.

What a patriotic group!

The mortar attack on his first night in Sa Dec hadn't caused any US casualties, but it had killed two Vietnamese civilians, whose house had been on the north side of the river, directly across from the ARVN Ninth compound. The barracks located just behind the headquarters building, four rows over from the air force hooch, had been hit, but everybody had gotten into the bunker by then.

The Kid suggested to Lieutenant Wilson that they were now combat vets, but Wilson only laughed and said that wouldn't be so until they got shot at with rifles and such in a situation where they could fight back. "We were in a mortar attack, not combat," he said. "There's a big difference."

The Kid hadn't bled from the bump with Herrick, so the argument for a Purple Heart was moot. He was surprised that his head still kind of hurt. He rubbed the spot while looking out the door of the chopper, which was winging along in an easterly direction on the way to Tra Vinh.

While getting their gear together and taking care of administrative stuff within the ARVN division, the soldiers had had a chance to talk with a couple of officers who had been to Tra Vinh. Interesting town, they said. It was also known as Phu Vinh, but the South Vietnamese government of President Thiệu had changed the name to Tra Vinh because Phu Vinh was recognized as the birthplace of the Vietcong. It was where the VC held their first recorded meeting, after it became clear that the election mandated by the Geneva Accords, which followed the 1956 victory by the North Vietnamese at Dien Bien Phu, was not going to take place. It seemed that John Foster Dulles, Eisenhower's Secretary of State, convinced Ike that Ho Chi Minh was a communist and that if they held an election, he would win hands down. Can't have that, so no election! Instead, the United States helped the old traditional hereditary emperor of Vietnam, the Bao Dai, to reclaim the throne in Hue just long enough to call for aid because "South" Vietnam was being invaded by those dirty communist bastards from the "North." Now he knew how the British soldiers must have felt when they got assigned to Boston after the Tea Party.

Between him and Wilson, on the chopper floor, there was now a total of five duffle and laundry bags full of gear. Mainly it was extra ammo, which didn't really make the Kid feel all that secure.

He adjusted his butt on the seat, looking for a little relief from the gamma globulin shot the two of them had gotten while they waited to fly out of Sa Dec. The Kid hated needles, and he had never seen a bigger needle in his entire life; it looked like something that a veterinarian would use on a horse! In fact, the gamma globulin shot was so big, it had to be shot into both cheeks of a person's ass over a period of two days! Supposedly, it protected against hepatitis and a bunch of other evil stuff to which they would be exposed out in the hinterlands of the Delta.

As the chopper arrived over Tra Vinh field, the Kid could see runways for a regular airport, not the small "international heliport" like in Sa Dec. The bird came to rest on a yellow *H* adjacent to a small one-story terminal building that was situated just off the road that ran on into the town.

A modified International Land Rover, open like a convertible with no top, sat nearby, with one jungle-hatted GI visible sitting behind the steering wheel. As they touched down, the Kid looked at his watch: 0900 hours on June 6, the anniversary of D-Day.

They had their gear off the chopper in an instant, and just as quickly, the bird was gone in the cloud of machine-generated dust. When the dust had settled, the Land Rover drove over to where the men stood with their bags, and parked.

"Howdy." The staff sergeant stepped out from behind the wheel and down onto the ground. He sported one of the most amazing blond handlebar mustaches the Kid had ever seen! "Welcome to Tra Vinh. I'm Sergeant Spencer." There were handshakes all around. "I'm here to take you to the compound."

150

A yellow Lab waited, its tail wagging in the back seat of the Land Rover. "That's Rusty, the unit canine," Sergeant Spencer said, having seen both men staring at the dog.

"Thank you," Lieutenant Wilson replied as they began to throw the baggage into the back. Just as he hefted the last bag in, he stopped and looked strangely alert. "Was that a shot I heard?"

His saying that made the Kid show some surprise, but Spencer kind of rolled his eyes behind his clear-lensed glasses. "Oh, that," he said. "That's just the Tra Vinh Airport sniper."

"The what?" the Kid asked, clearly perplexed and on guard.

"The Tra Vinh Airport sniper. Don't worry, he never hits anybody. Ever. Yep, he's here almost every day, mostly right around this time; he takes a few shots and goes home. He doesn't shoot anybody, and we don't go look for him. Kind of like an unspoken contract."

"You've got to be kidding!" Wilson couldn't believe what he was hearing, but the Kid could see he was amused by Spencer's story.

"Nope. God's truth." Another couple of shots rang out. Two men working on the flight line, about five yards away, jumped down to the ground as if they'd just been missed. "He likes to come close every once in a while to scare you a little, but in all the time I've been here, going on eight months, he's never hit a soul. Ready? Let's go!"

Wilson took the front. The Kid gladly took the back with the dog, remembering what the dude who'd driven him from Bien Hoa to Saigon had said about sitting up front.

"Yeah, we like to joke about the airport sniper," Sergeant Spencer said as he drove. "We think the position is hereditary, passed down from father to son, one of the safest jobs in the whole VC army. We think his great-grandfather sniped at the French, his grandfather sniped at the Japs, his father sniped at the French again, and now he's sniping at the Americans!"

Right across from the Tra Vinh airfield, there was a huge Vietnamese cemetery. As the Land Rover drove past it, the smell just about floored the Kid. The graves were all aboveground, like those in New Orleans, where the ground was too wet to bury people in. The Kid could see that many of the tombs were cracked and slightly open, emitting that strangely pungent and sickening odor of rotting death in the tropics. Bad, but still not as bad as the Cholon Fish Market. What a strange day this was turning out to be.

Tra Vinh airfield sat on the western edge of the town, and in about a minute, they were in it. It was a quaint-looking burg judging by what the Kid had seen so far.

151

He and Wilson had walked around Sa Dec a little, looking into shops and whatnot. It must have been twice the size of Tra Vinh. Tall trees lined the main drag, making it a regular shady lane. Lots of bicycle and foot traffic and noticeably fewer vehicles than in all the towns they'd been in so far.

Turning a corner, they saw a massively dug-in structure of logs and sandbags sitting in the middle of an area that looked as if it had once been a park. "That's the tactical operations center [TOC]," Spencer said as he shifted gears. "That's where they coordinate all the field operations when we're out fighting. During Tet, the VC actually came into town and attacked it, but they didn't get in. We lost twelve ARVNs—KIA—in its defense and took out about twenty VC in the process."

Ow. The Kid winced. *Fighting right in town! Not good, not good.*

"Here's the compound," Spencer said as he pulled into a driveway between the pillars of an eight-foot-high gated wall. The compound was another old French plantation house. With its surrounding grounds, it appeared to be about one-fifth the size of the plantation at Sa Dec. The main building was three stories tall, and the Kid could see that it was once a thing of beauty. A broad veranda graced the front, and the driveway went under a portico that was formed by a row of service buildings that ran down the right side of what had once been clearly the fanciest estate in town. A pair of very dark-skinned soldiers stood guarding the front gate. Although they were Asians, they did not look Vietnamese.

"Our compound is guarded by a bunch of Cambodia mercenaries, as tough a bunch of sons of bitches as you'll ever meet," Spencer said as the Land Rover came to a stop. "This is home!"

Walking through the portico, they found themselves in a courtyard that was formed by the big house, the service buildings, and the servants' quarters at the rear of the estate. It had a real lawn of green grass that took up the whole courtyard except for a dirt area that was set up with a volleyball net and a white- lined court.

"Officers sleep in the big house, and EMs are out in the servants' quarters." Spencer pointed as he spoke.

Big surprise there, the Kid sarcastically thought.

"The mess hall is in there, and so is the club." Spencer gestured to the one-story row structure that had a bunch of different entrances. "The compound is so small here, the officers' mess hall and the EM mess hall are only separated by an archway. And we actually have to share the club," Spencer said offhandedly, "which is through the last door down there."

At that, the Kid quickly looked at Wilson to get his reaction, which he read as a one of disgust. *Oh, boo-hoo, no big exclusive officers' club again! Bummer! Hmm, the trend with the club's is holding,* the Kid noted. *Smaller and smaller!*

"We've got a little PX here too, but it ain't got much, just cigarettes, some booze, razor blades, toothpaste, soap, paper, and envelopes. And occasionally batteries and stuff like that. But anything you need, you can usually find downtown in one of the shops. Oh, by the way, do either of you play volleyball?"

"Well, I've played a little, in high school," the Kid volunteered. "I was on the gym class coed championship team when I was a senior."

Wilson said nothing.

"That's good, Stocker. We need some help. The main form of evening entertainment here at the compound is Vietnamese and any other Asians versus Americans at volleyball, and recently they've been kicking our asses. We could sure use some fresh blood."

"Sure, I'll play." He gamely smiled. "What the fuck? Looks like it's the only game in town!"

"OK, let's see." Spencer pondered his next move. "Stocker, let's find you an empty bunk down here in the servants' quarters," he said as he moved that way down the sidewalk that ringed the lawn.

Inside the L-shaped building, Spencer commenced to look into each of the cubicles, analyzing each one, until he found a bunk that appeared to be empty.

"This ought to do for now. And yes, here's an empty locker that …" He stopped in midsentence as he began to open up the locker for a look inside. "Oh, this was Kelly's space. Yeah, I guess they shipped his stuff home. Got killed last week, with Major Dugan, out on the road to Cang Long."

"That's too bad," Wilson cut in. "How'd they buy it?"

"They were in a jeep and they were going out with a convoy, but the major forgot something and came back to get it. And when they left again, they got picked off before they could catch up to the rest of the convoy. Stupid mistake, really. Paid the ultimate price for making it."

The Kid got an eerie feeling in the pit of his stomach. *That's all it would take in this country, one stupid mistake, and you'd pay with your life.* It apparently didn't bother Lieutenant Wilson.

"Stocker, you can go ahead and get squared away, if you want, while I find a place for Lieutenant Wilson," Spencer said. Then he and Wilson left.

The Kid sat down on the bunk and lit up a smoke. Conveniently, the other occupant of the cubicle was a smoker and had an ashtray in play. Another room, another locker, another week of living out of a bag. He hated it. Pulling out his trusty transistor radio, he turned it on and sat it in a favorable place on a trunk that was next to the other lockers, listening as he stowed his stuff.

"Oh, when the sun beats down and burns the tar upon the roof, and when the tired streets are so hot, they're like fire too, under the boardwalk, down by the sea, on a blanket with my baby, that's where I'll be," the Drifters melodically sang as the Kid picked up his M16 to see how dirty it might have gotten at the helipad. *Not too bad. Certainly not bad enough to clean again yet.* He'd heard so much about M16's jamming that he wasn't scrimping on keeping his piece clean.

"Under the boardwalk, out of the sun. Under the boardwalk, we'll be having some fun. Under the boardwalk, *boardwalk.*"

Then the AFVN disc jockey announcer came on, saying, "This special news bulletin just in: Senator Robert F. Kennedy has been shot and is in critical condition in California, where he had just won the California primary election and apparently had the Democratic nomination for president within his grasp. Again, Senator Robert F. Kennedy has been shot and is in guarded critical condition at a hospital in Los Angeles. We will have more details for you as they become available."

The radio then played some nameless big band–sounding instrumental as the Kid sat stunned, his mouth hanging open, on his bunk. *RFK has been shot! My God! First the president, then Martin Luther King Jr., and now Robert Kennedy!* His reaction was to jump up and run out into the middle of the compound and yell it: "RFK's been shot!" But the only person he knew here was Lieutenant Wilson. How ironic. When they'd been killing some time in Sa Dec, they talked politics once over a beer, and the Kid said he liked RFK but that he liked Eugene McCarthy better. Wilson had responded that RFK and McCarthy were both just liberal do-gooders who couldn't stop telling other people how to live their lives, or words to that effect.

The Kid immediately wondered if there was a TV in this compound where they might see Armed Forces News from Saigon. Rising up, he went out the door and over to the building where Sergeant Spencer said they'd find the club. Opening the screen door, he passed through a front room that was apparently the mess hall. He could see Vietnamese kitchen workers getting ready to serve the noonday meal by setting out condiments and silverware just on the other side of an archway with an opening so wide that it separated the enlisted mess from the officers' mess only on a token basis.

Seeing a doorway at the left in the back of the room, he went through it and found himself in the club. There was a chest-high L-shaped bar to the left as he stepped down to the floor. A pool table took up a quarter of the club to his right, and he could see a rack of cues up against the screened wall of the back of the establishment. A few tables and that was it. No TV. The place was empty except for a Vietnamese barmaid whom the Kid had not seen upon entering because she was sitting down in a chair reading a book.

"Hi, GI. What you want?" She smiled at him, her black hair cut a little bit longer than shoulder length. She work a dark skirt and a flower-print blouse, like an American woman would wear, as opposed to the type of clothing the Kid had thus far observed on natives of the country. Her very slim body and very attractive delicate face presented a most pleasing aura.

"Oh no!" He was a bit surprised when she rose up out of nowhere. "I'm new here and just kind of looking around. You speak good English?"

"Pretty good."

"Is there a TV, a television, around here?" "TV?" She had a quizzical look on her face. "Yeah, you know, like radio but with pictures!" "Ah yes, I know what you mean. No got!"

Rats. He walked back into the mess hall and through the arch. The two rooms held fewer than twenty of the long folding tables between them, meaning the troop contingency here was extremely small. The room was filled with the aroma of a hot lunch being prepared.

Walking out of the officers' mess door and into the yard, the Kid looked up at the back of the three-story old French mansion. A bunch of bunk beds were visible through the screened-in porch at the back of the house. Upon entering, he passed through a room where he figured many of the officers must sleep and into an area that might have once been the living room. It was set up with four couches and a bunch of folding chairs, which indicated that movies were shown on the far wall. A grand staircase led to the upper floors. As the Kid stepped up the marble risers, he could hear AFVN playing at the top of the stairs. As the room came into his view, the Kid could see a half dozen men huddled by the radio, bent over and intently listening. One of them was Wilson. When he noticed the Kid coming up the stairs, he immediately said, "RFK's been shot."

"I know! I heard it on my radio! What a shock!"

"Boy oh boy, is this ever gonna fuck up the election!" a major exclaimed. "Who do you think is going to get the Democratic nomination now?"

"Is he dead? They didn't say he was dead yet," the Kid said.

155

"He may not be dead, but from what we're hearing, the wounds are life-threatening. And if that's so, ain't no way he's going to be well enough to campaign. The Democrats will nominate somebody safe, like Humphrey," the major said, voicing his opinion. "Anybody but Mc Carthy!"

"PFC Stocker, this is Major Gillmore, compound commander," Wilson said, introducing the Kid to the man with whom he spoke.

The Kid snapped to and saluted out of force of habit.

"Can the saluting, PFC." The red-haired Major Gillmore stuck out his freckled- covered hand. "That can get an officer killed in the field," he said, repeating what Wilson had earlier said to him.

"Yes, sir. I'll can it, sir!"

The radio announcer recapped what was known at the time: Kennedy had just won the primary and had given his victory speech, thanking all the Californians who were helping him secure the nomination at the convention, which was coming up in Chicago. After the speech, he had left the hotel through the kitchen, where he was shot and badly wounded, apparently by a kitchen worker who was of Arab descent.

"The suspect, a Palestinian named Sirhan Sirhan, is being held without bail."

Everybody in the room was an officer except for the Kid and one other GI, who looked at the Kid with a very sympathetic stare before walking over and introducing himself.

"Hey, I'm Paul. Welcome to Tra Vinh." "Hi, I'm Curt. So, what do you do here?"

"Not much of fucking anything, I'll tell you that for sure." Major Gillmore immediately turned around and took a shot at the dark-haired specialist 4. Everybody but Wilson and the Kid laughed.

"I'm the major's personal aide." Paul grinned at his boss. "I'm in charge of getting it for him wholesale!"

The name on his uniform said "Heineman." "Where you from, Heineman?" the Kid asked.

"Pontiac, Michigan." "Tigers fan?"

"You bet. Denny McLain is going to win thirty this year."

"Bullshit. Nobody's won thirty since Dizzy-fuckin'-Dean!" the Kid declared. "If Whitey Ford couldn't win thirty with the Yankees, no Tiger is gonna do it."

"Word has been given at the hospital," the AFVN announcer's voice said, coming through loud and clear, "that Senator Kennedy has been taken into surgery, where a team of doctors is attempting to stabilize his condition."

"Wow. Too fucking sad! Where were you when President Kennedy got shot?" the Kid asked Heineman.

"In school. The teacher got called out of the room, and when he came back, he told us. And then we listened to a radio they played over the PA for about an hour, then they said, 'You can all go home.' Where were you?"

"I was in a car traveling from Boulder, Colorado, to a speech meet at Trinidad, and we were south of Pueblo, where there wasn't any radio reception. So, when we got into Trinidad, my debate partner, Larry Ryan, walked up to me and said, 'The president's been shot.' And I said, 'Oh yeah, what's the punch line?' Because there'd been a joke going around the month before: 'Hey, did you hear Jackie broke her arm?' 'No, how?' 'She was helping Jack off a horse.' So I thought it must be a joke. But he said, 'No joke. He's been shot in the head.' I couldn't believe it!"

A few more "where I was when Kennedy got shot" stories followed: "I was in a school ..."; "I was in a car ..."; "I was doing laundry ..."—each introduction followed by, "And I'll never forget it."

Now, they all shared an event like that, them in the room, only the Kid had had his moment in private a little earlier. The sheer circumstances of their situation dictated to them that RFK's being shot wasn't going to change their lives; they were deep in the war zone, and even if the next president, who wouldn't take office for another seven months, stopped the war on his first day, they'd all be halfway through or done with their tours of duty. So, that quickly, things went back to business as usual.

"Ready for lunch?" Heineman asked the Kid.

"Sure. I was just down there. It smelled pretty good compared to a lot of the shit in this fuckin' country!"

"Sir, may we be dismissed for chow?" Paul requested of Major Gillmore.

"Sure, Paul. And what the hell, go ahead and take the afternoon off, I won't be needing you until tomorrow morning."

"Thank you, sir!"

"Uh, Lieutenant Wilson, could I get the afternoon off too?" the Kid asked while the asking was hot.

"Sure, I guess. I just moments ago found out we can't meet Lieutenant Troung until tomorrow, so go ahead. But report to me after dinner tonight."

"Yes, sir." The Kid went to salute, but he caught his right hand with his left and pulled it down, as if it had a mind of its own.

Walking down the stairs, the Kid asked, "So, how long have you been in- country?"

"Just about nine months on the money," Paul said. "In fact, I've got ninety days left today. Tomorrow, I'm in the eighties!"

"Wow." The Kid was très jealous. "I've been here almost two weeks! I'm so long that if I were a dick, I'd be in a carnival sideshow!"

"It's not chow time yet," Paul said as they exited the main building. "Let's go to the club and get a beer. You can meet Wen."

"Oh, if she's at the bar right now, I just met her. I mean, I didn't meet her; I talked to her when I was looking for a TV. … Is she your girlfriend?"

"She's a friend who is a girl." Paul grinned. "A bunch of us frequently go over to her family's house. She was Captain Pratt's girlfriend, but he got killed like four months ago. Really nice guy."

They walked into the club. Wen was standing at the bar. "Hi, Heineman. How are you today?"

"Fine, Wen, except there's bad news from America today. The brother of President Kennedy has been killed—shot in California! Very sad."

"Ah, sad. We know 'sad.' So, you want beer?" "Yes, please, two of them."

Opening one of the two fridges behind her, she pulled out two cans of Budweiser. Pulling the ring tabs off, she set them before the GIs, who stood at the bar lighting up cigarettes. Paul slipped her a brown one-dollar MPC note.

"Wen, this is PFC Stocker. Uh, what was your first name?" "Curt."

"Curt, this is Wen."

"Nice to meet you." The Kid extended his hand to her extended hand and gently shook her fingers. *Too pretty,* he thought.

The two men sat down at a nearby table. "You said her boyfriend got killed a few months ago?" the Kid asked as he exhaled.

"Yeah, what a bummer. Got ambushed out on the Cang Long road. Bad story. You don't want to hear it." Heineman took a big, long swig of Bud. "So, you and Lieutenant Wilson are psyops?"

"Yep. I'm a foreign-language announcer who doesn't make any announcements; I'm here to advise some Vietnamese dude who is going to do it."

"Then you're a *covan.* That's Vietnamese for 'adviser.'" "Covan?" the Kid repeated.

"Yeah, that's right. Vietnamese isn't so hard. As soon as you pick up a little, use it whenever you can. The Vietnamese really appreciate it when Americans try to speak the language. It's a sign of respect. Like this." He said to Wen, "Co Wen, an beaucoup dep hoa!" Wen beamed a smile from behind the bar.

"Hashi Paul, an beaucoup dinky dau!" "What'd you say?" the Kid asked.

"I said, 'Miss Wen, you are very beautiful,' and she said, 'Corporal Paul, you are very crazy.' *Co* is 'unmarried woman,' *ba* is 'married woman,' and *beaucoup* is French for 'a lot.' There's lots of French words in use in Vietnamese because the French were here so long. And *dinky dau* is 'crazy.'"

As they sat and drank and smoked their cigarettes, men began coming in to the club and mess hall in anticipation of lunch, which was now only fifteen minutes away. Two men in air force uniforms walked over to their table.

"Hi, Paul," the more burly of the two sergeants greeted Heineman. "What's this shit we're hearing about Robert Kennedy getting assassinated?"

"Hey, Ernie. That's what we heard on the radio. Last thing we caught was that he was in surgery and they thought they had a chance to save him."

"New guy?" Ernie stood looking at the Kid, as his companion, a blondish sergeant with a mustache and a fairly good crop of hair for a serviceman, let out what could only be described as a gasp.

"I don't fucking believe my eyes!" the blond exclaimed with a broad grin. "It's the fucking Kid! The Kid from Colorado!"

"Say what?" Heineman looked puzzled.

"The Kid! From WKDA in Nashville! Good Guy Curt Stocker!" He stuck out his hand. "Hello, Kid. I'm Pete Johnson. I was stationed at Stewart AFB in Smyrna, just outside Nashville, and used to listen to you all the time! And I even saw you out at the WKDA Good Guys Summer Splash at Pine Springs last August before I got sent over here. You had the cutest fucking girl in the whole place! All of us air force guys were salivating over her and getting ready to hit on her, but you showed up and she went running to you. We hated you and wanted to kill you!

But we always loved your show! I can't believe it! The fucking Kid is here!"

Needless to say, the Kid was taken with the moment. It was like how an author feels when he finally hears that somebody has read his book.

"Pete, nice to meet you." They shook hands. "Yes, she's pretty hot. In fact, we're engaged now." He pulled Flo's picture out of his breast pocket and flipped it onto the table for the others to see.

"Oh yeah." Johnson picked it up first. "She had on this little pink bikini, and we were all sprouting woodies over her!" He sat down as Ernie stepped over to the bar and ordered them a couple of beers. "I was actually listening to your show the night you announced that you'd been drafted, and I said to one of my roommates, 'Hey, what are the chances that the Kid and I will end up in the same place?' I already had my orders for 'Nam in my pocket, and I actually fuckin' spoke those words—and look at you!"

"Let me see." Heineman pulled Flo's picture out of Johnson hand. "Wow, she is cute. What's her name?"

"Flo, short for Floretta. She has a twin sister, and her name is Loretta."

"She's got a fucking twin? Damn!" Johnson nearly screamed, "Where was she at the Splash?"

"She was there. Remember the slightly hefty one in the blue bikini? They're not identical, and she's engaged to a marine."

"Ah fuck, what the hell! Ernie, this is the Kid!" Johnson said as Ernie returned with their beers and sat down with them. "That DJ I mentioned who played all the long versions of the songs and the cuts from the albums that weren't in the Top 40. You know, the one I was talking about who had all the voices and little subshows going on?"

"The one you have been waiting for to come on AFVN?" Ernie looked at the Kid with a quizzical gaze.

"Yeah, this is him!"

"Well, you can stop waiting for my show to debut on AFVN, because I got stuck in psyops instead, and here I am, appearing in Tra Vinh, live and in person! Ta- da!" The Kid spread out his arms.

"Ladies and gentlemen, it is my pleasure to present to you, live from the twelfth floor of the Stahlman Building in beautiful downtown Nashville, the hardest- working man in radio from midnight to six, the Kid, Curt Stocker!" The Kid was flabbergasted. Johnson had his radio show opening committed to memory and just did it right there. "What was the name of that song that played in the background of your intro?" he asked.

"'Can't Sit Down (Part Two),' by Phillip Upchurch."

"We have to take the Kid over to Wen's," Johnson exclaimed. "Oh, wait!" he said, jumping up and running out of the club, only to return less than twenty seconds later, holding a copy of a record album. "Look what I've got!" It was a copy of *Sgt. Pepper's Lonely Hearts Club Band,* the Kid's favorite record.

"I'll be fucked! I have been wanting to hear that album since I left the States!" The Kid took it and held it in his hands.

"We can take it over to Wen's when she gets off work and listen to it over there," Paul said. "Hey, Wen, when do you get off today?"

"Fourteen hundred hours." Wen used military time.

"Great, we *de choi* at your house!" Paul said, then immediately translated for the Kid. "*De choi* is 'Go play'; *de lam* is 'Go work'—and bring your M16."

Chapter 13

Tra Vinh was, on the surface, a quiet little town. The Kid did not feel that he was in any danger as the group of four soldiers and Wen left the compound and walked down the shaded street past the TOC, their M16's slung over their shoulders.

"Wen lives four blocks over this way," Paul commented. They all puffed cigarettes as they walked. "Her parents are really nice, and they let us use their house like a club away from the club, where we can smoke the *can sa.*"

"How do you say it?" the Kid asked.

"*Can sa,* Vietnamese for marijuana."

"I remember when *Sgt. Pepper* came out." Peterson had the album tucked safely under his arm. "Johnny Wailin said you all at WKDA were the first station in the country to play it. Is that true?"

"Well, that's what they told us. Supposedly, some guy who used to work at Capitol Records had a bootleg copy and offered it to Dick Buckley as an exclusive to play the day before the release, but Buckley turned him in to the Capitol Records rep and they busted him. As a thank-you, they said we could be the first station in the country to debut it."

"Groovy!" Peterson said as he followed along.

"And then, Wailin played almost all the tracks, but he saved me one, the reprise of the Sgt. Pepper theme on side two. Thanks a lot, Johnny. So, I was the first DJ in the United States to play that cut on the radio!"

A massively large pig that must have been the size of a grown Saint Bernard dog contentedly ate some sort of refuse off the street in front of them. "Holy fuck! Look at the size of that porker!" the Kid exclaimed.

"That our neighbor's pig," Wen said. "He's only got another month or so to live, then he's breakfast, lunch, and dinner!"

Wen's family lived in a modest two-story house in a middle-class neighborhood of Tra Vinh. Her father was a merchant and had a store downtown that sold hardware and farming supplies. As the group entered the home, he was there to greet them, along with her mother.

"Ong Nguyen, this is our new friend Curt," Paul said, introducing him. "Ba Nguyen, this is Curt!"

Bows, handshakes, and smiles ensued as Pete moved straight over to the old console record player that was up against one wall and put *Sgt. Pepper* right on. As the Beatles cranked it up, the men all sat down at a round table of dark wood inlaid with beautiful abalone shell in a design including flowers and birds.

"Fuck, this table is beautiful!" The Kid ran his hand over it.

"Yeah, I'd like to buy it and take it back to the States with me," Paul said as he pulled out a pipe and a small black 35 mm plastic film canister. "And look at that armoire!" He gestured with his head as he packed a load of can sa into the bowl and lit it.

"It was twenty years ago today that Sergeant Pepper taught the band to play. They've been going in and out of style, but they're guaranteed to raise a smile. So, let me introduce to you the act you've known for all these years, Sergeant Pepper's Lonely Hearts Club Band!"

The pipe went around the table. The GIs smoked as the Vietnamese looked on, all smiles. Just to hear the Beatles was uplifting to the Kid; they didn't play enough of them on Armed Forces Radio. When the pipe came to the Kid, he took a deep hit and held it in as long as he could before coughing it up.

"Smaller hits, Kid. Take smaller hits!" Johnson laughed as he received the pipe.

"So, Lieutenant Wilson has volunteered us to go out to some fortified hamlet at Tan An." The Kid turned to Paul. "Is this a good thing or a bad thing?"

Paul took the pipe from Pete and drew a hit as he considered how to answer the Kid. "Well, there's really not much going on out there, so from that viewpoint, it's a good thing. But there is nothing there—no electricity, no running water, no PX, no movies, no whores, no fuckin' nothing. You'll be bored to death before you'll be KIA in a battle, so in that respect, it's numba ten!"

"What about that big attack they had a couple of nights ago?"

"Oh, that. That wasn't much at all. The Vietnamese commander reported that they killed one hundred twenty-five VC, but that is so much bullshit! Talk about inflating body count numbers. The colonel needed some body count to look good after taking the beating he did a month ago—lost thirty-two men in one day, a bloodbath. That's a lot for down here in the Delta."

"And the singer's going to sing his song, so let me introduce to you the one and only Billy Shears of Sergeant Pepper's Lonely Hearts Club Band."

Wen's mother appeared at the doorway to the kitchen with a round of Cokes, which she sat before the Americans.

"Cam on u am," Paul said. Turning to the Kid, he explained, "That's 'thank you very much.'"

"Cam on?" the Kid repeated.

"Com quotche!" the mom responded.

"That means 'You're welcome' or 'Think nothing of it.' Fuckin' A, you'll be learning Vietnamese all day long out at Tan An, Kid."

As the pipe circled the table and the Kid got high, he sat there in the living room of his Vietnamese hosts and marveled at the fact that even twelve thousand miles from Nashville, he was still the Kid! Were things looking up? Not really. He still had fifty weeks to go, but today was turning out OK, except for the fact that Kennedy had gotten shot! It came back to him. "I wonder how RFK is doing?"

"They ought to tear the asshole who shot him from limb to limb!" Ernie fumed. He was from Boston and was a huge Kennedy fan. "I just hope nobody shoots him like Oswald, so they can fry his fuckin' ass!"

"I get by with a little help from my friends. I get high with a little help from my friends," the four of them all sang, singing along with the last line, and then commenced to laugh their asses off over the fact that they'd all had the idea to do it at the same time.

As the Beatles got to the end of "Lucy in the Sky with Diamonds," Wen's mom sat a big plate of fried potatoes in the center of the table. They looked like potato chips but were thicker, done to a golden brown. The Kid tried one and found they were delicious! That he had a killer case of the munchies was no big surprise as the pipe had gone around and around the table and Paul just kept filling it up when it got toasted.

"So, you and Wilson will make it five Americans out at Tan An," Paul said between hits. "The captain in charge out there, Captain Morris, is really short. He's supposed to rotate back to the States next week. There's a lieutenant from Ohio there, Jim something or other, and an E-5 career man named Sergeant Matt, who is dumber that a box of fucking rocks! This guy has been in the army for fifteen years and he's only an E-5! Can you believe it?"

164

"Wednesday morning at five o'clock as the day begins, leaving a note she hoped would say more, she silently slips out of the living room door, and she's free!"

"Is the place really surrounded?" the Kid asked Paul.

"Oh, fuckin' A. Yes, totally! Cang Long Province is a hotbed of VC activity. They are everywhere out there!" Paul laughed. "They say the VC killed the nuns and priests who lived there in the abbey and blew up the cathedral as a statement of what happens to anybody who opposes them. Blew it up all but the steeple. I've been out there once, to deliver some supplies and mail, and that thing sticks up about eighty or a hundred feet in the air. The VC use it as an aiming device, so they haven't ever knocked it down."

"For the benefit of Mr. Kite, there will be a show tonight on the trampoline. The Hendersons will all be there as Mr. Kite flies through the air. Mrs. K. and H. assure the public that their performance will be second to none. And of course, Henry the Horse dances the waltz!" Wen came back into the room after changing from her Americanized work clothes into something more Vietnamese: black pajama slacks and a pink top. She kept staring at the Kid with a tiny smile on her lips.

"She thinks you're cute," Ernie kidded the Kid.

Just then, Wen's little sister, who wasn't more than eight or nine years old, came in from school.

"Men yoi, Quan," Paul greeted her.

"Men yoi, Heineman," Quan returned the greeting.

"Wen's little sister," Pete said, stating the obvious. Reaching into his pocket, he flipped her a piece of yellow-wrapped Juicy Fruit gum.

"Can on u lam. Trung shi." She smiled at him.

By the time the Beatles got to "A Day in the Life," the men were all righteously toasted to the gills. And when it ended, Pete rose up, went over to the record player, flipped the record over, and started it again. Worked for the Kid.

When it finished playing for the second time, the men rose up and, stretching, announced they were going back to the compound. Fishing around in their pockets, they each dropped a couple of dollars in MPC on the table. Seeing this, the Kid did the same.

"Cam on u lam, Mama-san," Paul said, with an arm around her shoulder. "Wen, we will see you tomorrow, OK?"

"OK. Bye now!"

Gathering up their M16's, they tumbled out into the street and began the four- block walk back to the compound. Clouds appeared to be building into something of a storm, so they all picked up the pace. By the time they reached the compound, it was starting to rain. Walking through the portal and into the courtyard, the Kid saw Lieutenant Wilson standing in the doorway of the servants' quarters, as if he had been in there looking for him.

"Lieutenant," he said as he walked up to him. He stopped as the other three men made their way on past him and into the billet.

"RFK died. He didn't make it out of surgery."

Just then, the sky opened up with a monsoon rain, and the two of them stood in the doorway, watching it come down in sheets. The Kid had never seen it rain that hard in his life. There would be no volleyball tonight.

Chapter 14

The Vietnamese Ninth Division's Fourteenth Regiment had its own compound in Tra Vinh, located on the north edge of the small town. Like the US compound, it was an old French building complex made over into a military position. And this was where Lieutenant Wilson and the Kid went the next morning to meet their counterpart, the Army of the Republic of Vietnam's political warfare officer Second Lieutenant Troung. The Army of the Republic of Vietnam, or ARVN as it was commonly referred to, did not have psyops units. They called their propaganda branch "political warfare units," POLWAR for short.

As Lieutenant Wilson and the Kid walked through the front gate, the helmeted guards eyed them but knew for certain, since they were Americans, that they need not worry about them. The ARVN uniforms were olive green and very similar to those worn by the Americans in the States, but not similar to the trendy jungle fatigue cut of the US Expeditionary Forces. The ARVN soldiers were armed with M16's, just like the Americans.

Immediately inside the gate, Lieutenant Wilson turned to one of the guards and said, "We're lookin' for Ti Ui Troung, the political warfare officer." The guard looked at him as if he was from Mars and speaking Martian; he clearly had no grasp of English on any level. "Aw, forget it!" the lieutenant said, turning to the Kid. "That looks like the main office over there in that building. I'll bet somebody there speaks English."

Crossing the compound and entering the front room of the structure, they found a group of Vietnamese officers sitting in chairs, listening to another officer speak as he pointed to a map. Wilson said in a very loud voice, "Does anybody here speak English?"

The man who was leading the group stopped and grimaced, apparently pissed about having been interrupted. "Yes, I speak English, Lieutenant. May I help you?" he asked, dropping the tip of his pointer from the map, which had a bunch of red and blue squares on it like the map Lieutenant Colonel Atkins had back at Sa Dec.

167

"We're looking for Ti Ui Troung, the political warfare officer. Can you help us find him?"

"Oh, Ti Ui Troung's office is next door." He lifted the pointer in the proper direction.

"Thank you," Wilson replied, turning and leading the way out of the meeting, the Kid in tow. "Fuckin' ARVNs. I hear they are the most worthless pieces of shit in the whole war," he droned to the Kid as they made their way to Troung's office.

Walking up the three steps that led onto the small covered porch of the building, Wilson stopped and knocked on the doorjamb, even though there was no door to stop them from entering. "Hello, Ti Ui Troung?" he said to a man who sat at a desk in the middle of the room, smoking a cigarette.

"Yes, I am Ti Ui Troung. Please come in," he said in perfect English. He extinguished the butt. "You must be Lieutenant Wilson!" He rose and stepped out from behind the desk to shake the lieutenant's hand.

"Pleased to meet you, Ti Ui Troung. And this is PFC Stocker, my foreign-language announcer, my right-hand main man from Nashville."

As the Kid stuck out his hand, he could see that Troung was wondering what in the hell a "right-hand main man" was.

"Pleased to meet you, Stockah." They shook hands and exchanged smiles, the Kid noting that Ti Ui Troung had the slightest trace of a cleft palate. He could see the telltale harelip.

"*Mein yoi,* Ti Ui Troung." The Kid put a Vietnamese-language spin and little bit of a bow into his greeting, feeling more than a little Asian after hanging out with a Vietnamese family the day before. The lieutenant was about Wilson's height, which was a couple of inches shorter than the Kid. His uniform was starched, pressed, and creased to the nines.

"Mein yoi!" he responded to the Kid as his face broke into a huge smile. "An bic Vietnam Cong Hoa?"

"Say what?"

"I said, 'You understand Vietnamese?' *Bic* is 'understand.'"

"Oh no, not really. I've just learned how to say 'hello' and 'thank you.'" *And marijuana,* he thought. "I've only been in-country for two weeks now."

"That's very good that you are trying to learn the language. I will gladly help you!"

"Well, we meet at last," Wilson said, cutting into the conversation. "I'm looking forward to getting started working!"

"OK, we talk now, Lieutenant Wilson. You want coffee? We can go to shop across street and talk there."

"That sounds really good," Wilson said. He looked at his watch, seeing that it was still a few minutes before 0900 hours.

Troung grabbed his hat, and the three of them headed out the door. They walked across the compound and out the gate to a small but bustling street-side coffee shop that catered to the members of the ARVN Fourteenth Regiment.

A dirty white cloth canopy was suspended from poles over the half dozen rickety wooden tables that filled the room between the corrugated tin shack, where the coffee and foodstuffs were prepared, and the dusty street. A line of Honda motor scooters were parked immediately adjacent. The three men pulled up stools, and Wilson and the Kid propped their M16's against the edge of the cable spool table.

"What you want, coffee with cream and sugar? Maybe iced coffee?"

"I'll have iced coffee, black," the Kid said. He liked his coffee black, and he was quickly learning that if there was ice to be had in Vietnam, then one should have at it!

"And I'll have mine hot with cream and sugar," Wilson said.

A barefooted Vietnamese girl of about twelve or thirteen, clad in unlaundered white pants and a light blue top, came over to their table. Troung spoke to her in a rapid tongue before turning to his guests. "Hungry? They have Chinese noodle soup." He pointed to a bowl a Vietnamese officer was enjoying at the next table, lifting it right up to his mouth and directing noodles the short distance to his jaws with his chopsticks.

"Oh no, we just ate before coming over here." Wilson had answered for himself and the Kid. He pulled out his Winstons and offered one from the pack to Troung, who accepted it.

Quicker than lightning, the kid whipped out his Zippo and lit Troung's cigarette. Then he pulled out one of his Kools and lit it. Without closing the top of the lighter and dousing the flame, he offered to light Wilson's cigarette.

"No, no, no. Third man on a match, very unlucky!"

"Lieutenant. This is not a match, it's a lighter, and I daresay, nobody is going to shoot you lighting a cigarette in broad daylight!"

"That may be, but don't tempt fate, that's what I always say," he said. He brought forth a book of matches from his pants pocket and lit his own smoke.

"Now, Ti Ui Troung, it's my understanding that you don't have any loudspeakers yet."

169

"That's right, don't have yet. May not have for two, maybe three weeks."

"OK, so, since we can't do that, I've made arrangements for us to go out to the fortified hamlet at Tan An," Wilson said, informing him of the plan.

The expression on Troung's face changed from happy to sad as if somebody had just thrown a switch. "Tan An? What for? There is nothing out there but VC!"

"My point exactly. Since we're here to fight a war, I say, let's go fight!"

"Man, Lieutenant, you say all kinds of stuff, don't you?" the Kid cut in. "No third man on a match. Let's go fight. Stocker, you can take the day off now—"

"Stocker, you had half a day off yesterday, so don't go thinking that's going to be a regular deal. Now, Ti Ui Troung, as I heard what our options were at division headquarters in Sa Dec, it seemed to me that working the fortified hamlet would be the best use of our time for psyops reasons. You don't agree?"

Before he could answer, the girl arrived at the table with the coffees, set up in tall, thick glasses cut in a hexagonal pattern, and placed them in front of the men. Lifting the glass to his lips, the Kid took a sip and experienced a jolt as the superstrong cold liquid coated his tongue.

"Wow! That is some strong coffee!"

"Ti Ui Troung, don't you agree?" Wilson asked for his concurrence again.

"If we do not have loudspeakers to accompany the infantry, I think it would be a better use of our time and energy to perform hamlet pacification rather than try to convince the unwilling to enter into a fortified hamlet."

A meeting of the minds. The Kid looked back and forth between the two lieutenants as Wilson digested what Troung had to say.

"What do you mean?" he finally asked, seeking clarification.

"Hamlet pacification is where we visit hamlet and teach political lessons." Troung stirred the huge sugar crystals at the bottom of his tan-colored iced coffee with a long-handled spoon before taking his first sip.

"Well, I think the VC should be pacified with bullets." Wilson was resolute in his comment. "Quite frankly, I'm glad you don't have any loudspeakers right now, because I don't think the VC deserve a chance to surrender!" It struck the Kid that these two men were starting out their relationship on the wrong foot. Troung wanted to convince the VC to come over to the ARVN side with logic, and Wilson wanted to persuade them with ballistics.

170

"This is very good coffee." The Kid attempted to defuse the situation with a change of subjects, but to no avail.

"Lieutenant Wilson, our mission is to win their hearts and minds. That is the only way we will triumph. We cannot kill them all, for then, what will we have won?"

"Ti Ui Troung, if we did kill them all, the war would be over, right?"

"The French and the Japanese could not kill them all, and never will the Americans, not with all your jet planes and tanks and artillery. The only way is to teach them that communism is not the way!" The Vietnamese lieutenant was very articulate.

While the pair argued, the Kid drank his coffee, smoked some more cigarettes, and thought about how he wished he was back in the States with Flo. And since that was not possible, he wished he were over at Wen's house, eating fried potatoes, smoking weed, and listening to *Sgt. Pepper* with his newfound friends and Johnson, his new Asian fan club.

Finally, Wilson decided to wrap the meeting up. "Ti Ui Troung, I tell you what: let's go out to Tan An and see what we can get done for a couple of weeks, and then we can reappraise our situation and see if we want to change what we're doing. OK?"

"OK. By two weeks, maybe we have the speaker team equipment here, so I agree. Then, we try pacification. You arrange chopper for us tomorrow?"

"Yep, it's all set up. We're leaving from Tra Vinh field at zero nine thirty hours. So now, PFC Stocker and I are headed out to the firing range to get in a little target practice. We want to be ready just in case the opportunity to shoot some VC should present itself. Isn't that right, PFC Stocker?"

"Yes, sir. I sure as hell don't want it to be the other way around!"

"What do we owe the girl?" Wilson inquired as he fumbled around in his pants pocket.

"One hundred fifty piasters," Troung said, "or two dollars MPC."

That would be 256 piasters at the Taj exchange rate, the Kid quickly calculated to himself, *a 75 percent tip. What the hell, the little girl deserves it. But what she really needs,* the Kid thought while watching her pick up the empty glasses, *is a bar of soap.*

Parting company with Troung, the Kid and Lieutenant Wilson walked out the front gate of the regiment and stopped as Wilson apparently was pondering their next move, or at least the direction, if indeed they were going to the rifle range to keep up their M16 proficiency.

"Let's see, from what Sergeant Spencer said, the rifle range is about half a mile down the road from regiment headquarters, so it would be that way." He pointed in the direction leading away from the compound.

Just as they began walking, a one-ton truck, with Americans driving it, came and stopped.

"Yo, Lieutenant," the driver addressed him. "Where y'all headed?" "To the rifle range," he replied.

"Would you two like a lift? That's where we're headed!"

"You bet!" Wilson's face lit up. He was pleased to be getting a break and not having to hump his gear around in the killer heat as the clock pushed 1100 hours.

"One favor we would ask of you, however," the driver said, his arm leaning on the window of the truck as he flipped ashes off his cigarette. "We're here to pick up some VC prisoners who are going to do a work detail out at the range, and we need some help guarding them. Would you two be game to help us out?

Otherwise, we'd have to wait around for somebody in regiment to assign us some ARVNs to do it."

"Sure! No problem. Be glad to do it!" Wilson volunteered their services without as much as a look at the Kid.

Once they'd climbed on board, the truck carried them back through the compound gate and drove over to a fenced-in enclosure on the far side of the complex topped with barbed wire that was clearly designed to keep people in.

The driver stepped out of the cab with a clipboard and turned to his newly enlisted guard detail. "Now, when we bring them out, I want you to let them see that you've chambered rounds, and then they'll know you mean business. And if they do try anything, like jumping out and taking off, just shoot 'em."

"Gladly!" said Wilson. "Uh how should we do it? Us in the back and them up by the cab, or vice versa?"

"You guys get up by the cab and let them load into the truck at the back. That way, if they rush you or jump out to run, you can shoot them without shooting us! They'll have their hands tied. They've been cooperative in the past, but still, they are VC, plain and simple, so don't let your guard down."

With the warning, the Kid became more than a little bit apprehensive; he was about to see his first live Vietcong. *Just shoot 'em.* OK, if it came down to it, he guessed he could do it. He'd certainly be more willing to shoot them if they rushed them and tried to take their M16's, rather than shooting them in the back as they ran away.

The driver walked over to the two guards at the enclosure gate. The Kid could hear him saying "Men yoi"—hello in Vietnamese. They apparently knew him and why he was there. The passenger, meanwhile, never got out of the cab and never said hi or boo, just sat there smoking a cigarette.

Soon, the driver emerged with a string of four men who were clad in shorts and tattered shirts, barefoot, with haircuts that made them all look as if they shared a barber with Moe of the Three Stooges. The driver directed them by pointing the way to the truck. As they stood by the tailgate waiting to load, Wilson chambered a round into his M16. The Kid did the same, drawing the pull assembly bar back with two fingers and releasing it, thereby placing a brass-encased shell into the firing chamber. The VC prisoners immediately became noticeably uncomfortable as they exchanged nervous glances.

"Ha!" The driver grinned. "They think we're taking them out to shoot them! That's good. We want them to be nervous!"

"Mau-mau." The driver spoke to them initially in Vietnamese, then switched to English and sign language. "Hurry up. Come on, hop on up there." He gestured.

One at a time, while eyeing the weapons being pointed at them by the officer and the PFC, the VC climbed into the truck, the task made slightly more difficult by the fact that their hands were tied in front of them.

Once they were squatting on their haunches, Wilson said, "OK, hit it!" and the driver slowly began to maneuver his way out of the compound.

The Kid studied the VCs as the truck rolled through the gate and took a left turn down the dirt road. One of them had flecks of white in his hair at the temples.

Another had a really bad case of buckteeth. The third one had a nasty gash on his left leg, where he had a recent injury that looked to be healing, and the fourth one couldn't have been more than fifteen or sixteen years old. Say hello to the enemy!

None of them appeared to be that mean or vicious. *How many Americans did each of you kill before you got captured?* the Kid had to wonder. As the truck bumped along the uneven dirt roadway, the prisoners continued to talk quietly amongst themselves. The youngest one was visibly upset.

"I think they really do think we're taking them out to shoot them," the Kid commented to Wilson.

"Good!"

The rifle range was located right on the edge of town. There were two signs, one in Vietnamese and one in English: "Firing range: Danger beyond this point." is what it said in English, and the kid assumed the Vietnamese sign was the same. The truck stopped at the far side of the parking area, next to a partially completed shelter hut where, once it was completed, anybody practicing at the range could take shelter when it rained.

Jumping down over the side one at a time, the Kid and Wilson backed far enough away to give the four room to unload and to prevent the possibility that one of the prisoners would leap on them. The passenger finally got out of the truck and, flipping his most recent cigarette away, chambered a round in his own M16. "I'll take it from here," he said to the pair of temporary guards. "Thanks a lot." Turning to the prisoners, he gestured with the barrel of his weapon, directing them to the structure where they would be working. He said, "Come on, you gook fuckers, let's get the lead out before I put some more into ya!"

Visibly relieved once they saw where they would be working, the VC all smiled and nodded their approval at not being the targets for today's rifle practice. They lined up to have their bonds removed.

Wilson and the Kid walked over to the firing line, where nobody else was currently practicing. Off in the distance were some upright plywood boards that had silhouettes of humans, white within black borders, attached to them, some at 590 meters, and a few more at 100 meters.

"So, PFC, are you any kind of a shot?"

"I'm a much better shot at pool than I ever was with a weapon, sir." The Kid was only being truthful.

"Well, a little bit of practice sure can't hurt. You never know when the time is going to come in this country when it will be for real, especially where we're headed." With than, Wilson flipped off his safety, put his M16 on full automatic, and emptied eighteen rounds into one of the targets. Wood chips and splinters flew everywhere as his bullets ripped up the middle of the target.

"Wow, not bad!" The Kid looked at the smoking barrel of Wilson's gun as he hit the button to pop out the empty magazine and slam in another.

"I should hope to fuck it's not too bad! I was rated 'expert' in our Airborne rifle qualification tests," the lieutenant proudly bragged. Stepping back, he waited for the Kid to take his turn.

Stepping up to the mark, the Kid went to chamber a round, but then realized one was already in there. So, flipping off his safety and carefully placing the selector switch on full automatic, he lifted the weapon into position and let it rip. He only hit the target twice, but both rounds were in the region of the head.

"That was plain fuckin' pathetic, PFC." Wilson shook his head in disgust. "What you want to do is aim for the fattest part of the man. You don't wanna go for head shots. You want to raise the probability that you'll kill the fucking bastard by going for the thickest part of his meat!" With that, Wilson stepped up and let fly with another burst, this time blowing to hell the part of the target that would have had genitalia had it been a real human.

"Ouch! That's gotta leave a mark!" The Kid laughed as he stepped up for his second clip. "I can do better on single shot," he said as he drilled the target right in the chest with one bullet.

"Try that with semiautomatic, like three or four short bursts," Wilson coached him. "That way, you might have more control, and then when you get better, you can use full auto more effectively."

"Yes, sir," the Kid answered. He commenced to comply with his instructions, placing well-controlled bursts into the target.

"Well, Stocker, you appear to be coachable," the lieutenant said, critiquing his performance. Stepping back into position, Wilson let go with another burst, first into one target and then, quickly changing his aim, into the one next to it. "If two guys are rushing you, you gotta be able to get 'em both!" He stepped back, clearly proud of his work.

"Nice shooting, sir," the Kid paid him a compliment.

"Yep." Lieutenant Wilson looked the Kid in the eye. "I volunteered to come to Vietnam because I've always wanted to find out what it was like to kill somebody. And the only place you can do that, without any legal reprisals being brought against you, is in a war zone," he said cold-bloodedly.

The revelation sent a snaking, quaking shiver down the Kid's spine. From the even tone of Wilson's voice, there was no doubt that he really meant it.

Chapter 15

The Tra Vinh compound was home to a very eclectic group of Americans, some in the army or the air force, and some not. The "not" group included a few CIA agents, a Navy SEAL, and some members of USAID, or to the uninitiated, the United States Agency for International Development, allegedly a civilian organization designed to promote business opportunities, but in reality, or so everyone believed, an organization manned by more CIA agents. There were also a number of Asian civilian workers there, from Korea and the Philippines, who were on contract to do a wide variety of tasks, such as engineering, compound maintenance, and the training of Vietnamese to do such jobs.

In all, the smallness of the compound's population and the fact that there wasn't a separate officers' club forced fraternization of the ranks on a level previously unexperienced by the Kid. And he wasn't so sure he liked it. In fact, he was sure he didn't like it when Lieutenant Wilson, with a hand gesture, took him away from the table where he was drinking beer with Paul, Ernie, and Pete by beckoning him over to where he stood at the bar.

"Stocker, tomorrow we are choppering out to Tan An," he said, ashing his cigarette as he stood at the bar nursing a glass of whiskey on the rocks. "I just wanted to have a drink or two with you and talk about some of the stuff we might encounter and what we're going to be trying to accomplish out there. Did you hear that they got mortared last night?"

"No, I didn't!"

"Yeah. It could have been a lot worse than it was, but this shell that came through the roof of the building turned out to be a dud!"

"Wow!"

"Uh-huh! It hit right on the new radio bunker they're building. And if it hadn't been a dud, the entire US contingent would have been killed. Buy you another beer?"

"Sure, why not? I've got nothing else to do," the Kid lied. He and his newfound friends had just been discussing scoring some pot from the

Cambodian guards who could be seen in their billet area, located right out the back door of the club in a covered courtyard.

"Tell you what, let's make it a beer and a shot!" Lieutenant Wilson said to the Kid. "Barmaid!" he said jokingly to Sergeant Spencer, who was manning the bar that night, as civilian Vietnamese workers had to be out of the compound and home by sundown, when the curfew went into effect. "A beer for Stocker, and two shots of Jack in the Black!"

"You got it, Lieutenant!"

The Kid hated bourbon. When Spencer poured the shots before them on the bar, he eyed his suspiciously. "I've had a couple of bad experiences on bourbon, Lieutenant. I don't know if I want to drink this!"

"Stocker, what are you, a fuckin' pussy?" He lifted the shot glass. "This is one lousy shot as a toast to the success of our mission!"

Tentatively picking up the shot glass full of caramel-colored booze, the Kid tapped Wilson's waiting glass, closed his eyes, and threw the liquor down, gasping for breath in the aftermath. It never ceased to amaze him that anybody liked this foul-tasting, debilitating beverage.

"All right!" Wilson smacked his lips, obviously enjoying it. "So, since we're going to be joined at the hip for the next few months or so, I thought we should get to know each other a little better. Your girlfriend back in the States, Flo? Is that her name?"

"Yes, sir, Flo."

"I was thinking you might want to write her a letter and give it to me to give her if, God forbid, something bad should happen to you."

"In case something bad happened to me?" Yes, the Kid thought for a second as the bourbon worked its way through his system, *I guess something bad could happen out there at Tan An, like death or dismemberment.* But there was something about the idea of writing such a letter that didn't sit right with him. "I don't know, Lieutenant. I remember reading about soldiers in the Civil War having letters like that in their pockets when they went into battle. But as I think about it, it occurs to me that if you want to prevent a letter like that from ever being read, the first step would be never to write one in the first place."

"That's an interesting take on the situation. I never thought about it like that." In their earlier conversations, Wilson had said that he was married, but he'd never mentioned the name of his wife.

"Have you written a letter for somebody to give to your wife, sir?" "Yes, I have. I left it with Captain Smith, in Can Tho."

177

"Where did you meet your wife?"

"I met her at the University of Denver."

"You went to the University of Denver? You never told me that! I grew up in Boulder before I moved to Nashville!"

"Oh, really?" he said in such a theatrical tone of voice that it caught the Kid's attention. "I spent a bunch of time in Boulder while I was at DU. What a great place!" Turning to the bartender, he said, "Sergeant Spencer, set us up with another couple of shots, and this time make them Wild Turkey!"

"Oh no, Lieutenant, with this beer, I don't think I can do another shot."

"Stocker, you fucking wimp! Now, we should take advantage of this night because out at Tan An, the way I hear it, there ain't no club and life is going to be plenty spartan. So, let's just let our hair down and have some fucking fun! How about a game of pool? My marker's up next; be my partner, and let's take those two on and wax 'em!" He gestured with his head to a pair of majors who had been dominating the table all night long. "You do play pool, don't you?"

Did the Kid play pool? Was that the question? The answer was an unequivocal yes. In fact, the Kid's father had bought a table for their basement in Boulder, once he realized how much time the Kid was spending at the local pool halls. From then on, the Kid had worked relentlessly at his game. "Sure, I've busted a rack or two." He smiled. But the reality of the situation was that, on top of the two beers he'd had with the boys before Wilson got friendly, the pair of shots he'd just drunk were starting to affect his coordination.

The Tra Vinh club pool table looked as if it had seen a bit of combat. The fabric was both stained and ripped in more than a couple of places, and the covering had worn off the rails, showing black rubber behind green felt running for a couple of feet up one side. The cue rack held a selection of aluminum and wooden cues, but only three of them still had tips, and they were all as crooked as a barrel of snakes.

"Jesus, is this bent, or am I?" the Kid joked as he selected his stick.

"This is a hardship tour, PFC!" Wilson drawled in his Texas accent as he examined the available cues. "We just have to make the best of whatever gets thrown at us!"

As one of the majors put away the eight ball with a long shot down one of the rails, the Kid could see that the table was also not anywhere near the condition known as level.

"All right, Boar Hog! Way to shoot! Who's next?"

178

"We are," Wilson said. He stepped forward, grabbed the rack, and began to gather the balls being pulled from the pockets.

"This should be interesting," the Kid quietly said to Wilson. The lieutenant set the balls and removed the triangle, placing it back in its storage location.

The majors who were teamed against them both wore West Point class rings. The one known as "Boar Hog" had one of the flattest flattops the Kid had ever seen. The graying of the hair at his temples indicated that he was older than a career man would want to be when he reached the rank of major. His real name was Boarz. His partner, who lined up for the break, was blond, younger-looking, and much less intoxicated than the Hog. The name visible on the patch above his pocket was Howell.

"You are the man, Howler!" Boar Hog hollered as his partner sank a solid ball off the break. Howler nodded his head in controlled reassurance as he looked over the table to determine his next shot.

"Seven in the side," Howler said matter-of-factly. He bumped in the easy shot. "Five in the corner." He took a longer shot and missed. "Fucking rat's ass!" he swore, turning away in disgust to take another slug of his beer.

"All right, lieutenants go first," Wilson said as he walked around the table, checking out the lay of the stripes. "Eleven in the corner." He stroked it in. "Thirteen in the corner." He lined up his next shot and missed it, knocking in a solid ball for the opponents on the slop. "Fuck!"

"Thank you! OK, you psyops boys are toast!" Boar Hog declared as he stepped up to the table. "One ball in the side off the fifteen." He missed it badly.

"All right, PFC, let's see what you can do!" Wilson encouraged his partner as the Kid devised his plan.

"Fifteen in the side." He shaved it in. "Nine in the corner." He smoothly put the nine away and bounced off the rail for position. Checking the bare and slightly flared wooden tip, he wondered how anybody could get any good English with an instrument as flawed as his cue was, but still he continued. "Fourteen in the corner off the six." Boom. "Ten in the corner." No problem for his fourth in a row. Now, the majors were paying a little closer attention.

"Damn, Stocker, leave me something!" Wilson admonished him.

"How about I leave you the eight? Thirteen straight down." He hit it soft, recalling that the table was tilted toward that pocket. The ball hit the rail, came off, and still rolling, curved into the pocket.

"Go, Kid! You're on fire!" Peterson called out from their table, which had an excellent view of the match.

179

"Twelve in the corner," he called his shot. It was the last stripe remaining in play. He shot, only to have the ball change directions when encountering the biggest rip on the table. It missed by an inch but came back nicely off the rail.

"Ooh, too bad!" said Paul, who was now standing to watch what was going on.

"Come on, Howler, the table is wide open now! Do your thang!" Boar Hog rallied his mate.

"Beat these fuckers," Paul whispered in the Kid's ear as he stood to the side watching. "Boarz is the biggest flaming asshole in all of Vinh Binh Province."

"OK, but I'm getting a little tipsy. The lieutenant is buying me shots, and I usually don't do hard booze."

"Hang in there!"

"Hoo, a miss!" Lieutenant Wilson yelled out, loud enough for anybody in the club to hear. "For my shot, make it the twelve in the corner." Then in the twelve ball went. "Well, fuck me in the ass, I can't get to the eight ball!" Wilson looked at his poorly left cue ball, stymied behind three solids. "Safe." He hit two rails, leaving it tight on the second one.

"Ho, that's a scratch!" Boar Hog laughed as he picked up the cue ball and walked to the breaking end of the table.

"What the fuck do you mean? I hit two rails!" Wilson immediately got hot under the collar.

"That doesn't work here. House rules are if you didn't hit a ball, that's a scratch— and one of yours comes out." The Hog pulled the fifteen ball out of the side and spotted it. "Three in the corner." Having picked a very easy shot, he made it. "Four in the corner." That one he missed. "Fucking piece-of-shit table!" he said, blaming the equipment.

"Get 'em, Kid!" Peterson was now also standing as the Kid walked up to the cue ball.

"Fifteen off one rail in this side." The Kid tapped the designated pocket with his hand and neatly parked the fifteen right in there. Turning to the eight, he saw it was sitting toward the drain hole in the far corner. "Eight ball there." He gestured across the table with his bent stick. Once he hit the ball hard enough to get it rolling, it curved in.

"Kid, Kid, Kid!" Peterson slapped him on the back.

"Nice shooting!" Wilson stuck out his hand in congratulations. "Show me a good pool player and I'll show you a misspent youth!"

"With a capital *T.* And that rhymes with P, and that stands for pool!" the Kid said, quoting "Ya Got Trouble" from *The Music Man.* "Thank you. Thank you very much!"

The majors tossed their sticks in the general direction of the cue rack and looked at the Kid with contempt. They had won six matches in a row leading up to this, and they were not good losers.

"Next!" Wilson bellowed as he walked over to the vanquished pair of officers. "Sirs, I believe you owe us a round; make it Wild Turkey shots, if you please." This lieutenant was the standard table bet: a drink per team member.

"Yeah, you're right," Howler said, motioning to Spencer. "Set 'em up, Spence!"

"Not another shot," the Kid lamented as Wilson brought the drinks over from the bar.

"To victory!" the lieutenant said, hoisting up the shot and downing it.

"Victory." The Kid choked his shot of liquor down. Now he was walking over his own personal line. He didn't enjoy hard booze; it had a tendency to make him sick.

Their next opponents, it turned out, were the pair who had been driving the truck to the rifle range when the Kid and Wilson were guarding the VC prisoners on work detail earlier in the day.

Wilson broke the balls and sank nothing. The PFC passenger, who was dressed in civilian clothes and had no name tag, promptly sank three solids.

"Watson is hot now!" Peterson exclaimed. "Come on, Kid, show them your stuff!"

The Kid stepped up to the table and called, "Eleven in the corner." Stroking the cue ball, he missed, much to the delight of their opponents and the majors, who remained to watch.

Walking slowly around the table, the driver, whose name was Hicks, selected his shot. "Five ball in the corner," he said. He quickly stroked the cue ball but mishit it. In turn, the five hit the twelve, which nudged the eight ball into the side pocket.

"Woo-hoo!" Wilson yelled. "We win again! That'll be two shots of Turkey, gentlemen." The lieutenant demanded immediate payment of the table bet. As soon as the pair brought the two shots back, the lieutenant was on the Kid to belt them down.

"Talk about your major buzz. I got one going!" The Kid drunkenly grinned at Wilson. Deciding to go with it, he called out, "Who's next?"

181

"We are." A pair of black sergeants rose up and prepared to do battle as Wilson pulled out the few balls that had been knocked in.

Placing his newly lit Winston in an ashtray on the two-by-four framing to which the window screening was nailed, Wilson broke the rack and failed to get a ball down.

The first of the black team shot at a stripe and missed, bringing the Kid to the table. "Open table?" The Kid looked it all over.

"Right," Wilson said. "That seven looks tasty."

"Ah, I see what I want. The three in the corner." The Kid lined it up, but when he made his shot, the tip slipped off the cue and he missed the three completely, shaving the eight ball into the side pocket.

The unpleasant look on Wilson's face was accented by his jaw dropping open in disbelief. "What the fuck was that?" he lamented to the Kid as their opponents high-fived each other.

"All those shots, sir," the Kid said, feeling a little wobbly. "I told you, I don't get along with hard booze."

Wilson eyed him, apparently a little bit pissed. "You pay for their drinks then!" The Kid complied and got them the beers they said they preferred.

"Oh well, at least we beat the shit out of the majors!" Wilson was happy about that. "Hey, if you don't cotton to liquor, let's get a couple of beers and go outside and talk for a bit."

Picking up two Buds from Spencer, Wilson handed one to the Kid and led the way out the door of the club, through the EM mess hall and out into the hot, humid night air. Finding a bench outside the servants' quarters, they sat down. The Kid lit up a Kool.

"So, Stocker, what did you think of Ti Ui Troung today?" "Well, he seemed like a nice enough guy."

"Too nice. He wants to coddle the VC. No good. We need to wipe them out—the sooner, the better!"

"I thought our job in psyops was to get them to defect?"

"Yes, that's true, but we need to kill a bunch of them along the way to show the ones who surrender that we mean business!"

"So, how long do you think it will take us to get the loudspeakers?"

"Do you really care, Stocker? Think about it: would you rather go up to a VC with your loudspeaker blaring or your M16?"

"Neither, given a choice."

"Don't tell me you're one of those bleeding-heart liberal doves!" Wilson seemed to be upset.

"I do have my reservations about this war," the Kid said, sipping his beer, "but I'm not a CO or anything like that." To the uninitiated, CO stands for conscientious objector.

"It's a good thing! Otherwise, we'd be at odds, and that wouldn't be a situation I'd care to experience."

"Uh, Lieutenant, I don't feel so good." The Kid was overtaken with a wave of nausea. In the next instant, he threw up. Some of the chunky vomit splashed on the lieutenant's boots. Jumping to his feet, the Kid ran for the latrine just inside the door, trying to get the next batch into a shitter, which he did. When he was done retching, he slowly walked back outside, where Wilson sat smoking.

"I gotta go lie down, sir. Mixing beer and whiskey is the kiss of fucking death for me. I should have known better. I apologize for your boots," he said. Then he turned to leave without waiting for Wilson to reply.

"OK. See you at breakfast," Wilson said in a slightly irritated tone as he rose and headed back to the club.

Staggering into the servants' quarters, the Kid made his way to his bunk and flopped down on his back. The room began to whirl, like water going down a commode. To stop it, the Kid plopped one foot onto the floor. *Thank God I got a lower bunk,* he thought as the nausea continued. He could hear AFVN on a radio a couple of cubicles away: "Wild thing, you make my heart sing. You make everything groovy." *How appropriate.* He had to laugh to himself. "Wild thing, I think I love you." He made up his own lyrics for the next verse: "Flo thing, you make my heart sing." His stomach continued to heave. "Flo thang, I love you." *God. Oh God, oh God. How fucked am I? he thought. How did I come to be here? I cannot believe that tomorrow I am going to be in some fucking hellhole in the backwaters of the Mekong Delta, totally fucking surrounded by VC! This has got to be one of those wild-ass dreams of mine. This can't be real. If I wake up, I will never drink shots again! My God, I barfed on the lieutenant's boot! I am fucked like a duck!*

"Kid?" he heard somebody softly calling. "Kid, you OK?" It was Pete, with Ernie and Paul. "Shit fire, Kid, you were throwing down the shots! How many was that? Four or five?"

"Oh, hey, guys. Don't get too close. I already threw up on the lieutenant's boots!"

"Yeah, we saw you do it!" Paul said. The three of them belly laughed. "I guess you were too drunk to see the look on his face! It was priceless!"

"Here, Kid, we brought you something to cure the whirlies," Ernie said. "Try to sit up for a second."

The Kid struggled to a sitting position, only to see Paul holding a pipe in front of his face. "Take a couple of hits on this and you'll feel better. Con sa has a way of curing the nausea." He struck a flame on his Zippo.

"OK. What have I got to lose? Only my life," the Kid said. He bent down, put his lips on the pipe, and inhaled, feeling immediate effect.

"This is that Cambodian shit we were telling you about," Paul said. He took a hit himself and passed it on while the Kid held his down. "This will straighten you right out or, if you're already straight, give you the bends!" More laughter. "Here, have another!"

The Kid complied. After the second hit, he felt much better, but far from perfect. "You wouldn't happen to have a little bit of this I might take out to Tan An, would you?"

"Oh sure, no problem!" Pete said. "We'll get you all set up in the morning."

"Thanks, guys!" the Kid said. Then he keeled over and passed out, still dressed and with his boots on.

Chapter 16

"Stocker. Yo, Stocker, reveille time! Rise and shine, PFC." It was Lieutenant Wilson gently shaking his bunk.

"Ak, not so loud, sir," the Kid moaned. He opened his eyes and saw that it was indeed morning, his watch reading 0700 hours.

"Come on, we've got a lot of stuff to do to get ready to go out to Tan An. Sergeant Matt is coming in this morning to get some supplies, and we're going back out with him at one thousand hours, so let's get moving. Oh, I see you're still dressed. That should save us some time!" Wilson laughed.

Lying there on top of his sheets, the Kid realized that he had passed out with his clothes on. At some point, he must have gained enough consciousness to remove his boots. And where were his glasses? He always knew exactly where he put them, but this morning, he didn't. "My glasses are missing," he said. "Oh, wait a minute, I'm lying on them!"

"You gonna live, lightweight?"

"Apparently, but not without some pain," the Kid said. He fought with his mosquito netting enough to give himself some room to swing his feet onto the concrete floor. Somebody must have tucked it in for him after he passed out.

"I'd recommend some hair of the dog, but the dog bit your ass so bad last night that you'll probably need a rabies shot!" Wilson continued to have fun at the Kid's expense.

"I'll be OK. A shower and breakfast and I'll be good to go." Then he remembered where they were going that day. "Or not," he said, lying back down.

"Whatever. Tell you what, you don't need to bring all your stuff with us today. We aren't going out there forever, and as I understand it, there aren't any lockers or anything. Spencer said you could leave some of your stuff locked up here and that they'd keep this bunk for you when we come in, so bring a couple of changes of fatigues, lots of socks and underwear, and all your field gear. The rest, you can stow here."

Hmm, the Kid thought, *some mention of returning.* That was a positive sign.

"I'm going to breakfast, and I suggest you hurry up and do the same. It's going to be the last American meal we'll have for a while."

No more American food? That was a negative sign. The forecast for today was mixed "Yes, sir, I'll hit the shower and be right there," the Kid said, finally rising up and looking for his shaving kit. As he got up from the bed and proceeded to undress, he could see it was going to be a back-assward kind of day.

Once out of the shower, the Kid began to feel better. Standing in front of the mirror and brushing his teeth, he eyed his tube of Colgate. He knew that stuffed into the end, his stash from home had dwindled down to a couple of joints and three or four roaches. He had to find Pete or Paul before they left. Hopefully, they would be at breakfast.

Walking out the door of the servants' quarters, the Kid spied traces of his vomit on the ground by the bench where he and Wilson had chatted last night before he got sick. Thinking about Wilson's boot, he wondered how pissed the lieutenant was.

Entering the mess hall and moving through the serving line, the Kid quickly looked the diners over to see if any of his new friends were there. They weren't. Bummer. But there was Wilson, sitting on the enlisted side of the arch, eating with a sergeant E-5. Upon seeing the Kid, he motioned him over to join them.

"Stocker, this is Sergeant Matt. Sergeant Matt, this is my team, PFC Stocker, my main man from Nashville! Although, judging from the way he didn't hold his liquor last night, I might have to change that to 'my main pussy from Paducah'!"

"Sergeant Matt." The Kid sat his tray down and extended his hand.

"Hello," the thin, wiry-looking, square-headed E-5 greeted him.

Sergeant Matt was the epitome of a lifer. The army was all he knew and would ever know. He had enlisted when he was seventeen, in early 1953, and caught the tail end of the Korean War. The man had been subjected to one war and hadn't gotten out of the military, but in fifteen years, he had only attained the rank of buck sergeant, which was only two ranks above where the Kid had gotten to in nine months. This led the Kid to believe that what Paul had said about Sergeant Matt was true: he had to be about as smart as a box of rocks.

"So," the Kid said, taking a sip of coffee, "I hear y'all lucked out there night before last."

"Yep, we sure did! If that round that came through the roof would have gone off, I wouldn't be sitting here now. Look at this." He used his fork to point to a red chaffed spot on the side of his forehead, just below his crew-cut hairline. "A piece of tile from the roof hit me in the head, and although the blood didn't gush out, you can see it sorta made a scab. I think I deserve to be put in for a Purple Heart, but Captain Morris says he won't put me in for it. I don't think that's fair!"

"Well, last week in Sa Dec, we had a mortar attack and I bumped heads with this guy going into the bunker, so maybe I should get one too!" The Kid smiled at Wilson, who continued to eat without looking up.

"Yeah, but I got hit with a piece of tile that was loosened by the enemy shell, and I actually bled, so I deserve it. You can't get one for bumping heads with somebody in our army!"

"Gentlemen, if you would finish up, we've got some shopping to do. Sergeant Matt has been telling me about some of the stuff we need to get, like kerosene lanterns, that is, if we want to write letters or read at night; and cigarettes and booze, if we wanna drink or smoke; and any kind of snack foods we can find. Things are pretty thin out there, right, Sergeant Matt?"

"Real thin," he said with his mouth full. "We eat every night with the Vietnamese, and they fix some really weird stuff, so if you want anything like candy or crackers for a midnight snack, you gotta bring it out with you. And we don't have a fridge, so it's gotta be stuff that won't go bad in the heat."

Once breakfast was over, the three of them borrowed Spencer's Land Rover to drive to downtown Tra Vinh. It was a bustling area about six blocks long and three blocks wide that surrounded an area of outdoor stalls serving as a farmers market. In one food store / drugstore, they found a selection of Vietnamese candy and stocked up on some strange-looking stuff they Kid had never seen before, some of it hard, and some of it puffy sugary-looking confection balls in pastel colors.

Then, standing in front of a hardware store, the Kid spotted Wen's father.

"Men yoi." The Kid bowed and smiled to Nguyen, who recognized him. *Ha! I already know a local!*

"Men yoi, Stockah!" He threw an arm around him. "You come to buy from me? I give you best price, you bet!"

"Yes, Nguyen, we need kerosene lanterns and kerosene; we're going out to Tan An!"

"Stocker, come here." Lieutenant Wilson immediately motioned the Kid over. "Do not discuss troop movements with the civilian population! Jesus, that's privileged information! Loose lips sink ships, for Christ's sake!"

"Oh, sorry, sir! This is Nguyen, Wen the barmaid's father. I met him when Heineman and the guys took me over to Wen's house. He's on our side."

"You don't fucking know that! Don't ever again tell a gook where you're going. That's an order!"

The shopping trip took about an hour. Then the Kid and Lieutenant Wilson hit the compound PX and bought about five cartons of cigarettes each. At a dollar and a half per carton, that was more than seven bucks in smokes. And of course, Wilson bought whiskey, and the Kid got himself some extra batteries.

Finally, they were ready to roll. The Kid was already throwing his stuff into the Land Rover for the drive to the airport when Wilson materialized, wearing his steel pot.

"Stocker, you don't want to have your helmet in your bag if you need it. Isn't that right, Sergeant Matt?"

"In a chopper? Nah, fuck, jungle hat is good enough for me!" the diminutive sergeant answered, contradicting the lieutenant. "If the VC flip in a round or two when the helicopter arrives, we'll be dead meat anyway. Helmet wouldn't do ya much good in a chopper crash. And it hasn't happened for the last five trips, so we're overdue."

Just then, Sergeant Spencer walked up with a pair of flak jackets in his arms. "Here, Lieutenant, I got these for you and Stocker. They might come in handy." He passed the two heavy bulletproof, shrapnel-proof garments to the pair.

"Thank you very much!" Wilson responded, relishing the prospect of danger in their immediate future and putting his on to see how it fit. "What do you think?" He styled it "the latest rage in Saigon!"

"Yeah, right." The Kid took his and put it on. It was really heavy and hot; he'd rather not wear it. But what the hell; better safe than sorry. He pulled his steel pot out of the top of his gear bag and, removing his jungle hat, plopped it on his head. Now he was starting to feel like a soldier, something he had fought against from the very first day of basic training. Pulling a small plastic bottle of insect repellent from his pocket, he stuck it into the elastic band around his helmet. "This is the way you see it on TV back home!"

"All right, we've got to pick up Ti Ui Troung, and we're supposed to meet the chopper in thirty minutes. Let's head out!" Wilson gave the order.

Troung was ready to go. He was traveling light, only one bag, but he too wore his steel pot and a flak jacket.

"Men yoi, Stockah." He smiled at the Kid. He didn't smile at Wilson.

On the ride out to Tra Vinh field, the Kid's mind again wandered back to Nashville. He thought about the reason he'd gone there from Colorado back in February of 1967, to see the first long-distance love of his life, Donna Nadeau. If he hadn't been so gone on Donna, he never would have left the University of Colorado and traveled to Nashville determined to find a job in radio. So it was her fault, he decided, that he was in a jeep full of guns, flak jackets, steel pots, bayonets, canteens, bullets, and grenades, on his way to a fortified hamlet smack-dab in the middle of VC country. Or was it his dad's fault? If he hadn't been working with Donna's grandfather Frank Nadeau at the *Denver Post,* it never would have happened. It was his dad and Frank, after all, who had introduced the pair at the end of the summer in 1962, at Lakeside Amusement Park on Carrier's Day Out. The Kid remembered it like it was yesterday:

He and his brother, Scott, were waiting in line at the roller coaster with a bunch of the other paper carriers, when Frank and his dad walked up with two girls in tow. "Hi, boys," his dad said. "This is Donna and Diane, Frank's granddaughters from Tennessee, and the two of you are going to show them a good time. Period." Diane was the older sister, who was actually the same age as the Kid, and Donna was the younger sister, two years younger than the Kid. Diane was paired with Scott, and Donna ended up in the roller coaster with the Kid. She was too cute! She had that Natalie Wood thing going. Or was it Elizabeth Taylor in *National Velvet?* Didn't matter, the Kid was floored by how pretty she was. Then, when they kissed in the tunnel of the roller coaster on about their third ride, it was all over for him. He was a week shy of fifteen, and she was thirteen. They rode the coaster and kissed in the tunnel about twenty-five times, serious and curious tongues touching, playing, and seeking. For thirteen, she was hard at work developing some amazing breasts.

Pulling into Tra Vinh airfield, Spencer drove over to his waiting spot by the chopper pad and, shutting off the engine, cocked his head to listen. He didn't have to wait long before he heard it: the report of a gun fired by the Tra Vinh Airport sniper. "Right on time!" He smiled.

They began moving their gear from the vehicle to a spot close to the helipad. As they did so, they heard another half dozen shots, but none of them seemed to be in their vicinity.

"Someday, we ought to hunt that fucking gook down!" Wilson swore contemptuously, his hands on his hips below his new flak jacket.

"Oh, no way!" Spencer protested. "We don't want him replaced with some sniper who actually shoots people!"

"Good point," the Kid said, noting that Troung had winced when Wilson used the word *gook.*

189

In less than five minutes, the chopper had arrived and settled down onto the pad, its blades churning up the inevitable dust storm.

"Gentlemen, good luck!" Spencer hollered over the engine noise. Giving them a half salute, he jumped into the Land Rover and took off.

The four of them, assisted by the door gunner, quickly loaded the gear and secured it. Once they were belted in, the bird went airborne. Sitting by the door in the nearly overloaded chopper, holding his M16 and wearing his steel pot and a flak jacket, the Kid was awash with emotion. *How did I come to be here? Oh yeah, it's Donna's fault! Her and those amazing lips!*

On the short flight to Tan An, the Kid became nervous. Would they get mortared upon arrival? And if not, would they be attacked that night? He hadn't been able to find Paul, Pete, or Ernie before he left and, consequently, hadn't gotten any of that Cambodian pot. Now that was a real tragedy!

He didn't have long to wait to find out the answers to his questions, because by chopper, Tan An was only fifteen minutes from Tra Vinh. As they arrived, the chopper pilot spiraled down over the fortified hamlet, giving the Kid his first good look at the old bombed-out cathedral that was the centerpiece of the position.

The roof was completely blown away over the main part of the destroyed church, and the walls at the back and on the right side had been pounded into rubble.

The remnants of the roof were splayed in jagged pieces over the area where the congregation used to sit. As described, the steeple still stood. The Kid could see that the balcony behind it was still partially there. From out of the low-slung building that was between one hundred fifty and two hundred feet to the left of the spire, he could see four people emerging to welcome the chopper, all of them Vietnamese except for one rather large white guy.

When the chopper touched down, everybody rushed to off-load the gear; the pilot wanted to get the hell out of Dodge. In fact, Dodge City most likely had never seen violence of the scale that had been visited upon that church, so in a matter of seconds, the supplies were off and the chopper quickly became a speck in the distance as the occupants of the building came up to greet the new arrivals.

"Welcome to Tan An!" The big white guy, wearing black horn-rimmed glasses and a green T-shirt, came forward and shook hands with Wilson and the Kid. "I'm Lieutenant Jim Hollings!"

"Hello. I'm Ross Wilson. This is PFC Stocker, and this is Ti Ui Troung, our RVN counterpart!" Wilson made the introductions.

Ross? The Kid was caught off guard. "Ross?" He turned to Wilson.

"Ross is my middle name." Wilson could see that the Kid was surprised by his apparent change of names from Herschel. "I never liked Herschel, and I prefer Ross."

"Pleased to meet you, Ross! Sergeant Matt, I trust you made a successful trip!" Hollings turned to the sergeant who, obviously, had done some shopping for him.

"Pretty much, Lieutenant. I got your smokes and a bottle of vodka—and a packet of mail with three letters from your wife!" Matt said. He immediately began moving bags.

"All right! That makes it a *good day*!" Jim beamed.

The Kid, Ti Ui Troung, and Wilson did a 360-degree turn as they looked over their new temporary home. Tan An had, at one time, been a community of Catholic priests and nuns who worked among the peasants of the region. A wide round open window, easily ten feet in diameter, accented the church steeple, and a broad sidewalk ran right through the middle of the chopper pad from the nonexistent front door of the church and led to a large canal at one end of the compound. In addition to the church, a dwelling for the clergy sat on the other side of a small creek that cut through the middle of the compound about thirty feet from the sidewalk. An ornate little wooden bridge spanned it, but anybody who could run could have easily jumped over the small waterway, which wasn't more than three feet wide.

"Ever been here before, Ti Ui Troung?" Wilson asked.

"No. But I heard the story of how the Vietminh killed the priests and raped the nuns here in 1953. Very brutal!"

"Let us help you with your stuff," Jim said. He directed the three Vietnamese men with him to carry the newly arrived gear. "Captain Morris and the unit are out on an operation right now and most likely won't be back for another couple of hours. I'm in radio contact with them, and things have been pretty quiet out there today."

Crossing over the bridge, they approached the clergy building, which was one story with a high red-tiled roof sloped at about a forty-five-degree angle and rising up about again as tall as the walls. A hole was clearly visible in the middle of it, halfway to the top.

"That's where the mortar round came in night before last." Jim stopped and pointed. "Thank God it was a dud!"

The building had a front porch recessed back beneath the roof that was about ten feet deep and was one step up from the ground. The pillars that held it up must have once had tile on them, but were now showing only raw plaster.

Stepping inside, the Kid switched from his prescription shades to his regular eyeglasses. They found themselves in a large room that ran all the way from the farthest wall at one end of the house to the farthest wall at the other end of the house. Looking up, the Kid marveled at the large exposed beams of the structure. A massively huge tabletop, easily twelve feet long and four feet wide, set on cinder blocks, took up much of the space to the right. Taking off his steel pot, the Kid rested it on the table and removed his flak jacket, draping it over a stool.

Two doorways led through a wall to the back half of the building. Walking through one door, Jim waved for the two new guys to follow. "This is our new radio bunker." He showed them a sandbag-walled edifice about ten feet square that was built up to six feet in height and had a round-beamed roof covered with plywood but not yet protected by sandbags. "We were all in here when that round came in." He pointed up at a two-foot-wide hole that showed blue sky above. "It hit right on the corner of the bunker there. By the grace of God, it was a dud!"

"Wow!" said the Kid, reaching up to touch the broken plywood. "You are a bunch of lucky fuckers!"

"No fucking shit! Sergeant Matt here got grazed with a piece of tile, but it wasn't bad enough to medevac him. And he didn't bleed, or else he would've earned himself a Purple Heart. But that was all that happened from it."

The group drifted back into the main room. Sitting down on the stools that lined the table, everybody lit up smokes.

"Coke, anybody? It isn't cold, but it's wet," Jim offered. Just then, the radio popped with some traffic in the back room. "Oh, excuse me for a minute," he said. He trotted back to the half-finished bunker to receive the incoming communication.

The room had big wide-open windows with no glass or screens. The Kid could see some army-issue sleeping cots stacked in the corner, and after having also seen a half dozen others set up on the far side of the room, decked out with mosquito netting, he figured that was what he'd be sleeping on that night. No electricity, no running water, no club, no steam bath, no massage parlor, no Cambodian pot, and now no bed.

"Hey, men." Sergeant Matt stuck his head out of the back room. "Let me show you the facilities!"

With Wilson in the lead, the Kid and Troung followed into the back, beyond the radio bunker to another side door. Waiting inside was Sergeant Matt. "This is the latrine," he said, pointing to a single porcelain john with no seat and no flush tank. "The way you use it is you get a bucket of water from the canal and hand- flush it when you're done."

"That's it? That's the 'facilities'?" Wilson was incredulous. "Where's the toilet paper?"

"Oh, I should have had you bring some," Matt said sheepishly. "Oops! Well, you can use some of mine."

"Add no shower, no sink, no toilet seat, and no toilet paper to the list of what Tan An doesn't have," noted the Kid.

"Yep. That's it. We don't have much out here. And every night, we eat with the Vietnamese officers at their mess."

"Well," said the Kid, "when they said this was a hardship tour, they weren't farting Dixie out their assholes! How do we shower or wash up out here, Sergeant Matt?"

"We shower when it rains. There's a couple of gutter spouts, one at each corner off the front porch. It actually works pretty well, especially now, since we're still in the wet season. The potable water is over there in the jerricans." He pointed to a row of green five-gallon containers lined up by the bunker. "It's rainwater that we've treated with iodine pills."

The ultraspartan accommodations were apparently a little more rustic than even Ti Ui Troung had been expecting, the Kid sensed, watching the Vietnamese POLWAR officer exhale a deep sigh.

"With no movies and no club, it looks like we'll have plenty of time for language lessons, Ti Ui Troung," the Kid said. "And I'm anxious to get started. How do you say, 'Get me the fuck out of here'?"

With a smile, Troung replied, "Di di mau. That mean go or leave, really fast!"

"Di di mau!" the Kid repeated as the group walked back into the front room. Passing the radio bunker, they could hear an electronic statically punctuated conversation taking place between Jim and the unit out in the field.

"Roger that. Out." Jim emerged from the bunker. "That was Captain Morris. The unit is almost back to the perimeter. They didn't see any action today, and they didn't find anybody to talk to about moving into the hamlet."

"How many families live here now?" Troung inquired.

"About two dozen." Jim lit up a cigarette. "I hate to say it, but this area is pretty solid VC. The families who won't move in, they for sure have relatives fighting with the VC, and they are staying out to aid and support them. If we can catch them doing it, we punish them by burning down their huts and arresting them. But it's pretty rare we even see 'em, if they don't want to be seen."

"What's the troop strength of Charlie Company?" Wilson asked.

"Right now, we've got about ninety-five ARVNs here. A third of them are new assignees right out of ARVN boot camp. We got our asses kicked about a month ago—got ambushed and lost thirty-two men, some KIA, and others wounded so bad that they're either still in the hospital or released from service because of missing limbs. The captain has half the new troops out on this patrol for training, and we're going to take the other half tomorrow."

"There's an operation tomorrow?" Wilson's face lit up like the tip of his Winston.

"Can we go?" "Sure! Why not?"

The Kid did not like the sound of any of this. Back in the front room, they saw the three Vietnamese men who had helped carry in their stuff squatting out on the front porch smoking cigarettes. Dressed only in loose-fitting shorts, their bodies were lean, but their feet were huge, very broad across the front as if they'd never been restrained by shoes or boots in their lives.

"There's the unit now," Sergeant Matt said, pointing to a line of black silhouettes emerging from around the corner of the church. Their exact location was neatly marked by three radio antennas bobbing back and forth over the heads of their operators.

"You'll like Tu Ta Van," Jim said, "the Vietnamese commander. He loves to party. In fact, I'd be willing to bet that he'll want to have a big welcoming dinner for you three tonight!"

"*Tu ta.* That's Vietnamese for 'major,'" Troung translated for Wilson and the Kid.

"So, *ti ui* is 'second lieutenant'?" the Kid asked.

"Yes."

"Then he's Ti Ui Wilson!" The Kid pointed at Herschel "Ross." "Very good, Stockah! Your Vietnamese soon be numba one!"

Standing in the shade of the porch, the men watched the returning troop filing over the bridge. An American and three of the ARVNs continued on toward the priests' quarters while the rest of the men began to fan out, looking exhausted, on their way back to their respective hooches. A number of Vietnamese women had come forth to greet various soldiers.

"They let them bring their wives and children out here, if they happen to be from around here," Jim said. "It's sort of a reward that they can be together at any point during their service. But the ARVNs are trying to keep soldiers from the Delta in the Delta, and soldiers from the highlands in the highlands, because they know the territory and the way the people think."

"I see," Wilson said as the group of four arrived at the porch.

"Captain Morris," Jim said to the American officer, "this is Lieutenant Wilson, PFC Stocker, and Ti Ui Troung, our new resident psyops team!"

The captain's uniform was totally dripping wet and liberally smeared with mud up to his knees. As he removed his steel pot, he revealed a smallish oval face and dark hair, the latter matted by the helmet. One of the Vietnamese men squatting on the porch came forward and took it and his M16. "Welcome to scenic Tan An!" The captain stepped onto the porch and shook hands all around.

"This is Dai Ui Dong, Charlie Company's executive officer," Morris said, introducing the Vietnamese captain, whose face sported a scraggly black mustache that looked as if he'd swiped it from Adolf Hitler. "And this is Tu Ta Van." He gestured to the Vietnamese major, an older-looking gentleman with a very round head and a bit of a gut hanging over a tightly cinched army-issue belt that looked awkwardly funny above his somewhat skinny lower torso and legs.

Neither man carried a rifle, but both wore a standard US Army–issue .45 pistol on their hip. The major unbuckled his holster and handed his pistol to one of the other Viets, who had jumped up to do his bidding.

"Welcome!" he said. "This calls for a party! We celebrate your arrival at very special dinner tonight!" Then he turned to the man who had taken his pistol and rambled off a series of what could only have been orders in Vietnamese.

"What did he say?" the Kid whispered to Troung.

"He tell the man to kill a dog and have the cooks prepare it for dinner tonight." "Dog? We're having dog tonight?" The Kid's mouth fell open.

"Oh yes, Vietnamese eat lot of dog, Stockah," Troung said in a matter-of-fact tone. "There will be other food as well, chicken, maybe fish and vegetables. You eat dog yet?"

"Uh, no."

"Maybe you like?"

Entering the building, Captain Morris peeled off his sweat-soaked uniform shirt and threw it on the floor by one of the cots, quickly thereafter removing his boots and pants. The Kid noticed something black stuck to the calf of his left leg.

"Fucking leeches," Morris said. He sat down on his cot, picked up a plastic bottle of insect repellent, and squirted a stream of clear liquid onto the bloodsucking parasite, causing it to curl up and drop from his leg. A rivulet of bright red blood poured from the round circle where the leech had been attached and ran down Morris's leg. He picked up a green handkerchief from his cot and used it to apply pressure to the spot.

"They have an anticoagulant that they inject into the wound when these leeches grab onto you," he commented to the Kid, who, he saw, was intently watching the process. "When you're out in the paddies, you always pick up a couple, so be sure to check every once in a while. The sooner you remove them, the better."

"This is Trung Ui Minh," Jim said, introducing one the other ARVN with the command element. "He's Charlie Company's first sergeant."

Minh had a graying goatee beard to match the gray hair that showed when his helmet came off. Smiling broadly, his mouth flashed with a number of gold fillings. "Welcome," he said, nodding his head in the Asian style while shaking the hands of the newcomers. Then he made some comment to Troung in Vietnamese, to which Troung replied. At that, the first sergeant barked some orders that set the other squatting Vietnamese man into motion.

"He is sending his man out to cut us sticks so that we may string mosquito netting on our cots tonight. The mosquitoes are quite bad here during the monsoon season," Troung said, translating what had just been said.

"Oh, I offered you all some Cokes and never got them! Excuse me," Jim said. He moved to bring them forth out of a wooden box of supplies set up against the back wall. "And now that the unit's back in from the field, it's lunchtime! *Om, ancom!*" He put his hand to his mouth to mimic the act of eating.

With that, the Vietnamese aides, minus the one who was out cutting sticks, sprang into action and produced the elements for lunch—a couple of cans of Spam; a couple of cans of Vienna sausages; some crackers; some fruit; and greens, primarily mung bean sprouts—and spread it out on the table.

After lunch, First Sergeant Minh invited the three new members of the unit on a tour of the fortified hamlet, beginning with the old church. As they approached, the Kid could see the walls riddled with bullet holes, as if somebody had punished the church itself. Inside the broad arch of the open doorway, there was a rickety-looking bamboo ladder that led up through a jagged hole in the wall and into the balcony above. Minh motioned for them to climb it. It was a good fifteen feet high. Once they were all on the landing, Minh motioned them over to the large round window, where they stepped up on a riser and peered out at the perimeter.

"Our defenses run from there to there." He pointed out the concertina wire barrier that was supposed to hold off the VC long enough to allow firepower to be brought against them. His English was every bit as good at Troung's. "Be very careful up here," he cautioned. "The floor is weak in some places, and if it gave way near the edge and you fell, you get hurt beaucoup!"

They could see the tops of bunkers that were placed around the compound, most of which had sandbag coverings, but some just had loose dirt piled up on them.

Standing as near to the edge as he dared, the Kid peered down into the rubble that was once the cathedral. Twisted rebar was visible protruding from much of the blown-up cement, and he could see that, indeed, one would most likely suffer if one should happen to fall off the balcony into the morass below.

The front of the church, from which the spire rose up, still had much of its wall, especially where the ladder was, but looking off the open back, which was actually where the altar had been, the Kid could see the boundaries of the hamlet beyond the crumbled church walls. It occurred to him that possibly this was the sanctuary he sought, where he could come later and smoke a joint.

Hmm, this place does have an EM club.

Climbing down the ladder, they exited the front door and stood briefly on the sidewalk, deciding what they might look at next. Just then, Minh gave a cry of surprise and dashed about ten feet off the sidewalk and into the six-inch-high grass, reaching down with his hand.

"Ho! Cong loon!" he cried, and with that, he raised up his hand to reveal that he had a grip on the tail of a humongous snake! He whipped it up and swung it around like a lariat over his head. The thing was easily seven feet long!

The Kid just about crapped his pants. "Holy fuckin' bat shit! Look at the size of that thing! Is it poisonous?"

Troung rambled in Vietnamese to Minh, who was now working his hand forward to get the snake behind the head. "No, he says it is just water snake, not cobra!"

Once he got the head, he brought it over for them to look at, its forked tongue visible in its mouth, held open by Minh applying pressure behind its skull. *"Ancom,"* he said. "Food. We cook for tonight!"

Knowing that both dog and snake were on the menu that night, the Kid felt his appetite fading completely away, like an ice cube melting in the tropical sun. *How did I come to be here?*

Chapter 17

It was just past 1800 hours and the sun was going down behind the building, casting heavy shade across the front of the priests' quarters. Even though it was the wet season, it didn't appear as if it was going to rain that night.

A long, low table had been set up outside the main room on the covered porch of the priests' quarters, and a bevy of ARVN wives, daughters, and sons scurried about setting it up for Tu Ta Van's welcoming dinner. The diners would be sitting on the concrete.

The group of dignitaries relaxed on the edge of the porch: Tu Ta Van; Captain Morris; Lieutenants Jim, Herschel "Ross," and Troung; Dai Ui Dong; Sergeants Matt and Minh; and the Kid. The Kid noticed that he was the lowest-ranking man in the group. They sat in a row, and not surprisingly, every single one of them was smoking a cigarette. Lieutenant Wilson and Dai Ui Dong were already drinking whiskey, and Jim, with Sergeant Matt, was enjoying a warm beer.

All of them had taken off their uniforms and were in T-shirts, shorts, and flip-flops. The junior officers of Charlie Company, who were trickling in for the dinner, all still had their uniforms on. Each of the four platoon commanders and their highest-ranking enlisted men had been invited to the fete. The table was set for eighteen people, nine on each side.

Aromas from the cooking drifted on the air from behind the building where, the Kid had discovered upon doing his own investigation, the Charlie Company mess kitchens were located. Although he knew dog and snake were two of the dishes being prepared, it smelled pretty tasty.

As soon as the table had been set, Tu Ta invited everyone to sit down. The Kid ended up between Troung and Minh, sitting directly across from Morris and Dong. *If I had a name like Dong, I'd change it,* the Kid silently amused himself. He was beginning to take a liking to Minh, whose soft brown eyes and pleasant expression and demeanor exuded an aura of friendliness.

Bottles of cheap California wine and PX whiskey were positioned around the table. Three of the ARVN wives began pouring it into waiting glasses.

Once everybody had some, Tu Ta lifted his glass and proposed a toast. "We drink to welcome our new arrivals." He gestured with the glass to the three. "And we drink to Dai Ui Morris, who leaves us to go home tomorrow!" Everybody drank when Tu Ta drank.

"Oh, you're leaving tomorrow?" Wilson asked the captain in a surprised tone of voice.

"Yep. I've got a week left, and I decided today that I've conducted my final operation. I don't want to chance it anymore, being so short, and Major Gillmore said I could come in tomorrow and begin my out-processing. So, I'm gonna di di mau this fucking bandstand!" Then Captain Morris made his own toast. "I raise my glass to Tu Ta, my friend, and Dai Ui Dong and Trung Ui Minh, some of the finest soldiers I've ever served with in any army. I drink to the success of our endeavor!" Down the hatch.

The Kid mulled the taste of the rosé wine on his tongue: fruity, yet unpretentious. Still not feeling too good about how drunk the lieutenant had gotten him the night before, he had vowed to watch it that evening. But when Jim raised his glass in yet another toast, the Kid could see that it might be a little on the difficult side to remain sober if he was going to appear to be polite and honor each and every toast.

"To Captain Morris, the best CO I've ever served under, and to his pending reunification with his wife and kids!" Gulp, gulp, gulp.

Thank God we're going to eat now, the Kid thought, as the wives began bringing out platters of exotic-looking cuisine. Large bowls of steaming rice hit the table and were passed around, along with a bowl of leafy greens and fresh bean sprouts. Cut fresh cucumbers and tomatoes were piled high and put within everybody's reach. A pot of stew was next. The Vietnamese began ladling it on top of the rice, and the Americans followed suit.

"Is this the dog?" the Kid asked Troung, spooning the thick reddish stew— vegetables and strips of meat—onto his rice.

"Yes, this is the dog. And there is the snake." He pointed to a platter of fried roundish tidbits of serpent, cut into two-inch chunks. "Try some of each for politeness," Troung instructed.

Other dishes followed: a chicken that was all cut up and likewise stewed, including the head and the clawed feet, and also a plate of darker meat strips that were not stewed. "That is buffalo," Troung said as he picked up his chopsticks. "You know how to use chopsticks, Stockah?"

"Yeah, a little." The Kid picked up his pair and fumbled with them in an awkward manner.

As the wine and the whiskey flowed and as the platters went around the table, everyone was having a good time. The stewed dog wasn't half bad, the Kid decided. But looking at the head of the chicken, its beak still attached and its empty eye sockets staring up at him, made a little queasy. The Vietnamese cook the whole chicken, including the yellow clawed feet. He decided to take only a wing of that delicacy. The snake, however, was surprisingly good.

"Are there cobras around here?" the Kid inquired of Minh.

"Yes, there are many poisonous snakes, including cobra."

"What do you do if the VC shoot and you have to jump into a bush before you can check for snakes?" It was an issue that had been lately on the Kid's mind.

"Are you afraid of snakes?" Minh looked at him with a cocked head.

"Sort of, yeah. Aren't you?"

"In Vietnam, we say that you need not fear snake if your heart is pure." Minh took another piece of snake off the platter and put it on his plate. "Is your heart not pure?"

"What do you mean?"

"Do you steal? Do you lie? Do you ..." Minh stopped in midsentence and turned to Troung, saying something in Vietnamese, to which Troung answered by supplying the word *cheat*. "Do you cheat or wish harm to others?"

"No."

"Then you need not worry about snakes; they will not harm you."

While that was good news to the Kid, in the back of his mind, he now knew there were cobras around here. And krait snakes—don't forget those little bastards.

But he had answered Minh's question truthfully. He was not a malicious person, so he began to accept the concept as he sank his teeth into another well-done piece of the serpent's ass.

"Snake have more to fear from you!" Troung laughed as the Kid chewed.

Captain Morris was packing away the wine and was getting a little tipsy. "Ya know, now that the year has passed, I gotta say, it went faster than I thought it would when I first got here."

Right, easy for you to say, the Kid thought; he hadn't even finished his first month yet. To even think about being short made him want to cry, and here he was sitting across from a man who was leaving tomorrow to go home.

"So Jim," Morris continued, "beginning tomorrow, you're in command, for a couple of days anyway. How about that?"

201

"How about that, sir? Well, there's no replacing you in our hearts."

"That may be, but I guess, from what Gillmore told me over the radio earlier, they're sending out a new captain in a couple of days, a Japanese American named Yamato."

"If you're going in tomorrow, I guess that means I'm running the operation tomorrow."

"Roger that, Jim. But I imagine that Lieutenant Wilson, being an alumnus of the Hundred and First Airborne, will gladly assist you."

"You can count on me, sir," Wilson immediately responded.

The Kid munched on his snake and thought about what Wilson had said at the rifle range the day before.

As it got darker, the dinner party continued. Four kerosene lanterns were brought to the table to provide light. The brighter the lights got in the dark, the more insects they attracted, and soon, the partiers adjourned to inside the building. There was continual toasting, and the Kid noticed something interesting about the Vietnamese. Whenever a toast was made, they would just take a sip from their glass, not down the whole drink. Then, they would generously pour half their drink into the closest American's glass and propose another toast, then repeat the whole process until the Americans had drunk two drinks to their two sips.

Once all the glasses were empty, they would all be filled again, the process beginning anew. It turns out that the Vietnamese were always amazed at how much Americans could drink and had made a game of trying to get them drunk.

On the far side of the front room, the newly arrived three men could see that their cots had been prepared by the Vietnamese aide who had found the sticks from which the mosquito netting was now strung. All manner of flying insects were now being attracted through the open windows to the flickering lamps. The Kid could see the nets were a total necessity. Pulling out his bottle of insect repellent, he applied some to his bare arms, legs, face, and neck.

The Kid finally got out his own new lamp, which he filled with fuel, preparing to write Flo. He placed his transistor radio on the table and turned it on. "There is a house in New Orleans they call the Rising Sun. It's been the ruin of many a young man, and God, I know I'm one." Eric Burden and the Animals melodically emerged from it. All the Vietnamese in the room, to the Kid's surprise, rushed over to listen as soon as they heard it.

"That is best American song!" Troung said with a smile. "Numba one! Everybody love 'House of Rising Sun'!"

"Well, the group that sings it is British, not American," the Kid said, correcting

Troung's error.

"You say, but any song that American radio play, to us, is American song."

OK, *have it your way.* The Kid smiled back at him, nodding, as he got into his letter.

Dearest Flo,

Well, today I finally got about as far away as possible from civilization and everything I've ever known on earth! We, meaning Wilson, Troung, and I, are now at Tan An, the fortified hamlet. Talk about being in the boonies! This is unreal. I'm writing to you by the light of a kerosene lantern as there is no electricity, running water, or plumbing in this place, and we will be sleeping on cots. We are staying in an old Catholic church complex that was destroyed by the VC some seven years ago, and, not to scare you, we are completely surrounded! The only way in or out is by chopper. The Vietnamese commander had a welcome dinner for us tonight, and they served dog and snake! I saw the guy catch the snake. It was seven feet long but not poisonous. Looks like I've fallen in with a real bunch of gourmets! Tomorrow, I'm going on my first operation. We still don't have any loudspeakers, so I'll be at the back of the pack, or so Lieutenant Wilson says, but the thing about this country and the war is that there is no back or front.

I've been here for two weeks now, and soon, I hope that I will start receiving your letters. Haven't gotten any mail yet, but since I can't go any farther out into the boonies, some of it ought to start catching up with me pretty soon. I am missing you like nobody's business, Parnelli. I've got your picture out in front of me. Hey, dig this! An air force guy at Tra Vinh was stationed in Nashville and he used to listen to my show! Not only that, but also he was at Pine Springs at the Good Guy Splash and he said he was going to hit on you before I got there! Is that a scream or what?

His name is Pete Johnson. He had a copy of Sgt. Pepper's, and we went over to some Vietnamese friends' house and listened to it. They made these thick homemade potato chips that were dynamite! Needless to say, I did have a case of the munchies at the time, if you get my drift.

The captain who is in charge here is going home tomorrow, so I can send this letter out on the chopper that will be coming for him. Jeez, I hope I get a letter from you soon. The suspense is killing me about you-know- what.

Whatever happens, know that I love you! ISYL.

Love,

Curt

As he finished his letter and placed it into the envelope, Sergeant Minh walked up to him and Wilson, who had sat down while the Kid was writing. "This is Xuan. He will be your houseboy. Anything you need—laundry done, boots shined, weapon cleaned—Xuan will do!"

"Well, that's really nice!" Wilson looked Xuan over. He was wearing a pair of faded red shorts, was no more than five feet, three inches tall, and had big eyes, ears that stuck out slightly, and kind of square jaw dominating his grinning face. "You numba one houseboy?"

Xuan looked at Minh with a blank expression on his young face, apparently not understanding. An exchange in Vietnamese took place, followed by a lot of nodding and smiling.

"Yes, Xuan numba one houseboy! English not too good, but hard worker. I help you talk to him," Minh said. "Anything you need?"

"Ah yes, there is," the Kid said. He rose up and, carrying his kerosene lantern for light, went into the latrine to fetch the water can. "Would he go fill this so I can take a shit?"

"Sure, no problem!" Minh said, handing Xuan the can. With a nod, Xuan was gone. He was back in a flash, with the container full of canal water.

"Cam on u lam," the Kid said, grinning as he took the water can.

"Com quo che." Xuan nodded.

"Yo, Sergeant Matt, where's that TP you said we could use?"

"Over there, in the supply box," the lifer replied. "That's where we keep all the communal goods."

Returning from the john, the Kid saw Lieutenant Wilson, Ti Ui Troung, and Tu Ta Van out on the porch, pulling from a box some metal devices with wires attached.

"What are those?" he inquired of the three twelve-inch-wide, three-inch-thick curved metal shapes, each about the size of a license plate, with pointed legs apparently designed to be stuck into the ground.

"These are claymore mines." Wilson smiled. "You set 'em into position in front of you, and if the VC break through the first two lines of defense, you can blow these things, and they'll spray shrapnel out in an arc, killing everything within seventy-five meters in front. See the way it's curved? That creates a widening kill field. And you set them up to overlap. Plus, you gotta stay away from the thing because it's got a backwash explosion that will kill everything within fifteen meters behind it."

"Wow!"

The Kid sat on the edge of the porch as Tu Ta, Minh, and Wilson placed the claymores just this side of the little creek and ran the wires back into the command's quarters, connecting the wires to small switch boxes.

"Quite the invention!" Wilson marveled.

Back inside, the Kid, smoking, sat and talked with Lieutenant Jim and Captain Morris for a bit. They watched as Van, Minh, and Dai Ui Dong broke out a set of ivory dominoes and commenced to play a very spirited match, badgering each other in Vietnamese as they slapped down the spotted tiles into crossword-like mosaics. Dai Ui Dong was still putting away the whiskey at a pace close to that of Lieutenant Wilson.

"Got a big day goin' tomorrow," Wilson said, as he sat cleaning his M16 by lantern light. "If we're lucky, we may see our first action!" The lieutenant appeared almost too excited to sleep.

You got that one wrong, Lieutenant, the Kid thought. *If we're really lucky, we won't see any action at all!* His hand gravitated to the Canadian beaver nickel hanging from his neck.

Taking his toothbrush and canteen to the front porch, the Kid did his teeth. Looking at the crushed tube in his hand as he brushed, he knew there were no more than a couple of joints left in it. Damn! He wondered when he'd be able to get some of that shit-kicking Cambodian black pot. For a moment, he considered walking out to the church to sneak a joint, but deciding he didn't want to walk out among the claymore mines, he chucked the idea. It was about 2230 hours when he turned in.

Crawling into his netting and feeling the heat bringing forth the sweat, the Kid stretched out on his back atop his camouflage poncho liner; he wasn't used to sleeping without a pillow. Looking up at the huge beam directly above his head, he contemplated if maybe he should move his cot. If a mortar were

205

to come in and knock the beam down, it would kill him! But what if he moved the cot to the place where the beam, or the mortar round, eventually fell? A guy could go crazy trying to preguess shit like that. He finally had to laugh at himself for even going anywhere near such irony.

From the back room, he heard the hourly radio check come crackling through. It was a call from the TOC in Tra Vinh, just checking all the outposts to ensure everybody was well. The Kid was glad he didn't have radio watch that night.

Tomorrow, he would have to pull a two-hour shift in the middle of the night, waiting for the call, or being the one to make the call should they get attacked and need support. When all the lanterns in the front room were extinguished and even Wilson and Tu Ta had climbed into their racks, the Kid's mind began to float off into the strange realm of the half dream and half conscious contemplation.

Tomorrow, they were going out with the unit on a real operation, and according to everybody who had spoken of it tonight, chances were fifty-fifty that they'd see action. How would the Kid act? Would he be a chicken when the first live round screamed by his head? Would he run away, or just run and look for someplace to hide his head in the sand—make that mud? Would he be wounded? Would he live? Would he ever see or hold Flo again? Spilling over the edge, he entered the dream state. He was in a cart and his hands were tied behind his back. People were jeering at him and the other people in the cart. He was dressed in a dirty white ruffled shirt, ripped open at the neck. As the cart came around the corner of a street and into an open square, he could see it looming up in front of him: the guillotine! Fucking French!

Chapter 18

It was the roosters that brought the Kid out of his fitful attempt at slumber. There must have been half a dozen of them competing with each other to claim the sunrise. The Kid could hardly detect the first hints of the dawn out the two large windows facing the east. But from over at the long table, a single kerosene lantern threw a soft light that showed him the silhouettes of the two dozen mosquitoes that hovered and rested around his netting, smelling his breath, but not finding any way to sample his blood. He could tell that the person at the table was Minh.

Rising up, the Kid pulled his glasses out of his boot. He put his feet into his flip- flops and shuffled outside a few paces off the porch to take a piss. He could hear the unit began to stir, getting ready; they were going out today.

Turning, the Kid went first to his cot for cigarettes and his Zippo, and then to the table, where he sat down across from Minh, who was reading a typed letter.

"Om, Trung Ui Stocker," Minh said.

"Isn't *trung ui* 'sergeant'? I'm not a sergeant!"

"You are an American, so you outrank me, even though I am a sergeant. You even outrank Tu Ta!"

Interesting, the Kid thought, as he lit the first cigarette of the day. In a way, I do outrank Tu Ta! So I'm like better than a major in the South Vietnamese army now—and the day has barely started. "What's that, Minh, a letter?"

"Yes, it is from my daughter My, in Danang. That is where I'm from. She is trying to get work as an interpreter with the Americans, and she is in classes right now. She writes me letters in English for practice. Would you like to read it?" He turned the letter around on the black surface so that it now faced the Kid.

"Sure," said the Kid. "How old is she?" "You say 'how old' Vietnamese— 'Bon u.'"

"Bon u?" the Kid repeated as he pushed his glasses up the bridge of his nose.

"She is twenty Vietnam, nineteen the way Americans count." Then he began to read: "'Hi, Pop. How are you doing? Work at the base is going pretty good with my part-time job. I have been trying to get much sewing done to help Mom as well. Grandma lost her ID card last week, and we have had trouble getting her a new one. Meanwhile, one of us has to be with her when she goes out, or they would pick her up as a VC. My brother and sisters are all OK. Minh got a bloody nose and a broken finger in a fight at school, but it was his fault. Now he knows what you say about karma is so! I know you cannot come home before Tet, but do you think that after what happened, the army will let any soldiers go home for Tet in 1969? That would be so sad. Since you didn't make it home this year, it will be two years since we have seen you. Mom cries a lot, but I tell her to be strong. And the other kids. Love you, Pop.'"

"Want to see picture?" He already had it out with the letter. "I like to look at it when I read her letters. It is more like I can be with her."

Taking the black and white wallet-size shot, the Kid looked at My's picture and was floored. She had her head tilted and wore her hair the same way as Flo's in the picture he carried most of the time in his pocket. Rising up, he went back to his cot area to retrieve the photo and show it Minh. "Look, Minh, my fiancée looks like your daughter!"

"Ooh, yes, she does!" he said quietly; there were still some in the room trying to sleep. "In Vietnam, very easy to remember. When things are alike, you say, 'Sem sem.' Is like *same* in English, only say twice!"

Groovy! the Kid thought. *I'm in a language immersion class!* "So, Minh, how do you say in Vietnamese, 'What is that?' or 'What is this?'"

"You say, 'Kai ye?'" "Kai ye?"

"Ya. You point and say, 'Kai ye,' and I give you Vietnamese word for it, OK?" "OK! You number one! How you say, kai ye, you number one in Vietnamese?" "An mot!"

"So, Minh, do you think we'll see any action with the VC today?"

Minh lifted his eyes from his daughter's picture and the one of Flo, which he had been comparing, and peered deep into the Kid's eyes. "Action could start before we leave this table. Or we may not see VC for one week, maybe two. We wait. All the time we wait, they plan. We will see them eventually, maybe today, maybe not."

"So, what yer sayin' is sem sem, fifty-fifty?" He mixed his Vietnamese and English.

"Oui!" Minh answered in French.

208

Suddenly, there was a great commotion from outside. A shrieking, ear-piercing squeal split the morning stillness, erasing completely the sound of any roosters within a mile.

"What the fuck is that?" The Kid jumped up and whirled around.

"That is just breakfast and lunch." "What?"

"The pig they are going to kill to feed the soldiers for breakfast and make something for the unit to take along on the operation. We have no refrigeration, so we must kill our meat fresh and use it that day."

The Kid walked out the front door as the rest of the occupants of the cots began to stir. There, being dragged along by a rope wrapped around its middle, was a young pig of about a year in age kicking and fighting for its life as if it thought it actually had a chance. Two cooks, a male and a female, coaxed it along.

"Why don't they just knock it in the head? They're going to kill it anyway."

"Yes, but they want to cut its throat and drain out the blood so it is not wasted. And if it is killed with a blow to the head first, the blood does not flow out properly."

OK, sorry I asked. The Kid followed the fighting around the corner of the building to where the kitchen activity took place. He watched as the male cook pulled a huge-ass butcher knife out of a storage area. A fire was already roaring in the big square cinder block enclosure below the grill where they cooked. Then, the pair shortened their grip on the rope and got a hold of the pig by the legs, lifting the creature up onto a two-square-foot platform built about two feet off the ground.

The woman straddled the pig's back and gripped its ears firmly, pulling its head back and exposing its throat. Now the pig grew suddenly quiet, as if paralyzed by its fear.

Stepping up with a bucket in one hand and the foot-long blade in the other, the male cook placed the bucket beneath the pig on the ground and, in a flash, slashed the porker's throat with one smooth motion. He had apparently done it hundreds of times, maybe thousands. Incapable of bellowing in pain with its air passage severed, the pig's body violently contorted in its death throes. As the Kid watched, his dream from the night before popped back into his head, instantly flashing back.

Weak of stomach, the Kid turned away as the blood flowed in spurts into the bucket. The pig's heart beat its last. *What a way to start the day.* This had been a mistake, he knew, as nausea swept over him. Making his way out of the mess area, he knew, *No breakfast today for the Kid.*

Entering the building, he found everybody had risen as a result of the pig's execution. They were going out today. There was an electrical current in the air.

The male cook followed almost immediately behind the Kid. As he passed, the Kid could see he had a cup of blood, which he took over to Tu Ta. Grossly revolted, the Kid watched Tu Ta take the cup and belt the blood down like a cup of coffee. Now he was really feeling like tossing the contents of his stomach.

"What was that, Tu Ta?" Wilson asked as he lit a Winston on his cot.

"Fresh pig's blood!"

"I'll have to try that someday!"

The Kid was sure he would.

Soon, the smell of coffee wafted into the room and Xuan appeared with three cups, one for the Kid, one for Wilson, and one for Ti Ui Troung.

Sergeant Matt came out of the back room, where he'd pulled the last two-hour radio watch, and went over to his cot. "You don't need me out there today, right, Lieutenant Hollings?"

"Well." The lieutenant stretched his big arms, having just risen. "I guess not. We got two extras today, and one of 'em is Airborne, so go ahead, catch some shut- eye."

"Thank you, Lieutenant," Matt said. He climbed into his cot and tucked his netting in. "Am I ever looking forward to this!"

It was now getting light in a hurry. Once dressed, the Kid picked up his M16 and looked it over, opening the chamber and angling his thumbnail to reflect up the barrel to show if it was dirty or not. It was OK. Sitting on his cot, he took his steel pot with its inserted helmet liner and held it in his lap. Taking his ballpoint pen, he began drawing on the right side. He wrote "Flo" in block letters about three inches high. As he looked at his artwork, he took the pen and changed the *O* into a peace symbol. *Cool,* he thought. Lacing up his combat boots, he walked over to the jerrican that had the potable water and filled his canteen. While he was doing that, Wilson came up to do the same.

"Here, Stocker." He handed him a small bottle of dark brown pills. "These are iodine pills to purify water if we run out of the safe stuff."

"Thanks."

"And here." Wilson handed him another small bottle of white pills. "These are salt pills. We'll be sweating our balls off today, and you need to replace the salt you lose to keep going."

"OK." The Kid put them both into his pants pocket. "How many clips you figure we'll need?"

Wilson pondered for a second. "Uh, one bandolier ought to do it. If you need more than that, we'll be in shit so deep, it probably won't matter."

"In other words, save the last round for yourself, like the boys of the Seventh Cavalry, huh?"

"Sure, if you don't want to get captured. That scares me worse than the thought of being killed," Wilson said.

"Me too," the Kid agreed. He had devoted some thought energy to this very question recently. But whether or not he could actually off himself was something he figured he'd only know given the particulars of some specific, totally drastic situation. "You gonna wear your flak jacket?" The Kid eyed his lying at the foot of his cot.

"Stocker, it's going to be hotter than a hundred and ten degrees out there today. Can you imagine trying to run with that thing on?" Wilson replied, with a condescending look on his face. "That thing is for mortar attacks and defensive stuff, not for maneuver operations out in the paddies."

"OK. Just asking." The Kid frowned, having thought a bulletproof garment would be a good thing in a firefight.

As Tu Ta, Captain Morris, Dong, Minh, Lieutenant Hollings, Ti Ui Troung, and Wilson sat down at the long table for breakfast, the Kid went outside and sat down on the porch with his second cup of coffee. The bloodletting incident of earlier that morning still had him off his feed. Sitting there, he thought about what they were preparing to do: venture outside the compound into VC-held territory, where they were going to supposedly try to convince some of the inhabitants to move their homes into the fortified compound and, of course, fight the VC should they surface and contest their presence on their turf. *How did I come to be here?*

From deep inside the building, the Kid could hear radio traffic coming through. It was a heads-up for Morris; the chopper that was to transport him for the first leg of his journey home was on its way, and the captain was being alerted to be ready to go. He was already packed.

"I can't believe this day has finally come," he said to Lieutenant Jim. The two of them began hauling his duffle and equipment bags out to the landing spot on the sidewalk in front of the church. "You guys can have all my foodstuffs—C rations and all that shit!"

"Thanks!" Jim said.

"Uh, Captain." The Kid walked up to them. "Would it be possible for you to take these letters in with you and mail them for me?"

"Sure, Stocker, not a problem!" He tucked the three of them into the large front pocket of his jungle fatigues. "So, this is your first operation today?"

"Yes, sir."

"Good luck. You're going out with a solid bunch of well-trained guys."

"Thank you, sir. It was nice meeting you, sir." The Kid smiled, knowing that what Morris had said was not necessarily the truth; a dozen of the ARVNs were going on their first real operation today too, he knew from conversations the night before. But what else could he say? "See ya"? "Cover your ass"? The Kid shook the captain's hand and went back to the porch so he wouldn't be in the vortex of the chopper's dirt storm.

Looking at his watch, the Kid noted the time was 0730 hours. Taking off his clear- lensed army glasses, he switched them for his black-framed prescription shades.

Off in the distance, he detected the *pop-pop-pop* of the approaching Huey, and soon he picked it up visually, coming in from Tra Vinh to the north. It was June 9. The Kid had only been in-country for two and a half weeks now, so he still had more than eleven months to go on his tour, and today, combat was a very real possibility. He wanted to cry. *Why can't that be me?* he thought as the chopper set down on the ground. He watched Morris and Hollings load Morris's bags and hug, before the captain climbed into a seat and put on his belt. He had a huge fucking grin on his face as the chopper quickly di di mau'd, up and out of the compound, returning the place to relative quiet.

By 0800 hours, the soldiers of Charlie Company scheduled for the operation had begun to gather on the chopper pad. The command element was collecting the last of the gear they needed, and everybody was about ready to depart. Radio antennas whipped around behind the heads of the men upon whose backs they were affixed. The machine gunner was doing some last-second maintenance on his M60, and a number of the ARVNs were dripping with grenades affixed to their pistol belt harnesses. About a dozen wives, nearly all of them holding babies, spoke in quiet tones to their husbands, who were about to venture out into enemy territory.

The Kid smoked as he stood waiting, his M16 slung over his right shoulder and his steel pot tilted back at a jaunty angle. It was subtle, but he thought he could feel the ground shaking, like an earthquake. Although he'd never felt an earthquake, he imagined this was what one would be like.

Lieutenant Hollings, who was standing about ten feet away, turned to him. "You feel that, Stocker? That's from a B-52 strike about fifteen kilometers away from here!"

"No shit?"

"No shit!" he replied. "Look! There they are!" He pointed upward. Sure enough, the Kid could pick them out: three B-52's flying high overhead in a triangular formation, headed east.

"That's incredible!"

"Di di mau!" Tu Ta Van gave the signal that it was time to move out. He punctuated his orders with gestures from a white walking stick that was about as tall as he was. At the command, the wives gave their husbands one last hug and stepped back as the men shouldered their gear and prepared to depart.

The unit that day was operating with two platoons of four squads. As they walked past the east side of the church and made their way to the compound perimeter, Wilson, the Kid, and Troung fell in behind Tu Ta, Lieutenant Hollings, and Dai Ui Dong, smack-dab in the middle of the whole shebang. This was the command element.

"At least you don't have to walk point." Jim smiled at the Kid. They passed between a pair of defensive bunkers and crossed through an opening in the concertina wire, making their way outside the compound. "If you were a PFC with an American unit, you'd have to walk point, but the ARVNs do all our point work."

"Fine with me," the Kid said. He observed a couple of ARVN privates moving out into the point positions, rippling the surface tension of the water in the paddies. They were now going out into the expanse of the open rice paddies, which seemed to stretch for at least a couple of miles before there were any tree lines. The Kid took his rifle off his shoulder and held it in his hands, being careful not to point it at the back of anybody's head. Such futility he felt; he didn't have a clue about what he was actually going to do when the shooting really started.

All the soldiers walked in the water of the rice paddies, next to the dikes that separated them. "Why don't we walk up on the dikes and out of the mud and water?" the Kid inquired.

"Well, quite often, the VC sneak up here at night and put foot mines in the dikes. Walking on them can sometimes be very dangerous, especially right around here, where they expect us to be a lot, and them not," Jim explained.

"That's why ya have to be so careful around this place, what with the ones they put out to get us and the ones we put out to get them. It's only a matter of time until one goes off."

In front of them, three squads fanned out as they moved forward. "Should I chamber a round?" the Kid asked Wilson. Their feet made squishy noises every time they took a step and pulled their boots out of the mud.

"Might as well. But be sure to keep your safety on." Wilson at this point chambered a round in his own M16.

Placing a round into the firing position, the Kid felt a little more secure; at least he was armed and dangerous! Turning around and looking back, he sensed that the Tan An church steeple was slowly growing smaller as they moved farther out into the rice paddies. He had seen them from the air, and now to be down in them, M16 in hand, boots and fatigue pants soaking wet up to his knees with water, and T-shirt soaking wet from his neck down with sweat, the reality of where he was swept over him. Here was the Kid on combat patrol in the Mekong Delta!

How did I come to be here? He felt so thoroughly fucked for having taken an extra year to get out of the infantry that he felt most like shooting people in his own army!

It was eerily quiet, except for an occasional radio transmission between Dai Ui Dong, Tu Ta, and the front squads, which were opening up more distance between themselves and the command element with every step. The sky was nearly cloudless, and its bright blue contrasted with the muted green of the growing rice shoots and the tree line, which steadily crept closer and closer.

That's obviously where the VC are dug in and waiting for us, the Kid thought as he walked along in silence. He thought back to his pheasant-hunting days in Nebraska and to the times when he and his buds at Northeastern Junior College, in Sterling, Colorado, used to go poach ducks on the Tammarack Game

Preserve down on the South Platte River outside Crook. Now, their quarry was also armed and dangerous. The Kid had always gotten a little buzz from doing something he shouldn't have been doing when they were poaching, but it was nothing like he was feeling now on his first real combat patrol.

As he again and again pulled his one foot after the other out of the mud, he thought about Robert Kennedy and the national mourning taking place back in the States about another funeral just like JKF's. Politics, he scoffed, swatting at a chopper-sized fly and missing. *It's the parlor sport of the rich. They sit around in their suits and ties and send young men off to die here in the jungle.* Only that very instant, there wasn't much jungle anywhere near the Kid. He had read in one of his indoctrination guidebooks on Vietnam that the average elevation of the Mekong Delta was five feet above sea level. *Fuck, it is flatter than Kansas!*

Staying even with him as they walked, the Kid looked at Ti Ui Troung, who was sweating like the breakfast pig. Troung still had his M16 slung over his shoulder and wore a somewhat disgusted look on his face. Ahead of them, the Kid could see various soldiers in the front squads bending over and picking something up and dropping it into a sack or something as they walked.

"What are they doing, Troung? Looks like they're collecting something?" Curiosity finally got the better of the Kid.

"Yes, I see, but I don't know," Troung replied. "This is my first operation too!"

A soldier with a red cross on his helmet was suddenly walking along with the pair. He said to Troung in Vietnamese, "Om, Ti Ui," and then to the Kid in English, "Good morning!" Although clearly Vietnamese in his skin tone and army uniform, his features were almost Western as his eyes were nearly devoid of the Asian stretch.

"Good morning," the Kid replied. "Are you the medic?"

"I am a medical doctor," he said in perfect English, "but yes, today, I am the medic on this patrol."

"Oh well, that's great! A real doctor instead of just a medic!" the Kid said with a smile. "I'm Curt." He stuck out his hand.

"Pleased to meet you, Curt. I am Bauxi Mui." He didn't have any rank on his uniform, but on his collar, he wore a little stickpin with the caduceus.

"*Bauxi* is Vietnamese for 'doctor,'" Troung said, translating and teaching the Kid a new word.

Mui must have been fresh out of medical school, because he didn't look very old.

"Bon u?" said the Kid.

"How old am I?" Mui asked for clarification in English, appearing somewhat surprised that the Kid was trying to speak Vietnamese.

"Yeah, how old?"

"Thirty," he said, "but the way Americans count, twenty-nine."

"My uncle is a doctor back in America." The Kid made small talk with the doc as the unit moved along through the wide-open expanse. "And my mother works for a bunch of doctors at a clinic!"

215

"So, your family has a medical background. And what about you?" Bauxi Mui inquired.

"Well, the only time I have anything to do with medicine is when I *take it!*" The Kid made a pantomime like he was swallowing a pill and, in rapid succession, giving himself a shot in the ass, to which the doctor laughed. "Yes, I hope today that my only function will be as observer!"

As the morning progressed, the Kid could feel the water getting hotter in the paddies. When they had first stepped into it and it rushed through the little brass ports in his boots, it had a cooling effect on his feet, but now it was up to lukewarm temperature and his toes were starting to feel wrinkly, as if he'd been in the swimming pool too long.

Walking along, his mind wandered back to the States and that night, New Year's Eve 1966, just after it had become 1967, when he had taken LSD for the first time in Aspen. Sitting there in the living room of Rob Roy's house, looking at the embers of the fire, he had a hallucination, seeing soldiers wearing steel pots somewhere in the jungle. And now, here he was. *I wonder if I'm now somebody else's hallucination.* He toyed with the reverse of the image. After that night, he'd seen the image in the end of his cigarettes even when he wasn't stoned. Now he was living it.

All he could do was pull his foot out of the mud and move it forward, then pull the other foot out of the mud and move it forward. They were moving so slow! It was like watching a movie he didn't like; he wished there was some way he could walk out of the theater or shut it off! *Think of something cold,* he thought, and in his brain, the song "I Am a Rock" by Simon and Garfunkel began to play. "A winter's night in a deep and dark December. I am alone, looking out the window at a freshly fallen silent shroud of snow ..."

With the tree line growing taller at their approach, the Kid could now make out a couple of grass huts at their base, but he couldn't see any people. The rice paddies looked pretty well tended to for having no people who are working them. *They are probably looking at us through their rifle sights right now.* The Kid got a chill, which surprised him here in the tropics.

The lead elements were now at the huts in the tree lines, and he could see them moving around, looking for who knows what. They came and went from inside the low-slung grass structures. Reaching the edge of the paddies, the Kid stepped up out of the water onto the solid land that ringed the huts. In front of one of the huts was a rectangular-shaped pond about twenty feet long and ten feet wide. Behind it, in the shade of an overhanging roof, sat an old woman on a platform. She was dressed all in black and had a red and white checkered scarf over her head from which scraggly strands of gray hair had

216

escaped. As the Kid got close to her, he could see that her mouth was ringed with a red color, like a really bad lipstick job. When she saw him looking at her, she smiled at him, showing off her gums, which were equally red, and her teeth, or what was left of them, with their very visible decay.

"Ti Ui Troung, what's that stuff around her mouth?" the Kid asked.

"Oh, she chew betel nut. Many old people do because it has a narcotic in it that numbs their teeth, which are very bad. Even though the betel nut make pain go away, they do not understand that it is to blame for their bad teeth. Very bad habit."

"I see," said the Kid. The use of the word narcotic had caught his attention. Maybe he would have to try this betel nut thing one time just to check it out. He had tried most everything that he'd been offered in the way of drugs up to this point, except he swore he'd never shoot up.

Looking at his watch, he noted that it was now 0900 hours: it had taken them an hour to cross the wide-open area. *It must be wider than two miles,* the Kid thought, as Tu Ta walked up to the old woman.

"Men yoi, Ba," he said, which the Kid understood. Then Tu Ta launched into a stream of Vietnamese the Kid couldn't follow.

"What's he asking her?" The Kid turned to Troung, who was listening intently.

"He asks, 'Why haven't you moved into the fortified hamlet yet?' And she says, 'Why should I? This is my home. It has always been my home. When I die, my children will bury me here.' Tu Ta asks, 'Speaking of your children, where are they?' And she says, 'They are not here. They have gone away.'"

One of Tu Ta's soldiers came out of the woman's hut with a black pot in his hand. After some fast talking, another couple of soldiers began to make a fire in the woman's small firepit, which had a rack for hanging pots over it. Then, it became clear what the soldiers had been picking up as, one at a time, they came forward and emptied their pockets of snails. Half the troops were looking for the VC, and the other half had been looking for snails. Uncorking his canteen, the soldier who had found the pot filled it up with water, and soon it was boiling over the fire. Tu Ta sat in the shade on the platform with the old woman and offered her a cigarette, which she accepted. *Well, hell,* the Kid figured, *they are cooking her snails in her pot with her firewood, uninvited, so the least Tu Ta can do is give her a smoke!*

Looking up, the Kid chanced to catch Lieutenant Wilson coming from the back of the hut. "What's up, Lieutenant?" he asked as he pulled out a Kool and lit it.

"There's fresh shit in the outhouse, and I'd bet you money that that old lady never shit a turd as big as the one I saw. There's men around here, and they must be VC! Otherwise, they'd show themselves."

"Oh," the Kid said, "so you're an expert in old lady's shit? You can pick crap out of a police lineup? How do you know it's fresh? You didn't study that at DU, did you?"

Wilson stood still and looked at the Kid, not knowing for sure how to take his sarcastic attitude toward the whole situation. This was serious, but at the same time, there was something to be said for the ability to let off steam under pressure. "You'll be laughing out of your new asshole if the VC jump out from behind the bushes or up out of a hidey-hole and spray us down with their AK- 47's," Wilson said, a little ticked that the Kid had made fun of his observation.

"A hidey-hole?" The Kid's mouth fell open. "You actually called it a hidey-hole?"

"Well, yeah. What the hell? That's what they call 'em in the Hundred and First, like in 'Spray down the hidey-hole'; 'Drop a grenade in that there hidey-hole'; and 'Barbecue the hidey-hole—if y'all got a flamethrower, that is.'"

A bad fucking movie. That's where I am, the Kid thought decidedly. *I'm caught in a bad fucking movie!* He watched as the ARVNs hovered around the pot full of boiling water while Tu Ta fanned himself, his steel pot sitting top down at his feet, as he spoke to the old woman. *Oh well, this is better than being in some bullshit commando operation like in* The Dirty Dozen *with Lee Marvin and Jim Brown.*

Ha! They were completely surrounded! Wait a minute. The Kid quickly realized something. *I'm completely surrounded! How the fuck did I come to be in this place?*

And worst of all, the Kid couldn't listen to music. Finding a place in the shade of a stand of sugar cane to the left of the house, he sat down on the ground and took off his steel pot. If Tu Ta could, then he could. The Kid propped his M16 up on top of it, kind of as if he'd parked his chopsticks on the little chopstick holder the Vietnamese had at each table setting last night. Troung came over and sat down beside him, clearly winded from the arduous walk.

"Whew, this hard work!" Troung said. He unscrewed his canteen and took a long drink. "And what we find? One old lady!" He was clearly agitated, but on a subdued level; he couldn't change his lot any more than the Kid could change his at this moment they were sharing.

"Kool?" The Kid offered him one from his pack.

"Oh, cam on u lam!"

"How do you say, 'You're welcome' or 'No problem'?" "Com quoch che!"

Suddenly, the ARVN command element became excited. The snails were done.

"Hey, Stocker," Wilson hollered, "you gotta come try these! They're great!"

After the dog, snake, water buffalo, and chicken feet of the night before, the Kid rose reluctantly and walked over to the elevated platform where the ARVNs had the pot of snails within easy reach of Tu Ta, the old woman, Dai Ui Dong, Jim, Wilson, and a few of the ARVN NCOs. Walking up to the pot, the Kid could see that there were about five or six brass-colored needlelike probes, each about five inches long with a ring on one end, with which the snails were being pried from their black shells.

Taking one off the point of an offered probe, the Kid popped it into his mouth. It was hot. He jockeyed it around with his tongue as he took a little sip of water to cool it off; he'd had his canteen ready just in case the thing tasted rotten. But when he bit into it, the snail released some very pleasant flavors. And the texture was very interesting to his palate.

"The French couldn't get enough snails." Tu Ta smiled as he consumed another one. There were plenty to go around. Wilson was all over them.

"Oh, gawd, this is the life!" Wilson said, reveling. "Do you know what a plate of snails costs in New Orleans? Five dollars!"

The escargot feast continued for about twenty minutes. The Kid ended up eating about half a dozen of them and decided it was one of the tastier things he'd had since leaving Tra Vinh and the last American mess hall.

Soon, the order was given to move out. The little old woman would be staying behind. Again. It turned out that Troung had discovered from Bauxi Mui that Tu Ta's idea of an operation outside the fortified hamlet generally came down to this: walking out here and eating the old woman's snails. It was her punishment for being the mother of at least three or four Vietcong.

Leaving the house, the unit moved down the tree line to what had been its right. Now, they moved along just inside the trees, looking out at the wide-open expanse and the dinky little steeple of the church back in Tan An.

To their left, Wilson and the Kid could see that the foliage got thicker as one moved deeper into the tree line.

"Do you know how thick this tree line is and how far from the paddies on the other side?" the Kid asked Jim, who was now walking right in front of him.

"Well, right here, I'd say it's anywhere from twenty-five to fifty yards wide at the most. Then on the other side is another stretch of paddies just like the one we came out through." Jim turned his head a quarter turn to talk to the Kid, keeping one eye peeled and focused on where he was going.

The immediate feeling of danger, being inside the tree line, struck the Kid as being less than when they walked up through the paddies. At least there, if something started, there were trees to hide behind. The last thing on his mind was snakes.

After what seemed like an eternity, when at one point their path took them a little deeper into the trees and back away from the openness of the rice fields, the Kid caught a glimpse of the church and realized how close they were to being back in the hamlet. Then, they were suddenly in a clearing where there were three houses, all about three times the size of the house of the old woman where they had the snails.

"This is where the hamlet chief lives," Troung informed Wilson and the Kid, who came up behind the commander and his entourage. "We have been invited for refreshments!"

"Well, I like the sound of that!" Wilson wiped the sweat from his brow with a tan handkerchief. He held his steel pot in one hand and his M16 between his knees. "Better clear your weapon if we're going inside, Stocker," he said, as he went and took his own advice.

The house where they were gathering had a tall roof and was primarily open on two sides. Inside, there was another one of those low, long tables that required sitting on the bamboo mats that covered the mud floor. In addition to Tu Ta, Jim, Wilson, the Kid, Troung, Minh, and Bauxi Mui, there were at least a dozen Vietnamese men with the hamlet chief, who crowded and huddled around the table, while easily a dozen children hovered as close as they could get to the hut. As if by magic, a bottle of clear liquid appeared on the table in front of the hamlet chief. Two women came from near the rear wall of the hut and began passing out shot glasses.

"Kai yie?" The Kid pointed to the liquid in the glass bottle, asking Troung what it was.

"Bossey dai," Troung said. "It is a very strong local liquor made from rice."

As soon as there was a glass in front of each man, the bottle went quickly around the table, and then they sat, looking across the table at the head man, who grinned from ear to ear. He spoke as he lifted the glass, making what was obviously a toast, and then, along with everybody else at the table except the Kid, he threw down the drink and reacted to it.

220

"Stocker, drink. That's an order," Wilson said quite seriously.

"I don't know, sir. I've had way too much booze over the last three nights, and I was thinking about not drinking today."

"For God's sake, Stocker, drink it this instant or you will be insulting the hamlet chief!"

"He is right," Troung advised from the other side.

Looking at the swirling clear liquid, which seemed to shine like a diamond there in the shot glass, the Kid bit the bullet and threw it down. It was like drinking kerosene. The fire of the liquor, which was more than 100 proof, lit a trail directly to his stomach. As the Kid gasped for air, the Vietnamese roared with laughter and slapped each other on the backs. The Kid was a hit. He shook his head in mock tremors, seeing even through his watering eyes that this was more entertainment than they'd had in months.

"I'm on fire!" The Kid fanned his mouth as he watched his shot glass get filled up again. "Oh no!" He feigned pushing it away, but Wilson pushed it back.

"Now they want you to make the toast." Troung smiled, clearly having fun, as the other glasses were filled.

"OK." The Kid thought for a few seconds, then lifted the glass and said in a loud voice, "To victory!"

Troung translated, and again the glasses were raised to a rousing cheer. As the Kid belted down his second shot of Bossey Dai, he noticed the Vietnamese were not draining their glasses, just like the previous night. Then they poured some of theirs into the Americans' glasses, and instantly, another Vietnamese rose and made another toast. Again they drank, but now the Kid was only sipping, like the Vietnamese, while Wilson was throwing down the shots. The Kid realized that it was what he did; Lieutenant Wilson was a heavy drinker.

A huge plate of mung bean sprouts appeared on the table, but as soon as the Kid munched a couple down, he noticed that his digestive tract was starting to send him a subtle message.

"Uh, sir." He turned to Wilson. "How do you think they say 'Montezuma's revenge' in Vietnamese?"

"Say what?"

"I think I'm coming down with diarrhea, sir."

"Oh, that's just great! Well, Private, you'll just have to deal with it!"

Turning to Troung, the Kid moved close to his ear and said, "Ti Ui, I've gotta take a wicked shit. Does the hamlet chief have a latrine?"

221

After a discreet inquiry, Troung turned to the Kid. "It is out behind the back wall, at the edge of the clearing, by the fishpond."

Rising from the table, the Kid made his way outside. As he walked quickly around back, looking for the outhouse, he noticed that all the kids were now following him. *Thank God Troung's directions are solid,* he thought as he found the outhouse. Going up to it, he realized that it had no door. *Doesn't matter anymore. I have to go so bad.* Inside the small three-walled enclosure, the Kid, seeing there was nothing to sit on, realized that he would have to squat over the opening that the Vietnamese shit through and do his business right into the fishpond.

Remind me to skip the fish dish the next time they serve it, he thought, as he undid his belt and dropped his pants, much to the delight of the kids, who jockeyed for a look. But when he let loose with the pent-up gas and liquid shit that coursed through his lower bowel, making possibly the most vulgar noise on the planet, the Vietnamese children plain howled! Many were laughing so hard that they fell on the ground and rolled. *Ah, blessed relief!*

Fuck. No toilet paper! Pulling some grass off the thatched wall of the commode, the Kid wiped his ass with it as best he could. More than a little scratchy. *Yes, this truly is a hardship tour!*

As he rounded the front of the building, the men were emerging from the hut, and it appeared that Tu Ta was ready to go. Courtesies were being paid to the hamlet chief by the command element. The Kid went up and bowed and extended his hand to shake. "Cam on u lamb," he said, much to the delight of the hamlet chief, who slapped him on the back.

"Com quo chi!" He nodded.

Walking off, the Kid was perplexed. "Don't those people live inside the fortified hamlet?" he asked Jim.

"Yes, they do, at night. During the day, they like to come out here to the houses they left and use them while they tend their paddies. The VC have burned them down a couple of times in the past, but for some reason, they've quit doing it lately."

"The VC are more than likely sleeping in these huts at night," Wilson speculated. "The hamlet chief and his people use them during the day, and the VC use them at night! Kind of a symbiotic relationship!"

The hamlet chief's house was not too far from the compound. Soon, the unit was traipsing through the opening and back into the confines of the old religious quarters. The Kid had completed his first patrol: not a shot had been fired, nobody stepped on any land mines, and all they'd done was eat snails and get drunk.

Entering the priests' and nuns' house, the Kid went over to his bunk, put his rifle down, and sat down himself. First he took off his shirt, then his boots. When he peeled off his socks, he found it: his first leech! "Fuckin' A! Look at this." He pointed to it as he pulled gently at it to see how firmly it was attached. "Cigarette or insect repellent?" He grinned at Wilson.

"Which is closer?" the lieutenant replied.

"Cigs!" the Kid said. He pulled a Kool from the pocket of the shirt that lay on the floor. Standing, he got his Zippo out of his pocket and lit up, getting a good, hot ember going at the end of his cancer stick. Sitting down, he crossed his left leg over his right knee, presenting the best shot at the bloodsucker that had attached itself to the inside of his left calf. As he touched the leech with the ember, it recoiled and retracted, then fell off and onto the floor amid the Kid's blood, which had dripped onto the tile. "Gee," the Kid said, staring at the droplets, "wouldn't it be nice if that was the only blood I ever shed on the soil of Vietnam!"

Well, the joke was on the Kid, because the blood was fairly rushing out of the spot where the leech had been attached. It continued to run down his leg and onto the tile floor at a pretty good clip.

"Try a little direct pressure," Wilson suggested. He stood by and watched, dripping with sweat. "Hey, maybe I've got some too!" He got excited, as if it were something war buddies should share, and quickly set down his gear and unzipped his boots. He had the ever-popular laced-up trick zipper rigs affixed to his. Sure enough, he had two leeches!

The Kid went to the community stores and got some toilet paper to hold over the dime-sized red spot that continued to ooze blood thanks to the leech's anticoagulant saliva. He was filthy. "God, what I wouldn't give to take a shower!" he said, wiping his sweaty hand across his equally sweaty brow. Just as he made the comment, Sergeant Minh came into the room.

"You may be in luck, Stockah. Looks like monsoon is forming up. We might get rain in maybe one hour!"

"Well, all right!" he said enthusiastically, but feeling on the inside that he was now getting screwed by the army on a whole new level. There were guys in Saigon with showers, PX's, bars, clubs, whores, and grass! What did he have?

"Hey!" Sergeant Matt hollered from over at the community stores box. "Look at all the stuff the captain left us from his last care package!" He pulled out a box still covered with brown wrapping paper that Morris had gotten from home a couple of days earlier. "There's half a dozen cans of Spam in here!" Matt said in a tone of voice that would have convinced you he had just

223

discovered gold. "And Jiffy Pop popcorn, and Shake-a-Pudd'ns. And look, a bunch of hard candy—Fire Stix from Jolly Rancher!"

"Hey, Fire Stix. Those are from Colorado!" The Kid walked over to look at the newly discovered treasures. "But what I could really go for right about now is a cool pop, you know, those things you used to stick in the freezer in the plastic tube. Know what I mean?"

Matt looked at him with a blank stare. Apparently, he had not had that experience as a child and, being a dedicated lifer in the army, his horizons were not much broader than the gate of whatever post he was living at that year. "His mom sent him some Snickers once. You should have seen them; they were like little bags of liquid chocolate shit! Oh boy!" Matt continued to dig around in the captain's late stuff. "Look at this! A cache of chicken noodle soup C ration meals!"

Now that was a real find. Some of the C ration meals, such as the ham and lima beans, were bad enough to make a guy contemplate suicide.

"I know what I'm having for lunch," Wilson sang out from over on his bunk, where he was treating his own leech wounds.

Walking back over to his cot and reaching under his poncho liner, the Kid pulled out his transistor radio from the place where he had cached it and turned it on.

"Soldiers from the sky, men who jump and men who die." Barry Sadler blared out at him. *Oh well, he thought, it'll be over in two minutes.*

"Ooh!" Sergeant Matt dropped what he was looking at and ran over to the Kid's cot. "The Green Beret! Turn it up!"

"Two hundred men they'll test today, but only three win the green beret."

"I tried out for the Green Berets," Sergeant Matt said with a trace of a frown on his square jaw, "but I didn't make it. But my boys, if they can't be Green Berets, I don't even want them to be in the army!"

"Really?" said the Kid, his head cocked to one side. "You can do that, not go if you don't get what you want?"

"Well, my dad was in the army, and I'm in the army, but if my boys can't be with the best, I don't want them in at all!"

"How old are your boys?" the Kid inquired.

"Fourteen and twelve."

"Do they even want to be in the army at all? I mean, if they don't want to be in the Green Berets, why should it make a difference to you? They've gotta live their own lives, don't they?"

"Oh, they'll want to join up. There's nothing greater you can do than fight for your country."

"What if your country's wrong? Are you a 'my country, right or wrong; better off dead than Red' kind of guy?"

"You bet I am!"

"So, whatever your country says is right?" The Kid went for a setup.

"Absolutely!" Matt replied with a firmness that left do doubt as to his feelings. But the look on his face indicated that he now harbored suspicions about how the Kid apparently felt about their mutual country. "You don't believe in supporting your country, right or wrong? It's still your country."

"That may be true, but remember, slavery was once legal in our country, for almost seventy-five years after it was founded for 'life, liberty, and the pursuit of happiness,'" the Kid said, quoting the Declaration of Independence. "Because it was the law of the land, slavery, right?"

Sergeant Matt didn't answer right away. He took a couple of seconds to think about it. The Kid could see that he was straining his gray matter, as if inwardly he knew slavery was wrong, but he was trying to find some way to justify his simplistic stand.

"Well, slavery might have been wrong, but I still believe in my country, right or wrong!"

"*Might* have been wrong?" the Kid questioned, his mouth open in mock shock, his eyes big and round, and his head shaking from side to side. "Might?" He could see how uncomfortable he was starting to make the sergeant, whose pea brain was just beginning to grasp the ridiculousness of his statement.

"Well, OK, that's a bad example. But we have to support our country in this war, right or wrong, because a lot of soldiers have already died!" There, he was satisfied that put the Kid in his place.

The pair was distracted from their argument with the arrival of Xuan, who had just entered the building, no longer dressed in the olive-green uniform he had worn on the operation they had just completed. He was back in his faded red shorts with bare feet as he padded over to the Kid's bunk and took his wet, muddy boots off to be cleaned, along with Lieutenant Wilson's. Xuan and Troung exchanged comments, and Xuan added Troung's boots to his armload, taking them outside on the porch, which was now in the shade.

Checking his watch, the Kid saw that it was 1400 hours. All the Vietnamese, he noted, Tu Ta, Dai Ui Dong, and Sergeant Minh, were stretched out on their cots.

"You know where the country of Mexico is?" the Kid inquired of Troung, who was himself stripped down to his boxer shorts and sitting on the edge of his cot.

"Yes, south of America."

"Yeah. … No, actually, it is still in North America. Anyway, they have a thing they do there in the afternoon where everybody takes a nap. It's called a siesta," the Kid said. "Is that what's happening here? Everybody's taking a nap in the hottest part of the day?"

"Yes, Stockah," Tu Ta spoke up. "It is too hot, and lying still in the shade helps keep you cool. Why not try it?"

Walking back over to his bunk, the Kid looked down at his shaving kit, which was partially open. Upon pulling out the Colgate and his toothbrush, he said, "Hmm, I've got a really bad taste in my mouth. I think I'll brush my teeth." Picking up his canteen, he slipped his bare feet into his flip-flops and padded out onto the porch. Once there, he set down the canteen, put some of the white paste on his green toothbrush, and commenced to brushing away. As he did so, he dropped the crumpled tube into his pants pocket. After spitting and rinsing out his mouth, he sauntered back inside, where Lieutenant Wilson was also now going the siesta route.

"Uh, Lieutenant, I'm going to explore the church some more. It's pretty interesting."

"OK, but don't go anywhere else!"

"Roger that. Like, where would I go? Into town?"

"No, I mean don't go walking around the perimeter or anything. Don't forget that there's lots of defensive mines and stuff around here."

"No sweat," the Kid said. He checked his pocket to make sure he had his Zippo and cigs with him as he plopped his jungle hat atop his head and headed out the door. Walking toward the church, he noticed for the first time, off to his right, a wooden-framed cage enclosed in barbed wire. It was about six feet square but only about two feet high. Curious, he thought, *Maybe that's where they keep the pigs before they kill them.*

Walking slowly in the radiating heat, he crossed the little stream and the grass, and then walked up the sidewalk to the four stairs that led up to the nonexistent church doors. He went inside through the bullet-scarred arch where the doors once hung. Stepping carefully around the chunks of rubble that littered the floor, he made his way to the ladder. The base of the bamboo poles, to which the rungs were lashed, was firmly wedged into a place between a couple of the bigger chunks of concrete that used to be the ceiling directly

226

above where they now rested. The bamboo contraption had a certain camber to it as the Kid climbed the dozen or so rungs and emerged from the hole in the corner of the building, where he stepped onto the landing. The tower rose up another forty feet from where the Kid stood. He had his head tilted back, gaping upward, marveling at the sheer reach of the Catholic Church, its having the money and time to build something like this in the middle of a sea of rice paddies.

Stepping up on the riser that ran beneath the round window, the Kid looked out upon the scene. Nothing was going on with everybody inside for siesta. A couple of chickens scratched for bugs, and it looked that Minh and Bauxi Mui were sitting on the porch and smoking cigarettes next to where Xuan was polishing boots. The landing itself had been fairly well cleared of rubble right around the window, but off to the left, there was a partial wall and the remains of a room that was still filled with the slag that had once been its top and sides. The Kid sat down on the riser and pulled the Colgate from his pocket. Unraveling the end of the tube, he pulled out his cache and papers. He had three papers left, along with a pinch of reefer and a couple of roaches. He would have to ration carefully. He dumped the green leaf carefully into his hand and placed it on top of the plastic baggie. Then, he ripped up the roaches, paper and all, and spread the mix together, at which point, he divided it into three equal piles and commenced to roll three joints. As he struck his Zippo and lifted the flame to the tip of the third joint, he thought back to the joint he had smoked in the john of the jet on the way over and how cramped the quarters had been. Now, as he sat on the riser and looked out behind the nonexistent church walls and ceiling, he could see for miles, just like the Who song. *Hmm, next time, I'll have to remember to bring the transistor radio up with me.*

The Kid leaned back against the wall and took another deep hit. He felt very secure because he could keep an eye on the only way up to where he was. Nobody could sneak up that ladder without making it move. And looking around, the Kid could tell that nobody could see him from any spot on the ground. *Bingo! Instant enlisted men's lounge! Not quite Top of the Mark, but it's got a real private, homey feel to it.* There was no TV, no movies, no PX, no whores, no bars, no snacks, no mess hall, no friends, and not much more pot. What else was left? Being a student of religion, the Kid briefly pondered the ramifications of beating his meat within the church's hallowed walls. Quickly realizing that this was in all likelihood the only place on the compound where there was enough privacy for the activity, he pretty much decided that's what he'd do as soon as he finished the joint.

Being that he was in a place that was surrounded by VC and likely to be, at some time in the foreseeable future, attacked, and given that his lover was thousands of miles and light years away and he might never see her again, he figured he might as well entertain himself with the hand he had been dealt, so to speak.

Another hit on the joint and he was beginning to get off, but he decided that he was going to burn it to the end and stick the roach into a Kool and finish off every last molecule. Once at the end of the joint, the Kid pulled out a Kool and, spinning it between his fingers and thumb, knocked just enough tobacco out to house the roach. Ceremoniously raising the Zippo up, he fired it up and pulled the hit deeply into his lungs. Closing his eyes, he held it for as long as he could. Slowly blowing it out, he thought about the day he had taken the picture that he carried around of Flo. A nippy breeze had been blowing in off the Pacific last December, when he'd driven all the way from Indianapolis to Vista, California, to see her. He wanted to swim, at least get her into a bikini once while he was there, but it was just too cold. Then they had gotten up and walked down the beach, the waves rolling in, the seagulls calling in the air as they floated past on thin, pointed wings. He was beginning to hear somebody calling him off in the distance. "Stocker! Stocker! Hey! Yo! PFC!" *Wait a minute, it's not a dream. That's Wilson's voice, hollering for me!*

Rising to his feet, the Kid peered through the round window to see Wilson walking his direction. He was crossing the creek and soon stood beneath him on the sidewalk in front of the church steps. Looking up, his face was painted with a grin so big, his immense mustache could not conceal it.

"Stocker!" He stood there openly excited, shirtless, with his hands on his hips above his fatigue pants. "Great news! We've been invited to come on a search and destroy operation with Major Boarz and Able Company!"

"Say what?"

"I said, we have been invited to chopper in to Tra Vinh tomorrow and go on a search and destroy operation with Able Company the day after tomorrow! Isn't that great news?"

"Well, yes and no!"

"Whaddya mean, yes and no?"

"I took an extra year to get into Armed Fucking Forces Radio so I wouldn't have to be involved in shit like this!"

"Tough shit is what you're involved with, PFC. You'll just have to learn to live with it."

"Yes, sir," the Kid replied with drooping shoulders. Wilson turned and smartly huffed off back toward the parish house.

228

Dejectedly, the Kid stepped back down off the riser and took an angry puff of his Kool. Shit. *Plain old everyday shit, shit, shit! How did I come to be here?*

He paced to the edge of the precipice. Standing at the jagged drop-off to the shattered flooring, he recalled Minh's warning from the day before: the edge was weak and undependable. The Kid stared down at the big crumbled pieces twenty feet below him. *Hmm,* he thought, *if you fell off here and broke your ankle or leg, you'd certainly get medevacked out of the field. Yes, everyone knows the edge is unsafe. I could say that I was standing close to the edge, trying to see over, when it broke. Why, if I sat of the edge and really picked my place, chances are I could break an ankle and not do too much other damage! What will it be, your ankle right now or your life the day after tomorrow on some dumb fucking search and destroy mission?*

Out in the center of the old destroyed cathedral, where the sun hit directly most of the day, the cement remains of the destruction were partially covered with moss and plants that had begun to grow up amid them. Flicking the butt of his Kool off the balcony, the Kid watched it curve down and arc off the flat surface of a big piece that was tilted at forty-five degrees. *Gee, if I hit like that, I might break not only my ankles, but also my ribs, arms, and skull. What if I never skied again? If I got killed on the search and destroy, for sure I'd never ski again, or make love to Flo, or eat a hot dog at a ball game, or do any of that sentimental shit it's so easy to take for granted. If I was hanging off the edge, it'd only be fifteen feet. What if I did it and they figured it out and busted me for self-inflicted wounding? Am I a coward if I don't have enough courage to jump off a building to keep from getting shot?* The Kid wavered on the edge, listening, wanting to hear the siren call to dash himself upon the rocks. *Just enough. No. I could never jump.* He backed away. *I gotta play the hand.*

A gust of warm, moist air hit him in the face and made him look up. A massive dark and menacing cloud formation was bearing down on the fortified hamlet. *It looks like the monsoon is on its way. Hot damn,* he thought, *it's going to rain hard enough to take a gutter pipe shower!* Cautiously, he mounted the ladder and made his way safely to the bottom.

Chapter 19

The next day, when the chopper didn't come to pick them up, Lieutenant Wilson was pissed. On the radio to the TOC back at Tra Vinh, he was informed that the operation had been postponed and that he would be told in plenty of time when to come in and be a part of it when it finally happened.

The next day after that, and the day after that as they sat waiting, Wilson's growing frustration at being trapped in some backwater black hole, where absolutely nothing was happening, was driving him to grind his teeth and cuss under his breath as if he had Tourette's syndrome. *He must have been expecting Tan An to be some kind of Khe Sanh when he consented to come out here,* the Kid mused as he watched him pacing and smoking on the front porch of the rectory.

The Kid, on the other hand, could have cared less. Every day that he heard the reply come back over the radio—"Not today!"—he rejoiced secretly in his heart. For as much as he had feared coming to Tan An, nothing had happened since their arrival that even hinted at danger. He was content to take his transistor radio and Kools up into his hideout in the church, where he would listen to Radio Saigon and doze, or read a paperback book, or write letters to Flo, his parents, and his friends back in Nashville and Boulder. He was accumulating quite a little stack since he couldn't mail any of them until a chopper came out.

Ti Ui Troung took the opportunity to fulfill one of his other appointed tasks. It was his job to deliver lectures to the South Vietnamese troops on the political philosophy of their government and why the war must be fought and won. He would get about twenty-five of the troops together at a time and lecture them in the shade of the priests' quarters, one session in the morning and another in the later afternoon.

There weren't any more snail-scarfing operations out into the hinterland as Lieutenant Jim, Sergeant Matt, Tui Ta, and Dai Ui Dong were content to wait, using the absence of a commander as their excuse for inactivity. Tan An had become the most boring place in the entire war zone!

One night, the Kid accompanied Troung on a visit he made to troops living in a hooch out by the perimeter. Crawling into the opening of the sandbag-lined combination hooch–bunker, the Kid's eyes adjusted to the soft candlelight inside. The place was about six feet wide by eight feet long, with the ceiling no higher than five feet. Over in one corner, the two occupants had a little cooking alcove set up, and a Sterno can fire was heating a small pan of rice soup. The troops offered small bowls to each of the visitors.

It was now approaching a week since the Kid had eaten any US Army mess hall food, and the steady diet of rice, chicken, and strange meats was beginning to get to him. He was literally in a constant state of lower-intestinal distress, and he had Xuan fetch the many cans of water needed in his duel with the great emperor Montezuma.

The Kid looked at the cup of soup and smelled it. The aroma seemed to be far more pleasant than the stuff that was coming out of the common mess area behind their building where, every day, a pig was given the coup de grâce. The Kid tasted one of the small bits of meat that floated among the rice and veggies. *Frog legs,* he silently bet. "Kai Yi?" he asked. "What's this?"

The two hosts just looked at each other and then at Troung, then spoke a word that the Kid, of course, did not understand. Then they pointed to a hole in the wall of their bunker.

"Kom bic?" the soldier said. When the Kid again failed to understand the words or gestures they used, he turned to Troung.

"It is rat, Stocker. The meat in the soup is rat. In Vietnam, we have a saying," Troung began with a smile. "Country rat and city dog. Country rat is very clean because they eat rice out of the farmer's bin. Country dog is kind of skinny because the farmers do not have enough table scraps to make the dogs fat. City dogs are very fat because there is more food in the cities, but city rats eat garbage out of the dump and are dirty. *Bic?*"

The meat tasted bland, but the soup was quite good. The Kid ate it and enjoyed it, at least as much as he enjoyed the dog! *Can't wait to write home about this.* He chuckled as he bestowed Kools on his hosts and fired them up with his Zippo. *You boys got any of that kick-ass Cambodian shit cached out here?* he wanted badly to ask them, but he knew he couldn't tip his hand to Troung.

Finally, on June 14, word came in the late morning that the chopper back to Tra Vinh would arrive around noon. All of a sudden, Wilson and the Kid were rushing around gathering their gear.

"I can't wait to take a shower," the Kid exclaimed.

231

"I can't wait to get out there tomorrow!" Wilson was single-minded in his quest for action. "All this fucking sitting and picking shit with the geckos! If we didn't go today, I think I would have bloody fucking flipped out!"

"I can't wait to eat in the mess hall!" The Kid's eyes lit up with irony. "Guess I thought I'd never hear myself speak those words!"

Now Troung had not himself been invited, nor did he inquire about being included in the operation upon which the Kid and Lieutenant Wilson were going, but he was inviting himself in on the noon chopper out of Tan An. "I cannot wait to sleep in my own bed!" He beamed.

Lieutenant Jim and Sergeant Matt just kind of watched with a small bit of circumspection since they would not be going. "Hope they put our mail on this fuckin' chopper," Sergeant Matt lamented.

What I wouldn't give for a letter from Flo. The Kid pined briefly as he stuffed his gear into his laundry bag. He was going on one month in-country and had yet to see a single piece of mail. The suspense was killing him. Was she or was she not pregnant? That thought occupied his mind the whole time they were dragging their gear out to the pad and waiting on the porch for their Huey. As the distant *pop-pop-pop* drew closer, the Kid switched from thinking about whether or not he had knocked up Flo to thinking about what would happen if the VC were to pick this chopper as the one to knock down with a mortar round, as they occasionally did, like Sergeant Matt was always talking about.

The second the chopper touched down, the men moved quickly to load their gear. The door gunner flipped a canvas pouch to Sergeant Matt, whose eyes lit up: US Mail!

Smooth as an Indy 500 pit stop, they were quickly back in the air and Tan An was becoming a speck behind them. Up in the cool air. *This gunner dude has it made.* The Kid smiled at him as he leaned over his weapon, surveying the terrain that flew by beneath their beating rotor blades.

Settling down onto the Tra Vinh helipad, the Kid quickly spied the International from the compound, with Sergeant Spencer at the wheel. As soon as they had off-loaded and the chopper lifted up and left, Spencer moved out to pick them up.

"Is your buddy here today?" Wilson asked Spencer as he shut off the motor and stepped down to help load.

"Yep! And he put one right over my head not ten minutes ago. I didn't move a muscle! He's here working now. Listen!"

232

"That cocksucker! He has to be in those bushes right there!" Wilson pointed. "I'm going to put a few rounds in on *him,* and then we'll see what *he* thinks!" He picked up his M16 and chambered a round.

"No, no, no, Lieutenant!" Sergeant Spencer was instantly adamantly opposed to the suggestion. "Major Gillmore has given specific orders that nobody is to do anything that will upset the Tra Vinh Airport sniper in any way! If you shoot in his direction and change the status quo, I'll have no choice but to report you directly to the major himself! Then you can bet your ass you won't be going on no fuckin' operation tomorrow—or maybe ever!"

It was easy to see that Wilson did not cotton to being threatened by a lower-ranking person, but he complied by ejecting the shell onto the ground, picking it up, and putting it in his pocket. There were no more rounds fired by the sniper while they loaded up and began their drive the mile back into Tra Vinh.

Before going to the US compound, Sergeant Spencer consented to drop Ti Ui Troung at his post. But rapidly wheeling through the streets lined with tall trees, they were soon pulling into the compound.

As they parked the International in the portico and began pulling out their gear, Paul Heineman walked out of the back door to the main house. "Hey, Kid, welcome back!" He smiled. "What did you think of Tan An? Isn't that church awesome?"

"Yeah! And what a view! Why, you can see trees at the other end of the paddies!"

"Well, I've got something you might find just a little bit more exciting." Paul brought his hand out from behind his back and held out to the Kid a pastel yellow envelope. "I almost put this in the mail bag that just went out to Tan An, and then I remembered that you all were coming in for the operation tomorrow. You'd most likely have shot me if I had!"

It was a letter from Flo! A smile broke across the Kid's face as he reached out and took the envelope from Paul and lifted it to his nose and deeply inhaled the aroma of her perfume. Intoxicating! "Oh my gawd! Have I been longing for this!" The Kid was so excited that his hands were shaking just the slightest bit as he kissed the envelope. Another whiff of the envelope and he had to fight the urge to rip it open on the spot. No, an event of this magnitude required a little more planning for maximum enjoyment. Slipping it into his breast pocket, he continued with the unloading and moving of his gear out of Spencer's International.

"If you want to eat lunch, you'd better hurry, 'cause the mess hall closes in about fifteen minutes," Paul said. "I'm going right now, if you want to join me."

"Sir?" The Kid turned to Wilson. "Is that OK? If I go to lunch now?"

"Sure. That's sounding like a good idea to me too," Wilson replied as he hefted up his gear bag and M16. "What say we meet in the club at about fourteen hundred hours? That way, you can take a shower and get cleaned up too."

"Thank you, sir," the Kid said. He picked up his gear to deposit at his area on the way to the mess hall. His heart was beating at an increased rate as he could feel the letter burning a hole in his pocket. Now that he had it in his possession, he was in no real hurry to open it. He would choose a moment when he could give it his full attention. Right now, the prospect of enjoying some American chow was foremost in his mind. "You wouldn't believe the shit we've been eating out there, Paul: dog; the heads and feet of chickens; snake; and believe it or not, rat! I don't care what's on the menu today, I'm going to fucking *love it*!"

"Let me give you a hand." Paul reached down and picked up the Kid's M16 and ammo bandolier as the Kid hefted his bag over his right shoulder.

"So, you going on this operation tomorrow?" the Kid inquired as they walked across the lawn to the servants' quarters.

"No, I'll be over at the TOC with Major Gillmore, monitoring the whole shebang on the radios."

"I can't believe we have to go out with Boarz's unit. What an asshole. Anyway, that was my initial impression when we shot pool with him and his buddy last week."

"Roger that! Boar Hog is, without a doubt, the biggest ignorant fucking asshole in the entire province! Or maybe all of IV Corps!" Paul grimaced as he opened the screen door for the Kid. "Be fun if he got his dick shot off! Not kill him, but leave him to live life without his cock!"

The mental picture of what Paul had wished for established itself in the Kid's mind, causing him to laugh. "Funny what passes for entertainment here in the war zone!"

After locking up his stuff, the Kid put Flo's letter, which had "No. 4" written on the bottom right corner, on the pillow of his bunk lest it get sweaty in his pocket. The aroma emanating from the mess hall when he walked in the door was almost as sweet as Flo's perfume!

"Ah, chicken-fried steak! One of my fav'rites!" the Kid exclaimed as they picked up their plates at the head of the chow line. "Look at that! Mashed potatoes and gravy and peas and carrots and salad and rolls and butter! I'm

234

dead and in heaven!" The Vietnamese women who were serving them had to laugh at his facial contortions as he egged them to fill his plate a little fuller than their initial offerings at each pan of chow. "Beaucoup, beaucoup!" He grinned.

Once they were seated, there was little conversation as the Kid commenced to shovel it in. "You know," he finally said with a full mouth, "they kill a pig every morning out there. What a freaking loud and bloody mess! Right outside our quarters! Oh, does this shit ever taste good!"

"I guess it's true what Einstein said." Paul paused in the cutting of his meat. "It's all relative. Because I've been eating this shit for the last six months, and right now I fucking hate every bite!"

"Nectar of the gods!" the Kid said, following a swig of iced tea. "Ice! Fucking ice is now a luxury item!"

Once they finished, they both lit up cigarettes. "So, Paul, what's the deal tomorrow? What kind of an 'operation' is it?"

"Well, it's going to be big by our standards. All three Third Battalion companies are going out after the VC Tenth Battalion, which we've got located between Tan An and Cang Long. One company is going to be set up in a blocking position, and the other two companies are going to try to drive the VC right into them. Boar Hog's company is going to be driving on the left side, and Howell's company is going to be holding the right and bending around to cap the bottle. Anyway, that's the way Major Gillmore is drawing it up on paper. So, you and Wilson will be on the left flank. The thing you really gotta watch out for is our blocking position shooting at them as you're driving them forward. That 'friendly fire' will kill you as dead as any VC will."

"I'm fucked! Foreign-language announcer, my ass!" the Kid exclaimed. "I think I'm going to go read my letter and take a shower."

"Hey, we're going over to Wen's tonight after the briefing at sixteen hundred hours. Want to come along?"

"You bet, if the lieutenant will let me. Later," he said as he picked up his tray and headed for the busing window.

Back at his bunk, the Kid picked up the letter and sat down on his mattress. Time bomb? Was he about to find out that he was going to be a daddy? He rummaged around in his gear bag and pulled out his bayonet to use as a letter opener.

Slicing the top of the envelope, he reached in and withdrew the folded pages, of which there appeared to be four, and opened them up.

June 7, 1968

My Dearest Curt,

First and foremost, let me tell you how much I love you and want you and can't wait to be your wife and wake up in your arms every morning, darlin! This is the fourth letter I've written you since I got your address. I'm numbering them so you can tell if you have received them all or not. I have now gotten eight letters from you. I even found Can Tho on a map, so I've got an idea of where you are.

Things are so crazy here, you can't believe it! As you surely know by now, Robert Kennedy was shot and killed in LA. All of the country and especially California is in mourning. We always used to say things like that only happened in Texas and the Deep South! Now it is here in our backyard. It was an Arab that did it. Nothing makes any sense. RFK had just won the California primary and had the nomination in his hands, and then this. Who knows what will happen next?

On a lighter note, school's out for the summer, so now I gotta look for a job. Most likely waiting tables somewhere. It's been getting hot, probably not as hot as where you are (or as hot as I am for you), but me, Lo, Sandy, and Jacque have been to the beach a bunch of times already. I like to go to the spot where you took that picture of me and pretend you're here, taking it again! Lo's and Sandy's boyfriends are taking them to see a movie tonight and asked me to come along, but I'm just going to stay home and write to you. Why be a fifth wheel?

So, darlin', I got to tell you I'm a little bit nervous if Aunt Minnie is going to show up next week. That's when she is due to visit. But whatever happens, I wouldn't change anything! I love you so much. I kinda feel the way I usually feel before I get it, but a little different now that I'm not a virgin anymore. So you shouldn't worry! OK? I imagine you've got a whole bunch of other things to worry about. We watch the news every night, and now I kind of look for you when they say the film is from the Mekong Delta. Wouldn't that be something if I actually saw you? For now, I have your picture out on my pillow. I'm writing this lying on my bed. I've just gotten out of the shower and am like totally naked under my robe. I think about us at the TM at least a few times every day. I even drove by it last week.

I can't believe that you've only been gone for three weeks. It seems like an eternity! How will we ever last for a year? We will have to go check in at the TM the second you're back! On that note, it is late and I've gotta get some rest so I can get up and start my job search tomorrow bright and early in the morning. That's when my dad says you are most likely to find a job. We shall see!

Love and kisses and anything else you want!

Flo

PS: I'll see you later!

As soon as the Kid had finished reading it, he went back to page one and read the entire letter again. Slightly chagrined about the fact that there was no news on the pregnancy front yet, he paused over the sentence about nakedness under the robe. He looked at her picture and cursed the army, the war, LBJ, and everybody else who was responsible for keeping them apart.

Then he shucked off his clothes and headed for the showers. *My God, I am on a major roll: a letter from Flo, food in the American mess hall, and now a real live shower!* The cold water poured over his head, cooling him off from the tropical sweat bath that had been his day thus far. When he was dressed, he read Flo's letter again and put it away when it was time to go meet Wilson in the club.

Chapter 20

When the Kid entered the mess hall, he could see Major Boarz and Lieutenant Wilson sitting together at a table off to the left of the pool table by the back wall. Entering the club itself, he noticed Wen behind the bar and almost missed the step down that marked the boundary of the club proper, stumbling slightly as he waved hello to her. Smoke curled up off the cigarettes that the officers were smoking as the Kid stepped up to the table and said to Wilson, in a quiet voice, "Reporting, sir."

Wilson looked, not at him, but at Major Boarz, as Major Boarz turned his gaze from Wilson, with whom he had been enjoying a laugh, to the Kid, with an eye that indicated an appraisal.

"PFC Stocker, you remember Major Boarz, I'm sure."

"Yes. How are you today, Major?" The Kid kind of bowed Asian style to him since he wasn't supposed to salute in the field. "I'm, shall we say, mildly excited about tomorrow," he lied through his teeth. What he was, was fucking scared out of his constantly sweating skin.

"Well, *mildly excited* is an interesting choice of words, PFC." The major took an authoritative puff on his Winston and stared directly from his steel-blue eyes into the eyes of the Kid. "Maybe scared shitless out of your fucking breeches is closer to the truth!" he said as he looked at Wilson. They both laughed.

"Major Boarz is a West Point graduate," Wilson said in a tone of voice that dripped heavily with the perfume of sickening adoration.

"Well, actually," the Kid began as their laughter died down, "the major is pretty much right on the money. I am a little scared, I'll admit it."

"I like your attitude, Stocker." Boarz's square-jawed face, accented by his equally square flattop haircut, blossomed into a smile, showing gold fillings. "I'm sure you'll do fine tomorrow. Sit down. Let me buy you a beer! Wen, one for the private!" he hollered. Wen jumped to comply.

The Kid pulled up a chair at the end of the table so as not to sit next to either of the officers. "Lieutenant Wilson, will there be a psyops team with us,

238

and will we have speakers tomorrow?" the Kid inquired. Wen set the Falstaff on the table in front of him and picked up the blue one-dollar MPC note Boar Hog had flipped toward her hand.

Looking again at each other, the lieutenant and the major broke out into another overpowering fit of laughter, enjoying some private joke that apparently involved the private. The Kid took a log pull. Ah, cold beer. What a luxury!

"No, there are still no speakers in the province at this time," Wilson said matter- of-factly. "Tomorrow, our function will be primarily to observe and learn. We will be operating with the command element, Major Boarz here and his XO, Lieutenant Wallace."

"But don't worry, PFC." Boarz grinned. "I like to get right up front and see what's going on every once in a while, so you all will definitely see some action! The amazing thing is—and this is something you'll have to watch out for—the front has a tendency to swing quickly around when some gook jumps up out of a hole and opens up on your ass!"

Pleasant thought. The Kid took another long pull. "How long are we going to be out in the field?"

"Don't know," Boarz said as he snuffed out his butt. "Depends on how much contact we end up getting. We think there's a main-force VC battalion out there. If we hook up good, it could last a couple of days."

Kid's stock began plunging like the 1929 crash.

"The major has some C rations he's gonna give us, just in case we do end up out there for the night." Wilson smiled, as if it was a real big favor. Well, it would be, as long as it wasn't lima beans and ham!

"How long have you been here now, sir?" The Kid turned to Boarz.

"On this tour? Seven months. This is my third tour," he spoke while watching the Kid's face to gauge his reaction to the information.

"Third tour?" the Kid exclaimed.

"Yep. What else is a West Point grad going to do if he doesn't fight wars? Tell me that!"

"You like getting shot at?"

"I fucking love it. There's nothing like it."

The Kid, able to see that the dark-complexioned, square-headed, set-jawed, muscle-rippled professional soldier meant what he'd said from the bottom of his soul, felt a chill run up his spine.

239

"You don't have to come to the briefing." Wilson had spoken the words of freedom that the Kid so sorely wanted to hear. "I guess it's already going to be a little crowded, so I'll brief you myself later, say, around twenty hundred hours right here, after chow?"

"Yes, sir. Thank you, sir," the Kid said, turning to see Wen smiling at him. "Men yoi, Co," he said in Vietnamese, and then quickly changed to English. "Did I get it right?"

"If you were trying to say, 'Hello, young lady,' then yes, you did! How are you, Kid?"

She had called him Kid! It made his heart soar to know that in spite of the fact that he was looking at being in a combat situation in less than twenty-four hours, he was still the Kid!

"I get off work in an hour. Want go to my place?" Wen asked the Kid. "Johnson left his record *Trung Ui Mui*. That is how you say *Sergeant Pepper's* in Vietnamese!" She flashed him a smile with the whitest teeth, which made him broadly smile back.

"OK, you numba one!" he said, having run out of Vietnamese. "I go back to my bunk next door. You come get me when you get off, OK?"

"OK! For sure!" She had continually been wiping the bar as they spoke, and now she declared herself done as she flipped the rag she was using into the sink by the refrigerator that held the club's precious supply of cold beer.

The servants' building enjoyed the cover of a high canopy of palm trees, and thus it did not get hit directly by the sun during the hottest part of the day. The Kid watched a gecko scurry off the wall and onto the screen that let in some moving air as he entered his cubicle and, at once, got out the letter from Flo. He read it again and then, with it open in his hand, he lay back down on his mattress with one boot on the floor. This was the first real mattress he'd been on in more than a week. He closed his eyes and tried as best he could to latch onto an image of Flo and ride with it. Nearly naked in the Traveler's Motel, lying on the bed before he'd taken her panties off. Shy little look. He remembered a dozen of their kisses, the first in Nashville, their last in the San Diego airport, the one at the drive-in, in Vista, a couple of nights before New Year's Eve, right before he proposed to her. Now that had been quite the kiss! He recalled the electric feel of her tongue against his. It was as if she had sucked the proposal right out of his mouth!

He dropped off to sleep. The letter slipped from his hand and fell to the floor as he tumbled into a dream. There were soldiers standing in the jungle. Were they South Vietnamese? They were all wearing the exact same steel pot. The

Kid was almost close enough to see their faces. *Wait a minute.* It wasn't soldiers in the jungle he was looking at; it was the hallucination he had seen in the embers of the fireplace that New Year's Eve in Aspen. It was the same soldiers he had seen in the ember of his cigarette countless times! But now, he could almost see their faces, but their backs were turned to him! *Who the fuck is it?*

"Kid." A gentle voice and a hand on the shoulder brought him back. Wen had come to get him after work. "If you'd rather sleep, that OK. Oh, you drop you letter," she said as she bent over to pick up the folded yellow pages and the envelope that had bounced a little ways under his bunk. "Gulfriend letter?"

"Wen." The Kid blinked, took off his glasses, and laid them in his lap so he could rub his eyes. Taking the pages from her hand, he put them back envelope. "Yes! The first I've gotten! And no, I don't want to sleep. Let's go to your house and listen to *Trung Ui Mui!*" Plopping his jungle hat on his head and picking up his M16, he said, "Let's di di mau!"

Stepping out of the building and into its little courtyard, the Kid spied Lieutenant Wilson standing and talking to a group of officers over by the volleyball court, getting ready to attend the briefing. Wilson immediately picked him out, and when he was even with them, he called out, "Stocker," stepping away from the group to address him. "Where you think you're headed?"

"Over to Wen's house, sir. I've been invited over to listen to records."

"Where the hell is Wen's house?" he asked with an edge of displeasure to his voice.

"Oh, don't worry, Ross," one of the other officers called out, "it's just four blocks over. He can't get lost, and what the fuck, he's armed. I used to go over there myself before Wen's boyfriend got killed." He waved to Wen. She waved back. "And, PFC, she's not a whore, so don't go thinkin' you're gonna get in her panties!"

"Yes, sir. I mean, no, sir," the Kid said, correcting himself.

"OK, you can go," Wilson said. "I guess there's no doubt you'll be back for chow!"

"You got that one right, Lieutenant!" The Kid waved in a half salute as he turned to follow Wen.

As they made their way past the Cambodian mercenary gate guards and began walking down the broad but tree-lined street, it occurred to the Kid that he was, in fact, alone with a woman for the first time in absolutely days, just walking along, smiling, and talking little as they made their way amid curious kids who, of course, never missed the chance to panhandle a GI when a target of opportunity presented itself.

241

"Gum, gum, cigarette, candy. GI, you give now. You numba one!" The chorus rose as the gang grew to almost ten.

"Di di mau!" Wen hollered at them, along with a stream of rapid Vietnamese the content of which the Kid could only guess at.

"What did you tell them?" he asked, once the group rapidly disbanded and let them walk off in peace.

"I say I know their names and their mothers and I bet they are all now supposed to be doing chores!"

Wen was beautiful by any standards. She was slender, had a shapely little body, had a tight little ass, and had an alluring face with black hair that cascaded down over her shoulders. *Sort of like Flo's,* the Kid thought, as birds sang in the trees and general quiet pervaded their stroll.

"You wear American-style dresses. I like beaucoup!" the Kid said.

"My boyfriend Roger have his mother send from home. He is dead now for five months."

"Yes, I have heard that he was a very fine officer from men who knew him."

"Very nice man. After him, I say cam bao ya—never again an American boyfriend. When he die, too sad!"

They walked in silence through the second block, the Kid's mind racing from one thought to another. *Is this the last woman I'll ever walk down the street with? Will today be the last time I hear* Sgt. Pepper? *Will I ever find out if Flo's pregnant?*

Could I possibly be lucky enough to get the million-dollar wound? How did I come to be here?

"How did he die?" the Kid's curiosity drove him to ask.

"VC ambush on the Cang Long road," she said. "No big battle, no hero's death, just shot in head. Four GIs die that day. Roger say he catch up with convoy to Cang Long, but VC kill him first."

The Kid thought about how quickly it could all end. If he could know how much time he had left, would he want to know it? No. The answer was a definite no.

Arriving at Wen's house, the Kid ejected the magazine from his M16 and opened the chamber just to make sure the weapon was cleared. Removing his jungle hat, he stepped through the door to the greetings of Wen's mother and one of her aunts. None of the others had arrived yet.

"Men yoi, Hash Shi." They nodded as they smiled, their faces framed by light gray highlights in their dark hair. "How are you today?"

"Excellent, now that I'm here!" he said as he sat down on the divan that took up one side of the low round inlaid teak coffee table. "Bauxi mui? S'il vous plâit!" He pointed at the record sitting beside the turntable.

"Ah, Beatles!" Ba Nguyen said, lightly stepping over to the Victrola to put the record on.

As the tones of the orchestra's tuning up came into the Kid's ears, Wen's aunt placed a Coke with ice on the table in front of him, along with a pipe and a small dish of marijuana. All of a sudden, he was as close to heaven as he could get in that part of the world. He took a long drink, picked up the pipe, tapped in a pinch, and struck fire on the Zippo. "It was twenty years ago today that Sergeant Pepper taught the band to play." He melted away as he quit thinking about the operation tomorrow and just listened to and felt the words come at him out of the little tin horn speakers. At least it was in stereo!

He smoked a bowl and was instantly toasted beyond belief; he had smoked the last of his toothpaste pot three days ago. Interesting, he marveled, *how much better the archaic record player sounds as my mind takes off.* As much as he had wanted to get stoned, once he ran out of pot at Tan An, there really was no physical discomfort with not having it. But in 'Nam, knowing that any second you could get shot or blown up, even if you weren't in a battle in the jungle, was mentally very unnerving indeed. Amid a wave of paranoia, the Kid considered for a second if he should keep his M16 loaded or not. *Might not be polite,* he finally decided.

"What would you do if I sang out of key? Would you stand up and walk out on me?" Ringo Starr sang. "I get by with a little help from my friends."

As if on cue, Ernie and Pete suddenly walked through the door and sang along with the record: "I get high with a little help from my friends!"

"Kid! Welcome back from Tan An!" Pete reached across the table and gave his hand a shake, the two men wrapping their thumbs.

"Pete! Ernie! Hey, guys! Oh gawd, thanks for leaving this stuff! I ran out, and I've been straight as an unfucking hammered nail for the last three days. But I'm off now!"

"So, we were worried about you, Kid, but you go out there, and then nothing happens!" Ernie said. "We've been keeping an eye on you. If they would've hit, we'd have had a brace of jets on top of them!"

"Well, thanks! It's nice that 'a little help from my friends' includes air strikes!"

"Men yoi, Ba dep." Pete gave Wen's mother a hug. "Hey, Wen, he's not getting fresh with you, is he?"

"No, he not getting fresh. Kid tell me he love gul back in America! Got letter today!"

"That's no lie. I've even seen her." Pete smiled. "Why, she's almost as good- looking as you!"

The pair of air force men sat down. The pipe was reloaded and passed as the Beatles played on.

"Fuck me," the Kid said. "I'm so not looking forward to this operation tomorrow. That fucking asshole Wilson had to go and volunteer us for this crap. No speaker team, just straight bullshit. I don't know. Fuck me, because I'm fucked! Plain and simple."

"Well, hey." Ernie exhaled. "It could be like Tan An: they're hitting it right and left, and when you go out there, nothing!"

"That was the rap on you in Nashville," Pete said. "Luck of the Kid! I heard it said more than once myself. Shit, when I saw you were here in Tra Vinh, I even felt lucky! Hell, there's plenty of times the units go out and don't get any contact with Charlie."

"I'd love to believe that!" the Kid mused.

"Picture yourself in a boat on a river with tangerine trees and marmalade skies …"

A plate of Ba Nguyen's scintillating fried potatoes arrived on the table as if on cue, just when the boys were hit with a massive attack of the munchies.

"Cam on u lam, Ba!" Pete bowed. "These are numba fuckin' one!" He picked up one of the hot chips and popped it into his mouth.

"Where's Paul?"

"Oh, the briefing is running long," Ernie said. "He is Major Gillmore's right-hand man, you know. If they change something, he has to redraw up all the maps, so he might not even make it before dinner, which they'll start serving in about forty- five minutes."

"God, the food at Tan An sucks really big donkey dick!" The Kid paused. "Wait a minute, donkey dick is the only animal part they didn't serve!" He wolfed down the homemade chips. "Jesus, these are great!"

They ate the spuds and blew another few bowls of weed. When *Sgt. Pepper* went into the final chord of "A Day in the Life," they rose and said goodbye to the Nguyen family and headed back to the compound for chow.

That night, after dinner, the Kid wrote to Flo and then his parents. He didn't say in either letter that he was going on an operation the next day, but the thought crossed his mind: *Will this be the last letter Flo, or Mom and Dad, ever reads from me?* His mind went back to when Lieutenant Wilson had suggested he write Flo a letter and give it to him to give to her, just in case he didn't come back. No. That idea was still poison; there was one letter he'd *never* write. *Cam bao ya!*

About 2100 hours, a poker game started in the servants' quarters. The Kid's vaunted luck was not with him at cards that night. At about 2200 hours, he finally folded his hand and went to bed. The welcome feel of the real mattress, after a week on the cot, put him out cold. But like everything else in Vietnam that had to do with hot or cold, hot finally won. About an hour and a half later, the Kid woke up with his arms spread out, soaking with sweat.

Was he dreaming? He must have been dreaming; he just couldn't remember what it was about that second. Voices, low voices, followed by a roiling kind of yell that was half victory and half defeat.

Someone screamed, "You son of a bitching muthafucking goddamned no-good sandbagging asshole!" It was a voice to which the Kid could not attach a face.

"Ha! I had the black deuce in the hole from the start, numb nuts. There was no way I was going to lose. And look, now I've got it all!" the equally faceless winner gloated.

The poker game seemed to go on forever, even though everybody knew it was going to be an early call.

"OK, this is absolutely the last fuckin' hand!" It sounded like Heineman was saying it. "And it's going to be seven-card stud baseball Chicago style, but with White Sox—because we can't split the pot on the last hand."

"Why doesn't any fucking body just play fucking poker anymore?" a voice lamented. Must have been one of the losers. "What does all that fucking 'baseball, Chicago, with or without White Sox' mean again?"

"It's seven-card stud, baseball rules, threes and nines wild—and you get another card on deuces. And the low spade doesn't split the pot. White Sox. OK? You in?"

The Kid chuckled as he rolled over and tried to find a dry spot on the bed to inhabit. Lying on his left side and looking out the door of his cubicle, he marveled at how good a mattress felt after sleeping on a cot for a week. A welcome breeze evaporated sweat off both his chest and back at the same time.

Chapter 21

He lifted the barrel of the gun and swung it up until the aiming bead was resting clearly on the center of his target's chest. With his finger wrapped around the trigger, he fired, and was actually shocked when his victim fell immediately from the tree and splatted in the mud of the half-empty irrigation ditch. He rushed up to the edge of the bridge and looked right at it. The poor little bird wasn't dead yet; it was still twitching in the throes of death. My God! He hadn't intended to kill it, merely frighten it. He had actually thought that the bird's feathers would stop the single BB from doing any damage. He hadn't thought that the BB gun he'd borrowed from his friend Billy Critchlow was really capable of killing anything! It was as if the dying sparrow had turned its head to look directly at its murderer and asked with a sad eye, "What the fuck did you do that for?" Then he saw it, some big bird coming to the sparrow's aid, its wings silently flapping as it settled down on the wounded creature. *Wait, it's not a big bird, it's a chopper coming in. Gee, I can't hear the engines making any noise. That's funny, Heineman was saying last night, "You never hear the one that gets you."* The Red Cross on the white background came into focus as the chopper drew closer. *Am I wounded? Is this a medevac? Am I dying?* Then the explosion happened! Or at least it sounded like one.

"Sorry, Kid. Hope that didn't scare ya!"

Unable to see any detail in the dim light without his glasses, the Kid could only guess from the tone of the voice that it was Hollis, who slept in the next cubicle over and whose bank of lockers made up one wall of his digs.

"What the fuck was that?" the Kid asked as he emerged from the sleep state he had finally gotten into after hours of tossing and turning.

"I knocked my steel pot off the back of my locker, and it fell down in your cubicle. Sorry, Kid. Really, I am!"

"What time is it?"

"About zero four fifteen hours. Chow starts in fifteen minutes. We all have to be with our units at zero five thirty, so you can probably sleep for another half hour if you want."

There would be no sleeping. There was an operation today. Except for the Kid's final passing out, there hadn't been any real sleeping all night long! He rolled over and picked up his canteen and took a long drink. Ever since he had been a paperboy, beginning at nine years old, and had to get up at two o'clock on Sunday mornings, he had dreaded alarm clocks. Consequently, the Kid had trained himself to almost always wake up before one went off. He could never go back to sleep now, because once before he had. He never forgot the morning when his dad came into his room, turned on the light, and asked, "Gee, are you back already? You must have set a new record today!" It was five o'clock in the morning and the Kid was still in bed when he should have been half an hour away from being done.

No sleep. Lighting up a Kool, the Kid then located his glasses and surveyed his gear that he had laid out the night before. Hollis's steel pot just missed his M16, as the latter sat, all cleaned and ready to go. *A pox on that cocksucker Wilson for volunteering us to do things we don't have to do and be places we don't have to be!* The Kid silently swore as he listened to other men begin to rise for the day, thanks to Hollis's faux pas, while he remained sitting on the edge of his bunk and let the nicotine start working. The next thing he would do in his life would be to go into combat with the South-fucking-Vietnamese infantry. The reality cloaked him like an ocean wave wrapping around a flat stretch of sand,. His total overall situation had become so pathetic that the Kid almost laughed at himself out loud. *How the fuck did I ever come to be here now?* Reaching up around his neck, he found his lucky beaver nickel—oops, right next to his dog tags. He remembered another of the conversations from the night before, between Wilson and Boar Hog, wherein the Hog was giving a recounting of creative ways he'd seen dog tags attached to a corpse. For that is the only true purpose of dog tags: to have something to jam in the teeth of the corpse so that Graves Registration could record the death, that is, if the dead guy had a head, or around a toe, Boar Hog laughed as he talked about it. Why, he had heard of a guy in World War II who had his dog tag attached to his dick, as it was the only appendage he had left. So how and where did they *find* the dog tag, if everything was blown off? Boar Hog hated it when people dinged his stories.

Walking into the latrine, the Kid took a seat on a shitter. He sat there and thought about what a massive huge flaming dickwad Boar Hog was. The man was the essence of the career lifer from the South. He graduated from West Point so he "could show some Yankee soldiers how it's really done" by the guys "who should have won the Civil War."

The Kid was almost totally dressed when Wilson stuck his head into his cubicle.

"Hey! Ready to go? Wanna get some chow?"

"Sure, why not? The condemned man ate a hearty meal." The Kid rose up to join him.

An air of excitement permeated the compound when they entered the tiny mess hall, which was already almost completely full. Men were preparing for battle by downing some bacon, eggs, toast, coffee, and peaches, and a big glass of milk.

"So, what do you think Charlie's having?" somebody joked.

"Don't know, but he's having lead for lunch!" There was a big laugh in the room.

"With a napalm chaser!"

"And we'll make sure he shares with his buddies!" another man said, keeping it going.

The Kid spied Paul sitting at the table with Major Gillmore and a couple of his staff. As the Kid nodded a greeting, he realized that he was still kind of stoned from the weed they'd smoked the previous night, which wasn't all that long ago. He'd have liked to sit with Paul, but it appeared that Wilson was "suggesting" they sit with Boar Hog. What a way to ruin a perfectly good meal.

"So, you cleaned that M16 up real good, PFC?" Boarz quizzed the Kid as he placed his tray on the table.

"Yes, sir! I only hope to keep it as clean as it is now, sir!" He smiled back at him. "A clean weapon is a happy weapon, sir!" Those West Point boys loved to be called "sir."

"Morning, Ross." The Hog continued to shovel in the chow.

"Morning, Major." Wilson took his seat. "How's everything looking?"

"Just fine. Spencer is going to drive us over to the regiment compound as soon as we all finish chowing down."

Judging from the way you're throwing it down, that won't be too long, the Kid silently surmised. Looking around the room as he chewed, the Kid saw that everybody who was going out was already wearing their pistol belt harnesses, and the officers, their sidearms. The number of Americans actually going out in the field with the South Vietnamese today totaled about a dozen. Four would be with Able, four with Charlie, and four with Delta. There would be another half dozen Americans in the TOC. And over at the table by the door sat Captain Gullen, who would be doing air recon above in a Cessna 150. His code name was Bird Dog.

248

"I gotta get me a pistol," Wilson said, as he, too, had been looking and noticed that he was the only officer in the room who was not carrying a sidearm.

"We'll find you one," Major Howell said from the far end of the table. "I know a guy who has a nine-millimeter Luger for sale. We'll see him when we get back, tonight or tomorrow."

"Tomorrow?" the Kid questioned.

"Yes, this little garden party could easily go two days!" Howell nodded. "If we get them stuck in somewhere, we won't come home tonight and let them di di mau! That's for damn fuckin' sure."

Breakfast was good, but the Kid's stomach had a certain amount of built-up churn going. He'd pretty much gotten over the diarrhea, but he hadn't felt totally right for days. Much of it, he figured, had to be the stress.

Breakfast ended, and the Kid went to prepare. Standing in front of his open locker, he took one last longing look at Flo's picture and put it away. He wouldn't risk it getting wrecked out in the paddies if he had to, for example, crawl around in the mud for some reason, such as if people were shooting at him. He grabbed two unopened packs of Kools and stuck them into his cargo pants pockets. *Wait, better take four, he decided, just in case all that two-day operation crap comes home to roost.* His Zippo he had loaded with fluid and flint the night before. Onto his pistol belt, he affixed two canteens, one above each hip so his arms wouldn't bang them when the walked. To the top of the pistol belt harness, he had Hollis hook up his small pack, where he had his C rations that Boarz had given them and his poncho, for when the rains came, and for something to sleep on should they really end up spending the night in the field.

Then, he attached his bayonet to his hip through the little grommet eyes that had been very cleverly designed by the Department of Defense. He still had some hard wrapped candies that he'd gotten out of Captain Morris's cache, so he put a bunch of them into his other cargo pants pocket, along with some Juicy Fruit gum that he'd gotten from Tra Vinh's little podunk PX. Over his shoulder, the Kid now slung a bandolier of M16 ammo. Eight clips of eighteen-round loads were encased, each in its own little socklike compartment of the surprisingly soft jungle green fabric, and tied off to form the loop. *These finely crafted .223-caliber beauties can all stay right where they are in their clips. That will be fine with me, he silently vowed.*

And then the crowning glory, his steel pot. Pulling a small plastic bottle of insect repellent out of his locker, he stuffed it into the canvas band that held the helmet liner tight on the outside of the metal. Then the whole thing was fitted over the helmet liner, which held the webbing that fit the rig to the head.

249

Plopping it on, the Kid felt the chin strap hit him in the jaw a couple of times as he looked around to see if he had forgotten anything.

Walking out into the compound, the Kid found it is bristling with firepower. Every swinging dick in the place was armed to the teeth. The men who weren't going out on the operation and the Cambodian guards were all on edge because, they always theorized, when the unit was in the field, it was a good time to hit the town. Made sense to everybody. Even Heineman, who didn't like to lug around any more weight than he had to, was taking his M16 over to the TOC. Be a shame to need it and not have it.

Artificial light shone out of the back porch area of the big house, where most of the junior officers had their bunks, and lit up the volleyball court. A throng of officers, mostly captains and lieutenants, along with a couple of warrant officers, stood there kind of pawing the sand with their combat boots as they smoked early morning butts and tried to generate as much optimism as possible.

Wilson spotted the Kid as he walked up. "Stocker! Here's a couple of grenades, if you want 'em."

"OK. Why not?" The Kid put his M16 over his shoulder to free his hands, then he took the dark green baseball-sized killers and held them in his hands, sort of juggling them. "Whoops! Ha-ha. Uh, what's the best way to deploy them, sir?"

"Well now, there's a right big military word from the PFC, yes indeed!" Wilson wryly commented. "If you mean use them, of course, you know from basic training that the only grenade you ever threw?" He changed the real subject of the sentence in the middle of it.

"Yes, it was—is, sir."

"Well, then." Wilson began to pay the Kid a little more attention, as if it would not be wise to give him something that could kill them all and not be sure he could handle it. "If you put these rubber bands on your harness real thick, you can hang them on there." Wilson pointed to his own rig. "Or you can go ahead and hang them on your belt."

"I think I'll just take one, sir. It's not like I'm going to be rushing up front to throw it while we charge the pillbox or anything. But one would be nice. Wouldn't want to come to the war and not have my own hand grenade, that's for sure." The Kid smiled as he handed one of them back.

Wilson didn't always know how to take the Kid. The more they were together, the more he realized that the Kid occasionally made fun of him and continually took more liberties as they established their professional working relationship, such as it was in the middle of the Delta. He was not about to let the Kid turn the whole thing into one big joke, which, given a chance, the Kid would do. Wilson knew he had to maintain command of the only man in his command.

"Stocker, I will not tolerate you doing anything out there today that will reflect badly on you as a man or on you as a member of the United States Army, *an bic?*"

Well, it looks like Wilson is picking up a little Vietnamese too, the Kid observed, which prompted him to answer back in the local language. "Toi bic, Trung Ui Wilson. Yes, I understand."

Just then, Major Gillmore came strutting out the back door of the villa and hollered, "Di di mau, gentlemen!"

With much snuffing of cigarette butts and picking up of rifle butts, and with a breaking-the-huddle kind of growl, the assemblage headed for their places in the grand dance that was called an operation. The one thing an infantry operation generally had in common with surgery was the spillage of blood and the need for transfusions and, occasionally, amputations.

Making their way over to Spencer's Land Rover were the Kid, Wilson, and Major Boarz, and his executive officer, Captain Wallace. His first name was Jerry, but Wallace was known around the compound as Wally. Captain Wally.

"Good morning, PFC," he said to the Kid as they all piled into the vehicle. "How'd you come out in the poker game?"

"Ah, I folded early, so I only lost twenty bucks. Man, I hadn't seen a real bed in a week, and I wasn't going to waste it. But they were still going strong at midnight. I know this because they kept me up. I never really got back to sleep."

The four men settled into the Land Rover as Spencer turned and looked them over. "Got it all? Everybody got their weapon? Nobody's is pointed at the back of my head, right? OK, we're off!"

There were three jeeps and the International going over to the Fourteenth Regiment headquarters compound to meet up with the ARVNs. The streets were not yet thronged with the early morning crowds because of the curfew, but they were certain to be there in another half hour when the time was up. The vehicles navigated with minimal light as their headlamps were mostly covered to observe blackout rules. The covers on the headlights allowed a beam about the size of half a pack of cigarettes to light the way.

They pulled into the Fourteenth Regiment's compound at 0525 hours, just as the ARVN soldiers were finishing loading into their trucks. Their officers stood in a little knot, surrounding Colonel Than, the regiment commander and counterpart to Major Gillmore.

"Wilson, you and your man throw your gear into that truck there on the end," Boar Hog said. He swung down out of the Land Rover and fairly bounded over to where Colonel Than and the others were smoking enough cigarettes to barbecue soe pork ribs.

"Good luck, Kid," Captain Wally said as he grabbed his gear to follow.

"Gee, thanks, Captain Wally," the Kid replied in the voice of Beaver Cleaver. Kid. He called me *"Kid"! I'm still the Kid! What the fuck is the Kid doing in a place like this? How did I come to be in this fucking place?*

Wilson led the way, and the Kid followed him over to the covered deuce-and-a- half that the Hog had assigned them to. When they approached, they could hear the ARVN soldiers playing grab-ass in the back. The Kid couldn't understand the words, but from the tone of the noise the pair heard, he figured it couldn't have been anything else.

The noise it stopped as soon as the ARVN soldiers saw Lieutenant Wilson.

"Mein yoi, boys!" he said as he stuck out a hairy hand and forearm and motioned for somebody to give him an arm up onto the end of the big truck.

Once up, he hoisted the Kid up into the tented back, and they mercifully took seats on the end. Even though the sun was not up, it was still cooking hot, and farther back into the covered truck, the air quickly got much worse. But they didn't have long to ponder that, because almost as quickly as they were seated, the truck rumbled into motion.

"So, Lieutenant," the Kid hollered across the four feet that separated them,

"where is it exactly that we are going?"

"Somewhere up along the Cang Long road. That's all I know."

The Cang Long road. With that, the Kid just sat there and thought about Wen's boyfriend and those three other guys who got killed up there. But too much of that was going to drive him crazy, so he started thinking about WKDA back in Nashville. Wouldn't his listeners shit if they could see him now, riding out to do battle with Charlie, the dreaded fucking Vietcong?

He remembered that night in early June when he had come into the station at a quarter to twelve and went into the control booth where Johnny Wailin was finishing up his shift. The Kid and Wailin had by this time become roommates in an apartment building with a pool north of West End and not far from the Vanderbilt campus. The Kid had learned that Wailin was one strange bird. He was brash and crude, but he acted this way with a know-it-all sophistication that people in general found nothing short of outrageous. That was his on-the-air shtick, that and the fact that he just sounded as if he knew a lot, not that he necessarily did.

"Hey, Kid, here it is! I got two hot dates. This one chick says she's ugly but loves to fuck. Sometimes when they say that, they're really cute! And I'm going over to her house so nobody'll see me and since I'll fuck anything. If she's ugly, I'll just fuck her and get on to my other date!" Now there was a man with a plan. It hadn't taken the Kid long to realize that cardinal rule number one of being a real hot DJ was that you didn't just go meeting up with anything that sounded good over the phone, because if you were to do that, you might live to regret it on the hog farm of life. Never settle for someone you can't be proud to be seen with. "Oh, by the way," Wailin said as an afterthought as he was almost out the door, "your dad called from Colorado and said he'd call back."

Sure enough, no sooner had the Kid sat down and done his midnight show intro, the studio hotline phone rang. When the Kid picked it up, it was his father on the other end. "Say goodbye to all your girlfriends, because you're in the army now!" The Kid was struck speechless. "Curt, are you there?"

"Yes, I'm here."

"Your draft notice arrived today. I saw it and had to open it. I figured you'd want to know."

As the truck rumbled past the rifle range, the Kid lit a Kool. The truck was already full of smoke from the ARVNs farther back in the canvas enclosure, some of whom had been smoking all along.

Now, they were out on the Cang Long road. *Which is scarier,* the Kid pondered, *going out to Tan An or coming out here on the Cang Long road?* Less than half an hour out of Tra Vinh, the trucks came to a stop along a stretch of road that was intersected by what appeared to be a small, old-looking, slightly elevated dirt road leading off through the paddies toward the trees to their left.

The troops quickly made their way out of the trucks and assembled into squads along the road. Point men immediately began moving ahead of the group as three pairs of soldiers trotted out to create the cushion a good point team was supposed to give the main unit to the left, right, and front. Wilson and the Kid walked from their truck at the end of the line up toward the center of the column and soon met the command element coming down the other way.

"The LD [line of departure] is just over there," Wilson said, looking at his map and pointing with a cigarette to a place between the two point teams.

"Excuse me, Captain Wally," the Kid said as they came together on the road, "I wasn't at the briefing last night, so I was wondering if you could explain to me, in layman's terms, sort of a *Cliff's Notes* version, what the fuck we are trying to do here today."

"Oh, OK, I guess I could do that," Wally said. The unit began to head up and move out, with radio telephone operators, or RTOs, tagging along close by the men to whom they had been assigned. Captain Wally's man was right behind him. If a radio call came in or Wally needed the radio, the mouthpiece was immediately slapped into his hand by his RTO. "Today, Able Company, operating with four platoons, is the left side of a pincer movement in conjunction with Baker Company, which is coming south from Vinh Long, and together we are going to try to steer the VC Tenth Battalion into Delta Company, which is going to be lifted to an LZ as soon as it is light out and will move forward to where they'll dig into a blocking position about ten clicks northwest of the LD. All clear now?"

As clear as the mud in the rice paddies that lay before them. "So, what you're really saying is that we are gonna walk out here until we find somebody who wants to have a shoot-out, at which time we will have said shoot-out. And we will chase them if they run."

"That's right, we're going to chase these little bastards all day, and they will run all day and most likely shoot at us all day, and we will never even once see them! We're code named Arrowhead. Baker is Bow; Delta is Shaft; and the TOC is Feather. On the radio, Boar Hog is Arrowhead One, I'm Arrowhead Two, Wilson is Arrowhead Three, and you are Arrowhead Four."

"I have a code name?" "Yep!"

The Kid pondered his new code name: Arrowhead Four. Not as cool as "the Kid." He checked the time and realized a skin rash was developing under his watchband. It was 0615 hours. Time to get started.

When the unit moved out, nobody walked up the small dirt road that led in the direction everybody was going, but rather all the troops stepped into the water- covered squares of rice shoots. Like the paddy dikes around Tan An, odds were quite high that the road was mined. The Kid's boots sank about three or four inches deep into the mud with every step. The palm trees loomed overhead, and the thick brush cloaking the bases of their trunks began to look sinister. It was finally getting light as the command elements of the company arrived at the first tree line, which was set back a little more than three hundred meters from the road. The Kid and Wilson had fallen in behind Boar Hog and Ti Ui Nguyen, Boar Hog's ARVN counterpart. They both had their own RTOs, and when the pair walked side by side, their two antennae made it look as if an eighteen-wheeler was coming down the road. *How ironic,* thought the Kid, *they don't want enlisted men to salute them in the field, but they walk along with an RTO, and his antenna sticks up in the air, marking them like the hole on a golf green. I'll never understand officers,* the Kid decided as he walked along, with every step he took moving farther out into the actual backwaters of the Vietnam War, looking for some VC. He was sweating mentally and physically as the command element stopped and stood there, all pointing, talking, giving radio messages, and making a whole lot of noise and commotion. *How could the VC not know we are coming today?*

Where the command element stood was like a crossroads. Except there were no roads, only paths. The tree line would mark the route the unit was to follow to the first checkpoint, where everybody commenced milling around, lighting up cigarettes, and acting pretty calm. *Apparently, we have a time-out,* reasoned the Kid. Then the radios came to life.

"Feather One to Arrowhead One. Over."

Boar Hog's RTO immediately supplied him the handset. "Feather One, this is Arrowhead One. I read you. Over."

"Roger, Arrowhead One. Are you online? Over."

"Roger that, Feather One. We have arrived on the LD and are deployed and ready to begin. Over." *Pop, crackle, squelch.*

"Roger that, Arrowhead One. I copy you are online at the LD. You should soon have support from Bird Dog, who is just now leaving with the light. Over," came the voice over the square boxlike PRC-25 radio strapped to the Vietnamese private's back. He struggled to stick with Boar Hog as he twisted and turned, examining the disposition of his troops. Turning to his counterpart, Major Nguyen, he spoke, "Move 'em out, Tu Ta!"

Rapidly rattling off some orders in Vietnamese, the ARVN officers and noncoms began motivating their troops.

"OK, Captain Wally." Boar Hog prepared to issue his orders. "Your two platoons go down there to where the trees run north. Sweep up through them and clear them up to where I will meet you, here." He pointed to some spot on the map.

"Roger that, sir," he said crisply, then turned to relay the word to his Vietnamese counterpart, Captain Nguyen.

"This is the real LD," Wilson said as he examined his map. "So, now we're right at the beginning of the operation!" He smiled and took a deep breath. The man was outwardly excited. "All right, Major, we're ready. Let's move out!"

Boar Hog turned his head slowly and looked at Wilson as if to say, *You're ready? Nobody gives a shit when you're ready. I'm the guy who calls ready.* Looking away into the distance, he waved everybody into motion with a gesture akin to cracking a whip.

The ARVN rifle squads now moved into the tree line and made their way like a multicelled beast, carefully advancing along the path that paralleled a little canal that ran down the middle of the foliage. Point men out in front were followed by riflemen, with a M79 grenade team behind them, more riflemen, and then the machine gunner, ready to move forward at a second's notice if needed. Boar Hog and Tu Ta were at the back of the first platoon. After they had gotten a ways ahead, the second platoon, with the Kid and Wilson, began to move forward with the same weapons deployment. Only the second platoon's point men were more at the rear than the front, it turned out, so that the unit had security on six points surrounding the group. The Kid and Wilson were literally at the back of the outfit.

"Shit, goddam, fuckin' crap!" Wilson fumed. "I wanna be at the fucking front!"

"Remember what Boarz said," the Kid softly said to Wilson as they carefully placed their steps.

"What's that?" Wilson asked without turning around.

"That when you least expect it, the back can become the front!" "Oh yeah. And don't you forget it!"

With every step, the Kid kept expecting the jungle to explode in an orgy of gunfire and artillery, but he and the others remained unmolested as they walked through the tree lines, out of one and into another, for about an hour, until they finally came to a collection of half a dozen abandoned grass huts. About that time, Bird Dog could be heard approaching from off in the distance. Soon, the Kid picked up the small, high-winged craft, flying at about two thousand feet off to their left. The psyops pair caught up with Boar Hog as he and the ARVN major were having a discussion of some sort. The Kid, feeling the rising heat, sat down on a patch of fairly safe-looking grass and, after taking a drink, lit up a Kool and tuned in on the conversation.

"The VC live here. We burn huts now!" Boar Hog was insisting. "Deny the enemy comfort!" he said.

"We burn huts, we send up what you Americans say 'smoke signal,' tell VC exactly where we are!" the Vietnamese major objected.

"Tu Ta, they fucking know where we are right now! But when we aren't here tonight, they won't be sleeping all nice and comfy in these huts, because they'll be piles of burnt ashes on the ground!"

256

"Is that your advice, covan?" Tu Ta used the Vietnamese word for "adviser." "Yes, Tu Ta, burn 'em to the ground!"

"OK." Tu Ta gave in and accepted the argument. "Burn huts!" He signaled with a shrug.

"Stocker, you got a Zippo, right?" Wilson turned to the Kid, who, of course, had just lit a cigarette with his lighter.

"Yeah, so?"

"Well, burn that hut!" "Why me?"

"Why not you, Stocker? When I give you an order, you don't go askin' me about it; you do it, PFC, understand?" By the time he got to the end of the sentence, Wilson was bristling, as if the Kid had disobeyed him on some important issue.

"Yes, sir!" The Kid jumped to his feet and, taking the Zippo from his pocket as he walked over to the corner of the nearest hut, flipped open the top of his lighter and cranked the wheel. Raising his hand to the grass roof's lowermost corner, he held the flame until it caught. Then he went to another corner and did the same thing again, working his way around. The blaze took off as if the hut had been treated with kerosene. It burned a very orange color, and the smoke built up with the flame until a black plume, indeed, told the Cong that their foe was certainly at the source.

ARVN moved swiftly among the half dozen huts, torching all of them. They had searched them all beforehand, finding only a picture of Ho Chi Minh and a homemade knife that looked as if it had been fashioned from an old auto support flat spring.

"Arrowhead One, this is Bird Dog. You copy? Over."

Boarz held out his hand, and his RTO fixed him up. "This is Arrowhead One. Bird Dog, I read you loud and clear. Over."

"Is that you burning huts, Arrowhead One?" "Affirmative, Bird Dog."

"Roger your smoke. I will be in the neighborhood for a bit, checking your front. Just came from the mine dump. The shaft should be set by now. Over."

"Roger your last transmission, Bird Dog. Out," Boarz said. He dropped the receiver from his hand and consulted his map. "Delta Company has arrived at their blocking position and are digging in right now," he said. "We need to get moving!"

The point men were long gone up front, the way the unit had to follow, and soon the smoking huts were behind them as they edged through the trees and bushes. In places, the foliage was really thick, but in other places it opened

257

up a bit and the Kid could see about thirty to fifty meters in distance. Now the psyops pair was right with Boar Hog and Ti Ui Nguyen when the radio again came to life.

"Arrowhead One, this is Bird Dog. Over." "I read you Bird Dog. Over."

"Five armed men are making their way just inside the tree line to your ten o'clock. I'm preparing to maneuver and fire rockets at them to mark their spot. Over."

"Roger, Bird Dog. That's not Arrowhead Two by any chance, is it?"

"Negative, Arrow One. I've got Arrowhead Two marked clear, tagging behind you in line. I am preparing to roll and fire. Over."

And with that, Bird Dog, who was visible from the ground, dropped a wing and kicked his tail around. A pair of rockets streaked off his wing pods and disappeared from sight beneath the tree line. The report of the explosion soon came back to the unit. Now the Kid was really sweating. The enemy had been spotted.

"Come on, come on!" Boarz waved to Tu Ta behind him. "Let's move it, Tu Ta. Get your men rollin'!"

The pace through the trees hastened as the unit moved forward to make contact with the armed men. *That is, if they have not all been killed by Bird Dog,* thought the Kid. He chambered a round as he and Wilson moved forward. Boarz turned to Wilson and signaled for him to come up to where he was.

"Ross, you take the right squad with Ti Ui Nguyen. We know there's Charlies on the left, but watch our right while we try to find them, got it? Stick close to Ti Ui and his RTO so we can stay in touch. Move out!" And with that, he turned and hustled off.

The look on Wilson's face was classic, like a boy who had come downstairs on Christmas and found a pony under the tree. "You heard the man, Ti Ui, let's get movin'," he said as he turned to the grim-looking ARVN lieutenant, who relayed the command to his troops.

The Kid decided he didn't want to stand next to Ti Ui, Wilson, and his RTO, so he moved down the line a little to his right, as it appeared to him that was the direction they were supposed to go. Not too far in the distance, he could hear rifle fire commence. The enemy has been engaged. His M16 was held at the ready in front of him, the barrel sticking up at a forty-five-degree angle as he strode along, wondering how worried he should be about trip wires and booby traps hidden within the boot-top-tall grass growing within the tree line. *It sounds like Captain Wally's platoons might be getting into it.* His breath was coming a little faster now, and his thoughts were ripping through his head like an 8 mm film projector on rewind: Flo. His first girlfriend. His first bike. The day he broke his ski at Winter Park. *Is this how your life flashes before your eyes before you die?* he actually wondered right before it happened.

It came from the front left, not with a bang or a real loud noise, but rather with the unique low sucking sound a bullet makes as it cuts the air. It whistled by his right cheek so close that the Kid felt its heat. *Holy fucking crap! I just about got my head blown off!* The Kid slammed his body to the ground. Lying there in the foliage on top of his M16, his breath came in gasps and his body was awash with a colossal adrenalin rush that simultaneously captivated and terrified him. It was the strongest physical reaction the Kid had ever experienced in his life! He was a cherry no more. This was not your Tra Vinh Airport sniper. The Kid had just been the intended target of a marksman. And for that matter, he still was!

Slowly lifting his head, the Kid watched a couple of the ARVNS rise to kneeling positions and begin to return fire. Rising to his knees, he tried to see what was going on. Bringing his M16 to his shoulder, he wanted to fire but had no target; all he could see was the backs of the ARVN's heads. So, he held off, but rose immediately to a crouch. A couple more isolated *pop-pops* took place, and then everybody on both sides opened up. The individual sounds of rounds being fired and passing overhead melted into a wavering clatter board of commotion unlike anything the Kid had ever imagined. He instinctively refound the ground. More rounds blistered right over where he'd ended up flat against the soil of 'Nam.

With that, the Kid realized he'd better move it or lose it! Crawling as fast as he could, he moved forward about fifteen meters to a group of three tree trunks in tight proximity. Wilson had gone for the same tree, and now the two of them lay there on the ground as more rounds ripped into the palm bark about three feet above their heads.

Chapter 22

"Are you fucking happy now?" the Kid half screamed over the din of fire. "This is what you fucking wanted?"

"Oh fuck yes! Yeehaw! We're in it now!"

And how! The Kid felt a bump on his back and, turning around, discovered that Ti Ui Nguyen's RTO was hunkered right down there using them for cover. *Ah, I see why.* Ti Ui Nguyen was himself there to their right, farther around the trees from the fire. Bullets continued to find the trunks of the trees that partially protected them.

Then the Kid saw a strange sight. Four ARVN privates came casually walking forward in the hail of bullets, calm as senior citizens on a dog walk. "Jesus H. Christ, take a look at that!" He tapped Wilson's shoulder and pointed to the men.

"You mean Jesus H. Buddha!" He laughed. "It's that Buddhist philosophy." Wilson hollered, "They don't care if they die, because they believe they will advance on the wheel of life to a better place."

Amazing. Look at that! Fuck. I'm a Buddhist, but I don't wanna die! The calmness in their faces is incredible! They have accepted their fate, whatever it might be. If they live after this day or die in the next second, they don't care. The Kid had considered himself to be a Buddhist since his senior year, when he'd taken the Boulder High School course on comparative religion, taught by Mr. Trow. But living in Western society, he had met few real Buddhists. And now this was a display of faith on a level he'd never before seen. Ha! He had to chuckle as he thought of Pat Bowen, the bespectacled, slightly petite redheaded teenage girl from Nashville who had designated herself as the president of his fan club. Once she found out he was a Buddhist, she never missed a chance to try to convert him back to Christianity.

"You're gonna need Christ in 'Nam, Kid," she'd bemoan. "I read where there's a lot of people who see the light in a foxhole."

"Pat; why can't you imagine that there is something going on in the cosmos other than what is written in one book?" is what he used to tell her. But now he was here and he was having a religious experience all right! *Thank all the Godheads of nirvana! I'm still alive and not gone on to that better life yet!*

Still, the four men amazed him with their expressions of complete calm. In fact, they looked plain fucking bored as bullets whizzed between them and where the group of men were huddled by the base of the tree. *Hmm, when you're time's up, it's up, and if it ain't, it ain't!*

Not returning fire, the four men stood, discussing among themselves, with pointing and other gestures, where they should go next.

Suddenly, Ti Ui Nguyen jumped out from behind the trees and began screaming orders to them. With his encouragement, they broke into a trot, but about twenty meters ahead, they dropped on their stomachs and began to lay down automatic fire in front of them. Taking advantage of the cover, Wilson motioned to the Kid, Ti Ui, and the RTO to rise up and move forward, away from the protective tree cluster, and lie down behind them. The Kid could still not see any of the enemy, who continued to shoot in their general direction. He was beginning to realize that it was possible that the enemy could not see them either and that all the lead that was flying every which direction might not be aimed at any one soldier in particular but rather might be a reaction to an unseen action.

After about ten minutes of firing, there was a lull. With much screaming of what could only have been Vietnamese expletives, Ti Ui Nguyen got his squad to advance another thirty meters ahead, at such an angle that they found themselves at the edge of the tree line looking out into the paddies.

"Arrowhead Three, this is Arrowhead One. Do you read me? Over." The radio spoke to them. Wilson rolled over and took the handpiece from the RTO.

"Arrowhead Three, I read you. Over."

"Roger, Three. A helicopter gunship should be arriving our location any second. When he lays down the fire, we need to move up and out into the paddies. Over."

"Roger, One, I read you. When the air cover arrives, we move up and out!"

"Roger, Arrowhead Three. Now, I know you're an artillery officer, but I hope your time in the Hundred and First got you ready for this. Over."

"Roger, Arrowhead One, I am ready. Over!"

"Roger, you're ready, Three. So, here's the skinny: my squad will cover you to advance one paddy dike, then you cover me while my squad moves one dike ahead of you. Got it? Over."

"Ten-four, One. Three, out!"

Above the sound of sporadic rifle fire, the Kid detected the *pop-pop-pop* of helicopter blades: the gunship was arriving. Casting his eyes skyward, he picked it up, coming from behind them at their four o'clock, about a thousand feet in altitude. It was a Huey. As it intersected the tree line they were in, it turned parallel and dropped down in elevation, then the door gunner opened up, the puffs of smoke from his M60 clearly visible from the ground. About fifteen seconds later, the group experienced a rain shower: brass shell casings falling from the sky.

"Let's go, goddammit!" Wilson rose up and screamed at Ti Ui Nguyen, "Shoot, move, and communicate! It's time to move!"

The Kid, looking at Ti Ui's expression, could see that he was not happy, but still the lieutenant ordered the squad to emerge from the tree line. Looking across the open paddies, the Kid shuddered as he saw a distance of about two hundred meters to the trees on the other side. The ARVN troops advanced, shooting from their hips as they rushed forward, trying to take advantage of the covering fire from above and from Boar Hog's squad on their left. When the gunship got to the end of the line, it did a 180-turn and flew back up the line with the other door gunner blazing away, pouring lead into the trees, hoping to make the VC take cover as the ARVNs leapfrogged their way across the deadly open space.

It felt like the suppressing fire was working to the Kid as he plodded along, running as much as his fatigued condition and the mud in the paddies would let him. He could see in front of him that Boar Hog's men had arrived and were getting into the trees.

When they finally caught up, Wilson and the Kid were surprised to find out that this particular tree line wasn't more than thirty meters wide and that staring out the other side was another area of open paddies with another tree line on the other side. Only the distance was more like four hundred meters— twice as far as they had just come.

"There's no way they could have gotten across there that fast without the chopper or Bird Dog seeing them," Wilson reasoned. "They gotta be hidden over here somewhere. We should search these bushes for them!"

"Arrowhead Three, Arrowhead Three, come in! This is Arrowhead One! Over." The amazing little RTO was still right there, looking scared but doing his job.

"One, this is Arrowhead Three! Over."

"Three, this is Arrowhead One. What is your location? Over."

"One, we are at the edge of the tree line. The VC here are gone. Over."

"Roger that. Arrowhead Two is moving up through the perpendicular trees to our left, and he thinks he's got them on the run in there. We are also at the edge, and we must move forward across the opening so we have a chance of cutting them off before they break into the next tree line. Do you copy? Over."

"Roger your last transmission, but I believe the men who were shooting at us are still concealed here. Request permission to try to flush them out. Over."

"Negative, Three. Our orders are to advance across the paddies and take control of the tree line to our twelve o'clock. The gunship will supply us cover once we're halfway across. Same MO as before, Three: we shoot, you move; you shoot, we move. Do you copy? Over."

With a clear look of disappointment on his face, Wilson accepted his orders. "Ten-four, I copy. Over and out." Dropping the handset, he turned to the Kid and Ti Ui. "Well, you heard the man. Let's get ready!"

After Ti Ui Nguyen commanded his charges to spread out, they moved from the trees back into the open paddies. This time, none of them were running, only trotting. Looking to their left, the Kid could see Boar Hog's squad coming out at the same time. Together, the line was making steady progress across the open rice fields. At the halfway point, right on cue, the Huey came flying parallel down the tree line directly overhead, and when the men on the ground could hear his M60 laying down the cover, Boar Hog's squad ran forward, ducked behind a dike, and opened up. Wilson and Ti Ui both hollered encouragement at the tops of their lungs as their squad broke into a run and quickly covered the ground up to the next dike, where they began firing their weapons, putting down some cover of their own. The Kid was lagging behind, feeling kind of flushed as he made steady progress to close the gap.

Sensing they were finally close enough to cause some hurt, the VC really opened up on the advancing ARVN line. The splashes of bullets fired at them could be seen hitting the water among the short, newly planted and slightly separated shoots of rice. *Or is that the brass falling?* About twenty meters off to his right, the Kid saw an ARVN get hit and fall to the ground, grabbing at his left shoulder as his M16 flipped up in the air and splashed into the murky water amid the rice. *Holy fuck! Is he dead? A medic is right there. It is surprising that more men aren't getting shot!*

Plodding along, trying to keep up, the Kid was becoming winded. *Got to stop smoking those fucking cigarettes!* The act of pulling each foot out of the mud to take the next step was making his thighs ache, as if he'd been skiing all day long at Arapahoe Basin. Now about six meters out, the Kid's left foot became stuck in the mud and caused him to stop in his tracks. *Shit!*

I'm stuck in some deep fucking shit! Now he knew how the ducks felt. Just then, a burst of rounds hit the water about two feet to his left. *Oh my God! Automatic weapon!* Desperately trying to free his foot by shifting his weight to his right foot, he was chagrined when his right foot, too, became stuck. Now a burst hit to his right. The gunner had overadjusted. Seeing this, the Kid dropped to his ass and, from the seated position, flopped down on his back in the brackish water. *Oh God! I hope I'm not sticking up too high because of this backpack and the canteens!* A burst of fire came directly over him. If he had been standing or sitting up, he'd be gone! *I hope the fucker thinks I'm dead! If those rounds would have been an inch lower, they would have gone straight up my nose!*

His M16 was completely submerged but still in his grip as he sort of twisted to his left side and rocked forward, finally freeing his feet. He crawled while trying to hold his rifle up out of the water as he frantically moved to take cover behind a paddy dike about ten meters in front of him. He was still three dikes, or easily sixty meters, from the tree line. Not more than fifteen meters to his left, an M79 grenadier knelt down and, in quick succession, popped three rounds into the trees right where the bulk of Boar Hog's squad was trying to get in.

Lying there half submerged in swampish water and covered with mud, the Kid reached to his side, unsnapped the canteen from his left hip, took a long drink, and then looked up and down the line. Boar Hog's squad was even now shooting its way into the tree line. The Kid watched Wilson, Ti Ui Nguyen, and the rest of the squad rise up and, shooting from their hips, follow them in. *This is fucking hard work!* Struggling to rise and catch his breath, the Kid knew he had to catch up with the squad. Nearing the spot where he estimated Wilson and Ti Ui had gone in to the foliage, he was ecstatically relieved that the firing from the tree line had stopped. Within the trees, he could see the command element squatting on the ground and talking on their radios.

"Roger that, Flint One. We got four Whiskey India Alphas." Boar Hog was there, breathing pretty hard himself.

"I read you, Arrowhead One, but do you have any body count in the tree line? Over." Major Gillmore's voice was recognizable over the radio.

"Well, it appears that we've got a couple of blood trails, but we haven't seen any results yet. Of course they're gone. But we need a medevac. Over."

"Arrowhead One, I'm having the gunship land and pick up your wounded. Over." Just then, a horrific explosion was heard from deeper within the tree line.

"What the fuck was that?" Wilson ducked even lower than he was already ducking when it went off. He didn't have to wait long to find out as the PRC-25 radio immediately supplied the answer in Vietnamese.

264

"Some of third squad set off a mine! It was suspended in a tree," Ti Ui interpreted. "We have four more wounded, two seriously!"

With a look of disgust on his square, sunburned face, Boar Hog signaled for his handpiece. "Flint One, we're up to seven Whiskey India Alphas. We might still need a medevac. Over!"

"Uh, Arrowhead One, maybe an ARVN in an hour. The gunship is all we've got right now, so you'd better find a way to fit them in. Over."

"Roger. Out." Boar Hog looked at Ti Ui and shook his head. "You should go kick some ass over at regiment so those helicopter boys will fly a medevac into a contested area! We both know they got three of 'em sitting back there, doing nothing but waiting for this. And then they don't want to come!"

Not understanding, the Kid looked to Wilson with a questioning expression.

"The ARVN chopper pilots won't fly into a contested area to pick up wounded," he explained. Hmm, the Kid hadn't known that.

"But don't worry." Wilson immediately sought to put the fear he saw appear across the Kid's face to rest. "We're Americans. We can always get a medevac."

"That's right," affirmed Boar Hog. "If you get hit, I'll have you out of here in twenty minutes!"

How reassuring, mused the Kid, who had recovered his breath enough to want a cigarette. As he lit up, it occurred to him that never at any point in his short life had he even seen a dead person. He had never yet attended a funeral or in any other way encountered death. In all likelihood, it appeared that fact might quickly change.

About fifteen minutes later, the medics had collected the wounded near the command element. The two ARVN privates who had been closest to the blast were messed up pretty bad. One had wounds on both shoulders; his steel pot had protected his head and saved his life. Whether or not he would keep one of or both his arms was another question. The second one must have been looking away, because he was lying facedown and his wounds were up and down his backside. Of the other two ARVNs who had been wounded by the mine, one was able to walk, and the fourth one had a bandaged knee. None of the three ARVNs who had suffered bullet wounds were in terribly serious of condition. The one whom the Kid actually had seen get hit in the shoulder was conscious. A second one was nursing a hand wound, and the third had gotten shot in the right calf and had a tourniquet tying off the loss of blood right above his knee. As the Kid's gaze worked its way down the row of men being prepped for evacuation, part of him wanted to be among them. *I'd take that hand wound! Fuck yeah, I'd pay a finger or even two to get out of this fucking hellhole alive!* But in the final analysis, he was plain glad he hadn't been hit. Yet.

The tree line appeared to be secured. The plan was to bring the Huey gunship down about two paddy dikes out and hustle the men out to it.

"Flint, this is Arrowhead One. Over."

"Arrowhead One, go. Over." The voice that came back was that of Heineman.

"Flint, we are prepared for the medevac with the gunship. Over."

"Roger, Arrowhead One. Why don't you go ahead and pop-smoke about twenty meters out of the trees to show your exact ten-twenty? The Bird is circling. I understand he has a pretty good fix already. Over."

"Roger, Flint. Out!"

"Arrowhead One, Flint Four, over."

"Flint Four, go. Over," Boar Hog replied to the transmission that had come back after he had said, "Out."

"Arrowhead One, how is Arrowhead Four doing? Over."

Taking a look at the Kid, who was sitting on his butt, smoking a Kool, caked in mud, and soaked completely, Boar Hog replied, "He's dirty but not dead. He's doing OK. Out!" Dropping the handset, he signaled for an ARVN with a pack to come over to his location. Then he dug out a smoke grenade and placed it in the soldier's hand. "OK, Tu Ta, tell him to go pop this bad boy on the first dike, then let's move 'em out!"

The ARVN trotted out of the trees out to the first dike and popped the smoke. It came out red.

Over the radio, the engines of the chopper could be heard behind the transmission. "Gunner one, I copy red smoke. Over."

"Affirmative, gunner one," Boar Hog spoke into his radio.

Seeing that the ARVNs could use some help carrying the four men who were currently incapable of walking, on makeshift stretchers fashioned from ponchos, the Kid slung his M16 over his shoulder and stepped forward to help. As they walked out into the water, the chopper came down. It was just like his dream that morning, the only difference being that the chopper didn't have a red cross on its nose. The ARVNs had taken the time to check an intersection of paddy dikes for mines and now directed the chopper to set down on it, so as not to mire its skids in the mud.

266

The blades whipped up a miniature storm of paddy dike water, which was raining sideways as the ARVNs struggled against it, advancing up to the doors, where they began pushing the wounded into the Huey as the two door gunners pulled. When they had five of them packed in, the gunner turned to the pilot, who nodded to go ahead and take on the other three; they looked pretty small and light compared to your typical US soldiers. Not waiting for anything, the chopper lifted off while the gunners still moved about, trying to secure and settle their hospital-bound load.

Walking back to the command element, the Kid could hear Boar Hog loudly swearing as the noise of the helicopter rapidly disappeared.

"Now, goddammit, Flint One. That's one of the main fucking reasons I wanted a medevac! Over!" Boar Hog was fuming.

"Don't go getting a case of the ass with me, Arrowhead One. I can't order those bastard ARVN medevacs to fly, and you know it. Over," came Gillmore's voice.

"What gives?" the Kid inquired, stepping up next to Wilson, who was now smoking.

"While the chopper was on the ground, four VC made it across the paddies to the next tree line!"

"No fucking shit? Did you see them?" "No."

"So you still ain't seen one, right? How you gonna kill what you can't see, sir?" "It's only a matter of time, Stocker."

Checking his watch, the Kid discovered it was high noon, the perfect time for a gunfight. Looking around, he observed many of the ARVNs eating the items they had brought for lunch.

"That looks like a good idea," he said loud enough for Wilson and Boar Hog to hear.

"Yeah, what the fuck? Go ahead, PFC. It's going to be fifteen minutes before we get it together to go after the fucking VC we could have killed if the fucking gunship hadn't been playing ambulance!"

Unbuckling his pistol belt, the Kid swung the pack around where he could get at it. Soaked and caked with mud, it looked more like Anasazi pottery than army issue, but inside, his C ration meal was still pretty clean. Taking the turkey and noodle meal out, along with the pound cake, plastic silverware, four-pack of Marlboro cigarettes, and little swatch of toilet paper, he took his P-38 can opener to the top of the main course. God, was he ever hungry!

"After lunch, better take a couple of salt tabs. We've sweated beaucoup today!" Wilson said between bites of his own C ration meal.

As the Kid ate, he kept seeing the faces of the wounded men as they were being loaded onto the chopper. The ones who were still walking had been kind of smiling as they clambered aboard. Then he thought about the four men who were walking through the bullets earlier when he, Wilson, Ti Ui, and the RTO were cowering behind the trees. Now he was a combat vet. He had faced enemy fire and hadn't chickened out and ran, but would the day ever come when he paid it no more mind than those four had today? *I doubt it.* Looking at his M16 lying there at his feet, he realized it probably needed a quick going-over to clean it back to a safe level. All the stories he'd ever read in *Time* and *Newsweek* about M16's jamming came flooding back to him.

While eating, they monitored radio traffic from Captain Wally's platoon, who were still chasing the VC through the trees. It seemed that the little bastards weren't running quite as fast as they had done earlier in the morning and might even have been showing the spunk to put up a real fight. Captain Wally now had two— no, make that four—Whiskey India Alphas, so the ARVNs had taken eleven casualties today to the VC's zero. The only thing going for the ARVNs was that none of the wounded had yet died. Only a matter of time.

"OK, Ross." Boar Hog came over to where they were resting. "Here's the deal. We're here on the map." He pointed to the spot. "Baker Company is coming down this way and is in contact. We need to get into this next set of trees, or the Charlies whon Baker is driving will just scoot on through and will hook up with Wally's Charlies and di di out the back door. We'll lose our one chance to drive them into the blocking position, which is set up in the next tree line to the west. Wally is back over here, but he's having trouble now keeping up his pace. He thinks they've figured it out and won't let him get to the bottleneck."

"OK." Wilson followed along with undivided attention.

"So, we gotta get moving right now and secure this next tree line. Ready?"
"You bet! Stocker, pack it up. We're movin' out now!"

Rising slowly to his feet, the Kid picked up his pistol belt and hefted it onto his back. "Shit! I gotta clean my M16? It's filthy!"

Boar Hog shot him a glance of disgust. "Well, PFC, you should have cleaned it before you packed your piehole. We've got five more minutes. Why don't you field-strip it to the barrel and dump some water down it to clear the mud, then check you magazine housing for mud, clear it, put the weapon back together, and let's get the fuck out of Dodge!" With that, he stepped off smartly, hollering orders to anybody within earshot.

268

Made perfect sense, and that is exactly what the Kid did. It took him less than three minutes. Soon, they were again walking to the edge of the trees and looking across to the next tree line. *This is fucking insane! Tree line after tree line! Does it ever end?*

The Kid could only think it was supposed to be the same deal as last time. "Shoot, move, and communicate," Wilson was ranting as they approached the edge of the sheltering vegetation. "We're working it pretty good!" He was loving it. "Hog says this one is going to be tougher because the blocking position is in the next tree line behind this tree line, and he thinks Charlie has figured it out."

"Why do you say that?" The Kid immediately seized on this new information. He didn't think it could get any hotter, in terms of either the temperature of the air or what they had experienced thus far today. *Anyway, I don't want it to get any hotter, but what am I gonna do?* "What's coming down?"

"Hog says Wally's meeting stiffer resistance; they've taken three KIAs! The tree line he's been working intersects with this one down there." Wilson pointed out of the trees, across about a hundred fifty meters' worth of wind-rippled rice paddies, to where the two tree lines came together at a right angle. As they crossed the opening, the tree line that Wally was fighting in was three hundred meters to their left. "See there, those tree lines are like a crossroads. Makes it possible to take one and run for miles and miles." This whole plan hinged on Wally's platoons getting to the crossroads, so Charlie'd have to go north, into the blocking position."

Oh, great! Three of the men I'm with just got killed. Imagine how I'd feel if three Americans got killed here today? Fuck, that is what Waterhouse and Imbach have to deal with. God! I can't imagine what it would be like to be going out as a private grunt having to walk point with an American unit!

Wilson and Ti Ui's RTO began receiving traffic. They paused to communicate.

"Arrowhead Three. Over," Wilson answered.

"Three, from recent radio traffic, it sounds like Wally's taken three KIAs and has a bunch more wounded. But he's still moving up! We gotta get over there and see if we can take some of the heat off Wally and his boys. Over." The voice of the Hog resonated. "We had our rest, so this time, instead of playing hopscotch, we are going across as a line, supplying our own cover all the way. Ti Ui is going to put down his machine gunners and M79'ers halfway to cover us on in. Got it?"

"Roger your transmission, Arrowhead One. We await your call. Out."

Somebody tell me that bastard Boar Hog didn't just say we are all going to go running across these paddies shooting our asses off until we get into the trees on the other side.

"Stocker, you ready? Isn't this why you joined the army?"

"Fuck no," the Kid said in the most calm and matter-of-fact tone he could muster.

"No fucking choice is what you got! We're goin', PFC. As soon as the word comes on the radio, we're goin' over there!" Wilson gestured by pumping his arm with his M16 grasped in a hairy fist.

"Arrowhead Three, this is One. Over." "One, I read you. Three, over."

"Go, go, go!" Boar Hog yelled.

"Di di mau!" Wilson hollered, dropping the handset and giving encouragement to Ti Ui to order his men to advance, which they did, pouring out of the trees and into the paddies, directing rifle fire in a high arc toward the tree line a football field and a half away.

When the Kid came out, he was already behind the phalanx on ARVNs, who were moving up rather quickly, given the heat, the mud, and the weight of their loads.

I feel like I'm in the fucking Seventh Cavalry! But at a quarter of the way across, the VC opened up from the tree lines and let it be known that somebody was home and not wishing to receive company.

As the rounds once again began buzzing around him, the Kid was wanting to hit the ground and low-crawl, but then Wilson and the squad would be too far ahead—and Wilson had been harping at him all day long about keeping up and not acting like some fucking chicken. So, he did keep up with Wilson, half slopping along, half trying to move with a purpose, dodging this way, dipping that. *This is fucking ridiculous! If I get shot, then I get shot! So be it! All this ducking and diving is a royal fucking waste of energy!* He should have been getting a second wind after lunch, but the Kid was instead fast becoming winded. Here it was, about three hours into his first real battle, and the Kid had come to a major catharsis; once engaged, it was not possible to be hysterical with fear for any length of time. *Hmm, if I got shot dead right now, it would actually be a relief! The only thing it would do would be to spare me more of this fucking bullshit! If I get killed, I'm free from this! Just don't let me get wounded and paralyzed from the waist down or neck down so I can't have sex anymore for the rest of my life. I'd rather be dead!*

Halfway out, the M60 machine-gun crew from Boar Hog's squads set up on a paddy dike and began to lay down some sweeping cover fire. Almost as quickly, Tu Ui's machine gunners threw down and followed suit. As they approached the position, slogging through the mud and heat, the Kid stood behind the machine gun and, along with Wilson, marveled at the smoothness of the crew who served the weapon. The gunner was blazing away, chopping jungle with his hot lead spray, while the ammo man kept the belt running clean. And when the can was empty, the ammo man hooked the gun up with another. A third guy was totin' extra cans of ammo. They were all a regular well-oiled machine!

The Kid gazed at Wilson and back to the gunner with a *Gee, I'm tired. Let's let them do the work* kind of expression. Then the pair almost simultaneously realized the volume of fire that was being directed at the machine-gun position by the VC. "Uh, sir, I think it might be safer if we got down behind the paddy dike."

"Oh yeah! That thing is so loud, you forget that some of the shit is coming back at us!" With that, they dove behind the fifteen-inch-high, two-foot-thick mud retaining wall about ten feet to the left of the gun and flat fucking belly laughed, juiced on adrenalin from the last, particularly close volley of bullets.

The Kid remembered thinking that from here on out, with the M60's in support, it should be easy. But no such luck. When the majority of the men arrived at the row of paddy dikes where the machine gun was set up, they stopped and took cover in response to a much increased volume of fire pouring out of the trees.

And so there they lay, half submerged in water, four squads of President Thiệu's finest, along with their four American advisers, a total of approximately fifty-four men, pinned down by absolutely not more than a dozen men inside the tree line.

Then came the escalations. Like most of the day, the Kid found this part to be scarier and more thrilling, in a warped sort of way, than it was damaging, when the RPG, that's rocket-propelled grenade, came screaming out of the woods. *The sergeant of the Charlie who shot it is probably kicking his ass because he missed everything!* Its smoking trail marked an arc, its highest point actually being where it crossed over the paddy dike behind which the ARVNs hid, and exploded what must have been twenty-five meters deep into the tree line from which they had just emerged. Well, the general feeling on the field was that a paddy dike could stop an AK-47 round, but it wouldn't be stopping no stinking RPG! Soon after the RPG flew, the radios crackled—and thank God that Ti Ui's RTO was right there for Wilson to get the word.

"Arrowhead Three, this is One. We got an air strike coming in on these boys, if they wanna play rough. It should be here in approximately three minutes. I suggest we view the shindig from the trees behind us. Over."

Looking up and down the line, they saw that part of the ARVN had begun to fall back as the machine gunners stayed to provide cover. Then, the M79 boys laid down a pattern of four rounds each at the edge of the tree line, which was stretching their maximum range, giving the M60 crews a chance to fall back.

Back inside the trees, the Kid was exhausted. Going for the canteen, he didn't think he would be able to take the water in as fast as he was sweating it out. Wilson had chosen to gravitate down about thirty meters to their left, to join in discussing the situation with the Hog and Ti Ui Nguyen. There commenced more looking at maps and pointing fingers. *Are they discussing what they're gonna do or who they're gonna blame?* Kneeling and using his M16 as a crutch upon which to lean, the Kid tried to recover his breath. He noted that most of the ARVNs were neither breathing as hard nor sweating as profusely as he. Most of them rested in the standard "gook squat" position. He tried it. Not bad! The ARVNs looked on, nodding their approval.

A lull came over the field. None of the ARVNs were shooting, nor was there any fire coming from the VC on the far side of the paddies. Wilson was hurrying back to his location as the Kid took out a Kool and lit it.

"Any minute!" the lieutenant said excitedly as he also took to the kneeling position next to the Kid, Ti Ui, and their RTO. "Two Thunderchiefs are on the way! This is going to be choice!"

Sure enough, from off in the distance, from across the ultraflat rice bowl of Asia, the faint roar of jet engines came approaching. Standing and searching the sky, the Kid picked them up, coming from the right, too high to be in attack mode yet. The pair of sonic blasters came across their front, behind the tree line that held the Charlies, as if to survey the situation.

"Be a crying shame if they fucked up and bombed us," the Kid ventured, a little bit nervous at the prospect of his first air strike in a real combat situation.

"Happened all the time in World War II and Korea." Wilson twisted to watch the jets peel off, first one and then, a little later, the other, and bank turn as if they were on a big oval, coming around for their first run. "When they come in on the attack, they'll be flying right over Delta Company."

All the ARVNs moved with them to the front of the tree line to watch. The Kid thought about where he had been just a few moments ago out there in the middle of the paddies, unable to advance. *Now, let's see, we've got airpower, you muthafuckers. Try this on for size!*

Now turning on the far right end of what would be their attack loop, and having achieved a spacing out, the first jet rapidly approached at an altitude of about five hundred feet. As it neared the place where it would need to release its bombs to hit the dug-in VC, the Kid could hear small arms fire coming up out of the trees.

The VC were trying their hardest to knock down that jet! When the bombs actually released from wing, the small arms fire stopped, and the company watched in awe as two black bombs fell as the jet pulled up. From their vantage point of 250 meters from ground zero, the Kid thought the explosions should have been louder. But what most amazed him was the fact that the instant the bombs had exploded, some of the VC were out of their holes, pouring small arms fire after the fading jet, and yes, some of the small arms fire they heard was being directed at the second jet, which was arriving very quickly on the heels of its partner to deliver its own ordnance. Another pair of bombs came off the wings, and more pulverizing of the tree line took place. But the VC were still kicking over there, the fire coming out hot and heavy as the jet roared off.

"Is this fucking cool or what?" Wilson was ecstatic. "Come on, boys! Kick their fucking asses! Yeehaw!"

The pair of jets each made another pass, dropping bombs. Then, on their third pass, when the first jet released its load, the projectiles looked much bigger than the earlier ordinance.

"Napalm!" said Wilson in an almost deadpan tone.

"How do you know that?" "It always tumbles."

Sure enough, the Kid watched the tumbling canisters of flaming death fall unerringly toward the tree line as the small arms fire stopped and the Cong went into their holes.

From his vantage point, standing behind a group of ARVNs who had edged a slight distance in front of him out into the paddies to observe the air strike, the Kid witnessed the napalm igniting in a horrendous fireball that at once seemed to grow to the height of a four-story building, while rolling in a wave of liquid fire for a good two hundred meters. Even in the heat of the jungle, and with the heat of sweat from exertion, the Kid and Wilson could only look at each other as they felt its pyrotechnic heat. Oh my God! Who could survive that?

But sure enough, the second the fire collapsed to the ground, there were VC on the other side up and dishing it out with small arms even as the next jet was this time even quicker upon them. Down in the hole they went—escaping the screaming jet, the tumbling nearly football-shaped projectiles. Then came the horrific roiling orange explosion, and this time when the fireball lit up the tree line, it silhouetted the soldiers who stood in front of the Kid, and he knew.

It's the soldiers in the fire! The ones I've been seeing since Aspen, when I took the LSD and saw this in the coals of the fire! This is it! This is what I saw and have been seeing in the tips of cigarettes and that dream!

The soldiers had their backs to him. They were black against the orange burning wall of fire. That was why there were never any faces. The Kid was standing away from it. *If I only had fucking clue one as to what any of this shit means! I don't know if I'm going to live or die, but I know I feel very much alive right now!*

The jets each made one more pass, this time both strafing the area with 20 mm miniguns, and the VC were still not ready to give it up and run, apparently not even from them.

"You gotta admire their guts," Wilson said. "Anybody who'd go after a jet with an AK-47 is pretty fucking ballsy! We know we've got our work cut out for us!"

No fucking shit! So you can only imagine how unhappy the Kid was when Boarz hollered out his orders. "All right, let's go! We should have been halfway across while they were doing that last strafing run, Tu Ta! Di di fucking mau, for God's sake!"

With that, the entire company charged out of the trees and dashed across the opening, firing madly with everything they had at their disposal. When the Kid finally arrived at the tree line on the other side about a minute later, there was no shooting and there were no dead VC, nothing there but limp foliage. The part of the tree line near him hadn't really been charred, but it steamed in the jungle humidity. "I wonder what it looks like at ground zero where the napalm hit," the Kid said to Wilson, who stood winded and catching his breath. On the edges of the napalm pattern, many of the broad leaves had spots on them from the droplets of flaming jelly, which had only spattered on them.

"Fuck! You'd think there'd be beaucoup dead VC over here after that, but there ain't shit! Over." The Kid listened to the Hog talk into the radio to the TOC.

"You mean to say you're in the tree line and there ain't shit, dead or alive? Over."

"Affirmative, Flint One. But you know, sir, that napalm sucks up all the oxygen out of the vicinity when it combusts, and there might be a dozen of 'em dead in their holes. Over." Boarz was acting as if he were a truant in trouble with the principal and was hoping that the man in charge would like his story.

"Just got word, Arrowhead One, that it appears Captain Wally's Charlies have also di di mau'd. Tell me they didn't all get away. Over."

For a split second, Boar Hog's hand dropped slightly from his mouth, and he looked at Tu Ta, who held up two fingers. "Flint One," he continued the transmission, "we just found some blood trails, two major ones, so I think we can officially say we've got two VC KIAs out of this. Over."

"Roger, Arrowhead One, two VC KIAs. I wish I could say good work. Over."

The Kid didn't see any blood trails, and certainly he saw no dead VC. But they were certainly gone and had broken off the engagement. In fact, he hadn't seen a Charlie all day. *Are they still hiding here in holes? Have they run away to a spot down the tree line to fight another day? Are they going to pop up out of the ground and start shooting at us in the next instant? Who the fuck knows?*

"Arrowhead One, this is Flint One. Apparently they have slipped containment. The plan is blown. Let's call it a day. Bring them back in. Out."

That was the first good news the Kid had heard all day!

Chapter 23

The old French plantation house looked pretty good to the Kid as Spencer's International pulled into the driveway at about 1800 hours. Riding with Boar Hog had been a pain in the ass because he was pissed that the operation hadn't worked as planned and he was sure that Major Gillmore was going to blame him for Captain Wally's shortcomings.

"Could have been worse." Wilson was trying to console Boar Hog as they began to unload. "We could have had American wounded." The lieutenant had stated a very powerful positive. "It was nobody's fault. Now I'll race you to the beer!"

With a sly look, old Boar Hog's ears definitely perked up at the mention of the sacred brew. Beer certainly sounded like a winning idea to the Kid. That and a bowl of Pete's green!

Out of the corner of his eye, the Kid spotted Hieneman approaching from behind the service building with a big grin on his face. "All right, Kid! You lived! We'll have to tie on one hell of a cherry-poppin' celebration for you tonight!"

The Kid's mind was racing from the experiences of the day, what with almost getting killed or wounded literally countless times. "Paul! What a mind fuck out there!"

"No shit! No way to explain it, is there?"

"Fuck if I know. Hope I don't get a lot more chances to find out. But don't look now, Wilson is jazzed out of his fucking brains for it!"

"Yeah, some guys are like that. I could see it in him even before you told us what he said about wanting to kill somebody but not go to jail. But what the fuck," he said, emphasizing that the Kid hadn't realized he had something behind his back. "I've got something guaranteed to take your mind off it. Not one"—he pulled out a pastel yellow envelope with his left hand and then fanned it—"but two letters from some broad named Flo!"

"Oh, wow!" The Kid let his rifle sag to the ground as he extended his hand to take the letters.

"But Jesus Christ, tell her to use a little less perfume! Handling those things is making my eyes water!"

The Kid held the yellow envelope to his nose and inhaled deeply. "Nectar of the goddess!" Over Heineman's shoulder, he spotted Ernie and Pete.

"Hey, Kid!" hollered Pete, as they came walking out into the early evening light.

"Did you enjoy our air strike? You were pretty close from what we hear!"

"Oh fuck, shit. Uh, wow, it was incredible! I was like across the street! And Charlies were shooting at those guys before and after every pass! Blew my fucking mind!"

"Yeah! We heard the pilots reported they took some hits there," Ernie reported,

"but they were minor! I'd hate to be around when one of 'em goes down!"

"That napalm is the scariest fucking shit I have ever seen in my life! Fucking death by cremation!"

"Or suffocation," added Pete. "And, uh, how many Charlies did they finally say we bagged for the day? Paul, what's the official number?"

"Well." Paul scratched his chin. "It's classified information, pertaining to only those who were directly involved. … Oh, that's you guys!"

"Right!" The three wanted to hear.

"The reported count says six VC KIA. Kid, how many did you personally see?" "None. I never even saw any of the blood trails."

"Odd, since four of them allegedly happened in your area of the field." Paul pulled at his chin as if he had an imaginary beard.

"I didn't see one Charlie, dead or alive. And if you'll excuse me, I've got a shower to take and some heavy-breathing reading to catch up on!" He saluted with Flo's letters and headed for the hooch.

That night, the beer flowed, the pot burned, the dinner was eaten, the pool was shot, and the two new letters were read and reread. And never were any of these things enjoyed as they were in light of the Kid's new status as a full-fledged combat veteran.

"Did you shoot off any rounds?" Paul asked at one point.

"Nope. Fuck, my piece was so filthy after the first time in the mud, I kinda cleaned the barrel and magazine port, but didn't want to have to shoot it." He paused and took a long pull on the cold beer. "Wasn't going to waste government-issue ammo if there wasn't a real target to shoot at. That and I

277

was just a touch back from the front of the squad, like at least a couple of feet," he said with a straight face, then burst out laughing. *It's good to be alive.* "But seriously, folks, with the way that that RPG came out of the woods and went over us all, I could've been back in the tree line and gotten it! One thing I learned is, who the fuck knows?

Why does one guy get it and not another guy? When the shit is just fucking flying everywhere, and I do mean ev-ery-where, you don't know what the fuck you're gonna do until you do what the fuck you do!" After a pause, he asked Paul, "Does that make any sense?"

"Yeah, I've asked myself those same questions! I just hope I never have to kill anybody." Paul paused. "I haven't had to yet!"

"Yeah, me too." The Kid nodded as the pair stood at the bar amid the celebrating crowd. "So far, so good. … Oh, look, I'm coming up on one month!"

"I used to go out every time Major Gillmore went." Paul got a weird look in his eyes. "And we saw plenty. I used to get pissed at Gillmore, like you're pissed at Wilson, for getting us into places where we could've been easily killed." Paul flicked the ash off the end of his cigarette. "I guess these officer types have waited all their lives for this, and they mean to have it."

"Yeah. He and Boar Hog were totally immersed! It takes a certain kind, I guess, to disregard safety and common sense. I can tell Captain Wally doesn't like it. But I will tell you this." The Kid indicated that he wanted Heineman to lean closer so that he would not have to convey this point to anybody else in the vicinity. "The rush I got off that first bullet singeing my cheek was bigger than any LSD experience or any pot or uppers or anything I've ever taken in my entire freaking life!"

"Oh, I know just what you're fucking talking about!" Heineman responded, his face lighting up under his dark, short, very curly hair. "Me and Gillmore were with Ti Ui Nguyen—you know him! The major who's out at Tan An—and we got caught out there without a perimeter because the Charlies were fighting us hard at sunset. So, when we first tried to set up our command post, we did it next to what must have been the equivalent of the VC command post because a half dozen of 'em jumped up out of their holes! I've never seen so many tracers going off in every imaginable direction. Ours were red and theirs were orange, and they were crisscrossing. That's how dark it was. When you can see the tracers starting to glow and you don't have a perimeter, that's a real adrenalin rush."

That was something for the Kid to think about. All day long, he had dreaded the thought of having to stay out in the jungle in a combat position in

278

the middle of the night, but now here he was, drinking beer and smoking pot over in the barracks.

"Stocker!"

It was Wilson who called him out of his thoughts.

"You didn't leave anything out at Tan An of great importance, did you?"

"Uh." He thought for a second. "No, sir, I didn't leave much of anything. Why, are we not going back?"

"Oh no, we'll be going back, but first we've been called into Sa Dec for a briefing on some things coming up in the near future of which we are surely a part."

Is this good news or bad news? "Yes, sir! When do we go to Sa Dec?"

"On the twentieth, in two days, so we're going to hang out here. Then we might be a week up there. So, there's nothing out there you can't live without for a week or two?"

"Nope."

"Well, you haven't had a day off in a while, PFC, so it'll sort of be like a break! Consider yourself on pass till the twentieth."

Good news! Very good news indeed!

"Hey, Kid! We're up at pool, and look!" Heineman said. "We're playing the Hog and Howler!"

Chapter 24

The paddies looked different today. From his vantage point in the door of the Huey chopper as it vibrated along at about three thousand feet above the rice fields, the Kid had a deeper understanding of what he was looking at. It wasn't just some flat open expanse of shining quilted watery paddies going off into the horizon; it was mud, snails, leeches, Charlies, mines, and booby traps.

His mind wandered, freed from the heat by the rush of cool air at that elevation. It was the only air-conditioning he had experienced in the past three weeks. The date was June 20, which, other than being the summer equinox and the longest day of the year, was also the last day of his first month of his tour. *God, is it hard to believe I've only been here a month! It feels like I've been here for fucking ever. So I haven't been laid for one month and two days. That also feels like double eternity! What I wouldn't give for Flo to be at the end of this chopper ride.*

While lolling around Tra Vinh for two whole days, the Kid had gotten another two letters from Flo. But neither of them had the news he was looking for. *Is she pregnant or not? When am I ever gonna fucking find out?*

He was looking forward to Sa Dec. He needed a bunch of essentials at the PX, such as toothpaste, razor blades, soap, cigarettes, and pot. He'd have to score some fucking pot of his own. He just never thought about it in Tra Vinh.

Everybody had so much and they all gave so freely that there was no need to have it, and the Kid, for some reason, just kept forgetting to buy some from Paul or Pete or Ernie. But he swore, his hand resting on the M60 door gun, that he was going to score some pot in Sa Dec. They had better everything in Sa Dec: better movies, better chow, better whorehouses. And Heineman had said that was the place to score!

The Kid looked across the chopper compartment to Lieutenant Wilson, whose steady gaze toward the ground indicated that he was off in his war comic neverland.

He'd have to shake the brass. Shouldn't be too hard since he hadn't seen an officers' club for nearly three weeks.

The Kid was starting to be an old hand at chopper flying. It was no longer such a big deal. It was just how you got around. You couldn't drive from place to place because the VC owned the highways in the rural areas. Good fucking luck out there, what with all the mines and snipers. So, as the chopper settled onto the pad at Sa Dec International, the pair smoothly exited the bird as some other men moved forward, dragging gear from the shack, on their way to who knew the fuck where.

"I'm going over to my billet, and you'll be in the same one you were last time," Herschel told the Kid once they were out of the backwash of the chopper's whirling blades. "As a matter of fact, I'm gonna go to headquarters and find out when we have to be present, so I'll just come over there and get you when I need you, OK?"

"Yes, sir," the Kid said, lighting up a Kool to smoke on the way over to the air force hooch. He even remembered some of the guys, including Herrick, the man who, until the Kid showed up, had never been beaten to the bunker, and Sergeant Redd with his black horn-rimmed Buddy Holly glasses. To the Kid's right was the Lucky 9 Club, and out in front of it was where they set up the movie projector when it got dark and showed some entertainment for the battle-weary troops. *Wonder what they're showing tonight?*

Walking in the door of the air force hooch, the Kid immediately found Herrick sitting on one of their three couches.

"Hey, if it isn't the Kid. It is the Kid!" he said, rising to his feet and extending his hand. He was clad in the standard off-duty shorts and flip-flops, with no T-shirt. "Good to see you again!"

"Good to see you again!" the Kid said, dropping his gear on the floor by the dark green couch.

"Oh, you can't sleep in the same bunk you did last time. Another one of your mates from the armor company has already grabbed it, Tom Roberts. Haven't met him yet, right?"

"Roberts? No, I haven't met him yet!" said the Kid, very much hoping that someday he would, from the things that had been said about Roberts back in Can Tho.

"Yeah, he's sitting outside on the bench over on the bunker side." Herrick indicated with a tilt of his head. "You can take that bunk there," he said, gesturing over his shoulder with his thumb.

Throwing his gear on the sheetless mattress of the lower bunk and laying his M16 behind it, the Kid walked on out the back door and turned to his left. Taking a couple of steps down the concrete walkway, he stopped at the edge

281

of the building, parallel to a still shaded wooden bench that faced the bunker, and saw a black-haired, clean-shaven man with a very strong chin stretched out and leaning back, his hands locked behind his head, listening to AFVN Saigon. "A- breakin' rocks in the hot sun. I fought the law and the law won." It was the Bobby Fuller Four.

"Hey!" the Kid called out. The soldier rocked forward and looked in his direction.

"Are you Roberts?"

"Yeah, I'm Roberts!" He rose to his feet.

"Well, I'm Curt Stocker, not only a member of your unit, but also a fellow graduate of the hallowed halls of DINFOS!"

"Wow! Imagine meeting a DINFOS grad here!" He laughed. "Pleased to meet you." They shook hands. "Don't tell me, you guys are in for the big meeting!"

"Yep, bigger than squat!" The two of them sat down. The Kid lit a fresh Kool. "So, how's things in the armor? I went out for the first time about three days ago, but there weren't any loudspeakers involved!"

"And there won't soon be!" The two of them laughed again. "We went out the other day, and I got wounded. Look at this!" He turned to show his left arm, which was marked by a horizontal red gash less than half an inch long across the meaty part of his shoulder. "I'm gonna get a Purple Heart!"

"Gee, do I say congratulations or 'That's too bad'?"

"Well, congrats is OK, considering that if it would have hit me in the throat, it could have killed me."

"No doubt. So, what happened?"

"Well." Roberts lit his own cigarette. "We were moving along, and we came to this spot on the road we were driving up. The VC dropped some mortars on the lead tracks and stalled everything else where it sat. They blew up the first one, killed everyone in it, and then hit the second one and set it on fire. The smoke was everywhere. I got off my track and stood there looking, when a group of seven ARVNs came staggering out of the smoke, uniforms and skin just flat fucking smoking and smoldering. They were in shock. And then a round came in and exploded a ways in front of us, and I got it in the arm."

"Wow." The Kid pushed his glasses back up his sweat-slicked nose. "That makes what we were in the other day sound tame."

282

"You must have been on that clusterfuck out northwest of Cang Long." Roberts apparently knew what was going on around the unit. "Where the VC Tenth got away again!"

"Yeah. It was snafu all the way. But I got shot at for the first time, so now I can quit worrying about that."

"So, what are you going to worry about instead?"

"Whether or not I knocked up my fiancée before I got on the jet just about a month ago. Should've heard by now." The Kid flipped his cigarette at the butt can, and it hit off the rim. "Not hearing must mean there's nothing to report yet."

"Fuck. That should be the least of your worries! She's pregnant or she's not. Either way, you still gotta even make it through your year. That's what I've been worrying about"—Roberts flicked his cigarette at the butt can, and it went right in—"ever since Tet. Things were pretty quiet until then."

Tom's transistor radio had continued to play on the bench next to him. As he picked it up, the Monkees came on, singing, "I thought love was only true in fairy tales, meant for someone else, but not for me …"

"Let's see." The kid unbuttoned his fatigue shirt and let it hang open. "I got to DINFOS in November of last year, so how many classes ahead of me were you?"

"Well, considering that it takes about four months to push guys through both the journalism school and the broadcast part of it, it must have been just two classes. Tony Dow was a couple of classes in front of mine!"

"They were still talkin' about him when I was there." The Kid nodded and had to push his sunglasses back up his sweat-slicked nose.

"Yeah! I'm a believer, I wouldn't leave her if I tried …"

"So, you got a picture of this chick you think you might could have knocked up?" Roberts said in a friendly manner.

"Sure." The Kid pulled the Polaroid out of his pocket and handed it over to him.

"She's cute. Wouldn't be the end of the world to have to marry her!"

"Don't I know it! That's my plan, even." He put the picture away. "Where you from?"

"New York. Long Island, actually."

"Oh, New York! I've loved the Yankees all my life!"

Roberts turned and looked at the Kid, caustically appraising him, his eyebrows raised as he stared. "I've hated the fucking Yankees all my life. I'm

283

a New York Giants fan, even when they moved to San Francisco. I'm still a Giants fan. Willie Mays is the best fucking player in the history of the world!"

The Kid knew immediately he had touched a nerve.

"And the 1962 World Series. Why couldn't McCovey's ball gone through? Why? The Yankees have won so many times. Why couldn't we win just that once?"

Sour grapes! "That was quite a Series either way, wasn't it?" The Kid appealed to their mutual love of the game.

Just then, Lieutenant Wilson appeared from around the corner, having come through the hooch, looking for the Kid. "Oh, there you are!"

It was the field, so the enlisted men did not have to rise for an officer. "And you must be Roberts! I'm Lieutenant Wilson." He extended his hand as Tom rose to his feet to shake with him.

"Nice to meet you, sir."

"Welp, Stocker, there's nothing happening until tomorrow morning, so you can take the rest of the day off—again. You're gonna get lazy and begin to think I don't know how to work an enlisted man, but what the fuck, just don't get into any trouble. I'll see you in the morning."

"Yes, sir. Thank you, sir." The Kid smiled. "What are you gonna do?"

"I heard that there's a pretty good whorehouse over on the north side of the river. I'm going over there with some chopper pilots." The lieutenant rubbed his palms together.

"That ought to be fun. Well, see you tomorrow after chow, sir." The Kid sat back down as Wilson disappeared around the corner.

The Kid looked at Roberts. "You got the day off too?" "Yep!"

"What do you wanna do?" "Got any pot?" asked the Kid.

"No, as a matter of fact, I don't."

"Then, I suggest we go find some!" The Kid beamed.

"Excellent idea. I tell you what, why don't we go out to the front gate and ask some cyclo drivers? If they're anything like New York cabbies, they can get you hooked up with just about anything you want."

"What are we waiting for?"

They went inside and got their M16's. After making sure their extraneous gear was locked up, off they went, out the door of the hooch, down the walkway, and out into the open area just inside the Fourteenth Regiment gate.

284

Just as they emerged in the area, they saw Lieutenant Wilson and two other men leaving in a jeep. Wilson apparently did not see them.

Immediately on the other side of the gate, there was a queue of cyclo drivers and their vehicles waiting for fares to emerge from the army post. Some had conveyances pulled by motor scooters; others were hooked to bicycles; and some had the passenger compartment in the front of pedaled conveyances, with the handlebars directly behind the passengers' heads.

The Kid and Roberts looked over the waiting drivers, wondering which would be their ticket to herbal bliss. Realizing that the two well-armed GIs were looking for a ride, a few of the drivers got up and began to motion them toward their rigs.

Roberts walked up to a small cluster of about four of them and said, "Can sa?" The drivers looked at each other and back to the GI, trying in vain to understand what he was saying.

"Can sa!" the Kid said to another cluster of drivers, making a smoking motion with his finger up to his lips. "Bic *can sa*?"

Then, one driver, who sported a scraggly mustache, a very dirty light blue shirt, baggy gray shorts, and ragged tennis shoes with no socks, stepped forward with a look of enlightenment on his face. Putting one hand to his mouth and holding the other as if holding a pipe, he said, "Tok fin!"

Looking at each other, the Kid and Roberts realized the man was making a smoking gesture.

"That's good enough for me," Roberts said. They smiled at the man, nodded, and stepped into his aluminum rig that was attached to a Honda motor scooter.

Stepping up over his bike, the driver stomped on the starter lever, and the little machine sputtered to life, expelling a sizable cloud of carbon monoxide into their faces. Gunning his engine with the hand throttle, he swung his rig around, and they headed out over the south bridge, leaving the island.

They passed by the businesses that lined the river's south side and rode along into the residential neighborhoods of Sa Dec.

Looking over at Tom, the Kid made the comment, "This fucker could be taking us anywhere, and all I've got is the clip that's in my gun!"

"Well, if it looks like we're leaving town, we'll make him turn around," Tom said. They bounced along over the rough streets of the river town, both of them knowing that a sniper could be anywhere, anytime.

Soon, the driver came to a stop by a rather large-looking house about four blocks back from the river and a few blocks down from the bridge. "You wait," he said in English as he stepped off his bike and entered the house. A minute later, he came to the door of the white-painted two-story rambling dwelling and, with the wave of an arm, motioned for them to follow him.

Rising from the cyclo, the pair crossed the street and walked up the three steps to the broad porch of the rather well-to-do-looking house by Vietnamese standards. There were four kids, two boys and two girls, their ages between three and four, and ten and eleven, watching them come up the steps. A mama-san woman and what must have been her older mom stood to the side of the door as the cyclo driver continued to motion to the Kid and Roberts to follow him.

Entering the house, they were led through a front living area and through a door into a large but dimly lit back room. There, the cyclo driver left them, closing the door behind himself. The Kid immediately switched to his regular glasses. As their eyes adjusted, he and Roberts discovered two old men reclining on a raised bamboo sleeping platform about ten feet square. One sat on his butt, almost upright but lying back against a mound of pillows. The other one was stretched out on his left side with his head resting on his hand. The platform bed had a canopy over it with while muslin mosquito netting tied curtain-fashion to the posts at its corners. In addition to the pillows against which the one old man reclined, there were more pillows lined the platform, making kind of a pit. The two old bearded guys motioned for the Kid and Roberts to take off their combat boots and join them on the platform. Placing their M16's to the side, the two sat down on the edge and took off their boots, then sort of crawled over to sit across from the old geezers, both of whom looked like the spitting image of Ho Chi Minh. A radio played music from one of the local Vietnamese radio stations very low in the background, the twangy, stringy kind of singsong Asian traditional thing, with a woman wailing at counterpoints to the music.

"Men yoi." The Kid nodded as he situated himself with his ass in front of the pillows, making sure his sunglasses were cached safely in his left breast pocket.

"Men yoi." The man on their left nodded to them, smiling slightly, as if it took an effort to move his lips.

The room around them was rather large and dark, but as their eyes adjusted to the light, it seemed like a storage area with the elevated bamboo platform taking on the feeling of an island floating above the white-tiled floor.

"Can sa?" said Tom, cutting right to the chase, mentioning the object of their search.

The two old men looked at each other, apparently not understanding the American's rough Vietnamese, but the man on their right pulled out an ornate wooden box from behind and, placing it between them and the Americans, flipped it open.

"Holy shit!" exclaimed Tom, looking at the contents of the box. "I think we're in an opium den!"

"Wow!" the Kid said slowly as he examined the box, "An opium den in Asia. Imagine that!" The box contained a row of five large, round wooden pipe bowls, each about four inches across, with a small metal-lined opening in the center that was about the size of a pencil. An ancient-looking wooden pipestem with metal screw fittings, which was about a foot long, lay in an angled grove in front of them. In the one of the box's compartments, there was a selection of wooden- handled needle probes, like the kind a student would use to tack down a frog for dissection in biology class. In another there were some small smoke-colored glass vial containers, each about the size of a tube of ChapStick.

"Have you ever done opium?" Tom asked.

"No, have you?" "No. Want to try it?"

"Yeah. What the fuck? We're here! They might still have some pot. We can try to ask them later." They looked at each other and laughed. "I've read about the Opium Wars and the opium culture in China and stuff like that. Shit, I say let's go ahead and see what the big deal is!"

"OK," Tom said. The two of them nodded their approval, indicating that the men should proceed with whatever it was they were going to do.

Watching with rapt attention, the Americans observed the Ho Chi Minh look-alike on their right lean forward and, with his skinny arm, take one of the bowls from the row in the box and screw it onto the pipestem. Setting it aside, he took a needle probe and a glass vial from the box, setting both these things in front of him. His buddy aided him by pushing over to him a small glass alcohol lamp that burned with a low blue flame. Unscrewing the little black cap, he set it aside and took the probe and dipped it into the bottle. Withdrawing a shimmering drop, he held it over the blue flame, and soon it began to bubble and cook. It looked like a miniature heart pumping and beating as it boiled on the tip of the needle. Then, he took the piece of fluff and kneaded it down on the metal part of the pipe bowl, rolling it on the edge until you could hardly tell there was anything there. Dipping it back into the bottle, he added another drop to the one he'd already cooked and proceeded to cook the whole thing again. This step he repeated six times, until he had a pea-sized glob on the end of the needle, which he then stuffed into the metal ringed opening of the bowl. Turning to his companion, he extended the pipe to him. Apparently, the second man was going to show the American boys how it was done. Turning the pipe over on the lamp, he hit it. His already shallow chest looked as if it was caving in completely, but soon it expanded as he drew the smoke into his lungs, where he held it for a few seconds before exhaling the oddly sweet-smelling smoke. He then turned and offered the pipe to the Americans.

"You first," said Tom.

"Oh, thanks," said the Kid. He rolled over onto his side and swung his body around to a position that would make it possible for him to place the bowl over the flame. "Here goes!"

Drawing on the stem, he could feel the smoke heating up as he persisted. Soon, the smoke was expanding in his lungs to the point where he coughed it up and commenced to have a hacking fit, which greatly amused Roberts.

"Cough, cough, gag! Gawd! I thought I wasn't getting anything at all, and then all of a sudden, it just sort of exploded in my lungs!"

The old men were slightly amused as they grinned at each other. *Rookies!* They didn't even have to say it.

"That's what happened to me the first time I smoked pot!" He grinned. But before Tom could try his first hit, the cooker had to do up another ball of opium, dipping and burning until he had a pea. This time, the pipe went first to Tom.

"I think I'll take it easy after seeing your experience," he cautiously said before he commenced to hit the load. He was pretty smooth, taking in the smoke and holding it for about fifteen seconds before blowing it out.

Then the pipe went back to the Kid, and this time, he succeeded in keeping his hit in.

"Feel anything yet?" Tom inquired.

"Nope. Did you get off the first time you smoked pot?"

"Yeah! It was right here in 'Nam, and I got off like a fucking space shot! Why, didn't you?"

"Yeah, I did, but it was awhile before I noticed it." "When did you first smoke it?"

"In October of 1966, in Boulder. Yeah, I got off that night. And later, it was the same with LSD. You can be tooling along after you take it, say, about forty-five minutes, and you don't feel anything, and then all of a sudden, at forty-six minutes, bam! You're tripping your brains out!"

"Wow," said Tom, exhaling another hit. "I've wanted to try LSD since I read the Timothy Leary interview in *Playboy*!"

"Ha! That's exactly what happened to us! Me and my friends, we read that and went out and found some in Boulder. That old joke 'I only get *Playboy* for the articles' was, for once, true—and I keep telling everyone it's true!"

The men kept cooking it up and passing the pipe. The Kid and Roberts continued to take hit after hit, until the Kid finally declared, "Yeah, I'm off on this stuff. I haven't had anything to smoke yet today, so I think I'm feeling what it is really like! What time is it?"

Tom looked at his watch. "Thirteen hundred hours! Funny, we missed chow. But I'm not hungry!"

"Me neither! Maybe that's why those guys are so skinny! Fuckin' A, it feels like we've been here for hours!"

"So, what do you think of the high?"

The Kid thought for a few seconds, evaluating it. Pot was nice and mellow, was music-enhancing, and generally made you feel good. The Kid was definitely off, but he was getting mixed signals from the drug. It was putting him in a place where he was wide awake, but way back into his mind, sort of away from his eyes.

"I don't know for sure yet. You know how your high can change after a while? I want to see what happens. It's like when I took LSD for the first time on New Year's Eve up in Aspen on a ski trip. I thought it should be over, and I wanted to come down after about six hours, but it just kept going!"

"So acid's cool, huh?"

"Oh, fuckin' A! It is so flipped out, the things you see and feel. The first time I heard 'For What It's Worth' by Buffalo Springfield, I was on LSD in the back of Greg Honeyman's car, which had speakers in every corner. Blew me fucking away!"

When Tom lit a cigarette, both Vietnamese men indicated they'd like one too, so the Americans lit them up. Soon, one of the mama-sans appeared with tea, and the pair sipped and smoked into the afternoon.

"I'll tell you one thing," the Kid said after a long silence. "The rush I got when that slug went past my head really close for the first time put all this crap to shame!"

"Yeah, I know what you mean! God, was that too fucking heavy or what?"

"You know all that shit about body count they're always talking about on TV back home?" The Kid hesitated. "Well, as no student of statistics, I can safely say that half the operations I've been on had a falsified body count!"

Roberts could only smile. "No shit! That's SOP! Being out here in the field has been a real eye-opener for me. Back in Can Tho, you don't see shit, so you want to come out here. But once you're here, you realize how fucking easy it would be to get killed and how good it is back in Can Tho."

"So, it's not bad, huh?" The Kid frowned.

"Well, I never once got shot at from November to Tet, when I finally saw some stuff that counted as real action. Fucking A, it was like the New Villa was the Alamo. We were completely cut off from the rest of the city and thought the Charlies were going to come and get us any second."

The Kid took a puff of his Kool as the old men fetched the third bowl in the box, retiring the second one so it could cool down.

"Look at that," said Roberts. "Gotta keep it cool, like the barrel of a machine gun!"

The Kid ascertained that, indeed, an opium high was quite different from any high he had previously experienced. His initial outing on opiates was definitely an event, not one that he had planned.

"So, you know they make heroin out of this stuff?" the Kid said, turning to reach for the ashtray to grind out his spent butt. Then he turned to Tom. "When I first smoked marijuana, I did it with the intention of proving a person could smoke it only once."

Roberts looked back at him, waiting to see if it was a joke, but the Kid kept a straight face. "Seriously?" Roberts asked.

"Yeah. I never even heard of pot until I was in eighth grade. Then a new kid in school from New Orleans, Ken Challier, bought it up in speech class when we were studying debate. The teacher was looking for suggestions for topics, and he said we should debate whether or not pot should be legal. So, I'd never even heard the word *marijuana* spoken until I was fourteen. Then, my best friend and debate partner, first at Boulder High School and then at CU, said to me, 'Hey, some of the guys got some pot, and we're gonna smoke it tonight. Want to try it?' Of course I said yes, but I asked him why he even wanted to try it. He said, 'Because I heard some people talk about it, and it sounds cool!' So, off we went."

Now the pipe was ready again, the Kid was offered the stem. He took the hit and held it for as long as he could. "Whoa," he said as he exhaled, "this shit is wicked! It's like when I talk, the words form in my brain and come out through my mouth, but there isn't any sound until the words are about two feet from my face!"

"Yeah, this stuff is something different!"

"So," the Kid began, "you know Boujold, right?" "Boujold? Yeah, of course. What about him?"

"He said you got busted for writing articles for your college newspaper. Where was that?"

"Lehigh University, in Allentown, Pennsylvania."

"And some ROTC army major turned you in to the Pentagon, and that's how you ended up out here?"

"Yeah, that's about the size of it. Poor fucking Boujold has been wanting to come to the field since I've known him, and he was about to get sent when I got busted and got sent instead."

"Yeah, the day I met him, he was fighting with the first sergeant about it."

"Ozelle?" Tom scoffed before he took another toke and held it in. "Now there's a shrewd muthafucka! He owns the whorehouse across the street from the New Villa, and he's making so much fucking money on the black market that it should be, and maybe is, a crime! That's who I worked for as company clerk before I got nailed. It was almost like a death sentence, being sent to the Armored Cav! God, were they pissed at me. When the captain told me, he said, 'Roberts, it looks like you've got too much time on your hands. I think we need to send you someplace where you'll be a little busier.'"

"So, Boujold got your old job?"

"Yeah. Can you imagine Boujold out here in the field? The first time he had to run for it, he'd probably have a heart attack!"

The Kid chuckled. "Yes indeed, he is a little on the hefty side of the scale!"

"For as smart as he is, why he wants to come out here is beyond stupid. I guess he just hates the standard bullshit of battalion so much that anything looks good to him. And of course, he wants to wear a jungle bush hat."

The pipe continued to come around. The Kid was amazed at how much he and Roberts had in common. "Well," he said, "they didn't even need a reason to send me out here! But what the fuck, here we are. What are you gonna do?" The Kid took the pipe and kept toking. Upon expelling his hit, he said, "I'll have to write the folks and tell them I've seen a little action. I've been sparing them that. So, you've seen a lot of action, huh?"

"More action than I ever cared to see, that's for fucking sure! We got into this one fight a month ago where they blew up five of our eleven tracks and killed about thirty-five ARVNs!" Roberts took a deep breath. "I thought I was going down that day."

"You came into DINFOS through journalism, and I came in through radio, and here we both are! The fucking shit the army will do to you never ceases to amaze me!" The Kid shook his head in despair.

All the while, the old men just kind of watched them, preparing new pipe loads when it seemed appropriate, and the pair just kept smoking the opium, getting more twisted by the minute. One of the mama-sans came and put a small electric fan on the corner of the platform and aimed it at the Americans. Contrary to the inclinations of their breed, it appeared they were no longer in a hurry.

After a long while of comparing notes about DINFOS, music, and politics, Tom took a hazy look at his watch. "Hey, we should be getting back. It's about seventeen hundred hours! Where did the afternoon go? We don't want to be out here when it gets dark. And we're so fucked up, a couple of VC third graders could take us!"

They laughed.

"Hey, let's try to see if they have any pot again!" the Kid said. Once again, he began to try out his Vietnamese-language skills. "Toi mun can sa!" (I want can sa!)

The men just looked at each other with blank expressions on their faces. Turning to face the GIs, they shook their heads no. Whether it was *No, we have no pot* or *No, I do not understand a word you are saying as you slaughter our language,* the message was clear: no pot! Only opium!

"Hey, let's see if they'll sell us any!" Tom said as he reached for his wallet. "I wonder what we owe them?"

"Yeah, let's see." Using sign language, picking up a small bottle and making like he was going to put it in his pocket, and then pointing at the pipe bowls, the lamp, and then his wallet, the Kid saw that the men clearly understood what he was asking: "How much?" He pulled out three ones in MPC.

"Here," Tom said, "give me two and I'll give them a five and see if they take it!"

The two old men thought that five dollars in MPC was a hell of a deal. It was, after all, more than one hundred piasters. So, the pair had smoked all afternoon and left with at least two grams of liquid opium, and it had cost them a total of two dollars and fifty cents each.

"I hesitate to think what this would be worth back on the streets of New York!" Tom said as he took custody of the bottle and slipped it into the breast pocket of his jungle fatigue shirt.

292

As he and the Kid came out the door of the house, they saw there on the street the same cyclo driver, waiting to take them back to the ARVN compound. He had a grin on his face about a mile wide, figuring that doing as good for them as he had was sure to merit a whopping tip!

And he was right. The Kid gave him three dollars MPC when he dropped them at the gate. The cyclo driver was as happy as a clam.

Walking across the compound, the Kid, as high as he was, took no time at all in spotting Lieutenant Wilson and another US officer, who were heading right for them almost as if they'd been waiting.

"That's Captain Brown from the Cav," said Tom as he, too, saw the officers striding directly toward them. "Fuck, I hope we're not in trouble!"

"PFC Stocker," Wilson said as the pair stopped in front of Roberts and the Kid,

"where y'all been?"

He doesn't seem mad. "We were, uh, at some little restaurant bar over by the sampan docks on the south side for a while. Why, have you been looking for me, sir?"

"Yes and no. It's you, Roberts, that we've been looking for."

Tom glanced at the Kid and back to his commanding officer. Detecting something of a smirk on Brown's lips, he saw the man was looking down, obviously trying to avoid eye contact. "What did I do now?"

"Well," Wilson said, "we got a phone call from Can Tho, from Captain Ronnie Smith, B Company commander, informing us to inform you of something." Now Wilson was grinning. Brown stepped right in.

"Roberts, may I be the first to inform you that you have been officially appointed as a cadet at the West Point prep academy, where after completion of one year, you will be admitted to West Point as a full-fledged cadet!"

Roberts's mouth fell so wide open that Tug Boat Willie could have ported there.

"West Point?" exclaimed the Kid with an expression of complete incredulity. "What the fuck?" He was confused after an afternoon of hearing how much Roberts hated the army.

"You chopper up to Can Tho tomorrow. You have to leave 'Nam immediately to be in Virginia in time to meet your orders," Wilson said. "Congratulations, Roberts, you're getting a four-month drop! That's really incredible!"

Tom was trying to digest what had just happened and what it meant. "I can't believe it! I'm going home?"

Well, Jesus, don't cry, for fuck's sake! "Excuse me if I seem a little out of the loop here, but what just happened?" The Kid nearly forgot he was stoned on opium.

"When I first got here," Tom began, "when I was company clerk, I got all my work done pretty fast and had a lot of time to read army regulations and publications. I discovered that you could apply to West Point through the ranks. So, I had pretty good grades, I was a high school athlete, and I had really high scores on my army exams, so I had time to put together an application. This was seven months ago!"

"That is fucking amazing!" The Kid was rife with jealousy. Here was a man who had just found out, as if being hit by a bolt of lightning, that his tour was over. He had just been handed a ticket on the Freedom Jet and would never have to ride into combat with the Armored Cav again!

"This calls for a drink!" Roberts feebly said, still shaking off the completely overwhelming experience of this moment. He began stumbling toward the Lucky 9 Club when he had a realization. "Oops, we gotta put away these first." He pulled the M16 off his shoulder, where it had been comfortably resting.

"We'll meet you there," the Kid called to Wilson and Brown as he moved to park his own weapon. "That's fucking incredible! How early are you getting out of here?" The Kid wanted the details as they walked toward the air force hooch.

"Four months! That's one-third of my tour!" Tom's face was lit up as the enormity of the news continued to sink in, his reality refashioning itself by the second. "I had totally given up on that after I got reported for writing stories for the civilian press. Shit, I hope that doesn't catch up with any of this until I'm out of here."

They pushed open the doors of the hooch to find Herrick still sitting on the couch, reading *Life* magazine.

"Say hello to the future Lieutenant Roberts." The Kid was backed by Herrick with a sweeping, twisting low bow. From that position, he threw his M16 onto his bunk.

"Lieutenant Roberts? Come on, it is not April Fool's Day!"

"No fucking shit!" Tom was grinning so broadly that the Kid thought his bottom jaw might fall off. "I've been accepted to the West Point prep school! I've gotten into West Point through the ranks, and I get to leave here tomorrow! Yahoo!" He threw his black beret into the air, where it was hit by the overhead fan and knocked onto the mosquito netting on the upper bunk over the Kid's. "I'm going fucking home!"

Over at the Lucky 9 Club, the drinking commenced. Tom was the center of attention. After all, everybody wanted to congratulate him for pulling off something so remarkable that it had gotten him out of 'Nam four months early!

"You're not serious about this West Point thing, are you?" the Kid inquired at one point during the evening.

"Well, when I first came up with the idea, I talked to Boujold about it, telling him that maybe the best way to implement change in the military was from within. But now, I don't think so." He took a swig of beer and a puff on his cigarette. "The chances of me ever going on to West Point and coming back here as a lieutenant are fucking nonexistent! But you can bet your sweet ass that I'm going to West Point Prep!"

The Kid didn't last long at the bar. The mess hall was open, but he didn't feel a bit hungry. *Must be an effect of the opium. I gotta lie down!* "If you'll excuse me," he said to Tom, "I gotta go lie down!"

Back at the hooch, the Kid discovered he was the only one there. Sitting on the edge of his bunk, he took off his boots, followed quickly by his shirt and pants. He pulled the netting down and took a deep breath, sort of like preparing for meditation, and lay down on his back, his thoughts drifting off. Once again, the song from *Revolver* played in his head: "Turn off your mind. Relax and float downstream. Is this not dying?" *Could it be that Roberts is luckier than me?*

Impossible. Nobody is luckier than the Kid. Anyway, nobody is luckier than me. He's going home four months early! I've always been lucky, but now I don't know. I don't know shit! Wow, this stuff is wicked! It's like my mind is on top of the hooch, and look! I can see right through the ceiling. And there's my body. Fuckin'

A. Kind of looks like I'm lying in a casket!

Floating on his opiate cloud, the Kid listened to the whirring of the ceiling fan and felt a little evaporative cooling sensation as the air fought to penetrate the mosquito netting. He needed to write a bunch of letters. He still hadn't told Flo and his parents that he'd been in the shooting part of the war. *I guess I should.*

Why not? They see it every night on TV. They gotta think shit like that is happening around me. I wonder if Flo got her period yet. Even though I don't know what it is, it is what it is. God, I hope she's not pregnant. I want to marry her, but I don't want a kid just yet—the Kid with a kid! He sort of snorted and laughed at the thought.

Evaluating the high, the Kid could sense the opium had a strength to it he had not previously experienced with pot, speed or LSD, the other drugs he'd experienced. *What is it about this shit? I have no sense of time! Where the fuck am I? God, I can't believe I'm still eleven months away from Flo and two years away from Nashville! I detest you, army. I hate your fucking guts and everything you stand for, and I hate your piece-of-shit war!*

As his mind floated, he could hear people coming in and going out of the hooch, having conversations with words he could not totally comprehend, and occasionally laughing. He mulled the word narcotic over in his mind. *What is it that makes it habit-forming?* At one point, he heard Roberts's voice.

"Is Stocker still out? What time is it?"

"It is now a little after twenty-two hundred hours," he heard Herrick answer. "The Kid has been out for four hours. If we get mortared, we'll probably have to drag him to the bunker!" More laughter.

"I can't believe I'm still up! Holy fucking A, did we get stoned! Fuck. If I weren't so buzzed by the fact that I'll be leaving tomorrow, I'm sure I'd be out just like him."

About two hours later, the Kid gained enough consciousness of his own thoughts to realize he desperately needed to take a piss. *Where am I? Oh yeah, Sa Dec! There are showers here!*

A piss and a shower now became the objects of all his desires. Opening his eyes, he looked around and saw that the lights were out and everybody had gone to bed. His watch indicated it was midnight. Swinging around to put his feet on the floor, he didn't bother with his glasses. He slipped on his flip-flops, located his shaving kit, grabbed a towel, and wearing only green boxers, headed for the latrine. His mouth was dry and felt like a road construction project. He stopped at the refrigerator by the door and took out the communal potable drinking container to have a big swig of cold H2O.

Down at the latrine, he was the only one there. After pissing, he picked the shower at the end of the line, which he entered, turning on the one handle. Cool water shot out of the showerhead and splashed his face. How refreshing!

Removing his soap from the plastic dish, he began lathering up, using the bar soap for shampoo and working his way down. There was plenty of water in Sa Dec, and he was in no hurry. When he got to his balls, his thoughts turned to Flo. As he soaped up his dick, a hard-on appeared. *What the hell, I might as well beat my meat!*

So he went to work on his cock, but after about ten minutes of effort, it dawned on him that he was not going to have an orgasm anytime soon, no matter how much he was in the mood for one. *Must be the effects of the opium! Now there's a bad mark against it!* Sex on pot was great, and sex on LSD was truly a trip, but he could see that opium was apparently a killer of the sex drive. After another couple of minutes of stroking, he gave up. That had never happened before!

After rinsing off, he climbed out of the shower, dried off, brushed his teeth, and ambled back to his hooch.

Once there, he pulled out his picture of Flo and dwelt on his sadness of their separation for a time. Then he lay down on his right side and drifted off into a fairly deep sleep.

Chapter 25

Off in the distance, the Kid could hear roosters and, then, helicopter blades. It was morning. As he awoke, the previous day's event flooded back to him. They had gone to an opium den! How cool.

Throwing up his mosquito netting and swinging his feet to the floor, the Kid spotted Herrick, who was just returning from the latrine with a towel wrapped around his waist.

"Hey, Kid, going to join up with the living?" The air force sergeant smiled, tossing his shaving kit into his locker.

"Oh yeah!" The Kid rose and stretched his arms over his head. "Is Roberts up yet?"

"Not only up, but gone! He was on that chopper that just flew out of here. He left you a note." Herrick pointed to a white folded piece of paper sticking up out of one of the Kid's boots.

Picking it up, the Kid could feel something wrapped up inside it. Unfolding the note, he found the small bottle of liquid opium. The note said as follows:

Curt,

You might as well take this. I don't want it anywhere near me when I'm trying to process out of here for the States! It was fun meeting a fellow DINFOS grad. Good luck on your tour. Maybe we'll meet up again someday.

Tom

PS: The Yankees suck donkey dicks!

298

"What's that?" Herrick asked as the Kid held up the little vial, looking at it in the light.

"Opium. We tried to find some pot yesterday and ended up in an opium den on the south side of the river! We scored some, and he left it for me."

"Oh, really?"

"Oh yeah, really! It was pretty fuckin' interesting!"

Just then, Lieutenant Wilson appeared at the door of the hooch. As he opened it to enter, the Kid sat back down and hid the vial in the mosquito netting.

"Good morning, sir," the Kid said with a smile, quickly standing up as Wilson stopped in front of him. In an instant, he could tell the lieutenant was pissed about something. "What's up, sir?"

"You'd better hurry up and get dressed if you want any chow. The mess hall closes in fifteen minutes. Then we've got some stuff to do."

"Yes, sir. What is it we have to do?"

"First off, we have to meet up with Roberts's replacement, who'll be down from Can Tho in about an hour. Then the staff briefing is at ten thirty hours."

"Yes, sir. Who are they sending down to replace Roberts?"

With a wry look of disgust on his face, Wilson spoke the name: "Boujold!"

"Boujold? No shit? Boujold is finally getting his wish to come to the field?"

"Yeah, and the worst part of it is that Captain Brown flat out told me they don't want his fat ass in the Armored Cav, so I've gotta bring him with us! Son of a fucking bitch! That fat bastard is going to be an albatross around my neck! And I thought Ronnie Smith was my friend!" With that, he turned and stomped out of the hooch.

"Who's Boujold?" Herrick was immediately interested in why Roberts's replacement would so totally tick off the lieutenant.

"He's a slightly overweight and occasionally pompous know-it-all kind of guy who's been trying to get out here to the field for nearly eight months! None of the noncoms or officers like him because they think he's a major-league screw-off, but he's all right."

"Sounds like he'll fit right in!" "You'll like him; he's a funny guy!"

At 1000 hours, a chopper indeed deposited one John Boujold at the Sa Dec International Heliport. As he clambered off the Huey, dragging a duffle bag and his extra gear bag, his M16 slung over his shoulder with his dripping bandoliers of clips, he sported a grin from ear to ear as if it were Christmas morning at the tree. *There's a man whose prayers have been answered.*

Be careful what you wish for! "Yo, Bouji!" The Kid smiled broadly as he moved to take his extra bag. "Welcome to the field!"

"Thank you!" he yelled over the noise of the big rotors. He stuck out his sweating hand, and they shook. Boujold was already huffing a little from the exertion of hustling his large ass. "I cannot tell you how happy I am to be here!" As soon as he was clear, the chopper lifted off, turned 180 degrees, and vanished.

"Well, Boujold." Wilson stepped up as the dust was settling after the Huey's quick exit. "Don't go thinking you've come to some summer camp in the fucking Adirondacks! This is serious shit out here, and I just want you to know up front that I won't take any of your standard bullshit!" His voice conveyed his displeasure at Boujold's mere presence.

"Yes, sir. I mean, no, sir. I've always done my job, and I won't let you down, sir!" He saluted.

"No saluting in the fucking field, soldier!" The lieutenant shook his head in disgust. "Jesus, you've got a lot to learn. And I hope to fuck you learn it before you get yourself or me or Stocker killed. Stocker, take him over to the hooch and cache his gear, then the two of you meet me over at HQ before ten thirty hours."

"Yes, sir." The Kid snapped to quasi attention, showing a straight face, but as soon as Wilson walked away, at least halfway out of earshot, he offered Boujold a flat five. "Slip me some skin! Fuckin' A, Bouji! Congratulations! But why you want to be out here is still beyond me! We went out on a combat mission last week, and let me tell you, the green issue boxers were a little browner before it was over!"

"You'll have to tell me all about it!" Boujold said as they began to haul his gear to the air force hooch.

"How about that fucker Roberts?" The Kid shook his head with a wry smile. "Can you believe it? A four-month drop! I meet him, and less than twelve hours later, he's going home!"

"Yeah. I remember when he was doing that paperwork after he stumbled across the regs that said you could apply to West Point through the ranks. I laughed at him and said, 'Fat fucking chance! What a waste of time!'"

"So, did you see him this morning?"

"Yeah, when he got off that chopper and I got on! Couldn't talk to him, what with the noise and moving his shit off and mine on."

"So, you didn't have a chance to talk? He didn't tell you what we did yesterday?" "No. Why, what did ya do?"

The Kid looked up to see a group of officers casually walking their way. "Now remember, don't salute," he said to Boujold out of the corner of his mouth. "Good morning, sirs," he said to the four lieutenants as they strode by.

"Morning, men!" one of them replied in a ROTC tone of voice.

"We went to an opium den!" the Kid said breathlessly after the officers were out of earshot. "And look what I got!" He pulled his hand out of his pocket and showed Boujold the small brown glass vial cradled deep in his palm.

"My dying fucking ass! Is that what I think it is?" His jaw dropped open. "I think I'm gonna love it out here!"

"Do you have any pot?"

"Uh, no, I never travel with it. Why? Haven't you scored yet?" He sounded almost as if he didn't believe that such a thing were possible.

"Not yet. Down in Tra Vinh, where we're headed, there's plenty, and the guys are so generous that I just keep forgetting to score some of my own until it's too late. Out at Tan An, there ain't shit. Nobody scores nothin'! So, we gotta get some shit before our asses end up back out there."

"Is that the place where you're surrounded?" "That's it."

"Fuck. But I don't give a shit! It's going to be so invigorating to be out of Can Tho and away from the petty-ass bullshit that nobody in a war zone should have to put up with!"

They arrived at the hooch and, upon entering, found it empty.

"The air force guys are really nice. This is where we stay when we're in here. And this is a good as it gets out here, so enjoy it. This is your bunk." The Kid indicated the one he'd slept in the night before, right on the aisle. "I'm over here in this cubicle. If you need to lock anything up, you can put it in my locker." He had made sure to move his stuff before Boujold showed up.

"So, what's it like?" Boujold inquired.

"What is what like?"

"The opium! I've always wanted to try it!"

"Man, it's hard to describe in a sentence or two. More of a body thing than a mind thing. But I still feel a little fuzzy today."

"How do you smoke it?"

"Well, they had all these elaborate pipe bowls and lamps and shit. I don't know how we're going to do it. But I'm sure we can figure something out! You can leave the M16. We gotta get going!"

The pair arrived at headquarters to find Wilson waiting for them out front.

"Thanks for being on time," he said sarcastically. They walked inside and headed for the briefing room, up the stairs from Lieutenant Colonel Atkins's office on the main floor.

Walking in the door, they found the rest of the group already assembled, crowded into the medium-sized room, making it a tight fit what with all the charts and map boards that had been brought up from Atkins's office for the discussion.

"Shit! He's fucking huge!" Boujold whispered to the Kid as the trio moved toward the last empty chairs, apparently reserved for them.

"Really!" The Kid smirked as his eyes wandered around the room, seeing if there was anyone he knew there. There was PFC Cleveland with Lieutenant Kazmarskij, whom he'd met briefly their first time through Sa Dec, and Captain Brown, commanding officer from the Armored Cav. Other than that, nobody.

Rising up to his full height of 6'4", Lieutenant Colonel Atkins picked up a pointer and began the briefing. "Good morning, gentlemen." His deep bass voice reverberated as he nodded greetings around the room, then had to push his glasses back up his rather large and sweaty nose. "As you all know, the VC have recently become more active here in IV Corps, and that has inspired us to come up with some new plans to try to counter their effectiveness."

Ignoring the colonel, the Kid's attention was attracted to a pair of geckos chasing one another across the wall right behind Atkins, near the ceiling, acting very territorial.

"Territory, that's what it's all about, gentlemen," Atkins was saying as he approached the chart. "It's really more important than body count. We need to control more of it on a full-time basis, so it is important that we keep our ARVN counterparts online with continuation and expansion of the fortified hamlet program."

Drone, drone, drone. Blah, blah, blah. I'm trapped in a prison from which there is no escape, except through the tunnel that requires I sit here and listen to this shit for as long as the big man wants to regurgitate it. ... I wonder what Flo is doing right now? She should be in bed. Please, please, please let her be riding the cotton pony! The Kid glanced over at Boujold to see if he was actually paying attention as Atkins continued to detail the new game plan at IV Corps level.

"But of course, gentlemen," Atkins said, "all the planning doesn't count for shit when you get out into the field and they're trying to kill you. To reduce their urge to do that, or to eliminate it entirely, is why we have officers like Lieutenant Kazmarskij and his crew, to supply us with the ways and means to win over their hearts and minds! Lieutenant Kaz, would you please continue by giving us the particulars of the new orders for psyops you've just received from your headquarters?"

First Lieutenant Kazmarskij, a tall, red-haired, blue-eyed, handlebar-mustached man, was about to talk about things that directly affected the Kid, so now the Kid decided to pay his undivided attention.

"Thank you, Colonel Atkins," Kaz said as he moved to the front of the group. Everybody called him Kaz because Kazmarskij was too hard to pronounce. "It's really easy," Kaz told the Kid when they'd first met three weeks ago. "Say 'Kaz,' 'mar,' 'ski,' then 'j.' Kaz-mar-ski-j."

"As you know, there is no sense in winning and losing the same ground over and over again. We kill them; more come to take their place. What we need to do is convince the local populations that what the ARVN government has for them and what the United States has for Vietnam is good, not bad. To this end, psyops is going to change its tactics a little bit. Instead of investing so much time and energy into troop support and loudspeaker missions, we are going to do more community-level work with the Vietnamese civilians in the hamlets and villages."

Well, I like the sound of that!

"We have some new equipment coming, a kind of media truck that has movie projectors, slide projectors, a loudspeaker setup, a typewriter, a little printing press to print instant leaflets, and a generator to run it all. So, we'll have that going for us. We haven't decided which area we're going to base it out of first, or which of our five lieutenants is going to get first shot. We'll figure that out when it arrives in about a month. This truck, as I understand it, will be the centerpiece of our psyops efforts when it goes out with ARVN POLWAR personnel and a medical presence. We show the local populations some movies, have the doc take a look at them, and leave them some really effective propaganda.

Eventually we hope to visit all the towns and hamlets we can drive it to."

A media truck! I want it! The Kid's imagination flew. This might mean no more slogging through the paddies!

"Until it arrives, we're just going to keep up with the leaflets and loudspeaker teams, where we have them operational. Then once we have the truck, we'll figure out who needs it most to start."

"Thank you, Lieutenant Kaz." Atkins rose and reassumed leadership of the meeting. After another forty-five minutes of dreary details meant more for the individuals to whom he was speaking than for the group in general, the colonel spoke the magic words: "Why don't we break for lunch and meet back here at thirteen thirty hours!"

As the officers filtered out the door first, the Kid, Boujold, and Cleveland stood in the background. *Hmm, we are the only enlisted men here today.*

Sa Dec was big enough to have separate officers' mess and enlisted mess, so the trio were glad they didn't have to eat with Wilson, Brown, and Kazmarskij.

"So, Cleve," the Kid inquired as they walked and smoked, "how are things going for you and Kaz?"

"Well, since I've been in Binh Minh, we ain't gone anywhere or done shit. No way when we flew down here did I think I'd ever be this bored." He smiled. "In other words, so far, so good! I hear you saw some action."

"Yes, we did." The Kid exhaled. "And believe me, I will take boring for the rest of the war if I can get it!"

"Not me!" Boujold piped up. "I can't fucking wait to get into some real action!"

Walking in the mess hall door, after the meal sign-in sheet, there was a table manned by a PFC, and in front of him sat a bowl full of pinkish-orange tablets.

"Ah yes," Boujold intoned, sounding like W. C. Fields, "filet of malaria pill! Come here, my little salmon beauty!" He took the pill and swallowed it in front of the PFC whose job it was to see that each and every soldier took his mandatory once-per-week malaria prevention pill. Not only did the pill protect you from malaria, but also it kind of acted as a laxative.

"Thanks." The Kid took his. *Oh yeah, malaria pill day. And I just got over diarrhea. Shit, shit, shit! I hate the fucking army and everything about it!*

At lunch, Boujold got into a bunch of talk about what was going on back in Can Tho and why he was so happy t finally be out in the field. The Kid just sort of tuned him out. In his mind, he suddenly had a vision of Flo in a maternity dress. *Fuck! I'm losing it!*

Chapter 26

They stood at the end of the bar, the Kid with a beer, and Boujold nursing a Drambuie, his drink of choice. The Lucky 9 Club had pretty much emptied out because the evening movie was about to begin. Tonight's cinematic treat was going to be a recent episode of Bonanza. Besides them, all who remained in the Lucky 9 were the six sergeants who were hunkered down at the poker table at the far end of the club. There was some serious jack in the pot, hundreds of dollars more than the Kid and Boujold made together in three months.

"So," Boujold began, "how do you think we should do it? Better yet, where do you think we should go to do it?"

"Well, I've been giving it some thought." The Kid snuffed out his Kool. "And what I think is, we could paint some of it on the outside of a cigarette and just smoke it like that."

"And where?"

"I found a place around the back of the club, down on the perimeter at the east end of the island. There's a bench, and we can see up the path both ways. If somebody came, we could ditch the shit in the foliage if we had to. Now might be a good time, what with everybody watching the movie."

"I think you're right," Boujold said. "Let's di di mau."

With that, they moved out of the club, trying not to look like they were up to something. The majority of the soldiers in Sa Dec that night were now sitting in front of the outdoor screen, right outside the club, getting ready to see the Cartwrights ride across the Ponderosa.

The Kid spied Wilson, sitting at the edge of those gathered, about ten rows back from the front, talking and joking with Captain Brown and the two warrant officers who had befriended him. He seemed fairly well occupied.

"Tell you what," the Kid said in a low voice, "I got some toothpicks from the mess hall tonight. Why don't we go over to the latrine, where there's some light, and I can paint up a couple of butts in one of the stalls."

305

They nodded their agreement and ambled off to the latrine, walking slowly in the muggy, still very hot air of early evening. Upon arrival, they found the latrine empty for the moment.

"Give me one of your 'grets, unless you want it on a Kool," the Kid said.

"Kool's fine with me." Boujold nodded.

Going into the stall and dropping his pants, the Kid figured he'd take a shit while he was preparing the opium cigarettes. *More diarrhea. I fucking hate those goddamned malaria pills!*

"Fuckin' A, what a god-awful stink!" Boujold hollered. "Is that you, Kid? Jesus, I hope we never get stuck in the same foxhole!"

The Kid laughed. *No shit. If you were in the hole, there wouldn't be any room for me!*

Pulling out his pack of Kools, the Kid tapped out a butt and then brought the small glass vial out of his shirt pocket and unscrewed the cap. Then he put the cap back in his pocket to reduce the chance of losing it. While holding the miniscule bottle between his knees, he dipped in the toothpick and got it soaking. Then he painted the liquid over about the first third of the Kool and set it aside on top of the roll in the toilet paper holder. Repeating the task, he made another, and let them continue to dry for a minute while he finished his dump. Then he put them both in his mouth, one on each side, as he wiped.

"Stocker, you didn't fall in, did you?"

"No. Is it clear?" he asked once he got his pants back up.

"Yes!" Boujold's voice came back.

Opening the stall door, the Kid quickly handed one of the opium-painted cigarettes to John. "Be careful, they're still kind of wet, so we should carry them like this." He demonstrated his palmed technique for concealment.

Soon, they were sitting on the bench and lighting up in the hot, muggy evening as the Mekong River flowed past them on its way to the Pacific.

"Hmm," Bouji intoned as he tasted the mix of opium, tobacco, and menthol. "Makes the smoke kind of heavy, and almost neutralizes the menthol. Ya know, I read once about Edgar Allan Poe that he used to put a pea-size glob of opium under his tongue every night before he'd start writing."

"Really? Interesting," said the Kid. "I heard of a book once called The Opium Eaters, but I never read it. I did read somewhere that there were all kinds of medicines used before the turn of the century that had opium in them, some that they gave to babies to make them stop crying. Maybe we should try that, if this doesn't get us off!" The Kid found that the sounds the Mekong River made as it rolled past the island were quite soothing with a gurgling liquid melody.

Why can't I be sitting on this bench with Flo?

"Feel anything yet?" Boujold inquired as the opium-painted parts of the cigarettes burned up.

"No, I don't," said the Kid. "How about you?"

"Nope. Nothing here to ever make me even think about giving up pot. What say we go the opium-eater route?" Bouji suggested. "Since it's liquid, we could put it in a Coke or something like that."

Back at the Lucky 9 Club, the pair could see Hop Sing chasing Pa Cartwright out of the kitchen on the screen as they came around the corner and entered the club door. The bartender pointed at them, acknowledging their presence and silently asking for their orders.

"Make mine a Coke," the Kid said.

"Me too."

"Two Cokes," the staff sergeant bartender repeated as he eyed them somewhat suspiciously. Or so they thought.

With Cokes in hand, they went back to the latrine. Once there, with the cups sitting on the back of a sink and with Boujold as lookout, the Kid dripped a single drop into each one. *Better to start slow. We can always add more.*

Stepping out into the heat of the evening air, they went back and sat down on a bench at the rear of the movie setup, where they calmly drank their Cokes. In about fifteen minutes, as Hoss and Little Joe were about to trick the bad guys into doing something stupid that would neatly wrap up the storyline, the Kid felt the opium wash over him from the inside out. He almost threw up, but succeeded in fighting it off by getting up and walking away. Boujold quickly got up and followed.

"Kid, you all right?" Boujold sounded concerned, talking in such a way so as not to attract attention.

"Yeah, I'm OK. Felt like I was going to hurl for a second, but I'm OK now. Shit! This stuff is coming on!"

"Oh, really!" Boujold all of a sudden reacted to a shiver that ran up his spine.

"Man! I'm really getting off! This stuff is wicked!"

It isn't the same feeling as I experienced when I smoked the opium yesterday with the two old men. This is stronger! God! It's like relaxing my whole body. My head feels like it's loose! Damn! High as I can be and nothing to do. No music to listen to, no girls to talk to, and no place to go for chow, only I'm not hungry. So, this is what those sick Victorian bitches were doing when they gave opium-laced formula to their babies to make them quit crying! An entire generation of Europeans hooked on opium. I can just see the babies. "I say, Mum, why is it I'm floating above me crib? Now I understand Mary Poppins*!"*

"Let's go back to the hooch and chill out. I gotta lie down," the Kid finally spoke, after just standing there for what seemed an eternity but was really only a couple of minutes. The movie crowd was now dispersing. "That's what happened to me last night too. I had to lie down or fall down."

The Kid and Boujold turned and made their way carefully through the crowd. It was dark, so nobody could really tell that they weren't walking straight. And with all the alcoholics, who could tell the difference anyway? It was dark all the way to the hooch because the Sa Dec compound practiced light abatement, except for when they showed the movie.

At the hooch, Herrick, Sergeant White, and Sergeant Redd were all there, just back from *Bonanza.*

"Hey, men. Psyching anybody out tonight?" Herrick jived.

"Yeah," Boujold deadpanned. "Two guys—us!" he joked as he sat down on one of the three couches that formed a *U* around the table made out of a used wire spool center. Opening his shirt all the way, he threw it back and tried to take advantage of the breeze from the fan.

The Kid went immediately to his bunk and, taking off his boots, shirt, and pants, lay down, leaving the mosquito netting up so as not to cut down on circulation. Removing his glasses and closing his eyes, his consciousness at first began to drift, but in a matter of seconds, it was more as if it were being tossed about in the surf. *It is so fucking hot! The Buddhists are right: hell is on earth, and this is where we suffer the most! Flo, Flo, Flo! Please, please, please don't be pregnant! How I hate this fucking war! How did I come to be here? Man, am I high! This is not right. Doing opium is not right. I can feel it gaining control. It is relaxing, gotta admit. Here I am, baking in the tropics and lying here thinking if I could feel like this for a year and wake up and have Vietnam be a bad dream. That would be OK! I wonder if the Yankees won today?*

As he drifted from one thought to another, he was aware that one of his air force sergeant hooch mates had turned on Armed Forces Radio Saigon and a song was playing from 1966 by the Outsiders: "Time won't let me, woo-hoo, time won't let me a-wait that long."

"And there you have the Outsiders, doing a medley of their hit 'Time Won't Let Me.' But time will let me. In fact, I've got all the time in the world, up until twenty- two hundred hours, that is. Until then, you're spinnin' free with Alan P."

The Kid sat up as if he'd been shocked with an electrical charge. "Alan P.?" he exclaimed as he tried to fight his way out of the opium-induced fog. "Alan P. is on AFVN in Saigon?"

"What are you talking about?" Boujold stood up from the couch as the Kid staggered into view around the corner of his cubicle.

"Alan P., that guy on AFVN Saigon right now. He was in the class behind me at DINFOS! Shit! He got my job!" With that, the Kid turned and collapsed back onto his bunk, suddenly in one of the biggest funks he'd ever been in, in his entire life.

Somebody he knew in the next class had made it to AFVN as it wasn't him!

Where is my luck? What is fucking happening to me? Overwhelmed by circumstances and the ingested opium, the Kid teetered on the brink of sleep, but with the unpleasant effects of the heat and troubling images of combat, napalm strikes, and loading medevac choppers with bodies intermixed with images of baby bottles and dirty diapers, he never really made it. *Is it a boy or a girl?* He could see Alan P.'s smiling face. *Good for Alan, but goddamn the muthafucking army bastards who put me here!*

Finally looking at his watch, the Kid discovered it was 0100 hours and, apparently, everybody in the hooch had retired. Again driven by the necessity to piss, he got up and made his way through the darkened compound to the latrine. Upon entering, he discovered that five of the sergeants who earlier had had the high-stakes poker game going in the Lucky 9 Club had moved the game into the shithouse when the club shut down. The three black and two white noncoms were so hard at it that they never even looked up as the Kid walked over to a urinal, his flip-flops slapping time to his gait across the cement floor.

"I see yo' three hundred dollars and raise your ass anotha' three hundred dollars mo," one of the blacks was exclaiming as he raised his hand high overhead to slap the Monopoly-colored cash into the pot on the makeshift playing surface, which was two benches from the shower area pushed together.

"I see you and call!"

"Full house, eights over treys!"

"Four queens! Ha! Finally! Come to Papa!"

"Shit!" the loser exclaimed as the winner raked in the dough. "Stick a fork in me; I'm done! I thought I had that fucking pot fer sure! Fuckin' goddamn shit!"

Walking out of the latrine, the Kid went back to the hooch, where he put on his fatigue top; grabbed his glasses, cigarettes, and lighter; and walked down the path to the bench behind the club by the river. Lighting up, he blew out the menthol smoke and hung his head in consternation. *Alan P., you lucky bastard! Oh well, maybe you can help me, if I can get in touch with you!*

Putting his hand into his left breast pocket, the Kid felt the little glass vial of opium. Taking it out, he held it in his hand and looked at it. *You're pure evil, you son of a bitch! And with that, he stood, cocked his arm, and hurled the container and its contents as far as he could throw it out into the Mekong River.*

Chapter 27

Nashville. I can't believe I'm actually going to Nashville. Here I am on the road with my thumb out! Is Donna gonna be shocked or what?! And even if the magic is gone and I don't connect with her, I might find a job in radio or in some city close by like. What was it, Murfreesboro? Where there's a college I can enroll in to save my 4-F draft deferment. I'm freezing my ass off. God, somebody please stop. Jesus, look at those mountains and all that snow on them. Why am I leaving Boulder? Oh, Donna, that's right. "Oh, Donna, oh, Donna, oh." The best dream of the night, of his best friend Larry Ryan dropping him off on the highway outside Boulder that would intersect with Interstate 80 eastbound, ended as the Kid finally could no longer ignore the discomfort from the heat.

Sitting up, he realized that he didn't have to get up, not until Wilson came to get them. *How fucking strange that I'm dreaming about Donna! I wonder if dreaming about Nadeau is cheating on Flo?* Just as he considered lying back down and trying to sleep some more, he could hear Wilson banging the door while walking into the hooch.

"Hello, Boujold." Wilson's voice carried loud and clear. "I'd say good morning, but it's too late in the day."

"But it's only zero nine hundred hours, sir," Boujold replied.

"That's way late in the army, Boujold. Maybe out here in the field you'll finally learn that. Yo, Stocker, rise and shine, PFC!"

"Yes, sir. I'm up, sir! Can't say I'm dressed. Only waiting to hear you say you got us a chopper down to Tra Vinh, sir!"

"Well." He came to stand in front of the Kid. "Not exactly. But I got us a ride!" "What 'not exactly' kind of a ride did you get us, then?"

"A truck!" He smiled as if he should be awarded a prize for winning a science fair.

"A truck, sir? We're going to drive to Tra Vinh?" He swallowed hard. "Tell me you're joking?"

311

"Nope. Our problem has been that we can't get a chopper with spare room enough to take us all three what with Boujold's gear, so I lined us up a spot in an impromptu three-truck convoy that's going from here to Vinh Long, where we can connect with a chopper or a truck convoy to Tra Vinh. Beats sitting around this fucking hole any longer."

"Hey now, watch it!" Sergeant Redd acted the part of the offended. "This is an air force hooch, and your jurisdiction is in question, as is your opinion!" he said from the couch, where he was attempting to tune his guitar.

"No shit?" A feeling of doom swept over the Kid as he looked at Wilson, whose eyebrows were knitted together in concern.

"Not a joke." Wilson looked at the Kid with a serious twitch in his handlebar mustache. "Get your gear together, you and your liqueur-drinking sidekick, and be ready to roll out of here at one thousand hours. Better go over to supply and grab some MREs for lunch today. And don't pack your ammo, because what we are doing in exchange for this ride is we're pulling shotgun duty." With that, he was gone, leaving the Kid and Boujold staring at each other.

"So, what does this mean in the King's English?"

"This is not good," the Kid said with a sincere air of trepidation that got Boujold's attention. "Three trucks isn't a convoy; it's a fucking target!" The Kid nervously lit up a Kool. "I'm beginning to question his judgment! This is not driving down to Eakin Compound. This could get dicey."

"Well, that's OK by me!" Boujold stoically said with a kind of glassy look in his eyes. "After sitting around for eight months, I'm ready to mix it up."

The Kid turned and stared at him hard. "Boujold, when the shit starts flying, you're gonna change your mind—and your drawers—in a New York second."

With that, the Kid grabbed his shaving kit and headed for the latrine. By the time he got back, Boujold was all packed and was paying extra attention to the ammunition in his clips. "Sitting around Can Tho, I never thought the day would come when I would need these." He held up a single round before inserting it into the black metal bullet case.

"You'd better fucking hope you don't need them today!" The Kid couldn't believe Boujold actually wanted to get some action. "You can fucking get killed when they shoot at you. Or does everybody back in Can Tho think this is a fuckin' movie?"

Soon, they were ready and sitting on the couch with Sergeant Redd, who was still trying to tune his ax.

312

"I tried to learn how to play once," the Kid said. "When I came into the army I'd learn how, you know, sitting around the barracks like in an Elvis Presley movie. But all I got was blisters once, then I quit."

The hooch door opened, and in popped Lieutenant Wilson. "Are you men ready?" "Yes, sir," the Kid and Boujold answered in unison, remaining seated.

Sergeant Redd just keep plunking at his slightly battered but functional brown wood acoustic guitar, squinting through black horn-rimmed glasses, his head tilted as if to seek the magic vibrations. Nevertheless, it all sounded pretty bad.

Making a wry face, Wilson extended his open hand to Redd. "Sergeant, let me show you how to tune an ax."

Looking relieved that there might actually be a chance that his guitar could again be playable, Redd handed it over, clearly prepared to pay attention to what it was that Wilson was going to do.

With little fanfare and minimal pussyfooting around, Wilson had it tuned in nothing flat and immediately launched into "Wabash Cannonball." His southern accent lent itself perfectly to the Acuff song.

Strong voice, pretty fucking well controlled. Sounds professional. I'll be damned, the sucker has some talent!

"Wow, you're pretty good, sir!" Redd said. "But would you go over that tuning thing again?"

"Sure. You tune this one first, then using it, you just go up the line!" He quickly fine-tuned the instrument. Clearing his throat, he began another song.

"Shine on, harvest moon, up in the sky …"

Beautiful. He'd played that song a thousand times. *Man, he's really good, but he'll never get anywhere unless he can rock and roll!*

Because the trucks in the convoy were late, Wilson ended up playing for a good half hour. The lieutenant was very entertaining, talking about jamming with So- and-So in some little club in Lake Charles, Louisiana, and around Austin. He did a great "Tambourine Man," a Dylan re-creation, but with more understandable vocal enunciation, which was incredible! And again, when he was done with "Tambourine Man," he told Sergeant Redd all the reasons he hated the Byrds for butchering the song.

The Kid lit up as he listened. *I've heard all this before. I'd be bored if we weren't leaving here to drive to Tra Vinh, for fuck's sake. Doesn't he know that's the fucking back way to Cang Long?*

"Wow, sir." Boujold gaped as Wilson handed the guitar back to its owner. "You're really good! That's more the kind of music I like, although there's a lot to be said for a good electric guitar."

"Why, thank you." Wilson grinned. Turning to the Kid, he asked, "So what did you think, Mr. Nashville?"

The Kid pondered for a second. *Lip service. The honest truth or fucking what? At least I don't have to tell him he sucks!* "Well, sir, I gotta admit, I've seen a lot of pickers, and that was damn good!" *Come to me, middle ground.* "Hell, you could get all the Music Row session work you wanted!"

"You really think so? Would you help me? You know somebody? If we all make it through this shit? I mean, when you get back to Nashville?"

As much as you are a redneck muthafucker who is doing everything he can to get us killed, I wouldn't help you lick the soles of boots in the restroom at the Ryman Auditorium. "Sure, I'll help you, introduce you to some people I know. You bet, sir. All we have to do is get through this shit. Uh, by the way, sir, did you happen to notice on the map that in order to drive to Tra Vinh from Sa Dec, we have to go the back way through Cang Long?" The Kid looked pensively at him for some sign that he might reconsider his plan.

"Yeah, so what?" Wilson looked surprised, as if he hadn't been expecting to be second-guessed by a PFC. "Ain't nothing gonna happen we can't handle," he smugly said. "Isn't that right, Boujold?"

"Yes, sir!" Boujold picked up his weapon. "Let's get the fuck out of Dodge! I'm itchin' to go, to do anything but sit around here and watch the fucking geckos eat bugs!"

Chapter 28

There are no good roads in Vietnam. It was an easy judgment for the Kid to make as the three-quarter-ton truck bucked and rumbled down the road from Sa Dec to Vinh Long. The asphalt had been torn up by mines planted by the VC, then had been repaired by the ARVNs and Americans, only to be mined again by the VC. The reason the trucks had been late was that the minesweeping hadn't been completed by the time they originally planned to leave. It was a job that had to be done every morning on every road that Americans and ARVNs traveled throughout the length of the country.

The road paralleled the Mekong River as it made its way the thirty miles southeast to Vinh Long, where it turned to the south on its way to Tra Vinh. From where the Kid sat in the back of the last of the three trucks, he was facing Boujold, and even though he couldn't see it, he knew the river was just beyond the tree line whose palms towered over the rice paddies that lined the highway. His M16 was locked and loaded. He had been on edge since leaving the city limits of Sa Dec.

Boujold, sweating like the porker he was, puffed on a big brown cigar he had broken out for the occasion. He held it between his teeth, working it with pursed lips, as he eyed the tree line behind and beyond the Kid through his dark glasses.

Looking at his round face and slightly bulbous nose, the Kid had to wonder if W. C. Fields had ever traveled through Ohio and possibly knocked up Boujold's mother! This concept took on a greater likelihood of being reality when the Kid saw the way that Bouji was able to imitate Fields's voice, something that he did quite often. "Ah yes, never give a sucker an even break! Must've been the suck- a-tash." *What a scream! I hate this fucking shit! We could hit a mine. VC snipers could open up on us. They could shoot at us with an RPG. They could blow a hole in the road, stop us, ambush us, and kill us!*

The Kid was so nervous about being out in the middle of nowhere with fewer than seven rifles in all three trucks that he plumb forgot about his main worry in life: whether or not Flo had a bun in oven. All he could think about was Wen's boyfriend having gotten killed on the Cang Long road driving in a one-truck "convoy." If Wilson's plan of driving on into Tra Vinh had life beyond Vinh Long, then they would have to drive right by that very spot along the highway.

Signaling to Boujold that he wanted to use his cigar to light a smoke of his own, the Kid pulled out a Kool and stuck it between his lips. Passing his stogie over, Boujold motioned for the Kid to just throw it away after he lit up.

Taking a deep drag, the Kid now lamented that they still had not scored any pot of their own while hanging out in Sa Dec. The air force guys didn't smoke, and they hadn't encountered anybody else on the island whom they trusted enough to ask for grass. *This being straight sucks! If I'm gonna get killed, I'd like to be high when it happens!*

The breeze caused by their forward movement was not cool; it was like being driven through a hair dryer, the motion serving to accent the heat, sort of like a windchill factor in reverse—a heat buildup factor. Every once in a while, they would fly by little concentrations of huts that made up the various fly-speck hamlets that were all that existed on the highway between the two delta towns. Vietnamese children would stand in front of the grass houses and wave at them as they passed, causing the Kid to wonder which one held the grenade they all had planned on flipping into the Americans' vehicle. Occasionally they saw peasants planting rice, almost exclusively old women and young kids, bent over and walking in rows, pushing the shoots into the mud beneath the water of the paddies. In one paddy, an old man plowed with a water buffalo yoked to a wooden share with two young boys, both looking to be younger than ten, riding on the buffalo's massive back, whacking at its flank with long wooden switches. *God, that'd make a great picture. I've gotta get a better camera!*

Being out in the middle of the country between towns without any troops was the most exposed the Kid had felt since arriving in-country. Civilian traffic was on the move, but it was sparse compared to the volume the Kid had witnessed on the drive from Bien Hoa into Saigon. Mostly buses and motor scooters, with very little other American or ARVN traffic, were on the road.

The Kid had the drawstring on his jungle hat pulled tight under his chin. *I wish I had my steel pot on!* Even on the operation before coming to Sa Dec, in combat, he hadn't felt this vulnerable. *At least then we had air and artillery cover and hundreds of ARVNs around. Now, we don't have jack fucking squat!* He could picture himself under the trucks, like the pioneers with their covered wagons circled, shooting away at the VC who were waiting to ambush them. *We don't have enough trucks to even make a frickin' circle!*

Adding to the covered wagon motif, the Kid recalled that the truck had a canvas top with sides that rolled up, giving them some shade from the high noon sun while still letting them see what was going on and catch some wind. Lieutenant Wilson was sitting up front, but they couldn't see him because of all the stuff that was packed into the truck. The Kid had no idea what their load was, but he hoped it wasn't ammunition or anything that would explode if they got shot at.

For a few moments, the Kid was lulled into a semitrance as he began to digest some of the articles he'd read in the copy of Newsweek back at the hooch in Sa Dec, especially the article about the looming peace talks in Paris. *So, they're actually arguing about the shape of the table!? I can hardly fucking stand it.*

That's so sad about RFK. What's the fucking point of working for anything worthwhile if somebody is just going to come along and blow shit away? If Humphrey wins the nomination, the party is gonna go down so big! Ha, Nixon! Who'd have thought? I would have bet my fucking life he was gone for good when he lost that election for governor of California! Can't believe I was for him the first time around. Sorry, Mom, I'm not a Republican anymore. And I'm not a Johnson Democrat. What the fuck am I? McCarthy can't win it. McCarthy has to win it! What the fuck am I doing here? Ooh, look at those four white cranes lifting up off the paddies against the trees! Wow. How will I describe them in my book? The pure white cranes lifted above the trees into the inviting blue sky, free to come and go as their needs and desires direct. Up, up into the towering white, billowy cloud formations that indicate that later this afternoon, it's going to pour monsoon rain like a muthafucka! I wonder if I should write it in first or third person?

Boujold was beginning to dig into his rations and was jostling to get into some sort of position where he'd have a place to put his M16 down but still keep it handy while he chowed. As Boujold ripped open his C ration box, the Kid could tell from the look on his face that he had gotten the dreaded ham and lima beans.

The Kid wasn't hungry. He looked at his watch: 1300 hours. *One o'clock,* his civilian side defiantly told him. He would eat in Vinh Long. Suddenly the convoy skidded to a stop.

Immediately, Boujold dropped his yet unopened can of ham and beans and picked up his weapon, throwing the sling around his neck. The Kid kind of stood up and held on to the end support while attempting to see over the top of the load and out through an opening between the cab roof and the canvas to find out what was up. He saw Wilson, who had climbed down out of the cab and was now walking forward, his right hand wrapped around the pistol grip of his rifle.

"Can you see what it is, sir?" the Kid hollered. Wilson ignored him.

"What is it?" Boujold was getting excited.

"Don't know yet. Don't hear any shooting though," the Kid said, swinging down out of the truck and standing on the pavement. "But if something starts,

317

I'm gonna feel better under this truck than in it, or maybe over there in the ditch off the road." He started checking out their surroundings. The truck engines were still idling, but as he stepped a few feet back from the end of his truck, he was surprised that it was this quiet way out in the middle of nowhere. Stepping to the edge of the road, seeing Wilson coming back, he walked up to the front of the truck to meet him.

"Just some Ruff Puffs sayin' they had some Charlies plinkin' at' em about an hour ago from up where those trees come closer to the road. But they think they're long gone now and say we can go on ahead if we have a mind to."

"Or words to that effect," the Kid added.

"Right. Get back in the truck. We're moving right out."

"So?" Boujold asked as the Kid hoisted himself back into the olive-drab truck.

"Nothin'. Some Ruff Puffs say they had some VC here about an hour ago, but they think they're gone, and we're gonna be gone out of here right now."

"Ruff Puff?" Boujold questioned, not understanding the term.

"That's 'regional force' and 'popular force'—RF's and PF's." *Hmm, I know more about what's going on out here than Boujold, and he's been here for seven months!*

"Now, Bouji." The Kid decided to play the devil's advocate. "If you were a VC, could you think of better cover than being a Ruff Puff? I wonder how many of them are? Gotta be some, don't you think? We give them weapons and everything!"

"Yeah. Maybe we'd better just shoot these guys as we go by!" he said. The truck lurched into motion. He was so ready that he was making the Kid nervous.

"Bouji, no taking your safety off unless somebody really fires a shot at us," the Kid warily reminded him.

As the truck began rolling forward, the Kid decided he should shift position and get on the same side as Boujold. After all, that's where the Ruff Puff had said they were, and the trees on the riverside were much farther back at this particular spot in the highway.

From where he was now propped up against some nondescript boxes, the Kid, through the slot over the cab, could see the other GIs riding shotgun behind the truck in front of them, trying to find a way to feel as if they had some cover. The drivers were not accelerating that fast, kind of as if they thought it was safer to go slowly into it.

Fucking A! Just go as slow as you can so that we'll be easier to hit! "Shit!" the Kid exclaimed. "They're going too slow!"

318

"Maybe they figure if they go slow and look like targets, if the VC are going to hit us, they can bait them into doing it now. At least we'll be with these Cocoa Puffs." Boujold pointed back at the dozen RF's and PF's who were continuing to walk up the road in the direction from which they'd just come.

The road angled to the left, toward the river, as it went by the bulge from the tree line that was within fifty meters of the highway. Even with the trees, the Kid decided it would be better to crouch down at the end of the truck by the tailgate. He knew this wouldn't stop an AK-47 round, but just as he got down, the truck sped up with a jerk, and Boujold, who was standing looking over the load and out the front, almost got flipped out! He nearly lost his weapon as he released his grip and snagged the support strut of the truck. The rifle would have been on the highway if he hadn't had the strap wrapped around his neck.

"Jesus God! Hold on, Boujold!" the Kid said, half laughing and half yelling it. "Is the safety still on that thing?" he frantically questioned as Boujold started to get his act together, waving the barrel of the M16 all over the place. "See? Ya gotta be careful all the time out here!"

As they were pulling away, the Kid and Boujold were looking straight back at the tree line. Glancing down to his left, the Kid saw a little puff in the dirt at the side of the asphalt. It made him think of how the dirt had looked at the Tra Vinh Airport when the sniper shot at a spot right near them. *Nah, couldn't be. I didn't hear any shots, but the trucks are pretty noisy. Well, yes, it could be a shot. But I don't hear any rounds coming by. We're getting farther away from this spot every second. If I open up on those trees, will the driver stop or keep going? I'd rather keep going. Please don't be somebody shooting at us. Come on, drive, you fuckers! Shit! I don't know if they were shooting at us or not. That might not have been a bullet. It could have been mud falling off the truck. I'll look and see if the wheel wells are muddy when we get to Vinh Long.*

Soon, the truck was far enough removed from the incident that the Kid again slipped into a road trance.

Wow, what a vivid dream about Donna. Looking at a picture in a dream—that's a strange way to see somebody. What is it about Flo that made me drop Donna? I'm not sure. Except I knew when I saw Flo that my future was tied to her in some way. Even if Donna might be a little bit prettier; hard to tell, really. Donna was there in Nashville, but what the heck difference did that make? I wish she would have let me have it. O how I wanted her! But if we'd've been doing it, maybe I'd have been with her that night and never even met Flo. Who am I kidding? Flo and I are meant to be. Reaching into his pocket, he pulled out the picture of Flo and let it fill his eyes for a few seconds before tucking it safely away.

The rest of the ride into Vinh Long was, by war zone standards, very uneventful. They pulled into town about 1330 hours.

The Vinh Long Airfield was on the edge of town, which was where the trucks were headed. As they pulled in, past the formidable system of bunkers and fences that guarded it, the Kid spotted a bunch of armored personnel carriers parked over to the side of one of the runways. Roberts had said that this was where the Armored Cav was stationed.

Once closer, the Kid and Boujold could see a collection of hooches a small distance behind the nine APCs, which were parked a suitable distance apart, but still forming a line. Arriving there, the trucks came to a stop. The pair climbed down to the ground as Captain Brown came out of the largest hooch.

"Ross! I didn't expect to see you here! What's up? Where you headed?" the bareheaded, sunburned, and green-T-shirt-clad soldier asked, standing with one hand on his hip, using the other to block the sun from his eyes.

"Hey, Bob! I heard these gentlemen were driving down here to bring you guys some ammo and stuff, so I thought I'd hitch a ride and see if I could find better luck getting back to Tra Vinh out of here than out of Sa Dec. There's just no spare choppers out of Sa Dec these days."

"Well, come on in and have a cold drink." Brown motioned to the group of eight men, who were dusting themselves off, most of them also lighting up.

The inside of the Cav headquarters hooch was pretty nice. The front part, covered with a tin roof, was fairly spacious, and at the end of it, a door led to a sandbag bunker where they could take cover when the shit came in. It wasn't air- conditioned, but they had three big fans going, so it wasn't too bad in terms of heat.

"Rollie!" Brown bellowed. "We got enough Cokes to go around?"

"I imagine," Rollie said as he opened the door to one of two refrigerators. It was loaded with Coke, Pepsi, and two kinds of beer: Falstaff and Hamm's—almost as well stocked as the club in Tra Vinh! Since he was stripped to the waist, the newcomers couldn't tell what rank Rollie was.

"Beer, Ross?" Brown offered.

"Sure!"

Taking out a Hamm's, he popped the top and handed the foaming beer to Wilson, who took a long, appreciative drink.

"Ross," Brown said, "you're not going to have any better luck getting a chopper for three with gear out of here than you were in Sa Dec. In fact, it might be harder."

"How about catching a convoy down to Tra Vinh?"

Brown looked at him with his head cocked to the right side. He sat his ass down on the edge of a substantial table made out of two-by-fours, then laughed. "Ross, the fucking Cav doesn't drive down to Tra Vinh through Cang Long and not get attacked. There ain't no fucking Punch-and-Judy convoys going to Tra Vinh. Did somebody tell you that?"

"Yeah, he did!" Wilson pointed at Staff Sergeant Hicks, a fixture in the high- stakes poker games at Sa Dec.

"Sergeant Hicks." Brown turned to him. "Did you tell Lieutenant Wilson he could get a ride out of here just so's you'd have a couple of extra guns on this run?"

"Yes, sir, I did exactly that!" He smiled and snickered. "I admit I gave the lieutenant a false promise of hope just to make sure he'd come and bring his boys." Hicks gestured at the Kid and Boujold. "Hell, they ain't doin' nothin' up in Sa Dec, but if they found out it was volunteer duty, they wouldn't volunteer, would ya, boys?"

"He's got that one right," the Kid said in an instant. "No fuckin' way!"

"You could have just asked, Hicks." Wilson took another long drink. "I don't mind volunteering my men! OK." Wilson mopped the sweat off his brow with one hand and then ran the cold can of beer across the same track with the other. "I'm gonna go over to the airfield control tower and see if I can't find a chopper to Tra Vinh. Y'all can rest here."

"I'll show you the way," Captain Brown volunteered, reaching for his jungle hat. The pair were soon out the door.

Finding a place to sit on a stool made out of an old crate, the Kid noticed a copy of *Stars and Stripes* lying on the table and picked it up. *Stars and Stripes* was the army rag that kept morale up, parroted the army propaganda, and put the government's spin on things in the war. Opening up the paper to the middle, the Kid flipped a couple of pages and came to a long list of names. "Casualties for the week of 6/14/68: Killed in action, 285." *That many?* It gave the Kid an eerie feeling as he read down the list, hoping that there would be nobody he ever knew listed here, especially him!

Throwing the paper down, he turned to Rollie. "So, you knew Roberts, right?"

"Tom? Yeah," the black man replied. "Can you believe it? Roberts in West Point! Ha! Well, I always thought he was one pretty smart muthafucka. But he was a Giants fan. Being from LA, I'm a Dodgers fan."

"Yankees fan." The Kid raised his right hand and did a little index finger salute.

321

"Yankees?" Rollie raised his voice in exasperation. "Yankees suck donkey dick!"

"That is exactly what Roberts said." The Kid smiled. "Wasn't it the Dodgers who had that perfect game hung on them by Larsen?"

"I wasn't a Dodgers fan until they moved to the coast," Rollie said. He reached for a smoke. "Hey, there's supposed to be a game on today—Dodgers and Cubs, I think. Let's turn on the radio!"

The Cav bunker had a pretty big radio, sitting on top of a bookcase that was full of paperbacks. As Rollie turned the dial, AFVN came on. It was during the Big Band Hour of the block-formatted station, music the Kid couldn't stand.

Somebody like Tommy Dorsey or Artie Shaw was playing.

"Must not be time yet." Rollie fine-tuned the dial for the best reception.

When the song ended, a familiar voice came on. "And that was Les Brown and his Band of Renown. And I'm Alan P., with you today for another twenty minutes, when AFVN Saigon will bring you the baseball game of the week, from LA, where the Dodgers take on the Chicago Cubs. Of course, the game has been over for hours and it's on tape delay. Until then, here's Frank Sinatra!"

Oh well, the old lifer geezers need their music too. It was a little bit of sweet revenge for the Kid, having to listen to Alan P. on the radio, knowing at least that he was forced to play music he hated. The Kid had figured out that Alan P. was the utility man and there was no telling what show he'd be doing when. Still, jealously raged within the Kid every time he turned on his radio and heard him, knowing that Alan P., and not him, was the lucky one in Saigon. *There's gotta be a way to get there. Gotta find a way!*

A half hour later, Wilson and Brown returned to the hooch.

"Oh, so you don't mind volunteering to ride shotgun on the way back to Sa Dec tomorrow?" Hicks cracked a broad grin.

"No, Sergeant. I think we'll wait at least another day to try to find a ride from here." Wilson wasn't going to give in that easily after finding out he'd been jobbed by Hicks.

"Suit yourself. You could be here a week!" Hicks smugly replied.

Chapter 29

July 2, 1968

Dear Mom and Dad,

Happy (almost) Independence Day from the front! Up where the fireworks are for real! I must admit, it feels a little different celebrating the Fourth of July when you're in a war zone.

Sorry I haven't written for a few days. We've been on a road trip, trying to get back to Tra Vinh. Since we couldn't get a chopper out of Sa Dec, Lieutenant Wilson got us on a convoy down to Vinh Long, another town in the Delta, where we were stuck for a week! We went down there in a three-truck convoy and ended up coming back on one truck! That is as nervous and scared as I've been since I got here! One truck and five guys. I think I used up a bit of my luck on that one! No amount of Right Guard could have taken the sweat out of that trip!

Talk about living out of a suitcase. That would be a luxury compared to living out of a duffle bag and traveling with only one change of uniform and two changes of underwear and socks. Stinky! This sucks big-time in a way I cannot begin to tell you, because I know Mom hates it when I cuss. Worst part of it is, all my mail is being sent to Tra Vinh, and I'm not getting it. We've been gone from there nearly two and a half weeks now. Boredom on top of boredom, baking in the tropical heat day and night; I could almost go for a little action. That word has a lot of meanings in this place! I should have a ton of mail when we get back to Tra Vinh!

So now I'm writing you from Sa Dec, where we are supposed to, finally, have a chopper take us back to Tra Vinh tomorrow. I need a letter from Flo (OK, and you guys, so bad I can hardly stand it. Mail is morale!).

I'll close for now. Boujold and I are going downtown to do some shopping. Sa Dec has lots more stores than Tra Vinh, and we need some items to take back out to Tan An, where we'll be stuck way out in the boonies again for a while, as I understand it.

Love,

Your no. 2 son

Sealing the envelope and adding it to the stack of letters he'd written over the last night, the Kid kicked off his flip-flops, picked his hand-laundered socks off the fan where he had them stuck to dry, pulled them on, and laced up his combat boots.

"Ready?" Boujold was impatiently waiting on the couch with Herrick.

"You guys are gonna love this! Mama-san Quyen has some of the hottest-looking girls in all of Sa Dec!" Herrick said as they picked up their M16's and headed for the door.

"Now this isn't the whorehouse where the officers go, is it?" the Kid asked, not wanting to run into Wilson on this mission, because it was grass, not ass, the Kid was really after.

"Oh no. They go to An's, so no sweat, GI!"

"And you're sure they're gonna have what we want?" the Kid asked, attempting to confirm.

"Kid, if GIs spend money on it, Mama-san Quyen has it!" Herrick assured him.

Mama-san Quyen's place was on the north side of the Mekong River, in an old hotel about a block off the waterfront, in what must have been the main French hotel back in the day. Her place was up on the third floor. Well, actually the whole third floor was hers, what with her girls each needing their own room in which to ply their trade, but Mama-san Quyen's own personal space was at the end of the hall in the back, and her room looked out onto a balcony, where there was a pretty view of the river. Wicker chairs surrounded the ubiquitous old cable spool table. Only Mama-san Quyen had hers sanded, had had the hole in the spool filled in with wood, and had the whole thing shellacked. She had also gone to the trouble to have the bottom part of the six-feet-in-diameter spool sawed off so that the chairs slid nicely up to the table.

324

Mama-san's room was huge by Vietnamese standards, at least thirty feet across the entire back of the building, with a classic hardwood floor, like a loft in the city. Her desk and a couple of couches lined the walls on the side of the room facing the building's exterior wall, and a shrine to Buddha was over in one corner on the side of the room facing the river. A stick of incense burned in a cup at the base of the display, which featured a lot of foliage and flowers.

Mama-san's big double bed stuck out into the middle of the room like an island in the Mekong. It was placed in such a way that its center was exactly beneath the ceiling fan.

"Mein yoi, Mama-san!" Herrick greeted her as the three walked into the room. They all respectfully removed their, and then placed their M16's in a rack specially made for the purpose, set up next to where a double french door opened out onto the balcony. Herrick had taken the time to explain to the Kid and Boujold that the accepted way was to have at least one guy in the room at all times to watch the weapons and their backs, so as not to present any freelancing VC with the opportunity to catch all the GIs with their pants down, so to speak.

"Men yoi, Herrick!" Mama-san rose to extend her hand to him. She was casually dressed in white pajama bottoms with a flowery top and had her partially gray hair pulled back in a bun. She apparently liked flowers a lot and had real ones around the place, many of which decorated her religious alcove. "You bring me new friends, Herrick. Thank you!" She and Herrick mutually bowed as they clasped hands in a four-hand shake.

Boujold sat down on one of the couches right in front of a floor fan that was whirring away as he mopped his brow with a green handkerchief. Seeing that the Kid was looking for a convenient place to sit, Mama-san moved over by her massively large bed and motioned that it was more than all right for the Kid to sit on its edge. It was covered with—what else?—a flowered bedspread.

I like it! This woman is pretty cool; what a big mouth she has when she smiles! Well, we know she isn't chewing betel nut yet. ... So, this is a whorehouse! Hmm. I love Flo. She said it was OK, but I know that's woman speak for "I'll be really hurt if I find out you did." And she'll always think I did, even if I didn't. So what the hell, I might as well! But it will have to be something pretty hot to make me want to do it.

No sooner had Boujold sat down than two young women came into the room from the hall side. One went to Herrick, and one settled next to Boujold on the orangish couch. They were not bad-looking, attired in short, simple sundresses and wearing high heels. They both had the same short haircut, not what the Kid liked. He appraised the women as he mentally tried to hold on to his picture of Flo. The one who had gone over to Herrick was apparently the one he visited on a semiregular basis. He had said to the Kid one night that seeing a whore regularly made her feel more like a girlfriend and less like a whore. And seeing how hard as it was for a GI to start a real relationship with any Vietnamese woman who wasn't a whore, to a multitude of GIs, anything was better than nothing.

Smiling broadly, Boujold welcomed the young woman in the pink dress to his couch, looking her over like a man who, if he was going to spend his hard-earned combat pay, wanted be sure he was going to receive full value. She had a cute face, but not anything that made the Kid feel like he wanted to go for it.

"Stocker." Herrick welcomed the young woman onto his lap. "This is Lanh!" "Men yoi, Stocka?" Lanh struggled with the Kid's name.

"Just call him 'Kid.'" Herrick smiled. "Everybody does, sooner or later. So, how you been, darlin'?" Herrick laid his right hand on her leg and immediately ran it up under her dress as she used her left hand to begin rubbing his neck.

"You say name you, Kid?" Mama-san played off of Herrick's comment with a bright, questioning expression on her slightly wrinkled face. If it was one thing the Kid had learned, it was that he couldn't tell what age Vietnamese people were. She looked as if she could have been anywhere between forty and sixty. Hard to pin down, as she fanned herself while sitting about three feet away from the Kid on the same side of the bed.

"It's a nickname—*bic*?" "Nickname?"

"Sem sem VC and Charlie. Hey, look, I'm speaking Vietnamese!" "Ah!" Mama-san's face lit up. "An bic Vietcong hoa beaucoup?"

"Ti ti." The Kid smiled and made a tight pinching motion with the thumb and forefinger of his right hand, denoting a very small portion. "Ti ti, Mama-san!"

"You numba one, GI!" she said to him. Then she let loose with a string of Vietnamese that the Kid had no chance of understanding, although he got the gist of when it apparently summoned a young woman from off the balcony, who rushed over to a small refrigerator that sat humming in one corner of the room and began pulling out soft drinks.

"I think I found what I want," Boujold said. He rose, took his new acquaintance by the hand, and assisted her to her feet. "Ah yes, my little jungle flower, you'll have to allow me to demonstrate that old medicine show

326

trick known as hiding the snaaaaake," he said, imitating the voice of W. C. Fields as the pair headed for the door and were off down the hall.

The girl-child served Herrick and then the Kid with relatively cold cans of Coke. *I wonder if their love of Coca-Cola will make them fight any harder? Is that how the United States is going to do it? ... Herrick's girl is pretty cute. Cuter than I thought when I sat down. I wonder if that's all Mama-san has. But here I am, sitting on her bed. Wait a minute, I wonder if she thinks she's gonna jump me?*

That thought flew from the Kid's head the instant after he thought it because into the room walked a young woman with long hair and an incredibly pretty face, dressed in white pajama bottoms and a light blue blouse, wearing sandals, not high heels—and she sat down on the bed right next to the Kid. Glancing from her face, then over to a broadly grinning Mama-san, then back to the young woman, the Kid was taken by how good she looked. *This girl is a whore? Incredible. What am I gonna do? She's too fucking cute not to fuck!*

"This Co Din!" Mama-san introduced them.

"Din?" the Kid repeated with a quirky look on his face.

"Easier for GI. Call me Pam if you like," she gently explained.

"Yes!" Herrick said. "I was thinking Co Din would be the one for you! Come, Lanh, time for boom-boom." Herrick slid her off his knee and stood up. As he did so, her dress rode up, showing a glimpse of her white panties.

Looking back to Din, she smiled warmly at him and began to rub his leg with her hand in a very friendly manner. As he drank his Coke, Din and Mama-san exchanged comments in Vietnamese for a couple of minutes. Then Din reached down and unlaced the Kid's boots.

"You feel betta without!" She let him help her remove them and his socks.

Reaching into his pocket, the Kid pulled out his pack of Kools and offered one to Mama-san, which she took, and one to Din, which she did not take. An ashtray was immediately brought by the young girl, who couldn't have been more than ten years old. The Kid eyed Din: high cheekbones, pleasing face, bronzed skin, very unpronounced Asian slant to her eyes, and a pretty little nose that led to a bright smile. Her dancing eyes would catch his and then look away and over to Mama-san.

Rising up off the bed, the Kid walked out onto the tiled balcony to check out the view over the river. Din followed in a leisurely manner to stand next to him when he settled in a spot at the railing made of cinder block and masonry. At three stories above the river, one could see much. There must have been a dozen boats of various sizes within easy view. An armed US patrol boat was cutting a wake up the far side of the river, its twin fifty-caliber barrels glistening in the afternoon sun. The Kid could see that the sailors manning it all had their life jackets on—or flak jackets; it was hard to tell. Maybe both. If you went into the water with a flak jacket, you'd sink like a stone!

A Huey helicopter came flying down the river and executed its landing maneuver at the Sa Dec International Helipad.

Finishing his cigarette, the Kid flipped the butt into the morass below at the end of the building. It looked just like the kind of junk he recalled seeing at the bottom of the balcony railing in Can Tho, at New Villa.

He took a long, hard look at Din's face. She knew he was studying her, and he had to wonder what she thought about having to do this to make a living. *But hell, by Vietnamese standards, this is pretty high on the scale. It's no wonder they're going to do it when there's so much money to be made. Oh, how about that!*

Boujold is done already! Ha! He didn't last ten minutes!

Seeing that Boujold was done and had returned, Din turned to the Kid. Taking his hand, she said in a soft voice, "You love me now?"

It's war. I could die tomorrow—or later this afternoon, for that fucking matter. I love Flo with all my heart, but Din is too cute and we are headed for Tan An. "Yes, I make love to you now."

Taking his hand, Din led the Kid off the balcony; through Mama-san's room and past a smiling Mama-san, who was making sure Boujold had something to drink after his session; and down the hall, three rooms to the right. Opening the tall louvered door, the pair entered a slightly narrow room that had a bed with a very plain brown wooden headboard parked at the end of the room. There was a vanity stand with a very strategically placed mirror opposite it and a tiled corner by the window where a sink and plumbing fixtures showed that in the past, this place had been a very swank French hotel by provincial standards.

Once the door was closed, Din turned to the Kid. "You give me five dollars MPC," she said, stating her price, and stuck out her hand.

Five dollars, less than the price of a movie and dinner, and I get to fuck you? "OK." The Kid pulled out his wallet, extracted a brown fiver, and handed it to her. She took it and put it into a drawer on one side of the vanity. Turning around, she began unbuttoning her blouse.

"No, no," said the Kid, stepping forward and taking her hands off the buttons, "I'll do it!" He led her over by the bed, where they sat down on the edge.

This is a switch, from meeting the girl, taking her out, and first getting to first base, then getting to second base and, weeks later, third base. I know this baby is going out of the park for a round-tripper, and I haven't even kissed her yet!

As the third and fourth buttons were opened, the Kid slipped the blouse off her shoulders and looked at her heavily padded bra. As he reached behind her, it surprised Din a little that he could unsnap her bra so quickly with just one hand. When it was off, he found small but interesting breasts with larger nipples than one would have expected to see on such small buds. *Oh well, it's not tits I want, it's pussy.*

Motioning for her to stand up, the Kid pulled down her white pajama bottoms and left her to step out of them as they lay on the floor, leaving her in nothing but a pair of full-sized red panties that came all the way up to her navel. *Gawd-awful ugly panties! Something you'd see on a Nebraska fan! Really cute legs and butt!* Bending over, she picked up her pajama bottoms and flipped them over to a low stool that sat in front of the vanity. Then, motioning for the Kid to stand, she went to work on his buttons. Off came his fatigue shirt. Open came his army-issue brass-buckled cloth belt. Opening his button, she took hold of his zipper and slowly lowered it, then dropped his pants to the floor, to find his erection fairly popping out of his green boxer shorts in her face. It made her laugh the way the thing came poking through the opening like a soldier called to attention.

With a hand on the elastic of his green army-issue boxer shorts, she pushed his swollen dick back against his belly and worked them off. Turning to the bed, she pulled down the bedspread, revealing some very white sheets.

"You lie down," the Kid said as he motioned with a sweeping gesture of his arm. Din immediately complied. Elevating his face over hers, while holding himself up on one elbow, the Kid kissed her. It was awkward, as if their lips didn't fit. He slipped her a little tongue, and she seemed not to care to slip hers back. It made it really awkward and, at the same time, apparent there was no way to hide the fact that neither one of them had any genuine passion for what was about to happen. It was a transaction, an exchange, nothing more. She lifted her hips to facilitate his removal of her panties.

The Kid sat cross-legged next to her and ran his hands up and down her slim brown body. Transaction or not, he was digging seeing and touching a naked woman who was more than casually attractive. He had never seen anybody naked who wasn't white, so his curiosity was almost as hard at work as his meat. Din had a mildly confused look on her face, as if she knew she should be working him over, but he was into working her. *Now there's some foreign muff!* He took the palm of his left hand and laid it on her mound. Only there ain't no mound.

There's no pubic hair up front! He parted her legs to expose her labia. *Wow, look at that. All the hair on this Vietnamese beaver is down between her legs! Now that's different. Looks like little Brillo pads!*

Suddenly, Din rose up off the bed and went to the vanity drawer. She came back with a Sheik condom in her hand. "Now you lie down, GI," she said, kind of pushing him over and giving him room to straighten out his legs. Sitting next to him, she opened the prelubed condom and dropped the wrapper by the side of the bed. Lifting his dick up off his belly and standing it straight up with one hand, she used her other hand to place the condom on the end of his penis, carefully rolling it down into place. Then she straddled him, up on her feet, as if she were preparing to sit down in the gook squat position. Holding his dick straight up, Din lowered her pussy down to where it touched the tip. Wiggling it around slightly to spread the lube on her outer labia with its tip, she seated it in the opening and then slowly lowered herself down until his rock-hard member had completely disappeared inside her.

The Kid let out a big sigh as he felt her hot vagina engulf his cock; it had been six long weeks since he'd been laid. *This feels great! Oh, how good would this feel without a condom! Forgive me, Flo, you're twelve thousand miles away and I'm in the war. It's too much to think about being twenty and never getting laid again, if something should happen to me like I get my dick blown off, or I'm killed, or who knows the fuck what! ... Look at her smile! What a cute little babe! I'll have to see how long I can hold out. I wonder if the Yankees are playing today?*

Din was not shy when it came to fucking the Kid. She directed his attention to the mirror, which he found quite entertaining, watching her pert little ass going up and down on his cock. He had left his glasses on for just such a look. She rocked back on her hands, giving him a great view of how his penis looked as it slid in and out of her.

After about five minutes, Din got off his cock and took a look at the reservoir tip of the condom to see if he'd come yet and she just hadn't noticed. Nope. She looked at the Kid, and he grinned back at her. She grinned at him and climbed back onto his cock, proceeding to bump and grind his meat as if she was going to churn it into an Oscar Meyer wiener.

After a couple minutes of this, she got off and looked again. Still no cum in the tip. As she let out a breath as if she was exhausted and discouraged, the Kid had to chuckle at her. Now he took her by the hand and motioned for her to lie down on her back. He spread her legs, and she welcomed him into her. As he penetrated all the way to the base of his cock, he shut his eyes and tried to convince himself that it was Flo whom his dick was in. As he pumped, he wanted to open up his eyes and see Flo. Slow pokes, deep short pokes, long smooth pushes into her slick and surprisingly tight pussy. Put it in deep and wait for it to cool down. In his mind's eye, he saw the Traveler's Motel, and finally, after holding off until he couldn't stand it a second longer, he released his pent-up load and spasmed on top of her as the last drops ejaculated out. He opened his eyes and stared into Din's brown eyes, which were looking questioningly back into his. *Do whores ever cum? I wonder.*

He rolled off and lay spent next to her. On his back, he was looking up at the ever-present ceiling fan. She immediately rose up off her back, removed the condom from his cock, and threw it in a small white wastebasket by the side of the bed. *Must not look. Must not see how many condoms are in there.* Taking a towel, she wiped the goo off his dick, handling it with a show of great respect.

Then she padded over to the corner and, squatting over the tile enclosure with her legs spread wide apart, used a cup to splash water onto her vaginal area with one hand while washing it with the other, and finally wiping it with a washcloth that was sitting nearby. Sort of like a poor girl's bidet. Picking up a towel, she dried herself off and put on a shiny yellow robe made of light fabric that was hanging on a convenient hook.

The Kid lit a cigarette and leaned back while he watched her clean up and slip into the kimono. Now that she was done, she sat down on the bed next to him, looking as if she were anxious for him to get dressed and shove off.

Back in Mama-san's room, the Kid found Boujold waiting for him.

"I thought you'd never come back, and I feel like going again. It's been awhile." He smiled.

"Go ahead, I'm in no hurry," he said. "Is Herrick done yet?"

"No." Boujold snuffed out his cigarette. "He's still in there banging away."

Once Boujold and his girl had left the room, the Kid turned to Mama-san. "Mama- san, *toi mun can sa?*"

"Can sa? I got can sa!" she replied. "You wait, I get!" She left the room and returned about a minute later with a white plastic bag that had Vietnamese newspaper peeking out of it. She set it on the bed in front of the Kid. "Here, can sa."

Opening the bag, the Kid lifted out the newspaper bundle and sat it in front of himself on the bed. Unfolding it, he looked at its contents: about a

331

half pound of the finest buds he'd ever seen. Or so he thought. Having never seen more than a couple of ounces, he was mostly guessing at the weight. But as for the buds, he'd never seen anything like them. They were tight little flowers, clumps of dark green pot, oozing with what could only be resin. Each one was on a tiny little stem, as if it had been cleaned up real nice. The first time he'd ever bought his own pot, he'd paid five dollars for a matchbox on the Hill in Boulder.

"How much?" he asked with a quizzical look on his face, not sure what she was going to say.

"You make me offer," Mama-san shot back.

Well, fuck. At ten dollars a lid, I imagine there's about a hundred dollars' worth of pot here. I mean, I'd pay a hundred for this in the States, but here, less than half that maybe. He looked in his wallet: he had sixty dollars MPC left. "I'll give you thirty dollars!"

"OK, GI! You give me thirty dollars MPC!"

He peeled off the twenty and then the ten, handing them over. Then he ran his fingers through his newly acquired cache. *What a deal! I can't wait to try it out!*

Just about the same time, Din, Herrick, and Herrick's girl all came back into the room.

"Oh look! The Kid finally scored!" Herrick smiled as he walked past the Kid on his way to the fridge, acting like he lived there at Mama-san's.

"Yes, I sure did!" Taking a Kool out of his pack, the Kid twirled out some tobacco and pulled a bit of free leaf from the bottom of the bag, which he stuffed in, using a piece of stem to pack it. Lighting it up, he took a long pull and held the smoke in his lungs, feeling it go straight to his brain. "Not bad!"

"I tried it once," Herrick commented. "Didn't like it."

"Too bad." The Kid mimicked a frown before exhaling a horizontal column of smoky exhaust. After another couple of puffs, he was flying. Taking one look at Din, who sat next to him on the bed, he rose and, extending his hand for hers, motioned that he wanted to return to the room for round two. She smiled coyly as they walked past Mama-san. Herrick's girl said something to Din that made her laugh as they exited into the hall.

Back in the room, this time they both quickly took off their own clothes. The Kid reached into his wallet and got out another five dollars before tossing his pants aside. As the Kid lay down on his back, Din went to the vanity to put away the money and get another condom. When she came back, the Kid motioned that he wanted her to blow him. With a disappointed look on her face,

Din at first pretended that she didn't understand, so the Kid put his finger in his mouth, relying on sign language, because he had no idea what the Vietnamese word for *blow job was. Suck mai? "Suck" surely doesn't mean suck.*

Reluctantly, Din sat down next to him. Taking his cock in her hand, she gave him something closely akin to a dirty look and put the head of his dick in her mouth. After about five seconds, in which no more than the first inch of his unit went into her mouth and he never felt even the slightest presence of a tongue, she turned to him with a pouting expressing. "This numba ten. You love me now!" She picked up the condom and motioned that she wanted him to fuck her.

"Well, OK." The Kid gave in. Din's face immediately lit up with a smile. Before the Kid knew it, the rubber was on and she was sitting once again on his cock, giving it the buffing of its life! She wasn't wasting any time. Definitely wasn't interested in any blow job, that was for sure. Oh well, it felt pretty damn good to be inside a hot-looking woman, condom or no condom. Closing his eyes, he continued to try his best to pretend it was Flo. *Now, how do I explain to Flo how it is that I know a move I want her to try out on me? Please be a bunch of letters for me in Tra Vinh. I think I'm finally going to find out tomorrow if she's pregnant or not.*

Motioning to Din that she should climb off for a second, the Kid got up on his feet and positioned her on the bed so she was down on all fours. Again, she was obviously wondering what the Kid had in mind, but she seemed to like it fine when he slipped it into her from behind. It made him think of the first time he and his first lover, Karen, had had a chance to experiment with all the positions one night shortly after they had just started doing it. Up until then, they'd only done it in the back of the Kid's 1955 Chevy station wagon in the missionary position.

When one of the Kid's friends had come up with the idea that a bunch of the high school guys could rent an apartment in Boulder, pretending to be college students, the Kid was in. And thus, the "Key Club of 12" was born. And what a boon it was to the Kid's sex life. The first night he and Karen had one of the bedrooms, they tried every position they could think of: her on top, the two of them in a chair, him entering her from behind, her on top of him, only backward, the two of them standing with him lifting one of her legs, both of them in the shower sitting on the edge of the tub. *No time for any of that,* the Kid realized, as he lost his control and shot his load. Stepping back from Din's shapely little ass, he looked to see if she was smiling or frowning when she turned to face him.

Was it good for you?

Again she peeled the condom off his cock, washed and wiped his dick, and then tended to her pussy. When she was done and once again had donned the yellow robe, the Kid pulled out a hundred-piaster note he had in his pants pocket and pressed it into her hand. "Cam on u lam," he said, using his weak but growing Vietnamese vocabulary.

She smiled and took it to the vanity.

Back in Mama-san's room, the Kid found Boujold examining his cache, and through the french doors, he could see Herrick and Lanh sitting at the table on the balcony.

"Hey, Kid, look at this! Mama-san's got pot! It was lying here on the bed when I came back. I said I'd buy it from her and offered her ten bucks, but she said to wait. Maybe she figures to sell some of it to you, too."

"Make that all of it," the Kid said. "I just bought all of that half an hour ago."

"Oh well, let me have half. Here's five bucks." Boujold stuck up a fat paw with a brown fiver folded in half between his fingers.

"Uh, no." *Shit, how much did I overpay?* "I gave her thirty dollars for this stuff, and I don't want to sell half. Tell you what, Bouji, I'll sell you a third of it for ten dollars."

"Fuck you, Kid! The whole bag is just worth five bucks!"

"Not to me, it isn't. It is in fact worth thirty dollars, because that's what I just paid for it. And if you want a third—and we are going to Tan An, where there ain't no pot; and you don't know anybody in Tra Vinh; and I don't know if we'll have time to score before we fly out—I'd be willing to bet that a third of this might even cost you more out at Tan An."

Boujold looked a bit perturbed, but he said, "OK, ten dollars. Here's your money." He handed the Kid a ten. "Hey, Mama-san, you got?" He tugged at the plastic bag the pot was in to demonstrate he needed another one. She knew exactly what he meant.

The pair spread the pot out on the newspaper it was wrapped in, and the Kid eyeballed its division into three piles. "Take your pick." He motioned to Boujold as soon as he had them situated in such a way that he didn't know if one was bigger than the other two.

"I'll take this one." Bouji slid the one he'd chosen over to his side of the paper and proceeded to put it into the white plastic bag that Mama-san had supplied.

The Kid looked at his two piles. *What the fuck am I going to do with all this pot? I can't cache it anywhere, because you never know when you're leaving a spot in this war or if you'll ever go back. Fucking A. I'm going to have to carry this around in my pocket all day, every day!*

Situating the pot in the bag, the Kid used the excess plastic on top to wrap it back around and thereby double bag against breakage, before twisting the top into a little slipknot. He fit it into the right-leg cargo pocket of his fatigue pants and was mildly surprised to find it fit in there quite neatly.

"Hey, look at this!" He modeled his concealment technique for Boujold, Mama- san, and Din, who were all sitting on Mama-san's bed. "You can hardly see it. And this is as big as it's ever gonna be, because I'll be smoking it smaller on a regular basis!"

"Yeah, that pocket looks a little puffy, but who the fuck doesn't have puffy pockets in this fucking place? From what I've seen of our little extralong excursion down to Vinh Long, I think you might be right about keeping it on the person."

"Hey, Herrick." The Kid stuck his head out the door. "Do you know where there's a tobacco or pipe store anywhere in Sa Dec?"

"Actually, I do," he said, turning to look at the Kid. "You about ready to di di mau?"

"Sure, let's go. Ciao, Lanh." Herrick kissed his girl and grabbed his M16 off the door rack. Soon, the Kid, Herrick, and Boujold were back on the street.

"Look," the Kid said, marveling, "the same cyclo driver who brought us here is waiting to take us back, sort of like he owns us!" The three of them laughed.

Chapter 30

They watched him struggle along with his gear, a bag over each shoulder and his M16 slung on as well, as they waited for him at the Sa Dec International Helipad.

"You tell him anything about the Tra Vinh sniper yet?" Lieutenant Wilson looked at the Kid with a cocked head and half a grin.

"Nope."

"OK, then, here's what we're gonna do. If the sniper shoots, we'll hit the ground like it's the real deal, OK?" Wilson seemed delighted to the point of having a rough time concealing it.

The Kid pondered. *Fuckin' what got into him? Lieutenant Wilson wants to play? Good clean, if not slightly devious, fun? Sure, why not?* "Count me in! But the guy has to cooperate. What if it's his day off, or he worked earlier?" The Kid brought up the uncontrollable aspect of Wilson's plan.

"Yeah, that's certainly possible, but it's his favorite time of the day, so if he's there, let's make Boujold think we're pinned down and really milk it!" He actually chortled.

"Sure! I'm in all the way!" The two knocked fists, hidden from Bouji's view, as he was almost there with his load. "Hey, sir, if I could ask, sir, a couple of weeks ago you wanted to open up on the Tra Vinh sniper and waste him, and now you want to work him into the act? What gives?"

Wilson made a glance off into the sky, as if evaluating the question, and then said in a serious tone, "Well, hell, since I can't shoot him, everybody's gotta have a little bit of fun now and again, don'tcha think?"

Boujold was definitely not having fun as he humped his baggage up to the heliport. "Hey, Stocker, thanks for the help, but when I asked, I wanted you to take one of the heavy ones, not the lightest one!"

The Kid looked at him and shook his head from side to side. "Bouji, I took one! What the fuck more do you want? I didn't take the right one? Shit, I'll take the fucking thing back to the hooch and you can hump it over here yourself!"

Yeah, come on Tra Vinh sniper man, be working. This will be great!

"OK, OK, you're right. Thanks, really!" He took to the shade of the little square shelter on the helipad.

With three bags of gear and clothes, Boujold had it all with him. The Kid and Wilson, on the other hand, were traveling light, with most of their stuff strung out between Tra Vinh and Tan An. The nearly three weeks in Sa Dec and Tra Vinh had been a bit much on the little bit of stuff they'd brought for three or four days.

The bulk of the stuff the Kid had that he cared about was locked in the cubicle he used while he was in Tra Vinh. He actually had an air check tape with him, should he ever get a chance to make it into Saigon and drop by AFVN. You never know.

The Kid and Wilson could have hitched into town, but Boujold was going to need some help.

"Is anybody meeting us at the Tra Vinh Airport, sir?" the Kid inquired of Wilson.

"Oh yeah, I almost forgot, Ti Ui Troung is coming out to get us. I meant to tell you guys. And we've got a surprise waiting for us down there!"

"Surprise?" The Kid's curiosity was piqued. "What surprise?"

"Well now, if I told you, it wouldn't be a surprise then, would it, PFC?"

Yes, the SOB is in a very playful mood for some reason. Is he a head and stoned out of his mind and just concealing it from me because he has to? Maybe I should smell his breath and see if he's been drinking this morning. Surprise?

Hmm.

It was not a minute after Boujold had gotten his shit collected that the bird showed, settling on to the pad in the usual debris-whipping way, almost blowing the fat boy's new jungle hat away.

Once squeezed into the bird, Boujold was in the middle, with the Kid to his left and Wilson to his right at the doors. The lone gunner made sure all the bags were tied to some strap or another in front of their feet, and then he signaled the pilot to di di mau.

Lifting up off the pad, the Kid held his M16 between his legs. He was able to feel the big bag of pot in the leg pocket of his pants pressing up against Boujold's leg. In his other pocket was the Kid's new pipe, a small-bowled and straight-stemmed piece, the smallest one to be found in the Vietnamese tobacco and smoke shop Herrick had taken them to down by the river. It has cost him two dollars MPC. He could have gotten a better deal if he'd had some MPC converted into piasters.

Make a note: get piasters.

As the chopper zoomed down the Mekong, gaining speed before popping almost straight up into the air, the Kid checked his outside pocket to make sure his new pipe wasn't about to fall out into the river. *Now that I've got a cache, I don't think I'll even mind going back to Tan An. God, I hope I've got some mail in Tra Vinh. This no getting mail shit has got to stop! Is today finally the day I get to find out if I'm on my way to daddy land?*

Pregnant. Not pregnant. That was all the Kid could think about on the way over to Tra Vinh. A couple of times, he caught glimpses of Wilson, smirking beneath his windblown handlebar mustache, his little practical joke locked and loaded.

Boujold rode along, occasionally trying to see something of the landscape below, but mostly leaning back, his head against the engine compartment housing, alone with his private thoughts. His new jungle hat, upon which he hadn't even written yet, was clutched firmly in the same hand that held his weapon.

The too few minutes of the coolness at three thousand feet of elevation were quickly over. The chopper was now in the pattern to settle onto the corrugated pad painted with the yellow *H* in the circle, there in Tra Vinh. Pulling all Boujold's gear off as expediently as possible, they cleared the chopper to depart, and soon they were standing there in relative silence. Nothing. No sniper yet.

At the side of the airport terminal building, there was an American jeep painted with a South Vietnamese flag, with yellow and red stripes, on the bumper. Straightaway, the jeep came forward to meet them. It was Ti Ui Troung driving, and with him was another young Vietnamese soldier sitting in the passenger's seat.

"Ti Ui Wilson, Stocka, welcome back," Troung said as he stepped out of the jeep and commenced to help load the gear. "I thought you gone for good. You take so long to come back!"

"Nope, here we are, back and ready to do whatever it is we end up doing." Wilson shook Troung's hand. Still no sniper.

Now the young Vietnamese man, dressed in what appeared to be a brand-new uniform with hardly any patches of any sort sewn on to it, had climbed down from his seat and stood by Troung.

338

"Lieutenant Wilson," Troung addressed the lieutenant. "This is Corporal Ba, your new interpreter!"

"Corporal Ba, pleased to meet you." Herschel shook his hand. "Corporal Ba, this is PFC Stocker and PFC Boujold, the rest of our team," he said, completing the introductions. "We look forward to working with you in the days to come!"

"Wait a minute, is this our 'surprise,' that now we have our own interpreter?" the Kid asked.

"Yep. Our own interpreter, to go with us everywhere we go. We'll never have to sweat the language barrier again!"

The nervously smiling young-looking soldier with extremely white teeth half bowed and half stuck out his right hand to shake with the Kid and Boujold. "Hello. How are you!"

"Corporal Ba has just graduated from US Army language school in Saigon, and this is his first assignment!" Troung explained.

"Bon U?" the Kid asked, wanting to know Ba's age.

"Oh, you speak some Vietnamese?" Ba answered in English.

"Ti ti," said the Kid. "But tell you what, you teach me Vietnamese and I'll teach you more English!"

"Yes, I think that is very good idea!" Ba smiled as if he were happy. "I am nineteen."

How could anybody nineteen, in any army, be happy being stuck in Tra Vinh or, worse yet, Tan An? *Let's get this show on the road. I want mail call!* "So, gentlemen, what say we get into the jeep and get over to the compound? I've got to believe that Heineman has some mail for me today! Di di mau beaucoup!"

The group piled their gear into Troung's jeep, which precariously began to drive out to the short bit of road between the chopper pad and the terminal, connecting with the road into Tra Vinh. Still no sniper. Nothing but a quiet ride into town.

Can't wait to hear that Sgt. Pepper! Right after mail call.

Heineman had mail for the Kid all right—a three-inch-thick stack of it, and a package the size of a shoebox from his dad! The Kid felt that he had died and gone to heaven.

There were five letters from Flo; three from his mom and dad; one from his brother; two from his best friends Dave and Patsy in Nashville; one from his best friend Larry Ryan from Boulder; a letter from Pat Bowen, his official "unofficial" fan club president; and seven fan letters from WKDA listeners in Nashville whom he didn't even know. Twenty letters!

Sitting in the shade of a palm tree on the bench out in front of the servants' quarters, the Kid eyed the letters from Flo. They were numbered 11, 14, 15, 19, and 20. Flo was up to twenty, and he now had only eight. *There's twelve missing Flo letters out there! One of these has to have the news.*

Nervously, the Kid used his P-38 to open Flo's letter no. 11.

June 10, 1968

My Dearest Curt,

Hey, darlin', hope this finds you safe. I love you too much to think that you aren't in a place that's safe. I can't imagine what it must be like to not know when you go to bed at night if you're going to get attacked before the sun comes up.

I got two letters from you yesterday! That's pretty funny that Mr. "I'm Not a Christian" you is staying in an old Catholic monastery and hanging out in an old cathedral!

Honey, I know you're not Christian, but I've been praying for you at church. What can it hurt? Lo and Jacque said they'd pray for you, too. And Lo and I also prayed for Aunt Minnie to show. Jacque doesn't know if there is anything I should be worried about. If she did, she'd probably tell Mom. Yesterday was supposed to be the day, so I guess I'm officially a day late. Lo got hers, and we have been almost like clockwork since we both started. It's that twin thing, I guess. Anyway, Lo said she was reading that being stressed can make you late. I still don't think I'm pregnant. Linda M., my friend who got knocked up last year, said she knew the day she was late that she was preggers. She said that it was like somebody threw a switch. I don't feel like that. What I feel is bloated. I think I've gained weight since you left because I get nervous and I eat to take my mind off it.

Last night, Lo, John, Sandy, and I all went to see 2001: A Space Odyssey. It was every bit as good as you said it was! But some of it I didn't understand. And of course, when they showed the big baby at

340

the end, Lo gave me a shot in the ribs so hard that I wanted to deck her! She can be such a bitch sometimes!

So, my job at the Discount Food Co. is going OK. I think calling people on the phone is better than waiting tables, but I'm not making as much money as some of my friends who are waiting. Sometimes, I tell the people that my name is Mrs. Stocker! I love you!

Well, gotta go. It's my turn to do the dishes.

All my love,

Flo

PS: I'll see you later!

Rats. Not the news he wanted. *Well,* the Kid thought, as he picked up letter no. 14, *four more chances!* Taking a deep breath of hot air, he opened it.

June 12, 1968

Dearest Curt,

Well, I'm not pregnant. You don't have to buy me anything for Mother's Day. Auntie Minnie came today while I was at work. I was sitting there talking on the phone, and all of a sudden, I felt a gush. I thought it was going to spot my shorts. Usually when I get close, I wear a pad, but I wasn't. Thinking I wouldn't because I didn't want to jinx us by having it stay white. It was like I decided I'd rather get it and not be ready than be ready and not get it. Get it? Silly, but hey, it worked! I love you so much. Someday I want to have our baby, but not in high school!

I hope you still love me. I gave you my best at the TM. Sometimes, like a lot of the girls I know said, when they told their boyfriends finally got it, they went away. Well, you went away—but only because you were ordered to by the army! So I won't hold that against you. The only thing I want to hold against you are my naked breasts! Does that make you hot? I'm trying to think of some more sexy stuff to write ya. I know you like it.

But don't write any to me! I think Mom sneaks a read every now and then. Now that I'm not pregnant, I've been thinking about doing it some more. I so wish we didn't have to wait! One month down and eleven to go. I know guys have needs, and I don't expect you not to do it while you're there.

But I don't plan on it, even though you said I could if I wanted. I don't know, I'm sort of confused. Not about if I love you, but just about things in general. This guy Ralph keeps asking me out, and I just kind of laugh him off. He's a nice guy, though. I wish I could just be his friend and him not want to get in my pants. But that's how all you guys are, isn't it?

This weekend, we are going to camp out at the beach. It's really getting hot here, and I'm loving it. Almost as much as I love you!

All my love always,

Flo

PS: ISYL!

The wave of relief that had washed over the Kid when he read the opening words of letter no. 14 was so satisfying that he put the other letters and the package on his bunk for later enjoyment and went to lunch.

The uncondemned man ate a hearty meal!

Walking in the mess hall door, the Kid saw the bowl full of orangish-colored tablets in front of him, with Staff Sergeant Mixx sitting in verification. Mixx was a Detroit-bred black man who was of medium build but who, after being in Vietnam for nearly eight months, was starting to look a little on the skinny side. *Malaria pill time already? Damn, I just got over diarrhea! I so hate the entire concept of armies, especially this fucking army and everything about it!*

"Hey, Stocker," Mixx said, reading the Kid's name tag, "I get to check you off now. You ain't been around much for being listed here."

"Yeah, I know. We went to Sa Dec, Vinh Long, and couldn't get back." The Kid choked down the pill.

Paul and Boujold waved to him as he came through the chow line of the mini mess hall, indicating they had saved him a place.

"So," said Paul, taking a sip of iced tea, "any news?"

Sitting down, the Kid tried to look serious, as if something was wrong, but he couldn't keep it up for long. "Not fucking pregnant!" H finally broke into an ear-to- ear smile.

"Well, all right!" said Boujold. "This calls for a celebration!"

Any good news was a ready excuse for a celebration in 'Nam, but this one, the Kid thought, savoring the idea, was going to be sweet!

"My man," said the Kid to Paul, "I've got some killer bud!" "Yeah, well, who doesn't?" He smiled back.

"Ah yes, but his is the expensive stuff!" Boujold mockingly commented à la W. C. Fields. "He paid thirty dollars for half a pound!" Then he laughed his ass off.

Just then, the far door on the officers' side of the mess flew open, and through it came a pair of muscle-bound soldiers wearing broad jungle hats, reflective sunglasses, and camouflage T-shirts, packing forty-five calibers on their hips and laughing their asses off too. It was Boarz and Howell.

"It was the shot of a lifetime!" proclaimed Major Howell, who was trailing Boar Hog through the door and slapping him on the back. "We were just out flying with Jackson in the Huey about ten clicks west of Cang Long when we flushed about four of them and the Hog." Howell paused briefly to make sure all the thirty-odd soldiers having lunch were paying attention. "He pops this guy with the M79 grenade launcher and hits him right in the head, and it just flat explodes! I've never seen anything like it! Blew his fucking head right off!"

343

The mess hall erupted with a suitable level of admiring comments and good- natured laughter at the report of success from the front.

"No shit!" Boarz took over the narration of his shot. "We caught 'em maybe two hundred meters out in the paddies from the trees. We could see that they were armed. As Jackson pulled up approaching the trees, they were on my right. I fired a shot that kind of arched like a Sandy Koufax curveball and just impacted right in the back of this guy's head!"

Wilson, sitting nearby, rose out of his seat to high-five the Hog, then joined in the general hand clapping and foot stomping, which went on for a good fifteen seconds. The sweaty men made for the iced tea table, still laughing at what was, apparently to them, a funny sight.

Sick bastards.

The Kid looked first to Paul and then to Boujold. *Grim. This kill-or-be-killed bullshit is disgusting! How and why did I get stuck in this place and time? Who can laugh at blowing a guy's head off? I know this is a war, but that seems like they're getting a little bit too much enjoyment for all the wrong reasons.* "That's just not my idea of fun," he finally said.

"True, but then you're not a washed-up, alcoholic, forty-year-old West Point graduate who's only made it to major with no future in the army either." Paul acted like it was something to mourn.

"Who are those guys?" Boujold asked, being new to Tra Vinh.

"Two of the company commander counterparts in the battalion." Paul filled him in on the still celebrating majors. "They love each other so much that they might as well get married!"

Chapter 31

From his vantage point in the circular window of the Tan An Cathedral, the Kid watched Boujold come out of the priests' and nuns' quarters and slowly work his way across the courtyard. Just before he reached the tiny footbridge over the little ditch, Corporal Ba came out and apparently wanted to accompany him, but Boujold waved him off. So, with drooping shoulders and hanging head, Corporal Ba returned to the shade of the building's ample porch.

Poor kid. Gotta be tough on him. Just because he lives where the war is doesn't mean that Ba must not be pretty scared and lonely.

The Kid continued to observe the hatless Boulold, who was also stripped to his boxer shorts, as he ambled along in his flip-flops, his belly sagging. Because of his belly, the Vietnamese had immediately nicknamed him "Buddha."

He was now even with the low-slung wire cage, the one the Kid had thought was for pigs the first time he'd noticed it. But it wasn't. Its real purpose was now being graphically demonstrated to them. It was a tiger cage and a tool for the punishment of ARVN soldiers who displeased their superiors. And it presently had an occupant, an unfortunate private who had not paid very close attention to the lessons being taught in Ti Ui Troung's civics classes. Or a man who'd had the balls to ask a politically sensitive question during the class, if Corporal Ba was to be believed. Either way, the poor ARVN private had been ceremoniously stuffed in there before sunrise, in front of a company formation, and told that his penalty was to remain in there until sunset. That was supposedly a light sentence, a single day in a barbed wire cage that was barely two feet tall and not long enough to really stretch out in. And, of course, a place where the sun always shone.

The Kid looked at his watch and figured that what with its being 1500 hours, the poor stiff had another two or three hours to go. Boujold stopped and was apparently saying some words of encouragement, not that the Vietnamese conscript was understanding him.

When Boujold got to the sidewalk and strode toward the church doors, the Kid turned and sat down on the riser to touch the Zippo to the bowl of his pipe, which he'd been packing while standing there. Nursing a good ember to life, he inhaled a deep toke and held it in. When he saw the bamboo ladder begin to shake with Bouji's weight, he grabbed a really big new blast and held it. A couple of seconds later, when Bouji's round head emerged through the hole, he blew it all out in his face.

"I can see I certainly came to the right place! At least I think I can see." Boujold coughed as he clambered up the last couple of steps onto the landing, pushing his black-framed glasses back up his sweaty nose. The Kid passed him the pipe and the lighter. "I think it's safe to say you've found your calling, Kid." He prepared to hit the pipe. "You can become a bong!" He took a hit and passed the bowl immediately back, then the two of them sat down and finished it.

"Jesus, I almost forgot what it was I came out here to tell you," Boujold said after a couple of minute of hot, humid silence. "They've got some mail for us. Bird Dog is flying out past here, and he's going to drop it out his window! Cool, huh?"

"Yeah!" More stifling hot silence. "So, Boujold." The Kid moved to pack the bowl again. "How do you like the field now?"

"This fucking blows chunks," came his low, deadpan reply without hesitation. "When people talk about this place and use words like *surrounded,* you can almost see human-wave attacks in your mind's eye. But *action*? Hard to believe we are the action."

"No fucking shit! Is this the most boring place you've ever been? And is this the most boring shit you've ever done? Or sat around while somebody else did?"

What they were doing was accompanying Ti Ui Troung, the man whom they were supposed to be advising, as he worked on his current hot project, sent down by the masterminds in Saigon. It was a South Vietnamese troop indoctrination program called "Willing Hearts." Troung would be visiting all the various companies of the ARVN's Fourteenth Regiment and essentially giving them motivational pep talks.

Of course, Lieutenant Wilson, the Kid, Boujold, and now Corporal Ba just sat around on the periphery, smoking cigarettes, while Troung worked away, doing his best delivery of the message of the Thiệu regime.

"I can tell Lieutenant Wilson is getting antsy." The Kid lit up a Kool. "He wants to be out in it so bad that I'll bet you that he makes a deal with Boar Hog or the Howler, or even one of the fucking captains in the other companies, to go with them on some bullshit battalion operation or another real soon. I can just feel it."

346

"All right! I can't wait!" Boujold enthused for the very thing the Kid was dreading.

"And I'm torn between staying out here, where there is nothing and where virtually nothing ever happens, and going back in to Tra Vinh, where I know I'll have to go on combat ops. But I can go over to Wen's house and listen to *Sgt. Pepper* and eat friend potatoes and shoot some pool the day before."

"That's what I want—out of here and potatoes! Yeah. I want some fucking combat experience! I didn't come over here to tell my grandchildren I was a clerk and that the closest I ever got to a gun was cleaning it over and over again, even when it wasn't dirty. I'll tell him that I'll go, and you can stay here," Boujold volunteered.

"Thanks, but it won't work. He doesn't like you, Boujold, don't you get it? He likes me, wants to think I'm his buddy in all of this and that I'm going to get him a record contract when we get out of the army and I'm back in Nashville."

"But I *want* to go! Why won't he take us both?"

"He told me, Bouji, that he doesn't think your fat ass would last out in the field on a combat op. He says he'd eat his fucking hat if you didn't get your fat ass medevacked at the earliest possible convenience once any real shooting or running started. His words."

Just then, "Bread and Butter," a song by the Newbeats, came on the radio that the Kid had been playing not too loudly sitting off to the side on a piece of rubble. "Ooh, my buddy Larry!" The Kid hurried to turn it up and commenced to sign along, including the high part. "I like bread and buttah. I like toast and jam. But I found my baby eatin' with another man. No, no, no mo' bread and buttah, no more toast and jam." The chorus enjoined, "I caught my baby eatin' with another man!"

"You know him?" Boujold asked incredulously when the song ended.

"Yeah. Larry Henley, he's friends with my fellow DJ Good Guy Dave Allen. In fact, Dave wrote the flip side of 'Bread and Butter' and made a pile of money because the A-side was a hit! 'Tough Little Buggy' was the name of it."

"Really?" "Yeah, really."

Then the Kid turned off the radio so they could listen for the airplane engine. Nothing but silence. A light breeze that had been blowing an hour earlier now had seemed to die off completely.

"Listen." Boujold cocked an ear. "I think I hear him! Bird Dog's engine."

347

Sure enough, off in the distance, directly out of the round window, the Kid could see a speck of black on the horizon. It was far, far away, across the paddies that stretched out before the bombed-out shell of a holy place, going for a couple of miles before the tree line looked no taller than newly mown grass on the far end of the gallery.

They watched as he dropped in elevation and grew in size, from a grain of sand to a period at the end of a sentence, to a fly, to a bird, and then to something bigger, a plane. *That's it, a plane!* he drew near to the church, which he had certainly been using to guide his approach.

"If I were a Cong, I'd open up on him right about now." Boujold put Bird Dog in his imaginary sights.

"And from where would you open up, say, out of a submarine duck blind built down there in the rice paddies?"

Bird Dog was buzzing them now. From an elevation of no more than a hundred feet, the pair saw a black container come plummeting out of the pilot's-side window, just over the perimeter. The object hit well inside the barbed wire and bounced like an unfielded punt, coming to rest after nearly hitting the tiger cage. The green-camouflage-painted Cessna 150 pulled up while passing directly over the steeple, climbing quickly to gain altitude before arriving at any of the surrounding tree lines.

By this time, a throng had emerged from the building and off the porch to watch the drop. The Vietnamese were hanging back, and the Americans were now hurrying across the little bridge.

"Well, that was exciting," Boujold deadpanned.

"I'm gonna go down and see if I got anything!" The Kid headed for the ladder.

"You going in, or are you coming back?"

"Coming back. I just dragged my radio, a canteen, and all my shit up here to really get toasted before dinner tonight, and I'm not there yet."

Bouncing down the bamboo ladder and out the church door, the Kid hopped down the seven steps, being careful not to trip in his loose flip-flops, and on to the sidewalk as Lieutenant Wilson, Lieutenant Jim Hollings, Sergeant Matt, and the new American commander, the man who replaced Captain Morris, a Japanese American named Captain Ken Katanaki, converged on the load. *There are only six American advisers at Tan An, and look, five of us are now together, a lucky shell. And Boujold is in charge of this chicken outfit!*

Standing back a little from the knot of Americans were Corporal Ba and Ti Ui Troung, who grinned while attending to the goings-on, even though they likely would not be getting anything in this most likely Americans-only mail call. It wasn't easy getting mail at Tan An. Nor was it easy to send any. In fact, the Kid had about twelve letters ready to go on the next conveyance in. He'd had plenty of time to write letters during the past four days since they'd arrived. Sitting around, they were doing nothing that resembled work—not running any ops with the new commander, as "Ken" seemed to be the kind of ROTC officer who wasn't interested in looking for extra ways to get killed. Lieutenant Wilson didn't like that.

Big Jimbo Hollings had been the one to end up opening the drop container, which was an M16 .233-caliber ammo can. The Kid saw the yellow envelope as soon as the lid flipped open, and Jim reached in and took it out. Twisting it upright, he read in his best mail call voice, "Stocka!" and flipped it Frisbee style to the Kid. "Hollings, where are you?" He looked around.

"Oops, here I am!" He stuck the white envelope into his pants pocket. "Look! Hollings again!" He laughed.

"Matt!" came the next one.

"Yo!" the skinny, flattop-cut lifer called back.

"And another and another!" Jim continued. "Wilson! Ha! Looks like a bill! Boujold, a little bundle!"

"I'll take his." The Kid stuck up his hand. Turning, he saw Bouji watching out the round window. He gave him the thumbs-up and pointed at the bundle and then back to the church.

"Stocker!" Hollings pitched him another letter from Flo and one from his brother.

Two Flo letters! All right!

"And yes, Katanaki! A bundle!" He handed the prize of at least five letters to the captain. "Nobody gets shut out! A good mail call!" Jim turned the can over to show it was empty.

"You get letters from girlfriend?" Corporal Ba came up to the Kid and pointed at the envelopes with one hand, while shading his eyes from the sun with the other.

"Yep! Two of them. And one from my brother! I tell you what, Corporal Ba, I'm going to take this bundle back up to Boujold and read these letters in the shade up there, and then before dinner, we could read some out of that Life magazine. How's that?"

"OK!" The young Catholic boy recently forced to turn man smiled as the Kid turned and headed back to the church.

The Kid was taking a liking to Corporal Ba. For a graduate of the American language school, Ba's English was not all that strong, but the Kid could sense that he was an attentive student. Plus, Ba was helping him with his Vietnamese beaucoup. *There's sure a lot of French words in Vietnamese. What is it with the French? Hey, I think I'm going to try to sneak this poor guy a stick of gum.* The Kid looked around to see who was paying attention. With his left side turned toward the building as he walked past the tiger cage, he eased a piece of Juicy Fruit out of his pocket and let it slip from his hand; it fell within easy reach of the punished one, whose hand quickly gathered it up. *Maybe I should have taken French. Non!*

Hefting the weight of Flo's two new letters, numbered 22 and 23, the Kid reckoned that they seemed lighter than usual. *I wonder what Scott has to say.* The Kid was also anxious to read news from his brother, who was now in medic school at Fort Lewis in Washington State.

Climbing carefully up the ladder, he found Boujold still staring out the round window at the tiger cage.

"I saw that. What if they give that poor son of a bitch another day because he's chewing gum in the cage?"

"Hmm." The Kid underhand-tossed the bundle of letters over to Boujold.

"Thanks!" Bouji began to take off the rubber bands that held the letters together.

"If I was him," the Kid said, "I'd swallow the gum and toss the wrapper as far as I could from the cage and blame it on us!"

"You think he could think that fast after cooking for almost a day in the tropical sun?"

"I don't know. You gotta admit, as a group, the Vietnamese are pretty smart. He's not in there because he wasn't paying attention."

"What was it Ba said? Refresh my memory: why is he supposedly in there?" Boujold looked up from his mail.

"Because he suggested that the possibility of negotiating with thT North Vietnamese might prove better than fighting them in this war." the Kid encapsulated what he thought Ba had been trying to say. Of course, many more words had been involved in the conversation between the ARVN in the cage and Ti Ui Troung.

"You're basically saying Ba said that the guy had an antiwar attitude."

"Yes. In a nutshell." The Kid sat down on the riser with his back to the round window and opened the letter from his brother first, while Boujold delved into his own mail.

June 25, 1968

Dear Lil' Brother,

From what you said about the rain there, you've got nothing on Seattle! It rains here all the time, and boy, can it get depressing. But most of our classes are inside, so we don't have to crawl through any mud or dig any foxholes right how.

So, see any action yet? I watch on TV and look for you, but from what you said, you aren't anyplace where there's anything going on they'd want to put on TV. Too bad you didn't get the radio gig. I know how much you wanted it. Who knows? With your luck, it's possible something will change. I don't know how you do it, but if anybody could fall in the Vietnam shithouse and come out smelling like a rose, it's you!

Well, little brother, it looks like Nancy and I are going to be married at Christmas. I know, being trained as a medic, I'll be coming to 'Nam right after you get home in May, and I figure, what the hell. I love her, and I'd rather have her here in Washington for five months before I ship out than just think about it.

I know we both said we'd be each other's best man, but I just can't wait. I hope you'll understand. I feel like I've got to marry her, sort of like how you told me you felt you had to propose to Flo. And how is Flo? Are you getting lots of hot, steamy letters from her?

Hope this finds you someplace where the beer is cold.

Love,

Yer bro

"Well, what do you know?" the Kid said. "My brother is getting married at Christmas! And I won't be there to be his best man. Too bad. We always had this deal that we'd be each other's best man. Oh well, I hope I fucking live to meet the bride." The Kid folded up the letter and returned it to the envelope.

"So, check this out! My parents just bought a color TV. The fuckers! I wanted one so bad when I was growing up, and now that I'm not there, they fucking go and get one!" Bouji seemed genuinely pissed.

"Take it easy, Bouji. Have another hit and chill. I'm sure they'll let you watch it—if you don't get killed, that is." The Kid passed him the pipe, but for himself, he tapped out a Kool and lit it before going on to the first letter from Flo. No. 22. I wonder what is in lucky 21?

June 29, 1968

Dearest Darlin',

Things haven't been too much fun around here lately. Lo and I have been working a lot, and now today, Lo found out her boyfriend John is going to Vietnam in two months! Now we'll both be glued to the TV every night.

Only difference is, as you know, the marines always want to go, so he's excited. It's so hard to watch the news anymore. I think I'm just going to quit watching TV because the news from Vietnam is so bad. Sometimes I think if things were bad, you wouldn't write and tell me, to kind of save me from having to worry. I hope you know that I love you because you always tell me you will tell me the truth and I believe you. So let me know. I can take it.

The beaches are really jammed this week, and everybody is getting ready for the Fourth of July. There's all kinds of dances and stuff. It's going to be lots of fun. Work hasn't been any fun. I hate this telephone thing, and I think I'm going to quit. My friend Sandy says she can find me a job waiting at a place down by the beach in Oceanside. Lo and I are both going to check it out tomorrow. Now we'll both be without our men when John goes to war. Gulp, I just had a TM minute.

I'll write again tonight.

All my love,

Flo

The Kid folded up the letter and stood up for a minute to look out over the scene, more to make sure people were still where they had been and that nobody was getting the idea that he or Boujold wanted any company. *Looks good. There's Wilson, still reading his mail, and Sergeant Matt sitting there. The rest of them must be inside.* He took the hot burning pipe and hit it, then passed it back to Boujold.

"Her letters are getting shorter, and she writes a brief part about beaches and Fourth of July parties and how much fun they're going to be without a boyfriend."

"Did she say 'without a boyfriend'?" Boujold inquired, looking up from his page.

"No, she didn't say it. I said it. You could tell that she had to be thinking that when she brought up big parties and then said nothing about them." The Kid took another toke. "I don't know, maybe getting engaged before coming over here wasn't such a good idea."

As if on cue, Boujold turned and addressed the Kid. "You know, Curt, from what I've been able to figure out from what you've said, you barely know her. You had more time apart than together. You had some time in Nashville, and you went and saw her at Christmas, and then you saw her before you left for Vietnam.

Three times."

"You never close your eyes anymore when we kiss …" The Righteous Brothers came over the little radio, the song wafting through the old church.

"Ooh, I like this song. May I turn it up?" Bouji motioned to it.

"Sure, go ahead." The Kid was a little surprised that Boujold would be so bold as to reveal that he had analyzed his relationship and then make a comment about it. "Well, we've exchanged hundreds of letters and telephone calls." He held the smoking pipe in his right hand. "And who are you to say I hardly know somebody? You don't know what I know."

"You've lost that lovin' feeling …"

"True enough." Boujold nodded in agreement. "I was just making an observation. I do that from time to time, try to put some things together and figure out where a person is really coming from."

"I see," said the Kid as he touched the Zippo again to the bowl. Passing it to his comrade, he took a drink out of his canteen, which was sitting by the radio.

"Medley and Hatfield. Do you know them too, Kid?"

"Nope, never met them," he said as he stared out into the paddies, past the priests' building on his right and the poor ARVN in the tiger cage, serving his sentence in front of them in the tropical sun, and then off to the trees that may or may have been filled with VC waiting to kill him.

Hmm. Boujold sort of sounds like he doesn't believe that I know some of the people I said I know. "You know, Boujold, I just want you to know one thing. I don't go around saying I know people when I don't. If it's one thing I hate, it's a lyin' bullshitter. I just want you to know, I'll play straight with you if you play straight with me."

"Whoa." Boujold was taken aback. "What brought that on?"

"Well, first you tell me that you think I hardly know the girl I'm engaged to marry, and then you ask me if I know Medley and Hatfield in a sort of sarcastic way that led me to believe that you don't believe me when I say I know Roy Orbison or that I met Roy Acuff or smoked pot with the Lovin' Spoonful."

"All right," Boujold said, "fair enough. Yeah, I guess there was a little of that in there." Now he paused and looked off into the same space as the Kid for about thirty seconds. "It was the part about you and Ronnie and the Daytonas smoking bananas that I thought was you maybe pulling my leg. Can you blame me?"

"There were no 'Daytonas,' and yes, the story is totally true. Bucky Wilkin and I had both read an article about the mellow yellow craze that was supposedly the subject of the Donovan song—you know that line, 'electrical banana, gonna be the very next craze.' So, I went out and got some bananas and dried the peels in the oven of my apartment and smoked the results." Silence. "Before Bucky got there. Didn't get off, so I actually spared him. But that's how we revealed to each other that we did both indeed smoke pot. I need to be stoned enough to think I can eat the dinner the ARVN mess tonight." Dipping the dark brown pipe into his thigh pocket, he repacked the bowl again.

"Yes, this is some good shit." Boujold chuckled. "Guess I shouldn't have given you any flak about paying thirty dollars for it."

"That's right! I forgot about that! Why have you got a case of the ass for me?" the Kid demanded.

"Jealousy, I guess," he offered straightforwardly. "Look at me. I'm fat. People have always made fun of me all my life. You, on the other hand, are not fat. You've led a charmed life, you're great with the women, you're lucky at getting jobs, and things always seem to break your way."

"Bouji, am I not standing on the second floor of a blown-out church with you in the middle of fucking Vietnam? Are we not out in a place where we are both cut off from the entire fucking world as we know it? Except by helicopter? We are cut from the same cloth, my man. But yeah, Bouji, I have had the breaks, and I hope I keep gettin' them! Bouji, that's like us standing here and arguing which of our Sa Dec whores was cuter! Mine."

From behind them and off to their right, at a forty-five-degree angle from where they lounged on the balcony of the destroyed church, the sharp sound of an explosion resounded and came at them. They turned, and when they did so, they observed a puff of dark gray smoke rising in a single cloud above the perimeter, on the bit of breeze that had just started blowing.

"What was that?" The Kid craned his neck and stared at what was a growing commotion. Vietnamese were all of a sudden coming out of the priests' quarters, along with Tu Ta, Dai Ui, Sergeant Minh, Big Jim, Lieutenant Wilson, and Commander Ken.

From their vantage point, the Kid and Boujold now observed some ARVNs running toward the headquarters building from a spot out toward the perimeter where the explosion had taken place.

"Are we under attack?" Boujold looked questioningly at the Kid.

"I don't think so. There's nothing happening, nobody yelling. One isolated explosion and nothing after that. Not much of an attack. But I don't know." The Kid tried to find a place on the bombed-out balcony where he could get a better look without putting himself in danger of accidently falling off. He was looking down on the tops of their heads when the two groups met about fifteen yards away from the corner of the church. A heated discussion took place among the Vietnamese, with a lot pointing in this direction and that. A couple of English comments sent Ken and Big Jim back in the direction of the priests' quarters in a fast trot.

"Lieutenant Wilson," the Kid hollered down. "What happened, sir?"

Turning his neck and raising his right hand to shade his eyes from the setting sun, Wilson visually located the voice out of the blue that had called his name. "Looks like one of the ARVNs accidently triggered one of the perimeter mines and killed himself!" he said, relaying the news he himself had just heard. "Ken's going to call in a chopper to come out and pick up the body."

"Say what?" Boujold called to the Kid from behind. "What'd he say?"

The Kid worked his way back from his observation point on the corner of the balcony. "He said that some ARVN stepped on one of his own mines and bought it, and that a chopper is coming in to pick up the body."

"What a stupid fucking way to go." Boujold shook his head.

In about ten minutes, four ARVNs came walking in from the perimeter from the direction of the accident. Between them, they carried what could only be the body. *Is that the poor soul who was just killed or the lucky soul who has just been released from his earthly suffering?* "I wonder if the guy was a Buddhist Vietnamese or a Catholic Vietnamese."

"We could ask Corporal Ba to ask for us, if you really wanted to know for some reason." Bouji seemed puzzled, unable to figured out why the Kid would care.

When the small party got to the front of the church, near where the helipad with service to Tan An was located, the four men laid the body down to await its aerial hearse. It was wrapped in a regular army-issue rain poncho. Tan An didn't rate having its own cache of body bags on hand.

"Well, I've never seen a dead person in all my life," said the Kid as he stared at the wrapped corpse, which was in a package that clearly had lumps on one end of it. "We took three KIA on the operation, but I didn't see them."

"I've seen a couple." Boujold reflected. "During Tet, there was one body we could see from New Villa, just lying in the street out there in Ben Xe Moi. Roberts and I looked at it for days. We thought they'd never come get it!"

"I don't know if this counts or not since I can't really see his body." The Kid pondered what exactly constituted seeing a dead person. "I helped load a bunch of wounded guys on the chopper on that first operation, but none of them were dead. And I never heard if any of them did die or not."

"Look at that guy in the tiger cage." Bouji picked up on the forgotten miscreant who was still serving his time. "I wonder if the dead guy was his friend or somebody he couldn't stand?"

"Or owed him money."

Bad sign. Here comes Wilson out of the priests' quarters. He's headed this way. He's got that look. "Shit, fuck, piss. Here he comes."

"Say what?" Boujold turned to look at the Kid, whose gaze was locked on Lieutenant Wilson, who was striding purposefully toward them.

"Wilson. He's walking like a man who has someplace to go," the Kid said. The lieutenant came to stand beneath the circular window that framed the pair.

"Yo, troopers," Wilson, standing up, hollered up at them.

"Yes, sir?" they answered in unison.

"Get down here and come inside. We've got some army business to conduct." "Yes, sir," they said again in unison, equally dejected.

356

"What do you think he wants?" Bouji probed to see if the Kid might know anything as they picked up the radios, their canteens, their packs of cigarettes, and their mail.

"I got no fuckin' idea. What the fuck shit difference does it make? We will be here tonight, tomorrow morning when we wake up, and the next night, and the next, until he cracks and we go in to do something stupid with those major fuckheads the majors."

As they came out of the church and walked down the sidewalk toward the body, the Kid's eyes fell upon the body. *Give it a wide berth? What the fuck. It's just a dead guy; everybody dies. I hope I don't die anytime soon, but what are ya gonna do if you get killed? Who ya gonna bitch to? Hard to believe that the stuff in that poncho was a person with a life just a few minutes ago. That's how it goes. Life here goes on. Happy Buddhist on to a better life, or unhappy Catholic who he didn't the last rites and is now stuck in purgatory?*

Looking beyond the dead guy, the Kid made eye contact with the poor Vietnamese offender, propped up on one elbow inside the tiger cage. Without smiling, the man gave the Kid the slightest nod of appreciation as he slowly chewed. The Kid ticked a finger of recognition to the man without lifting his arm from his side.

"That's pretty fucking brutal, don't you think?" Boujold was chagrined as they passed over the little bridge.

"No shit. Talk about your Article 15!" the Kid answered.

Sitting on the edge of the porch, Lieutenant Wilson, Ti Ui Troung, and Corporal Ba were all smoking shirtless, a fashion statement. Squatting gook style behind them in front of the big window was Xuan, their houseboy, who was also smoking a cigarette. As the Kid and Boujold walked up, Wilson rose and motioned for them to follow him into the building.

Over at the long table, he sat down opposite them. "What I've got here, gentlemen, is some paperwork for 'rations not available,' known in the military as RNAs. Since we're out here in the boonies eating in the Vietnamese mess, we are entitled to be paid an extra two dollars and fifty cents per day so that we can buy our rations on the local economy. And once this paperwork is filled out, when we eat in Tra Vinh, you gotta pay for your meals. Understand?"

The Kid looked over the army forms. "No, shit rations are not available! Sounds simple enough. But does it say where we can spend the two fifty out here?"

"No, Stocker, it doesn't. But this will mean about an extra seventy-five dollars a month in your pay envelope. If you don't want it, that's fine with me, but why wouldn't you?"

"I do," Bouji said. He picked up the pen and began filling out the forms. "Uh, what is for dinner tonight anyway?"

Big Jim, having heard the question, turned to Minh. "Trung Ui, what are we having for dinner tonight?"

"Hmm, rice of course. And chicken, I think. That and rice." Minh smiled a yellow- toothed grin. "Did I say rice? We fresh out of dog and snake and all the good stuff!"

Eating with the Vietnamese was getting old, and having to fill out documents such as the one sitting on the table in front of him was a solid indication that there was more of it to come.

"Oh, and we can stick our mail on this chopper coming out to get the body, so any mail, get it ready," Wilson informed the pair.

Corporal Ba came and sat down next to the Kid. "How come you and Boujold spend so much time up in church? Some of the soldiers say you lovers!"

Well, that got a big laugh around the table.

"Now we know." Sergeant Matt was all over that one. "I always figured there was something odd about you, Stocker." He smirked with a crooked smile messing up the symmetry of his nearly square head.

"That's interesting," the Kid said, waiting for Sergeant Matt to ask what was interesting before he went on. And sure enough, he did.

"What's interesting, Stocker?"

"That you know what odd is. A guy has to know how to count to two before the concept of odd can be clearly understood and explained."

"I know how to count!" Matt shot back insistently.

"Oh, right, it's *reading* that you don't do!" The Kid counterpunched the hapless Matt and turned to chortle with Boujold as the skinny lifer wracked his feeble brain for anything that might resemble a comeback.

"OK, children, just sign the fucking papers so we can get the package ready for the chopper."

The Kid complied and then went over to his cot and pulled out his pack of letters, written in front of the kerosene lamp at night because that was all there was to do. *God, what I wouldn't give for a pizza, or a McDonald's hamburger and a bag of fries. Talk about a raging case of the munchies!*

Off in the distance, the rhythmic thropping of the approaching chopper could be heard. An extra chance to send out mail was a bonus to the men of Tan An. It wasn't like Saigon, where every day mail left for the States and

358

arrived from home. *Living in the rural United States in the 1700s must have been similar to this shit. No plumbing, no running water, no stores, no TV, no cars, no fucking nothing. And a bunch of Mohawk Indians surrounding your house, waiting to kill you. But what the hell. If we keep not getting shot at, I can handle this shit.*

Soon the chopper was settling onto the pad. Once it was down, a group of four ARVNs passed the body up to the door gunner. When they were through, Ken moved forward and handed the gunner the packet of letters, forms, reports, and requisitions he was sending in to Tra Vinh. Then, in an instant, the chopper, the body, the letters, the noise, and the dust were gone.

Almost as an afterthought, Ti Ui Van remembered the poor trooper who had been punished by spending a day in the tiger cage and gave the order to let him out.

It had been quite the busy day at Tan An.

"Hey, Boujold, looked skyward. It's starting to rain! All right, we are going to get showers today after all!"

Chapter 32

The Kid'ss head snapped up. Whoa! He had fallen asleep at the switch! It was a quarter after three o'clock in the morning. There the Kid was, sitting in front of the WKDA control board doing his show, and he had actually nodded off. *Thank fucking God the record didn't run out! ... Coffee. Need coffee. I gotta quit staying up all day and trying to make it through the night to the next day, and then get caught staying up so late the next day that if I go to sleep, I won't wake up in time to make my air shift.* He pulled open the thick wooden insulated sound- dampening control room door and walked down the beige-carpeted and wood- paneled hallway to the announcer's lounge, where he checked the pot. *Thank God! There's a cup left. ... Phone ringing! Better take it in the control room.* The Kid hurried back down the hallway and into the control room, trying not to spill the coffee, and picked up the phone. "KDA. This is the Kid."

"Hey. Hello. Say, I want to talk to the FM DJ, please."

"There is no FM DJ. It's all automated. It's just a machine in there, running along like a big tape recorder, with some other tape recorders that automatically kick in and play the commercials."

"Gee, too bad. I was hoping he'd take a request like you do." "No such luck, sorry." *Click.*

From where he was sitting, the Kid could see past his control board in the WKDA AM studio into the newsroom and out the other side, into the room that held the automated FM equipment. *Gee, that really is a waste. They have four FMs in Nashville and all of them are automated. WKDA ought to unautomate and play rock and roll like we're playing here on the AM! Wouldn't that be cool!* The Kid cued up his next record: "Light My Fire" by the Doors, a really hot new group out of California. The music director, Baby Bill Craig, had given him the album the song was from. Since it was six minutes long, WKDA had made a shorter version to play in its Top 40 format that was only three minutes long, but the Kid could play the longer version on his midnight-to-six gig and nobody cared. He played a lot of long cuts like that. As the chords to "Light My Fire" started, the Kid had to laugh to himself. *It's so funny that Dick Buckley said he wouldn't play "Light My Fire," because it is clearly about a couple of people doing it. And then he said that WKDA has never failed to play a song that made number in Billboard magazine, but here it is the middle of July and it's headed for number one!*

"Hey, Private, shake a leg! Come on, let's go!" Lieutenant Wilson rattled the edge of the Kid's bunk, rousting him out of his deep sleep. "We gotta be at ARVN digs by zero six hun, so get your shit together!" He turned and left, leaving the Kid to ponder the pros and cons of breakfast.

He had been sleeping great in the bed. *I hate Tan An and that cot. I hate the army. I hate fucking Vietnam. I hate going out on combat ops. I fucking hate that we'll probably get shot at today. How the fucking A did I ever get to be in this frickin'-frackin' war?*

The Kid reached to turn on his radio, which was resting on the floor beside his bunk, but he stopped in midmotion. No. Alan P. might be on, and I don't think I can take it.

God, what a vivid WKDA dream! I thought I was really there! Air-conditioning. The control room was air-conditioned. Sweat rolled off his back as he made his way into the latrine. *Good news, bad news: Good news is there's commodes here to shit in that flush! Bad news is, since I'm sitting on this crapper, I'm going out today. Gotta remember to drop those letters off with Paul before we leave for ARVN land.* As the Kid sat there on the toilet, he nodded off again, and when he snapped back, he thought for a second he was dreaming again. Then the reality of the heat brought him around. *Yeah, wouldn't it be great if this was the dream and I was going to wake up back in the world!*

As he brushed his teeth and looked at his bloodshot eyes in the mirror, he contemplated what was supposedly going to happen today. Ti Ui Troung was actually going to show up with loudspeakers. *Or so he says! I'll believe it when I see it. So far, I haven't done one thing I was trained at DINFOS to do, and I don't think that's going to change anytime soon.*

When Wilson and the Kid arrived at the ARVN compound to catch up with Company A, they met Troung and Ba at Troung's office.

"So, Ti Ui." Wilson looked at him through early morning cigarette smoke.

"Where's the loudspeakers?"

"In this box, Lieutenant!" Troung reached into a container at the side of his desk and pulled out a white bullhorn about a foot long with a small square power unit attached and a strap so that it could be placed around a person's neck. He was smiling broadly as he clicked it on and carefully said, "Chieu hoi," almost in a whisper, fearing the effects of voice amplification.

"You gotta be kidding!" the Kid spit out. "I thought our speakers were supposed to be so big that you had to carry them on a rucksack frame!"

"Oh, we no have those!" Troung shook his head. Corporal Ba, standing behind him to his left, shook his head in unison.

My God! I'm advising announcements over a bullhorn! How the motherfucking hell did I ever get here? The Kid took the bullhorn out of Troung's hands and examined it. "If you took this thing and pointed it in a VC's ear, say, from the distance that dude in Saigon did when he shot that Cong in the head during Tet, he might hear you!"

The call came from outside that the unit was ready to depart. Soon, they were rolling down the road as the sun lightened the sky and gave definition to the rice paddies right on the outskirts of Tra Vinh. They were getting a late start today.

The Kid noticed that they were going the opposite way from Cang Long, which made him a happy camper.

As the soldiers climbed down out of the trucks at the end of the line, the Kid lit up a butt and took a deep drag. Major Boarz walked up with Tu Ta.

"Mornin', gentlemen," the major said. "Ross, you and Ti Ui Troung and your speaker team are going with Captain Metzger here today." He motioned to the man who stood slightly behind him, holding an operational map encased in plastic, with the arrows of direction encoded on it in red.

"Captain Metzger, how are you today?" Wilson nodded in his direction.

"OK, I reckon," Metzger replied with an accent that revealed he was from some place in the South.

Lots and lots of southerners in this man's army, the Kid mused as he puffed his Kool. He'd gotten a different take on southern since he'd gone to Nashville, but he was still amused that so many southerners were in the army.

"Well." Metzger got out his own cigarette and lit up. "Let's hope we get a chance to deploy the speaker today and get us some Hoi Chans," he said sarcastically, mimicking a third grade teacher in cadence and oral punctuation, "that is, after we rack up some body count. Pickings have been slim here lately," he seriously lamented.

As the troops left the road and entered the paddies, the radios began to crackle, the singsong Vietnamese language permeating the electrically charged air.

362

Wilson fell in behind Metzger, whose nickname around Tra Vinh was "Mets," while Ti Ui Troung fell in behind Mets's RTO, with the Kid and Corporal Ba bringing up the rear of their little command element.

It was already hot when the sun peeked up over the horizon, instantly kicking up some more heat. The men walked through the first set of paddies and entered a tree line that turned out to be fairly narrow. Out into the open on the way to the next tree line, the Kid watched as Boarz moved off to their left with two squads.

"So, what's the plan here today, sir?" The Kid caught up to Wilson and sought some information on the day's operation.

"As near as I can tell from the map," Wilson spoke as they continued to walk along, "there's a sizable tree line area down here a couple of clicks away. We're going up this side, and Boarz is going up the left side, while Wally takes a couple of squads right up the gut. We're going to try to flush them out into the open where the trees finally peter out down there about another three or four clicks."

"Seems simple enough," the Kid replied. "What's the rub?"

"The rub, as you so accurately put it," Wilson said, smiling at him, "is that we and the Hog's units gotta stay ahead of Wally so we can put in supporting fire. But that means we'll be even, and if Boar Hog's squad shoots into the trees at them, we'll be in line to take some friendly fire!"

"Shit!" exclaimed the Kid.

"Hey, it happens from time to time. Actually, too much, to tell you the truth," Metz added. "In fact, we've made up our own medal for when it happens. If you get shot at by your own troops, you get the Paddy Medal! And every time it happens after that, you get a Xin Loi device to put on it."

Xin Loi, the Kid now knew from his rapidly increasing Vietnamese vocabulary, roughly meant, "So sorry about that!"

Half an hour passed as they made their way forward outside the tree line to their left. The trees on the other side were at least a half mile or more away. The unit had taken to walking along the top of a paddy dike to keep out of the warming waters of the paddies. Looking back, the Kid could see that the ARVNs were spread out in a thin line along the dike, easily a hundred men trailing behind them and another fifty or sixty in front.

Suddenly, way back down the line, where the Kid's gaze happened to be looking, he saw two soldiers sort of pop up into the air and fall to the ground as the report of an explosion swiftly came after.

"Holy shit!" Metz exclaimed. "Looks like somebody triggered a booby trap!"

The radio crackled, and sure enough, word came up from the rear that, indeed, a soldier had stepped on a mine embedded in the paddy dike and two men were badly wounded!

"Fuckin' A!" The Kid breathed the words to Ba. "We all passed over that spot on the dike! Any one of us could have stepped on it!"

The young Vietnamese interpreter appeared to be shaken up, realizing that his foot could have missed the mine by mere inches. He started scanning the ground around his feet nervously, suspicious of every inch of the large dike that ran parallel to the woods.

When the first *pop-pop* of rifle fire wafted in from in front of them to the left, the Kid was not really even startled.

Shit, here it comes. Here comes the fucking insanity of combat! A couple of bullets here, a couple there. Hmm, it doesn't seem as bad as the first time. Ha! Ain't that the way with everything! Fuckin' A! It's picking up; must be Wally in there. Glad I'm not in there with Wally. I thought Wilson was going to volunteer us and that fricking joke of a speaker to take the inside. I wonder why he didn't?

More rounds could be heard, and for the first time, some of the lead was coming out of the trees and toward the men. Like a row of dominoes falling, the ARVNs and their American counterparts began diving behind the paddy dike upon which, until seconds ago, they had been walking. The Kid took a look behind him at

Corporal Ba, Ti Ui Troung, and their speaker operator and saw they had all hidden themselves as more rounds whistled by.

"Wally's squad's got it goin'!" Metz hollered as he dropped the handset of his PRC-25 radio into his RTO's waiting hands. "Let's move! We gotta work our way up the line so we can bring some fire into the woods without shooting Wally's guys up." He waved the men forward along the paddy dike with the battle map in his left hand. He was up and running, his army-issue .45 pistol held in his right hand. Of course, Wilson was right behind him, and the Kid could do nothing but follow suit.

After about fifty meters, a new hail of fire came at them out of the woods. Their little command element fell to the ground behind the protective dike.

"Hear that?" Wilson hollered at the Kid. "You can hear the clack-clack-clack of the AK-47 action!"

"Hey! Ya can!" The Kid marveled for a second at the distinct sound signature of the AK before the individuality of the shots from the communist weapons were lost in the volume of return fire the ARVNs began pumping out. The Kid still couldn't see anything to be gained by jumping up and blazing away with his own M16. In fact, he wasn't carrying that much ammo and decided not to waste what he had. The frickin' thing was becoming more and more of a burden as the sun rose up the into the sky and its geometric angle caused everything below it to get hotter. The Kid looked at Wilson, whose own M16 had gotten more the slightly muddy in the last couple of seconds.

"We gotta get us some pistols like Metz!" Wilson turned and said.

"You said we," the Kid said. The firing kept up. They lay tight by the black loam of Vietnamese earth. "You mean I can get one?"

The lieutenant smiled a wry smile. "Sure, why not? I don't give a shit what kind of weapon you carry!"

Cool! I can't wait to stop lugging this piece of shit around!

As the minutes passed like hours, the firing continued, and soon, Wilson, the Kid, Ti Ui Troung, Corporal Ba, and the cowering speaker operator were huddled near Metz and his RTO, listening to radio traffic, as Wally's boys worked up the inside.

"Wally's got a couple of US Army senior NCO infantry advisers in there with him today, a couple of E-7's who really know their shit!" Metz, exasperated, listened to them call the shots on the radio.

They lay there in the mud, monitoring the progress of Wally's unit, as enough round flew over their heads to keep them aware that they were on the periphery of the engagement. The voices of the two NCOs, both so obviously southern, gave the orders and controlled the movement of the ARVN rifle squads.

"I think we got 'em! Yeehaw!" the voice cracked over the monitor. "That's some of the prettiest work I've ever seen these ARVNs do with the M16! We got us three VC KIAs here!"

With that announcement, a lull in the firing set in, and immediately Metz and Wilson were up. "Let's go check it out!" Wilson grinned. Rising up and over, and then jumping off, the dike, he headed for the tree line thirty meters away.

As Troung, the speaker man, and Corporal Ba walked by, the Kid looked at Ba. "We could've gotten us some Hoi Chans, but it sound like they killed them instead," he said grimly.

"They can kill them every last one of them for all I care," Ba spat out in stunted English.

Walking toward the trees, the Kid could feel that Ba, like him, and Ti Ui Troung, and especially the speaker operator, would have preferred to be anyplace but where they were, doing what they were doing, except for Wilson, who looked as if he were having a great time!

Entering the trees, they discovered they were in line with men from Wally's flank. Knowing this, they made their way into the growth in the general direction in which the soldiers had pointed them.

We're going to see dead men. Holy mother of fucking pearl, looks like I'm finally gonna see a corpse.

Soon, they came upon a well-worn path that led out into a little clearing inside the tree line where there were three thatched-roof huts strung along the far side, their backs up against the foliage. ARVNs were coming out of and going in to the huts, looking for whatever they might find. Another knot of soldiers, including Boar Hog, Wally, and the two NCOs, stood in a group in front of the huts over to the Kid's left. At their feet lay the bodies of the three freshly slain VC. Boar Hog was examining one of the newly captured AK-47's.

Oh my God! Look at that! My first real body count. Seconds ago, they were alive and trying to kill us! I wonder if any of them knew they were going to die today? Wow. Three dead Charlies at once! I wonder which one, then, is the first dead person I've ever seen?

The Kid's eyes fell upon the body nearest him as he walked up. The trio had been laid out face up, and the man was surprisingly tall, much taller than the two men who lay next to him. His body was dressed in tan shorts and a cotton shirt that had a faded flowery pattern on it and was closed across his narrow chest with just one button. The Kid's attention was attracted to a hole just above and in front of the man's right ear. *I don't see any other holes on his body. That must be where he got it.* The expression on the dead man's face was quite serene, more than suitable for the position he now found himself in. But as the Kid moved around to the side of the three corpses' heads, he made a grisly discovery. The tall man no longer had a back to his skull!

I think I'm gonna puke!

One of the guest infantry NCOs noticed the Kid's queasiness and snickered. "His brain's over there, if you wanna take a look at what's left of it. It fell out where we picked him up to move him over here. This is almost where the shorter two fellas fell."

Fight it! Fight the urge to hurl. Do not embarrass yourself. Do not give in. Take a couple of deep breaths. Om, om, om.

The other two bodies both had numerous bullet holes in their legs, arms, and torsos, kind of as if they might have had four or five riflemen zero in on

366

each them at the end. *Just like Bonnie and Clyde!* Judging from the size of the exit wound in the first guy's head, the Kid could only try to not imagine what the backs of the two shorter VC looked like. He could see blood pooling around their torsos.

"Son of a bitch, he was a tall muthafucker!" Wilson said, now down on one knee, examining one of the slender man's hands. "Don't look like he was the one cutting the firewood or nothing. I'll bet you he's a Chinese adviser! They got 'em, you know."

"Well, we didn't find anything on his body to tell us that's what he was, but shit, I don't think I've ever seen too many Vietnamese that tall," Boar Hog spoke up. "What about you, Tu Ta?"

The Vietnamese major nodded his head, his mirrored sunglasses catching a ray of sun peeking through the trees and flashing it upon the body as he looked it up and down. "No see like this! This man beaucoup tall! Chinese for sure!"

The Kid pulled out his canteen and took a swig of water to try to dilute the bile that had almost made it out of his mouth. He rinsed and spat out a mouthful of water before taking a long drink and then offering the canteen to Ba, who stood immediately to his right. The young interpreter looked a little queasy too. Taking the container from the Kid, Ba also rinsed and spat before taking a drink and handing the canteen back.

"Come on, ladies," Boar Hog chimed in, "we gotta keep moving if we're gonna get some more of these fuckers to add to our tally today!"

"Ya dang sure as hell got that right!" the freckle-skinned guest NCO hollered.

"Let's see if we can reestablish contact. I think there were more 'n three of 'em."

The Kid, Troung, Ba, and the speaker caddy turned to Wilson to see what he was going to do.

"Tell ya what, Ti Ui Troung," Wilson began, "why don't we keep the speaker in here with Wally's boys instead of going back out with Metz? This way, we'll most likely get a better chance of using it!"

When Ba turned and obviously informed speaker man that the group was staying in the trees, the expression on his face spoke volumes: the prospect of having to use his little toy bullhorn scared the living piss right out of him.

When Ti Ui Troung began giving him a raft of shit, the speaker man's eyes fell to the ground in shame, and when Troung laid off him and turned

367

away, the speaker man's eyes turned toward heaven with a begging, pleading look.

Just then, all hell broke loose again, and in that split second, everybody was crawling around looking for cover. The radios came to life. Two southern NCOs began rushing forward and moving low, crouching in rifle-ready urgency, toward where they were apparently needed, their frantic RTO in tow.

Crouching appropriately, the command group began moving forward behind the rifle squads. They alternately appeared and disappeared through the foliage.

If a VC jumped up out of a hole now, he could just shoot in every direction and cause all kinds of frickin' hell! I wonder if we'll ever see any of the little bastards who aren't dead. Haven't seen that yet. Now I've seen a dead guy—a couple of dead guys. They're dead and the war goes on! Who's next?

As they worked their way through the brush, it seemed as if it were a rolling engagement with the VC running in front and the ARVNs chasing, until the VC would stop and lay down some serious shit, thereby stopping the ARVNs while they got up and ran some more.

At one point, the command group came up to a canal that cut through the tree line. It looked man-made and was only about six feet wide with very steep banks. The advance squads had already crossed it.

Welcoming the break as a chance to catch his breath, the Kid noticed that the clouds had been building and the sun was not gone. It was starting to look more like a storm was coming in.

"Ti Ui," Metz spoke to his ARVN counterpart, "have one of your men look out there, up and down this cut, and see if they can see a bridge device of any sort. I don't think the RTOs can jump this thing too easily."

The Vietnamese lieutenant signaled one of the ARVN riflemen to emerge from the trees and take a look. As soon as he stuck his head out of the tree cover, a hail of fire came screaming down the canal line as if it was a shooting gallery and he was the duck. The ARVN didn't get hit, but the closeness of the miss had taken his breath away.

"Whoa, daddy-O!" Wally proclaimed, "Up there?" He got the ARVN's attention and pointed to his right, inquiring if that was the direction from which the fire had come. The shaken man nodded, indicating that it was. Taking up the handset on his PRC-25, Wally put in a call to Metz. "Poppa Two, Poppa Two. Over."

"Poppa Three. Go," came the reply, crackling over the radio.

"Poppa Two, we are at the little canal you should see on the grid, and we are taking fire from a spot between you and us. Do you think you can work in a little and see if you can find the little fucker and neutralize him? Over."

"Poppa Three," Metz's voice responded immediately, "if you can get him to shoot at you some more so we can get his ten-twenty, that would be a great help! Over."

Wally got a cockeyed look on his face. He said, "Poppa Two, what we want you to do is get him to stop shooting at us, not shoot us while you look for him. Over."

"Three, just do something to draw a little fire. I don't know what, but make him shoot off a few rounds, like, right now. Out!"

Wally looked at Wilson and Ti Ui Troung. "Hey, get that goofy fuckin' speaker guy to holler at the bastard!" he suggested, as if it were something that had come to him out of the book of Revelation.

"That might work!" Wilson immediately agreed. Troung turned to the speaker man and spoke in rapid-fire Vietnamese, causing the guy to turn an even paler shade of yellow.

"Yeah," said the Kid, "tell 'em we're surrounded!"

"No, you stupid shit!" Wilson exclaimed to the Kid. "Tell 'em we've got them surrounded!"

"Oh, right. Then why do I feel so surrounded?" The Kid felt the need to continue questioning in light of the fact that the lieutenant had missed the joke.

Ti Ui Troung and speaker man moved off to the right through the trees parallel to the little canal. Once they were about twenty feet away, they could no longer be seen. Wilson and the Kid cocked their ears to see if they could hear the speaker at all, even if its horn was pointed away from them. They heard little scratching singsong noises going out, but nothing coming back.

"Rats!" Wally slapped his map on his thigh. "The fucker isn't going for it. We've gotta draw some fire. Ti Ui." Wally turned to his lieutenant. "Have one of your men run out of the woods and dive across the canal and get on the other side," he said.

After taking a couple of seconds to explain what he wanted, the lieutenant got a private to find a path and an opening where he could launch. He ran up the ten steps he could reach by running and jumped across the canal, clearing it by a good two feet. As soon as his boots hit the dirt on the opposite side, the VC opened up, late. Clearly the sniper had not been expecting that, but he did fire off some rounds.

"Let's have somebody else jump over and make him shoot again!" Wally got excited. "If we do it sporadically, he won't know when to draw a bead!"

Peering across the canal, the Kid could see the first ARVN crouching safely within the cover of the trees and shrubs. Another one took the jump, and again the same thing happened: the volley came, but it was way late.

"I'm going!" Wally proclaimed. Without waiting to discuss it with Wilson or anybody else, he got into position and bolted, jumping the canal, again drawing ineffective fire. Not wanting to be left too far behind his leader, Wally's RTO followed almost immediately, arcing across the opening, but stumbling on his landing with the heavy radio on his back. He barely cleared the canal, making it by less than half a foot, crawling frantically the last bit to get himself to safety.

Wilson and the Kid turned and looked at each other. "Your turn," Wilson coldly said. "I'll be right behind you!"

"Uh, sir, why don't you go first and show me how?" The Kid was stalling.

"God fucking dammit, Stocker, jump over the fucking canal! That's an order." He fumed.

"Oh well, since you put it that way, sir, and not a 'turn' I can take if I want, OK, sir!"

And with that, the Kid backed up, gripped his M16 by the top handle in his left hand, and took his ten steps. At the spot he'd picked to launch, his right foot slipped in some mud. It was more that he fell forward than jumped and failed to clear the canal. He landed chest first against the bank, knocking considerable wind from his lungs. His reaction was to hold onto the bank as he valiantly spread his arms and tried to use his M16 to claw his way back up it. He couldn't get a grip with his boots as they slid off the muddy side of the canal. And when a volley of bullets screamed up the canal, he let go and, tumbling the six feet, landed butt first, splashing into the muddy brown water in the bottom of the ditch. It went over his head. Desperately trying to hold his breath and hold onto his weapon at the same time, he ended up pushing the M16 down into the mud in his initial attempt to get up.

Stunned and coated with mud, the Kid rose to find he was up to his waist in water. Oh, he still had his M16, but it had so much mud caked on it that he couldn't see his hand where it was gripping the weapon by the handle atop the trigger housing. The Kid was scrambling to get some footing on the grease-trap- like bottom when he looked up to see Lieutenant Wilson come flying over the top of him. Once again, bullets filled the air above the canal ditch. Not having anywhere else to take cover, the Kid sucked in as deep a breath as his aching chest would permit and ducked back under the oily water.

Pflugg, pflugg, pflugg. The noise came to his water-filled ears. *Bullets being shot into water? Mud clots falling in? Oh God! Where are my glasses?* His hand instantly moved to the bridge of his nose to feel for his prescription shades, but he couldn't find them on his face. *I've lost my glasses!* The Kid needed air, so he struggled to his feet. Luckily, the shooting had stopped. His breath came ingasps, and he was spitting mud and whatever else he could out of his mouth. Looking up, he spied Lieutenant Wilson smiling down at him.

Wally was on the radio when the Kid walked up to stand by Wilson at the edge of the canal. "Roger that, Papa Two. You got the SOB. That's great! Out. Well." He tilted back his steel pot and wiped his brow. "Our body count today is up to four!"

Wilson's attentions turned back to the muddied Kid whose head was still three feet below the top of the ditch. Kneeling, he aid, "I believe your order was to jump over the fucking canal, not go swimming, PFC." He tried to look stern before he broke into laughter. Then the Kid heard more laughter. It was Ti Ui Troung, speaker man, and Corporal Ba, on the other side of the ditch, also looking down and quite totally entertained by the Kid's entire misfortunate incident.

"I lost my glasses!" the Kid screamed in anguish.

"Oh no you didn't. They came off up here when your face hit the bank!" Wilson held them up. "You OK? Fuckin' A, Stocker, it looked exactly like you got shot, the way you fell in there! Let me give you a hand!" With that, Wilson extended his paw downward to take the Kid's chocolate-dipped M16 up first. Then he grabbed the Kid's wrist and hoisted him up out of the canal.

They could hear the action moving on ahead of them as the Kid tried to catch his breath. *Holy fucking shit pile! Look at me! This M16 isn't a weapon, it's a plastic spoon in a hot fudge sundae! How am I ever gonna get this mud off?*

Just then, the clouds opened up and the monsoon rains began to fall in hard driving sheets. *Well, there's your answer!*

Chapter 33

The American compound club in Tra Vinh was rocking! Sergeant Spencer had a new tape recording system and speakers he'd just gotten shipped in from Tokyo all set up and blasting Buck Owens's "Tiger by the Tail," of all things. The beer was flowing, the ivory on the pool table was rolling, and Wilson was the center of attention in the room as he described the "event" from earlier in the day.

"It was like when he got up to the bank, he wanted to stop but was past the point of no return. And then when he could see he couldn't stop, he tried to glide across like Rocky the fuckin' flying squirrel!" Wilson regaled the crowd, and everybody roared with laughter at the Kid's expense. The Kid sat at a table nearby with Paul, Pete, and Ernie, smoking and drinking beer, having almost as much fun as Wilson. After all, he hadn't gotten shot, and being the center of attention was never a problem for him.

"And then he's hanging there like a Christmas piñata, legs flailing, looking to get busted open, but the Charlie misses him by less than half a foot! So he throws his arms up like, Sweet Jesus, take me, and falls into the canal! And from as near as we can all figure, when the VC gets up from his spot to try to finish him off down in the water, that's when Metz's boys shoot him in the back!"

"We should use the Kid for bait more often!" Pete piped up, to a rousing round of supporting yells.

It was a pretty tight group there in the Tra Vinh compound out in the middle of the Mekong Delta, basically in the middle of nowhere, guarded by a bunch of Cambodian mercenaries. It was definitely the size of a compound that could be taken, as it almost had been in the recent Tet Offensive.

The Americans who had been sentenced there—and most of them viewed it that way—were a truly mixed group, knowing that whatever happened, they were in it together.

First there were the army guys, who essentially had control of the compound. Major Gillmore was the top-ranking officer, and therefore, he was

God incarnate. First Sergeant John Vickers was the top enlisted man, and he was a no-bullshit World War II veteran who was near the end of his career in the army.

There were all kinds of civilian types hanging out there, some clearly in the CIA, because they were Air America pilots. They flew in and out and rotated around. You never got to really know any of those guys before they were just gone.

"Hey, Stocker," Boar Hog said, getting into the mix, "how'd you stay alive under water? Did you have an air pocket in your helmet, or did you get some air out of your ass?"

The room just fell down laughing at that one, but the second the laughter died down enough for a retort, the Kid replied, "No disrespect, sir, but I'm personally not familiar with the technique you just mentioned about breathing the air emitted from your ass. Perhaps you could demonstrate for us how it's properly done by the numbers, like they taught you at West Point?"

A gasp escaped from the crowd, followed by dead silence; the Kid had insulted West Point. As the crowd waited for Boar Hog's comeback, which was not delivered with the swiftness of a Western Union telegram, the pressure on him grew. Finally the Hog blurted out, "Well, you can just kiss *my* ass!"

The Kid desperately wanted to say what he was thinking, which was one of his father's favorite lines: *You're all ass! Mark the spot!* But instead, he bit his tongue and replied, "No, thank you, sir!" snapping off a sarcastic salute. Boar Hog was not somebody you wanted mad at you.

Mercifully, the Buck Owens song ended. Spencer got up on a chair and hollered, "OK, who's got another tape we can play?" An anonymous hand supplied him with one to thread on. It turned out to be Cream's *Disraeli Gears.* Sweet!

The Kid looked around himself, once again feeling a wave of "lucky to be alive" sweep over him. It was a relaxed moment, sitting, talking, smoking, and nursing a relatively cold Miller High Life, when Wilson motioned that he should come to him.

"I've been waiting so long to be where I'm going." The Cream song was cranked up as the Kid rose from the table and made his way past the pool table and out into the dining room portion of the building, where Wilson had joined a sergeant at the table. They were looking at a pair of pistols. The sergeant was one of the NCOs who'd been advising the ARVNs in Wally's squad earlier. Sergeant Tanner was his name.

"Hey, PFC," the red-haired, freckled Mississippian said, "you clean up right nice! Now, I can only hope your M16 is as clean as you are!"

"Oh, thanks, Sarge. Yeah, you can dress me up and take me out. Not you, of course, Sarge, but the right people, I mean."

"Hear you're in the market for a pistol and the lieutenant is going to let you carry one. I'm going back to the States in three weeks, and I'm getting rid of a couple. I got a nine-millimeter Luger and a .38 snub nose. They're both for sale for a hundred dollars each."

"You can have the one I don't get," Wilson said as he fiddled with the Luger, which looked like something right out of Erwin Rommel's holster. "I really like this!" He hefted it in his hand and then drew a bead on about ten different things around the mess hall.

"It has a nine-round clip." Tanner pointed out its main advantage over the .38.

"I'll take it!" Wilson smugly declared.

The Kid picked up the .38 and held it in both hands. Flipping open the cylinder, he checked to make sure it was unloaded. Then, looking into his wallet, he discovered that he had about one hundred twenty-five dollars left to his name, but it wasn't long until payday. "A hundred, huh? Does that include any ammo?"

"It does. I got two boxes of thirty-eight-caliber ammo and three boxes of nine- millimeter bullets for the Luger," Tanner said, lifting it up off the seat beside him, where he'd had it cached in case he needed it to close the sale.

And before he knew it, the Kid was the proud owner of a .38 snub-nosed pistol. Just like Sergeant Joe Friday on *Dragnet*! It reminded him of a cap gun he once had.

"Plus, for the .38, I got a leather shoulder holster that you can have." Tanner tossed it onto the table as he rose to go.

"Hey! Thanks!" the Kid expressed his delight. *A shoulder holster! I am fuckin' stylin' now!* Slipping his right arm through one loop, he found that the strap fit across his back and the holster was hanging essentially in his left armpit. "Do you think I should load it?" he inquired of Wilson.

"Well, yeah, unless you plan on throwing it at somebody." The lieutenant smirked.

"Leave the one chamber you rest the hammer on empty," Tanner advised. "Not that it's gonna go off or anything. It's just somethin' I've always done."

"OK, Sarge, if you say so," the Kid replied. He pushed shiny silver rounds into five of the chambers. Checking the safety, he then pretended to draw a bead on a gecko scurrying across the mess hall's back wall. "Pow!"

He verbally blasted it and blew the imaginary smoke from the barrel before placing the pistol into the holster—a fully armed dude. Rifles weren't allowed in the club, but guys wore their sidearms in there all the time. The Kid had to take it in and show the boys. "Thanks, Sarge," he said as he rose to go, interrupting the man's counting of his money.

Back at the table, the Kid's new sidearm was a hit! If he'd been in an American unit, this kind of behavior by a specialist 4 would never have been tolerated, but out in the boonies, men didn't give a shit. Just like the "no saluting in the field" stuff, nobody cared what kind of weapon a person felt he might want to carry.

Sergeant Tripp, a skinny twenty-one-year-old from Sacramento, carried a sawed- off shotgun in combat. He hated the M16 and felt the sawed-off shotgun was a better choice to have in the foliage of the jungle.

Lieutenant Chester, an artillery officer adviser with regiment, wore two army- issue forty-five calibers. His opinion was that if he needed to, he was going to blaze away with both barrels!

And of course Boar Hog, who liked to do his hunting from a helicopter with a grenade launcher and a fifty-caliber machine gun mounted on a truck tire with a makeshift 2" × 4" tripod, also never went anywhere without strapping on his .45. "I'm gonna go lock this thing up so I can shoot pool." The Kid almost immediately decided to take the thing off for the night. "We're up next," he said to Paul.

Chapter 34

The chopper dropped them off at about 1600 hours, which was pretty close to dinnertime. From the second they stepped off the Huey in the Tan An compound, Boujold was all over Wilson; he wanted to go on a combat operation; he wanted to go back in to Tra Vinh for a shower; and he needed some stuff from the PX. No doubt about it, Bouji was totally fed up with Tan An and would do anything or blow anybody to get out. After Wilson handed him a big pile of mail, he took it and immediately walked off.

Dumping their gear inside the priests' quarters, Wilson, the Kid, Lieutenant Jim, Boujold, Corporal Ba, and Captain Katanaki sat down on the front stoop, where Wilson proceeded to tell them the details of the operation they'd been on the day before while the table was being set for chow.

Again the Kid endured the story about how he ended up in the canal and almost got shot down in the water before emerging as a mud pie. Bouji was especially entertained.

"So, Corporal Ba," Captain Katanaki said, "how was your first taste of combat?"

Smiling, Ba was visibly searching for the right English words to describe his experience. "It was too much exciting! No like! Next time, I stay here with Boujold!"

"Cam fuckin' bow ya!" Boujold swept he right arm in an erasing gesture. "Next time, sir," he said, turning to Wilson, "I deserve to go! I've waited for my chance long enough, dammit! I want to go on a fucking operation!" His insistence bordered on a juvenile temper tantrum.

Wilson looked at him sideways, his mouth crooked, as he contemplated his response. Taking a big hit on his cigarette, he blew out a stream of smoke and snuffed the butt out on the step. "OK, Boujold, since you're making such a big stink about the whole thing, I imagine that you're just gonna get that wish!"

"Really?" he replied cautiously, his eyebrows rising above the black frames of his glasses, waiting for the punch line. "You're not shitting me, are you, sir? You're gonna let me go?"

"Negative fecal material, Specialist," the lieutenant said in a reassuring tone of voice. "In fact, we're all going back in on Monday or Tuesday. Wednesday, the regiment is starting a two-day operation. And, Boujold, you can come along!"

This was news to the Kid, so he was immediately as sad as Boujold was happy. *Of all the fucking shit! A two-day mission. This time I think he means it!*

"All right!" Bouji hollered, rising up off his ass, pulling his boxer shorts out of his crack. "I can't fucking wait!"

"Be careful what you wish for, Bouji," the Kid cautioned him, "you might regret it. You be *beaucoup xin loi*!"

"Gentlemen." Sergeant Minh emerged from the building and stepped onto the porch. "Ankong! Eat now!"

After the meal, it didn't take long for Boujold and the Kid to head on out to the old church, transistor radio in hand, for the privacy of the upper floor.

"Who wants to buy this diamond ring?" The lyrics of Gary Lewis and the Playboys greeted them as the Kid turned on the radio and set it in its standard position, above them in the round window.

Dipping his pipe into the cache pocket, the Kid lit the pipe with his Zippo and inhaled deeply of the pungent herb, then passed it to Boujold. As the aura of stoniness engulfed him after the second hit, the Kid closed his eyes and floated. *I'm losing touch, Flo. It's all too much. I try to think of you, and all I see is the blank look on Tall Chinese Guy's face.*

"Well, I've seen my first dead guys for real now," he opined, giving Boujold a hard stare. "Why you are so hot to get out there in combat is beyond me. It is not a good thing, Bouji, don'tcha see?"

"Easy for you to say." Bouji took the pipe and inhaled a giant hit. After holding it for nearly fifteen seconds, he exhaled in a long, measured breath. "I feel like a coward hiding out, not getting a chance to really experience combat. Look at you: you've already got two operations under your belt."

"They were dead, Bouji. The one guy had his brains blown out. We took nine casualties on booby traps alone. That could be waiting for you. Fuck. I'd get out of it any way I could, but Wilson seems determined to keep volunteering us for this shit."

"Yeah! And for once, I'm on his side!"

"Traitor! He's trying to get us killed, and now you're volunteering! It's a dumb shit thing to do. Don't you remember the basic training mantra? Never volunteer for *anything*!"

"Maybe so, but I'm bored stiffer than a horny dick out here. While you were gone, I almost shot myself, having to listen to that jack-off Sergeant Matt talk!"

They laughed.

Once the song by Gary and the Playboys ended, the DJ stepped in. "And that was Dean Martin's son Gary Lewis and 'This Diamond Ring.' It's eighteen hundred hours, and you've got Gary W. Gears on the Armed Forces Vietnam Network, coming to you live from Saigon. I know some of you are out there in secret positions and I'll bet you're tougher to find than a needle in a haystack!" he said, as Dusty Springfield broke into "Silver Threads and Golden Needles."

The very deep-voiced Gary W. Gears was some new announcer the Kid had not previously heard on AFVN. *Another fuckhead getting in there while I rot in the frickin' boonies! Shit, shit, shit!*

"That's some cornball schtick." Bouji had a sour look on his face. "I must say, you are far more entertaining just sitting around!"

"Why thank you, Bouji! Although I thought the line about Gary Lewis being Dean Martin's son was pretty funny."

"Say what? Ha! I didn't register that!" Boujold snorted, taking the pipe from the Kid's outstretched arm.

"And Jesus fuck!" The Kid continued his critique, saying, "His voice is so deep, he must be standing in a pit!"

When they were done with the pipe, Boujold stood on the riser looking out the big round window and lit a cigarette.

"Whoa!" The Kid pulled on the leg of his boxers and cautioned, "You'd better get down. It's almost dark enough for that to make an attractive target!"

"Oh, fucking bullshit!" Boujold stepped off the riser, but was incredulous. "I'll give you five dollars if you can prove there's a VC within a hundred miles of this stinking hole! Come to think of it, let's see!" He stepped back up on the rafter, lit his Zippo, and waved it around like he was in the Old North Church giving the signal to Paul Revere. "Yo! You jerk-off douchebag Charlies," he shouted, "here we are! Come get us!"

"Jesus, Bouji," the Kid said in a cautionary tone, "you're starting to attract attention! What if that's the secret signal to attack, you fuckhead? Didn't stop to think of that, did you?"

"I hope it is!" he hissed at the Kid in such a tone of voice that he broke down. The two of them laughed until they couldn't stand, but then just as they were catching their breath, Boujold jumped up and resumed with a vengeance.

"Hey, you chickenshit asshole fucking VC," he literally screamed from the top of his diaphragm, "here we are! Come get us, you muthafucking sons of pig- humping goat dick suckers!"

"Not cool!" said the Kid in a calmer voice. "You're gonna make somebody come up here."

And sure enough, almost as the Kid spoke the words, they could see a couple of men walking across the open area in front of the priests' quarters, crossing the bridge and heading their way, but they couldn't make out who they were.

"Way to go, numb nuts," the Kid said, scoffing. "Now the smoking lamp is out!"

When the two men got to the bottom of the church steps and looked up at the Kid and Boujold, the pair saw it was Dai Ui Dong, the company's executive officer, and Corporal Ba.

"Hey, Stocka," Ba hollered up at them, "we come up now, OK!" "Sure, come ahead," the Kid replied.

Soon, the pair stepped off the bamboo ladder and walked onto the flooring of the bombed-out church balcony. There was just enough light in the rapidly fading sunset that they could see a little detail in the faces of the men as they walked over to where Boujold and the Kid now sat on the riser, smoking tobacco and listening to the stylings of Armed Forces Radio Saigon.

Once standing in front of them, Dai Ui Dong said something to them in Vietnamese that the Kid completely failed to get any part of. So, turning to Ba, he was told, "The captain wants to know what he yelled out the window."

"So, tell him," Boujold insisted, an impish grin apparent.

"No!" Ba nervously laughed. "I too embarrassed to say! I can hardly believe what you say!"

"You mean the 'pig-humping goat dick sucker' part?"

"Yes." You could almost see the poor kid blushing in the poor light.

"Go ahead," Bouji said to Ba, "tell him what I said."

As Ba searched for the words, the Kid eyed Dong. Of all the Viets they lived with at Tan An, the pockmarked and Hitler-mustached face of Dai Ui Dong was perhaps the most unfriendly. It was as if he had some kind of supersized bug up his ass and he was disagreeable with everybody, his troops and the American advisers alike. He also drank like a carp and even gave Lieutenant Wilson, who could hold more booze than any man the Kid had ever met, a run for his MPC. And it appeared the captain was more than a little

379

bit down the road to alcohol oblivion on this yet young evening. In fact, the Kid had to wonder how he had managed to climb that rickety ladder!

Finally, Corporal Ba spoke to the captain. After his tentative explanation, a slow smile spread across Dong's face. Dong started to laugh, and it infectiously spread to the Kid, Boujold, and Ba. Soon, the four of them were all laughing together.

The Kid offered Dong a smoke from his pack of Kools and lit it for him when he took one. Again Dong spoke to Ba, who translated for the pair. "Dai Ui Dong say we go down and he buy you drink now!"

Looking at each other, the Kid and Boujold could see they were each in agreement; it wouldn't be a good idea to refuse the captain's invitation. Rising up, they gathered their stuff, and the four of them headed down the bamboo ladder one at a time, with Dong going first.

Once back at the priests' quarters, Dong hollered for his boy to bring him a new bottle of Old Grand-Dad and some teacups. Wilson stopped cleaning and messing with his new used Luger and walked over to the table.

"So what's cookin'?" He smiled, eyeing the bottle of bourbon.

"Dai Ui Dong is, uh, buying us a drink." The Kid smiled back, nodding in Dong's direction as he cracked the seal on the bottle. *God, how I hate bourbon!*

Ti Ui Troung was writing letters and chose to ignore the proceedings. Sergeant Matt, always anxious to be included in anything, came right over, apparently ready as ever to throw down a couple of shots. Tu Ta Van and Captain Katanaki were busy with some paperwork at the far end of the table and seemed mildly annoyed by what was unfolding. Lieutenant Jim was reading a paperback by his kerosene lamp but closed it and indicated he was in a drinking mood, too.

Once the shots were poured, Dong lifted his little white cup and said something that caught Tu Ta Van's attention, as well as Sergeant Minh's. Bauxi Mui's mouth fell open, showing his total shock, as the group lifted their cups and drank the toast.

"What'd he say?" Boujold inquired of Ba, who was sitting immediately to his right.

"He say what you yell out window: VC make love to pigs and eat penis of goat!"

"That's not quite what I said," Bouji commented, mopping some sweat from his brow. "I said they suck goat dick, not eat it!"

380

"Yes, I know, but no want to say to him!" Ba expressed his apprehension at talking about acts of homosexual goat fellatio to a superior officer.

"Come on, chickenshit, tell him!" Boujold egged him on.

"No can do!" Ba refused.

Another shot followed the first, and another and another, although the Kid was now not drinking and slowly removed himself from the table. "Well, I gotta write some letters. I'm falling way behind," he said, apologizing to the group as he extracted himself.

Sitting on his bunk, the Kid lit the lamp on the crate by his cot and, taking up his pen and paper, began a letter to Flo.

My Dearest Parnelli,

This is quite a scene tonight here at the old fortified hamlet. Captain Dong came out to the church because Boujold was yelling insults at imaginary VC, and now he and Wilson, Matt, Jim, Katanaka, and Boujold are doing shots of bourbon while I'm writing to you. They made me do a couple, but now they are cracking open their second bottle.

Flo, I miss you so much that I can hardly make it through the days. Just to feel your cheek next to mine is all I want on earth. Gawd Almighty, it's only the twenty-eighth of July; I can't believe I've only been gone two months and a week. Can't forget the week! You know, tomorrow is the anniversary of the day we met at the Leroy Van Dyke premiere in Nashville. Some days, I still can't believe I'm here and expect to wake up—hopefully next to you!

We've been on some more operations. No, we haven't gotten any VC to defect yet. You should have seen the joke of a loudspeaker that Troung brought with us. It makes me so pissed that I'm in this psyops thing. I could personally shoot the asshole who ever thought loudspeakers were a good idea.

So, when we were running through the trees (getting shot at), I slipped and fell into a canal. I got the wind knocked out of me and got wet and muddy, but not really hurt. It was pretty funny to everybody but me. Kind of like when we were laughing about the gorilla throwing the shit at all those people at the San Diego Zoo. It wouldn't have been so amusing if we'd been hit with the crap, so what the hell! At least I didn't get shot.

Hey, you said you wanted to know the truth. But now I say to you, don't worry. You know I've got my lucky beaver nickel strapped on, and you and I are meant to be together, darling!

Boujold is still bugging Wilson about going out on an operation, and tonight, Wilson said he was going to bring him on the next one. Stupid bozo. If I didn't have to go, I sure as hell wouldn't ask to go! Wilson said we're going on a two-day operation in a couple of days.

Hey, guess what? I bought me a pistol, and now I don't have to carry an M16 on operations anymore! That piece of plastic shit is more trouble than it's worth. I got a .38 snub nose and a shoulder holster. I'll have to send you a picture! I'll get Boujold to take a Polaroid tomorrow.

Well, I have to sign off now and write the parents and Larry Ryan. I've gotten way behind writing to everybody but you, my dearest, sweetest lover. Ooh, a TM moment!

I'll see you later!

All my love,

Curt

The Kid continued to write letters, and the men continued to drink until the second bottle was all gone. By that time, Dong was smashed to the point of staggering when he tried to walk.

Wilson laughed at him. The Kid could see it pissed off the Vietnamese captain. Dong grabbed a pack of smokes and walked out the front door and into the darkness. Nobody paid him any mind, as the standard domino game and letter writing and reading continued on into the quiet night.

About 2200 hours, the Kid was ready to turn in. Just as he had lifted his bare feet up off the tile floor and began tucking in the mosquito netting around his bunk, automatic weapon fire erupted out in front of the building. Immediately, everybody who was sleeping in the front room of the priests' quarters jumped up out of their cots in a frenzy.

Rushing to the windows, they discovered it was Dong doing the shooting. The stinking-drunk Vietnamese captain was standing on the front steps of the church shooting his M16, loaded with tracer rounds, on full automatic, off toward the perimeter, holding it at a forty-five-degree angle to the ground. Between bursts, he was spewing something in Vietnamese, the content of which the Americans had no idea about.

Psychedelic! I hope that drunk fuck doesn't shoot any of us!

Tu Ta Van went nuts! He yelled at Sergeant Minh to run out there and get Dong to stop, but the old sergeant was very apprehensive about going out while the inebriated captain was spraying rounds all over hell and back. Instead, Minh went out behind the building and circled around, approaching Dong from the side, not from the front. Soon, he had talked the captain into handing over his M16. He supported him as he staggered back to the building, babbling incoherently, where he dumped him on his cot.

"Dai Ui Dong needs to learn his limits," Wilson said sarcastically, slurring; he was as tipsy as the Kid had ever seen him.

"Just another typical night at the Tan Alamo," Boujold whimsically said, sitting down on his own cot. He, too, was more than a little twisted from the drinking bout. "They oughta stick Dong in the tiger cage for that," he further suggested.

Outside on the porch, in the hot, humid tropical night, with no breeze blowing, venom flowed from Tu Ta Van's mouth as he berated the wobbling Captain Dong, who was trying to be frozen at attention but who wavered back and forth like a drunk failing a roadside sobriety test.

"He in trouble beaucoup!" Ba commented in an intense whisper. He prepared to climb into his mosquito netting on the cot next to the Kid's and Boujold's.

The Kid had sprayed the inside of his netting with insecticide again and shooed away the hangers-on before quickly jumping into his cot and redoing his tuck.

Lying there in his boxer shorts, he tried to find a comfortable position, but it was, as always, impossible for him to like sleeping on the army cot. Especially out at Tan An, because there was no electricity and, consequently, no fans.

Soon, the rest of the residents of the priests' quarters were also settled back into their mosquito nettings for the night. Except for the Sergeant Minh, who was on radio watch, they were soon a snoring bunch.

Tossing and turning, the Kid was trying to zero in on a pleasant Flo memory to take him away from it all. It was his Christmas leave when he had visited her in California, the night they went to see *Gone with the Wind* at the

Vista Drive-In, that captured his focus. *What a great movie,* the Kid thought when he heard the epic was playing at the Passion Pit. *We can make out for four hours without getting interrupted!* They kissed and kissed while the Kid fondled her breasts. At one point, she let him open her blouse and slip his hand inside, where he could feel her swollen little nipples through her bra, which he soon lifted above her breasts so he could suck those darling nipples. *This is getting good!* And then, for the first time, when he made his move to get up her dress, she let him run his hand up her inner thigh and spread her legs ever so slightly, allowing him access to rub her pussy on the outside of her panties, culminating in a soaked cotton crotch. Ooh! *Sweet wetness! Maybe she'll let me in! I'll just put my finger over here on the elastic on the outside of her leg, run it over the top of her leg and down the inside, sort of push it over, and bingo! I'm in! She likes it! She's repositioning so I can get it in deeper.* More kissing, more fingering. Now little kisses. Hand out of the panties and cupping her face. He looked into her brown eyes, illuminated by the burning fires of Atlanta raging on the screen. "Flo, will you marry me?" She gasped in total surprise. "Yes!" she said, hugging him as hard as can be. Explosions went off; mortars were coming in; and there was automatic weapon fire. *Wait a minute, there were no automatic weapons in the Civil War.*

"Incoming! Incoming!" Sergeant Matt yelled out. In a flash, everybody was out of their cots, scrambling, trying to find their pants, weapons, flak jackets, and steel pots at the same time.

"We're under attack!" Lieutenant Jim came rushing out of the back room.

The Kid was looking for his glasses when two more mortar rounds screamed in and creamed the old church to the right of the steeple. Automatic rifle fire punctuated the confusion.

"Tu Ta! Have you figured out where they're hitting us yet?"

"Yes!" the near-naked Vietnamese major, clad only in his boxers, hollered. He was standing over the shoulder of Sergeant Minh, whose radio now crackled with calls. "They are coming at us on the east side!"

Commander Ken was on the US radio set calling for support as the men frantically got dressed. "Spooky's on the way!" he yelled out. "Jim, light the arrow and point it east!"

"Everybody get ready!" Katanaki was pulling up his own pants. "Get plenty of ammo. We are the reaction squad! We have to be ready to support anyplace they break through the perimeter!"

The Kid, already into his pants and shirt, quickly wrapped himself up in his flak jacket before pulling on his boots without socks. He grabbed his M16 and saw Wilson do the same thing. *No pistols tonight!*

384

Boujold was up and looking confused, as if unsure if this was real or a fabrication of his overdrunk imagination. But quickly, as the level of firing on the perimeter grew more intense, he realized it wasn't an alcohol-induced dream. "Is this some real shit, or are more ARVNs blowing themselves up on the perimeter?"

Bouji's answer came in the form of automatic weapon fire striking and creating masonry shrapnel out of the wall in the back room on the other side of the radio bunker. It sounded to the Kid like really huge spitballs, about the size of basketballs, impacting on a blackboard, but what with the echoing gunfire bouncing back off the church and with the reports from outgoing fire, it was suddenly a very noisy evening in Tan An.

Jim and Ken were in the radio bunker frantically calling for support. The rest of the command element, Lieutenant Wilson, Sergeant Matt, Tu Ta, Ti Tu Troung, Corporal Ba, Boujold, and the Kid, quickly gathered themselves and were now waiting, their M16's locked and loaded, a little sweat of the non-heat-generated variety beginning to show on their faces.

They monitored the radio traffic on Tu Ta's PRC-25 as the landscape outside the priests' quarters was lit up by floating illumination flares that were drifting toward the ground on their parachutes, in an attempt to peel back the cover of darkness over the enemy.

Off in the distance, between the explosions and sporadic shooting, airplane engines were coming to within earshot.

"Spooky's here!" Sergeant Matt proclaimed. "Now they're goin' to get fubared big- time!"

Holding his M16 in his sweaty hands, Boujold's eyes were about as big as the Kid believed they could get without flat falling out of their sockets. "Do you think they're going to use us?"

"Fuckin' A if I know!" The Kid drew a deep breath.

In addition to the fire going into and coming out of the compound on the ground, the air was now filled with the streaming red lead of the Spooky gunship's three minicannons as it poured out of the dark and chewed up the ground. From inside the headquarters building, however, none of this could be seen, only heard.

Burrrrrrruuuuuupppppppp. Burrrrrrruuuuuupppppppp. The miniguns fired.

When the Spooky completed its first pass, it sounded as if most of the ordnance was now flying out of the compound and not coming in. After Spooky circled over one more time, Tu Ta shouted into the radio the command for the compound troops to cease fire.

And then all was quiet. As quickly as it had started, it was over. Spooky's twin engines faded quickly as the aircraft flew off into the distance. The command element would not be required to perform the duties of the reaction force and seal the perimeter tonight. The enemy were standing down.

Tu Ta and Commander Ken immediately left to go out and check on casualties and damage. All the rest of the men in headquarters lit up cigarettes.

The Kid just happened to look up as Boujold walked by his cot and dropped something from his hand onto it.

Strolling over to see what it was, the Kid found a five-dollar MPC note lying there.

Chapter 35

For Lieutenant Wilson, it was a love-hate thing; he hated giving in to Boujold's whining and having let him come, but he was anticipating seeing the look on Fat Boy's face when the first lead bee came flying by. He had the previous night confided in the Kid that he did not expect Boujold to complete the operation.

Wilson was betting that if he didn't get hit, he would jump at the first chance he had to extract himself from the field.

"Boujold, remember our deal. If I have to medevac you for any reason other than you are WIA or dead, you are to never ask me to go on another operation as long as I'm in charge of you, bic?" the lieutenant said, pressing for confirmation of their arrangement.

"Bic, Lieutenant. You won't need to worry about me. I'll be OK. I'm ready for this. In fact, I've been forced to wait too long!" The bravado came through loud and clear as the group finished buckling up their pistol-belted web gear and assembled on the roadway around the drop point in the predawn tropical air.

The Kid eyed Bouji from head to toe in the early morning light: his steel pot band held the obligatory bottle of insect repellent; a pistol belt and harness draped his Oliver Hardy body; and he was equipped with a backpack setup. In addition to the ammo in that, he had chosen to drape himself with another pair of green cloth M16 clip bandoliers that he wore X style. Two canteens and a bayonet were attached to the belt itself. Boujold's cargo pants pockets were stuffed with extra cigarettes and a C ration meal that he had removed from the box to make it fit better in his clothing.

"Boujold," the Kid said, "you've got more stuff on you than a Yankee peddler!" He snuffed out his Kool. "Did you ever stop to think for a second about what it's going to be like trying to run lugging all that shit? Later, for example, when the temperature rises up over a hundred and somebody is shooting at us? Got any salt pills?" he asked, noting that Bouji was already sweating and they had not yet stepped across the line of departure.

"You bet! I got salt and iodine water purification pills." He retrieved both from his pocket to show that he was truly prepared.

The Kid, on the other hand, had packed very light. Now that he no longer had to carry his M16 and the associated ammo, he was stripped for speed! The .38- caliber pistol tucked neatly in his shoulder holster rode above his pistol belt, and he no longer carried a backpack. *Screw the poncho. I'll already be wet, so who gives a fuck?* He had returned the grenade Wilson had given him, so the belt carried a clip pouch containing his box of .38 slugs and just one canteen. In his jungle fatigue pockets, his C rations were split up among them. He also carried an extra pack of Kools in one of his pockets. When the time came to run in the rice, he was not going to be weighted down by any extraneous equipment, unlike the rotund rookie.

Corporal Ba, who had up until his first taste of combat eschewed cigarettes, was now smoking like a grizzled veteran. He held a Salem between his fingers, Asian style. The look on his young face was one of distraught and deep anxiety.

Ti Ui Troung was not with them today, nor was any loudspeaker equipment. It appeared to the Kid that Wilson was completely blowing off their psyops mission. What he really wanted was to get up front and possibly collect his first VC scalp. Now that Wilson was no longer armed with a rifle, he had found himself a walking staff, known affectionately as a "du mai" stick, which translates into "dumbass stick," meant to prod unwilling soldiers into action by striking them.

As the line of soldiers moved out on the mission, following the little arrows that had been drawn on maps the night before, the Kid, Boujold, and Wilson walked casually in a group, with Ba about twenty-five meters back from Captain Wally, his counterpart, and their RTOs.

They were behind the advancing three squads of ARVN infantry in the center of the operation and today had been given "Jade" as their call sign. Major Boarz, who was with the element on the right flank, was calling the shots for the overall show. His radio tag was "Obsidian 1." Captain Metz's squads, which had the far left flank, were designated "Quartz." The tactical operations center, back in Tra Vinh, today was going to be "Turquoise."

"So, Kid," Boujold began, "you're going to be sorry when you need some firepower and all you have on you is that piece capable of not much more than putting a bullet in your own head."

Wilson laughed. He thought that was pretty funny.

"I do believe the man has insulted my choice of weapon," the Kid responded. "Lieutenant Wilson, is it our mission, purpose, or place to be acting with the ARVNs in an assault capacity?"

"Nope." The lieutenant confirmed what the Kid had said. As he walked along, he was taking great pleasure in the performance of his new du mai stick.

"See, Bouji, what we're supposed to be doing is winning the hearts and minds of the people. So we don't want to appear warlike; we want to appear with an air of authority and command, to instill a sense of trust in the new traitor. Kind of like that 'good cop, bad cop' thing, right, sir?"

"Yep." Wilson stopped. Turning to face the two, he said, "That's right, Stocker, we are here for psyops. But, if Specialist Four Boujold wishes to participate with the assault troops, I will authorize such activity."

"You will?" Boujold seemed excited at the prospect.

"Sure, Specialist. If you want to go right up front when the shooting starts and even talk to Captain Wally, I'll bet he'll let you assault a tree line with the ARVNs if you really, really want to! In fact, Specialist, it might even be required!" With

that, he made an evil little laugh, unlike anything the Kid had hitherto heard issued from the lieutenant's lips.

"Anyway," the Kid continued, "the only reason I'm carrying a pistol is Lieutenant Wilson said I could. And so far, we've never even seen an active Charlie, let alone been close enough to shoot one with an M16, without shooting an ARVN first, so what the hell? Believe me, Bouji boy, when the shit starts and you gotta run, you can't decide to quit or stay back and rest; it's not an option. You gotta keep up, and you'll be dumping stuff like those bandoliers. Bet you five."

"No bet."

The Kid could see that Boujold was contemplating the possibilities as the group moved steadily into the tree line that was defined by the paddies that stretched endlessly out before them.

The operation today was due west of Tra Vinh and then concentrated to the north, where the VC held sway over territory reaching out to the Mekong River, some eight miles away.

The VC Tenth was out there, concealed, armed, and waiting. *This is the part I hate, before it starts. This sucks so bad. That fucker Alan P., I gotta get a hold of him. If only I could get out of Tan An and be in Tra Vinh on a regular basis. At least they have regular mail there and an American mess hall. God, this diarrhea is killing me. I hate the chow at Tan An. I hate the cot. I hate Dai Ui Dong. But whenever we come in, it just means more of this shit! God, I hope I get some more care packages from home so we've got some munchies out there. No refrigeration, no running water, no movies, no regular mail, no whores. I'm getting kind of horny.* The debate raged in his head: *Should I remain faithful to Flo, or get laid because I could die tomorrow? Oh well, excuse me, in the next second I could die. Still can't believe Boujold wants to do this when he doesn't have to.*

He's fucking nuts!

After about an hour of walking and stopping, walking and checking the maps, Boujold was getting antsy as more perspiration soaked his jungle fatigues. "This is going to be another boring no-action clusterfuck hike, isn't it? That's the only reason you let me come along, isn't it, Lieutenant Wilson?"

"No. You aren't paying attention, are you, Specialist Boujold?" Wilson addressed him formally. "We have excellent intelligence that the VC Tenth is right in our path, so if you just keep your green boxers on for another few minutes or clicks, whichever comes first, I'm pretty fucking sure you are going to get what you came for!"

The way he said it sent a chill down the Kid's spine. The Kid had no desire to mess with the VC Tenth. He did not want to look for the VC Tenth, much less find them, but he knew the odds were far better that the opposite of that would be true: *The VC Tenth will find us!*

The smell of the Delta, humid and earthy, filled the Kid's nostrils as the group slowly plodded along, with his mind bouncing between memories of his now distant life in the States and the growing suspense of when the lead was going to start flying, as he was 100 percent certain that it would. *All I wanted was to be in Armed Forces Radio, and now look at me! How did I fucking get into this situation?*

Upon arriving at the compound, the Kid had found that among his mail was a letter from Larry Ryan, his best friend from Boulder: "Curt, if you want, I can send you some of the 'Timmy goods,'" which was code for Timothy Leary's favorite, LSD.

"Don't do it," the Kid had written back, "because if I took it and some kid pointed a toy gun at me, I'd hallucinate it as real and shoot him."

The sky was relatively clear of clouds on this early August morning, not that it meant the monsoon rains wouldn't eventually come that day. *Please, not a rainy night, if we have to sleep in foxholes while this operation goes two days. The thought of staying out in the jungle overnight is freaking fucking insane!*

"Well, it's been over an hour," Boujold said, stopping to take a sip from one of his canteens. "Where are the little fuckers?"

"One thing is for certain." The Kid stopped next to him and likewise took a drink. "You can bet your sweet ass they know where we are! They're just waiting for an opportune time to start the party."

"Speaking of MIAs, I wonder where Bird Dog is." Lieutenant Wilson searched the skies for the air spotter's Cessna 150 that was usually buzzing around them on operations. Removing a cigarette from his right breast pocket, he reached into his pants and pulled out his Zippo to fire it up. The rest of the command element took this to mean that now was a good time for them to light up as well.

No sooner than they had all taken their first deep puffs, a burst of automatic weapon fire creased their position. Instantly, Wilson, the Kid, and Ba hit the deck, leaving Boujold still standing, looking inquisitively, head cocked to one side, as if to analyze the report. But when the second volley registered on his consciousness, he dropped to the ground so quickly that his helmet was left suspended in midair, like Wile E. Coyote before he plunges off the cliff in a *Road Runner* cartoon.

"Holy shit!" Bouji screamed as he scrambled, crawling across the ground to retrieve his helmet from where it had rolled. He quickly put the helmet back on his head. "That was fucking close!"

"No it wasn't!" Wilson yelled at him. "That was a good five or ten feet over our heads!"

The three squads in front of the command element immediately responded. Once they had received more return fire, everybody realized that the unit was now fully engaged with the no-longer-elusive VC Tenth. Looking over to where he flattened had his body against the dark earth, the Kid noted that Boujold was as white as a sheet!

Intense radio traffic communicated the situation to Captain Wally It appeared that the VC had opened up on all three elements of the operation at the same time!

"Jade One, Jade One, we're taking fire. Do you read me? Over," the voice of Boar Hog crackled.

"Obsidian One, I read you. We are taking fire too. Over." Wally returned his page.

"Roger the fire," came Metz's voice over the frequency.

"Jade One, press your counterpart to get his boys moving. Now that we have contact, we do not want them to get away! Over."

"Obsidian One, I read you and roger that last transmission. Out!" Turning to his troops, he said, "OK, boys, let's go!"

With that, Wally and his RTO jumped up and moved forward, in pursuit of the squads, which were mostly obscured by the foliage that surrounded them.

Pulling himself up off the ground, Boujold rose to a kneeling position on one knee, chambered a round, and flipped off the safety of his M16.

"So, who ya gonna shoot?" The Kid smirked, still lying on the ground next to Boujold. "I know you can't even see all our guys up there, let alone a real target!"

"At least I'm ready!" he said, scanning the field of vision in front of him that, indeed, did not contain any of the VC who continued to shoot at them.

"For Christ's sake, Boujold, put your fucking safety back on until you're going to use it. The last thing I want on earth is to be accidently shot by W. C. Fields!"

"Come on, ladies!" Wilson yelled, Luger in one hand and his du mai stick in the other. "Let's go!" The chase was on.

Clambering through and around the trees and bushes amid the thick foliage, they began moving forward, alternately taking cover and then rising and rushing as the opportunities presented themselves. The area they were in was punctuated by paths and by rows of banana trees and tall palms that were full of large green coconuts, with little gardening plots of vegetables next to fishponds by a collection of four huts they encountered as they dodged bullets and tried to figure out where to take cover next.

This must be some of the houses where the VC Tenth live! I'll bet they hate this! With all the ordnance and bullets flying at them, it again amazed the Kid that he and the others couldn't see any of the enemy. Being that this was his third major engagement, he was starting to feel a certain air of acceptance, if not actual calm. *Your time's up is when it's up, but I don't get the feeling mine is up yet!*

The combat action was having a bewildering effect on Boujold, who apparently thought the deal was going to be a shoot-out between two groups of soldiers, à la the Revolutionary War, exchanging fire across an open green. All this running was not something he would have agreed to do up front had he any real idea of how far they were going to have to march. After less than fifteen minutes of this, the Kid noticed that his compatriot was breathing fairly hard with labored breath, something that resembled an asthma attack.

"Bouji! You all right?" the Kid inquired as the two of them lay prone on the ground behind a row of banana plants, following a particularly close volley.

"Yeah." He panted. "I think so!" But the tone of his voice revealed that he was not entirely sure if he was buying it himself. All traces of his earlier bravado had been erased by the AK-47 rounds that peppered them as if he were the meat du jour.

"And now you have your wish!" the Kid exclaimed. "You wanted combat, and now you've got combat! How do you like it?"

Boujold had no answer as bullets ripped green bananas off the plants above their heads and the debris rained down on them.

"Yo, Fat Ass." Lieutenant Wilson chose to insult Boujold as he also took cover at a distance of about fifteen feet to their left. "No passing out from exhaustion.

Things are just getting started!" Up he jumped and with Ba in tow, moving forward into the engulfing bush.

"Come on, Bouji!" the Kid hollered as he rose into a crouching position and prepared to take off after Wilson. "We can't stay here!"

They followed behind the ARVNs moving forward, taking fire from and giving fire to an enemy that remained expertly concealed among the lush green tropical foliage. Then, as inevitable as the noontime heat, the monsoon rains, and rice with dinner, they came to the edge of the tree line and were left standing, confronted by an open area of rice paddies that was flanked by the trees on all sides.

The shooting in their area of the field had stopped, although they could hear, farther down the tree lines to both their right and left, Metz's and Boar Hog's boys still fighting their way through the woods that hooked around and bracketed the open expanse in front of their formation. A totally winded Boujold finally caught up to them about five minutes later.

"Bouji," the Kid addressed him as Boujold did a near-collapse on the ground, "you don't wanna hang back. You see, the VC who were shooting at us are not out there." He pointed to the wide-open stretch of paddies that now confronted them. "That means they are probably in hidey-holes behind us." He turned to Wilson. "Isn't that what the rangers call them, sir?" Addressing Boujold again, he said, "And they could jump out and cap your ass just like that!" The Kid used his finger and thumb as a pretend gun held to Boujold's head.

"That's affirmative, Specialist. Hang back at your own peril!" Wilson calmly asserted before he chuckled under his breath, amused to see Boujold teetering on the edge of heat exhaustion.

Sweat poured from Boujold's forehead as he gasped for breath; this was likely the most exercise he had gotten the entire war. Deep concern painted the expression on his round face as the reality of their situation unfolded. It was barely 0930 hours, so the day was far from half over, and it was certainly not anywhere near as hot out as it would eventually become. Boujold had apparently just about shot his wad of physical reserves. The barrel of his M16 was propped up on his left thigh, muddied, grimy, and nearly worthless, as he struggled to get out his canteen.

"See now why I wanted to carry a pistol so bad?" The Kid pointed to Boujold's weapon. "That thing is supposed to be as light as a feather, but it's getting heavy, isn't it, with a little mud added to the equation, don't you think?"

Boujold nodded his agreement, being too winded to speak, let alone argue.

"Obsidian One." Wally was on the radio. "You take any casualties yet? Over."

"Jade One, that is affirmative. We have two Kilo India Alphas and four Whiskey India Alphas. What about you? Over."

"Obsidian One, so far we've been lucky and haven't taken any of either, although Jade Four is looking a little on the fried side. Over."

"Jade Two? Are you there?" Boar Hog called out Wilson's code. "Didn't I tell you not to bring that fat-shit candy-ass out here? Over."

Looking up to the Kid and then down to the ground, Boujold was chagrined by the insulting disrespect he continued to reap from everybody around him.

Wincing as he took the handset from Wally, Wilson responded, "Affirmative, Obsidian One." He eyed Boujold. "And like I said, it's either going to make him a better man or kill him. I don't care; whichever comes first! Over."

After exchanging their opinions, Wally and Boar Hog decided that Wally's squads had no choice but to cross the open paddy to continue and maintain the integrity of the operation.

"Spread out!" Wally commanded. His instructions were relayed to the ARVNs by his counterpart. "OK, move out!"

With that, the three squads stepped out of the trees and into the open. The Kid could see nearly the same amount of fear etched into the faces of both Boujold and Ba as they began crossing the three hundred meters of open space that was easily as wide. The shooting had lessened but was still sporadic amid the trees on both sides of them.

"Into the valley of death rode the six hundred." Alfred Lord Tennyson came to the Kid's mind as his boots sank into the warming water and mud of the paddies. They made a sucking sound as he pulled out first one, and then the other, to step ahead. *Sure as shit, they'll wait until we are halfway and then open up.* The Kid recalled the other times he'd been put in this situation in the last month.

Checking his new ten-dollar Seiko watch, the Kid noted the date was August 3. *Hey, in one month from today, I'll be twenty-one! I hope to fuck I live to see it!* He looked at the back of Wilson's head as they eased out into the full view of any VC who might have happened to be waiting on the opposite side. *I should just shoot you, you reckless muthafucker! We don't have to do this, you bastard! "Well, Your Honor, it was like this: it was self-defense because that cocksucker was trying to get me killed. You'd have shot him yourself, Your Honor." This is not our assignment! And if I could get my hands on Gil for getting me to sign up for DINFOS for an extra year, I'd shoot him too! I'm in a shootin' mood today!*

From the sound of his breathing, it seemed that Bouji had recovered a bit and possibly had gotten his second wind. "You doing OK?" the Kid pensively asked, walking next to him.

Boujold nodded. "Yeah, I think so."

"Just wait till we get to that paddy dike about five meters up from here. I see that's about halfway, Bouji. Once we get past there, it's only a matter of time until they'll open up on us. Bet your sweet ass on that!" The Kid made his prediction. "Fuckin' A, I'm surprised they're not shooting at our flanks! They must be too busy with Boar Hog and Metz's boys!"

Sure enough, as the last of their squads stepped over the dike that the Kid had estimated was the halfway point of the crossing, the tree line in front of them exploded as eagerly awaiting VC began pumping out rounds at the exposed soldiers of South Vietnam.

Diving back behind the paddy dike, the squads took cover. *This is so stupid, crossing the open spaces like this! What is the point?* The Kid's thoughts questioned the sanity of their tactics from the paddy dike behind the front squads, where the command element had all ended up.

"Wally!" Wilson hollered from his prone position in the mud. "Can you get us some air support?"

"Maybe!" Wally answered, lying propped up on one elbow behind a dike, consulting his map and making the call to the TOC. "Turquoise One, this is Jade One. Do you read? Over."

"Jade One, go," came the reply.

"We're pinned down in the open, and we could sure use some air support on coordinates two, papa, thirty-five, one, hotel, twenty-four. Over."

"Roger your call, Jade One. Let me see what I can do for you!" the TOC assured the men.

After what seemed like an eternity, but was only a few seconds later, the TOC was back on the radio. "Jade One, Turquoise One. What I can get you is artillery out of Soc Mau if you want it. Over."

"Turq. One, I gave you the coordinates, two, papa, three, fiver, and one, hotel, twenty-four. Over." Wally flashed the group a thumbs-up.

Wet, muddy, and apprehensive, the center element hunkered down as the AK-47 fire continued to harass them for another minute. Then it arrived, a barrage of three 155-millimeter shells from an unseen firebase, riding on the sound of whistling wind, their trajectories at the end punctuated with fire, smoke, and debris catapulting into the sky upon impact.

"Goddamn!" Boujold exclaimed, rising up to peer cautiously over the paddy dike behind which they lay. "That's really fuckin' close!"

"Not close enough!" Wilson yelled. "It's too deep in the trees! Wally, do you know if that firebase is behind or right or left of us?" Wilson hollered over the din.

"Soc Mau firebase is east of us, Ross. Near as I can tell, they'd be shootin' parallel across our front!"

"Then have them knock it half a cunt hair to their left. The distance is good, but those shells need to hit right up front, where the Charlies are!"

Being that Wilson was actually an artillery officer, Wally took his advice and made the observation. "Turquoise, be advised that our FO, Jade Two, advises the artillary knock—uh, 'half a cunt hair' is the measurement—to their left! Over."

"Roger your adjustment. Will relay verbatim," a snickering voice came. It sounded to the Kid that Paul was on the switch.

Less than a minute later, three more shells came hauling ass into the very spot Wilson had suggested was the point of attack. The men could feel the ground shake as the resonance from the concussion rolled over them, barely two hundred meters back from the trees.

At impact, Wally jumped up and, waving his pistol in a big circle, motioned the squads to mount the assault. "Come on, men, we gotta use the cover! Charge!" he screamed at the top of his voice.

The ARVN rifle squads took their cue. At the urging of Dai Ui Than and their noncoms, they rose up out of the mud and advanced, doing the leapfrog run, providing support with fire, then running some more. Wally had gotten slightly ahead of them, but the Kid, Wilson, and Ba were sticking close together, moving up to the next set of dikes and ducking for cover while the next squad moved up.

Boujold was falling farther back, along with two ARVN infantrymen who, it appeared, were showing some reluctance to get with the program of the tree line assault. The artillery had not stopped the enemy fire from streaming out from the tree line.

The jets don't get them. The artillery doesn't get them. Are these little fuckers bulletproof? The Kid marveled at their tenacity. Goddamn, *if they had an air force down here in the Delta, they'd be unstoppable!*

Boujold and the two ARVNs had taken cover, but the tops of their three steel pots could be seen peeking over the low dirt wall. "Come on, you slacker!" Wilson spat back at Boujold. "Get your fat ass up here now!"

The trio rose up, stepped over the dike, and began to run forward. They had taken a dozen strides when a barrage of AK fire came directly over the Kid's head and into their midst, causing all three to hit the deck, Boujold face-first. One of the ARVNs tumbled backward, and the other fell first to his knees then keeled over to his right. He had been looking back, right at them, but the Kid couldn't tell if any had been hit or if they just took cover. He could see Boujold lift his head slightly and look quickly to either side of him, but the ARVNs were not showing any signs of life.

"Medic!" Boujold let out a desperate cry. "Medic!" He waved his arm over his head.

Oh, shit! The Kid rose up and immediately began high-crawling back to where they lay in the water of the paddy. "Bouji! Bouji! Are you hit?" he frantically called out when he was within earshot.

"I'm OK, but I think these two guys bought it!"

An ARVN medic came running past the Kid, hustling over to the downed soldiers with a complete disregard for the amount of fire that continued to flow from the tree line. Rolling the first man over, the medic shook his head and quickly moved to the second, to whom he began to administer first aid. He signaled to Dai Ui Than with a slicing motion across his throat that both men were *het roi.* Dead.

Finished. KIA.

When the Kid reached him, Boujold was dazed and stunned; the men on either side of him had just been killed, and he had been spared. "Missed me by less than a fucking inch!" he declared, shaking like a leaf in a monsoon windstorm.

"Come on! We gotta at least get up behind the next dike!" The Kid battled his own fears as ordnance continued to coat the battlefield. Half supporting him and half dragging him along, the Kid moved Boujold up to the dike, where they concealed themselves.

Boujold's breaths were coming in wheezing gasps. His glasses and the Kid's were spattered with mud and lying half submerged in the blades of rice shoots

rising up out of the stagnant-smelling water. The sounds of rifle fire and miniexplosions from the ARVN's M79's punctuated their conversation.

"If we lie back too long, we'll never hear the end of it." The Kid was trying to work up his nerve to rise up and follow the unit toward the tree line.

"I don't know if I can!"

"Bouji, do you want Wilson to tell everybody at Tra Vinh you're the biggest pussy in the regiment?"

He thought long and hard before he answered. "No!"

"Shit! Then, let's go!" the Kid yelled. Je rose up and dashed off toward the tree line, or at least the next paddy dike; he'd see how the atmosphere was before making the decision as to which to enter. As he neared the next paddy dike, which was the third out from the tree line, he looked back to see that Bouji had followed his lead. Once he reached the dike, it seemed to him that the fire from the trees had died down, so the Kid kept going. Plodding along, falling into a trot, in about a half minute, he was at the beginning of the tree line where Wilson and Wally were standing, waiting. When, a couple of minutes later, Boujold finally walked up, Wilson didn't waste any time letting him have it.

"Specialist, you're about on time as much as the troops who relieved Custer," he began. "I thought you were worried about getting your share of Charlies in this tree line, big talker." The lieutenant's words dripped with sarcasm.

"Yes, sir. Sorry, sir. I'll do better as soon as I get my second wind." Boujold's body oozed sweat and mud.

"You'd better take some of those salt tablets," Wilson suggested. "You too, Stocker."

About ten meters inside the tree line, Boujold and the Kid stopped to look into the smoking holes made by the 155-millimeter artillery round. In a day, they would be full of water, and in two days, full of mosquito eggs.

Looking back out over the paddies, the Kid watched as six ARVNs were bringing in the bodies of the two soldiers who had ben shot next to Boujold, two holding each of the casualties' arms, and one carrying the legs. Down to their left, looking back, they could see Boar Hog's men bringing their dead and wounded out of the tree line and to an obvious collection point.

"They've called in two medevacs," Wally said, monitoring his radio. "In addition to the four dead, we've got nine wounded."

At the mention of the choppers, Boujold seemed to suddenly perk up. And then, when he took his next three or four steps, the Kid detected a newly noticeable limp in his left leg; he was sort of waking without bending his knee as he made his way toward Wilson, who was about twenty meters away, standing with Ba, talking to Dai Ui Than. The closer he got, the more pronounced his limp became.

The Kid hustled up behind him, curious as to what the sweating, mud-encrusted, whipped, and exhausted Bouji had to say.

"Uh, sir?" Boujold said, interrupting the lieutenant.

"What the fuck is it, Boujold?" came the terse reply.

"Sir, I think I've pulled a hamstring," he began. "I'm not sure if I can run anymore."

Wilson just stared at him through his sunglasses as an expression of wry disgust spread across his face. "Pulled a hammie, huh? What, exactly, is it you are trying to say, Specialist? That you want to go out on this medevac? Is that it?"

"Well, sir, it's starting to stiffen up," Bouji began slowly. "Yes, sir, I think I might have to." Seeing the disbelief in the lieutenant's face, he tried to become more convincing. "Really, sir, no shit. I pulled it coming in off the paddies, and I'm hurt. And I don't want to be a liability to the unit, sir, but I really need to go in. I can't run anymore."

The lieutenant looked over Boujold's shoulder to the Kid, who now stood a couple of feet behind him, taking it all in. "He look hurt to you, Stocker? He sure as fuck didn't look hurt to me!"

"Not my call, sir. I'm not a medic and I'm not an officer, so I've officially got no comment on this one, sir." The Kid declined to be sucked into the discussion.

The expression on Boujold's face was becoming desperate; he was making his move to get out of the field, and he could comprehend that nobody among the present company was buying his tale of woe. "Sir, I wouldn't be asking if I wasn't really hurt. And I know what this means, that you won't let me come on any more operations, but shit, I'm hurt!" he insisted.

Lieutenant Wilson turned to Wally. "What do you think, Captain? Is there gonna be any room on the choppers for this particular sack of worthless shit?"

Wally paused to consider, looking at the collection of wounded and dead that was being assembled. "If it was one chopper, no, but since it's two, I imagine there's gonna be some room on the second one, if we don't get any more wounded or KIAs before they get here. Shit, fuck! Ross, let the poor bastard go in. He's sure as hell not helping us!"

"You're right, Wally." Turning to Boujold, he said, "Specialist, I'm gonna let you go in because you are a worthless piece of shit. And I guess it wouldn't be fair to your mama to get her little baby killed to prove my point."

Boujold slumped down to the ground. "Yes, sir. Thank you, sir," he said in a tone that contained all the elements of regret, gratitude, and relief.

"No fuckin' fair!" the Kid hollered, holding up his right pinkie finger. "I wanna go in! I broke a nail!" His mock outrage got a laugh from everybody but Boujold.

When the choppers arrived, the Kid again helped load the casualties. The eight wounded ARVNs went on the first one. The four KIAs and Boujold went onto the second. *Dead guys are getting to be less and less a big deal,* the Kid thought as they hurriedly strapped down the bodies so the chopper could get out of Dodge. *Fuck me! Am I battle-hardened or what?* He looked at Bouji as he clambered aboard the medevac, apparently trying to maintain the delicate fantasy that his leg was hurt. *Boujold, you're never gonna hear the end of this!*

Once belted into the bird's back seat, Bouji took off his steel pot and wiped the sweat and mud from his forehead with a fat paw. *Is he crying?*

Chapter 36

They sat in a semicircle, in front of the grass and thatched-roof hooch that was going to be their command post and shelter for the night. Tu Ta, Dai UI Than, the five American advisers, and Corporal Ba attempted to relax as they ate the various rations each had packed for the night, enjoying the first lull in what had been almost continuous action for the last six hours.

The headquarters element had chosen a set of three huts in the middle of a tree line that was about two hundred meters long by fifty to one hundred meters wide. Surrounding it was nothing but paddies. The Boar Hog felt fairly confident, after a nearly thorough sweep, that it was internally secure.

The ARVNs had taken the smallest of the three huts and were scurrying about hanging ponchos to make it lighttight for their radio operations and communications center for the duration of the night. If things got dicey, this was from where they would call in Spooky.

Behind them, the doorless entrance to the largest hut yawned open, exposing a spartan are that featured no furnishings except for a bamboo sleeping platform, two feet up above the dirt floor, that was about as wide as a king-sized bed. It was covered with a couple of thinly woven reed mats that were tattered to the point of being nearly nonexistent.

The choices for the five Americans were to sleep tonight on the ground with whatever snakes or nocturnal crawly insects might happen to come across one's hopefully unconscious body or, as the Kid understood the conversation, to stretch out on the sleeping platform shoulder to shoulder like a family with one bed in the Middle Ages.

At least it doesn't look like rain. Is that the only good thing in my life right now? How did I ever in the fuck come to be in this place? The cot at Tan An would look pretty good tonight! Thank God I've got a lot of insect repellent, what with no mosquito net. I should've brought some pot. Ha! What am I thinking? Even if I had brought some pot, there sure as hell isn't anyplace I'd dare to go and try to smoke it. But shit, could I use a hit right now!

Most of the dinnertime conversation centered on disparaging the member of the operation who was no longer present.

"That wimpy-assed mass of jelly." Wilson scoffed. "The expression on his face when they first opened up on us this morning alone was worth it! Talk about your epiphanies. That was sure as hell his!"

Turned out there had been a pool on how long Boujold would last, a buck apiece among almost all the officers at Tra Vinh. Boar Hog had won the twenty-three dollars with 1130 hours. They hadn't told the Kid about it because they didn't want him telling Boujold and, thus, taint the results.

"Fuckin' A, I thought he was going to scream for his mommy right there where we came to the rice paddies and had to go out in the open." Wally grinned between bites of his MRE.

"And I'd be willing to bet he crapped his fucking pants big-time when those two ARVNs got shot on either side of him!" Wilson chortled. "I thought he was burnt toast when he fell!"

"In all fairness," the Kid interjected, "that would have made quite a few people crap their pants."

"Never should have brought him, Herschel." Wally shook his head slowly from side to side.

"Well, I told you why I did it, Wally. And now I don't have to listen to his crap anymore. He's done. Stick a fork in him. I'm sending him back out to Tan An, where he can cool his heels until his DEROS for all I care. Besides, Stocker and I got a new assignment coming down the road anyway."

"Say what, sir?" The last statement had caught the Kid's attention.

"Yeah, Stocker, I meant to tell you. Before we left, I got a message from Can Tho that tomorrow or the next day, our MSQ-85 truck is supposed to arrive, along with a new specialist 4 from DINFOS, and we're taking it out to do psyops in Cang Long."

Sitting on his steel pot in the middle of hostile territory with the sun setting on the prospect of being mortared or attacked all night long without a bunker to hide in, the Kid hadn't really considered things getting any worse, and now he was hearing that they were being sent, not just down the Cang Long road, but to Cang Long itself! *I'm fucked, beaucoup!*

"Look at the bright side," said Metz. "If Buddha Belly were here, there wouldn't be enough room for all of us on that sleeping platform, which means since Fat Boy is a specialist 4 and he outranks you, PFC Stocker, you'd be on the ground!"

Bite me, Metz. "Well, sir, the first time you get fresh, I'll be going for the ground anyway."

402

"Don't worry about that, Stocker." Metz grinned. "You're not my type!"

"Oh, then the rumors are true?" The Kid laid the setup.

"What rumors?"

"That you like your women Rubenesque and that Fat Boy actually turns you on!"

Even Boar Hog, who usually scoffed at the Kid's humor, got a good laugh from that mental picture.

"And the rumors I hear about you must be true too, then." Metz was going to try for the comeback.

"OK, sir, fair enough. What rumors are those?" The Kid played along.

"That you've only got one ball and that your dick is less than two inches long."

The Vietnamese just kept eating, not really comprehending the flavor of the insults that flowed between the Americans. Ba, who knew some English and was most advanced among the three, smiled broadly at the exchange as a couple of privates waited on Tu Ta and Dai Ui Than like servants. When Tu Ta finished eating, one of them was right there with a hot cup of tea. Tu Ta thanked him and handed him his pistol to clean.

"Gentlemen." Boar Hog rose to the standing position. "Shall we tour the perimeter now before dark, so that we'll have an idea of what we're doing when they attack us tonight and we have to plug a hole?"

When they attack us tonight?

Having just finished eating, every man there lit up a cigarette, with a flurry of flicking and clicking Zippos.

Wally, Metz, Tu Ta, Dai Ui Than, Wilson, the Kid, and Corporal Ba set out like a line of chicks following their mother hen, in this case Boar Hog, to inspect the perimeter that had just been solidified in preparation for the night.

As they walked, Corporal Ba, the Kid noticed, was sticking to him like a puppy, afraid that a bigger dog was going to jump out of the shadows and bite him on the ass. Ba would bump into him every time they stopped to check something out, his anxiety level growing noticeably in direct proportion to the darkening of the night.

The day had been exasperating. Chasing and being pinned down, then more chasing, never seeing or engaging the VC in a major way, the unit had been continually under fire all afternoon. Boar Hog had ordered a fallback from the front-most position to this location, which had invitingly beckoned to them with its obvious defensive advantages.

403

The unit had taken sixteen casualties, eight of them KIAs, and had very little to show for what they'd done. Boar Hog had claimed eight VC dead, based on fiction he pulled out of his ass, almost as if he'd feel better about everything if the score for KIAs were at least tied on that day.

The sun had been down twenty minutes, the yellow clouds turning orange, broken into steep canyons and appearing again, reflecting off the water in the paddies that stretched out in front of the first field-of-fire foxhole the ARVNs had prepared at the edge of the trees.

God, what a beautiful country!

"This is our twelve o'clock," Boar Hog said, informing the group of his layout. "We were lucky to find this place. It's really got a nice setup, being isolated the way it is. The only real place I think we might have a problem is at zero three hundred, the place we had gotten to when we fell back, so we'll walk around the perimeter clockwise."

On their way around the tree line, as they followed a very well-worn path just inside the foliage, they came to some ARVN rifle pits, each manned by two soldiers, about every thirty meters. It made for very tight overlapping fields of fire. The plan and the manpower inspired confidence. Eight of the sixteen soldiers who had been wounded or killed had been replaced by a squad of reinforcements who had come out on the chopper that took away the last four casualties, so there were plenty of ARVNs to go around.

And there were four extra M16's stacked up behind the command hooch, collected from the casualties, for use by the Kid, Wilson, Ba, and even Boar Hog, should the necessity arise during the night.

Arriving at the 0300 position, the group saw a much more substantial collection of ARVN defenders.

"Here, as you can see," Boar Hog lectured the group, "the tree line on the other side of the paddies is only about a hundred meters off. So, I've got two of our four machine guns over here, offset twenty meters to either side, with a brace of five claymores set up in an arc at thirty meters out. If the VC come at us out of those trees, we'll filet them!

The group continued the tour until they had circled the entire island of foliage and arrived back at the three hooches. Darkness was settling upon them, and the Kid was growing more apprehensive about a lot of things. First off, he was a light sleeper, and the thought of having to sleep shoulder to shoulder with four other men on a hard wooden surface couldn't have been any less inviting. Second, the chance of a night assault by Charlie, or at least a mortar attack, seemed highly likely.

Might as well just sit up all night. Ain't gonna get any sleep no matter what I try. Wait till I write home about this! "Dear Flo, please forgive me. I've been sleeping with men!" "Dear Larry, OK, so I slept with some guys. At least I kept my pants on." "Dear Mom and Dad, the accommodations here are really quite rustic, but we are saving money by bunking five to a bed." "Dear Scott, being that you are up there in Seattle, you really might want to reconsider that Canadian option, if you know what I mean."

Inside the ARVN radio hooch, they were lighting candles to check the efficiency of their cloaking procedures. It was now dark enough that the light leaks would show so they could be plugged. Before long, the poncho wall was apparently tight.

"Well, at least we can all go in there and have one last smoke before lights out," Wally commented with a sigh, gesturing at the hooch with his head. The Kid could tell he wasn't looking forward to this night either.

"Hashee Ba." The Kid turned to the interpreter. "Where is it you are bunking tonight?"

"In the hut with Tu Ta and Dai Ui Than." He pointed to the hooch between the ARVN radio shack and the American Hilton.

The Kid and Ba shared a unique brotherhood; they were the only two enlisted men who were hanging with the officers, the Kid because he was an American, and Ba because he was their designated tongue. The Kid had gotten the impression from body language and facial expressions that some of the ARVN lieutenants and other senior noncoms resented Ba and the fact that he was privileged. If he had been a regular ARVN grunt, he would have been, at this instant, sitting a hole with an M16, peering out at the paddies, waiting for the VC to spring upon them with whatever surprise they had in store for them on this night.

"I still can't believe that Boujold tried to sell us all on a pulled hamstring." Metz began to revisit the controversy of the day. "Limping around like Chester. 'Ma lag's hurt, Marshal Dillon.' What a stupid fuck!"

"Yes, that may be," said the Kid, "but we're here and he's not. How stupid does that make us?"

"Stupid maybe, but chickenshit, no!" Metz retorted, slightly miffed that the Kid would in any way say anything positive about the man who had taken the easy way out.

"Fuck Boujold!" Wilson emphatically stated. "He's the biggest blowhard I've met since I joined up!"

"Damn straight. Fuck him and forget him!" Boar Hog said with contempt. "Stocker, or 'Mouth,' as I like to call you behind your back, I'm giving you an order to entertain us by telling us some jokes. I hear you've got a few of 'em, and they had better bloody fucking well be funny!"

A command performance. "OK, sir, let me think for a second. All right, here's one—one with a military flavor, sir, in honor of fighting men everywhere. It's a tale from World War I. There they all are in the trenches, and every so often, one of them will jump up and fire off a round or two. When this one soldier does, he gets shot right between the eyes and falls dead in the bottom of the trench. The man next to him takes a look and exclaims, 'Oh my God, Schwartz is dead!' The man standing next to him hears this and says to the man next to him, 'Oh no, Schwartz is dead!' So it goes up the trench: 'Schwartz is dead'; 'Schwartz is dead'; 'Oh no, oh no, Schwartz is dead.' So finally, it gets up to the general: 'Schwartz is dead!' The general says, 'Who the hell is Schwartz?' And so it goes back down the trench: 'Who's Schwartz?' 'Who's Schwartz?' 'Who's Schwartz?' Until it gets back to the man who is standing next to Schwartz's body, and he looks down and confirms it: 'Schwartz is the man with the twelve-inch cock!' And so it goes back up the line—'Twelve-inch cock'; 'Twelve-inch cock'; 'Twelve-inch cock'—until it gets to the general. And when he hears this, he's got to go see for himself. When he gets there, sure enough, he discovers that Schwartz has the biggest dick he's ever seen! It is so stunning that he pulls out a bayonet and whacks it off and sticks it in a jar of formaldehyde. Then, everywhere he goes, he pulls it out and just blows everybody away, showing them how big this guy's dick was. Well, the war finally ends and the general goes home. When he gets into his house, the first thing he does is set the jar on the mantel over the fireplace.

Then he calls to his wife, who was upstairs when he came in, 'Honey, I'm home from the war!' She comes running down the stairs and into the living room.

Taking one look at her husband, and then seeing the jar over the fireplace, she stops cold in her tracks and starts to sob. 'Oh no, Schwartz is dead!'"

Everybody laughs, even Boar Hog. Then, about fifteen seconds after the joke was over, Tu Ta and Dai Ui Than started to laugh their asses off; it had taken that long for Ba to catch them up with the translation.

"That's pretty good," Boar Hog said. "I got one." He composed himself and began: "What's the difference between a lady track star and a pigmy?"

The Kid immediately responded, "One's a running cunt, and the other is a cunning runt!"

406

Laughs abounded, but not from Boar Hog, who was slightly pissed that the Kid had stolen his punch line. The Kid immediately fired off: "What's the difference between a lady preacher and a woman in a bathtub?" Silence. Nobody stepped up to steal the Kid's punch line. "One has hope in her soul, and the other one has soap in her hole!"

Big laughs.

"Tell us another one!" Wally chuckled.

So the Kid told about five jokes, much to the amusement of all. The whole scene momentarily had a Boy Scout camp feel to it, although there was no campfire, no s'mores, and no singing kumbaya. It wasn't like they were at war, out in the middle of enemy territory, doing what passed for relaxation, waiting for the VC to make a move; it was the classic male soldier bonding situation, the men sitting there swatting mosquitoes, talking about things back home and how many days they each had left in their tours, reliving incidents from the fighting earlier in the day, and sharing memories of back home. All the while, the sky was getting darker.

When the urge for tobacco hit, they adjourned, in two- and three-man groups, to the ARVN radio hooch, where they could smoke without having the light from the Zippos or cigarettes draw any fire.

Soon, there was nothing to do but lie down and try to get some sleep. The Kid checked his watch: 2100 hours. *If I was back in Nashville, I'd just be getting up to go to work. How am I ever going to make it through this night?*

Entering the hooch, the Americans' eyes were adjusted to it just enough to see their way around. They were all very aware of where the M16's were cached, leaning up against the hooch wall at the foot of the platform. At this point, each man was making his own decision on where he was going to put his piece.

Everybody kept their pistol belts on except the Kid, who had his .38 in his shoulder holster and had a bayonet and canteen on his pistol belt, which he removed. He held the canteen in his left hand and placed the belt and bayonet right under the platform's edge.

Boar Hog crawled up first. "I get the wall," he said, working his way across the matted surface and placing his steel pot down as a pillow. Lying on his back, he said, "Hey, this ain't so bad!"

Metz and Wally were next, followed by the Kid and Wilson, who took the outside edge. After much jostling and wiggling and settling in, they were all lined up, ready to sleep.

"Hey," Wilson suddenly said, "does anybody think that if a mortar round came in here and hit us, we'd all be dead? Who'd run the unit? Does anybody think one of us ought to go dig a hole in another part of the area? Just for safety?"

There was silence as the group digested what the lieutenant was suggesting. Then, Boar Hog spoke up. "So, you wanna dig a hole, Wilson. Is that it?"

"Well, no."

"Ain't nobody else here gonna dig a hole. We all outrank you, except for Stocker, and he's not in command of anything! Herschel, if we get killed, we'll be dead and it won't make any fucking difference. We've got a good perimeter, and if the VC will let us sleep, *I'm* sleepin'. If they wanna fight, I'll get up and call in some goddamned Spookies, and *then* we'll get some rest."

Again, the men settled into place as much was humanly possible on the hard surface in the middle of a battle zone in tropical heat amid the stink and wetness of their filthy jungle fatigues.

After about a minute of silence, the Kid fake snored like the Three Stooges:

"Snort-wheeeeew …"

Wally answered with, "Bee, bee, bee, bee," and the five of them all burst out belly laughing.

Timing is everything!

"OK!" Boar Hog insistently hollered, trying to stop laughing himself. "Everybody, especially Stocker, shut the fuck up! That is an order, goddammit!"

After a few snickers, they settled down again. Exhaustion was universal, and soon a couple of them were actually snoring, but one of them wasn't the Kid. The helmet as a pillow thing was not working. He slid his helmet up a little and let his head rest directly on the mat, his body lying completely flat. The heat was stifling, and there was little circulation in the hooch. The mosquitoes buzzing overhead were obviously weighing their dislike of repellent against their desire for blood. *Only a matter of time before they come in for the bloodsucking.*

Having always needed a glass of water by his bed to sleep, the Kid had his canteen cached over his head behind his helmet but was reluctant to take a drink because the movement would disturb the others. So, he persevered. In light of his inability to actually go to sleep, his mind began to wander from one wild fatigue-induced scenario to another.

What to do with the glasses? Now here some major decisions were to be made. *Gotta have them if we are attacked. Can't lose the fucking glasses, fuckhead. If you lose the glasses, you're a dead man! Put them in your pocket and you'll roll over on them and break them. Put them in your pants pocket and don't roll over, or put them in your breast pocket and sleep on the other side. Sleep? Ha!* It was everything the Kid could do to keep from breaking out into a laughing fit! *Sleep? Ain't no sleep! OK, wear the glasses? Pants pocket and don't roll over wins!*

Lying there on his back, the Kid felt his heart pulsing blood through his brain. He also felt the sweat beads on his forehead. He began to see patterns in his third eye like the ones he'd seen the times he'd taken acid. *Talk about a bad trip!*

Imagine the worst possible scenario, and then when you open your eyes, you find that it's only a dream! When I open my eyes, I'm going to be in Nashville! No, California! He opened his eyes and blinked. Shit! I'm in the middle of the fucking rice paddies in the Mekong Delta in a hooch sleeping with four frickin' men, and I'm less than two hundred meters from the Charlies! I know they're fucking over there just waiting for us to go to sleep, and then they'll come rushing in and cut our throats!

The thought of having his throat cut triggered the Kid's recurring nightmare about decapitation on the guillotine, which he'd most recently dreamt in Tan An, dreaming he was going to the blade in the French Revolution. *"But I am innocent! I am but a child! I am barely fifteen! I have never done anything to harm anybody! Even my father the duke was good to our serfs!"*

"Aw, sorry, Keed, that's too bad. We gotta whack you anyway, or the council de revolution will whack us, no? As you know, this executioner's job is hereditary, and nobody in the Sanson family has ever not beheaded those sent to us for whacking, so the only thing we can do for you is get it over with as quickly as possible, so you don't have to think about it. Real fast! Here, first we strap you up to the board and lay you flat. In goes your head. We put the collar down, and instantly the knife comes down. Then, whack, it's over, monsieur. Next!"

The Kid's body jolted. He sat up bolt straight and took a real gasp, his hand grabbing his throat. The blade did not arrive! Hot, humid breath came slowly from his lungs. *Damn! Lucky thing I didn't suck in a bug!* He lay back down. Flo. First kiss. First time unbuttoning her blouse and actually sucking on her right nipple.

All of a sudden, she was on top him at the Traveler's Motel, the fourth time they'd done it that afternoon. *Holy moly! Oh my God! What am I doing? Stop, stop, stop!*

If I get a boner here, I'm dead meat! Yankees. Yankees. They must be playing right now. In Boston. Yeah, in Fenway. Mantle and Williams! Ford and what's his fuck? Hell, Boston never had any good pitchers. That's why they always lose!

Baseball. Shit. It's August and the Yankees are almost in last place! I can't believe it looks like the Tigers are going to win the pennant. And who is this Denny McLain fuck, gonna win thirty games?! Where the hell did he come from?

The Kid considered rolling over, but there was too little room. Each of the men could get up if they wanted to by crawling off the foot of the platform, but now it seemed that Wilson, to the Kid's right, and Wally, to his left, were actually asleep. The Kid looked around with his peripheral vision with his eyes closed and saw a scene. It was near the top of the roller coaster at Lakeside in Denver, and they were riding in the front car. The Cyclone! Donna was next to him, and his arm was around her, but he took it off her shoulder to hold it straight up in the air as the coaster crested the top of the first drop and thundered down the tracks and into the banking left turn! *Whee! Wha-woo! "Donna. I'm sorry, I've met a girl. Her name is Flo, and somehow I think she and I are meant to be. I'm swept away." Oops! Boulder Creek, 1965. The early summer runoff was very high. "Hey, Rick, we can tube it without our butts hitting any rocks!" Holy moly! The water is so cold and the creek current is so strong that it has knocked me over! It's ripped off my tennis shoes. There goes my inner tube. I'm being washed downstream.*

Willow! Willow! Grab the willow branches hanging down in the water! What fools we were. Sgt. Pepper! *That's it! Play the* Sgt. Pepper *album in your head!*

The night was still; there was no action, only the slightest hint of some off in the distance, as explosions or thunder could be faintly heard from far off. The Kid composed himself, lying there and spinning the disk in his head: the crowd noise, the band tuning up, then the music! "It was twenty years ago today that Sergeant Pepper taught the band to play …" As he relived the sounds, the album cover exploded in his inner field of vision, all Peter Maxish, psychedelic and everything. *If only I were at Wen's in Tra Vinh listening to this!*

His concentration couldn't hold. After he got through "with a little help from his friends," the Kid's thoughts strayed into politics. *Nixon is in for the Republicans, and the Democrats are in total disarray now that Robert Kennedy's been shot. Humphrey has been trying to distance himself from Johnson; McCarthy really doesn't have a prayer; and now the convention is coming up in Chicago.* Being a debater, the Kid had always followed politics quite closely, and now his mind didn't know what to think. *Mom will vote Republican, and Dad, the "independent," had better vote for peace. You'd think a man with one son in Vietnam and another on the way here would neither an elephant nor a donkey be. Gotta admit, they've both got their faults! Hell's bells, what the fuck does it matter to me? Here I am and here I'll stay until my tour's over or I get killed or catch the million-dollar- wound brass ring—whichever comes first! Crap, shit! Diarrhea! Wouldn't you know it?*

The Kid sat up and inched his way forward with his hands and on his butt until he could stand up off the end of the platform. The toilet paper from his MRE was cached in the same pocket as his glasses; he felt for it when he took the plastic frames out and put them on. *Pretty fucking dark! Can't see shit to go take a shit! I so break myself up!*

Locating his pistol belt, he got the bayonet and headed outside the hooch and into the still of the tropical night. Having known beforehand that this problem might arise, he had a plan, a place to go to dig his cathole and squirt the vile brown liquid into it, over behind the ARVN radio shack.

An ARVN guard standing sentry, or rather squatting sentry, right outside of Tu Ta's door watched the Kid as he shuffled past. Looking at his watch, the Kid learned it was only one o'clock in the morning. *Still four and a half hours to morning light; this is fast becoming one of the longest night's I've ever lived! Ha! Look at that! The sentry has figured out how to smoke on guard duty! Look at the way he holds his steel pot, concealing the ember. And then it shields the light when he takes a puff! I'll have to try that!*

The Kid made his way past the squatting sentry, who nodded politely to acknowledge his presence. Behind the radio hooch, the Kid found the area he had in mind. He'd had so much diarrhea lately that his asshole was totally sore from wiping. Everybody got it. There was no sense in doing anything but try to ride it out and build up some immunity to all the bacteria that must be causing it. Not to mention the malaria pills! *Shit, have to take a malaria pill when we get back,* the Kid thought. He dug in the dirt with the bayonet, trying not to have to handle the dirt with his hands. *Why bother to dig? Hell, it should just seep into the ground like water! And the rest of it is about the same color brown as the soil!* Squatting down, he placed his left hand behind himself for balance, and the brown liquid, mixed with little chunks of god-knows-what, went squirting noisily into the hastily dug cathole. *Outgoing! This will piss off the Cong! There is never enough toilet paper in these MREs!*

Returning to the hooch, the Kid felt his way back to his slot on the platform and, as quietly as he could, retrieved his steel pot from its place. Then he went out to join the smoking sentry.

411

As he approached the man, he could barely make out the features of his face in the darkness. The man's head had a certain squareness to it, with his hair cut in such a manner as to accent his highly exaggerated wide-set jawline. He squatted at the edge of the building as he held the cigarette in one hand and his helmet in front of it with the other. In this manner, when the light brightened on the tip of the cigarette with each puff, it was shielded from the front by the steel pot, from behind by his head, from his right by the radio shack, and from his left by the hooch where the officers and the Kid attempted to sleep.

"Chow, Ong," the Kid whispered as he came up and squatted next to the man. Taking out a cigarette, he pantomimed his desire to smoke along with the obviously well-seasoned ARVN veteran.

"Ah!" The man comprehended his desire. "You *sem sem* me!" He motioned for the Kid to hold up his steel pot, and together they made a double-helmet shield. Using the ARVN's cigarette, the Kid lit up. *If only basic training Drill Sergeant Smith could see me now! Out in the middle of combat, in a defensive perimeter, and learning there is a way to smoke a cigarette in the middle of the night and not get shot! They could have taught us this in basic, but nooooo!* The Kool smoke filled the Kid's lungs and the nicotine rushed to his brain, inducing its incredibly calming effect. It was a lot tougher not being able to smoke tobacco than it was not to smoke pot, the Kid was beginning to realize, just because of the limited smoking opportunities in combat, especially at night.

The pair smoked and listened to the stillness. Nothing was going on. Insect noises begat a calming effect on the psyche almost as much as the tobacco did on the body; as long as the insects were making noise, nobody could up and say, "Awful quiet. Yeah. Too quiet, pilgrim."

From inside the radio shack, sounds of transmissions and muffled replies could be heard periodically by the smoking pair on the outside. Of course, the Kid's Vietnamese, although it had been getting much better in the two-plus months he had now been attached to the Vietnamese army, wasn't good enough to allow him to understand anything being said. Besides, it was also in code.

Once the cigarette was extinguished by pushing it into the dirt, the Kid rose up shakily and made his way back into the hooch, deciding he should again try to get some sleep. This time, he tried his left side, facing Wally, who was facing Metz, who was facing Boar Hog, who was facing the wall. Wilson, lying on the end, was still on his back, staring straight up. With the helmet now under his head and his extra pair of socks acting as a cushion on top of the helmet, the Kid felt strangely at ease, almost instantly dropping off into a deep, fatigue-laden slumber and falling into a highly vivid dream.

Flo, there you are. I call, "Flo!" but you can't hear me. Where are you? Sitting by the ocean, with your hands clasping something. A letter. From whom? Me?

Her lips are moving, but I can't hear what she is saying. She seems to be crying and praying! Has something happened? I must get close enough to see the letter! Why, it's the letter Wilson asked me to write that he said he would give to her if I got killed! Wait a minute, I never wrote that letter! "Flo! I'm not dead. I'm right here! They can't kill me, not even with those machine guns!" Machine guns? Holy mother of Jesus, we are under attack!

The five men, literally in unison, rose up and tried to get off the platform as the twin M60 machine guns were open for business and pumping out the ammo over at the sensitive 0300 position! The Kid pulled his .38 from its holster and rushed outside.

Tu Ta, Dai Ui Than, and Ba came clambering out of the other hooch. Frantic talking was going on inside the radio shack as the firing continued.

"I haven't heard the claymores go off yet," Wilson observed. That was a good sign. *Poof, poof!* Up in the sky about six hundred feet, two illumination flares lit up and began floating to the ground, rocking gently under their miniparachutes, illuminating the area in front of where the machine guns were shooting. By the time the group had finished checking their pieces and making sure they had bandoliers, the shooting stopped.

Standing behind Tu Ta, who now had his head stuck inside the radio shack, Boar Hog anxiously awaited word of what the hell was going on.

Tu Ta finally turned. "False alarm," he informed the big man and the tense little group. "How you say 'itchy trigger fingers'?" He laughed.

"Fucking gooks!" Boar Hog cursed the race in general; he didn't know if it was the VC or the ARVNs who were responsible, but either way, it was gooks who had caused his slumber to be disturbed, that much he knew for sure!

You're not Boar Hog. You're Bore Pig, the Kid thought, secretly renaming him.

Chapter 37

The Kid dipped the pipe into his right front fatigue pocket and filled it with a good couple of hits as he walked leisurely down the shady tree-lined street leading from the American compound to the riverfront shopping district of Tra Vinh.

Walking as the lone American, he was also venturing out without the otherwise ever-present Corporal Ba, whom the Kid treated now like the younger brother he never had. He was even brazenly breaking the general rule never to leave the compound alone, but today the Kid just kind of felt like it. He had some shopping to do, and nobody was ready to go with him. Besides, he was speaking pretty good beginning Vietnamese now, having hung out with the ARVNs and Corporal Ba for the past two months.

The Tra Vinh shopping district was six blocks from the compound, giving the Kid just enough time to have two or three hits on the pipe, which was all it would take for him to stay high for the whole morning. He felt quite safe walking along, knowing there weren't any Americans close enough to hamper his desire to blow some weed, but at the same time also know that some were close by enough, by a couple of blocks, that if anybody were to question why he was out alone, he could say he was trying to catch up to the others.

Sheathing his pipe in the same pocket with his movable cache, the Kid soon arrived at his destination, the all-purpose supply and hardware shop owned by Wen's father, Nguyen, where it was his plan to buy a nylon mesh hammock. He wanted something small enough to wad up and stuff in his cargo pants pocket because there was no way he was ever again going to sleep on a platform with a bunch of guys, or on the ground out in the middle of the boonies on an overnight operation.

"Ciao, Ong Nguyen," the Kid said to the shop owner, stepping around a display of aluminum cooking pans. Smiling, he watched the middle-aged man's face as Nguyen came to recognize the man who was standing across from him. Nguyen smiled in answer.

"Ah! Ciao, Stocka! Da Kid! How are you?" Nguyen answered in English, bowing slightly from the waist and then extending his hand to shake.

When the Kid tried to speak Vietnamese at his stage of learning, it frequently turned out to be only a couple of words of speech followed by pantomime and charades to communicate his idea.

"*Toi mun* [I want]. Toi mun this!" the Kid finally blurted out, having spied the hammocks. He walked down the aisle of goods to his left, where a moderate selection of brightly colored nylon woven hammocks were on display. Looking through them, he found a green one that he liked: almost camouflage, he reasoned. Holding it up, he inquired, "Bon u?" He wanted to know how much it cost.

Nguyen put his hand to his chin, seemingly studying the hammock in the Kid's hands, before looking and saying, "Ba MPC." That was three dollars' MPC.

"Mot!" The Kid held up one finger, offering one dollar MPC, bargaining in good faith.

"Mot MPC? Cam bao ya!" Nguyen shook his head, indicating that one dollar was not enough—and not actually knowing if the Kid was joking with him or not.

"Hai." The Kid held up two fingers.

"OK, Kid! Hai." Nguyen nodded his lightly graying head in agreement. "You sure drive hard bargain!" He ribbed him good-naturedly.

As the Kid handed Nguyen a five-dollar note, the merchant pulled a bundle of MPC from his front right pocket and began to make change.

"Toi tic piasters!" The Kid requested that Nguyen give him his change in Vietnamese money. "Toi di choi, drink Kaffee nouc da!" He was going over to the marketplace, where he planned on ordering an iced coffee and sitting at a spot with a view of the river while he wrote a letter to Flo. So, back went the MPC, and out of the left front pocket of his tan pants came a role of dirty, well-used piasters. Nguyen pulled off three twenties, a ten, and a fiver, giving the Kid an exchange rate of twenty-five to one. Fair enough. "Cam on u lam. Thank you very much!

Ciao, Ong." The Kid bowed respectfully, then turned with his purchase and left.

Back outside the open-fronted store, the Kid made his way across the bustling market, amid a sea of conical hats, baskets of produce, hanging ducks and chickens, and fish, to the main cafe, which was in a building that had been built at a right angle to the river. A makeshift canopy shaded the dozen tables that were arranged out in front of the open cafe area under the roof that had easily another thirty tables. At 0830 hours, it was after their breakfast rush and there were a couple of empty tables, one conveniently on the edge of the patio exactly where the Kid wanted to sit.

A row of two dozen or more twenty- and thirty-foot-long boats, some high-sided with cabins, and others open and shallow with long motor shafts sticking a good ten feet out the back, were beached along the riverbank, with farmers coming in from upriver and downriver to sell their produce in the market. It was clear to see that some of the families had to live on their boats full time.

There were lots of females, from baby girls to old grannies; lots of young boys, from babies to nine- or ten-year-olds; and a few grandpas, but no men of military age in this market, except for the ARVN soldiers, mostly officers, who were sitting around tables casually eating and smoking.

Looking at the open table and sitting down, the Kid lit up a Kool while waiting for a pair of boys to sort out who was going to wait on him. Finally, the taller and apparently older of the two, a lad of about eleven, came over to his table.

"Ciao, Em," the Kid said, addressing him as a child.

"Ciao, Mai," the boy said, addressing him as an American and waiting for whatever was coming next with a puzzled look on his face.

"Toi mun caffee nouc da, kong sur, kong dur." Coffee, iced, black, no sugar or milk, was what the Kid ordered.

His Vietnamese must have been good enough, because the boy turned and hustled off. And before the Kid had gotten much past "Dearest Flo" on the stationery now in front of him on the table, the boy was back with his order.

"Cam on u lam." The Kid thanked him. He stirred the tall glass tumbler full of ultrastrong black coffee and ice and took a long drink of the cold liquid. Then, ignoring the abundance of stares around him, he turned his attention back to Flo's letter.

I'm writing this from the cafe down by the river, where I'm drinking iced coffee and smoking a cigarette. I've got a spot in the shade, and it's not half bad. At least the cafe has ice today. You don't really miss the little things till you can't get them. But I miss you all the time!

Well, today is supposed to be the day that the psyops truck arrives from Can Tho. It's coming in with a convoy from Vinh Long, if it makes it! Glad I'm not on it. Don't know how this new deal is going to change things, but if it means going on fewer operations with Lieutenant Wilson dragging us out where we do not need to be, then I'm all for it.

I'm really missing you bad lately, Flo. Without your letters, I'd be going totally nuts. All I wait for is to get one of your perfume bombs at mail call and hope it has new pictures in it (hint, hint). But really I just want to smell your scent, which is about all of you that you can fit into the envelope and send over here.

So, Bouji has finally gone back to Tan An. He left yesterday. Wilson and I took him out to the airport to meet the chopper at about eight o'clock in the morning, and finally the Tra Vinh sniper shot in Boujold's direction.

And was it ever funny! The shot came about twenty meters to our front, and Wilson started jumping around like it was a big deal. Bouji just sat there on his duffle bag, smoking a cig. I was playing along, so I kind of ducked down on one knee. Wilson was hollering, "Run, Boujold, run! Sniper! Sniper!" Bouji just sat there and said, "I hope to fuck he just shoots me in the head and saves me the trouble of going back to Tan An!" Then, just as the words were out of his mouth, the sniper put a round five feet behind his butt, and he flopped on his face so quick and lay so flat, I though he was a flapjack! What a scream! That's about as close as I've seen the Tra Vinh sniper come to anybody.

So now, after hanging with Boujold for two months, I gotta put up with a totally new guy. I hear he's a DINFOS graduate, so at least we'll have that in common. I'm pretty sure he won't be an ignoramus. His name is Sweet. Isn't that sweet? James Sweet. Dig this: he's driving the MSQ-85 down from Can Tho in the convoy! Imagine that! You're new in-country and you end up on a convoy from Can Tho to Vinh Long to Tra Vinh! He has to drive through Cang Long to get here, and when he does, we are all driving back out there tomorrow. Or the next day. You never know in this stinking place.

Just like last week, when we ended up out at Than Pu, pulling indoctrination duty, waiting for that convoy to get together for the trucks to come down. Don't get me wrong, honey, I don't like going out on combat missions, but I really hate sitting around baking in the heat while Ti Ui Troung blabs his mouth off in those stupid and endless classes. They are enough to make any good ARVN desert and go over to the Cong. It's worse than our army! So far, Than Pu wins my vote for the worst stinking hole in the country (again, I emphasize "so far"). I don't know what it's going to be like in Cang Long, but I do know it would be really nice to have a real bunk for a while. These last couple of days here in Tra Vinh are spoiling me again. I just bought a hammock to take out into the boonies the next time we have to stay out overnight on an operation. I'm never sleeping on the same bed with a bunch of men again!

Not that we get fresh news over here, but I do know the Democratic National Convention is coming up real soon. God, I hope they pick McCarthy, but you know it's going to be Humphery. "Hubie" doesn't have a clue or a chance, even against Nixon. I got registered to vote here two days ago. I hate LBJ, and Hubert didn't move too fast in distancing himself from the war machine. And I can't see myself voting for Nixon, so I went with independent. My dad would be proud, and Mom would skin me and everything. I'm finding it interesting that my first vote for president will be cast from a war zone. Can't wait to get my absentee ballot!

Well, my darling, I'd better close for now and get back so I can mail this and see if anything from you has come in today. I love you, and so believe me when I say,

I'll see you later!

Curt

Looking up from the newly completed letter, the Kid saw the boy standing quietly in front of him with his hand out, wanting to be paid for the iced coffee. Checking his watch and seeing that it was approaching 1000, the Kid pulled a twenty- piaster note out of his pocket and laid it on the table, not bothering to wait for change.

Approaching the compound, the Kid was hoping nobody would notice he'd broken the "don't go downtown alone" rule. Then, he saw something sticking up above the barbed-wire-topped front wall of the old French estate. Entering the compound, he discovered that it was, indeed, the MSQ-85. Mounted on the back of a three-quarter-ton truck, it looked like an olive-drab camper with no windows. The square box had a door in the rear, and above the door was a lift arm with a pulley configuration that looked like a little gallows. *Oh no! Lieutenant Wilson is right here!*

Standing there and looking under the raised hook of the newly arrived truck were Wilson, Ba, and the person who the Kid thought must have been the new guy.

"Hey! So this is it!" the Kid said, announcing his presence.

Wilson looked up and down, and then obviously behind him, searching for his companion. "Stocker. Where have you been?"

418

"Uh, I went downtown to buy some stuff." He pulled the hammock from his pocket. "Look, Lieutenant. I almost got you one too, but I figured you'd rather pick out your own."

"Oh. Who did you go with?" the lieutenant asked, not really noticing anybody with the Kid when he walked up.

"I walked down with Hopkins," the Kid replied, naming one of the mysterious Air America pilots who occasionally hung out at the Tra Vinh compound. "He peeled off and went over to the CIA compound a block back. So, this is it, huh? And you must be Sweet!" The Kid immediately changed the subject and introduced himself to the new guy all in one breath.

Sweet extended his hand. "Yep, I'm the new guy, Jim Sweet!" They shook hands while Corporal Ba looked on, smiling. Lieutenant Wilson grimaced, trying to determine if the Kid was telling him the truth about Hopkins or not. The Kid didn't know where Hopkins was, but he hoped he wouldn't walk up from somewhere inside the compound anytime within the next minute or two.

The MSQ-85 was filthy. "You just get in?" the Kid asked Sweet.

"Yeah. What a trip! We left Vinh Long this morning at zero seven hundred, right on the heels of the road sweep. I was pretty nervous the whole way, but we made it down without any incident. There were about fifteen trucks and jeeps in the convoy." The slim, blond-haired GI grinned with raised eyebrows, emphasizing his wonderment at their fortunate luck.

"I was just telling PFC Sweet that I want you and him to wash this thing up and get the mud off. And once you do that," the lieutenant said, "we can get inside and look at the equipment we'll have to work with."

"You'll never believe how loaded this thing is." Sweet mopped his sweaty brow and took a long drink from the canteen he was carrying. "It's got everything from a sixteen-millimeter movie projector to a typewriter and a little printing press!"

"Oh, really? That's just great!" the Kid said. *A typewriter! Hot damn!* "Well, there ain't no hose and running water here. What did you have in mind for washing this thing, Lieutenant?"

"Spencer is getting us some buckets and rags, and you guys can roll a couple of those empty fifty-five-gallon drums over here to stand on to reach the top."

"All right," the Kid said. "Corporal Ba, are you going to be our Gunga Din?"

"Your what?" Ba, of course, failed to get the reference to the old Cary Grant movie where Sam Jaffe plays the water boy for the Bengal Lancers.

"Our water boy. You bring us water and we'll do the rest!" the Kid said. Sergeant Spencer walked up with three empty buckets and a bag of rags.

"Here you go, gentlemen." Spencer dropped the equipment at their feet and put his hands on his hips. "Have fun! Oh, and when you're done, do mine next. And don't forget the polish!"

"Thanks, Sarge," the Kid said, "but I'd really rather you polished mine." He pointed to his dick.

"Cam fucking bow ya!" Spencer said. He turned and walked off. Sweet looked confused.

"*Cam bow ya* means 'never happen' in Vietnamese," the Kid explained. "Corporal Ba here will teach ya the ropes, like he's teaching me."

"You men had better get crackin' or you won't be done by lunchtime," Wilson admonished. As if they'd miss lunch if they weren't finished. "I'll be back to check on y'all."

"I'm sure you will, sir." The Kid nodded to him as he turned and walked off after Sergeant Spencer.

The MSQ-85 was parked in the shade of the high leafy trees that were in the front yard of the manor house. It was a perfect place to wash the thing, out of the sun.

"Ba." The Kid pointed to the buckets on the ground. "You go get us some water, and I'm gonna go get my radio so we can have some tunes while we wash this hog." Taking out his cigarette pack, the Kid turned to Sweet and offered him one, which the new man took.

"Oh, thanks," he said as the Kid lit them up, Sweet's first.

"Did anybody get you a bunk yet?" The Kid exhaled.

"No, not yet. Shit! I just pulled into the driveway about fifteen or twenty minutes ago."

"Well, come on while I get my radio, and we'll see what's available down at the servants' quarters. That's where the EM sleep. The officers sleep in the manor house here." He pointed to the tall, stately two-story European-flavored building behind them. "I hear you're a DINFOS grad, huh?"

"Yeah, like I heard you were one and this was where I'd find you. So, you can imagine how pissed I was to get this psyops assignment," Sweet said, overstating the obvious.

"Can I ever!"

"Is this place secure?" Sweet eyed the wall and the Cambodian guard who stood watching the street traffic from the front gate control bunker.

"Ain't noooo place safe, but this isn't bad," the Kid said. They came into the courtyard and started across the volleyball court. "Anyway, a couple of guys have told me about their experiences here during the attack at Tet. They held it because of the Cambodian guards. But we are not staying here, and where we are going will not be anyplace remotely as safe as this!"

They crossed the grass and entered the servants' quarters. Knowing that Carpenter had just left the day before to go home, the Kid escorted Sweet to Carpenter's empty bunk, in the cubicle next to the Kid's own, when he was in town.

"And another thing," the Kid said in a low, guarded voice. "Wilson may seem OK on the surface, but the fucker is nuts. He's been volunteering us for all this search and destroy bullshit because he wants to hunt scalps. He digs this shit, and we have to do what we can to make sure he doesn't get us fucking killed doing something we're not supposed to be doing!"

Sweet's mouth fell open, giving extra depth to his naturally long and slightly slim fair-skinned face. "You mean he's, like, reckless?"

"That's a nice word. You can likely sleep here in Carpenter's bed. He DEROS'd yesterday. Didn't really know him, but we're not staying long. Spencer will give you a permanent locker so you don't have to drag everything into the field. This is pretty much home base. It's got the only American mess hall in the whole province, but most of the time, we'll be eating native."

"Well, fuck me!" Sweet sat down and tested his new bunk.

The Kid ducked next door and grabbed his radio, then motioned Sweet to follow him back out. "Ain't no TV. Got one really bad pool table. And this place is so small that the officers and the enlisted men have to share a club." The Kid pointed to the club door as they passed by. "Yes, sir," he continued, "it's been a lot more Fort Benning than Fort Benjamin Harrison, I'll fucking tell you that!

We've been pulling a lot of operations, and there's been a ton of shooting and shelling, but to tell you the truth, now that you're here with that truck, I'm fucking praying that we won't be pulling so much boonie duty with the ARVNs. You play volleyball?" the Kid asked as they crossed the court.

"Sure!"

"Good. There's a game every night after dinner, between the Americans and the ARVNs, before we kick them all out, even Corporal Ba. The ARVNs have been cleaning our clocks. The place isn't much, but Tra Vinh is the best thing we've got out here, so enjoy tonight and maybe tomorrow, because we're headed out.

In fact, the plan is we're taking this truck and heading back up the way you came, to Cang Long."

"Ah. I remember passing through there. Wasn't anybody there but ARVNs." Sweet stood, looking at the truck he'd just brought down the Cang Long road. "Is that place safe?"

"Fuck no. Aren't you paying attention? Ain't no safe place!" the Kid replied in a

no-bullshit tone of voice. "Not in this whole fucking country. But once you're really out there in some combat, Tra Vinh does feel kind of safe. But we know it's not."

Once they had the radio situated on the front porch of the mansion, about ten feet away, and properly tuned, Ba was back with the buckets of water, and the trio got to work. Stripped to the waist, with Armed Forces Radio playing in the background, they slopped on the water and soap, carrying on a running conversation.

Through the course of the job, the Kid discovered that he and Sweet had a lot in common: Sweet had arrived at DINFOS about two months before the Kid shipped out, so they actually had been there at the same time. He had a fiancée, named Barbara; he was working for a radio station in Bangor, Maine, when he got drafted; he was opposed to the war; and he did indeed smoke pot.

When one particular song started on the radio, Sweet jumped off his fifty-five- gallon drum and ran over to the radio to turn it up. "Oh boy, 'Freedom Train' by the Rascals," he said. "Have you heard this yet? It's about four months old in the States."

"No!" replied the Kid, who also stopped to listen. "I saw in an old *Billboard* that they had a new song out. This is it, huh?"

"Yeah! You'll love this! 'All the world everywhere, it's easy to see, people everywhere just gotta be free.' Kind of an antiracism, antiwar thing, really. I'm surprised AFVN is playing this!"

The Kid loved the Rascals, and he was blown away by the new song. "Listen to my opinion and it's easy to see, people everywhere, they gotta be free! See that train over there? That's the train of freedom," Felix Cavaliere sang. "It's gonna rise up any minute! It's been long, long overdue …"

"Wow!" the Kid exclaimed. "I love it!" Then, with a disappointed look on his face, he said, "Jeez, I'm so out of touch. Music was my life. Being out here is like being musically dead! I got one buddy who made it to AFVN in Saigon, Alan P. That bastard. He's a nice guy, but I'm sorry, he's not half the jock I am! Luck of the fucking draw. Now that you say we've got a typewriter, I can start putting in 1049's, requesting a transfer to AFRN in Saigon. They say that never happens out here, but I'm more of a 'nothing ventured, nothing gained' kind of guy. This guy Tom Roberts, a fellow DINFOS grad, by the way, got out of here four months early by getting accepted to West Point prep academy!"

"Yep." Sweet stopped scrubbing for a minute. "There's a typewriter all right. I've been using it to write home to Barbara."

With the last two buckets that Ba had fetched, they splashed the cab of the MSQ- 85 to rinse it one more time, with each man drenching a door. No sooner had they dropped their buckets than Lieutenant Wilson was upon them.

"Almost a good job, gentlemen." He swaggered up and pointed to some mud on the rear passenger's-side tire rim, which Corporal Ba jumped up and immediately wiped off. He continued on around. "Not bad. Not bad at all, gentlemen. So, this is the MSQ-85, the latest in political warfare in Southeast Asia." Arriving at the back end of the army-green box, he stopped and rocked back and forth on his heels.

Must be the Prussian blood coming out ...

"PFC Sweet," the lieutenant began, "let's open up the back and take a look at what's inside!"

"Yes, sir." Sweet jumped to the task, turning the handle and swinging open the three-foot-wide door, revealing an inside that was a little dark, until the new man threw a switch, turning on an interior overhead light, as he pulled himself up into the van with a convenient handgrip.

"Here," Sweet said, pointing to his left, turning to face the trio, who peered in with wonder, "is the generator. The pulley system hooks up right here." He performed tasks as he explained them. "After you take up the slack like this, you jump down, pull it up, slide it out, rotate it on the arm, and drop it on the ground over here on the side that has the generator plug. With this pulley and arm, one man can handle it pretty easily." He smiled and gestured as if he were Carol on *The Price Is Right* showing off a prize.

"Once the generator is hooked up and running, it powers the speakers that are built into the front of the MSQ-85"—the PFC, who was stripped to the waist, strode forward to point to the speakers—"for making announcements to crowds. And here in the back, the generator powers the interior lights, so they don't have to run off the battery. Come on in!" Sweet gestured that the lieutenant and the Kid should enter the van, which they did, to discover they could almost stand upright. "Over here is the eight-millimeter projector in its protective case. In that rack up there is the eight-foot screen, on which we can project this selection of six Vietnamese-language propaganda films that, right now, I have no idea what they are about."

"Sounds like we'll have to sit down with Corporal Ba and Ti Ui Troung and figure out what we've got," the lieutenant casually said. "Go on."

"Yes, sir. And over here is a thirty-five-millimeter filmstrip projector and a selection of six filmstrips to show the Vietnamese villagers. And here is the keeping place for the typewriter, inside this case. And over here is the little printing press. It's really kind of cool. It has rubber movable type, and we can make our own leaflets!"

"Ah, I had one of those as a child." The Kid departed down memory lane.

"And there's also a slide projector, but there aren't any slides for some reason." The tour concluded with the Kid and Wilson quickly stepping outside, as it was stifling hot in the back of the van.

"And here in this plastic bag," Sweet said as he stepped down, "are the collected operating and instruction manuals for everything on the truck, including the truck itself."

"Very interesting!" Wilson took possession of the sack and stood back to admire his new machine. "There's nothing I can't run or fix if I have the manual." He grinned. "Only thing wrong is that this thing is a huge target! This is gonna attract attention out there on the road, bet yer ass on that!"

"Well." Sweet put one foot up on the step that led into the van. "We didn't have any trouble coming down. Everybody seemed to think we would, but nothing ever happened. Didn't disappoint me, I'll tell you, by Jesus."

Corporal Ba, who was feeling left out, piped up, "Now, anyway, we don't have to walk or ask Sergeant Spencer to use his truck!"

"Good point, Corporal," the lieutenant said, "but we gotta do something to beef up this truck's defenses." The proverbial light bulb apparently went off in his head. "I know! We could put some claymore mines on it, and if we got ambushed, we'll just blow the enemy off and drive on through!"

"No disrespect intended, sir, but are you crazy?" the Kid asked immediately. "Don't forget, sir, claymores have a backwash, for fuck's sake! If we set off a claymore attached to this truck, it would trash us too!"

"Oh well, we can put a bunch of sandbags in between the claymores and the truck. It could work. I know it!"

The Kid glanced at Sweet and caught his eye. *See what I told you? This man is fucking nuts!* he silently said with an upward glance. "Sir, we aren't going anywhere that we'd need to even think about doing something like that, are we? Like without a convoy or extra protection?"

"In all likelihood, sooner or later, Stocker. This is a war, you know." He cocked his head and pursed his lips in his signature "Boy, are you stupid" pose.

"Fuckin' A!" The Kid stuck his head back into the van for another look around.

"This thing's got more gadgets than the frickin' Batmobile!"

"Yeah!" Sweet jumped right on it. "I got a Batmobile feeling too driving down here!

That was it; from that point on, the MSQ-85 was the Batmobile.

Just then, Paul Heineman came walking into the compound, returning from the TOC with Pete Johnson. "Hey, kids and Kid! What have you got here?"

"We think it's a Batmobile, but the army calls it an MSQ-85," the Kid explained their new ride.

"Nice. What the fuck does it do?"

Since he'd only learned about it a few minutes earlier, the Kid, instead of launching into a spiel, turned and introduced Paul and Pete to Jim Sweet. "Guys, this is a fellow DINFOS grad, Jim Sweet, who just drove it down here with the convoy from Can Tho by way of Vinh Long and Cang Long!"

"Wow!" said Paul. "Kudos, man!"

"It's got audio and visual capabilities, movie projectors, and tape recorders, along with a generator that can be used with lots of things too numerous to mention!" Sweet put it in a nutshell.

"And we're going to take it to Cang Long and do psyops with it tomorrow or the next day," Wilson said, reassuming his command position.

"Aw, that's too bad!" Paul turned to Wilson. "That means you guys are gonna miss a big-ass operation two days from now, with one element of the assault to be landed by Vietnamese navy junks!"

"Say what?" Wilson's ear pricked up like a German shepherd guard dog that had just heard somebody jump over his fence. "Junks? No shit?"

"No shit, sir. Battalion-sized operation with three companies. We're going to try to bag them up by Loc Da."

"I gotta be there! A river-borne assault. This may be our only chance to experience this, Stocker."

"Wait a minute, sir, is this an MSQ-85 sitting here or chopped liver?" The Kid tried to control his complete surprise at the turn of events. "They're expecting us in Cang Long, sir. We've got a psyops mission to do, sir!" He then suddenly turned to Paul in a cinematic huff. "And I thought you were my friend!"

"Sure, Kid. You know I'm you're friend. Think he wouldn't have found out? Major Gillmore is laying the plan out at the briefing this afternoon, so it'll be public knowledge in the officer corps by fourteen hundred hours."

The Kid knew that Heineman was right. Wilson would have found out. "Sir, what about Sweet, sir? Is he coming?"

Valid question. Wilson looked at Sweet and asked, "Sweet, do you want to go? You can if you want, but since you're new, I won't make you go on this one."

"I'll pass, sir," he shot back without hesitation, letting out a silent but highly visible sigh of relief.

"OK, that's your option until we get an opportunity to do some training. All right! Hot damn! A water landing! I thought I'd never get to do that! Well, gentlemen, looks like Cang Long can wait!" Wilson excitedly stormed off.

"Shit!" the Kid screamed. The second Wilson was out of earshot, he said, "God fucking damn it!"

Ba reacted too, knowing he would be going wherever the lieutenant and the Kid were going. "Mothafuck! Son of bitch!" he said, trying to cuss like an American.

"You teach him that?" Sweet asked.

"Yeah. Me and a couple of hundred other guys!"

Chapter 38

The Kid got to use his new hammock much sooner than he had expected. Turned out that the river assault was part of a two-day operation, but he got to use it even sooner than that!

The night after the arrival of the MSQ-85, instead of being in Cang Long, the Kid found himself over at the Company A compound down by the river, which was the main reason they'd been selected to make the river-borne assault. Along with the lieutenant and Corporal Ba, they were spending the night there because they would be boarding the junks before sunup.

The Kid had found a nice place to tie up inside a fairly large enclosure the company used as a training room, meeting place, and staging area. There were four-by-four posts that held up the twelve-foot-high ceiling. The distance between them was perfect. The hammock was more comfortable than he had ever dreamed, far superior to any of the cots he'd been exiled to during his tour.

He awoke almost refreshed at 0400 hours, when the unit was mustered out, and began preparing to board the ARVN navy junks that were arriving to pick them up in forty-five minutes.

As always, while the ARVN troops assembled, the wives and children of the soldiers who lived on and near the compound came to say their tearful goodbyes, babies on hips and other children clinging to pants legs, praying that this wasn't farewell for the last time.

I wonder if any of them are dying today. Him? Him? Me? Wilson? Ha! I only wish that fucker was dead! Where the fuck does he get off volunteering us for this shit? We got no psyops equipment or mission on this operation. Hell! Ti Ui Troung isn't even here. Hmm, I wonder if this is within regulations. Imagine if I pulled some army-regulations shit on him and stopped him from going on these operations. Would he be pissed or fucking what? Nah. He'd probably shoot me with the Luger or make sure we went someplace where I would for sure get shot. God! What am I thinking? We are going someplace where I could get shot!

"Isn't this exciting, Stocker?" Wilson was in his happy place. "I've always watched the old news reel footage of D-Day and wondered what it would be like to make a landing with the door flopping down, then charging out into the surf and hitting the beach!"

"Don't go getting your hopes up too high." Captain Brad Dalton, the top-ranking American adviser with Company A, punctured his balloon. "These things aren't landing craft, they're fucking junks! And as for hitting the beach, there ain't no fucking beach. I've done this twice before, and if we're lucky, we'll get to walk down a plank from the boat to the land. If we aren't lucky, we'll have to climb over the side and get into water up to our chests and wade ashore and hope to fuck we aren't getting shot at while we do it."

"Oh well, if they aren't going to be shooting at us, we don't want to go, right, sir?" the Kid sarcastically said to Wilson.

Wilson gazed at him in the weak light of the training facility's overhead naked bulbs, which offered barely enough illumination to read by. "Someday, Stocker, you're gonna have to get with the program, or you're really going to piss me off!"

"What'd I say? You want to be in the action, sir? Isn't that a correct statement on my part?" The Kid wasn't in the mood to take his "get with the program," WETSU ("We eat this shit up") crap today.

"Stocker, it's not what you say; it's the way you say it that sometimes pisses me off."

The Kid stared back at him in silence. *It's a good thing you can't read my mind, you fucking bastard, or I'd already be in the stockade. Because I hate your fucking guts and I'd love nothing better than to kick your redneck ass for doing this to us to satisfy some sick desire you have to take a life.* "Yes, sir, you're right, sir. I really do need to get with the program. I don't know, it's just a bad habit to be so sarcastic. I need help. Perhaps the army should send me back to the States, where there's some competent psychiatric assistance that could realign my consciousness to be more congruent with the 'program.' Sir."

Wilson shot him one of the dirtiest looks he'd ever seen, then chose to drop the issue. "So, Captain Dalton, how long have you been with A here?"

"Three months now," the crew-cut, black-haired, muscularly built man answered. Dalton was a former college football player type in his late twenties who looked as if he'd become addicted to the Charles Atlas bodybuilding plan.

Bet nobody kicks sand in his face!

"It's a pretty good company, for ARVNs. They'll fight, that's for sure. Sometimes B Company doesn't want to fight, and that's hurt a couple of operations I was on with them," Dalton said, reminiscing. "But not A Company. Tu Ta Kim is an ass kicker; you wouldn't want to be on his wrong side." Lighting up his first cigarette of the day, he exhaled a huge puff and continued. "Anyway, what the fuck, today is today, and it's the only day that counts."

Profound. You wouldn't think anybody in that kind of shape would smoke. "Ah, yes, sir," the Kid cut quickly cut in, "but yesterday, today was tomorrow, and tomorrow, today will be yesterday. And I think most people agree, 'Yesterday' is one of the best Beatles songs ever written!"

Dalton looked first to the Kid with a wry smile painted across his wide jaw. "OK, so I now see why Major Boarz calls you 'the Mouth.'" Then he looked at Wilson. "You have to put up with this?"

"Yeah. All the time," Wilson said, pulling on his boots. "But the Mouth has never let me down—yet."

"Yet?" the Kid shot back. "What do you mean, *yet*?"

"Well, you just never know, do you?" Now Wilson was getting profound. "It is probably a safe bet to say we haven't seen the toughest shit we're going to see on our tour yet, because it's only the middle of August."

The Kid made no reply, realizing that, unfortunately, the lieutenant was probably right.

"Hello, Lieutenant Wilson." Corporal Ba approached the group of three Americans, who were in the company of a skinny, short, and almost frail-looking Vietnamese radio operator, which was obvious because of the PRC-25 strapped to his back. "Lieutenant Wilson, this is Con," he began. "Con, Hashi Stocka.

Stocka, Con." Then, switching to Vietnamese, he said to Con, "Stocka bic Vietnam Cong hoa beaucoup!"

Amazingly, the Kid actually understood what he'd said. He replied in Vietnamese, "An trot Sai. Toy bic Vietnam cong hoa tee tee," which means, "You are untruthful. I only understand a very little bit." He used his fingers to show the international sign language gesture for a pinch.

Con's eyes lit up. He said, "Ah, numba one!" and gave the Kid a thumbs-up and a wide, yellow-toothed grin.

"Lieutenant Wilson," Ba said, "Con has been assigned to us. He is your radio operator now for keeps. He come with us alla time!"

"Really? Well, all right!" The wiry lieutenant was pleased that finally he was getting some respect. "To whom do we owe the thanks for arranging this?"

"You have Major Gillmore to thank," Dalton answered. "In fact, he was over here yesterday checking preparations, and told Tu Ta Kim to find you

429

a guy you could have for keeps, no matter who you're operating with in the regiment. Con is now your RTO!"

"Speaking of which," the Kid cut in, "what are the call signs today?"

"Ah, good question." Dalton opened a leather map folder he was carrying and consulted his notes. "Well, Company A is going to be Dolphin. Major Boarz and Company B are going to be Catfish. Ain't that fittin' for the redneck? Captain Metz and D Company are going to be Marlin, and the TOC today is Jonah."

That made Captain Dalton Dolphin 1, Wilson Dolphin 2, and the Kid Dolphin 3.

How cute. TOC always has their little theme. I guess I should have expected water-related bullshit today of all days.

Then, looking up to see a flurry of ARVN officers and NCOs entering the facility, Captain Dalton pointed. "There's Tu Ta Kim. Looks like we're almost ready to go."

over to where the little group of Americans stood with Corporal Ba and Con the RTO.

"Men yoi," Dalton greeted the very serious-looking Vietnamese major, who was one of the more muscular-looking Asians the Kid had ever seen. "We lift weights together," Dalton proudly said as he made a subtle flex of his pec muscles. "Dai Ui Kim, this is Ti Ui Wilson, Hashi Stocker, and their interpreter, Hashi Ba."

Kim shook hands with Wilson and then the Kid. *What a firm grip! I think he tried to hurt my hand! I can see this guy is a major fucker! What a cold expression. Couldn't be more than early thirties—pretty young for an ARVN major. He must be on the fast track.*

"We di di mau?" Dalton looked to Kim for confirmation that the unit was ready to load up.

"We go now!" he curtly replied. His XO and NCOs swiftly motivated the troops to pick up their gear and head out.

The unit made its way out of the compound gate and quickly covered the hundred meters that led down to the canal that connected to the river. In the traces of the first morning light, the Kid could see four junks tied up at the dock, upon which the lead elements of the company were beginning to load.

Unlike what the Kid thought of when he heard the term *junk,* a rather large ship with a turned-up bow, a cabin on the stern, and bamboo masts with sails that stuck out to one side, these, he discovered, were smaller. About forty

430

feet long and roughly fifteen feet wide in the middle, they did have bows and sterns turned up, but there were no sails to be sure. *Ha! They kind of look like Mike Fink keelboats!* The Kid could hear the engines idling as the four-man crews of each craft assisted the troops in boarding.

The Kid could see the silhouette of the junk's operator as he peered out of a fortified pilothouse at the back of the boat. One platoon of roughly thirty soldiers fit nicely on the deck area of each boat. Sitting on the gunwale, the Kid ran his hand over the smooth, well-worn wood of the craft, trying hard not to think about the fact that this tub was going to carry him into combat.

The air was what passed for cool in the tropics, that is, as cool as it ever got down on the Mekong River before sunup. Soon, the company was loaded. The Kid checked his watch: 0500 hours, straight up.

Almost in unison, the crews cast off the lines and shoved the junks back before jumping aboard and securing the ropes. The motors drew them in reverse away from the dock, and as each found the room, it turned out toward the middle of the canal.

The ARVNs were now sitting on the deck, lighting up cigarettes all over the place, and of course the Kid, Wilson, Ba, and Dalton all joined in the smoke fest. There wasn't a man there who wasn't outwardly a little bit nervous, except maybe

Lieutenant Wilson, who was grinning from ear to ear, although the corners of his upturned mouth were hidden by his bushy mustache. He chose to stand, rocking gently with the junk, on sea legs that obviously displayed his nautical experience.

"This sure beats the truck ride." The Kid smiled back at Wilson. "Remind you of your time with the merchant marines?"

"No. This is nothing like the freighters I was on," he said. "On them, once you get a little used to it, you can hardly feel them move. Now in a Nor'easter, those freighters could be bucking sons of bitches! These look like they hardly ride down in the water more than like three feet."

"That's about right," Dalton said. "These are really shallow-drafted so that we can get really close to shore. In fact, they'll try to find a place where we can hold and run out a gangplank for deboating. I sure hope we don't have to get in the water to start the day."

I second that emotion! the Kid silently agreed. Once the four craft were out of the canal and into the river's current, they turned upriver and fell into a line, about twenty meters apart and at least a hundred meters from the shoreline. The junk that carried the Kid and his group was third in line as the little convoy cleared the limits of the town of Tra Vinh. They were now flanked by nothing but open shoreline all the way up to Vinh Long, forty miles to the west. It was like boating on the mighty Mississippi, only it was the deadly Mekong. The Kid couldn't even begin to make out the shore on the far side. But it was becoming light enough for them to see how silt-laden the waters of the Mekong were.

As they motored upriver toward their destination, the Kid turned to Dalton and attracted his attention to ask a question. "Are we there yet?"

Dalton chuckled and smirked. "If you ask again, I swear to fucking God, I'll make the captain turn this boat around."

"Are we there yet?"

"In about half an hour. And don't bother asking again, because I'm not answering." Dalton nipped the Kid's next one in the bud.

The tops of the high tropical clouds were beginning to catch some color—faint oranges and reds. Ba came over and sat on the deck next to the Kid, who offered him a Kool as he prepared to light a fresh butt. The young Catholic had become quite the smoker. "Stocka, you scared?" he asked.

"Yes, a little," the Kid truthfully replied. The time between departure to go on an operation and when the action actually started was always the worst. *How bad is it going to be today? I hope I can find a good place to tie up my hammock tonight; at least I won't have to sleep on the ground or in some fucking hooch with Wilson and who the fuck knows. I wonder what Flo is doing right now? She should be coming home from school. Did I make a mistake asking her to marry me? I mean, how much fun can high school be if your boyfriend is out of the country for the whole year? ... I wonder if we're gonna be shot at when we land? There's sure not much fucking cover out here in the middle of the fricking goddam Mekong. I wonder how big the biggest fish is in this river?*

"Hey Lieutenant!" the Kid hollered across the deck at Wilson, his voice rising over the noise of the junk's powerful engine. "We should've brought our fishing gear and done a little trolling up to the jump-off spot!"

He laughed. "Who needs fishing poles?" He tapped on the top of one the hand grenades attached to his pistol belt. "Yeah, I don't mind fishing when somebody else is going to clean them!"

"We're quite a ways out now," the Kid hollered over the wind and the noise of the engine. "How far you reckon to shore, Lieutenant?"

"Hmm, I'd say not more than three hundred meters. I don't know what the ARVN navy tactic is, but I sure as hell hope they've got something tricky to do so as not to tip the unit's hand."

No shit, Sherlock!

In what the Kid deemed to be all too quick, the four junks began executing a left- leaning U-turn to make for shore. The time was 0530 hours. It appeared they had traveled past the landing site and were now circling back to it as they angled for the foliage-laden green bank of the river. *Those fucking woods could be full of frickin' Charlies just waiting for us. God, how I hate the army, the war, and you, Wilson, because we don't have to be here, you son of a fucking bitch! Ha! This will be great shit for my book! If I ever live to write a fucking book—or another letter home, for that matter. Well, I've got the lucky beaver nickel. How fucked are you when your lucky necklace is your ace in the hole? Wow! The closer we get, the taller those palm trees get! Shit, mutha! This looks tricky! I wonder how they'll ever find a place to land and pull it off with the current. It looks like a swirly, moving kind of thing. Ooh, feel the adrenalin, and nobody's even fired a shot yet!*

"Hey, Lieutenant!" The Kid shuddered as if he were cold. "Didn't a big bunch of guys die at D-Day by drowning when they stepped off the landing craft into deep water and sank with their loads of ammo?"

"Yeah, I read that." He grimly nodded his head, weighted by his steel pot. "I guess we'll have to watch out for that. But you aren't traveling too heavy, are you, Stocker? I see you brought a poncho this time, that and your MRE and your fifty rounds of .38 shorts. I doubt if you'd sink. Got your chin strap on? If your steel pot fell into the water, it would be flat gone! I wouldn't wanna be out here without a steel pot." He flicked his cigarette out into the river. "Well, they haven't opened up yet. This is a positive development. In a minute, you should be able to see for yourself what the plan is, Stocker. It's damned clever!"

Being so pointedly told, the Kid became observant, as tension among the ARVN riflemen noticeably mounted around him. Then he spotted it: an opening in the tree line where a sizable canal or tributary vented onto the Mekong. The junks were now quickly motoring for it.

"Major Gillmore reckons this is the most dangerous part." Wilson chose to let the Kid in on information he'd been holding back. "He says when we enter this canal, if we don't get caught in a crossfire, that will mean that the VC did not find out our plan of battle. If we do, that means the VC got tipped off. And man oh man, what a plan B Gillmore has in case that happens!"

"Say what, sir? Are you jiving me that there is a good chance when we go into that canal that we're going to be in an ambush?" The Kid was now tingling with trepidation, fearing what might be preparing to pounce on them.

"Yep, that's affirmative, PFC. And if that happens, TOC has airborne, right now, two flights of Phantoms. If the VC are waiting to ambush us, the jets are going to ambush them instead by hitting both sides of the canal almost immediately! What a brilliant plan!" Wilson's admiration for the major was beyond generous.

"OK, sir, now let me get this straight." The Kid continued to seek clarification as now Ba and Con, the new RTO, were quite interested as well. "The chance we are going to get ambushed is so high that there are fighters on call hoping it happens? And if it does, there's going to be air strikes on both sides of us? I don't believe it!"

"That is affirmative, PFC." The lieutenant was now steely in his demeanor. To accent his assuredness, as the first of the boats entered the waterway, he drew his Luger and checked to make sure a round was in the chamber. "Kind of makes you wish you'd brought your M16, doesn't it, PFC?"

It was still not yet bright enough out to require sunglasses, so the Kid had been looking at the lieutenant. He looked him right in the eye when he made that last comment. "You didn't bring yours," he immediately fired back. "I kind of look at that as a bellwether: is where we're going bad enough to make the lieutenant want *his* M16? And if you're not bringing yours, then I'm not bringing mine." Then he quickly added, "Unless of course you tell me to," seeing the lieutenant was possibly reexamining his decision to let the Kid carry a pistol. "Like I told you back when I found out we don't have any stinking loudspeakers, sir, so we can do our job, I don't plan on putting any ARVN infantrymen out of theirs!"

Now their boat was entering the canal. No shooting had yet welcomed them, but the ARVNs were all ready for the worst. Safeties were off and rounds were being chambered all up and down both sides of the deck. Ba was on a knee with his left hand touching the deck for balance, while on the floor behind Wilson.

Prepared to hand Ba his microphone was Con, the RTO. *The little shrimp looks like he's ready to go! He has a new job as personal radio telephone operator to an American lieutenant, and he's going to make the best of it! Carry your radio, sir? Clean your boots, sir? Help you call in an air strike, sir?*

The Kid nodded and smiled when he caught Con's eye. The radio operator's face lit up as he smiled and nodded back. *Con, you skinny, narrow-jawed, bug-eyed little scarecrow, you're going to be a character in my book!*

The bows of the junks sliced through the morning-calm water of the canal, which at its confluence with the river was at least fifty meters wide, but it quickly narrowed to no more than thirty meters as it ran in a straight line to infinity. With their motors cut back near idle, the boats let their momentum carry them deeper into the estuary off the main river.

That's right, here we are, dangling like ripe fruit to be picked off by the VC Tenth or any damn VC who comes down the pike. Sweat poured off the Kid's face. He couldn't tell if it was from the heat or the situation.

The Kid could see that a path apparently ran down one side of the waterway to the junks' left. Huts were visible through the trees. On the right side of the four boats, the bush, which came right up to the edge of the bank, looked kind of wild and uncultivated.

The lead boat soon angled for the left bank, and following suit, the four junks pulled over as if they were a train. They made it up to a position a scant two meters from the shore, where the boats lurched to a stop, stuck in the mud. Very quickly, the crewmen slid out gangplanks, flopping their ends onto the land, which was no more than two feet lower than the junks' gunwaless. Soldiers hustled off decks as ARVN lieutenants sent point men out to scout the area.

No shooting, and we aren't going to have to get wet! This ain't so bad. So far, so good!

Since there was no opposition, the men disembarked with speed but no real urgency. The landing area, the Kid noted as he bounced down the plank and stepped off onto the dark soil, was surely the hamlet of some collection of families in the middle of their farm complex. Towering palms lorded over recently tended gardens, clearly visible in the early light amid the vast tree line. The palms hung heavy with coconuts that appeared ripe for the taking. A prosperous- looking operation.

The junks, now empty and again floating above the mud, wasted no time in effectively pulling a major-league di di mau. When they disappeared out into the river, it really sank in for the Kid: now they were in the middle of the jungle with no transportation and were preparing to fight their way wherever the fuck it was they were going. *How did I ever get in this position?*

It was now fully light, and the radios were popping with traffic for everybody but Wilson, it seemed. But then, he and his charges were tagalongs. It was nice to have a PRC-25 to listen in, even though the four were not truly involved in the execution of the plan. Feeling left out, the lieutenant motioned his band to follow him over to where Captain Dalton was confabbing with Tu Ta Kim.

"Looky over there." Dalton pointed with his right arm to the thatched house to the extreme left of the immediately visible huts. "See the little wisp of smoke?

Somebody stayed here last night and had a fire this morning, and I'll bet they're not long gone or even gone at all!"

"Dolphin One, this is Jonah One. Do you copy? Over." Dalton's radio crackled to life. His RTO handed him the mike.

"Jonah One, this is Dolphin One. I copy. Over," he replied.

"Dolphin One, it appears we'll have no need for the air strikes. I'm releasing the boys. Just so you know, your counterpart should now be receiving orders to proceed with your maneuver. Please confirm. Over," Major Gillmore's voice ordered.

"Dolphin One, roger that. Out," Dalton responded, seeing that Tu Ta Kim was on his horn.

After a spirited exchange with the ARVN colonel, who was probably sitting next to Major Gillmore back at the Tra Vinh TOC, Kim wheeled around and waved all his subordinates into action.

The four platoons of the company had already begun to spread out down the canal, back toward the river and, up to the right, deeper into the very massive tree line complex. A look at his watch revealed to the Kid that things were getting under way at a little after 0600 hours.

Without fail, as it was on every ARVN operation the Kid thus far been a part of, as soon as the skirmishers moved out front, some of the men began collecting foodstuffs. A half dozen men were picking through the biggest garden, securing tomatoes, snap beans, and a bunch of other vegetables the Kid couldn't immediately recognize. One ambitious ARVN had taken off his combat boots and was barefooted, climbing up the tilted trunk of a healthy palm with a machete held in his teeth to drop down some coconuts.

The Kid stood and watched him climb. He was obviously skilled, going up the thirty-foot-tall tree quite quickly. *That's a pretty stupid thing to do.* How exposed is that? "Look, Lieutenant." The Kid tapped Wilson on the shoulder and pointed up at the trooper, who was now trying to secure a handhold so he could begin hacking at coconuts. Taking the machete from his mouth with his left hand, the ARVN delivered a well-aimed southpaw blow, and coconuts began tumbling to the ground.

"Cool!" Wilson endorsed his activity. "Ba, bring me one of those. I could go for a little coconut milk this morning!"

No sooner had Ba taken his first step to comply than a single shot rang out from the woods. The coconut scavenger instantly fell, tumbling from the tree.

"Holy shit!" Wilson screamed. In the next second, the entire company was sprayed with AK-47 fire from at least a half dozen positions!

The ARVN response was immediate. When they opened up with their M16's in a deafening roar of return fire, the platoon was wholly engaged! Or so they thought.

Fuckin' shit is flying everywhere! Not only had the Kid found himself on the ground, but also he had gotten down so quickly that Con actually sat on his head before the weight of his back-mounted radio pulled him rolling over on his right side. He slickly held the radio microphone up out of the dirt as he went.

The ARVN barrage continued for another thirty seconds, and then there was a lull, during which it was determined there was not any incoming. After about ten seconds of harrowing silence, the Kid lifted his head and looked up to see ARVNs rising off the deck, but with a measure of caution.

Tu Ta Kim was on his radio, then he relayed the information to Dalton. "We think maybe four, five men shoot and run! We try to reestablish contact di di mau!"

From the left, over by the first platoon, came a call for a medic. "Bauxi! Bauxi!" At least three men were waving, indicating that someone was in need of immediate help there. Another pair of medics were already headed for the base of the coconut palm from where the coconut picker had gotten himself picked off.

Tu Ta received a series of radio communications. He turned to Dalton. "We have three wounded and one KIA," he said, pointing to the scene of the palm tree incident. "If he not dead from bullet, fall kill him. *Het roi* for sure!"

With that, the command element began moving over in that direction, roughly fifty meters to their right, with Dalton and Kim moving forward much more quickly and with more urgency than the psyops men and their Vietnamese entourage.

As they slowly walked, the radio squawked, "Dolphin One, Jonah One, what is your casualty situation? Over."

Lieutenant Wilson heard the message. Seeing that Captain Dalton had left his RTO and was jogging up to check something out, he signaled Con to hand him the mike, then he responded to Major Gillmore's call.

"Jonah One, this is Dolphin Two. That figure you are looking for, as I understand it, is three Whiskey India Alphas and one Kilo India Alpha. Over."

"Roger your transmission, Dolphin Two. Do you have any idea of the seriousness of the wounds? Over."

"Negative, Jonah One. That information is still being determined. Over."
"Roger, Dolphin Two. Jonah One, out."

Ahead of them, the Kid noted something of a commotion where the soldier had fallen when he was shot out of the tree, but he couldn't quite make out the nature of it. *Hmm, an awful lot of yelling and hopping around. I wonder what the hell the deal is.* "Hey, Ba, what are those soldiers yelling about?"

Craning his neck to hear, Ba listened to what was being hollered by the soldiers. And now Dalton, who ran over, was standing and waving for help.

"They say that soldier not *het roi*! He's alive!" Ba blurted out the news as soon as he comprehended what all the shouting was about.

Sure enough, when the four of them got to the base of the coconut palm, they discovered the tree barely leaning out over a fishpond with the soldier having landed in the shallowest part of it. The depth was nevertheless sufficient to break his fall. He was lying on the ground, dazed, soaked, and muddy, while the medic, who had cut away his pant leg, was tending to the bullet wound in the outer portion of his left thigh. Apparently, the bullet had not broken the bone, but the medic was swabbing out one nasty-looking flesh wound.

Just then, the radio popped with another call from Major Gillmore. "Jonah One to Dolphin One. Do you read me? Over."

"Dolphin One here. I read you, Jonah One. Over," Dalton answered.

"Dolphin One, can you confirm your casualties? And do you require a medevac? Over."

"Jonah One, this is Dolphin One. We have four Whiskey India Alphas, at least one serious, so yes, lay one on us. Over," the sweating muscle-bound captain called in.

There was a strange radio silence, followed by a perplexed Major Gillmore calling, " Uh, Dolphin One, you have no Kilo India Alphas? Over."

"Affirmative, Jonah One, we have negative Kilo India Alphas. Over."

"Roger, Dolphin One. I copy three Whiskey India Alphas and one resurrection. Is that right? Because Dolphin Two told me you had a KIA. Over."

"You told him we had a KIA?" Dalton turned to Wilson with a questioning look.

"Well, yes!" Wilson stammered. "Even Tu Ta Kim said if the guy wasn't shot dead, the fall would have killed him! I copied the radio send on the other figures and called it in." Wilson was slightly embarrassed.

"Hey, guys!" The party could hear someone yelling over the radio in the TOC, which was being keyed open on purpose. "A company has three Whiskey India Alphas and a resurrection!" Howls of laughter. "Is that a Roger India Alpha?"

Dalton looked at Wilson, who seemed flustered by being laughed at, then over at the Kid. When the Kid burst out laughing, Dalton, Ba, and Con followed suit, with Wilson almost immediately joining in.

"Resurrected in action! What a scream! Shit! I too would have sworn the guy would have had to be dead just from the fall! I can't wait to write this one to Pat Bowen!"

After he caught his breath and wiped the tears of laughter from his eyes, Dalton put in a call: "Jonah One, Dolphin One. Do you read? Over."

"Jonah One here. Go. Over," came the return, with laughter still continuing in the background. The Kid picked out Paul's voice. "Ask him if the guy bounced when he hit the water!"

"Jonah One, it could take us a fight to work our way out to the paddies from here to a place where we could even land a chopper. Tu Ta Kim thinks since we have this place secured, it would be a good idea if you had one of the junks return to pick up our wounded, so we can press the fight in the right direction. Over." He cocked his head to one side as he awaited Gillmore's decision.

"Dolphin One, in fact, two of the junks are already on the way back. Jonah One out."

And with that, Kim issued orders for a squad to stay and maintain security over the canal landing until the men were medevacked. Then he turned his attention to the front, where he knew there were at least a few VC up there who had already bloodied them this morning.

As A Company moved forward out of the orderly neatness of the little hamlet and into the bush, the Kid began to understand the size of the particular tree line they were in. From the Mekong River to their left, it was at least a thousand meters to the first open section of paddies to their right. *Why, that's a kilometer!* Whenever the Kid looked at a battle map, he could see the arrows, squares, and lines drawn but could never translate that into where they were in the field.

I might as well be in a frickin' gunnysack as in these trees. Can't see the lead squads. Can't see the flank protection. Wonder if any of this is booby-trapped or if Charlie moves around in here enough to keep it clean? Goddamn! It was just 0630 hours, and now it's 0700. How time flies when you're having fun!

Trailing Lieutenant Wilson and Con through the woods, the Kid and Ba walked cautiously along, waiting for the inevitable, when Charlie couldn't stand it any longer and would hit at them. Then, it would start: the running and ducking and crawling and hiding and running and running, trying to catch the VC and make them stand and fight. Or if they chose to run, Tu Ta Kim would chase them into the waiting arms of Boar Hog and B Company, who were now pushing through the same said tree line, but from five klicks off in the opposite direction.

Meanwhile, Captain Metz's D Company had it the easiest; they were pulling seal duty, out in the paddies along the edge of the trees, to make sure none of the VC were coming out as the vise closed down on them.

Hmm, I wonder who's guarding the river. If I were a VC and this was what I was getting, I'd be down to the river to make my getaway! Like John Colter breathing through a reed while the Blackfeet walked by looking for me!

The Kid's thoughts were punctured by the *clack-clack-clack* of AK-47 fire coming not very far from their front and flying by their position close enough to make them once again seek the ground.

Then it fell into the routine: get up and move until there was too much fire, then get down while another part of the unit brought pressure and caused the antagonists to change location. And so on and so on. Before the Kid knew it, his watch said 0900 hours; they'd now been under fire for more than two hours.

Following in the paths of ARVNs in front of them, the Kid and Ba had ended up getting shuffled over to the right, while Wilson and Con, following another set of ARVNs, were now slowly drifting to their left. Whenever their squad would get up and move, the Kid and Ba were right with them; neither had any desire to be at the tail end of the formation, where a counterattack could very likely happen.

Running in a hunched-over position, the Kid was about three meters directly behind an ARVN rifleman when suddenly a bright yellowish light flashed to either side of the man. Instantly, the Kid found himself knocked to the ground with his ears ringing from the explosion. The man in front of him had triggered a booby trap and blown himself up, but his body had shielded the Kid from the jagged fragments of shrapnel. And even though the Kid had been knocked down, he was unhurt!

Rising up off the ground, the Kid steps forward to see the condition of the man who had triggered the device. He had been tossed back and to the left of the trail and was lying on his back, one foot mangled and black, his arms flailed out. The Kid looked up the body to see a black-charred face with eye sockets that were nothing but open red holes. The soldier's steel pot was still strapped in place, but his chest was cloaked with a shredded uniform shirt, exposing a myriad of jagged holes that looked black against his Asian skin. The smell of burnt flesh permeated the Kid's nostrils.

"Bauxi! Bauxi!" the Kid frantically shouted for a medic. The man was not breathing or moving, and when the Kid looked down, he saw that the man's crotch was a red mess. Jesus H. God! His junk has been blown off!

The Kid staggered back at the sight of seeing another man's manhood shredded.

I'd want to be dead if my dick and balls were blown off!

With the medic approaching, Ba turned and pointed to the man's dropped M16, still lying on the ground. "Bring it?" he asked the Kid.

"Shit yeah! Can't leave it here!" the Kid yelled back as he began to move away from the scene. *Where's fucking Wilson? Can't believe I've lost sight of him so completely! OK, I got guys to the left and right and guys up front. Fire from the front!* The Kid dove down to the ground as a particularly heavy volume of rifle fire picked up in the air around his head. It continued for another minute while the Kid lay there facedown in the mud of Vietnam's Mekong Delta and breathed in, gasping adrenalin-driven inhalations, putting him on the edge of hyperventilation.

This is not fucking good! I can't see what's going on around me. If I get up at the wrong time, Charlie's fire might get me, and if the ARVNs behind me open up, they could get me too! He lay there with his head on the back of his hands, aggravation and frustration beginning to well up inside his psyche, where they collided with the fear of death, and particularly of dying before he even made it to twenty-one and had a chance to truly experience life and the many enjoyments it offered. *Is this how it's going to end? I'm going to stand up in some stupid senseless no-name firefight, and some random bullet is going to be in my space and cause lights out? Is that all I have to look forward to? What if I should never decide to stand up again in my life? Oh, fuckin' a, man! It's getting heavier!*

Then, amid the rifle fire that filled the jungle arena, the Kid, from where he lay, picked out another sound that he had come to recognize in Vietnam, and quite well from afar after being in Tan An and other isolated places such as Than My— the unmistakable aerial vibrations of approaching rotor blades! *From my right, a chopper is coming!*

The Kid twisted on the ground and turned to look skyward, as well as he could without exposing himself, to see if the increasingly loud report of whirling blades was bringing medical or military help. *And there it is, a Cobra gunship!* It was visible ever so briefly through an opening in the forest canopy, then it broke off to turn and unleashed its devastating attack, strafing

441

with miniguns, which were mounted in the little turret at the base of its razor-thin nose. The Kid could sense that the rifle fire that had pinned them down had suddenly ended.

Rising up, he looked back to see that Ba was right there. And now the rest of the ARVNs who'd been pinned down with them were getting up. Seeing that Wilson and Con were close by, the Kid and Ba moved quickly over to their position.

"Man oh man, did I ever just dodge a bullet!" the Kid exclaimed.

"Stocker, we've all been dodging bullets all fucking day." The lieutenant almost yawned! "So, what are you talking about?"

"Well, sir, we were running along on this path over here to the right, and this ARVN in front of me tripped a booby trap and blew himself up. I was right behind him. It knocked me down, but I didn't get a scratch!"

"Oh, too bad. No Purple Heart for you!"

"Fucking fine with me. I'm sure as hell not looking for one in any way, shape, or form!" the Kid swore.

"Hot enough for you today, Lieutenant?" Captain Dalton walked up and extended his canteen to Wilson.

Wilson took a decent drink and handed the canteen back. "You talking temperature of the air or the action?"

"Take your pick!" the captain offered, but their conversation was cut short by Tu Ta Kim, who was obviously ordering the company forward.

The unit continued to advance while the deadly Cobra stuck around. It made a number of strafing and rocket runs from a couple of different attack points, cutting figure eights over what they'd identified as ground zero. From one angle, the Kid could see sun flicking off the brass shell casings as they rained to the ground from the Cobra's miniguns, dropping all over the battlefield. Still, when the company swept into the real estate the VC had occupied, not to anybody's surprise, the woods were not full of dead Vietcong.

There are never any dead Charlies from that shit! Go fucking figure! What do they do to get away? Hide in convenient spider holes? Or hide the dead and wounded guys in holes too? I know there's always a few left over to shoot at us, that's for damn sure!

Company A was moving forward at a quick clip in the tropical heat, a wearying pace, as they maintained contact with the quarry. But they never succeeded in racking up any verifiable body count.

I've still never seen one of the sons of bitches who wasn't captured or dead. If I could only tell one guy coming in to DINFOS that this could happen to him,

I'd feel like I'd done my duty. Foreign-language announcer! Get cornered and broadcast appeals to surrender or die? Get 'em cornered? Ha-ha-ha!

The Kid's mental state was becoming jumbled in the continuing combat; he would alternately feel invincible, as he was missed by round after round of rifle fire, and then frightfully vulnerable, lying in the weeds, catching his breath, trying to find the toughness to jump up and advance again in the face of enemy fire.

Talk about being in a position where you can't quit! Shit, what am I saying? Boujold quit! Maybe I should pull a hammie! No. I wouldn't want anybody talking about me the way they talk about Bouji.

The Kid, Ba, Wilson, and Con the skinny and slightly bowlegged RTO had hunkered down behind an almost imperceptible low berm of earth that ran in front of their path. It may have once been the bank of a small canal that fell into disuse and was then overgrown. *Hmm, it's almost lunchtime. I could sure as hell go for a break in the action, that's for damn sure. Doesn't Charlie have to eat lunch sometime too? You'd think anyway.* A flurry of AK fire hammered the foliage above their location. *Damn! Looks like they're not ready for lunch after all.*

Exhausted, the Kid lay prone on the ground behind the earthen lip of protection. With his head hanging down from the weight of his steel pot, and with the front part of his body propped up on his elbows, he could feel a slight breeze on the back of his exposed neck. Ironically, at that exact moment in time, he felt at first the lightest touch of something landing upon his neck, like a leaf or a bug, followed almost immediately by the deepest, most shocking bolt of pain he had ever felt!

"Aaahhh! Oh my God!" He writhed on the ground as his hand slapped at the source of the pain, right on the vertebra that connected his head to his spine. His fingers felt a gooeyness as they instinctively moved to its source. "Am I hit?"

"What is it? What is it?" Wilson reacted to the earsplitting scream of the Kid, who was in real pain. "Are you OK?" He pulled the Kid's hand away from his neck so that he could see what kind of damage he had sustained.

"Oh well!" The lieutenant didn't seem too panicked. "Here's the problem: that's not blood, it bug guts! You've been bitten by a big-ass red ant! Look!" He pointed upward. "There's more of them on that frond, and it looks like some of 'em are thinking about dropping down on us! We'd better get the fuck out from under here, at least down a few feet!"

They all moved over. Looking back, they could see the palm-like tree they had been under was alive with red ants, big, burly-looking specimens with pincher jaws the size of tiny nutcrackers. The Kid's neck was becoming stiff from the pain.

"Holy mother of God!" he exclaimed. "I've been bitten by ants before, but these ants are from another planet!" The commando ant had gotten a pretty good chew before the Kid smashed it. "When I looked at this trace of red on my fingers, I was sure I was hit! *Hey! Am I bleeding? If I am, does it count for a Purple Heart?*"

All this time, shooting had continued around them, and it wasn't stopping now.

"I thought you said you weren't looking for a Purple Heart, Stocker," Wilson half hollered over the din of fire.

"I'm not!" he said. "But if I do get hit, I'm not going to turn one down! And I'd bet you a ton of money that this ant bite hurts a whole hell of a lot worse than a lot of wounds people have gotten Purple Hearts for."

"Oh, I doubt that!" Wilson scoffed, and almost on cue, as if it had been waiting for the lieutenant to say that very thing, an ant that had earlier landed on him finally sank its pincers into the side of his neck. He howled as if he'd been bitten by a werewolf, slapping and bucking in pain, to which the Kid, Ba, and Con could only respond with roars of laughter.

The Kid began composing the letter in his head: "Dear Flo, you'll never believe this. There we were, pinned down and dying—of laughter. And wait until I tell you about the resurrection!"

Wilson's response was to advance. "Come on, you pussies! Let's go!" he hollered as he up and bolted off over the protective berm and into the bush beyond. Con was hot after him, sticking to him just like a really good RTO should. The Kid and Ba gave each other a telling look, knowing they had no choice but to follow.

Gotta keep Wilson in sight. Gotta keep the pace! Seems like the firing has abated somewhat. Still not taking any chances. What the fuck am I saying? I don't know if I've even got any chances left to take, like that guy who bought it in front of me back there. Ah, there's some fire. Where the fuck do they go? Shit, are they good! It's like the Yankees against the Washington Senators! Except, who are the Yankees and who are the Senators? I mean, we're the Yankees, but the Cong are kicking our butts! Imagine combat baseball: you're running along like this—you're the batter—and the pitcher jumps up out of the bushes and tries to throw one at your head. An out is when you're out cold. You have to find first base with a compass and a guide—and a machete. Ha! That'll be a great radio bit when I get to Saigon, or back to WKDA, whichever

444

comes first! Oh, man! Hit the deck, Wilson! Ow! Shit! That ARVN just got shot in the head!

The Kid crawled up behind Wilson and Con. "Jesus H. Christ! Did you see that? That guy get shot in the head!" He exhaled forcefully, having just witnessed a bullet passing through a man's head, traced by the conical spray of red matter coming out the other side.

"Fuckin' A I did!" The lieutenant's eyes were about as big as half-dollars, and he had one grim look on his Texas panhandle face. "But it didn't look like it hit him in the brain. Looked more like he got hit in the jaw!"

Sure enough, when they moved forward the fifteen meters to where the head shot victim was lying on the ground, he was very much alive. It appeared that the bullet had passed right through both cheeks!

My God! What a lucky SOB!

A medic rushed over and began to treat the poor soldier, who had a look in his eyes that could only be described as a combination of shock, pain, fear, and disbelief. The medic determined that the bullet had taken some teeth but missed the main part of his lower jaw; he had a hole in each cheek.

"See?" said Wilson. "That's the difference between an AK-47 round and an M16. An M16 bullet would have made an exit wound that'd rip off the whole side of his face, while that jacketed AK-47 round just sails right through ya!"

The wounded man was sitting up as the medic started to treat him with a white sterile pad and some tape. *He must be in terrible pain!* From what Ba said was going on, it seemed that the man had a couple of teeth knocked out on his lower right jaw and had had his tongue almost shot off.

No time to stop and watch the medic work. Dalton and Kim could be heard coordinating unit movements over the radio, but they were somewhere unseen up ahead. Wilson was bent on catching up with them.

The foursome moved as swiftly as bodies could in the jungle, while being intermittently shot at, with heat and humidity adding effort and draining will with every step. The Kid's lungs were burning with the fires of hell. He was reminded of the long hours training with the Boulder High School track team. Running and running. He had been a half-miler. He wasn't fast enough for the sprints and didn't want to suffer the pain of the mile, so the half mile had been his perfect event. In fact, his track training had come in quite handy in basic training; he'd always gotten a hundred points on the mile-run part of the physical training test. Today, however, the distance was considerably longer. He estimated they must have covered at least a couple of miles thus far, but the unit hadn't really been moving in a straight line.

Now this is pretty funny. I'm out of breath, but I'd give anything to stop and smoke a cigarette! The Kid knew when he started smoking at age sixteen that it wasn't good for his track-and-field aspirations. In fact, he finally had gotten kicked off the track team as a senior, for skiing and smoking, when he showed up for his lecture with the coach about smoking on crutches from a skiing mishap.

But now, muscle fatigue and the burn had a new significance. To fall behind was not only to lose the race, but also quite possibly to lose one's life. There was no end-of-training session and no welcoming shower.

This is going to go on all day long and will go on again tomorrow. Talk about cross-country! Sure glad I'm not toting that M16 and all that related shit! Now I've got Corporal Ba to caddy for me. Ha! Didn't even have to Tom Sawyer him. And look at Con! That little bastard is as cool as Jean-Claude Killy in the downhill. Oh God, what I wouldn't give to be up in the Rocky Mountains right now this second! A Basin! Winter Park! Remember the snow! Remember the icy wind! ... Whoa, babies! *That one was close! Hot wind of an AK-47 round!*

Down once again on the ground, lying as low as they could get in the best available bush, the four men of the psyops representation waited for the fire to cool. And again they ran, a fast forty or fifty strides, where they fell for safety again. *This is a Sisyphean deal if there ever was one! The never-ending task. Talk about rolling rocks up hills; that'd be easy compared to this!*

"Hey, Lieutenant, how many of 'em do you think we're chasing?" the Kid asked, panting as they lay in wait.

"Hell, I don't know. Maybe a dozen or more."

"Or less," the Kid speculated. "What if it was just a half dozen, or even three or four? Shit, what would we do if we ever hit a bunch of them when they had as many men as we have here today?"

"You're right on that one, Stocker!" The lieutenant had to laugh a nervous chuckle. "They'd kick these ARVNs' asses!"

Chapter 39

"So tell me," Sweet began, sitting across the rickety wooden bar table from the Kid in the Tra Vinh Club, where they'd both sat down with cold beers that Sweet had just purchased from Wen before the Kid walked in. "How was the operation?"

The Kid, dressed in shorts, flip-flops, and a green T-shirt, lit up and did not yet start to speak. He pushed his cigarettes and Zippo off to one side and lifted his can of Budweiser. He was freshly showered and just beginning to really unwind. They had been back about a half hour, and it was still forty-five minutes to chow time.

"Did you find a nice place to hang your hammock?" Sweet was naturally curious, figuring his turn was coming.

"Well, yes, yes I did! And thank you for the beer." The Kid ashed his butt. "I found these two trees that were perfect, and I was able to run another line and string my poncho over it like a tent. Had it open on the ends for ventilation. It worked out great! You gotta get one! Wen's father will sell you one for a dollar." The Kid craned his neck to see if Wen, who was tending bar, was listening.

She was. "You bet! He give best deal in Tra Vinh!" The Flower of the Orient smiled as she waited for her next customer.

"I take it you two met yesterday," the Kid said, having already heard that Paul, Ernie, and Pete had taken James over to her house for an afternoon session on the pipe.

"Indeed. Jeez, don't you just love their table? Paul was trying to buy it from Mama-san. Says he wants to take it home with him when he goes in sixteen days. Lucky fucker!"

"He goes on my birthday. His DEROS is September third. I'll be twenty-one and one of my best friends goes home. Good for him, good for me. If I live to twenty- one."

The sparsely occupied club was beginning to fill up. Officers who had washed off the two-day operation were starting to trickle in. There was generally a gridlock at the two officers' showers in the main house after an operation; it was one time when the enlisted men actually had it better, because they had six showers in a near-regulation-style latrine tacked onto the end of the servants' quarters.

"Oh, you know what I heard today on AFR? It's looking like a senator from my home state of Maine, Edmund Muskie, might get the pick to be vice president on the Democratic ticket with Humphrey! That's pretty cool because he is a really good guy!"

"Muskie? Never heard of him," the Kid replied. "When I think senator from Maine, I think that woman Margaret Chase Smith."

"People are still laughing about the resurrection!" Sweet grinned. "I've heard bits of it, but you saw it? You lucky dog! I've heard you're lucky. What the fuck happened? I'll bet this is going to be a great story!"

The Kid was getting ready to tell the story when into the club stormed Sergeant Mixx, with a major case of the ass for somebody. Spencer was trailing him, trying to calm him down.

"That fucker owes me three hundred dollars, and I'm going to collect it! Where is the little son of a bitch?!" The slightly built black sergeant was looking through the screen wall of the club, which was right off the end of the bar that made visible an old porch area, beyond where the Cambodian mercenaries bunked on a row of cots. A knot of about five of them were huddled in conversation in one corner.

The object of Mixx's scorn was apparently among them.

"Now, Sergeant Mixx." Spencer made a nice move to get between the belligerent noncom and the door. "You don't want to go out there and start anything. I'm not going to let a poker debt disrupt the peace and quiet of what I like to consider *my* compound. You *bic*?" He looked a bit more nervous than "old hand third-tour Spencer" normally looked in most situations. "He's out there with his five buddies, and you know everybody's armed, so what are you going to do? Shoot him? How big of a dumb son of a bitch are you? Trying to start something with the goddamm Cambodian guards. What, Charlie's not tough enough for you?" Spencer challenged him and stared him down.

Mixx seemed deflated, as if he had had a plan, had had a couple of drinks, and was now ready for this confrontation, as if he had had it all played out in his mind and now he saw that Spencer was not going to let the play go down. "Goddamn, Spence, they ought not to play poker if they can't afford to lose. But I know this Cambodian cracker has got the dough, and muthafucka is plain old not payin' off!" Turning to leave the club through the mess hall, apparently not ready to throw in the towel, Mixx said over his shoulder, "I'm not lettin' that fucker off the hook!"

Leaving in such a huff and trying to deliver a parting over-the-shoulder shot at Spencer, the sergeant collided in the doorway between the mess hall and the club with Lieutenant Wilson, who was just arriving.

"Hey! Watch the fuck where you're going, Sergeant. I'm mean, shit! What's the rush?" Wilson actually stopped him for redress.

"Sorry, sir. Won't happen again, sir," Mixx quickly spat out, staring past Wilson and immediately continuing to exit the building.

"What's wrong with Mixx?" Wilson asked of Spencer, who was apparently looking

to see if Mixx had, in fact, left.

"Oh, he won some money from one of the Cambodian guards in a poker game, and he let the fucker put an IOU in the pot on a call, and now the guard won't pay him the three hundred dollars. He's pissed, that's all."

"Should've never let some gook fucker put an IOU in the pot! What the fuck was he thinking? At least it's nothing major. That's good," Wilson said, as he arrived in front of Wen, who waited at the bar to take his order. "A beer and three shots of Turkey back, honey!" He smiled sweetly. As she began to pour the drinks, Wilson motioned Sweet and the Kid over to the bar.

"Yes, sir?" the Kid asked inquisitively as the two of them joined him, just as Wen poured the third shot.

"I propose a toast," Wilson said, indicating that he expected the Kid and Sweet to hoist shots of whiskey with him. "To the new team and the new assignment in Cang Long!" He clinked with the pair and threw the whiskey down, slamming the empty shot glass on the counter. The two PFCs followed suit, lacking the lieutenant's relish, but having no graceful way of refusing. From the look Sweet made, squinching his face into a pucker as the Wild Turkey burned his throat, he apparently disliked whiskey as much as the Kid.

"So, it's set. We're going out tomorrow with an escort of two MP fifty-cal jeeps. Ti Ui Troung is bringing a jeep too. We're leaving at about zero eight hundred hours or right after they finish the morning minesweeping, whichever comes first." Wilson took a sip of beer. "Make sure you got what you need from the PX, because we probably won't be back until payday at the end of the month."

"Bummer!" said the Kid. "I don't suppose there's a pool table in Cang Long. In fact, I'll bet there's not, so, sir, since the table's open, how about it, you and me, *mano y mano*?" He motioned toward the old battered green-felt arena with a thumb over his shoulder. Just as he was doing so, Metz and Wally came into the club and beat them to it.

"Well, I think I'm going to try to write a couple of letters before chow. Uh, thank you for the shot, sir." Sweet excused himself and left.

"Hey, Wally," Wilson called to the captain. "After you guys play this game, Stocker and I have a grudge match that we want to finish. You can have the table back after if you want, but would it be OK if we played it? We were heading for the table when you guys rushed in and cut in front of us!"

"Likely story, Ross, you snoozin' and losin' mutha!" Wally finished racking as Metz sorted through the miserable selection of cue sticks, finding which ones were still serviceable. "Tell you what, after this game, we'll let you guys have it for one, then we'll play you doubles for the table. Deal?"

"Deal!" Wilson agreed.

"If you get choice of stick, then I get to break!" The Kid quickly began laying down the ground rules. As the lieutenant pondered for a second the choice, a disruption boiled over on the porch outside the screened wall to the Kid's immediate right. It was Sergeant Mixx! Since Spencer had not let him out onto the porch, he had worked his way around to the back and had come up behind the five Cambodian guards in their bunk area, having circled around the latrine.

"Hey, you! Yeah, you. Muthafuckin' gook of a punk-ass bastard!" He pointed with his hand. "I want my money, and I want it now!" Mixx screamed. He reached down and pulled from his waist a .45-caliber standard army-issue pistol, which he pointed at the group of guards. Seeing the piece come out, the five wide-eyed guards immediately jumped about four feet in the air in every direction. Cots, small tables, dishes, chopsticks, footlockers, and a clothesline with uniform shirts began flying up in the air as they looked either for cover or their own weapons with which to respond.

Holy fuck! He's got a gun, and he's going to start shooting!

Whenever he would look back on it, the Kid would always see it in slow motion. But when it happened, it was over in a heartbeat. The Kid sprang out the screen door and, after taking three strides, hit Sergeant Mixx, with his left arm wrapping around his waist. As he swung around behind the man, whose concentration was solely focused on trying to draw a bead on one certain guard in the frantically scrambling pile of humanity, the Kid pulled him down backward, falling upon one of the guard's sleeping cots, while reaching up with his right hand and grabbing Mixx's right wrist and pointing the pistol straight up in the air. *Where's the noise?*

450

Immediately on his heels, Lieutenant Wilson had followed the Kid out the door. As the Kid kept Mixx's right hand and his gun pointing skyward, he ran up and ripped the .45 from the sergeant's sweaty grip. At the same time, Wally and Metz had jumped over in front of the Cambodian guards with their arms up like crossing guards, forbidding them to fire and alternately making the international sign language gesture for "calm down" by moving their arms toward the floor.

A rush of people followed them out the door. Among them was Sergeant Spencer, who, along with Captain Dalton, each grabbed one of Mixx's arms, pulling him up off the Kid and holding him in custody.

"Whoa, whoa, whoa!" Spencer yelled. "What the fuck happened to your senses, Sergeant Mixx? Now I gotta arrest you! Come on, Captains, let's take him up to Major Gillmore's office while we find the major and figure out what we're going to do."

With that, the two men strong-armed Mixx off the porch, through the club, out the mess hall, and to the left, toward the plantation house.

"What happened?" A new arrival to the scene sought information.

"Mixx pulled his piece on these Cambodians, and he likely would have shot some of them if Stocker here hadn't disarmed him!" Lieutenant Wilson reached down and extended a hand to help the Kid up off the disheveled cot. "Goddamn, Stocker, I can't believe you did that!"

Dazed, the Kid stood there, slack-jawed, his head literally spinning with adrenalin, as he tried to comprehend himself what it was he'd just done. "I broke up a gunfight? What the fuck was I thinking? Those Cambodians could have opened up on Mixx!" He hit himself in the forehead with an open palm.

"Hey!" Wally walked over to the Kid and slapped him on the back. "That was fucking spectacular! I caught the whole thing, like right out of the movies! It was as if you'd done something like that a hundred times! How did you know to do it that way?"

"Man oh man, I don't know! I have no idea why I did anything, except I thought he was going to shoot right then. All the while I was pulling him down, I expected to hear his gun go off!"

"And you, Ross." Metz turned to Wilson, who still held Mixx's .45 in his hand.

"What a well-oiled machine you psyops boys are!"

Just then, Sweet came rushing onto the porch. "What happened? What did I miss?"

451

"Stocker and I just broke up a gunfight!" Wilson was fairly beaming but finally realized that he should jack the .45, unload it, and eject the clip. "You ready for another shot of Wild Turkey, Stocker? That didn't seem to slow you down much there."

"And I missed it?" Sweet exclaimed in disappointment.

"Look at it this way, Sweet," Wilson waxed. "If Mixx had started shooting, you'd have been happy not to be here!"

The crowd began to drift back inside the club. "Don't that beat all?" Sergeant Johnson, one of Mixx's closest associates, said. "They'll have to get him out of here. Those Cambodia guards will kill him first chance they get. Those people cut off heads and eat the liver of the slain foe. I would not want a bunch of gun- and knife-toting Cambodes havin' a major case of the ass on me! That's for *damn* sure!"

Chapter 40

August 17, 1968

Dear Larry,

So much is happening around this place that I don't hardly know where to start. First off, how do you like the typed letter? Pretty good, huh? I know how you hated my handwritten index quote cards in debate, so this is good news and bad news.

The good news is that now I have access to a typewriter! The bad news is that it's part of the gear on this new psyops truck that just arrived, and I and Wilson and this new guy, whose name is Jim Sweet, no cracks, are taking this truck out in the field to do mind games with the gooks. It has its own generator, movie projector, slide projector, and filmstrip projector, and a big-ass screen, a loudspeaker system, and a little hand-cranked printing press where we can print our own leaflets! How efficient! We are going to this place called Cang Long, up the road about twelve miles west of here, specifically because it is a hotbed of VC activity along an important road down here in the Delta. Not looking forward to this. It is a small town that's near the ARVN compound where we did troop indoctrinations week before last, the one where that major was shooting rats running to and from the outhouse as his only form of recreation. And we were so bored, we watched!

Anyway, dig this! I broke up a gunfight last night in our club here at Tra Vinh! This black sergeant was going to dust this Cambodian guard who owed him money, and when he whipped out his pistol, I was standing just inside the door from where this all was happening, and I ran out and tackled him! No bullshit! What a stupid fucking thing to do. I got around behind him somehow. Coach Pagano would have been proud! I should have just gotten down on the floor, but before I knew it, I had this guy down. And then Wilson ran up and took the gun out of his hand! Kind of cool? No, it's major fucking cool! Major stupid, but now that it's over, it's cool.

So, we are all excited here about the Democratic National Convention and are still pulling for McCarthy. The peace candidate makes a lot of sense to us all over here in the mud and rice getting shot at. I'm afraid it's going to be Humphrey and it will just be more of the same. Nixon says he has a secret plan to end the war. He ought to tell us what it is. We here at the front would like to know if his plan is for shit or just plain shit. Perhaps, based on our firsthand knowledge, we could say if it has a feasible chance of succeeding.

Well, there's no women where we're going. I've still only banged the one whore I told you about. Part of me wants to be loyal and true blue to Flo, and the other part of me says, *I'm so horny that the crack of dawn looks good!* If a really cute whore came along right now, I'd trip her and beat her to the ground! Oh well. Damned if you do, cursed to eternal horniness if you don't. Flo wrote that she knew I wasn't a virgin when she met me and says a couple more won't matter, so just don't ever tell her about it.

So, how's your love life? Did you get it on with that girl Marcia yet? Still nothing from the draft board? I can't believe your luck! And you call me lucky! Shit, I transferred schools and they got me. You've dropped out and nothing yet? Amazing. Well, I'm pulling for you. I wouldn't wish this shit on anybody. OK, maybe Johnny Wailin and Dan you-know-who, but that'd be about it.

We went on another operation and made an assault yesterday off Vietnamese naval junks on the Mekong River! What a trip. As soon as we landed, this ARVN climbs a tree to whack down coconuts and gets his ass shot right out of the sky! And the funny thing was, everybody thought he was dead and they called it in on the casualty report. But when it turned out he was still alive, headquarters wanted to know if we'd had a resurrection! Who said war is not funny?

That thing I bought, the one I carry around in my front pocket, it's only half used up! I can't believe how little of it, it takes to perform the necessary mental adjustment. It's the *only* good thing about this fucking place.

Take it easy, amigo!

Curt

The letter to Larry was one of a half dozen the Kid had fired off on the typewriter the night before, including a five-pager to Flo, so they'd all be put in the mail right away and not have to come back in from Cang Long. Because occasionally, the Kid had heard, it was three or four days out there between mail calls.

At least Tra Vinh has mail call every day. The Kid's thoughts wandered as he rode along in the cab of the MSQ-85, bouncing down the pockmarked road, rolling ever closer to Cang Long. *Why do I get the feeling that something really bad is going to happen in Cang Long? Must be that first night I went over to Wen's house and she told me about the captain gettin' ambushed and dying out there on the Cang Long road. Wherever it was exactly, we'll have to pass it to get to Cang Long. I think she said it was by the My Though cutoff.*

The Kid sat in the shotgun position, sleeve rolled up with his bare, very tan arm hanging out the window. His M16 was propped up between his legs, its clip inserted and ready for action. Next to him, on the fairly broad canvas-covered seat of the three-quarter-ton army-issue Batmobile truck, sat Jim Sweet, sweating profusely because he was in the middle. And on the driver's side sat Lieutenant Wilson, whose arm was starting to get that "drove to Las Vegas" look, like the Kid's dad used to get from hanging his arm out while driving in the desert.

Although it was breezier sitting by a window, the trio were all equally eating the dust of their five-vehicle convoy as it flew down the rustic pavement that was the Cang Long road. As soon as the roadway reached Cang Long, it became the Tra Vinh road, going back, or the Vinh Long road, going northwest. One thing the Kid had learned was that anything with pavement in the Mekong Delta was called Highway 4, no matter where it went, so people spoke of roads in sections of where they went next.

In addition to the Batmobile, the convoy included another three-quarter-ton supply truck with food and ammunition for Cang Long; Ti Ui Troung in his own personally assigned jeep, with whom Corporal Ba was riding, both armed to the teeth; and two fifty-caliber Rat Patrol jeeps pulling security. The jeeps were so named because of their big-ass fifty-caliber machine guns mounted on the back of each one, which made them look like those jeeps on the TV show *Rat Patrol,* which was set in the Sahara Desert. The jeeps had crews of three: a driver, a gunner, and an ammo man. One of the jeeps was in the front of the convoy, and the other brought up the rear. There was some comfort in having a pair of fifty- calibers with you; nothing said security in Vietnam like a crew-served weapon.

But just knowing that you might need them and then wondering if they might not be enough by themselves was a scary thing to contemplate. *I wonder if the Yankees are playing today. Why do I care? We could die any second. And they're eliminated. Looks like the Tigers and St. Louis is my bet.*

Before the town of Cang Long, the group drove past two postage stamp–sized settlements along the road that were large enough to have names. The first one, about seven miles out, called Nguyet Hang, was just coming into view. It could be seen lying in front of the elevated bridge that crossed the canal upon which it was situated. The village actually was bisected by the small canal, which had a bridge that was so small enough, the ARVNs didn't even bother to guard it. If the VC were to blow it up, they'd throw up another one in an afternoon. A bus was coming over the bridge from the opposite direction, and when sitting atop the bridge, it stuck way up high in the air. The silhouettes of the people riding the roof made it look even taller.

Sitting in the middle seat, Sweet was in a position to light up a cigarette. When he did so, both the Kid and Wilson grabbed his lit stick and lit their own, sitting in the draft of their respective windows.

Look at how thick that tree line is here, the Kid thought as they approached the Nguyet Hang bridge. *That place could be full of Cong, and they could open up on us any second! God! To be someplace really safe! Somewhere I wouldn't have to worry if we were going to be ambushed in the next second. What a relief that would be! How did I come to be in this fucking place?*

The convoy crossed the Nguyet Hang bridge and were now on the outskirts of the village beyond. Soon they arrived at the north cutoff, where Highway 4 shot a branch straight up toward My Tho, where Dave Waterhouse and John Imbach were stationed with the US Ninth Division. "How far up to My Tho, you reckon?" the Kid hollered to Wilson.

He answered without taking his eyes off the road, "About thirty-five miles, I imagine. You wanna drive up there? We'll drive up there."

"No, thanks. I wasn't asking for that. Just curious, sir." *I wonder how the boys are doing up there? It must have been somewhere right around here where they got the captain,* the Kid thought as the truck continued on past the turnoff.

They continued on toward the second flyspeck of a village on the road, My Hue, no more than three miles past the cutoff. As one approaches My Hue traveling north, the first thing that comes into view is the Buddhist monastery. At three stories high, it sticks up noticeably in the Delta. It was quite old in appearance and was rather imposing for being out in the middle of fricking nowhere. Kind of like the old Catholic church. As they drove past, they could see standing at the rail on a balcony a group of about a dozen monks, all wrapped in vibrant yellow robes, some young and others old, observing them. *Hello, Messers VC.*

Then the road took a sweeping curve, eventually resulting in an almost ninety- degree turn to the right. Located on the far end of the turn, where the road straightened out, was an artillery firebase with three 155 mm Howitzers sitting within a square perimeter of protective sandbags. The convoy pulled to a stop by the entrance to the guns; the lead fifty-caliber jeep had some mail to drop off for the US artillery crews manning the position.

Wilson, Sweet, and the Kid took advantage of the stop by jumping out to take a piss by the side of the road. When they did so, an artillery crew appeared, looking as if they were preparing to fire one of the guns in some supporting capacity, so the three of them walked over and stood back to watch the crew work.

The big gun was aimed and calibrated. Then, in rapid succession, a crewman delivered the shell into the open and waiting breech; the door was slammed shut behind it; and the mechanism was pulled that fired the shell. The port opened, and the smoking casing tumbled to the ground. The process was repeated two more times with a smooth, nonchalant rhythm. The Kid was amazed. *You can actually see an artillery shell leave the barrel of the gun and visually track it to its zenith before it disappears from sight!*

"Wow!" exclaimed the Kid. "I didn't know you could see a shell leave a gun!"

"Oh yeah!" chimed in Artillery Officer Wilson. "Isn't that something? Plus they've got all kinds of shells to shoot, antipersonnel, Willy Petes, antitank. Artillery is really cool!"

"Then why didn't you stay in it?" Sweet asked the obvious question.

"I said it was cool, but not that cool. There's just not enough action. You never see the guys you're fighting."

"So, Lieutenant?" the Kid cut in. "We never see them when we're with the infantry either! They are, without a doubt, the most elusive bunch of motherfuckers on the whole planet!"

Ti Uri Troung and Corporal Ba came up to stand with them. They watched the firing of another three shells.

"Who are you shooting at?" the Kid hollered as soon as it looked that the crew was standing down.

Turning to see who had asked, the helmeted—but naked from the waist up— loader responded, "Fuckin' A if we know. They call in the coordinates, and we fire the gun. We don't know who, or if we ever hit them or not," he drawled as he pulled out a smoke. "If they call back and give us an adjustment, we figure we can fire for effect. Sometimes, we shoot all night, every fifteen or twenty minutes, into a quadrant, doing 'H & I,' harassment and interdiction fire. We could be killing VC, VC children and wives, or VC water buffaloes, or blowing up VC shithouses and ammo dumps. Fuck, we don't know, and we don't care! You guys brought mail, right?"

"Yep!" Wilson responded. Without another word, the artillery crew walked off.

"Come on, time to didi."

Turned out their destination was barely half a mile from the artillery position. In less than a minute, the convoy was pulling up to the front gate of the Cang Long District Headquarters Compound, which they found was open.

They made the left turn and slowly drove through an open twelve-foot-wide steel- plated double swinging gate, each half of which was hung on a square white masonry column that was easily ten feet tall, one on either side. They appeared to be rather weatherworn and old. *This place has been a fort for a long time.* The Batmobile drove under a banner that was strung above the gate connected to poles that stuck up another ten feet above the columns. It was canvas that had been written on in Vietnamese, with the yellow- and red-striped South Vietnamese flag on one side. Along the top of the compound wall was a barbed wire extension that stuck up another ten feet and was encased in rolls of razor- sharp concertina wire, stacked roll upon roll, all the way to the top.

"I wish Ba was here so I could ask him what the sign says." The Kid looked around at their new surroundings.

To the right of the driveway, which apparently continued straight on through the compound, the barrel of an M60 machine gun protruded from a bunker that was manned by two Vietnamese guards. Immediately behind the bunker was the front of the Cang Long District Headquarters Building, home of the Thiệu government in this neck of the Delta. The South Vietnamese flag fluttered over the center of the porch, one side of which had also been turned into a sandbag-bunkered position. More sandbags were visible blocking a window in the building behind it.

The one-story-high civic building, with a yellow plaster and red-tiled roof, ran down the right side of the sandy driveway, and a row building, obviously broken up into compartmental rooms, ran down the left side, leaving a forty-foot-wide avenue between the structures.

The spacious compound had plenty of room for the five vehicles of the Tra Vinh convoy to easily pull well into the yard and park. The supply truck pulled out of line and moved down to the end of the long, low building on the left, stopping at a spot where four ARVNs emerged from a door to greet it.

A group of men, three being ARVNs and four being Americans, emerged from a doorway halfway down the civic center building and walked toward the newly arrived personnel.

"Bueno días," a rotund Latino lieutenant called out, waving a hand over his thick dark hair from fifteen feet off. "Welcome to Cang Long, the outpost you'll most likely want to be posted out of! I'm Lieutenant Luis Reyes." He extended his hand to the Kid, who stood closest to the arriving group. "Pleased to meet you!"

"I'm Curt." The Kid shook his hand and looked into his roundish, smiling, friendly face. "Nice to meet you too!"

Continuing with the introductions, Lieutenant Reyes went down the row: "This is Captain Bowersox, our CO for another three days. This is Lieutenant Jones, our XO. This is Master Sergeant Doc, our medic."

"Everybody calls me Doc," he said after first pushing his army glasses back up his nose, shaking hands all around. His large, rounded head was nearly bald, but he had healthy growth above his sweat-soaked ears, from which his army-issue glasses continued to slip.

"And this is Dai Ui Phan, our ARVN CO. Then Trung Shi Thoi, our ARVN first sergeant; everybody just calls him 'Top.' And Ha Shi Binh, our driver." Reyes completed the introductions.

There were handshakes all around, along with nodding and smiling.

"Welcome to Cang Long," Captain Bowersox said, flashing a broad smile. "We'll get you squared away here and moved in. I don't reckon we'll be going out to do any psyops today. There'll be plenty of time for that tomorrow or the next day.

Oh, wait a minute, not the next day for me! I'm going home!" He turned to the ARVN captain. "Dai Ui, will you show Ti Ui Troung and Hashi Ba where they'll be bunking? *Cam on u lam.*" He bowed the slightest bit.

Troung and the Dai Ui must have had something in common because, after that exchange of greetings, they started acting like long-lost buddies. The Kid thought, *Well, the atmosphere seems pretty casual. Place doesn't look that bad; at least it's not another Thanh My—on the surface anyway. I wonder where we'll be sleeping?*

"Lieutenant Wilson," Doc began, "our officers and senior ARVN personnel sleep in the main building. I got a bunk ready for you." Turning to address the other American lieutenant, who stepped forward and was at the ready, he said, "Jeff, if you could be so kind as to show Lieutenant Wilson here where he'll be bunking, I'll take care of the EMs."

Doc started walking toward the screen door on the left end of the long, low building. "I think you two will like it over here in the infirmary. There's plenty of room for two of you in there. You'll find some cots stacked in there you can set up with mosquito netting. You all can bunk in the main building if you want, but this has a lot of privacy that you wouldn't have over there."

"No shit?" The Kid's face lit up. "Privacy?" He had been wishing for a real mattress, but there was a lot to be said for privacy. "Let's check this place out!"

Leading the way through a screen door, Doc walked into what was essentially his office. "I keep my stuff in here, but there's plenty of room for your gear. And I've got this fan that you can turn on, and it swings back and forth, so you'll both get its benefits. Not bad in here, really."

"Yes!" Sweet took off his steel pot and sunglasses and looked around at the cluttered medical storeroom. "This looks like it'll do nicely."

"Yeah! This looks great compared to some of the places I've been recently," the Kid said.

"So, let's go bring in our stuff, set up the cots, and take a look around the place. Whaddya say?" The Kid began to make his move for the door. Just then, a boom attracted their attention, followed quickly by another.

"Oh, that's just the artillery up the road a piece. Guess you had to come by them fellas to get here." Doc noticed they had noticed the firing. "After a while, you get used to it. Hell, you know as well as I do how easy it is to tell incoming from outgoing, so don't worry about them. When they shoot this certain type of shell, they have to put the powder load in a bag, and when they do and they're shooting down our way, the wadding falls on the roof of the infirmary." He cocked his ear upward and, sure enough, could easily hear the sprinkling noise of something falling on the roof. "There's some now!" he said, then walked off.

"Shit! That means we're right in line with it," Sweet exclaimed. "Maybe we should move?" He looked seriously at the Kid.

"What's the point?" the Kid quickly responded. "The line of fire changes. You could be under it anywhere when the short round happened. That's what you're worried about, isn't it? If there's one thing I've learned in this place, it's that if it ain't gonna get you, it ain't, and if it is, it is. All I know is that I'm sleeping here tonight." He stood by the door and waited for Doc to get a little farther away.

460

Then he dipped his pipe into his right pocket leg and, with a flourish, took out his Zippo and lit up a bowl. After taking a big, powerful hit, he passed the bowl to Sweet, who did not find it necessary to relight. He quickly took his hit and passed the bowl back.

"Yeah," Sweet said, holding the hit in, "I guess you're right." He exhaled and blew out most of the smoke when he got to right.

They each took two more fast hits and, in their newly toasted state, went out to fetch their gear and take it into yet another billet, hooch, hole, or compound.

There'd been so many of them, they were starting to melt together in the Kid's mind. Kind of like his companions. Not that anybody was dying, they were just being left behind when he moved on. First there was the DINFOS boys, then the guys in Can Tho. Then there were the guys at Tra Vinh and the guys at Tan An. *Boujold isn't around anymore. God, I'm barely hitting three months in this hell.*

Well, that's one quarter done anyway. Now Sweet and these guys here I'm going to get to know. For how long? Of all the people who've come and gone, Wilson never goes away. That's one thing that is for sure. I wish that fucker Wilson would go away from my life. I know that bastard is going to do something to get us killed!

Back at the Batmobile, Sweet opened the compartment door. He and the Kid pulled out their duffle bags and humped them back to the infirmary. After assembling their cots, they stowed their M16's and headed for the main building.

Crossing the driveway, they threaded their way through a row of three jeeps that were parked in a line between the two long buildings. The drive was covered with a heavy kind of sand that let people walk around the compound without getting their boots muddy during the monsoon season—and it was still monsoon season in the Delta during August.

The obvious door to enter led them into a large, open room. The ceiling was higher than the adjacent portion of the building, as if the Americans had added the latter half of the structure to the old traditional building. They could hear a generator purring in a courtyard that they could see beyond the screened confines of the large orderly room. They also saw the fans to which the generator was supplying power, along with feeling the cool air blowing from them.

"Not bad," said Sweet. He strolled over to a box of paperback books from the Red Cross to see if there was anything worth reading. He picked up a

461

Perry Mason novel and cracked it open to the middle before tucking it into his right cargo pants pocket.

"We're gonna be having lunch in about twenty minutes, back in the dining room off the patio," Lieutenant Jeff Jones said to the two PFCs. "The mama-sans here are pretty good cooks, and y'all won't have to be pulling any KP." His friendly smile brightened his well-chiseled face beneath his black hair, which was combed back and kind of long for the army, close to Everly Brothers style. Jones was short, coming only up to Lieutenant Riuz's shoulder, and he looked like somebody the Kid had seen before.

"I got it!" he exclaimed, pointing to Lieutenant Jones. "Roger Miller! You're the spitting image of Roger fucking Miller! Don't you think? Lieutenant Wilson? Roger Miller's twin—or near twin anyway!"

"Sort of. ... OK, I see it," Wilson replied, sounding bored.

"Yeah," the embarrassed Lieutenant Jones responded, "I get that a lot! Too bad I can't sing."

"Oh well, the lieutenant here can sing." The Kid nodded to Wilson. "Too bad he

doesn't look like Roger Miller!"

"Hey! I don't need to look like Roger Miller. Someday, I'll be bigger than Roger Miller, you just wait!" Wilson cajoled. "'King of the Road'? I got your scepter right here." He grabbed his crotch. "And 'England Swings'? Who gives a shit?"

Jones seemed a little perplexed that Wilson was attacking the celebrity he resembled. "Uh, come on. I'll show you where the shower is."

Along with Wilson, Sweet and the Kid were escorted past the dining room adjacent to the indoor courtyard and out the back of the makeshift building, where a wooden plank walkway led to a latrine area and the shower. The shower consisted of a green Plexiglas stall behind a poncho shower curtain. It was set square beneath a fifteen-feet-tall tower with a fifty-five-gallon barrel drum on top of a plywood platform, the showerhead operated by a pull spigot somehow adapted and sticking down out of the barrel.

"It's pretty nice, even if we have to hoist water up to the tank on top with this bucket to make it work." He picked up an old galvanized steel bucket with a length of yellow nylon rope tied to its handle. Pointing, he said, "The well's over there. You soap up, and then you pull the cord with one hand to bring the water. Makes rinsing your hair difficult," Jones said, "but what the fuck? It's better than nothing."

"And nothing is what we had out at the old Tan An church," the Kid added.

"You were out at the old church with the bombed-out steeple?" The comment caught had Jones's attention. "Hell, that's only five miles west of here!" he said.

The tour continued around the Cang Long compound. The kitchen was next, and it was a place humming with activity as lunch was just being readied.

"Ciao, Ba An," Jones said, greeting one of the three Vietnamese cooks working feverishly over the food prep table, where they were making sandwiches. As he passed, he reached down to snatch a carrot off one of the plates.

Ba An playfully slapped at his hand. "No, Jones! You dinky dau beaucoup!"

At the back of the compound on the perimeter, there was an old guard lookout and a gun position made of brick. It had a round base and a small square shelter- like enclosure at the top. "The French built this," Jones said, leading the way up a small three-step ladder. "They put together this whole compound, the walls and all. Cang Long has been the head of the district for years and years."

Standing there with a gentle breeze blowing just enough to evaporate some of their sweat, the men all stared out into the netherworld of the war zone. The Kid was amazed by how much better the view was at as little as an extra ten feet high. The compound looked out over miles of endless rice paddies, stretching off into the heart of the Mekong Delta. Way off in the distance, the silhouettes of a dozen or more peasants could be seen working the rice paddies. It was quiet.

But not for long.

A series of artillery reports came booming their way from the gun emplacement up the road. They had about them a hollowness that made the Kid think of the gun barrels from which they issued. *Hard to believe somebody could be drawing their last breath, with a shell on the way and not even knowing it.*

"Well," Jones said, breaking the trance, "I suppose after lunch y'all'll want to go across the street into Cang Long village and see your office." He moved to go down the ladder.

"What office?" Wilson asked.

"Vietnamese POLWAR and you psyops guys have an office set aside for you over in town across the street." Jones stepped off the ladder onto the dirt. "You know, a place where the VC can come if they want to *chui hoi*. Nothing fancy, just one room. Of course, we've never manned it yet. We've been waiting for a psyops team for months. You guys are the first!"

Chapter 41

All through lunch, the Kid spent his time hating Captain Bowersox, who had a continually giddy-looking, goofy expression on his face. Being short three days can do that to a guy. And he never missed a chance to work it into a conversation.

"Yep, in just three days I'll be eating steak in the returnees' steak house!" He grinned. "I think I'll spend the rest of the day packing. I've still got some stuff I said I'd give to the boys," he said, referring to some of his ARVN charges.

"Only four days till I see my wife! My God! I'm so fucking horny! I told her I wouldn't fuck any whores over here, and I kept my word. But God Almighty, am I ever horny!" His smile seemed almost too wide for his narrow face to contain it.

"Are you bragging or complaining?" Lieutenant Wilson asked in a tone of voice that indicated he didn't really want to know.

"Damn good sandwich, this one here!" Sweet said as he examined his bacon, lettuce, and tomato sandwich on a French baguette. "It's not real bacon, but more like fresh uncured pork strips crisped up, isn't it?"

"Yeah." Lieutenant Reyes picked his teeth with his little finger. "Captain Bowersox taught Co An there how to make them like this." He indicated the woman who could have been anywhere between twenty-five and thirty-five years old; it was hard to tell. "So, we have BLTs like clockwork, two, three times a week, and," he said, turning to the nearly glassy-eyed captain, "we shall think of you every time we have them after your departure!" He raised his red plastic cup of iced tea to Sox, as he called him, and then returned his attention to the newbies. "Our mess is pretty good because of the fact that there's a lot of really good produce in the Cang Long market, as you will see!"

After lunch, it turned out that first there was siesta; at Cang Long, nobody worked in the very hot part of the day. That suited the Kid and Sweet just fine. They retreated to their new digs and proceeded to take another couple of hits before lying down for a few winks.

About 1500 hours, the five newest citizens of Cang Long assembled at the gate of the compound with Reyes and prepared to leave its apparently safe confines.

"OK now," Reyes began, "although they rarely attack the compound with anything like an all-out assault, the VC here are very close by and active. And by close by, I of course mean some of the villagers are surely VC, or at the very least, at any given second, a VC sympathizer is in the area." The rotund Latino took one last puff on his Winston and flicked it out into the street. "We can usually go to town and not have any trouble. I don't think they want to attack us in town, because they'd probably end up shooting up a lot of their own people. But as soon as you get a little bit away from things on either side of town, look out!" He nodded his head for punctuation.

Wilson had instructed both Sweet and the Kid to bring their M16's. Ti Ui Troung was wearing his pistol, and Corporal Ba was the only person in the group who wasn't armed. Other than that, dress was casual, with no extra ammo and no steel pots; jungle hats would suffice.

The Kid had been making greater attempts to crack Ti Ui Troung's cards-close- to-the-vest personality. As they walked through the gate, the Kid said to Troung, "Chun ta de lam!" (We go to work!)

"Very good, Stocker." Ti Ui Troung engaged the Kid in conversation only in English. "Your Vietnamese is getting beaucoup good." They were all at the point where among the ARVNs and the Americans, everybody spoke a form of pidgen Vietnamese and pidgen English, switching back and forth as happened naturally given the limited scope of each group's mastery of the other's tongue. "It is very true, Stocker, whenever we meet the people, we are working!"

The Cang Long road now looked to the Kid more like a regular street as they came out of the compound and walked along it toward town, which was to the compound's left. Directly outside and opposite the Cang Long compound was the helipad, which sat in a wide-open area, much closer to the road than it was to the tree line down by the canal. There were two new buildings being constructed next to the helipad, one of which was apparently going to be at least three stories high. The far side of the open area was bordered by the long row of buildings that made up the Cang Long mercantile center, but all the commerce apparently took place on the far side.

"That long strip of buildings is the village center. For some reason it just kind of grew up as a row of added-on buildings that run from the Cang Long road, here, down to the big canal." Lieutenant Reyes gave them some of the local history. "The French built it, mostly as warehouses for produce and some housing for the workers needed to ship it up to Saigon via the canal to the river. Once the French left, the storehouses became a bunch of different businesses, but for some reason, none of the stores have ever done business out of their back doors. But now some Can Tho businessmen have come in to develop this plot of land. They started construction before Tet, and that was a setback, but now they're back at it." Workmen could be seen moving about in the construction area.

"Your office is about in the middle." Reyes pointed it out to Wilson with a brown arm as the group continued to walk. "But from what we hear, you're gonna be doing a lot of fieldwork with Doc and the boys on civic action programs, up and down the road."

"That's affirmative," Wilson said, with emphasis on the a. "I don't know what the fuck who-the-fuck was thinking when they got us an office after they gave us that fucking truck."

"Allow me, Lieutenant Wilson," Troung cut in. "The office is being provided for me by the ARVN Political Warfare Department."

Wilson stopped walking and turned to Troung. "You knew about this? And you didn't tell me?"

"Yes. Well, I tell you now. This program was planned before we knew you Americans had such thing as 'MSQ-85.' We propose that, to be effective, political efforts must have presence in town and in hamlets. Now we drive into countryside I no like! Too dangerous! Not do all the time. Still want office in town."

Up ahead, peeking around the corner of the row of buildings, a small throng of kids had spotted the Americans headed their way. They were quick to alert their buddies down the way. Within the space of thirty seconds, a mob of about two dozen kids came tearing around the corner and down the road toward the Americans and their Vietnamese companions, yelling, *"Mai! Mai! Mai!"* Americans! Americans! Americans! "Chocolate, cigarette, you give me! Mai! Mai! Mai!"

"OK now," Reyes began, "watch out for these little fuckers. They'll sure as hell try to pick your pocket." The little wave of humanity engulfed and surrounded the men.

The Kid could feel tiny hands touching, feeling, and trying to determine what was in his pockets. He'd gently brush them away, like shooing flies off. There were boys and girls ranging from four and five up to nine or ten, almost all of them barefooted, wearing shorts and tattered shirts and dirty as could be.

"All right, time for the secret weapon," Reyes said under his breath to the Americans as he rolled his eyes at the growing flock of children. He reached into his fatigue shirt's lower right-hand pocket, from which he pulled out a healthy handful of wrapped round peppermint candies. "Beaucoup!" he hollered as he heaved them back over his head behind them.

Instantly, the puddle of kids evaporated from around them as they lit out to retrieve the candies, yelling in delight and scuffling with each other to get the first one, then maybe two or three!

"Tried the same trick with a bag of M & M's once." Reyes smiled. "Got the same result!"

As the men turned the corner, the front of the Cang Long market area came into view. It was relatively busy for being at the tail end of the afternoon break. Lots of women of all ages. *Lots of young children. And look at all the pregnant ones, and the babies and toddlers. There's men around here, that's for fucking sure; we just can't see them.*

As they meandered down the row of shops, pausing to look at the wares of some, the Kid was conscious of a wave in front of them, people who had stopped their activity to watch the soldiers from a distance, then had made sure to move out of their way as they arrived at that spot and then, the Kid noted as he looked around, closing in behind them.

The Cang Long cafe and coffeehouse was located smack-dab in the middle of the long row of buildings. It was typical, with tables out front, some under an awning, some not, and with more tables inside under the roof of the open-air establishment.

"Corporal Ba and Ti Ui Troung, we must come enjoy coffee tomorrow morning," the Kid suggested.

"And two doors down, that's where your office is." Reyes pointed. "It'll be easy for you to have coffee here."

The group moved ahead. As they approached their space, Lieutenant Reyes cautiously stuck his head in through the large, screenless window to right of the doorway before he walked into the room. Following him through the door, the Kid checked out the office's spartan furnishings: one desk and two chairs, with no phone, no filing cabinets, and nothing decorative on the whitewashed walls other than a trio of medium-sized geckos. Then, along the left side of the room, the Kid spied a bench than ran nearly half the length of the twenty-foot-deep, twelve-foot- wide room. *Looks like it could have come out of a church!* It had the usual tile floor and louvered ceiling line.

"We need a shingle, sir," the Kid said as he slowly turned, looking the place over, "something like 'Hearts and minds saved while you wait!'"

"How about 'Hearts and minds pressed while you wait'?" Sweet suggested.

"Hmm, we could open up a bar." Wilson had been in a strange mood since lunch. "And we could have a stage over there where I could play guitar. And we could run a string of whores out the back and just get stinking rich!"

"And who would be your customers?" Lieutenant Reyes lit up a butt. "Charlie and his pals? There isn't a whorehouse here in Cang Long. Sox closed the only one that we ever knew about, about a week after he found out it existed, months ago. We tried to talk him out of it, but since he wasn't ballin', nobody was goin' ballin'."

Exiting the office, the Kid took a look to his right, down to the end of the buildings. From where he stood, he could see the canal and the boat landing at the end of the walkway. "Let's go down to the canal," he said to Reyes.

The normally jovial lieutenant gave him a serious glance and locked onto his attention. "Uh, no way you want to walk down there and stand at the edge of the canal. Here in Cang Long, that's just plain asking to get shot. The VC are absolutely, without a doubt, right on the other side of that canal."

"No shit?" queried Wilson. "What you're saying is, we walk down there, we'd be 'I' action?" He pointed to where the brown water was visible between the half dozen boats landed on the canal bank.

"That's affirmative, Lieutenant," Reyes replied. "And over there, that tree line that faces the town, they are most likely watching us from there too. If we went over that way, we'd be in a firefight in about a half a minute."

At that suggestion, the Kid noticed Corporal Ba's face suddenly displaying a very worried expression, as if he knew Wilson was the kind of soldier who would want to walk over there and find out.

"However, they apparently have some unwritten rule about shooting up the town, because they never have done it. But when we do inspection in the morning on the Vinh Long road bridge, not more than a quarter mile beyond the other side of those trees," Reyes continued, "they fuck with us every once in a while."

"Then I wanna go with you some morning," Wilson said with a silly-looking grin. If he wanted to convey the impression that he was some kind of loon, he was doing a pretty good job of it.

Smelling the aroma of roasting beans, the Kid said, "Hey, let's us all get a cup of coffee now—for something to do!"

There was immediate unanimous approval of the idea. Seeing a table open, the group sat down, much to the surprise of the two older men drinking tea at the next table over. *Ha! Those jokers look just like the guys Roberts and I smoked opium with!* the Kid thought.

Ti Ui Troung ordered from a girl of about ten or eleven, dressed in soiled white pajama bottoms and a faded tiny-flower-patterned top. Soon, the five of them were sitting there smoking cigarettes and drinking very strong coffee out of very small cups.

"Looks like these must have been left by the French." Sweet examined one of the delicate pieces of crockery.

"They only use them because you are Americans." Troung smiled as he prepared to pay the waitress. "This way they give you very little coffee!" Troung laughed. "Today will be my treat to celebrate the opening of our office!"

"Tomorrow night is Captain Bowersox's last night in Cang Long." Reyes ashed his Winston. "So, we're having Co An fix up a special meal, and we're going to have a little party. We don't have anything too special, but we'll have to drink up the rest of his whiskey!"

"That sounds like a plan to me!" Wilson was all on board with that. "But I'm getting kind of sick and tired of coming to places where the guy in charge is on his way home in a day or two. That's what happened to us out at Tan An, and the new guy wasn't too anxious to do anything. Hope we don't have to sit around while the newbie figures it out."

"As I understand it, Captain Bowersox's replacement is a captain who is pulling his second tour," Reyes said, supplying them with the inside dope. "So, he's not some guy who's going to have to get used to being in-country."

"So, Lieutenant." Reyes lit a new cigarette and addressed Wilson. "You psyop guys gonna go out tomorrow? If you want to, I'll tell Doc and we'll get you a security detail, and you can go for it!"

Wilson was inscrutable in his sunglasses and pulled-down jungle hat. "Hmm, what the hell! That's what we're here for. Shit yeah, tell 'em we're going out tomorrow!"

The Kid glanced over at Sweet, who it seemed was swallowing kind of hard, but he still spoke his mind. "And which way do you think we'll go? Not that way, I hope." He gestured with his thumb to the tree line behind him, which he'd just been told was packed full of VC.

"Oh no," Ti Ui Troung cut in, "we need to go back toward My Hue. We have a plan for how we wish to visit the hamlets along the Cang Long road, and tomorrow, if we go out, we will go back there."

When they finished their drinks and rose to leave, the Kid reached into his pocket and pulled out a couple of extra piaster coins to leave on the table for the girl, whose dark face lit up with a bright white smile.

"Cambode blood in her," Ba said. "Beaucoup Cambode blood all around in Mekong Delta," he said.

470

Chapter 42

That night after dinner, the Kid stretched out on his cot in his new hooch, in his new compound, and within the field of the airflow from the whirring fan, watching as his new roommate and field team companion, Jim Sweet, sat at Doc's s desk and clacked out a letter to his fiancée, Barbara.

While puffing on his pipe, the Kid listened to Armed Forces Radio Saigon. A new guy was on, somebody he'd never heard before, named Scott Manning. Not a bad jock at all, apparently out of Chicago. Much better than Gary W. Gears. The Kid had a good solid buzz going, so good that he didn't even mind when the artillery pieces fired down the road and the wadding fell onto their roof with a sound like that made by spitballs hitting the blackboard back in junior high school. The combination of sounds was, however, too much for Sweet.

"Argh! I can't write a letter with this fucking artillery shooting directly over our heads!" He turned and motioned to the Kid that he'd like a hit on the pipe, which the Kid immediately supplied. "Wait until I write Barbara about this artillery thing."

"Are you sure you want to do that?" the Kid questioned. "That'll just upset her. I make it a rule not to write things that I think will really make them worry."

"Hmm, well." Sweet pondered. "The way I figure it is, they're already worried, so what the fuck difference does it make? Anyway, I don't know what it is that they're shooting at down there, but they shoot over us a lot! Remind me not to go there."

The Kid reloaded the pipe. As he began burning another bowl, the first notes of Stevie Wonder's "I Was Made to Love Her" came over the radio's tiny speaker. "Here's a little something for all the brothers in the Seventh Air Cavalry up at a certain place in the Highlands that I can't mention, or else Charlie'd know you were up there coming to kick his posterior!" Scott Manning had said in the intro.

Once Sweet finished, the Kid twisted a clean sheet of paper into their machine and began to type.

471

August 18, 1968

Dearest Parnelli,

Well, here I am in Cang Long! Just when you think things can't get any worse, they get a little better. Ha, fooled you, because you thought I was going to say it was getting worse again. But, first off, we've been put up in the compound clinic, and it's really not too bad. It's private, and we have generators here and a fan and electricity! Talk about uptown! The good news is that we have a shower! The bad news is that it's a chore! To use it, you have to haul buckets of water from the well up the tower. One guy has to hoist the water out of the well and dump it into another bucket for the other guy to haul up to the barrel on top, which is about twelve feet up. It's a fifty-five-gallon drum, so you do the math. By the time we got the barrel half filled, my arms were so tired, I could hardly lift them to wash my pits!

How I'm missing you, my peanut. I lie down, close my eyes, and think what it would be like to feel your skin next to mine, and I just want to cry ninety-six tears. The song "96 Tears" by Question Mark and the Mysterians is playing on Armed Forces Radio right now. They've got a new guy on tonight. Can't believe how I missed getting in there. Damn! I'm still working on figuring a way to get in to Saigon so I can take them my tapes. Alan P. will help me. We've been writing now, and he said the other day that if I could get to Saigon, he'd introduce me to the powers that be.

Hon, I've been doing some serious thinking. After all, there isn't much nightlife here in 'Nam, and I want you to know, if you want to date during your senior year, it's OK with me. I know how hard it's going to be not doing that and having any fun at all, so please, believe me when I tell you that I know you love me enough that you could go out with some other guys just for the fun of it and still love me. I love you so much that I could forgive you anything except having another man's baby.

Tomorrow, we are taking the Batmobile out on our first real psyops operation, back toward Tra Vinh. To tell you the truth, I don't know whether to be scared or not. After all, it's not a search and destroy operation, and we'll have security with us, but how are the local VC going to react? Ti Ui Troung is nervous. They are supposedly like across the street watching us.

This place sometimes is just nuts! We were getting a tour of Cang Long's little village market, and the lieutenant who was showing it to us said that if we went down to the canal about a hundred meters off, the VC would open up on us. We all thought Wilson was going to run down there and see for himself! Then he said the VC have an unspoken rule about not shooting at us when we're in the marketplace, but everywhere else we are fair game! So here we go to the hamlets, to show some propaganda films and let Doc treat their little skin rashes and lance a few boils, then blow back to the compound. Sounds simple enough, but it ain't at the market. But I am still so pissed about being hijacked into this psyops crap that I do not know whether to produce a pile of fecal material or cease my visionary functions. Does that make any sense to you, my dearest and hottest Parnelli?

My new teammate is OK. Jim and his fiancée, Barbara, are in the same situation we are, engaged and getting married when he gets back. We compared pictures. You're cuter (you are). I told you he was from Maine and he's all excited about Edmund Muskie being on the Democratic ticket with Hubert. By the time you get this, the convention will probably be just starting. If Hubie does not distance himself from Johnson and become antiwar, he will lose to Nixon for sure. I can't believe how far I've come, from being a Nixon and Goldwater Republican in 1960 and 1964, to being an antiwar McCarthyite in 1968. You think being here has anything to do with it? I still can't believe they shot RFK. He would have ended this war. I know it only happened two months ago, but it seems like it was forever ago. That's what everything in this place seems like. Forever. This year is taking forever. Hard to believe it was three months ago today that we were at Disneyland, showering each other with kisses and hugs and ... Be sure to say hi to your mom and dad.

"Yo!" Lieutenant Wilson's husky voice called from outside the clinic door. "Sweet and Stocker, get your asses over here for duty assignments. Bowersox is making them in five minutes!"

The Kid put the letter sown to finish later, and the two PFCs, both bare-chested and clad in fatigue pants, trekked out into the compound and across the main drag between the buildings. Looking outward in the fading light, they could see the compound gates had been closed and the ARVN guard detachments were manning the defense bunkers with their M60's. The entire football-field-sized compound was also protected with a claymore net on the three sides that faced away from the Cang Long road.

473

Through the two big windows on either side of the door, they could see into the lit-up main building. It was so situated that the windows were not visible from outside the compound, so they required no light suppression for safety purposes. Inside, the pair found Captain Bowersox and Lieutenants Jones, Wilson, and Reyes sitting on the sofas set back against the outer wall of the old Cang Long District Headquarters Building, which was now the inner wall of the American "extension."

Sitting at the compound's tactical desk farther back in the room, tending the various radios connecting the tiny outpost to its lifelines of air and artillery support, was Doc, who was also nursing a Budweiser. Next to him in chairs were Dai Ui Phan and Top, the diminutive ARVN first sergeant.

"Hey, Lieutenant Wilson," the Kid said as he sat down on a folding chair opposite the couches, "don't you think Top here looks a little bit like Con, that RTO they set us up with on the junk assault?"

Appraisingly, Wilson looked at Top, who suddenly became aware that the two Americans were talking about him. "Yeah, I can see it! You're right, he does!"

Addressing Top in Vietnamese, the Kid said, "Trung Ui Top, you sem sem Hashi Con, delam Tra Vinh!" He gestured to his face, as if putting on shaving cream. "Sem sem!"

Top had a questioning look on his face that in any language said, *I don't understand.* "Khong bic?"

Corporal Ba, who had just come out of the back of the old building into the extension, had caught the tail end of what was going on and jumped in with an explanation to Top, who then nodded his understanding.

"Yes, Stocka," Ba said, finding a place to sit, "he does look like Con! Same size; face *sem sem* for sure!"

"All right, gentlemen," Captain Bowersox, who was just north of half drunk, said, slurring his words, "let's make this short and sweet."

"Sweet's here, but Short couldn't make it." The Kid jumped on the line. When he did so, Bowersox quickly cast him a serious glance—*How dare you interrupt me?* And just as Bowersox's jaw was opening to speak, the Kid jumped out of his chair and slapped himself on the forehead with an open palm. "Oh, wait! *You're* short! Aren't you, sir? Ain't nobody shorter than you, sir. Well, OK! Short and sweet! We're all here! *Choi duc oi!* Without any further ado, may I present to you the man with the plan, the captain with the most, the man who taught Co An how to make toast. Give it up for the *shortest* working man in town, Iai Ui Bowersox!" As the Kid alternately

474

pointed and clapped and waved at Sox as if inviting him up to a lectern, the pure look of shocked confusion on Bowersox's face caused everyone else in the room, Vietnamese and Americans alike, to completely break out laughing. And when that happened, Bowersox followed suit. After about half a minute, he couldn't figure out if he wanted to laugh or cry. Finally there was a total moment of silence, and he tried to speak again.

"But seriously, folks …" was as far as Sox got before the room went down again, nobody more appreciative of the outburst of laughter than the Kid. *This is only easy because they're all drunk!*

Now Vietnamese from the kitchen and back in the bunk rooms were coming in to the extension's main room to see what could possibly be so funny. Any laugh is a good laugh in a war zone.

"Jeez! OK." Sox was catching his breath. "Well, I am short, and I've got to tell you, somebody said to me once, 'Sox, when you go to Vietnam, if you make it and finally get home, you'll forget all the bad and only remember the good.' I'll always remember the great team we had here at Cang Long. Anyway, we've got radio watch here tonight, and I must say, we are all pleased to have three more Americans in the compound to step into the rotation. Now, with the addition of you three"—Sox pointed at Wilson, Sweet, and the Kid— "we've got six men we can use in the rotation of five two-hour shifts, from twenty hundred hours to zero six hundred hours. So, now somebody will get the whole night off from duty every sixth night! OK, tonight, the order will be: Doc, you pull twenty hundred hours to twenty-two hundred hours; Jonesie, you get twenty-two hundred hours to twenty- four hundred hours; Sweet, you get midnight to zero two hundred hours; Stocker, you take zero two hundred hours to zero four hundred hours; and, Ross, you'll pull the last watch, from zero four hundred hours to zero six hundred hours, while the lucky man Luis here gets to sleep the whole night through—that is, if Charlie lets him."

Nods of understanding went around the room.

Rats! I didn't want the middle of the night! "Sir," the Kid addressed Lieutenant Wilson, "you'll have to show me where your bunk is so I can wake you up."

"OK." He rose immediately, and the Kid followed him through the door and into the old Cang Long District Headquarters Building, the back of which now was set up as bunk rooms for the American officers and the higher-ranking Vietnamese. The tiled floors had some rugs scattered in front of the various lower bunks that lined the walls of what turned out to be four rooms off a corridor that led to the front of the building, which, the Kid could see, had been completely fortified with an extra wall of sandbags. Each room had three bunk beds, accommodating six men. In addition to the Americans and ARVN officers, one room was reserved for the higher-ranking ARVN noncoms, two of whom had been kicked out to make room for Troung and Ba.

"This is me." Wilson pointed to an upper on the far left-hand corner at the front- most left-hand room. "Jones is on the bottom. Troung and Ba are over across the hall there."

"Well, sir, one thing you won't have to worry about is me waking you up on time. That's for damn sure!"

"Ha. No doubt, Stocker. In fact, you can hit me ten minutes early so I can take a leak and smoke a cigarette and wake up."

"Fair enough." The Kid nodded his head and reached into his left breast pocket for a cigarette as he walked back to the extension. *Wow! Sweet and I really lucked out with the clinic sleeping quarters. Even with real bunks, this place sucks! Those ceiling fans don't do dick compared to that floor fan we have! And shit fire, we have enough privacy over there to smoke pot. So far, so good!*

"Stocker, over here," Luis called, motioning for him to join with Sweet at the radio desk. "We're gonna do a quick training session for tonight, OK?" He held a clipboard with a yellow pencil dangling from it against his knee, the pencil being attached to the clip apparatus by a string. "The way we work it—well, maybe you know if you were out at Tan An, because they're on our network—is we have an 'all's well' call every half hour, just to make sure everybody's awake and nobody's been over run or anything like that, ha-ha." The hefty lieutenant laughed, but nobody laughed with him. "Anyway, when the call comes from the Tra Vinh TOC, they'll just say, 'Charlie Lima, this is Tango Victor,' and you respond, 'Tango Victor, Charlie Lima, over.' Then they'll ask for the report, and the report, unless we're under attack, is, 'Alpha, Oscar, Kilo'—A-OK."

"And of course," Sweet said, jumping right in, "if we are under attack, you guys will probably be awake, right?"

Sweet and the Kid exchanged wry smiles.

"OK, I'm going back across to the clinic." The Kid prepared to break from the group. "I'm in midletter home to the fiancée, and I have a few more to write before I try to get some sleep in before zero two hundred hours."

"I'm with you," Sweet commented. The pair exited and returned to their room. Picking up where he left off, the Kid typed as follows:

476

So, we just got our radio watch assignments for tonight. Mine is from two o'clock to four o'clock in the morning, right in the middle of the night. I never minded midnight to six at WKDA, but this is the watch I hate the most.

Well, my darling, I've got to sign off because I have to write my parents, whom I've neglected lately. And believe it or not, I still get fan mail from Nashville. Seems like Dave Allen reads the letters I send him over the air! I'll write you some more while I'm pulling my watch.

All my love. ISYL!

Curt

Chapter 43

Writer's block. He had been staring at the page for more than an hour and hadn't been able to make it happen. *Where is my muse?*

Taking one last puff, he snuffed out his cigarette in an ashtray made out of an MRE pound cake can, which was full to the hilt. Sweat beaded steadily upon his forehead in the heat. There was no generator running at night, so there was no fan. Since the noise of the generator would have hampered the perimeter guards' ability to listen for sapper assaults, it was a sacrifice they all willingly made after 2200 hours. By the light of the kerosene lamp, the Kid stared at the longhand words, "Dearest Floretta," which he had written in about the first three minutes after he sat down at the desk to relieve Sweet at two o'clock in the morning.

Then, nothing. The first radio sentry call came and went, followed by the second. Unable to concentrate, the Kid found his mind wandering outrageously in a fatigued fog. No listening to AFVN Saigon on radio watch duty.

Shit. I wish I wouldn't have written in the first letter that I'd write her again on watch. Maybe I should open up that envelope and rewrite the last page of that and not worry about writing another letter. God. I just can't believe we're going to finally do something that has to do with psyops. But damn, Troung is really worried about going out in the hamlets! Well, I've got the M16 all cleaned and lubed. Since there aren't going to be more than half a dozen ARVNs with us, Wilson didn't have to ask us twice! Hmm, I wonder what the chances are of meeting any of those Buddhist monks? If they are all VC like everybody believes, what better place could there be to do psyops? I could go down there, tell them I am a Buddhist and want to join up. They could shave my head, and I'd just throw on a robe and not come out. Be a conscientious objector. What a story that'd be in Life magazine! But since I'm a combat vet, they'd never believe me.

I can't believe the election is almost here and we aren't going to have any better choice than Humphrey or Nixon! Here we are, fucking hunkered down in the Delta with a bunch of Vietnamese. Concentrate. Between thinking about the possibility of being attacked at night and that thing tomorrow—ha! I object! Hell no, I won't go. What the fuck am I saying? Oh hell, I'm still here! Getting dingy.

What a serene look that guy with his brains blown out had on his face. If you get it like that, I reckon you don't know you're getting it until the light goes out, or comes on—whatever the fuck happens when you die. Fuckin' A, I hope I don't find out here.

Dearest Floretta. You might as well be on another planet. ... Hmm, I never write to her as Floretta. What is that all about? Why do parents have to do that with twins? "Loretta, here is your sister, Floretta." Maybe I should see if she likes being called Retta. She'd wonder what that was all about. "Don't you like my name? Flo?" It wouldn't make a difference what her name was, I'd still love her! Say Hortense, though. There's one you don't hear anymore. "I love you, Hortense!" Ha! "I love you, Hortense. And here's your twin sister, Dortense."

"Charlie Lima, Tango Victor, over." The radio popped to life and snapped the Kid out of his daze.

He looked at his watch—0330—and then pulled the desk set microphone over to his mouth and depressed the send button. "Tango Victor, Charlie Lima, I read you. Over."

"Roger, Charlie Lima. What is your report? Over." "Uh, the report is Alpha, Oscar, Kilo. Over." "Roger, A-OK. Tango Victor, out."

Next hour, I'm going to make it "Asparagus, Ocarina, Knucklehead" and see what he says! Another half hour. The dead fucking middle of the night. The Kid stared at the mike. In the last couple of years, he'd spent hours in front of one, but this one was only connected to a handful of listeners, and he didn't have one of the largest music libraries in all of Nashville at his fingertips. When he'd DJ'd midnight to six o'clock, the hours between 'hree o'clock and five o'clock were always the hardest. From five o'clock to six o'clock, the Kid figured his numbers had the potential to be the highest of his shift, and he really kicked butt. He came up with this theme thing called "The Happy Sunup Hour" and did an uptempo really rock-out show with all kinds of produced drop-ins and fancy audio tricks.

Staring at the mike, for a split second he considered breaking radio silence with a radio bit, just for grins. *Yeah, right, I'd most likely get an Article 15 over that.*

That's all I need.

Then, in a low voice so as not to wake anybody up, the Kid began to pretend that he had taken over the mike. Without depressing the send button, he began his stealth broadcast.

"And we're back! Well, here we are, all doing the very same thing, that is, waiting for the sunrise! Thanks for tuning in. Glad to have you along on KPDY. That's K- Paddy, the nice-as-rice spot on your radio dial. It's zero three thirty hours Asian Pacific Gone-to-Hell-in-a Handbasket Time, and now Paddy Radio, the pride of the Delta, with much, much more music for the Mekong, is proud to present the man you can count on to gong the Cong with his really big dong, the man with less scammo and more ammo, the one and only Sergeant Pepper with his Family Band Hit Parade Show! Yah, whisper, whistle, whisper, whistle, quiet clapping, stomping of feet." The Kid was really getting into it.

"All right, to the phones! This is Sergeant Pepper, the hardest-working noncom here, to screw the Vietcong. And who do we have on the line?" Then the Kid supplied the other voice, lapsing into a fake Asian accent.

"Uh, hello, Trung Shi Mui. This is Nguyen, please, to make request!" "Nguyen. Hey, baby, how's it swingin'? Who do you work for, Nguyen?"

"Oh, uh, I machine gunner for VC Tenth, the Long-Gone Battalion. I need a request for my girl."

"Hmm. Your girl, hmm? And where is she tonight that you aren't together?"

"She is spy. Works for steam bath massage. Make beaucoup money, but she blows it all!"

"Well, all right, Nguyen, baby! So, what are you wanting me to play tonight for you, hmm?"

"You play something by Cream, OK, GI?"

"You got it, big guy! And here it is! For hum-humming along with down there at the Scientific, a psychedelic little number called 'White Room'!" As the Kid began to hum the song—*Hmmmm, hmmm, a-hmmm, ah, a-hmmm, hmmmm*—the performance was interrupted by applause. Startled out of his skin, the Kid nearly knocked the chair over as he jumped up and spun around, to find Lieutenant Wilson standing in the doorway of the old building.

"Well, all right! Excellent performance!" He laughed. "I might make a request too. Turn down the volume on KPDY, OK?"

"Oh, Lieutenant! Did I wake you? I guess I was getting a little carried away."

"No. I had to take a leak, and the latrine is over there!" He pointed to the courtyard, where his plan was to just piss in the driveway, as the latrine was actually a far distance beyond. Shuffling by, he looked at his watch, which along with his dog tags and green boxers, was all he had on. "Shit. It's almost time for you to wake me up anyway. What the hell, yer show was pretty good. Tell you what: let me take this leak, and when I get back and dressed, I'll let you go a few minutes early. Kinda like I was putting money in your hat!"

"Well, thank you, Lieutenant. That's mighty nice!"

Chapter 44

The truck rumbled into the courtyard area of the hamlet and, when the driver, Lieutenant Wilson, realized how close the cluster of kids was to the vehicle, pulled to a jerky stop.

"Son of a bitch! Wouldn't be good psyops to run over any of these little bastards, that's for damn sure!" He laughed.

Sweet and the Kid exchanged mutual looks of surprise at the size of the gathering. Jim, who was sitting shotgun, opened the Batmobile door and stepped down into the little bit of space the children were giving him. All the while, the group of easily fifty grade-school-age boys and girls bounced up and down and kept up a steady excited yell, like any large group of kids in the United States on a sugar high the day after Halloween.

"They look pretty excited!" Sweet said, nearly having to yell in the Kid's ear, as he got out of the cab.

"No shit! I think somebody told them we were going to show movies!" the Kid speculated, pantomiming cranking an old-time camera, with his left hand cupped over one eye. "Either that, or they seem pretty jazzed up at the prospect of just getting Band-Aids and suckers."

Immediately behind them, Troung arrived in his jeep, with Corporal Ba riding shotgun. At last, the Tenth Psyop Battalion field team was preparing to perform actual psyop activity, known in the manual as a civil action program, or CAP for short. The Kid thought, *Well, I am truly amazed; I bet Wilson hates this!*

They had picked a community center area where they knew there was a civic building, which served dozens of nearby farming families as a school and meeting place. Troung and Wilson immediately confabbed in the middle of the parking lot to review their plan.

The people had constructed an open-sided building beneath a high sloping roof that ended in eaves that stuck out and created a covered area extending five feet past where two steps rose up to the floor. It was capable of accommodating easily one hundred people. In addition to being the neighborhood schoolhouse, it was where they held elections for hamlet chief. Because it was well shaded, Troung's plan was to show the movies inside the building right after the peasants listened to his lecture on the merits of the Thiệu government.

Before the movie and the lecture, as an added bonus, Doc would run a MEDCAP, short for medical civic action program. Sitting by a small army-issue folding table, Doc would have the patient sit directly across from him. He'd minister to as many of their minor maladies as was possible given his limited resources. In this way, it was hoped that the common peasant out in the hamlets would perceive that the South Vietnamese government was doing something for him or her personally.

Ahead of the troops, two jeeps with six ARVN riflemen had pulled to the far end of the commons area and were arming up to fan out and post up to guard the team as they performed their dog and pony show. In order to beef up as much as possible, all the Americans had also brought along their M16's today.

"So, what do you think?" Sweet turned to the Kid. "See Grace Kelly?" he said with a worried look on his face. "You think this is enough security for what we're doing?"

"No. Never enough fucking security, I'll tell you that." The Kid gazed across the tops of the bobbing heads in front of them as they stood by the front tire of the Batmobile. "But I truly think that when we're in a place like this. I mean, this has got to be their kids, don't you think? I feel OK in a place like this because of the marketplace factor. They don't want to kill their own kids and people."

"So, Ba." The Kid put his arm around the corporal's shoulder and asked him point-blank, "Other than these kids here, and some of them we're not yet totally sure of, you're the only guy who isn't armed. How does that make you feel?"

Before he answered, Ba saw that Troung and Wilson were apparently in agreement about what was about to down and were returning to the truck to tell everybody the plan. "Not too nervous," he offered with a somewhat nervous- looking grin that emphasized his thick jowls.

The last member of the team had now arrived. Doc did not stop until he straightly pulled his jeep around and came to park beneath some of the shade offered by a stand of four twenty-foot-tall curving palms at the right corner of the civic center. There, he sprang from the driver's seat, pulled his card table and two folding chairs from the back, and began setting up his medical shop.

"All right, listen up," Wilson commanded the group, "Sweet, you pull the truck around over there to as far from the building as the cord will let us get, then pull out the generator and set it up. Stocker, after you help Sweet get the generator down, you take the screen set up in the school over there, on the right side. Ba, you help us run the electricity for the movie. After that, get the leaflets and begin passing them out among the women and old men and whoever." He stopped to take a drink from his canteen; it was 0900 hours, and the heat was building.

"OK, now, Doc will first treat their ailments, then Troung will give his speech, followed by the movies. The second they're over, we pack right up and we're out of here, like a getaway in bank robbery!" Wilson smiled because he liked his metaphor.

Hopping into the seat of the Batmobile, Sweet gently maneuvered it the twenty feet to where Wilson had pointed, where he parked it and set the emergency brake. He grabbed his and the Kid's M16's and swung down. By the time he'd rounded the back, the Kid and Ba had it open, with the pulley hook already connected to the red-framed generator. After stowing the rifles, the trio quickly hoisted the generator off and swung it to the shady side of the truck.

Wilson and Troung were up in the front, with the driver's door open, working on the loudspeaker system. It was capable of operating off battery power, so while Sweet, the Kid, and Ba set up for the movie, Troung prepared to announce the agenda of the visit to the growing throng of people. Word had gotten out to the point that a number of elderly citizens were now beginning to arrive at the hamlet center to check out the unusual activity.

Sweet, with the help of Ba, began to unravel the cords needed to hook up the equipment to operate the movie projector. The Kid took the screen and, hoisting it up onto his shoulders like a pair of skis, began to walk toward the civic center building.

He worked his way carefully through the cross traffic of running, yelling schoolkids, some of them showing interest Troung, others in Sweet and Ba, and still another group in Doc and his table of medicines. Now a good many had begun to follow him and the load balanced on his shoulder; they knew it was the screen upon which the movies would appear! The Kid couldn't help but notice all the children were smiling, thoroughly enjoying a morning at their school and a moment of their lives that wasn't exactly like yesterday. They had new and exciting tattooed on their faces, and it made the Kid feel that he was possibly, at last, really doing something to make a difference.

These kids could give a shit less about communism or capitalism, Ho Chi Minh or Nguyễn Thiệu, the Yankees or the Red Sox, Koufax or Drysdale— none of the great issues of our time. They're only interested in the classics: what's for dinner and what's on TV. Oh, that's right, they don't have any TVs. That's what's going to make this day so special!

Entering the building, the Kid moved to the right and set the screen down on the cement floor. Then he wiped his sweaty brow. Switching from his dark to regular glasses, he checked out the surroundings; a stark interior greeted him. The only furnishings were benches with slanted tables in front of them at the part of the room closest to the black chalkboards attached to the end wall. There were no light fixtures, no fans, and nothing electric in the whole building, which was why they could only show movies here with the aid of a generator.

A very slim woman, seemingly in her forties, wearing oval gold-wire-framed glasses, with her hair pulled back into a bun, dressed in white pants and a short- sleeved blouse, approached him, bowing, smiling, and on the surface, apparently happy to see him.

"Mien yoi, Ba," the Kid greeted her.

"Ah, mien yoi, Mai," she responded, approving of the fact that the American had bothered to address her in Vietnamese.

Gesturing to the screen and moving his arm around to draw the eye to various locations, he asked, "Odau?" wanting to know where he should put the screen.

"Here." She pointed to a central location near the front of the room.

Expanding the tripod base, the Kid raised the telescoping armature of the screen upward and then, flipping the release, spun the tube down into the horizontal position so that he could pull it up into place, much to the delight of the children, who let out a collective "Aah" as the silver screen emerged.

Turning, the Kid saw that Sweet and Ba had strung the cord to its correct location. The three worked their way through the waist-high crowd and, once outside, walked briskly back to the truck. When Troung started his spiel on the Batmobile's loudspeakers, the milling rural throng literally stopped in their tracks to listen to what the young political warfare officer from the suburbs of Saigon had to say.

As Troung pointed to Doc, the Kid understood the Vietnamese word *bauxi,* or "doctor." He was starting to pick up more and more vocabulary; the longer they hung out in the sticks with the Vietnamese, the better he was getting. When Troung pointed to the main building, the Kid heard him use the English word, or was it a French word? *"Film" must mean the same thing the world over, I guess.*

To that end, Wilson had retrieved from the Batmobile the case that held the films available to be shown. The round cans bore the seal of the flag of South Vietnam, and the titles were in Vietnamese. *I wonder what these are,* Wilson pondered as they stood before the open case on the floor in the doorway of the truck box. There were three films and six filmstrips. They'd have to watch and see what all this stuff was about.

"Tell you what." Wilson stood back from the end of the truck where they were working. "I don't like the setup here; there's nobody guarding the front door and watching up and down the road. So, I want one of you to take your M16 and go down there and secure it while we're showing movies. If you want, you can take turns."

"Fair enough." Sweet looked at the Kid. "Do you want first or second watch?"

"I'll take second because I'd like to help Lieutenant Wilson set up the projector."

"Oh." Jim immediately climbed into the back to retrieve his weapon and an extra bandolier of ammo. "Any pointers, sir, on where you think would be a better place to establish my observation post?" he said, plopping his steel pot, which had also been stored in the back, squarely upon his head.

The lieutenant looked over the scene: irregularly spaced clusters of huts dotted one side of the roadway, which ran to the right and up to the artillery firebase and, in the other direction, to the left and down to the Buddhist monastery, both of which edifices sat on the opposite side of the road from the hamlet's huts.

Between these two landmarks, the delta landscape opened up into nothing but a wide gaping expanse of rice paddies, going clear off into the distance, where it ended in a quarter-inch-tall green tree line.

Of the two neighborhood landmarks that bracketed the My Hue civic center, the Buddhist monastery was, by far, the closer.

"Well, offhand, if it waere me, I'd go down there on the left and take advantage of the shade of that hut's porch, and kind of conceal myself in the doorway while I watched. But that's just me. When you get down there, PFC Sweet, I trust you'll use all of the skills they taught you in basic training to pick the best location."

"Yes, sir." Retrieving a canteen off the front seat, he was off.

Troung had finished his announcements, and as Wilson and the Kid lugged the projector, he went over and perused the films, considering in what order to play them. His government was putting great effort into programs to combat the teaching of the VC cadre, who would arrive in a hamlet unannounced, much like they were doing today, and teach their own class. Only their classes quite frequently included the execution of the hamlet chief, if he had cooperated too much with the South Vietnamese government.

The schoolteacher had secured for their use a small table of suitable size upon which they could set up the 8 mm Bell and Howell projector. It was brand spanking new and came complete with a set of two sound speakers.

Setting aside the case, Wilson took the plug from Ba and inserted it into the back of the projector. Hitting the switch, he said, "Oh yeah, gotta turn on the generator before this thing will work. Stocker? Hop to it!"

Walking briskly back to the generator on the shady side of the truck, the Kid could see that Doc's line was still rather long, but everybody else was packing into the schoolhouse for the show. Down by the Cang Long road, the Kid could see that Sweet had pretty much taken Wilson's advice and was sitting on the front porch of someone who was at the movie, smoking a cigarette.

Clicking the switch to the on position, the Kid pulled the rope, and the sparkling clean, brand-new generator kicked into life and took off running with a throaty roar that quickly settled into a strong purr. The Kid could see Wilson giving him the thumbs-up as the bulb of the projector lit up. Sensing from the noise that something was about to happen, many of the villagers who were still standing in Doc's sick call line abandoned it for the schoolhouse.

Wilson must have been the audiovisual guy at his school because Troung had given him the films, and he had the first film threaded through the silver gears and ready to go in the blink of an eye. But before the film, there would be a lecture by Troung.

His talk took about ten minutes, according to the Kid's wristwatch. All the while, the children fidgeted and played their own special versions of grab-ass with each other. Their mothers and grandparents appeared to be listening to the words that came out of Troung's mouth, punctuated with wide, sweeping arm gestures. Not understanding the language enough to follow along, but having been a public speaker and debater for years in school, the Kid thought that Troung must have been doing OK, but he could see from some of the elders' body language, whispering and slight shaking of their heads in a negative fashion, that it was a tough crowd and a hard sell.

Finally, Troung concluded his remarks to the polite applause of the group. *I wonder if they are clapping because of what he said or because he's done?*

Signaling Wilson, who stood ready to start the film, Troung stepped out of the way of the screen, and the images sprang from the lens onto the screen to the cheers of the kids. Although the shades couldn't be pulled, the wide

487

overhang helped to shade the screen enough that the images were clearly visible to the audience.

Lighting up a cigarette, the Kid watched as the black-and-white film opened up by showing a scene in a hamlet that was being portrayed as the archetypal Vietnamese village. A group of workers were processing the rice crop, some of them beating the husks with poles to which were attached little bludgeons that broke the coverings from the grains. A pair of young Vietnamese girls used large, shallow wicker baskets that looked a lot like snow saucers to pitch the rice into the air so the wind could blow away the husks.

Into this pristine scene, all of a sudden, came charging a half dozen actors who were obviously dressed more as North Vietnamese Army members than as the Vietcong, sporting AK-47's, complete with bayonets. They wore the nastiest- looking masks upon their faces—brutal-looking large eyes, sharpened teeth with gritted jaws—and they brutalized the villagers by pushing them around and kicking over their baskets. One actor, who was apparently the VC leader, so indicated by the fact that he waved a pistol around and wore no mask, pointed at a book and lectured the villagers. Then, when two of the VC went into a hut and emerged with babies stuck to their bayonets, the action turned into an Asian opera-style dance!

"Wow!" the Kid half whispered to Wilson. "This is fucking wild!"

All the while, the size of the crowd had been growing noticeably. It was apparently "a happening." Just as the Kid had that thought, the Supremes did the soundtrack in his head. "Is it real, the happening, oh, oh, oh!" But the Motown thing did not match the action on the screen. Now two other masked VC were playing tug-of-war with a young innocent girl, and then, for some reason, they cast her aside. The Kid hadn't known what to expect from the art of Vietnamese film making, but this was not something he had imagined. Of course, the Thiệu government's mission was to portray the communists as animals, and the film definitely had the audience's total attention. And it wasn't lost on them that cast- aside young girl spotted her chance to escape and bolted to get help. She ran through the tree line and across paddies until, lo, she came upon three young Vietnamese studs stripped the waist, planting rice. Like Lassie, she convinced them there was big trouble in the village. After the largest and most muscular one struck a chest-popping pose of resolve for roughly five seconds, he motioned for his compadres to join him. Grabbing their nearby rifles, they charged back to the hamlet. The scene cut to the hamlet, where the VC were now beating old women and grandpas. After a couple of well-placed blows knocked down this one particularly vulnerable-looking granny, the "boys" appeared and vanquished the villagers amid great dancing battles and fanfare. Of course, Mr. Muscle had a direct

488

confrontation with the masked communist cadre leader and kicked his ass. Then the scene dissolved to the South Vietnamese flag, forever waving in the name of freedom.

"How about that, *Birth of a Divided Nation,* by Ho Chi Griffith!" the Kid exclaimed as it ended. Wilson just shrugged his shoulders, then rethreaded the reels for rewind and began the preparations for the next movie. The crowd was now even bigger, all of them talking excitedly about the movie they had just watched. Some people stood on the two steps, and others stood below the main floor of the school, but under the shade of the eaves, all now jockeying for position prior to the start of the next movie.

"I'll go relieve Sweet," the Kid intoned to the lieutenant. Working his way out of the packed school, he headed for the Batmobile to retrieve his M16. Doc had continued to work his table, and even though the movies had started, there were still a dozen or so old Bas, most with red and black checkered scarves on their heads and betel nut red on their lips, who were more interested in soap than soap operas.

The Kid grabbed a canteen and checked over his M16 as he made his way down to the road. *Gotta clean this sucker. It's pretty dusty here in Cang Long! This should be a pretty easy place to toast a bowl. There ain't nothing happening here today. Maybe when we leave, but only if they aren't shootin' this place up.*

"Hey, Jim," the Kid said, announcing his presence to Sweet, who sat in the shade of the porch on a well-worn wooden bench with ankle-thick bamboo legs. "Your turn. Don't know what you're going to see, but the movie we just watched was wicked wild!"

"Oh, really?" He rose and put his steel pot back on; it had been sitting on the bench beside him. "Like how wild?"

"It was all Asian opera with scary masks, dancing, and baby bayoneting!"
"Say what?" Sweet responded, not sure what he had just heard.

"Oh, they were dolls. No real babies were apparently hurt in the making of the film, but it was something, all choreographed out, VC with babies on the ends of bayonets, all dancin' around. Really! Wait till you see it. Needless to say, the good guys win in the end!"

"Here, do you want these clips?" Jim pulled the green cloth bandolier over his head and offered it to the Kid.

"Sure, leave them," the Kid answered. He took Sweet's seat and proceeded to dip the bowl of his pipe into his pocket cache to ready a load. "Do you want one of these?" he offered as Jim was turning to go.

489

"Naw, later," he replied, and took off toward the school.

The Kid torched his Zippo and took a healthy hit off the pipe. *Might as well get stoned. Nothing else better to do stuck out in the fricking middle of nowhere. That's nowhere, man. "He's a real nowhere man sitting in his nowhere land ..." This pot I got in Sa Dec has lasted me a long fucking time.* He took another hit. *Doesn't take much of this stuff! One more of these and I'll be Melba toasted.*

Putting away the pipe, the Kid rose and casually walked into the deserted Vietnamese house whose porch they had made their guard post. It was about twelve feet by twelve feet and had a table with a couple of discarded small American wire spools as stools and a bench permanently installed on the table's far side. On the table was a washbasin with some dirty water in it, and against one wall was a bookcase-like shelf where the family kept their few dishes. There was a small Buddhist shrine on a small pedestal in one corner. Like the huts they had commandeered on their overnight missions, this one had a very large sleeping platform. Under it were some boxes with closed lids that the Kid chose not to look in. *Probably everything they own in the world they either are wearing or it's in those boxes under that bed.*

He went back outside and sat down. Taking a long pull on the canteen he had attached to his pistol belt, the Kid wiped the sweat from his brow and looked up the road toward the artillery base and then back toward the monastery. There was very little traffic moving on the road today.

Hmm, the monastery is barely a hundred meters away. If I get up and ease my way down a little, I wonder what I could see. The Kid rose, situated his steel pot, tucked his M16 under the crook of his arm as if he were carrying a shotgun on a walk to the duck blind, and began working his way down toward the monastery, all the while becoming more vigilant of his surroundings. Staying on the occupied side of the road, he went from porch to porch, finding nobody home; they were all at the movies. Soon, he was standing almost directly across from the monastery.

Its walls of old masonry were worn from years of monsoon delta rains. The eight- foot-high outer wall looked to have been painted with a mural of some sort once, a long time ago. It was topped with broken glass and stood between the ground floor and the Cang Long road. A yellow-painted balcony rose up behind the wall, apparently accessed from the second floor, with a pair of huge cobra statues guarding its corners.

There's a monk! Ah, he finally sees me! Look, he's calling to his buddies and pointing at me! Hey, this is just like I imagined last night on radio watch! I could go over there and join them! Here they come to see the American!

490

Wow, all of these monks are really into the teardrop aviation sunglasses, that's for sure!

The bright yellow of their saffron robes flashed in the sun as the first monk now waved to the Kid and smiled broadly beneath his shiny, olive-skinned bald head. The Kid, with his rifle still in the crook of his arm, sort of put his hands together and slightly bowed his head to the holy men, one at a time. *A VC, a VC, a VC,* he thought while doing it. They were young, virile-looking Vietnamese men, the only ones of military age he had yet seen in or near Cang Long who were not ARVNs or amputees. *You fuckers are VC, aren't you! All safe there inside your pagoda, knowing the army is not going to come in there looking for you or your AK-47's or your RPGs. You've got your robes on now, but you healthy-looking fucks are probably card-carrying members of the VC Tenth Battalion with a wardrobe full of black pajamas!*

Then, the first monk motioned for the Kid to cross the road, pointing to the gate to his left: *Come closer.* At first, the Kid thought it would be cool, but then he realized, *I'm on guard duty! I can't go over there and fuck around with those billiard balls! I gotta watch the road. I'd better get my ass back!* Shaking his head no, the Kid made one last respectful bow, then, waving goodbye, he turned and plodded toward the school building.

Chapter 45

Dear Mom and Dad,

Hope this finds you both doing well and the weather not too hot there in Boulder. Ask me how hot it is here. Wait, don't ask! OK, I'll tell you anyway: it is 105°. We finally had mail call out here today, and I got no. 8, and now I've gotten them all but no. 4! That one is probably long gone, and somebody has already eaten the Shake-a-Pudd'ns and the VC have made a booby trap out of the shoestring potato can! *Que sera, sera,* as Doris Day would say.

We've been real busy here in Cang Long with the Batmobile. We took it out for the last four days in a row, and today, it's a day off. We really earned it. We've been doing these medical civic action programs where we take the doctor—or in our case, our medic named Doc—to hamlets and we patch up the easy stuff, like giving them medicine for pink eye and stuff like that. Doc figures that in the last four days, he's treated 380 villagers. And of course, we pass out leaflets and propaganda materials and show the movies when we find a building dark enough to make it work. We sure as hell aren't going anywhere at night to show movies out here in the middle of the VC stronghold! At least, so far, ole Charlie has left us pretty much alone. What we're doing now is a hell of a lot better than what Wilson and I were doing before the army saw fit to give us, this day, our daily truck.

I've written Scott again to let him know that I understand about this "best man" thing. I just can't be there, and we all gotta do what we gotta do. At least he is getting somebody I know to do it. If I had it to do over again, I think I might have run off to Las Vegas and married

492

Flo, so she could come see me in Hawaii without her parents freaking out. I am trying to get enough money together to get her a plane ticket so she can come to Scott and Nancy's wedding and so you all can meet your other future daughter-in-law.

We have a new commanding officer here at Cang Long, and is he ever a jerk! His name is Captain Robinson. He is a black man from Maryland who is here on his second tour. He only got here three days ago and already everybody hates him, especially the kitchen staff because he can't keep his hands off this one cook whom everybody likes. He'd like it if she were a prostitute, but she's not. Now, you know that I am one of the least prejudiced guys in the world, but it wouldn't make a difference if this guy was red, black, orange, blue, or purple: he is a blowhard and one of the loudest loudmouths I've ever been around! He says he volunteered to come back for another tour because he made so much money on the first one that he couldn't afford not to. I've actually heard that a lot. Can't imagine what it would take to make me pull two tours in 'Nam. Anyway, he also says he came back because he hates being home with his wife and that every time he goes home, she has another baby, so there is always a crying baby to get away from. I can't imagine not wanting to be around Flo!

The Democrats are just about to do their thing in Chicago. None of us over here cares, because we know that whatever whoever does whenever isn't going to change the way things are for us. You can bet your buns that it'll be a long time before anybody ever finds out what Nixon's secret plan is!

The Kid stopped typing for a second and stood up to look out the screen door of the infirmary to see if anything was shaking in the courtyard before he pulled his pipe from under the pillow on his cot and dipped it into the cache pocket. It was nearly 1600 hours, and he had been writing letters for the past couple of hours, taking advantage of the day off. Sweet, Lieutenant Wilson, Corporal Ba, and Ti Ui Troung were across the street in the village, manning the psyops office, mostly for grins, and Sweet wanted to use the typewriter as soon as the Kid had finished his letters.

Taking a pull from the pipe, the Kid painted another layer onto the high that he'd gotten an early start on because it wasn't a workday. Mail call that morning had put him in a pretty good mood: he'd gotten five letters from Flo and really got stoned before he escaped to read them, each once and then all of them once again! He was going to do it again right before bedtime. After another hit, it was back to the typewriter:

OK, I'm signing off right now. All the guys are over in the village, and I have to go get Jim Sweet because it is his turn to use the typewriter! So, I can't wait to see what you send me for my birthday! Lieutenant Wilson said I could have my wish, to spend it in Tra Vinh, where they have a pool table and a bar! Oh, Dad, that's it! I know what I want for my birthday. If you could send me a new pool cue, a cheapie—but one that still unscrews in half, one with a real tip on it—I will kick some serious butt here!

All my love,

Curt

He put on his fatigue shirt, buttoned it up, and slipped on his shoulder holster, also making sure he had enough cigarettes. Plopping his soft jungle hat upon his head, he crossed the courtyard to the main building. Inside, he found Lieutenant Reyes, Doc, Top, Dai Ui Phan and Jones sitting and talking to Captain Robinson at the dining room table; all six were smoking cigarettes and enjoying a Victoria Bitter, an Australian beer they had been getting lately instead of American brews. Notebooks and writing pads sat in front of them.

"Hey, Doc. Hello, sir, and sir, and sir. Ciao, Top. Ciao, Dai Ui," he said, greeting them all as he stood up on the landing without going down the one step to their level. "I'm going over to see what's happening at the psyops office, just so you know where I am."

"OK, Stocker," Doc replied with a troubled, worried kind of look on his face. It must have been something about a staff meeting; nobody in the upper chain of command at Cang Long had been remotely happy since the departure of Bowersox and the arrival of Robinson. They apparently had some issues to address.

Out the gate and across the street, the Kid was able to make it to the corner of Town Row before the children spotted him. He was ready with the Reyes defense. As soon as the gang materialized, he pitched a handful of Dentyne gum over his shoulder and then walked unmolested down toward the psyops office, when he was surprised to see Troung and Sweet coming back the other way.

"Hey, guys! How's it going?" They stopped to talk at the corner of the coffee shop.

"Hi, Curt." Sweet had just finished lighting up. "You get your letters done?" "Yeah. The typewriter is still out on the desk." Turning to Troung, the Kid said,

"So, Lieutenant Wilson and Ba are staying? Or should I just go back with you two?"

"Oh, Wilson stay. Say he have some paperwork to do for Can Tho." Troung seemed impatient, as if he had to go to the bathroom or something.

"All right. I'm this far, so I'll go check the office scene out. See ya." The Kid continued on his way. As he approached the door to the office, his eye was distracted by something down toward the canal at the end of the row. A small boat was approaching the shore with one black-clad man aboard. He thought nothing of it.

Entering, the Kid found Wilson sitting at the desk and Corporal Ba sitting on the bench to the left of the door, reading a letter. When Ba saw the Kid, his face lit up. Poor Ba had to go everywhere Wilson went nearly every second of the day and hated it immensely.

"Ciao, Kid!" Ba greeted him, making Wilson look up from his writing and grunt a terse hello.

"What are you doing?" The Kid slid over to the side of the desk and looked down at Wilson's work, as it didn't seem to be proprietary.

"Filling out the monthly reports for Captain Smith back at Can Tho. I gotta give him a detailed accounting of where we've been and what we've done and all that shit, and request some supplies and on and on." He ashed his butt. "This is the part I hate about being an officer. Ordering enlisted men around? Great. Drinking at the officers' club? Love it. Getting officer's pay? The only way to go. But filling out these reports? Hey, why don't you do this for me, Stocker?"

"Sorry, sir, not qualified, remember?" The Kid smiled. "That's why I'm an enlisted man; get in, take a nap, get out!" Turning to the corporal, he asked, "What ya got there, Ba, a letter from home?"

"Ah, yes! It is from my mother. For some reason, my father, he never write, but he wants me to write him!" He chuckled at his dysfunctional family situation.

Bored, the Kid plopped down on the bench and lit up a fresh Kool, blowing a long stream of smoke toward the door, where it danced in the light streaming in from outside. And much to his surprise, into the smoky shaft of light stepped a man.

He was dressed in black pajamas and a red scarf, was barefoot, and was of slight build, almost skinny at first glance. The man from the boat! Neither his sudden presence nor his manner exuded any serious feeling of threat as his hands rested, fingers extended, at his sides. His Asian face was awash in nervousness as he glanced briefly at each of the three men, before choosing to address Corporal Ba.

"Toi chu hoi!" he said, punctuating the phrase with an unsure smile and upraised open palms.

"Chu hoi?" Ba's mouth dropped open. He looked at the man with an expression of complete and utter disbelief. "An Chu Hoi?"

Nodding so there would obviously be no mistaking his meaning, the man again repeated the phrase that a Vietcong would utter when surrendering willingly to the government of South Vietnam: "Toi chu hoi!" I surrender!

"Well, I'll be a son of a bitch!" the Kid exclaimed as the meaning of the phrase sank into his barely bilingual brain. "Lieutenant Wilson, can you believe it? We have actually got ourselves a real live Hoi Chan! This is our first Returned Brother!" He took a step toward the man and stuck out his right hand to shake hands with the man in a gesture of welcome. At first the man hesitated, unsure of what to do, before finally extending his hand to the Kid, limply shaking his hand, and bowing and smiling all at once. *Fucking A! I'm shaking hands with a real live, honest-to-God Vietcong!*

"Son of a bitch if it isn't true!" Wilson was now smiling from ear to ear. "Maybe you should go get Ti Ui Troung. No. Wait a minute. Fuck him. He's being a bastard about a couple of things." He turned to face his own private interpreter. "We've got Ba. Let's interrogate him first ourselves! After all, he's our Chu Hoi!"

The Kid immediately went behind the desk and brought out a chair. Putting it at the edge of the desk, he motioned for the new convert to take a load off and have a seat. Still smiling nervously, the man nodded his understanding as he complied. The Kid whipped out his pack of Kools and offered the man a smoke, which he unhesitatingly accepted, nodding in gratitude as it was lit for him by the always present Zippo. Taking a deep drag, he said, "Ah, Salem!"

"No, Kool!" The Kid showed him the pack. "*Sem sem* Salem!" *Would you look at me! Here I am conversing with a member of the Vietfuckingcong! Now does this count for seeing one in the wild? I don't think so. After all, by the time he stepped in here, he'd already laid down his weapon, hadn't he?*

"Uh, don't you think it would be wiser to frisk the man before you cater to his needs?" Lieutenant Wilson suggested, virtually reading the Kid's mind. "Corporal Ba, ask him if he's armed."

"Yes, sir," responded the corporal.

"But, sir." The Kid pondered. "If he was armed and meant to do us harm, he could have easily done so the second he walked through that door, don't you think?"

"Are you armed?" the corporal inquired in Vietnamese.

"No, I am not. Not even a pocketknife," Ba said, translating the man's answer. The man was now much calmer than he had been in the seconds immediately following his surrender.

The Kid studied his face: dark eyes intent, probing, wide open, and filled with concern. *That has to be a heavy thing for a man, to surrender to his enemy's cause!*

"What is your name?" Ba asked.

"Nguyen Than," the man replied. He took another puff on the Kool, holding it Asian style, between the thumb and index finger, palm up. His hair was matted and laying flat but, strangely, had a slight curl to it, as opposed to most of the ARVNs, whose hair was cut short US military style, making it rather bristly. His face had the appearance of that of a person with some Western blood, possibly French; his eyes did not have the pronounced Asian cut to them, and his nose was more aquiline than flat.

"Toi Hashi Ba, Ti Ui Wilson, and Hashi Stocker," Ba introduced the group to the new ex-Charlie.

"OK, Corporal Ba." Wilson now had a fresh page of his legal pad turned over and had dated it, prepared to take notes on the nature of this Chu Hoi's mental state. "OK, we got his name, Nguyen Than. Ask him where's he's from."

"Where are you from? Where is your home?" Ba asked.

"A small village south of Hanoi," he answered.

"He say he from village near Hanoi," Ba told Wilson.

"Ask him how long has he been here in the South."

"How long have you been away from Hanoi and in the South?" Ba put the question to him.

"I just arrived in the Mekong Delta within the last week. It took me more than three months to walk down here bringing supplies through Laos and Cambodia."

Turning to Wilson, Ba translated, "He say he come down Ho Chi Minh Trail and just got here last week."

"Ask him why he decided to Chu Hoi!" Wilson instructed Ba, without looking up as he continued to write.

"Dai sao an Chu Hoi?"

That was a phrase the Kid was capable of understanding: "Why did you decide to turn yourself in?" Than took a long pull on the Kool, looked up at the ceiling as if to compose himself, and began to speak. The words he said and their rapidity made it impossible for the Kid to follow. After about a minute, the man shut up and Ba began to relate his tale.

"He say he leave the North in mid-May and come down Ho Chi Minh Trail carrying a load of twenty-four mortar rounds: twelve tied to front of stick, and twelve tied to back of stick. They move at night to avoid American fighters and bombers. They fight hunger, exhaustion, mosquitoes, and malaria, and sleep on the ground and in tunnels to protect them from bombings. They get attacked by Green Berets looking to interrupt the flow of war materials to the South. Some of them coming down the trail are attacked by tigers and eaten! No good job! Many are killed in bombings and by snipers. He say when he finally get to South Vietnam, he takes mortar rounds out to a position, and when he put them down, after carrying them for three months, some men there picked them up and shot them off: *boom, boom, boom, boom! And never even said hello, and most important, never say cam on u lam!*"

Wilson, Ba, and the Kid exchange glances. *They never said thank you? This guy defected because of bad manners?*

Ba continued with Than's tale: "They do not even offer him a cup of tea! They have no place for him to sleep! They ignore him completely. He is so mad and bitter that when ready to return to the North, he make decision: anything better than going back north, bringing down more shells to ungrateful southern fighters who do not say 'Cam on u lam!' So, instead of going back, he come here when he hears that we are in Cang Long."

"Hmm." Wilson was writing furiously. "I wonder if he's telling the truth?"

"Well, two things." The Kid pondered Wilson's question. "First off, we'll probably never know if he's telling the truth, because we sure can't go back and ask the other Cong if they said thank you or not. And second, what the fuck difference does it make what he says the reason is, as long as he Chu Hois?"

"His words and tone have ring of truth," Ba said, defending the new convert. "And what possible reason could he have to lie?"

"Well, Corporal, up until ten minutes ago, he was a fucking VC who was trying to kill us. That might be one reason why he'd make up some story that he wasn't from around here. But, as much as I hate to admit it, Stocker is right: what the fuck difference does it make? Come on, let's take him over and surprise the shit out of Troung! Ha! We got us a Hoi Chan!"

Chapter 46

The next day after Than the Cong had turned himself in, Ti Ui Troung and Lieutenant Wilson, along with Corporal Ba, glommed onto a passing convoy and, in Troung's jeep, personally drove their prize into Tra Vinh.

The most welcome result of all this excitement was that the Batmobile crew got yet another day off. The first thing Sweet and the Kid did after breakfast was to adjourn to the clinic and get righteously stoned. After taking another nap in the cool of the fan, the pair made their way over to the main house, where they found Lieutenant Reyes reading a Zane Grey book and Jones cleaning his M16.

"Pretty boring day and still an hour till lunch," Sweet commented as he and the Kid sat down on the couch opposite Reyes. "Not that I want any excitement, mind you," he clarified.

"Yeah, things are pretty dull out here at Cang Long most of the time." The Chicano lieutenant bent a page, closed his book, and flipped it onto the coffee table.

"Hey, I got an idea." The Kid's face lit up. "I just got some Polaroid film from home. Let's go out and take some pictures around the place. I know I want to send a couple to Flo and show her where we're at and what Cang Long is like!"

"OK, why not!" said Reyes. "Hey, Jonesie," he called to the young black-haired lieutenant who was completing the reassembly of his weapon, "we're going out to take some pictures. Want to come?"

"Sure! What the fuck!" he said, rising to put away his newly cleaned piece.

The Kid hustled back to the clinic and returned with his Polaroid camera, into which he had just loaded a new film pack. "OK, now I want some of the place. And, Sweet, you take some of me. And whatever you guys want me to take of you to send to your people is fine with me!"

The group of four made their way out the main door and began a photo tour of the Cang Long compound. The first stop was out back, where the Kid wanted a shot of the old brick French guard tower.

After handing the camera to Reyes and showing him which button to push, the Kid and Sweet climbed up on the two-step log ladder to the top, where they stood with their arms crossed, defiantly looking down on Reyes, who snapped the pic. Then they switched positions, and Reyes and Jones went up and stood on the round bottom layer of the stacked-brick shelter. As the Kid snapped the shot, the Vietnamese civilian workers' family dog, a pet today and dinner tomorrow, came running into the viewfinder's area, announcing that the main maintenance man's two young daughters were arriving on the scene. The two girls, the younger one eight and the older one ten, were always looking for a diversion from the humdrum life of Cang Long. They were such cuties with their hair cut in bangs and with shy smiles on their faces.

From there, the group and their newly acquired entourage gravitated to a mortar position, where Sweet and Reyes posed as if they were loading the tube to fire, although Sweet smiled for the picture too pleasantly to make anybody believe he was performing any task that had something to do with the war. Of course, the switch was made, then Jones and the Kid acted out the role of crew-served weapon operators.

Moving up toward the front, the Kid looked at his watch: 1130 hours, soon time for lunch. When the two girls' father, Lon, came out of the main building to see what was going on, Sweet wanted his picture taken with him, the girls, and their dog, and the Kid obliged. *That dog really likes Sweet!* As the Polaroid delivered the picture from its plastic body, the Kid took it and peeled off the backing. Lon's girls rushed over to watch their images materialize on the little square.

Giving the girls the pic to hold while it continued to process, the Kid turned around and took a snapshot of the front of the Cang Long District Headquarters Building. As he lowered the camera from his eye to take the picture in his hand, he heard strange crackling and popping noises coming from outside the open front gate of the compound. It was like a far-off voice speaking Vietnamese, weakly amplified and wafting on the breeze that now blew in the late morning. *What the fuck is that?*

The electrical static of a cheap bullhorn now came clearly to them, conveying a voice that was shouting something that, of course, was too complicated for the Kid to understand.

Cocking their heads to one side, Sweet, Jones, and Reyes tried to listen. As the speech continued, the expressions on the faces of Lon and his daughters changed from ones of fun and frolic to ones of fear. And when the voice stopped, the clear sound of an AK-47 on full automatic apparently being fired into the air outside the front gate really got their attention.

"VC! VC!" Lon yelled. He hurried his daughters back toward the main building with a quick shove. They ran for the safety of the sandbagged building.

"What in hell?" Jones gasped. "Are we being attacked?"

But as soon as it had started, it was over. Cautiously, the four Americans and Lon made their way to the front of the compound to see what they might see. But before going out the gate, because none of them were armed, Reyes signaled to the pair of guards on duty in the front-yard bunker to come up and help out. With their M16's locked and loaded, the guards took up position on either side of the white pillars and peered cautiously around the corners at the field across the street, which was where the disturbance originated.

From out of the main building, Top and Dai Ui Phan came running, both toting M16's, having been alerted by the girls that something was going on. Upon their arrival, Phan directed the two ARVN privates to rush out, cross the Cang Long road, and take up position behind the low dirt berms on its opposite side. Nothing happened. There was no firing as they cautiously peered over their piles of dirt, seeing no movement. The four Americans stayed in the compound while Phan and Top went out and investigated.

Returning, Phan had in his hands some pieces of dirty white paper, upon which something was written in black ink.

"Look!" He showed the papers to the Americans. "They scatter VC leaflets!"

The Kid reached out and took one from the ARVN captain and read it. Sure enough, it was VC propaganda.

The VC leaflet had a drawing of a soldier at the top of a 4" × 3" piece of gray newsprint-like paper who bore an uncanny resemblance to the VC soldiers depicted in the film they were now showing the villagers! The artwork could have been done with a wood print, or even a potato, the Kid thought. The type on it was roughly about twice the size of standard typewriter type. Altogether, it was rather amateurish compared to the slick four-color leaflets produced by the Americans. The text said, "Members of the Allied armies! Do not continue to fight for Thiệu and the Bellicose Ringleader Band!"

"Wow!" exclaimed the Kid. "Can you believe this? Look at this stuff! Bellicose Ringleader Band. What a great name for a rock group! Now presenting the Iron Butterfly and the Bellicose Ringleader Band!"

Sweet took one of the leaflets from Phan and examined at it. "My God, they're mocking us!" He and the Kid stared at each other with open mouths.

"You're right, Sweet! They are mocking us! The bullhorn, the leaflets, the whole nine yards!" The Kid peered out of the open gate, knowing that the

502

VC had come within thirty meters or less of the compound to deliver their message. "They did everything but show a movie! Do you think it's because Than defected to us yesterday? Is that what made them so bold or pissed that they would come up to the gate and do that?"

"No shit!" Reyes reacted. "That's not like them at all. Usually, they don't mess with us in town! I'll bet you're right about that Hoi Chan, because sure as shit about a dozen VC symps had to see him go in there to surrender to you guys!"

"We'd better be a little more careful," Jones commented. "There's change in the air. Has been ever since you-know-who showed up. Speak of the devil, here he comes now!"

Sure enough, Jones had been standing and looking back at the main building as he spoke to the group, and he had indeed seen the figure of Captain Robinson coming out of the building, a .45-caliber pistol in his right hand.

Captain Robinson cut a dashing figure as he strode toward the group near the front gate; the dash came from the black feather he wore in his jungle hat, the mark of a unit he had served with during his first tour. It made him look like one of the Three Musketeers and was totally not part of the uniform, but out in the boonies, nobody gave a shit. The feather only served to accentuate his already tall stature; he was 6'3" or 6'4" if he was an inch, and even though he sported a little bit of a paunch, he was big, strong, and muscular.

"What's this shit goin' on here?" He gave the photo group a look of condescending scorn. "There's Charlies over across the road, no shit, and y'all ain't getting ready to do nothing about it?" He stopped walking and waited, his pistol pointed toward the ground, waiting for somebody to speak up.

"Uh, yes, sir," Reyes volunteered. "Looks like they were doing a psyops operation of their own!" He held out one of the leaflets for Robinson to see.

Robinson took it and looked at it through his dark glasses as flies buzzed around the plume in his hat. "Get this weak fucking shit out of here!" he exclaimed, throwing it to the ground.

The Kid picked it up and vowed to save it. *What great stuff! I'll have to send some of this to Dave Allen! "Dear Dave, not only am I up front next to and slightly downrange from the cannons, but also I'm right across the street from a VC country club." Gee, I wonder if they really think that a leaflet like this would be capable of changing the mind of an ARVN—or even an American for that matter—and make him come over to the North Vietnamese side. Unfucking real. They are right outside the gate! But you already knew that, didn't you? Now you're talking to yourself. You're goin' nuts, Kid. How about that! Their psyops is working! I'm talking to myself!*

503

"What do you think, Top?" Robinson turned to the diminutive ARVN master sergeant. "You think we ought to get together some of the boys and go out and get 'em?"

Top looked to be strategically considering the question, glancing to Phan, his commanding officer, for guidance, but he wasn't too quick with an answer. When he finally did speak, he uttered words the Kid understood.

"Dai sao?" the diminutive man asked, wanting to know why.

Why? I mean, we do not have to go out there and try the expose ourselves enough to let them get a good shot at us. Let 'em have their fun, Captain!

Robinson was still an enigma in many ways, being so new to the command, that the group could only stand and wait, wondering what it was he was going to have them do. "What do we know?" he finally asked after a pregnant pause. "Did they go back across the canal, or are they still at the edge down there on our side?

Anybody know?" He looked at the group with the kind of contempt one might show toward a collection of itinerate schoolboys. "Anybody? Shit! Where's that blowhard Wilson when you need him? Betcha that white boy would go over there and got right after 'em himself!"

"You got that one right, sir," the Kid spoke up. "You can bet your ass he's just looking for an excuse, because he doesn't like this psyops shit we're doing right now at all. But he's not here, and I for one, as someone who has been dragged all over the Delta by him, am glad, because you are fucking absolutely on the money!"

With a sneer on his lips, Robinson wheeled and took a series of very deliberately large steps over to stand in the middle of the gate. Lifting his army-issue .45 up to an elevated, complementary forty-five-degree angle, he emptied the whole clip of nine rounds in the general direction of the tree line down by the canal.

"And don't come back, you gook muthafuckas!" he screamed, and then turned, laughing his ass off, having succeeded at thoroughly entertaining himself.

"Oh well, look at the time." He held up wrist in an exaggerated manner. "Eleven forty-five hours—time for lunch." And with that, the Captain Robinson blew the smoke from the barrel of his gun and returned the weapon to its holster, then ambled off to chow.

Chapter 47

Double-edged sword. Cutting and getting cut. The Kid had gotten to come in to Tra Vinh for his birthday, but Wilson had made him go on an operation! The Kid took a long pull on his Kool as he waited for one of the daughters of the village mayor to bring him something to drink, along with the other five members of the command element of A Company, with whom he sat at the mayor's table.

Exhaustion was the only word for it. They had just emerged from the paddies after an overnight operation and were waiting at the last village at the end of the paved road for the trucks to come and take the company back in to Tra Vinh before sunset.

Just as the command element staggered into the village, the mayor, as Captain Dalton identified him, was there to invite them all to relax at his house. And so it was that the young and haughty Tu Ta Kim, Lieutenant Wilson, Master Sergeant Rammermen (an attached lifer weapons adviser), Corporal Ba, and the Kid became his guests.

A courtyard area with a pretty garden of orange and yellow flowers running down one side and a small Buddhist platform shrine in one corner was tucked in behind a waist-high cement fence. A weatherworn wooden table was set up in the middle of it all, and there were plenty of chairs around the courtyard, indicating that frequently the table have must been the center for discussions or business activities.

From his chair at the head of the table, the slightly plump mayor hollered orders at his wife and kids; he knew these were important guests and he wanted to help them take a load off their feet. After an overnight two-day operation in the mud, it was a pleasure just to sit at a table! In addition to the five guests, Con, the bandy-legged RTO, sat in a corner of the yard, with his PRC-25 taken from his back now leaning against the fence.

Meanwhile, two platoons of ARVN soldiers from Company D, numbering about fifty, were buying tea, getting served, relaxing, and smoking at the small coffee shop across the street from the mayor's house. The shop had a large patio-like deck area with multiple tables, which was built up off the ground by about a foot. Half the ARVNs were at the tables, and the other half were sitting around the base of the elevated deck. Most were seated on their steel pots, and some had spread out ponchos where they sat and drained paddy water out of their American-style combat boots. A group of civilian women and children stood back a respectful distance, observing the unexpected visitors.

Well, it looks like I am going to live to see my twenty-first birthday, if we don't get ambushed while we're waiting here for the trucks to come. Oh man, I can't wait to get a shower. I hope we get back in time enough to go over to Wen's house and listen to Sgt. Pepper. God, I hope to hell Wilson starts bringing Sweet on his share of these things. Why does it always have to be me?

"Lieutenant Wilson," the Kid said in a voice that indicated a question was to follow, "why don't you ever bring Sweet with you on one of these while I get to sit back at Tra Vinh, like he's doing?"

Boot off, Wilson looked up from his right calf, from which he had just removed a leech, which he had been closely examining. "Well, shit. I believe that PFC Stocker does not want to be here with us, gentlemen," he suggested to the assembled company.

"It's not that, sir. It's just that, well, fair is fair. I like Sweet and all and don't wish him any harm, but I think he should get to come on some of these, that is, if you're not going to start bringing us both."

"Now, Stocker," Wilson said, snickering, "if I start letting you stay home, maybe Ba will want to stay home. And what if Con wanted to stay home? I'm not going to carry my own radio or interpret for myself, just like I wouldn't want to be expected to do what it is that you do. Oh, wait, you don't do shit! What is it you're complaining about again, Stocker? You are the most complainy private I've ever commanded. Fuck, I can't believe how you complained yesterday when I told you to bring that M16!"

True. The Kid had complained about being ordered to carry the M16, after being permitted to carry only the .38 for so long, but he followed orders. And now, the rifle was propped up against the table next to him, still unfired in combat.

"I swear, I don't know why I bring you and not Sweet." Wilson considered the Kid's question; after all, it wasn't really unreasonable. "Force of habit, I guess. What the hell!" he concluded as the drinks arrived. The mayor was springing for Coca-Colas, which suited the Kid, but the mayor's wife followed on the heels of the two daughters with a tray of shot glasses and a tall bottle of clear liquid.

Oh shit! Here comes the Bosi Dai! Of course the mayor was a hip enough host to have known that he should set his special guests up with a drink of the local ninety-proof rice liquor.

506

"Ah, cam on u lam!" Wilson nodded his approval to the smiling mayor as a glass of the liquid fire was set in front of him. Once they had all been served, including a glass for Con, the mayor raised his in a toast, after which they all drank the contents of their shot glasses.

"Numba one!" Wilson exclaimed with a liquor-induced twist on his face.

Ba hacked like the teenager he was, and one who might have just swiped a slug from his dad's liquor cabinet. The Kid drank his shot and followed it quickly with a swallow of Coke for a chaser. His mind was elsewhere. When they had come in from Cang Long on the afternoon of August 30, he'd seen a fresh copy of *Newsweek* magazine that somebody had just brought back from R & R in Hawaii. It had details in it about the riots at the Democratic National Convention in Chicago.

It seemed that the antiwar faction, deprived of Robert Kennedy as a candidate, had gone ballistic when Hubert Humphrey, who won the nomination over Eugene McCarthy, still refused to distance himself from the hawks of the party. It was all the talk that the "yuppies," a group of Abbie Hoffman and Jerry Rubin loyalists, who were similar to hippies, but more given to mayhem than making love, not war, had gone nuts and taken on the riot-gear-clad Chicago police of Mayor Richard Daly in a good old-fashioned street fight. There had been mass arrests, and clouds of tear gas had descended on the city like a fog imported from London. *Will this war ever end?*

"So, Stocker," Wilson said, trespassing on the Kid's private musings, "bet you thought we bought the farm when we got targeted by that machine gun this morning!"

"Yes, sir, you've got *that* right!" the Kid said. "It was hitting pretty fucking close! I thought it was going to eat right through that paddy dike!"

"No shit!" Dalton said, cutting in. "I was thinkin' I should have packed a snorkel so I could get submerged under that paddy water!"

The image made them all laugh nervously. That had been one dicey moment. It always started with a shot or two, and then all hell broke loose out in the middle of the open like that, where there was no real cover but lowness to the ground.

The Kid snuffed his Kool in the 155 mm brass-shell-bottom ashtray that sat centrally located in the middle of the table. He looked around at his surroundings. The two main masonry buildings of the town had most likely been built by the French sometime before World War II. They sat on either side of a spur of pocked asphalt that ran off Highway 4 to this town at the end of the line, where rice was gathered for shipment. The road had pools of

507

water in potholes from the afternoon monsoon rains that had come and gone, leaving distant clouds and blue skies temporarily overhead.

The two-day ordeal the group had just completed started eight miles to the north. They had worked their way down through tree line after tree line, taking casualties on booby traps, getting shot at, and once again, never seeing a live Charlie or a dead one.

"So, Captain Dalton, what is our official body count?" Sergeant Rammermen, the lifer weapons adviser, wanted to know. He was new to the regiment, and this had been his first operation—but not his first rodeo as he was on his second tour.

Dalton looked at Kim, who cast his eyes skyward and then earthward before answering the sergeant. "Fifteen VC KIA," he finally concluded, in this case lying. There wasn't a man at that table who didn't know there weren't fifteen VC KIA on this mission.

"We must have gotten them right at the end," the Kid said sarcastically, eliciting a laugh out of Dalton. "Where are they? Let's go take a look! Maybe do a recount. We might have broken twenty, don't you think?"

Rammermen looked at the Kid with an annoyed expression on his face, as if he did not appreciate the manner in which the Kid was questioning the validity of the answer he'd just been given. The older lifer was an E-7, with gray showing in the hair cut short around his radar dish ears. He was near the end of his career and was 100 percent army with a major WETSU attitude that left no space for criticism of his beloved employer.

The Kid took note, but he could have given a fuck less about anything that this especially ignorant lifer had to say. The men drank in silence for a few moments, listening for the engines of the trucks that were coming to pull them out and drive them back to the relative safety of Tra Vinh. But the late afternoon idyll was suddenly interrupted by a very loud argument that ignited on the patio platform of the little coffee shop across the street.

At first, there was some shouting and loud voices that attracted their attention, but then, as they looked over to see what the fuss was about, the troops on the patio began to scatter, frantically looking for cover as if they'd found a skunk in their midst. And the reason became immediately clear. One of the soldiers who'd been arguing had risen to his feet, ripped a grenade off his pistol belt, and pulled the pin, and was now shaking the live explosive in the face of his opponent. Only his enclosed fist, which held the handle of the grenade in place, prevented it from arming, but it would arm the second he released it.

The belligerent ARVN was hopping mad about something. As the man with whom he was upset backed away slowly, he kept closing on him, shaking the grenade menacingly in his face as a means of emphasizing his point in the argument. Some of the other troops were attempting to reason with him and calm him down, but the ARVN private would have no part of it. With the grenade in his left hand and the pull ring still on his right index finger, he pressed his argument to the soldier with whom he was upset.

Holy shit! If that guy lets go of the grenade, no telling where it'll land!

The members of the command element were now on their feet because the pair at the focal point of the altercation were headed in their direction, the one man backing away as slowly and cautiously as possible, not taking his eyes off the man who continued to wave the deadly miniature pineapple in his face.

Suddenly, Wilson left the mayor's courtyard and approached the pair, walking slowly, his raised, open palms showing so as not to make the troop with the grenade feel any more threatened.

"Lieutenant!" the Kid screamed. "What the fuck are you doing? Don't go there!" He grabbed his M16 and took up a position at the courtyard fence.

Without turning around, Wilson used his left hand to gesture to the Kid that he wasn't listening to him and that he should shut up and stay out of the way. The troop who was being threatened with the live grenade had quit backing up and was beginning to stand his ground.

The Kid chambered a round, flipped off his safety, and drew a bead on the ARVN with the grenade. *Jesus H.! Wilson! Are you crazy? Don't do this! My God, if that guys throws the grenade, I'm going to shoot him before he can get his hands on another weapon. If he lets go of that grenade, I will shoot him! I can't shoot him now or he will drop the grenade!*

The Kid was in a cold sweat as he sighted down his piece, his finger wrapped around the trigger, aiming for the midtorso of the angry ARVN, who was actually getting red in the face as he screamed at the gasping, shaking man with whom he was having the disagreement.

I wonder what the fuck that guy could have said to him to make him want to kill him? I can't believe you are trying to calm them down, Wilson, you dumb shit! You could get killed! If that guy throws that grenade, I will shoot him! "Sir! Get away!" the Kid cried again to Wilson out of anguish. For as much as Wilson pissed him off, made him go places they didn't have to go and do things they didn't have to do, and put him in danger unnecessarily, the Kid did not want to see him blown to bits by one of their own soldiers having a bad day.

Dalton, Kim, Ba, Con, Rammermen, the mayor, and the mayor's wife all watched from the courtyard behind the Kid as Wilson got right up next to the arguing pair in the middle of the road, about twenty meters away from them. Using hand gestures and soothing tones, he tried to convince the angry ARVN to put the pin back into the grenade.

I don't fucking believe this! I swear to God, if he lets go of that grenade, I will shoot him!

Wilson was now standing right next to the pair. It looked that the madman was beginning to cool off and that maybe he realized that he should insert the pin back into the grenade and not become a murderer. Holding the explosive device in his white-knuckle grip, the skinny private came to the decision that he should cooperate.

Wilson didn't speak enough Vietnamese to reason with the guy, so it was all French mime and tone of voice, but who would have believed it if they hadn't seen it? The lieutenant actually got the man to give him the pin from his right hand. Straightening it out and pinching it down, Wilson carefully inserted it back into the hole as he and the nutcase nervously held the grenade between them, the situation successfully defused. Wilson took the disarmed grenade from the man, whose emotions had him nearly in tears, and a wave of relief spread through the whole collection of ARVNs and civilians who had witnessed the incredible scene.

An ARVN lieutenant now rushed up and knocked the man to the ground. Then another three ARVN privates rushed up, and together they hauled the broken, crying man to his feet and took him into custody.

"Jesus H.!" Dalton cried. "Did you see that? Goddammm, Wilson, you are a fricking hero or an idiot, or an idiot hero! I've never seen anything like that in my time here!"

Wilson, who looked incredibly calm, handed the grenade to the man in whose face it had been waved in intimidation, then turned and walked slowly back to the mayor's house.

Just then, the trucks rolled up.

Chapter 48

There was a point every morning when the sun had longest been departed and the air was at the lowest temperature it would be all day at which time there was some good sleeping to be had.

In one of those rare moments, the Kid, just returning to his bunk from taking a leak, drifted off with a sweet calmness. *So cool, so cool; ah, this is the time to sleep! And it's my birthday! A day off, so Wilson isn't going to come in here and wake me up to go do any dangerous bullshit! What a fucking deal! God Almighty! I'm twenty-one! I made it! I'm twenty-fucking-one! Oh man, nothing makes you appreciate a bunk more than spending the night in a hammock! Almost didn't make it how many times? I lost count yesterday! Don't leave me now, lucky beaver.*

The fans hummed around the Tra Vinh servants' quarters billet as the army and air force enlisted men snored away. It was very nice, in fact, that the fan actually made it a little cool. The Kid pulled up his camouflage poncho liner that had been kicked to the foot of the bunk. He could hear the kitchen crew stirring in the mess hall across the courtyard, banging pots and pans, jabbering in Vietnamese, getting breakfast on the stove for the compound. If they had to be up, everybody else might as well have to be up too! *Hmm, if I were in the States, I'd be going out to get blasted tonight! Oh, if only I could be with Flo today! ... Alert: mosquito in the net. In the net. Be still. Let it land. Slap!* The Kid hit himself on the temple, smashing the little winged sapper, and settled back down. *And now she's starting school. Rats. Her senior year without dating anybody. That was bad planning on my part. I don't want her to start hating me for what she can't do. I told her to do what she wants. I can only hope she does. I wasn't thinking very smart when I asked her to marry me. Never mind that. I still love her and want to marry her. If she didn't want to marry me, she'd say so. Oh! That was so good at the Traveler's Motel. Sex is so good when you love the person you're doing it with.*

Floating with thoughts of Flo, the Kid slipped into a deep slumber. It wasn't long before he collided with the dream state. He was on the air in Nashville at WKDA. It was three o'clock in the morning, and his ass was dragging. He wanted to be with Flo in California, but he couldn't because he had to work his air shift or be in danger of losing his job as one of the Good Guys. It was tormenting him.

I love you, Flo, but I have to work! It's my future. Our future. I'm going to be a huge radio star and make a ton of money, and we're going to have a happy life and kids. Oops, the record is ending and the phone is ringing. Well, I'll just do a twin spin and answer the phone. "WKDA. Good Guy Curt Stocker."

"Is this the DJ?"

"Yes."

"Curt, I've been listening to you, and it's so late at night. I'm all alone, and your voice is making me so horny that I'm having to touch myself."

"Uh, gee, your voice isn't half bad either. And I'm touching myself—on the arm. But, you see, I'm in love with this California girl, and I'm not shopping for any phone tang, OK? Why don't you call Johnny Wailin if you wanna bug a DJ? He loves it when you talk dirty to him on the phone. Bye."

Then he heard voices, whispering, apparently trying to stifle noise for some reason—forced whispering and shussing, hissing noises.

"He's talking in his sleep!"

"Did I hear him say he was touching it?" A voice snickered loud enough for the Kid to open his eyes. Before him, he saw four men seated in folding chairs around his bunk. They were, from his head to his feet, Paul, Pete, Ernie, and Jim Sweet. As the Kid's eyes actually opened, Paul produced from behind his back a joint that was easily six inches long and as thick as a man's thumb, like a magician pulling a rabbit out of a hat.

"Happy birthday, Kid! It took me most a whole pack of papers to make this baby," Paul said. As he stuffed the gigantic joint into the Kid's mouth, the other three came up with their Zippos in unison, from down by their boots, and sparked him with a triple flame.

"I know the third man on a light is bad, but I think three lights on one joint is OK." Ernie chortled, having spoken in his Boston accent. "We decree you shall be stoned or drunk or both for the entire day!"

Heineman smiled, grinning the grin of a man who had just awakened on the day he got to go home.

The Kid took a huge puff and held it, letting his eyes bug out a little, then let it go with a big exhalation, along with which came his words. "Aw, guys, you really didn't have to!"

"No, we do have to." Paul took the joint from his hand. "I'm determined that we will smoke the rest of my cache before I fly out for Saigon at fourteen hundred hours!"

That's right, I turn twenty-one today and Paul leaves to go home. "Ah yes, we get to stop putting up with your short-timer bullshit today, don't we!" The Kid made a move to swing his feet to the floor, but Ernie and Jim blocked him.

"Before you are allowed to put a foot on the floor today, we must smoke this entire joint." Paul passed the hotly burning pillar of reefer to Pete, who got a gob of spit from his mouth and did damage control on a run getting out of hand down one side. He was dressed in fatigue pants and a forbidden white T-shirt.

"Yes, Stocker," Pete said after he exhaled. "We've got it all planned out. First, cop this major buzz, then have a little breakfast in the mess hall. After that, we come back here and smoke some more of Paul's cache, and then we di di mau over to Wen's and have lunch and listen to *Sgt. Pepper's* about a dozen times. And then we come back here, send Heineman packing, and shoot pool. Maybe beat up a couple of officers and drink until we puke or pass out, or both."

"Hey! You fucks are coming with me to the Tra Vinh Airport, aren't you? Major Gillmore and I are flying up to Saigon on Air Dumai! It should be a trip!"

"Say what? Air Dumai? Is that wise?" the Kid questioned.

"Yeah, it'll be OK. I mean, what could possibly go wrong? I doubt that we need to worry about the airport sniper. I wonder if I'm going to miss him as much as he misses us!" Paul grinned from ear to ear.

The Kid scanned his friends' faces. *In the book, the joint will be a little longer and a little thicker.* Either way, the joint came around pretty quickly that morning, but by the time there was stirrings around the billet, they hadn't finished but half of it. It had been packed by hand using only the finest Cambodian tops from a strain that was so dark that it looked like coffee and was so full of resin that it was sometimes difficult to roll it into a joint. But by leaving it out to dry in the air overnight, it had become just dehydrated enough to break into smokable form.

Apparently, Paul had been preparing this blend for more than a week for its smokability.

"Uh, guys, I really gotta take a leak. I don't want to break the rules or spoil the fun, but I gotta get out of bed now, you know, put my feet on the floor and either hit the latrine or wet my bed, for which I am way too old. However, let me assure you that I am as stoned as I need to be to meet the stoned criteria you wish to establish for the day, sir!" the Kid spieled as he swung his feet down, sprang to attention, and clad only in green boxers, snapped off a salute.

513

Standing at the trough draining his lizard, the Kid was a little wobbly from the early intake of the Cambodian.

"Happy birthday, Kid," came a greeting from behind his back as Hollis entered the latrine headed for the showers.

"Oh, is it your birthday?" inquired Vineola, the relatively new PFC from Gardenia, California, who stood at one of the sinks shaving.

"Yeah, it's my twenty-first!"

"So, that's why you guys are wakin' and bakin', huh? Well, if I make it, I'll be twenty-one in eleven months," the dark-haired, skinny troop said as he pulled the razor across his right cheek.

"Really? Fuckin' A, Vineola, you don't even look old enough to shave!" the Kid commented. He shook off his dick and turned to go back to the cubicle. *Ha! I'm talking like a fucking old man!*

Upon his return, the Kid discovered that Sweet had turned on his transistor radio, and now the low sounds of Armed Forces Radio permeated the humid morning air. The joint had been relit and was handed to the Kid. He took a deep hit and, holding it in, sat down on the edge of his bunk to pass the reefer to Pete.

"It's zero seven ten hours," the voice of Alan P. himself came over the speaker, "September 3, 1968, and I hope he is up and at 'em and listening because I want to wish my good friend and schoolmate, the Kid himself, somewhere down in the Delta, a happy twenty-first birthday. And in honor of his birthday, I know this is the song he wants to hear." The notes of Van Morrison's "Brown-Eyed Girl" began.

"All right, Kid!" Pete slugged him in the arm. "You still got the radio suction like nobody I know!"

The Kid sat on his bunk and listened to his and Flo's song as the superjoint continued to make the rounds. "Do you remember when we used to make love in the green grass behind the stadium ...?"

A bunch of other GIs poked their heads into the cubicle, taking hits, extending their congratulations to Paul on his departure, and offering birthday wishes to the Kid. After the song ended, the Kid pulled on his pants and a green T-shirt in preparation for breakfast.

Stepping out into the courtyard, the Kid saw the sunlight cutting through the towering high trees on the front of the French plantation house, painting a latticed shadow on the green grass, as the group made their way to the mess hall.

The smell of American cooking tantalized the Kid. Things had been fairly good out at Cang Long, but the night before last in the boonies, pickin's had been pretty slim.

Inside the screen door, they stopped briefly at the sign-in table and autographed the log. The Kid paid his money: $1.15 MPC. Because he was on rations not available and not near a mess hall most of the time, he actually had to pay the army when he ate at a US mess hall.

Over at the common chow line, which served both the officer side and the EM side of the mess, they all loaded up on eggs and bacon, potatoes, toast and jam, and steaming hot coffee. *And what's this? Doughnuts!* Toss on some slices of pineapple, bananas, and fresh tomato wedges and the gang was ready to do some chow.

The atmosphere was jovial as an endless stream of soldiers came over and said goodbye to Paul through the course of the meal. It was like he was holding court. The man had what everybody there wanted: a ticket home today.

Officers and enlisted men alike had been beholden to Paul, who, as Major Gillmore's chief enlisted liaison and gopher, had held a lot of power. And he never let anybody down. Need a chopper? How about some cigarettes at one of the outlying locations, or to make sure the mail got out to Tan An? Paul had been the guy.

But for the Kid, Paul's presence had had an even deeper effect. Paul had introduced the Kid to Wen's family and made it possible for him to hang out there. He also showed him how to get around town. Paul had a copy of *Sgt. Pepper's Lonely Hearts Club Band* and knew which of the Cambodian guards had all the good pot. He told the Kid the lore of the Tra Vinh Airport sniper and let him know how low Boar Hog had finished in his class at West Point (tenth from the bottom).

Even the Vietnamese cooks and all the serving women came over and said goodbye to Paul, who could only shyly smile, look down occasionally, and shake his head to mask the emotion he felt upon leaving Tra Vinh after a year, in which he had experienced the Tet Offensive and been on enough search and destroy missions to qualify for the Combat Infantry Badge fifty times over.

Major Gillmore entered the hall, his flattop-cut red hair and freckles made a little more obvious by his sunburn. He was looking for Paul, whose four companions waved to their commander, indicating they had a chair for him next to his soon- to-be-gone aide.

"Come sit on the enlisted side and see how the other half lives," Paul called out to him.

"Well, well, well! The day when I first met you, you said you thought it would never come. And here it is."

"Yes, sir. I want to thank you, sir, for all that you've done for me and the opportunity you gave me to be my own man in that job."

"You were one of the best, Paul. You never let me down. And golly, after all, you did save my life that day out there at Phu Lon."

"Well, sir, I must say I was much happier in your command after you stopped going out so much after that little incident," Paul replied, an expression of seriousness painting his features.

Through the meal, Paul and the major shared stories about near misses, comrades lost, and hardships shared, and at the end, when Gillmore rose from the table, he flipped Paul the keys to his jeep. "Here. It's got a full tank. You all can use it today. Just be sure you and these miscreants are back from where the fuck ever you might go in time for us to catch the plane."

"Wow! Thank you, sir! We'll be back before thirteen thirty hours. I'm all packed and ready, that's for fucking sure! So we'll see you then." Paul picked up the key at the end of the yellow nylon cord and went to extend his hand to the major, who slapped it out of the way and hugged him, wet-eyed, with multiple pats on the back.

"Flying Air Dumai, sir. You think that's wise?" the Kid inquired.

"Sure! Why the fuck not? It'll be Paul's and my last adventure!" the major said. He quickly added, "I mean our last adventure together, not our last, as in final, adventure." He added as he left, "Oh, and happy birthday, Stocker."

"All right!" Paul held the keys over his head. "And we'll have fun, fun, fun till Daddy takes the jeep bird away!"

Once transportation had been secured, the day became a whirlwind of stops. The group of five started by doing a driving tour of downtown Tra Vinh, ending up where Paul wanted to have coffee at the canal side one last time.

Sitting at Paul's favorite table, the one nearest the canal water, they all ordered iced coffee and smoked their American cigarettes. A boy walked by selling the morning bread. Paul motioned to him and called in Vietnamese, "La dai, em" (Come here). The homemade French bread, *bon mi* as it was called in Vietnamese, was baked in long, slender loaves about two inches thick and a little less than two feet long. The scruffy boy had the brown loaves in a basket contraption he had slung over his shoulder. The loaves stuck up out of his holder, looking like arrows in a quiver. The fact that he gave the loaf to Paul by reaching over his back and drawing it out only sealed that vision in the Kid's mind forever.

Paul pulled a hunk off the end of the fresh, aromatic loaf and took a big bite as he passed it to Jim. "I think I'm going to miss this French bread, and remember you can eat it without butter and still think it's the best!"

The Kid couldn't agree more. He had been eating a lot of the bread out in the field.

"If there is one thing those Frenchies accomplished here, it was teach 'em how to bake." Paul waxed nostalgic.

"Ah yes, but think of the things from the States you've been missing. And in just a couple or three days, you're gonna have it all!" Ernie said.

They all rose to walk back to the jeep, which had been within their sight the whole time. Paul had also paid three boys to act as guards, a few piasters each, and they now anticipated his return and their payoff as they jostled for position to be the first to get the American's money.

Paul gave them each twice what he'd promised them, and they sang in chorus,

"Cam on u lam, cam on, cam on!" (Thank you, thank you, thank you!)

Paul fired up the engine, and dropping it into gear, drove the jeep only about thirty meters before he slammed on the brakes in front of Wen's father's hardware and general store. Than was standing out front, smiling at the antics of one of his favorite Americans, who ran up to him and gave him a bear hug, then quickly wheeled to return to the jeep. Than waved at the group still in the jeep, all of whom he knew all by name, as he also knew they were on their way to his house.

Twelve blocks back from the marketplace, the jeep pulled to a screeching halt on the dirt street in front of Wen's, who came outside to greet the men. She was wearing black capri pants and a very Western-style blue blouse with her hair pulled back in a ponytail.

"Mein yoi, Mai," she said as the group de-jeeped. They weren't really staggering, but their gait was that of a rugby scrum as they pushed and shoved the guy going home and the birthday boy, who were shoving each other, in typical locker- room style.

"Mein yoi, Wen!" Paul stopped and stood in front of her as she stood in the doorway. "Toi de Saigon, fini Vietnam, beaucoup fuckin' happy!" He hugged her, picked her up, and swung her around like a kid sister.

"Wah! Heineman, you put me down!" Wen screamed, half serious and half in theatrical jest.

"OK." He put her down, and she straightened her blouse, tucking it back into her tight black pants. "*Co dep,* put down your hair for me today. That is the way I want to remember you." She immediately complied, pulling out the yellow hair tie and shaking out her black shoulder-length mane, smiling at

517

him, purely happy for his good fortune to be leaving that day to go home to his family and girlfriend.

Then Wen's hair was down, it framed her face in such a way as to make her the one woman in Tra Vinh they all wanted to fuck but never would.

"OK, Paul, you and friends, Mama-san say, can only listen to *Sgt. Pepper* three times. That is it! Last time you listen ten times—too much! She go beaucoup dinky dau!"

"OK, Wen, where is Mama-san?" Paul put his arm around her as the group moved through the door and into the Than family's living room.

"She in kitchen, cooking potatoes for you and lunch. You and Kid getting royal treatment today. Numba one. We party big-time!" With that, she released Paul's arm and rushed off to help her mother. The gang of five sat down around the table.

The table was black wood, about four feet square, at coffee table height, and upon it and around its Ming dynasty curved sides and legs were inlaid abalone shells in designs of vining plants, fish, and dragons, a masterful flowing design that nearly gave the illusion of motion.

Ernie was over at the console record player. As he stood up straight from his bent-over position, the first chords of *Sgt. Pepper's* orchestra's tuning up filled the Than family living room. "It was twenty years ago today that Sergeant Pepper taught the band to play." But as the words came out, the Kid made up his own lyrics and sang them in unison with the music:

"It was a year ago today that Sergeant Heineman came to 'Nam to play. He went out on patrol for a while when jungle fatigues were going in and out of style. So let me introduce to you the man so short, it makes me wanna tear. Sergeant Heineman's the short-as-hell DEROS man."

As the horn section played the musical bridge, the bong was out. Pete loaded it and fired it up, then passed it to Jim, who passed it to Paul, who passed it to the Kid, who passed it to Ernie. And then it was back to Pete, who reloaded it.

Wen came in from the kitchen and sat down on the couch next to Paul.

"Beaucoup sad!" Wen said, taking Paul's hand and holding the back of it to her cheek. "You no go!"

"Toi xin loi." Paul said he was sorry. "You no be my girlfriend, so why I want to stay?"

"So, you're twenty-one," Pete addressed the Kid. "What is it you would say, in your twenty-one years, is your biggest achievement?"

518

"Well." The Kid paused to consider as the bong came around again. He took his hit and held it in as he searched his memory for an answer. "I guess getting the job at WKDA and being one of the Good Guys. But when I was in the sixth grade, we had a really big slide at Uni Hill Elementary in Boulder, and when it snowed, you could ride down the thing, sitting on a piece of ice so you really picked up speed. And you hit this track we had packed into the snow, and with the right leather-soled shoes, you could slide for twenty or thirty yards! And at one lunchtime, in front of the whole school, I was the first kid who slid all the way to the school building. And when I touched it, the crowd went bananas! I guess it was my first real taste of fame."

"And now," Paul cut in, "you're a combat vet!"

"Yes." The Kid nodded his head. "But that will only be racked up in the achievement category if I live to see the States, like you, you lucky muthafucka! In three days, you'll be in Michigan!" *How many days do I got? Let's see: it's September 3, and in twenty days, I'll have four months in, which means I am at about two hundred twenty days. My God! I'm not even under two hundred!*

Agony.

Soon, Mama-san brought out some of her famous fried potatoes, golden slices lying on a stark white oval serving plate. They were just like potato chips, but these were fresh and hot and had a taste that was superior to that of the contents of any bag of commercially produced chips back in the world.

"Ah, numba one!" Paul, the true guest of honor, commented as the plate was set directly in front of him. "La dai, Mama-san." Paul patted the seat next to him on the couch as Ernie moved over to ensure Mama-san that there was room to sit down. "Come, sit." Paul rose up and, with a smile on his face, took her by the right elbow, gently guiding her into the seat. Mama-san Than smiled broadly, and you could see there was a little tear behind her glasses starting to cut a track slowly down her tan, lightly wrinkled face.

"I miss you, Heineman," she said to him as Paul put his arm over her shoulder.

"Mama-san, you know when I say I want to buy your table," Paul began, "you always think I am joking, but I am not." With that, he pulled from his pocket with his right hand a roll of bills. Unfolding it, he began to count out blue twenty-dollar MPC notes in front of her, placing them onto the surface of the table he was trying to purchase. "One hundred, two hundred, three hundred! There, Mama- san, I will give you three hundred US dollars MPC for your table."

Mama-san looked down at the money, her mouth open, forming a silent O of surprise. Then she looked back up at Paul's face, which was painted with his best I'm-so-stoned-and-blown-away-by-what's-going-on-that-I-don't-give-a-fuck- about-anything grins. Any fool could see immediately that she was not happy with the thought of selling her table.

"No take your money, Paul." She pushed the pile of military Monopoly notes over to the spot in front of him. "Sell table? *Cam bao ya!* Never."

"Aw, come on, Mama-san, I want to own your table! I can't imagine not being able to sit here and stare at it and smoke pot and eat your fried potatoes and listen to your stereo. And did I say stare at it?" The bong arrived at Paul's location.

To make sure he understood without reservation, Mama-san picked up the money, rolled it back into a bundle, and stuck it back into Paul's left breast fatigue shirt pocket. "You keep, no lose!" she admonished him.

Just when the record got to the cut of "Lucy in the Sky with Diamonds," somebody called out a greeting from the entryway to the house.

"Yo! Anybody home?"

The voice was familiar to the Kid, but it didn't register who it was until John Boujold stuck his jungle-hat-clad head in the door. "Hey, guys! I knew I'd find you here!"

"Bouji!" The Kid stood up and grasped his hand in a welcome. "How the hell did you get out of Tan An?"

"Thanks to Paul." Boujold stood with his M16 still strapped over his shoulder. "He sent a chopper out with supplies this morning, and I told Yamamoto I needed some stuff from the PX. And after all, today is your birthday, right? He's not a hard-ass, and there is a party going on as I can plainly see!" He gestured for the bong to come his way. Ernie quickly handed it over. Taking a big hit, the slightly- less-rotund-than-he-used-to-be specialist 4 blew out the smoke and laughed a hearty and gusty "Buddha Boujoldian" laugh, the kind you would have expected to come out of Falstaff in Shakespeare.

"You look for the girl with the sun in her eyes, but she's gone …"

Boujold unslung his M16, put it with the other two propped up by the door, and found a seat on the couch with Pete and Ernie. Upon landing, he let out a huge sigh and fanned his face with his jungle hat, as he was sweating profusely from the walk over.

"How's things going in the Tan An enlisted men's club, or the TAEMC, as we fondly used to call it?" the Kid asked.

"We never called it that, fondly or otherwise!" Boujold responded in mock surprise, giving the Kid a look and shaking his head.

"Well, that's what I'll call it in my book, the TAEMC," the Kid went right on. "Tay- mack. Yeah, that's it. Anyway, how are things out there? I keep waiting to hear the news that you've fragged Sergeant Matt."

"You can almost read my mind, Kid," Boujold said with a tone that contained at least half a measure of sincerity. "So, what's the plan here today?"

"Well," the Kid began, "Paul is leaving at fourteen hundred hours. He and Gillmore are flying up to Saigon on Air Dumai. Can you believe it? I sure as fuck wouldn't fly on Air Dumai, especially if I was short!"

"Yeah, Air Dumai numba ten thou!" Ernie insulted the national airline of South Vietnam.

"The airport sniper is who's numba ten thousand! He almost shot me in the ass last month!" Boujold howled.

"But, Bouji, *almost* means he didn't!" Paul leaned forward to the edge of his seat to talk more directly to Boujold. "And he never will! Why spoil a good thing? I've said it before, and I'll say it again: the first day he kills somebody, they'll be over there beating the bushes for him like people on a tiger hunt in India! That's the last thing he—or she—wants. And until then, nobody gives a flying fuck."

"You don't for a second really think the sniper is a woman, do you?" Pete asked.

"Could be. Seen some killer hard-as-nails women VC." Paul nodded.

"Ah, we all know he rarely misses his opportunity to put a few rounds over the heads of the civilians getting on the two-o'clock Air Vietnam flight to Saigon." Pete brought up a good point.

"If he's not there today, I'll feel cheated!" Paul belly laughed.

"For the benefit of Mr. Kite, there will be a show tonight at Bishops Gate. The Hendersons will all be there. And of course Henry the Horse dances the waltz." John, Paul, George, and Ringo played and sang as the time passed not very slowly.

"What's this I was hearing over at the compound about Wilson getting some steaming-mad gook private to put the pin back into a hand grenade yesterday?" Boujold inquired of the Kid. "And you were there?"

"Was I there? Shit. Fuckin' A, yeah, I was there," the Kid answered. "I couldn't believe anybody would walk over next to a couple of men who were arguing with each other over a live grenade." The Kid shook his head to emphasize his disbelief. "Told ya that mutha was crazy and not right in the head. We were sitting down drinking some Cokes when these two privates got into an argument across the street. One of them pulled the pin out of a grenade and was shaking it in the other's guy's face. Wilson walked right up to them and got the fucker to put the pin back in! Well, Wilson actually stuck the pin back in while the ARVN held onto the grenade. Talk about fuckin' hairy!"

"Tell the part about where you were gonna shoot the fucker," Ernie cut in.

"Oh yeah, I had my M16 locked and loaded, a round in the chamber, safety off. When Wilson went walking over there, I drew a bead on the guy with the grenade. If he let it go, I was going to shoot his ass before he could get any more weapons. Glad I didn't have to do it," the Kid said with relief.

"I know why Wilson did it," Jim spoke up. "It was because of you grabbin' Sergeant Mixx when he was going to shoot it out with the Cambodian guards back there a couple of weeks ago. That was slick as hell, and he's been jealous ever since!"

"Naw! That can't be it. Shit, he isn't jealous of me. He thinks I'm a candy-ass. But frankly, I don't care what he thinks, as long as he doesn't get me killed."

"And did he come close yesterday?" Paul asked.

"Oh fuck yes," the Kid said, awash in private thoughts about some of the nearest misses. "Ya know, as scary as it gets out there, I still haven't fired my weapon yet. When we're out there in it, all I ever see is the backs of the ARVNs' heads. The army doesn't pay me enough for me to want to run out in front of the enemy if I sure as hell don't have to."

"So what?" Paul cut in. "You don't have to be in front of the ARVNs to have the VC come at you."

Suddenly, Mama-san and Wen were emerging from the kitchen, both with a plate in either hand, with their special lunch.

"All right! I arrived just in time!" Boujold said. The group, who all had the munchies, dug into the chow.

There was chicken, specially fried up American style; a plateful of shrimp, their red shells and heads still attached; a huge salad with cucumbers, tomatoes, mung bean sprouts, carrots, and a bunch of other greens not as easily recognized; more potatoes; and Cokes with ice! Mama-san had pulled out all the stops.

"Now this," said the Kid as he chewed, "is where I'll write the section in the book like Thomas Wolfe. He was always the best at describing food."

"Hmm," Paul said, "that is the third time today you've referred to your phantom book. Do you think you can really do it?"

"Hell, I don't know." The Kid shrugged his shoulders. "Guess we'll have to wait and see if I live long enough. But if I do, you'll all be in it! That's for damn sure!"

"And if you did write a book about Vietnam," Pete began, "what would you call it?"

"Well, I haven't really gotten to that yet, but yeah, I need a working title." The Kid screwed up his face as he considered what that working title would be. "How about *Catch-69*? It'll be 1969 before we know it."

"Should've figured, coming from you." Sweet chuckled. "You'd just better hope the title doesn't turn out to be *Caught Gonorrhea Sixty-Nine Times*!"

Soon it was 1300 hours and time to go back to the compound to pick up the major and get Paul's gear.

Mama-san gave many hugs and cried many tears. Even Paul had moist eyes as he said his final goodbye to Wen.

"Maybe we come back after Paul flies out," Ernie said, being the last one to climb into the jeep.

"OK!" Wen waved before turning and running back inside the house. Mama-san stayed to watch the jeep motor out of sight.

Major Gillmore was waiting with his overnight bag on the plantation house's front steps when his jeep pulled into the compound and parked under the portico.

Collecting Paul's gear didn't take that long because he was traveling quite light with only one moderately sized suitcase that he had bought from Than's store.

Of course, there were more goodbyes to be said to and by Paul, and he had to rough up Rusty, the unit dog, one more time. The yellow Lab and pit bull mix was sure going to miss him.

"Partner." Sergeant Spencer appeared from inside the officers' quarters. "You all will never fit in the major's jeep, so let's all pile into the International. Let's go!"

"Thanks, Spence." Paul shook his hand. "I appreciate everything you did for me."

"You picked a good time to leave," Spencer commented as they all walked toward his vehicle. "This place is going to start changing really fast. In fact, the engineers are coming in next week to begin building a new enlisted men's barracks here, between the volleyball court and the servants' quarters. We're going to have about another thirty men stationed here as soon as it's done, so everything, from the mess hall to the latrines, will be more crowded."

That item was news to everybody who was waiting to climb aboard the airport shuttle, except Major Gillmore.

"Got everything?" Ernie inquired of Paul as Spencer turned the ignition key.

"If I don't, I don't give a shit and I don't want it!" Paul declared.

With Spencer at the wheel, Major Gillmore riding shotgun, and Paul, the Kid, Sweet, Boujold, Pete, and Ernie crammed into the back, the International rolled out of the plantation compound, down the shady tree-lined street, and out to the main road that turned into Highway 4 to drive the two miles out to the Tra Vinh Airport.

"I wish to fuck I was leaving this fuckin' place for the last time!" the Kid shouted to Paul over the noise of the engine and the wind. Paul acknowledged with a nod and a goofy short-timer's grin.

The air was extra ripe on that hot and humid day, and the odor of the rotting remains of the deceased in the cemetery across from the airport dominated the air upon their arrival.

Making a left, the International turned into the parking area of the Tra Vinh Airport. Spencer pulled the vehicle into a parking space on the shady side of the one-story airport terminal building. A number of Vietnamese nationals had already gathered for the 1400-hours Air Vietnam flight up to Ton Sa Nhut.

The old DC-3 used by the in-country airline was set to arrive any minute from Saigon.

Filing out of the vehicle, the group ambled over to the waiting area by the helipad, with Sweet carrying Paul's one suitcase. Paul walked along, clearly in a daze over what was actually happening. Major Gillmore wore his army-issue .45 on his hip, and other than the Kid's shoulder-holstered .38, the group was not armed.

Paul turned and gazed in the direction from which the sniper usually fired. He waved his arms wildly in a strange hello and farewell gesture to the unseen enemy combatant.

"That's just about where I was sitting when he nearly ass-shot me." Bouji pointed to a spot.

A group of about thirty Vietnamese travelers, civilian and military, husbands, wives, and children, waited for the plane in the protective shelter offered by the

Tra Vinh terminal building, if you could call it that. Some gathered at the wide door, looking out at the Americans, wondering why they had chosen to tempt the fates by egging on the infamous Tra Vinh Airport sniper.

The group sat there in the sun at the hottest part of the day, listening for rifle fire, smoking cigarettes, and not talking much because, at this point, there wasn't much to say that hadn't already been said a couple of times that day. Five minutes passed, then at last the engines of the arriving flight could he heard in the distance.

"There it is," Paul said, pointing to the black speck that came into view, turning on its final approach. "He's savin' it for when the plane comes; I think that's one of his assignments."

After another two minutes, the DC-3 was setting down at the end of the runway. The three-man ARVN ground crew and the Vietnamese nationals who had been waiting inside the terminal began to emerge and walk toward the loading area.

By the time the plane rolled down to their end of the runway, the group had moved up and were now nearly even with where the Americans were sitting on the helipad bench.

The ARVN empowered with the clipboard used it to wave the olive-green aircraft over to its mark. The logo for Air Vietnam was nothing more than a yellow- and red-striped South Vietnamese flag painted on the fuselage over the wing and above the diminutive row of windows. The logo distinguished the DC-3 passenger craft from its identical military brother, the C-47, which had no windows.

When the plane stopped, the other two ARVNs rushed in from either side and flipped pairs of wheel chocks into place, securing its position. As they did so, the Tra Vinh Airport sniper, as dependable as Old Faithful, opened up. At least three rifle shots echoed across the field. They must have gone right over the departing passengers' heads because they all fell to the ground. And babies started crying!

"There he is!" Paul jumped up and pumped his fist, bowing low from the waist. "Right on time! "Yesssss!" He danced an impromptu jig. The seven other Americans began laughing their asses off at his antics. Waving their hands over their heads and clapping and bowing, the group, save Major Gillmore, paid kudos to their invisible, but always ultimately polite, nemesis.

Kid slapped Paul on the back. "There you go. He says goodbye!"

"Now, how can he never hit anybody and keep his job?" Sweet asked, incredulous.

"Maybe he's a high-ranking VC and he does this for entertainment. You know, guy doesn't have a TV and is looking for some fun. I mean, hell, the party pays for his ammo, he gets to take a healthy walk and nobody gets hurt," Paul said, speculating on the life of their unseen semi-enemy.

The confused looks on the faces of the Vietnamese passengers, who were now kneeling down at the waiting area, clearly demonstrated they had no clear idea of what they should do. For the moment, the sniper had stopped shooting. The three ARVN ground crewmen, knowing the sniper's routine, nonchalantly went about their business. They urged the group to get up and move forward, directing them with hand gestures to the spot from where they would load.

The engines idled and the propellers continued to spin as the rear door opened and a three-step ladder was positioned by one of the crewmen. The arriving passengers deplaned quickly as the Saigon-bound passengers prepared to load, their *áo dàis* flapping in the wind, all of them struggling to hold onto hats and other items as they were blown about by the prop wash of the DC-3 engine.

"Well, I guess this is it, guys." Paul stood with his back to the plane, looking at his crew. Then he went down the line, hugging each one, with pats on the back and wishes of good luck. Looking over, he saw that the other Saigon passengers were half loaded.

"Paul, let's go!" Major Gillmore called out. Together, the pair walked toward the steps leading up into the old airliner.

The remaining six took seats on the bench, long-faced, waiting to see their friend and commander take off. The Kid and everyone else lit up a cigarette, almost in unison, and they smoked in silence, each with his own thoughts of how much he longed to arrive at this day of departure, the day when he would actually get on a plane to go home.

Before he stepped out of the line of sight behind the tail, Paul waved to the men again. Now the only part of his body they could see was his feet as he walked up to and then ascended the ladder into the plane.

Once the aircraft was loaded, the ground crew closed the door, picked up the ladder, and pulled away the chocks in short order. The twin engines revved up as the pilot prepared to bring the Air Vietnam DC-3 around to taxi into takeoff position, but when it started to move, the right engine at first sputtered and then began emitting black smoke, before all of a sudden bursting into flames!

"Holy fuckin' shit!" The Kid jumped up. "Look at that!" *Oh my God! What the fuck is going on?*

526

"Fire!" members of the group yelled in unison as flames shot up out of the engine cowling, bright orange and burning with a vengeance.

"Shit, fire!" Ernie screamed. "I think the sniper hit that engine!"

Of course there was no fire equipment at the Tra Vinh Airport, not even a fire extinguisher on the flight line. The pilots must have completely shut the systems down, because the right engine stopped and two of the ground crew were rushing to get the ladder back to the door to evacuate the aircraft as the left engine continued to burn.

"Jesus Christ! Paul and the major are flying up to Saigon in that?" Ernie exclaimed with disbelief.

"I think not," Sweet replied.

Sure enough, less than two minutes later, the major and Paul were again standing next to them on the runway, bags in hand.

"Welcome back!" Pete said. "Did you guys have a nice flight?"

"You can thank your buddy. We think he hit the engine." Boujold smiled, seeing a certain moral victory in the fact that the Tra Vinh Airport sniper had finally shot something other than the ground.

"Meet any cute stewardesses?" Ernie inquired with a smile.

"Shit!" Major Gillmore screamed. "Can you believe that? We can always get a chopper up tomorrow morning, but there goes my hot night in Saigon!"

"Bummer!" said the Kid. "But it's a good thing your hot time here at the airport happened on the ground, before you were in the air!"

Chapter 49

The lone MSQ-85 rumbled down the road toward Cang Long. With four soldiers sitting shoulder to shoulder in the front seat, it made it a little crowded, but it had to be done.

As usual, Lieutenant Wilson was driving and the Kid was riding shotgun. Corporal Ba was sitting next to the Kid, and between him and Wilson was Lieutenant Bill Hilgers, a pay officer from Can Tho. It seemed that when payday rolled around at the end of August, headquarters had forgotten to include Jim Sweet on the Tra Vinh payroll. Consequently, they had to send Lieutenant Hilgers all the way down specifically to pay him. And since on the day he arrived Sweet had stayed behind, rather than come in on a supply run, Lieutenant Hilgers was obligated to ride out to Cang Long in order to pay him. Of course it was hot, but it wasn't too dusty because it had rained around 1230 hours. At 1300 hours, the road was still damp enough to keep the dust down.

Lieutenant Hilgers sat, sweating, with his valise on his lap, in which were located Sweet's hard-earned military payment certificates. For Hilgers, it was quite a unique experience because he had only been in-country for about two weeks.

This little excursion was his first trip outside Can Tho and into the countryside, where he might encounter some genuine danger.

Glancing over at him periodically, the Kid could see that Hilgers was nervous. And with good reason. The MSQ-85 was the only vehicle in their "convoy." The Kid and Ba were plenty nervous as well. Perhaps the minor confrontation between the Kid and Wilson before departure had contributed to this situation. The Kid had had the nerve to suggest to Wilson that they wait to go to Cang Long until they had some other jeeps or trucks with which to travel. Wilson at first laughed at him, and then berated him for showing his "chicken feathers," an insult the Kid felt was undeserved. *What, does somebody have to get killed to prove he's not chicken? There's a big difference between chicken and stupid!*

The sweat on Hilger's face and the bouncing of the truck kept making his gray army-issue glasses slide down his slightly bulbous nose. He was forever

528

pushing them back up. Hilger's hair, visible below his baseball cap, was a very dark red, and his face was darker in complexion and not as fair-skinned as many true bright redheads. He wasn't a big guy, but he was larger than either Wilson or the Kid. And the diminutive Ba was crushed into his seat, bookended by the Americans. They rode along in silence, save for the roar of the engine and the bouncing of the truck, as Wilson managed to hit a never-ending string of potholes.

A green cloth bandolier holding M16 clips was hung from the glove compartment knob in front of the Kid, who sat with his M16 between his legs, his arm resting on the open windowsill. Suddenly, it dawned on him that it was a special day: September 11. *Oh yeah! Today is the anniversary of the day I was inducted into the army. One year down and two years to go. I can't believe I took an extra year for Armed Forces Radio. Without that, today I'd be halfway done. And I'm in Vietnam in combat anyway, so what the fuck did I get for taking another year? Gil, if I ever find you, I will seriously kill you, you and your "Curt, I can get you into Armed Forces Radio" bullshit! Stupid, stupid, stupid! A year ago today, I was in Nashville, on my way to boot camp at Fort Campbell, Kentucky. And where am I today? In a fucking MSQ-85 in the Mekong Delta with no convoy, armed with one rifle and three pistols, driving out to Cang Long! I swear to God, Wilson, if you get us killed, I'll kill you! Maybe that bastard ARVN should have dropped that grenade on you. How the fuck did I ever come to be here?*

There had not been any traffic heading down the highway in the opposite direction for some time now. The MSQ-85 was approaching the hamlet of Nguyet Hang, nearly the halfway point of the trip to Cang Long, when the Kid decided he was going to see if he could manage to light a cigarette when they slowed down to go over the Nguyet Hang bridge. He was staring out the window, looking at the tree line, absentmindedly unbuttoning his breast pocket to get out a Kool, when he heard the now unmistakable sound of a bullet cutting past extremely close to his left ear.

To listen to any of the four of them tell it later, and from the physical evidence, the only thing that could have happened right then was that bullet came in the passenger's-side window, went past the Kid's ear, Ba's forehead, Hilger's nose and Wilson's eyebrows, and went out the driver's-side window without hitting anything. If the bullet's flight path had been six inches to the left, it might well have gone right through all four of their heads! But there was no time to think of that then, because the harbinger was followed by a burst of automatic weapon fire!

"Jesus H. Christ!" the Kid screamed. "Sniper!"

Wilson, who got the message loud and clear, downshifted and jammed his foot to the floor. The Batmobile jumped up and almost did a wheelie as he gunned it.

Hilger might well have crapped in his pants because this was, after all, his personal baptism of fire, and Ba was trying to hide on the floor—and doing a pretty good job of it.

The Kid hoisted up his M16, chambered a round, flipped off the safety, and leveling it at the tree line from which the enemy fire was coming, pulled the trigger back and held it there for full automatic, but the gun fired only once.

"Holy fuck!" The Kid couldn't believe it. "It's *jammed*!" *All the fucking stories I've ever read about the M16 jamming in combat, and the first time I go to fire mine, it's* jammed*!* "Oh, wait a minute! Oops! I only had it on semiautomatic!"

Throwing the selector to automatic, the Kid wheeled and, with his back to the windshield, almost sitting on top of Ba, opened up with a full burst of seventeen rounds. The M16 was spitting out hot brass all over in the cab. One of the shell casings went down Hilger's shirt, and he let out a scream as if he'd been hit. The Kid ejected the empty clip, pulled a fresh one out of the bandolier, and slammed it into the breech, firing another eighteen rounds out into the jungle. It was full mayhem in the cab of the truck. *I can't see shit! I just gotta spray everywhere to suppress and hope I get lucky!* Changing clips as quickly as he could, the Kid ripped off another eighteen rounds.

All the while, Wilson was driving like some crazy redneck mutha at Daytona. Before the Kid realized it, they had come to the Nguyet Hang bridge, and the lieutenant had to slow down. He saw there was apparently no traffic on the bridge, which was a good thing, so he drove ahead. But once the truck was up on the bridge, in an elevated position, he saw them and slammed on the brakes.

Two buses were pulled up to the bridge and were blocking the way off it. The drivers were out on the road in front of them, arguing about who was going to go first. And onto this scene arrived the Batmobile and its rolling gunfight. Right about then, the bus drivers and some of the passengers who were out observing the argument were starting to realize that hostile fire was coming in their direction.

The sniper continued to fire and the Kid continued to fire back as the Batmobile sat perched up on the bridge, a most attractive target.

Wilson leaned out his window, screaming and frantically gesturing with his arms at the same time. "Get those fucking buses out of the way! I'm coming down. You had better move those fucking buses *right fucking now*! Move it! Move it! Move it! You *assholes*!"

Now, in all likelihood, the Vietnamese bus drivers did not understand a word that Wilson said, but his foaming-at-the-mouth screaming punctuated by gunfire seemed to get the message across. The drivers fairly flew into their buses and, in a flash, had them backed up enough to allow Wilson to drive the MSQ-85 off the bridge and down to the lower level.

Once they were down off the bridge, the Kid stopped shooting. In the eerie ear- ringing silence, they determined there was no longer any incoming fire.

"Everybody OK?" Wilson checked for casualties as he opened his door and stepped down.

"My gawd!" Hilgers exclaimed. "That one bullet almost took my head off!" "Mine too!" said Wilson.

"Mine too!" said the Kid, adrenalin flowing freely through his veins. "I just fired my weapon in combat! Hey, I wonder if I killed anything?"

"I don't know! Too busy trying to hide!" Ba was still working his way up off the floorboards as the Kid cleared his weapon. He had shot a total of six clips.

"When I left Can Tho, Captain Ronnie Smith said this would be easy!" Hilger gasped as he gathered the valise that had Sweet's pay in it; it had been momentarily unguarded during the fracas.

Wilson inspected the truck as the Vietnamese residents and bus passengers began to emerge from where they had taken cover. "Hmm, I don't see a single bullet hole! I'll be fucking damned! We'll have to look closer at Cang Long. Can't stand around here. Those guys are still within range!"

Back into the truck once again, they were rolling down Highway 4. As they passed the Buddhist monastery, the Kid couldn't help but note that the boys weren't out on the veranda today. *I gotta wonder if it was one of them!* They arrived at Cang Long without further incident.

When they entered the gate and parked, Doc, Sweet, Reyes, Robinson, and Jones walked casually out of the main building, primarily anxious to get the mail they were bringing back.

"Hey!" Lieutenant Reyes called out as the men began to climb out of the Batmobile. "How'd it go?"

As the Kid stepped down out of the passenger door, Sweet noticed he had a particularly goofy-looking grin on his face. "You did get the mail, right?" he inquired.

"Yeah, we so got the mail. We also got hit by a sniper, right at the Nguyet Hang bridge."

531

"No shit?" Captain Robinson said. "Everybody OK?"

"Yep." Wilson lit up and began walking around the truck, giving it a more thorough examination for damage. "At first glance, back at Nguyet Hang, it didn't look like we got hit. Do you see any bullet holes, Stocker?"

"No, but I'll tell you, I swear to God, that first round came right through the cab!" the Kid exclaimed, still holding his M16 by the carrying handle.

"No fucking shit!" Hilgers said, looking quite shaken as he held the pay valise under his arm. "That was my cherry popper!"

"Uh, this is Lieutenant Hilgers." Wilson introduced the unknown officer to the others. "He's here to pay Sweet, and then as soon as he can, he's going back. Sweet, you still wanna get paid, don't you?"

"Yes, sir, I do!" responded Sweet. "And get my mail, too!" Then turning to the Kid, he asked, "Do I have any letters from Barbara?"

"Guess how many?" The Kid grinned at him.

"I'll be happy with one."

"Well, then you're going to be five times happy!" he informed him.

"All right!" He was cheered by the news.

Doc said to Hilgers, "We've got a bunk for you; I don't suppose you want to hitch back to Tra Vinh tonight."

"No, you've got that one right," the still shaking newbie intoned. "What I'd like is a stiff drink and a chopper to come out here and get me!"

"Well, we've got the stiff drink, but that second thing, that ain't gonna happen," Captain Robinson deadpanned. "In fact, it might be a couple of days before any convoys go back, so you are stuck here with us."

While they were talking, the Kid opened up the door to the Batmobile cab and looked inside. "Hey, Sweet, look at all the brass! I must've shot up a half dozen clips!"

Sure enough, there was a ton of brass on the floorboards and in the crack of the seat, and a couple more lying on the running board.

"That must have been some shoot-out!" Sweet picked up a spent shell and looked at it closely before tossing it aside.

"Yeah. When I first opened up, this thing fired once and quit. I thought it jammed on me, but I found out I only had it on semiautomatic. I guess I'll never know if I hit anything or not. I could have hit some VC, or chickens or pigs. I know I had to have hit some trees. And they kept shooting at us, so I think it's safe to say I didn't hardly suppress them either."

"Nope, I don't see a single bullet hole!" Wilson said, clearly amazed, once he had finished his walk around inspection of the truck. "That in itself is pretty fucking amazing! That first round, it had to have gone right through the cab. Swear to God!"

"Ahem." Reyes walked up to Wilson. "The mail, *por favor.*"

"Oh, right." Wilson walked around to the rear door of the truck, opened it up, retrieved a brown sack into which the Cang Long mail had been tucked, and handed it to Reyes.

Pulling out a handful of letters, Reyes held the mail call right there; it had been four days since the Cang Long boys had last gotten mail. As soon as Sweet got his letters, he and the Kid headed for the clinic.

Once inside, Sweet sat down on his cot and began opening his cherished letters from Barbara.

The Kid put his M16 in the corner. "Now I have to clean this fucking thing!"

"So?" Sweet questioned, "You got some other plans for tonight I don't know about?"

"No. I just hate cleaning the fucking thing," he said. He pulled the mail, which

he'd already read back in Tra Vinh, out of his lower left fatigue pants pocket and tossed it onto his bunk. "Not that this is a contest, but I got six letters from Flo and a bunch of birthday cards from a whole lot of people, including five from Nashville fans!"

"Aren't you special," Sweet commented, without looking up from the pink stationery that was Barbara's favorite.

The Kid unbuttoned his fatigue shirt and hung it on the corner of his cot from the mosquito net support. Sitting down on his cot, he dipped his pipe into his pocket cache, fired it up, and took a gigantic hit. "Fuckin' A. I told Wilson before we left that we should wait for some more trucks to go with us, but no fucking way he's ever going to listen to me."

Sweet stopped reading and looked up. "Why, Kid, I do believe your hands are shaking."

Chapter 50

An hour and a half before dinner, Sweet and the Kid walked over from the clinic to the main building to begin their nightly shower routine. The first part of the routine was the lifting of the water from the well to the fifty-five-gallon metal drum that was the shower's holding tank. This process usually took anywhere from half an hour to forty-five minutes, with a smoke break at the halfway point.

Then the second part was getting their showers taken first, so that they, the men who hoisted the water, would not suffer the possibility of being the ones left soaped up and in the lurch when the supply ran out.

Entering the main common area of the Cang Long American addition, the pair spied Lieutenant Hilger, who was sitting by himself on one of the sofas over by the radio table, trying to look absorbed in a copy of *Stars and Stripes*. He had performed his mission of paying Sweet three hours ago and, since then, had a total of zip to do except sit around and think about almost getting his brains blown out that afternoon.

The rest of the Americans were scattered. Doc was doing supply paperwork and making requisitions at the atrium table, across from Robinson, who was reading a *Life* magazine. Wilson was apparently still taking a nap.

"Hey, sir, how's it going for you here at our exciting outpost?" the Kid inquired in a genial tone of voice as he and Sweet came to stand by Hilger's feet, which were propped up on wooden spool coffee table.

"Oh, hi. Not bad, but shit," he said, laying down the newspaper, "you guys don't have jack out here, do you? No PX, no real town, no movies, mail only once or twice a week. God, I hope I don't end up here." Hilgers smiled nervously, knowing he was talking to men who had to stay when he left. "I mean, I would if I had to, just like you guys. It's the army!"

"Yes, no doubt," Sweet began, "but you're an administrative man, attached to accounting, aren't you?"

"Well, yeah." Hilger lit up a cigarette.

"Then you probably won't have to be out here any more than this, I'd imagine. But the way I understand it, after a few months in Can Tho, guys want to come out here. Isn't that right, Kid?"

"Oh, for sure! There's no place I'd rather be. I mean, Armed Forces Radio? Why would I want to do that? But here's the bottom line. All I know for certain"—the Kid leaned forward toward Hilgers, as if he were going to truly impart some secret knowledge—"is that me and Sweet are going to haul water to take a shower. That's the only way you can get one here. And if you don't want to be the one at the end of the line or have to haul the water up two levels by yourself, I strongly suggest you join me and Mr. Sweet in filling the barrel, which is the only way an interloper such as yourself is going to jump to the head of the shower line."

As it sank into the lieutenant's skull what the Kid was saying to him, a grin broke out across his face. "OK, I've got no problem with that." He rose to his feet and followed the two privates across the room and into the dinning atrium, where Robinson sat with Doc.

"Hi, Doc. Hey, Captain R.," the Kid said as they walked past them on their way to the shower. "Looks like we got us a recruit for water duty!"

"Uh," Hilger began with a flavor of uncertainty, "I wasn't planning on being out here, so I didn't bring soap, shampoo, a towel, or anything. I have my toothbrush, but that is about it."

"No problem." Doc immediately jumped up. "I'll get you a spare towel. And we've got all that other stuff, sir. And ya know, you don't really have to help those privates; you'll get a shower anyway."

"Oh, I don't mind." Hilger smiled. "I've got nothing else to do."

"My experience is," Robinson said, cutting in, "don't you go listenin' to any of this bullshit comin' out of Stocker's mouth. If you let those EMs get soft, they'll be too soft to help you when the chips are down; you oughta make them haul the water."

"Beg pardon, sir, and with all due respect, sir," the Kid said, sugarcoating his response, "don't go givin' our recruit any mutinous ideas. When we're here, we haul the water all the time for every Americans' shower, and he's got nothing on his hands but time. It's a match made in Cang Long! Come on, sir." He turned back to Hilger. "We'll go easy on ya!" he said, gesturing in such a way to indicate that they should all proceed to the task at hand.

Walking through the kitchen with Hilgers in tow, the Kid and Sweet greeted Co An and the two other Vietnamese workers, who were busy preparing dinner.

535

Arriving at the well, the Kid pointed to a dirty-looking white plastic bucket at the end of a yellow nylon rope. He explained to Hilger what the drill was going to be. "The water's in that there well, and the shower storage reservoir is up there." He directed the freckle-faced lieutenant's eyes to the barrel in the sky. "One guy here on the well, one guy there on the platform. The water comes up from the well and gets dumped into the up-bucket, here, and that gets hoisted up and dumped there. We usually do thirty-five buckets, but because of you, we'll do forty-five tonight."

Sweet handed Hilger the rope connected to the up-bucket. "You can start on top. And don't worry." Sweet smiled. "Nobody's been sniped at up there yet!" Hilger grinned back, at which time the Kid threw in a comment.

"But there's always a first time!"

The smile faded from the visitor's face.

"Only *kidding*!" said the Kid. "That's why they call me the Kid!"

"Yeah, I was wondering about that," Hilger said. He turned, mounted the ladder, and began his ascent to his position.

"Actually, that was my disc jockey nickname," the Kid explained as Hilger continued to climb. "I was really young at the time."

"Still young," Sweet added.

"Forever young, yeah, but a lot older after today!" the Kid shot back. "How about you, Lieutenant? Do you feel older now that you've been shot at in this war?"

Arriving at the top of the platform by the barrel, Hilger turned and gazed down upon the pair. "Without a doubt! I took ROTC in college, along with accounting, and I figured when I graduated, I'd have to go into the army but that I'd be in the clerk corps and never see any action. Wrong! Hope I don't see any more!"

By this time, the Kid had hoisted the first bucket up from the well and dumped it into the up-bucket. Hilger, putting his back and hands into the job, raised the bucket with minimal spillage.

"Very good, sir." Sweet, who had hauled up the second bucket, applauded, waiting for Hilgers to drop his from the top to continue to process. And on it went, the Kid and Sweet taking turns hauling buckets up from the well, and Hilgers taking them all on to the top, meaning the lieutenant was working twice as hard as either of the privates. When they got to fifteenth bucket, the Kid called for a break, and they all lit up.

"OK, now you can come down. Sweet will take your place up on top." The Kid took on the role of director of operations.

Hilgers climbed carefully down from the water storage platform and stood at the bottom of the ladder, sweat emitting from every pore of his body. "This is hard fucking work! I'm really going to enjoy this shower. You know, ya take a lot of this stuff for granted back in Can Tho, a shower and a meal and a safe place to hang out. This is fucking wild out here in the boonies."

Just then the artillery unit down the road fired a three-round salvo that went right over their heads. Hilger almost dove to the ground.

"Good thing you weren't still up on top!" Sweet joked.

"It takes awhile to get used to the artillery, sir, but hell, this is fucking paradise compared to Tan An." The Kid blew out a puff of smoke. "Over that way about five miles is this fortified compound built around an old Catholic monastery that is really the epitome of being way out in the boonies. We'd have killed for a shower like this out there. Where are you from, sir?"

"Iowa, a little town called Mason City, in the central part of the state. It is the town that *The Music Man* musical is patterned after—River City," Hilgers related to the pair.

"Oh yeah, I've seen the movie," Sweet said. He began to quote lines from a song in the show: "We got trouble right here in Cang Long city, with a capital *C*, and that rhymes with *V*, and that stands for Cong!"

"Ha! That's rich!" Hilgers chuckled before flicking his butt away and dropping the bucket down the well. Sweet turned and began climbing up the ladder.

Once Sweet was in position on the top, the process began again: bucket from the well poured into the bucket at the top. Fill and empty, fill and empty. On one of his turns, the Kid dropped the bucket down the well, and as he did so, his glasses slipped from his sweat-soaked face and almost went down into the well. But in a knee-jerk reaction, the Kid reached out and speared the glasses by the end of an earpiece, saving them from being lost!

"Jeez!" exclaimed Hilgers. "That was a stroke of luck! What a save! If your glasses went in there, they'd most likely be flat gone! I mean, how deep is this thing?"

"Whoa! No shit! Deep enough!" The Kid had impressed even himself with his wild lunge to grab the errant spectacles. "And this is my last pair of regulars; I got one pair broken about a month ago. If I'd have lost these, I'd be down to just my prescription sunglasses!"

After twenty-five more buckets with the Kid up on top, the barrel was nearly full. The crew judged there was enough water for all the Americans to enjoy a short shower, which at Cang Long was the absolute high point of the day.

Doc showed up with a towel, soap on a rope, and a bottle of shampoo for Hilgers to use. Sweet and the Kid prepared to return to their quarters to retrieve their gear.

"Now, no jumping the line, sir," said the Kid. "You're third, OK? And don't let Captain Robinson cut in here ahead of you. He thinks just because he's a captain and CO here that that gives him certain privileges." The Kid had noticed, when he began speaking, the flapping approach of Robinson's flip-flops as he walked up with his green towel wrapped around his dark frame, toting his gear and ready to step into the shower.

"What you spoutin', PFC?"

"Oh! Hi, sir." The Kid feigned surprise that the captain should be hearing his words. He turned to face the muscular man. "I was just saying that rank has its privileges, sir. And your shower is ready!"

"Uh-huh, that's what I thought you were sayin'." Robinson wasn't smiling as he pushed past the trio, showing them his broad back as he stepped into the shower, pulling the green canvas curtain closed behind him.

"OK, so you're fourth," Sweet said, stating the obvious to Hilgers with a shrug of his sunburned shoulders.

Back from the clinic, Sweet and the Kid played their nightly match of rock, paper, scissors to see who was going first. Sweet threw a rock, and the Kid threw scissors.

As Sweet went on back for his shower, the Kid stopped in the main area and picked up the old copy of *Stars and Stripes* that Hilgers had been reading earlier. He sat down to peruse it. Opening up the newspaper, his eyes fell upon the column that listed the casualties from the war.

The headline above the list of names, which took up nearly a whole page, was "285 Americans Killed in Action." For no specific reason, the Kid's eyes began drifting down through the columns, alphabetically listed, each name signifying nothing more to him than a faceless victim, a grieving family back home, and a funeral in a town that was offering another son as a sacrifice on the altar of the Vietnam War, so that others won't have died in vain.

Then he saw it. "Imbach III, John, NMI [no middle initial]."

A harrowingly cold chill ran up his spine. *My God! The Boy Scout! The Boy Scout was killed in action! Holy mother of God! Imbach is dead!*

The paper nearly fell from his hands. The Kid was stunned. It washed over him and sank in that one of his DINFOS classmates and even one of his roommates had been killed! He thought back to the last time he'd seen Imbach, waiting with Waterhouse to take the chopper down to My Tho for

538

their assignment with the American Ninth Division. The Kid looked at the date on the top of the page.

August 25. *Two-week-old paper. John has been dead for more than two weeks. He barely made it three months. But in my mind, he was alive until this second. I wonder how it happened? I gotta find a way to write to Waterhouse. I wonder how many of the other guys have seen this?*

Sitting there, the Kid was still in shock, staring at the newsprint that bore word of his friend's death, when Lieutenant Wilson strolled out of the bunk area and into the commons and encountered him.

"Yo, Stocker, I thought you'd be out of the shower by now. You look pale. What gives?"

"Uh." He pointed to the casualty list. "One of my roommates from DINFOS was killed in action a couple of weeks ago."

"Oh no!" the lieutenant sympathetically exclaimed. "Shit. That reminds me, I should take a look later, too. Ya never know in this business. Looks like Sweet is out. You goin' or stayin'?"

"Goin'," the Kid said as he rose and headed on back. Passing Sweet along the way, he stopped him and said, "I just read in Stars and Stripes that I lost a classmate from DINFOS!"

"Damn! Where was he assigned?"

"He was a roommate, one of those two guys who got assigned to the 9th Division Public Information Office that I was telling you about, just up the road in My Tho. Not the one who was one of my best friends, but the other guy, the one we used to call 'Boy Scout.'"

Sweet could see that the Kid was fairly shaken up. "That's too sad! But what can any of us do? Fucking nothing." He shook his head as he walked off.

Entering the shower, the Kid took off his green towel and hung it on the hook along with his shaving kit. Getting out his soap dish, he was ready to get wet. Pulling the cord, he felt the brownish cold water cascade out of the showerhead and collide with his hot, dirty body in a soothing double treat of cold and wetness. For six months, he had slept in the same room as Imbach, showered in the same latrine as Imbach, eaten in the same mess hall with Imbach, and attended classes with Imbach.

Funny the things you remember. Imbach was so funny on KP! Telling stories about how the Boy Scouts got him ready for the army KP because they all had to help in the kitchens on jamborees and had so much fun playing KP pranks. Ha! What a scream! I wonder if he knew we were laughing at him and not with him? Ah, jeez. Boy Scout het roi. Dead. I wonder how he got it? Did he get it in the head, or the heart, or the gut? Was he dead instantly, or did he suffer? Oh jeez! No; you gotta believe he's going on to a better place.

The Kid released the rope lever, and the water shut off while he soaped up his head, where his blond hair was starting to get a little of its length back. He remembered how blond John's hair had been—and how fair-skinned he was. That had to be trouble here in the tropics. The Kid left the shampoo in his hair while he grabbed the bar of Dial and began to lather up. Running a hand over his face, he determined his mustache was beginning to get pretty bushy, although it still had a couple of weeks to go to become a real one. As he washed his own head, he recalled the body of the first dead VC he'd seen, the one with his brains blown out. He couldn't help but imagine poor John lying somewhere on the jungle floor with a similar hole in his head. Or was he riddled up like the two guys next to him? *Shit! I remember the night field exercise at Fort Riley, sitting in the foxhole, waiting for the fake Cong to attack. I wonder if he could see his own death, just like I used to see those soldiers' silhouettes in front of the napalm strike. Well, he knows the answer to the thing we used to argue about, him with his Bible-thumpin' old-time religion. Is it heaven and a hell? Or is it reincarnation? Is there karma? Is Jesus the only way? So, John, you can now make your point from the position of having performed deeper research than me. Why do I feel this previous life thing so strongly? It may not yet, thank God, be my turn to find out. Or maybe it is. Maybe I'm next. But I know one thing for absolutely certain at this second in time and in this very spot.* The Kid pulled the rope, causing the brown water to spill down from the showerhead and splash all over him. *I'm fucking lucky to be alive!*

Chapter 51

September 17, 1968

My Dearest Beloved Parnelli,

This place is interesting because here you can go swimming without ever going to a pool. What I mean is, every pore of my body is oozing and I'm swimming in sweat! And the fan offers no relief, and it's two o'clock in the afternoon on a Saturday, but every day is just like every other day here. All I know is that it's another day without you, making it a day I'd just as soon forget.

This morning, we were scheduled to do a CAP to the north in a hamlet cluster out past the Vinh Long bridge. I've got to admit, for as long as I've known Ti Ui Troung, which is about three and a half months now, I've never seen him as nervous as he got this morning! What happened was, first our security detail didn't show up at the appointed time, but we went ahead and set up anyhow. Then, right when Troung was supposed to give his big speech, before we showed the movies, Lieutenant Wilson like just turned around and walked off because it was time for the country- and-western music show to start on AFVN. He never missed the morning country-and-western hour, so he was sitting over in the back of the Batmobile listening to his transistor, not paying any attention to security. I and Jim were fiddling around with the projector; Ba was talking to a bunch of kids; and Troung all of a sudden started screaming. He ran to his jeep, grabbed his M16, and chambered a round. At first, we thought he'd seen a Charlie. Then he started screaming at Wilson, and after thirty seconds of turning red in the face and spitting while talking, he jumped in his jeep and barreled out of town back toward Cang Long. So I went over to Wilson and asked him what that was all about, and he told me that Troung was upset because there was no security. Well, it wasn't like we weren't armed. I, Sweet, and Wilson all had M16's, and Wilson and I had our pistols, but when Troung left, I felt pretty exposed with just us three guys. And Troung was right: none of us had been paying attention.

So Wilson suddenly got antsy too, telling us to hurry and break it down. And he got out his M16 and chambered a round. So now Jim, Ba, and I were gettin' all nervous and hustling and puffin' to put the projector back in its case and get the screen and all back into the truck. And the kids and adults were all like totally puzzled because they were hot to see the movies. Then, just as we got it all broken down and were shoving it into the truck, the security detail showed up.

They were late because Captain Robinson decided he wanted to ride along, and he made them wait because he had to get some more gear or take a crap or some BS before they left. So he and Wilson got into a ginormous argument, and by that time, we figured there was no way we were going to do anything, so we kept loading the stuff into the truck. And when everybody decided it was a no-go, we were all ready to di di mau!

So here we are back at Cang Long, and we aren't going to do squat again today. Thank God we have a typewriter; it makes telling a long story like this easier!

And to wrap it up, Troung was so pissed off at Wilson that he drove in to Tra Vinh with the first bunch of ARVNs who came along. Nobody knows when he'll be back, so we are really handcuffed. Looks like I'll be doing a lot of reading, if I can find anything worth reading. Oh, and this letter might be sitting here for a couple of days after I write it before it goes out.

The Kid paused to dip the pipe into his cache pocket and fire off a bowl while he rocked back in the folding chair and contemplated what he was going to write next. Oh, he had given Flo a rollicking account of the pay officer sniper attack when he got to fire his weapon, but he was still depressed and upset over the news about Imbach and hadn't conveyed it yet to Flo, because he didn't want to unduly rattle her by bringing up the subject of death. Still, he had written her frequently from Indianapolis about funny things the Boy Scout had said and done.

542

I was reading the Stars and Stripes paper a couple of days ago and found out one of my DINFOS roommates, John Imbach (you also know him as Boy Scout), got killed in action about four weeks ago by the time you get this. He was up the road with Waterhouse at the Ninth Division at My Tho. Don't know what happened yet. I hope to get a letter soon from Dave about it.

I guess I don't have to tell you that it feels exactly like you're about ten thousand miles and a couple of light-years away. Sometimes it starts to make me a little crazy when I think how long it still is until we can be together again. Then I just click my combat boots together, kind of like Dorothy in The Wizard of Oz, and say, "I wanna go to the Traveler's Motel. I wanna go to the Traveler's." Hasn't worked yet, but I won't give up, I promise.

All my love,

Curt

PS: ISYL!

He finished the letter, pulled it from the typewriter, folded it up, stuck it in an US Armed Forces stationery envelope, addressed it—Miss Flo Stuckey, 1279 Wax Wing Way, Vista, California—and threw it on his cot. *I can only hope we have mail call tomorrow.*

Looking at his watch, he noted the time was approaching 1500 hours. He had been watching the clock because there was going to be a new music show on Armed Forces Radio that he was looking forward to listening to.

In fact, the Kid was prepared, with his radio, cigarettes, lighter, sunglasses, and canteen all ready to go outside and do exactly that. Since the clinic was stuffy in the hot afternoon, and since Wilson and Robinson were in the main building, the Kid's plan was to sit in one of the jeeps in the Cang Long driveway—one with the top up, of course, creating the shade he was seeking—and listen while reclining therein.

Walking out the clinic's screen door, he looked to his right and saw that the gate to the Cang Long compound was open, as it usually was during the day, to demonstrate to the people that the Thiệu government was open for business.

The jeep of his choice belonged to Doc, and it was parked at the back end of the row of four, closest to the gate. It was also even with the central window of the main building, which was now across the sandy driveway to the Kid's right as he sat down in the passenger's seat. He turned on his radio and, after adjusting the tuning, hung it by the strap on the knob of the glove compartment door.

"Good afternoon, fearless fighting men of the US Armed Services. This is Gary W. Gears coming to you from Saigon on Armed Forces Radio, and today we have a special treat. The new music is in from Special Services, and for the next hour, we are going to give you a taste of the songs that are working their way up the charts back in the world! We're going to start out with a very interesting number by Gary Puckett and the Union Gap, singing their new hit single 'Young Girl!'"

This is really amazing. I hate Gary Puckett. And new music? This piece of shit has been out since February.

Of course, being a DINFOS graduate, the Kid knew how long it took a song to make it from the playlists of US radio stations to the flat-disk collections of forty- fives and long-playing albums, then be sent to Armed Forces Radio stations around the world as the only music the stations were authorized to play it. The big records, each containing about twenty-four songs, were called *Tops in Pops,* and their musical timeliness ran as much as six months behind the curve. The Kid knew that back in the States, new music was being played that very second that he wouldn't hear for months.

"And there it is, 'Young Girl' by Gary Puckett. Some people say I play his records just because his name is Gary, which isn't totally without merit. And now, for all you Monkees fans, here's their latest, about a girl named Valerie!"

It was another relatively old song, which the Kid had been listening to, along with the rest of the country, since just after New Year's. He took one last puff on his cigarette and, spinning the ember out and letting the little bit of remaining tobacco fall to the ground, put the filter into his pocket. To throw it on the ground would be to invite the wrath of Captain Robinson.

The sun was beating down on the Cang Long compound. There was absolutely no breeze on this day, and the clouds, for some strange reason, were not forming up to deliver the main product of the monsoon season. The Kid shut his eyes and tried to pretend he was anywhere but there. He recalled the afternoon music meetings at WKDA when he and all the Good Guys would sit around in Dick Buckley's office and listen to all the new songs that the record hacks were pushing, crown the pick hit of the week, and decide what else to put on the playlist. There were a lot of record hacks and label guys in Nashville, working what they considered one of the most important markets in the country, and WKDA was the most important station.

"And now, here's a new song from the Box Tops, the follow-up to their smash hit

'The Letter.' Don't we all have a reason to cry like a baby!"

Now this was a little newer; the Kid had first heard this song in March, and finally it was one he really liked. "When I think about the good love you gave me, I cry like a baby. Living without you is driving me crazy …"

Well, the lyrics really fit my situation! I hope I get to meet Alex Chilton someday.

As the song was nearing its end—"Who left the water runnin'? I cry like a baby, like a little bitty baby"—the Kid heard some rifle fire that sounded like it was off in the distance. It was barely loud enough to attract his attention, but then his radio was cranked up to near its decibel maximum. *Must be some ARVNs doing firing practice off the back berm.*

Then he heard it again, but this time the sound of the firing seemed a little closer. As he turned his head to the right, he saw at the main building window that Sweet, Wilson, and Robinson were all inside looking out at him with puzzled expressions on their faces. As he attempted to decipher their apparent concern, more firing came, and this time, it was much louder. In fact, the bullets were flying right directly over the roof of the jeep in which the Kid sat!

"Hey! Stocker!" Wilson yelled at him from inside the screened window. "They're shooting at *you!*"

The Kid sat straight up in the jeep seat. *They're shooting at me?* As he turned his head to look back over his shoulder and out the gate, the yet unseen sniper put a row of rounds in the sand between him and the main building! The bullets came in like a zipper being pulled up shut, *brrrrruuuuuupppppp,* in a line rippling the sand, starting at the end of the building and making their presence known at the other end of the jeep row.

Holy fucking shit! The Kid jumped up out of the jeep and bolted toward the main building door, but halfway across the sandy driveway, he realized he'd forgotten his radio, one of his most treasured possessions, so he stopped and wheeled around to go back and get it. Just as he took that first step back toward the jeep, he experienced a number of rapid-fire revelations. The first was, *This is stupid! I'm a sitting duck!* Now, he was a duck standing stock-still in the middle of the driveway. *Wait a minute! If he wanted to kill me, I would already be dead!* With that thought, the Kid stopped panicking. *Gotta be as cool as I've ever been.* As normally as he could, with resolute precision, he returned to the jeep and collected his radio and canteen. Turning slowly to his right, he chose not to look out the gate. *Do not make eye contact with the tiger.* He began taking measured, unhurried steps as he walked over to the main building.

By this time, Reyes, Doc, and Jones had joined Wilson, Sweet, and Robinson at the door to the driveway. They had all watched the whole thing. As the Kid walked in through the screen door, their jaws were all slack in gapes of amazement.

Hey! I think I'm gettin' this Buddhist thing down!

Wilson spoke up first. "What the fucking hell are you doing? That guy could have killed you!"

"But he didn't, did he?" The Kid stated the obvious. "And it occurred to me when I stopped to go back and get my radio that if he'd wanted to, he'd have taken me out with that first burst."

"Shit, Kid, you're too much!" Sweet was exasperated. "God Almighty, you are one lucky mutha!"

"And a stupid muthafucka too," Robinson added. "You do shit like that, you're living on borrowed time. You should've gotten down or crawled out the other side of the jeep, where the compound wall would've given you some cover!" The captain punctuated his remarks with a definitive head shake, affirming everything he said. It was a Robinson signature, kind of like, "'Nuff said!"

"Damn straight!" Wilson got in on it. "You should've ran back to the hooch, gotten your M16, and returned fire!"

Dai Ui Phan now emerged from his private office off the bunk room, pistol already drawn. "What is happening?" He looked quickly around the room, waiting for someone to start talking.

"A sniper across the street was taking potshots at Stocker, who doesn't seem to care," Robinson said, "and from what I saw, I'd say the fucker was behind the dirt berm on the far side of the helipad."

"We go see," Phan said. Top came out of the back, clad in a flak jacket with his steep pot in place, his M1 carbine in hand. Following were three soldiers toting M16's, all of them combat-ready. With a wave of his pistol, Phan sent all of them out the door and into the driveway first, but seeing as there was no incoming, the *dai ui* followed after the advancing men.

Wilson now returned from his bunk area with his M16, flak jacket, and steel pot to join the excursion. "Come on, Bill!" he encouraged Robinson to join them.

546

"That's all right, you children go on and play now." The burly man dismissed him as a father would a kid inviting the dad to a cap gun fight.

As Wilson ran out the door, the Kid turned to Sweet and asked, "Do you want to go?"

"Shit! No way!" came the immediate response. "I didn't sign up for any of this extracurricular bullshit!"

"Me neither. I'm not going out there and risk getting shot just to take a look at some spent brass. But let's go outside and see where the bullets hit in the sand by the door here!"

Robinson joined the pair, and they walked out onto the driveway. Captain Phan's men made their move through the gate and across the roadway, closing in on the sniper's approximate location.

"Had to be from there for him to shoot right down the row!" The captain paused to really consider what he was seeing. "Hmm, I never noticed that before, that with an open gate, from the other side of the helipad, they could have shot anybody coming out of our main door anytime the gate was open. Maybe we should start closing half of it!"

The Kid was looking in the sand to find where the rounds had struck, to see how close his assailant had come, but some of the bullets had already been scuffed up by the ARVNs charging off. And now Reyes and Jones were milling about as well.

The Kid found one bullet strike of which he was certain, parallel with the end of the jeep and nearly dead center of the driveway. It had missed him by fifteen feet. Not even close. That last burst over the top of the jeep had to be closer, maybe two or three feet up, tops. The Kid stood there and pondered the imponderable. *I should be a dead man. That sniper had me dead to rights. Why would he let me live?*

"Maybe your beloved Tra Vinh Airport sniper got transferred out here to Cang Long," Sweet said sarcastically.

At the mention of the Tra Vinh Airport sniper, Robinson's head snapped around. He said, "You believe that Tra Vinh Airport sniper bullshit? I hear that crap, and I don't believe it."

"Oh, so you haven't personally been shot at by him yet?" the Kid inquired.

"No. But I know that all the Charlies are trying to kill people, but they are just poorly trained." He walked down to the end of jeep row and pointed with his arm, using it like a rifle, at the jeep in which the Kid had been seated. "Stocker, the guy who just shot at you? Hell, if he was over by that berm,

547

he was hiding and he wasn't rising up enough to get the gun barrel over the top and bring fire down on you in the jeep, because if he were, the guards would've seen him."

"No they wouldn't have, not if they were in the bunker," the Kid immediately said. "Let's walk up there. I'll show you ya can't see the berm from the bunker. I think sometimes they kill who they want to kill and don't kill who they don't want to kill."

Robinson stood in his spot and eyed the Kid with disdain. Without uttering a word, he had an expression that said, *You are so full of shit.*

"Well, think about it." The Kid prepared his argument. "Out in a big operation, I agree with you: it's all kill or be killed. No doubt, they are trying to kill you. But look at us here in Cang Long. We know they are all over the fucking place; they just dropped off a calling card. They could shoot us anytime we leave the gate, but they don't." The Kid stopped to let his argument sink in. "And in all likelihood, the Charlies could overrun this pop stand of a compound in about a minute and a half if they really wanted to, but they don't do it. Why? Because this is where they're farming, these villages are their villages. They say they're on the side of Thiệu, but they're really growing rice for Ho Chi Minh. This is the village where the goods get bought by the people who relay them to the VC. They don't want some bullshit firefight raging around here. Oh, they'll take us out if we get careless, but they have the luxury of picking their targets—and the time and the place."

Sweet confronted him as they walked forward. "No matter which theory you subscribe to, you'd better start being more careful, or you're going to end up like your buddy in My Tho. How could you do that? Take it like it's no big deal?"

The Kid pondered the question. "I don't know. If it ain't your time, it ain't your time? Don't you think if he wanted them to, any of those first three bursts could have come right through the back of that jeep?" He stopped and stood in front of the door to the bunker. "Now, sir," he said, addressing his remarks to the captain, "I know what you're sayin', that the sniper didn't want to show himself, but look, sir, you can't see the berm from here! And he certainly wasn't very worried if he got up high enough to put that burst in the ground between me and the building."

Robinson could see it was plainly clear that the Kid was right; the guards couldn't have seen the spot from which the sniper was working.

"Well, he could've thought that somebody was actually going to come out and confront him! Then he would've stayed down." Robinson put forth his rationalization, speculating about the sniper's emotional frame of mind.

548

"I think the fucker was playing with me, trying to scare me. Being 'psychological.'" The Kid formed quotation marks with his fingers as he spoke. "I think it was one of the monks from down at the monastery," he concluded.

"The monks?" Jim questioned.

"On this point, I've gotta agree with Stocker." Robinson continued to walk toward the gate. "I think them monks is all fucking Charlies. We ought to burn every single goddamned pagoda in the country to the ground!"

"Now that would be a public relations nightmare," the Kid flatly replied, "the burning of churches and books. Widely frowned upon in the civilized world."

Arriving at the gate itself, the three of them watched as the detachment of Phan, Top, Wilson, and the three ARVNs swept the area, looking for traces of the elusive enemy. Wilson and Phan were returning from the construction site next to the helipad while the trio could see the heads of Top and his men, who were over behind the berm. They kept popping up and ducking down as if they were picking something up.

There was not much traffic on the Cang Long road that day. After a couple of minutes, when it became clear that they could probably go out unarmed, the three crossed the tarmac and joined Phan's group, who were now comparing notes in the middle of the helipad.

"So, what do you think, Dai Ui?" Robinson inquired of Phan, who stood with his pistol still clutched in his right hand.

"One man with AK-47. Di di mau, over canal. Or they want us to go down by canal and look for him, and they shoot at us from other bank. If he wants us, he can come back!" Phan holstered his piece and laughed heartily at his own joke. Everybody else joined right in.

Wilson extended his hand to the Kid. "Here's a souvenir for you, Stocker, a jacket from an AK round, one he shot at you!"

The brass dropped into the Kid's left palm. He picked it up using the fingertips of his right hand and spun it around in front of his eyes, staring at it. *This bullet does not have my name on it.*

Back at the clinic, as the Kid sat on his cot, looking at the sniper's shell casing. Sweet pitched him a spent M16 shell. "Here, Curt, this is one of the ones I pulled out of the truck that you shot off. You could drill holes in them and put them together like a Taoist yin and yang thing—one you fired, and one fired at you!

"Sounds cool, but no. Not dumping the lucky beaver nickel anytime soon." The Kid's decision was instant as he brought the two shells up in front of his face.

"What was it really?" Sweet asked in a serious tone of voice as he sat on the corner of Doc's desk. "Were you just too stoned to give a shit, or what?"

After considering his answer, the Kid said, "Well, of course I was stoned. And if I am destined to die in this war, I certainly want to die stoned. But to say I was so stoned that I didn't give a shit, I think, would be stretching it. But now that you bring it up, I think we should make an effort to see if a person can get that stoned." And with that, he pulled out the pipe, filled it from his pocket, and hit it with his Zippo, after which he offered it to Sweet, who took it.

As soon as Sweet exhaled, the Kid continued. "So, at first, with the radio cranked up, I could hear shooting, but I couldn't really tell where it was coming from.

Seemed like a long ways off. Then, when the bursts got lower and you guys hollered at me and I realized what was going on, it was like I was a spectator. I had no control. I was just along for the ride. My living or dying was not turning on anything I was doing or not doing; it was turning on how the sniper guy felt at that moment. I still think it's the fucking monks, and I think the guy let me live because I always bow and wave at them when we drive by."

"Yeah, it could be." Sweet considered the idea on its merits. "Never hurts to be polite in a war zone where lots of people own guns, but who the fuck knows? They always get away because they can melt into the people. We can't melt into squat."

The Kid swatted with his hand and missed a huge fly that had gained entry into their private quarters. "Fuckin' A, they're as elusive as these goddamn flies! But with the right technology …" The Kid paused as he slowly picked up his swatter and held it down by his leg, waiting for the fly to land. When it did alight on the corner of his goody box, which was down to his right, he attempted to deliver a lethal blow. "We can win this war yet!"

"Jeez! You just got fly guts in your goody box!" Sweet pointed at the twelve-inch- by-twelve-inch cardboard box in which the Kid kept what was left of his munchies from home. "I guess I'll stop stealing your stuff!"

"No, I didn't splatter him. He was on the edge. I did knock him down in there, though. Shit!" The Kid picked up the box. "He might not be dead! I might have knocked him into the one place he wanted to go! Oh, those

550

wascally fwys," he said, imitating the voice of Elmer Fudd, as he reached out his left hand to take the pipe from Sweet.

"Be careful not to blow any smoke in there," Sweet warned. "If a fly that size ever got the munchies, your goody box would be history!"

Chapter 52

Later that night, as the seven Americans and Ba sat down at the rectangular atrium table and began to eat dinner, the subject of the Kid's close call came up for discussion again when he took a drink of Coke.

"Lucky for you that you're not leaking when you drink tonight." Jones chuckled.

The Kid smiled back. "Yeah, I agree. But if I'd've gotten that million-dollar wound, I'd be the one laughing out of the other side of your mouth."

"Say what?" Reyes was trying to follow along as he loaded up his plate with rice and covered it with a stir-fried vegetable dish that An had prepared for them that evening, made with a tomato base.

"Ah, I was just mixing my metaphors, sir." The Kid brought him up to speed. "I say 'laughing out of the other side of his mouth' because if my million-dollar wound was a shot in someplace that really hurt, I'd be happy to be gone, but I certainly wouldn't be laughing. Or maybe I would?" He shrugged and continued to eat his salad.

"He thinks it was the monks, so now this is his metaphysical act," Sweet said, passing the fresh cut pineapple slices to Wilson, who sat to his left.

"And I for one say that most likely ain't wrong." Robinson used his fork to punctuate his discourse. "We oughta keep a closer eye on that pagoda and see if we can catch those jokers coming out some night."

"That sounds like a good one to miss," said the Kid, "sitting out all night waiting, trying to watch in the dark. I mean, hell, they most likely have a tunnel, and the door to come out is a long fucking way from their wall. We should look for that!"

"And when we find it, you can be the tunnel rat to follow it back." Wilson was all over it. "Don't you want to go visit them? Isn't that what you said?"

"Yeah, I did say it would be nice to take a tour of the pagoda, you know, see how they live and all that, but I never said I wanted to creepy-crawl down any tunnels. I'm actually sort of claustrophobic, if you wanna know the truth."

"We could do it if we had a starlight sniper scope, 'cause with those babies, you can see just like it was daylight!" Robinson continued to work on his plan to catch the monks at their nefarious dirty work. "Those things saved our bacon more than once when we were out in the boonies at night!"

Dinner was generally a pleasant experience at Cang Long. With a garrison of just four officers and three enlisted men, the Americans all shared one table.

Separate messes would have made no sense.

Some nights, Phan, Top, Troung, Ba, and other Vietnamese would join them, and whenever they did so, the kitchen staff remained and acted the part of waiters. But tonight, An and her helpers had brought the dishes to the table, where the Americans could easily help themselves, and left. They'd be back later to clean up.

"So, Ba," Wilson spoke with his mouth full, "Troung didn't say anything to you about when he'd be back?"

"No, he did not." Ba seemed uncomfortable with the subject, as if he knew more than he was saying.

"All that means is a few more days lyin' around, not getting shit done." Wilson was chagrined, as if he were cheating the army out of a paycheck by not putting in a full day and felt bad about it.

"Yeah, what a bummer." Captain Robinson took a deep swig of Victoria Bitter and wiped the foam from the upper lip of his face, which bore a slight resemblance to that of Jim Brown, the Cleveland running back turned movie star, who had the same mustache and strong jaw, only his face was a little more rounded in the cheeks. "Only real bummer is, I wish I could get up to Saigon and check on my businesses. If you let them gook women run your business too long without checkin' on 'em, they'll rob you blind!"

Everybody knew that Robinson had three bars and four whorehouses and was supposedly making thousands of dollars every month; he never missed a chance to tell people all about it.

"I had this one bitch of a mama-san running one house, and come to find out, she's got her own string of whores. She was going one trick for me and one for her!" The captain paused in the story and glanced around the table to see who was or was not paying attention. "Yes, sir, I beat the holy shit out of her and said, 'Don't you ever try that fuckin' jive again or somebody will find you floating in the Saigon River!'"

Old story; heard it a million times. "Sir." The Kid looked at Wilson. "Do you think we could get a radio message to somebody back at Tra Vinh and have them get a hold of Troung so he can bring our mail back out when he comes?"

"I don't care if that little weasel never comes back." Wilson was also still hot about what had happened earlier that day with the aborted psyops operation. "And you didn't help out any either. Beggin' your pardon, Captain." He swung around to face Robinson. "Twenty minutes late on a security detail was not the operational plan. Sir."

Robinson gave him a measured look of disgust. "Don't go getting a case of the ass against me, Lieutenant. Your men could have turned on that projector and let it run. THen the hamlet would have been happy and you all could've watched out until we got there, no sweat, GI. And here you are still making a stink about it? It wasn't my fault, it was the ARVNs' who didn't show, and there is nothing we can do about it now. Case closed." Robinson lowered his head and commenced to once again stuff his face.

I wonder who it was that Robinson pissed off in Saigon for him to sign up for a second tour, get promised Saigon, and then end up in a boonie hole like this? God, I wish I were in Saigon!

"If you *hombres* are going to argue, you can take it away from the dinner table," Reyes admonished the pair of verbal combatants.

"Captain Robinson," the Kid said, catching his attention, "so the unit you got the black feather from was operating in Saigon? I thought it was a grunt unit."

"Oh, it was, a grunt unit nowhere near Saigon. We were in the boonies up in the Central Highlands for six months pullin' security detail for firebases and patrolling and ambushing around. That's where I got sick with a real bad case of dysentery and was medivacked to Saigon. While I was there, a major in the hospital out at Ton Son Nhut offered me a job in the Graves Registration Unit there at the airfield, where all the bodies get shipped back to the States, and I took it. Then in another four months, I got an early DEROS because I'm doin' this second tour, and here I am. I know I'll get back to Saigon; it'll just take a couple of months.

Hope I don't have to get wounded to do it this time!"

"You worked in graves registration?" Wilson stopped and put his fork down to pick up his knife and butter some bread. "What was that like?"

"You don't wanna know," Jones quickly interjected, "leastwise, not until after dinner."

"No!" Robinson suddenly seemed excited. "I'll tell you what goes on there. It's really quite fascinating."

"Oops, you've done it now." Jones gave Wilson such a look, but by this time, Robinson had launched into it.

554

"Graves registration at Ton Son Nhut is where all the KIAs come, those that are really blown to bits and shot through the head or the heart. Everybody who dies instantly comes straight to graves registration, where they get identified, put into a casket, and shipped home."

"Uh-huh." Wilson continued to look interested.

"If the remains arrive in a body bag, that's a good thing, 'cause then you've got a good chance of keeping it all together. Some bodies come in wrapped in ponchos and, worse yet, not wrapped in anything. I've seen some bodies and body parts roll out of choppers and land like so much beef on the runway. We had gather them up and bag 'em ourselves."

From a quick look around the table, it was easy to see that more than one diner was now queasy from the captain's recounted memories. Even Wilson appeared to be a little fazed.

"I opened this one body bag that I thought was a little light." He set it up, pausing to make sure everybody was not only listening but also watching. "All that was in it was a hand with this much arm." He grabbed his forearm about three inches above his wrist. "It was a left hand, and it still had a wedding ring on it. The rest of the guy had been blown away. I heard tell it was from a friendly fire air strike."

The rest of the diners just exchanged glances as if to say, *Is this really happening?* After all, it is difficult thing in the military to tell your commanding officer to shut up.

"I've seen bodies with their heads completely blown off, and some with their faces blown off and the back of the head still there, like they got hit in the side of the head by an RPG. Some families want to have open-casket funerals, you know, see their loved ones for the last time, but the army sends instructions that the casket is not supposed to be opened under any circumstances. That's because they couldn't embalm what was left because it was just so much meat. And by the time it gets to there, it's definitely stinkin' to high heaven."

"Uh, sir, that's really interesting, but we're eating here." The Kid ventured down the road with the only available tack. "Is it possible we could have this discussion at any other time, sir?"

He laughed. Robinson laughed at how seriously the others were being grossed out. He apparently relished it. Corporal Ba was plain stunned. Jones and Doc declared that they were full and left the table. Wilson continued to eat, but Sweet and the Kid just sat there, sharing a mutual stare of disbelief, as Robinson continued with true gusto.

"I look in this one body bag that came in on one of about a half dozen choppers bringing dead GIs out of this one particularly nasty fight and I see white and black body parts in it, mixed together." He paused for effect. "So, I know they didn't have the time to get it right out there in the field. We had to open up the bag and sort it out as best we could. And once we found two dicks in the same bag!" He smiled.

Nobody laughed. It wasn't a joke.

"Uh, sir?" Sweet raised his hand like he was a student in a class. "Couldn't we change the subject? We get the point, but do we have to keep discussing this stuff here at the dinner table, while we're trying to eat?" he pleaded.

Robinson looked Jim straight in the eye; they locked stares for about two seconds, but the second Jim dropped his eyes to his plate, the captain continued.

"Guts is the worst thing. They get all spread out …"

With that, Sweet, Ba, and the Kid all rose from their seats and left the table. Robinson kept talking, now to only Reyes and Wilson. Reyes was shoveling in his food as fast as he could because he wanted out of there too, but he was a big man and wasn't about to miss a meal.

Up front by the radio, the trio stopped to talk with Jones and Doc about their disgust.

"You know," Doc began with an expression of genuine concern, "for the first two weeks he was here, he never said anything about being with graves registration, and for the last couple of days, he's been going off on these mind-fucking trips about what he did there. Well, you heard."

"My God! It was way too graphic for me, even if I'm not eating, I don't want to hear a steady diet of that." Sweet glanced back toward the atrium, where Robinson continued to talk and Wilson continued to listen. "Fuckin' Wilson, he's almost as weird as Robinson."

"Yes, Watson, go on." The Kid struck the Sherlock Holmes pose, holding his pipe in the detective's signature manner.

"They deserve each other," Jones said.

"Well, gentlemen." The Kid stood up from where he had momentarily been sitting on the arm of one of the couches. "I'm going back to the clinic to write letters and listen to the radio."

"Me too." Sweet followed suit. "We trust you'll let us know what we draw on watch. Ba, you can come if you want."

"Thank you, but talk before dinner say I am playing in poker game tonight."

"Suit yourself. But if you lose your shorts to these sharks, don't come stealing any skivvies from us, *an bic*?"

"Toi bic, Em."

Chapter 53

It's a dream. Oh yes, it's cold out; that's how I know it's a dream. And dark. The darkness is pregnant with silence. Quiet. Too quiet. Yeah. The old way-too-quiet. If only the wind would kick up a little breeze; it's so still that when I exhale, the condensed cloud of my breath obscures my view of the tombstones in the graveyard. Gotta keep walking. What's that squeak? *Oh, whew, it's only the rubbing of my paper bags against the front wheel of my Schwinn. I swear, if I get past the graveyard this morning, I will never again go and see a scary movie with Boris Karloff in it on a Saturday night before I have to walk by this cemetery to do my paper route on Sunday morning. And this time, I mean it! I hate this graveyard. I love this graveyard. Wait a minute, do I hate it or love it? Oh yeah!*

This is the same graveyard that Jennifer Dobbert and I used to make out in, back in the seventh grade. Closed-lipped kissing is pretty hot when you don't know anything else. Carolyn Bunnegar changed all of that, in the back seat of her brother Freddy's car at the Twinburger. Tonsil hockey city. Hey, my cherry lemon-lime 7 Up is really icy cold! Oh. Right. This is a dream. The honking horns, the racing engines, and the yelling and frantic screaming: that is not a dream.

The Kid opened his eyes to the sight of Wilson with his steel pot bouncing on his head, sprinting toward the clinic with a bunch of stuff in his hands, and to the sight of jeeps and soldiers rushing back and forth pell-mell behind him. The lieutenant crashed through the screen door and urgently began yelling commands at the men.

"Stocker! Sweet! Get up! Get up! The VC set off a command-detonated mine at the Vinh Long bridge at the morning inspection, and Captain Robinson, Top, and two others have been killed! And a bunch more wounded. And Jones and the rest of them are still pinned down there."

Oh my God! Sweet and the Kid exchanged looks of disbelief, but they both knew they were no longer dreaming. They scrambled to their feet and began grabbing for clothes.

"They got 'em with a command-detonated mine! Me and Reyes are going down to help him. Dai Ui Phan is one of the wounded. Sweet, you man the radios.

Reyes is calling in a medevac right now. Stocker." He flipped the Kid an M16 bandolier and pulled a PRC-25 radio from off his back. "You go secure the helipad!"

"Alone?"

"Yes, you alone." Wilson made it clear. "All that's gonna be left here is the two men in the front-door bunker: you, Sweet, and the mayor. We're takin' everybody else—all six of them! The PRC-25 is already set to Sweet's frequency. You might have to call in a Spooky. They're looking for some support for us now. It's too close for the artillery!"

Doc now burst through the door, with two ARVNs close behind, and he hurriedly started gathering the tools of his trade while pointing the privates toward a bunch of stretchers stacked in the corner beyond their cots. All the while, Sweet and the Kid were frantically pulling on their clothes and boots.

Ba came through the door wearing his steel pot and looking for Wilson. As he is searching, he collides with the first of the ARVNs exiting with an armful of stretchers.

Reyes hollered from outside, "Herschel! Come on, we got it! Let's roll!"

Wilson had at least three bandoliers of M16 ammo draped across his body, and every muscle in his body was poppin' tense with anticipation. "Ba, you come with me. Gentlemen, good luck!" he called. They flew out the door, Ba being reluctantly towed along in Wilson's wake.

Quickly dressed and in his combat boots, the Kid climbed into a flak jacket, slapped his steel pot on his head, slung the bandolier, grabbed his M16, jammed in a clip and chambered a round, checked the safety, and hoisted the PRC-25 up by one strap. After a supportive but terrified look from Sweet, he was out the door, running for the gate, as the last of the three jeeps going down to the Vinh Long bridge roared out of sight.

Crossing the Cang Long road, the Kid rushed for the berm from which the Charlie had shot at him from the opposite side just the day before. Charging up to the berm, he hit the ground behind it. *Oh my God, could there be a Charlie on the other side of this pile of dirt just waiting?* Breathing in big breaths of adrenalin- laced air while still trying to be stealthy, he slowly raised himself up to where his eyes could just see over the berm, his rifle grasped tight in his grip, his finger on the safety. Nobody!

He scanned the area of the tree line a hundred meters off down by the canal. *Nothing. I can't see anything or anybody moving down there. if they come, that's probably where they'll come from.* Listening up, it was easy for the Kid to catch the sounds of the battle still taking place down at the bridge, less than half a mile past the village, which was barely fifty meters to his left. The echoing sounds of automatic weapon fire carried far in the early morning Delta air. *Wait! What about the buildings?*

The Kid slid down from the top of the berm and twisted to his right to look at the new construction. There were no workmen to be seen; it was early, and sometimes they didn't work every day. *But that would be a perfect position for the VC! Shit! If they're on the roof there or they come out of the ground floor, I'm toast! If I get on the other side, I'm exposed to the river! I've got no cover in this position. There're just too many fucking ways they could do one man! Too much to worry about at the same time! They've killed Robinson and Top! Holy mother of God! Phan is wounded, Jones is pinned down, and here I am holding the whole freaking LZ! If they're on the top floor, I'm dead meat. No. If they were on the top floor, I would already be dead. There's no place to hide, and I can't go back to the compound! Maybe I should go into the building! Maybe not.* The Kid's hand went to his throat, where he clutched his lucky beaver nickel tight in his fist. *Om, be lucky. Om, be lucky!*

Since the VC were almost certainly down by the river, if they were anywhere around the place at all, the Kid chose the best spot to establish a lookout over the terrain toward the canal. He arranged his radio and bandolier and put in a call to Sweet. Depressing the mike button, he spoke into the handset, "Sweet! Can you hear me? Over."

"I read you, Curt. Over."

"Well, here I am at the berm. Negative activity here, but I can hear the fight going on down at the bridge. Glad I'm not down there. Over."

"The medevac's in on the way, two choppers, with an ETA of fifteen minutes. You got a smoke grenade? The pilots are gonna need to see smoke. Over." Sweet sought information.

"Negative on the smoke grenade. Over," came the Kid's reply.

There was about five seconds of silence before Sweet responded, "OK, roger no smoke. I tell you what, when the time comes, I'll run up to the gate and wing one out there. If I throw it across the road, that should mark the LZ. OK? Over."

"Roger, you're bringing the smoke. About time!" The Kid choked on a nervous laugh. "Out." He then took another deep breath and stared through

560

his sweat- streaked glasses at the tree line in front of his position. The rifle fire continued to be audible at the Vinh Long bridge, but it had, within the last few moments, dissipated somewhat.

Jesus, I hope all the available VC are down at the frickin' bridge fight and not anywhere around up here! Oh please, oh please, don't attack me! Ha! Would old Drill Sergeant Willie Smith be amazed at me securing an LZ all by myself. Oh please, don't make it a hot LZ! "Om, no hot LZ, om, no hot LZ," he quietly chanted. Checking his watch, he realized that all of this was taking place prior to 0700 hours. *My God! Robinson was killed on the morning after he couldn't stop talking about the morgue in Saigon! And Top is dead! I don't fucking believe it!*

Time nearly stood still as the Kid held his position against an assault that continued to fail to materialize. *Fine with me!*

"Sweet to the Kid," Jim's voice said, coming over the PRC-25. "Sweet to the Kid. Over."

"Kid. Over."

"I just got the call from the bridge. They've got the wounded and the bodies, and they're coming back. We've got four KIAs and five WIAs. You should be getting sound or visual on the choppers any second. As soon as you can hear or see them, call me and I'll heave the smoke. Over."

"Roger your transmission. Over." The Kid craned his head, and sure enough, chopper rotor sounds were detectable, coming in from the direction of Vinh Long.

There was no more shooting to be heard from the bridge as the rotors of the approaching helicopters instead became the sound to which the Kid's ears were tuned. *When the choppers land, if they're going to try anything here, that would be the time to get the maximum effect—then get the commanders and a chopper! Please, no. Please, no!* "Kid to Sweet. Bring the smoke. Over."

Seconds later, a belching red smoke canister grenade came flying out of the Cang Long compound gate. It cleared the road and bounced like a squirrelly punt before it finally rolled to the left side of the open helipad area. As the Kid's eyes followed the scarlet smoke twisting up into the blue sky, they found the Huey choppers, circling overhead.

The jeeps arrived from the Hoc Bang bridge for the dustup, the lead one being driven by Wilson, with Ba riding shotgun and holding one end of a stretcher steady. They all had stretchers precariously attached to the hood and back. A couple of them had three.

The KIAs were on the front two jeeps, easy to tell because their bodies were completely covered. Reyes drove the second jeep; Jones, the third; and an ARVN, the fourth, as Doc hovered over a wounded man, holding aloft an IV bag.

Once they stopped about thirty meters from the corrugated metal of the helipad, four ARVNs began unloading the stretchers and lining them up for loading.

As the pair of choppers settled onto the helipad, the draft from their rotors blew the poncho off one of the stretchers. It was Robinson's body; the Kid could tell from the black arm that had flopped to the ground on one side. He wanted to look away, but he was transfixed, hypnotized by the gore. *I want to puke.* The captain had been blown completely in half. His entrails were entwined like spaghetti, blue and oozing from the body cavity. What was left of one of his legs, from below the knee, lay across the bottom of the stretcher, a bloody, dripping stump and jagged bone sticking out of a jungle boot.

The two closest ARVNs grabbed the poncho and recovered his body, this time tying the corners to the handles of the stretcher to keep the event from happening again.

The crews beckoned that they were ready to receive, so the three lieutenants and three ARVNs began to carry the stretchers out to the medevacs. As a pair of ARVNs hustled Captain Robinson's body up to the Huey, a couple of loops of his entrails spilled off the stretcher and dragged along the ground, collecting red dust along the way. When the men reached the chopper door, the crewman helped them slide the body inside. Picking up the guts, he stuffed them back under the poncho without a single emotion upon his face.

Wow, no telling how many times he's done this very thing. I wonder which one of those other three is Top. Poor Top! Poor Top's family! My God, what a tragedy!

Doc was busy in the door of the chopper with the five wounded, including Dai Ui Phan, who was obviously in critical condition. Once Doc and the chopper crew had secured the IV bags, the loadmasters waved to the pilots, and just like that, the bird lifted up and the occupants were gone, leaving Doc and the three lieutenants standing in place watching them disappear along with the noise of their rotors.

The Kid picked up the radio, his M16, and the bandolier and walked over to where they stood. Doc's hands and arms were bloody up to his elbows. The others were quite bloody as well.

"We couldn't find his other leg," Reyes said, lamenting. "Can you believe the kinds of things he was saying at the dinner table last night? Talk about fucking spooky!" He rolled his eyes. "Holy mother of God!"

Back across the street, Sweet was waiting for them with the mayor at the main gate, both with inquisitive looks on their faces.

Standing in front of him and lighting up a Kool, the Kid said, "You know how last night he said guts were the worst? He was fucking right! He was blown in half! His fucking guts were *all* hanging out. It is the grossest thing I've ever seen in my life!"

"Jonesie." Reyes turned to the concerned-looking first lieutenant. "We've had this discussion. You've got me on date of rank by four months, so that makes you the acting CO."

"Yeah." He paused as quite possibly now, for the first time, what had just happened began to sink in. "Yeah, bad way to get your first command. OK, gentlemen, let's go inside and regroup and figure out what we need to do right away. First off, close those front gates. Mr. Thiệu is not open for business as usual today."

The mayor barked an order, and two attentive ARVNs hastened to comply.

Jones was still way off on his pure adrenalin rush, which was understandable since he was just thirty-five meters behind the group that had been taken out by the command-detonated mine that the VC had waiting for them this fine Sunday morning. He had seen his commander killed in front of his eyes, along with the senior ARVN enlisted man's death and the ARVN commander's wounding. Then he and the remaining men had fought a thirty-minute-long contest over the bodies of the dead and wounded. "Mayor," he said, addressing the ranking Vietnamese person in the compound, "find out who is now acting ARVN commander and have him come to see me immediately."

The shocked group of Americans and Ba made their way into the main room as the mayor, who had been a colonel in the ARVN army until his retirement, was deciding semiofficially to unretire, because all their lives might depend on it.

Charlie could sense weakness, like any hunter with bloodied prey.

"Tell you what, Herschel," Reyes began, "that was some piece of command control down there when the ARVNs got up to retreat and you turned them around and made them stick their noses in there and fight!"

The sudden praise caught Wilson off guard. He looked up to see where it was coming from.

"If it hadn't been for that," Reyes continued, "we'd have had to leave those six wounded guys there, at least for a little while, and some of them, most likely Phan, would have died. And we wouldn't have been able to recover the captain's body. Wilson, you son of a bitch, I'm going to put you in for a Bronze Star with a 'V' device!"

"No shit! I'll sign off on that citation!" Jonesie asserted. "Fuckin' A, I thought we were all dead men until you guys showed up and saved our asses!" He took a long drink from the bottle of water he had just pulled out of the fridge. "God, I still can't believe it, the noise when that thing went off." He broke down a little bit with an episode of the shakes and had to struggle to get out a cigarette, which Sweet jumped forward to light with his Zippo. "I was just far enough back that none of the shrapnel came to me! Then they opened up with the rifle fire!" Jones looked up at the ceiling as if to acknowledge that God had had a hand in his deliverance. "What a fucking well-planned ambush!"

"I sure as hell saw a couple of them today!" Wilson said pointedly to the Kid, then turned back to Jones. "We got that one son of a bitch who was just at the top of the bank down there about seventy-five meters behind whatever that was, a bale of hay or a mound of dirt. I couldn't say who did, though I think three or four of us hit him when he got up to move. I can't honestly count him as my first kill."

"Sir," Doc cut in, addressing Jones, "I'll start gathering the captain's belongings for shipment to graves registration. Corporal Ba." He turned to the forlorn little interpreter. "Will you go and see if there is somebody from the ARVNs who wants to come and get Top's effects? It's best to get these things done right away and get them over with."

"Good call, Doc." Jones nodded his approval. The radio crackled to life. It was TOC in Tra Vinh.

"Charlie Lima, this is Tango Victor. Over," a voice called out.

Rushing over to the radio table, Jones slid into the chair and depressed the desk mike switch. "Tango Victor, Charlie Lima, go."

"Charlie Lima, has your situation stabilized? Over."

"Affirmative, Tango Victor. We are all back in the compound, and for now preparing to defend, but we are no longer in contact. Over." Jones glanced from face to face of those in the room as he awaited the reply.

"Roger, Charlie Lima." The voice sounded a little bit like Boar Hog's. "We have your situation under advisement. We will have resources available if you need them, and we will send you a new commander as soon as we figure out who it is going to be. Out."

The Americans stood in the silence of the terminated transmission and continued to absorb the emptiness that always accompanied the loss of any man in a unit, much less the commander himself. Captain Robinson hadn't been a crowd favorite, but the manner and abruptness of his demise was truly overwhelming.

The inability of any of the men to vocalize their feelings merely scratched the surface of what were becoming murky pools of emotional turmoil and self-doubt, filling each and every one of them.

Am I next? Am I going to end up meat on a slab? How in the mutherfucking world in which I live did I come to be in this place?

Chapter 54

September 21, 1968

Dear Mom and Dad,

Guess what happened? Do you remember the trip I took in the summer of 1963, when the Trinity Lutheran youth group went to Chicago? Do you remember the high point of the trip, when I lost something in Lake Michigan and had to send home for something? And then how we joked and talked about what it would have been like to lose them over here?

Well, I did. Since I've been here, I've lost two pairs of glasses. Last night, when we were pulling water out of the well for showers, my last pair slid off my sweaty nose and fell into the well! So, all I have left is my prescription shades. In the daytime, I'm OK, but when the sun goes down, I am seriously handicapped. And because of that, I'm on my way to Saigon to get a couple of new pairs made up!

But I have a favor to ask. If you could send me even another pair. What I'd really like is a pair of gold wire-frames. You know, like the kind that John Lennon wears, round ones, sometimes called "hippie glasses" or "grandpa glasses." My prescription that is on file at the medical center's optical department should still be good. I just want some that aren't black or gray plastic for a change.

I got two tapes from Dave Allen yesterday in the mail of his show on WKDA. Nobody out here has a reel-to-reel tape recorder, but now I'll be able to listen to them in a couple of days, when I get up to Saigon. This might be my big chance. Since Alan P. is at Armed Forces Radio there, I can go visit him, and maybe he can introduce me to the men in charge, and I can play them my air checks and (come on, famous luck!) talk them into a transfer! Nothing ventured, nothing gained!

Also, I read in *Stars and Stripes* last week that one of my classmates from DINFOS was killed in action. John Imbach. He was one of my three roommates, no less. He is the first (and hopefully the last) of us to get it.

Well, got some stuff to do to get ready to go to Saigon. I'll send you a postcard from the Paris of the Orient!

Love,

Curt

PS: I got promoted to specialist fourth class, which is the same as a corporal! But you can't call me Corporal Curt.

Chapter 55

As the landing gear of the Caribou transport prepared to touch down on the Ton Son Nhut tarmac, the Kid was ripe with anticipation. It was September 23; it had taken almost a week to get it all together to come in. First, his health records were kept in Sa Dec, at ARVN Ninth headquarters, so he'd had to chopper up there, where he got stuck for two nights. But now he could see Saigon spreading out below as he craned his neck to look out the Caribou's miniscule window.

Of course he needed to check in at the Fourth Psyop Group headquarters, park his M16, have the clerk make him an appointment for the eye doctor, and then find the quickest way over to Armed Forces Radio Saigon, where Alan P. would be surprised as hell to see him!

The shoulder holster of the Kid's .38, concealed under his fatigue shirt and next to his skin, was beginning to chafe. *Should've worn a T-shirt.* He had to conceal it because his rank did not authorize him to carry a pistol. And although nobody cared in the field, they'd care plenty in Saigon! Still, the Kid did not want to move around Saigon unarmed, and he didn't want to carry an M16, so he was happy he'd spent the money on the Dick Tracy piece.

Between his legs was a new valise of black faux leather that he had bought from Taj the tailor for this trip. In it was the Kid's last hope of getting into Armed Forces Radio and out of psyops. It was his audition, a one-reel collection of air checks and production pieces from WKDA and, most important, the wild-ass opening for a special show he wanted to do on AFVN: *The Sgt. Pepper Family Band & Hit Parade Show.* He had written an opening to the show, and Bill Berlin, WKDA's production wizard, jumped into the mix and, as a going-away present, backed it with an overproduced psychedelic fade that was a one-of-a-kind treatment that just kicked ass!

Aside from the going for the glasses, the Kid was on a mission: to crack Armed Forces Radio and make them want him. *"Good morning, Vietnam,"* *my ass. Get that one-trick pony out of here! Vietnam, ten-hut! Choi duc oi!* *Men yoi, Saigon! Toi di choi! It's time to rock! I've gotta figure out how to* *stretch this trip out to at least a week! A week away from Wilson and Cang*

Long and even Can Tho! Oh, this is gonna be hot! Showers. A major trip to the PX! Armed Forces Radio Saigon.

A driver from group was there to meet the Kid. As the jeep took them toward headquarters, through the busy streets of Saigon, he marveled at just how far out in the fucking sticks Cang Long was. *Maybe I can stretch this thing into two weeks!* the Kid thought as he eyed the incredible number of beautiful Vietnamese women who crowded the streets of the Paris of the Orient. *I could stand being stationed in Saigon. I could get used to this. No operations. No active VC battalions maneuvering in your neighborhood. Although they are here. That guy and that guy, they're VC. And that kid in the shop pretending to draw a bead on me as we drive by, his parents are VC.*

The jeep stopped in traffic at an intersection, and the baseball-capped specialist 4 who was driving that day for the group leaned over to talk with the Kid. "How's things in the field? Seen any combat?" He cut right to the chase.

"Oh yeah. I've been seeing it." The Kid took a deep breath of the city odors into his lungs. "Yeah, quite a bit, actually."

"I'd like to get out there." The driver spoke the words with a distant sigh of major disappointment.

"That's funny." The Kid smirked. "Because I'm trying like hell to get back in here! How long have you been here?"

"Oh, I've been in-country for a month and a half now," he said. "Here the whole time. Haven't seen a Charlie or heard a shot fired. Although I have seen some rockets get shot into the city at night from the roof of the Continental Hotel." His light-complexioned, moderately blemished face brightened. He had relatively a wide jaw and a broad mouth, his very thin lips giving him a real distinctive look.

"If you never have to go out there and get into any of the killing end of this thing, you should consider yourself lucky, pal!" The Kid emphasized the word *lucky.*

"Easy for you to say, since you're there. This place is a fucking drag! They're real strict at group. Lots of bullshit inspections and shit because the officers and the noncoms don't have dick to do. I'd give anything to get into combat just once since I've wasted all this time in the army, learning all this bullshit. Just one time while I'm over here, I'd like to see some action."

The traffic began to move as the White Mouse national policeman who was directing traffic waved their side through. The Kid looked at the reflection of their jeep in his mirrored sunglasses as they passed by. He had gotten good and ripped on his drive to the Can Tho airport just a couple of hours ago and was feeling mellow, and now this guy wanted to talk combat.

"Be careful what you wish for," the Kid cautioned. "I've seen guys like you before, guys who want to get into it. And when they did, their new pastime became looking for ways to stay way the fuck away from it."

Scooters kept passing them, making their drive slower, but there wasn't much the driver could do as he worked his way down the jam-packed boulevard.

"You must have learned your way around here pretty fast if you've only been here for six weeks and they're letting you drive to the airport alone," the Kid said, changing the subject.

The driver laughed. "Ha! I'm from New York! The airport here is easy! After you've done it a few times!"

"Do you know where Armed Forces Radio is?" the Kid inquired.

"Sure!"

"What are the chances of you driving me over there, after I sign in and call over to see if a friend of mine can see me?"

"Yeah! I could do that. Actually, it's not that far from here. Nothing is far from anything in this town. It's pretty easy to figure out, except for some of the twisted little neighborhoods like Cholon!" The driver laid on the horn at the pilot of one Honda 110 who had cut it a little close. "In fact, you could get in a taxi and go just about anywhere you want. The gook drivers all understand 'Tudo Street' and 'PX' and 'Ton Son Nhut'—you know, shit like that."

"Well, my name's Curt." The Kid stuck out his hand as once again the jeep stopped in the throng of carbon monoxide–spewing motor scooters. "But everybody calls me the Kid."

"Everybody calls me Stoney," the specialist 4 answered, removing his right hand from the gearshift knob to shake the Kid's extended paw.

"Pleased to meet you, Stoney."

Upon arrival at the Fourth Psyop Group headquarters, the Kid went straight in to the orderly room and signed the day log. It turned out the clerk already had his eye appointment set up for later that same day for 1400 hours. "Travis there will give you a ride out after lunch. It's at Ton Son Nhut. And, of course, you know where the transients' hut is, don't you?" The clerk smiled as he handed the Kid an official piece of paper for the medics.

"Building four. Thanks."

After lunch, Stoney drove the Kid back to Ton Son Nhut, where, over on one side, the army had an incredible medical and dental operation setup—row after row of barracks-like buildings. It was all guarded by American MPs, who had checkpoints and bunkers all around the facility.

The Kid was right on time. Since he had his prescription with him in his medical file, they quickly checked his eyes with a light and had him look through a couple of lenses, then ordered his new spectacles.

"How long will it take to get the glasses?" he asked expectantly.

"Oh, we'll have them for you tomorrow afternoon about thirteen hundred hours, right after lunch," the medical specialist answered. "I imagine you are pretty anxious, what with how bad your eyes are and only having those shades!"

"You got that shit right! Plus, I don't want to go interview out at Armed Forces Radio with nothing but sunglasses. They might think I have some kind of an attitude."

"Yes. They dispense them down at the pharmacy on the corner a block over," the specialist 4 said, gesturing with his pen over his right shoulder.

Once the Kid was back in the jeep and it was rolling, Stoney wasted no time in demonstrating to him how he'd so quickly earned his name by handing him a cigarette.

"It may look like a Winston, but it's a joint!" he informed the Kid.

"Ah! Thanks!" He took it and drew in a long hit before passing it back.

"All the guys are smoking it like this here now. You can't tell what it is! And the gooks will take a carton of cigarettes and return you a carton of joints. It's great!" He laughed as he shifted gears and gunned it down the road off the giant air base. "Buck and a half for a carton of joints!"

"That reminds me," the Kid said, "I need to hit the PX, too. Can we do all of that? You've got nothing else going? You're my driver?"

"Pretty much!" Stoney passed back the joint.

"Well, driver, let's hit AFVN first! I need to get in touch with my main man there and see what I can do to get out of psyops."

"Nobody gets out of psyops," Stoney said, echoing a sentiment the Kid had heard a time or two before.

"Never say never," the Kid responded.

Armed Forces Radio and TV in Saigon had its own little compound. It was easy to spot from a distance because of the antennas bristling around it. As an important installation in the country, it was adequately guarded by American MPs.

Pulling up at the gate, Stoney just sat still behind the wheel as the Kid leaned over and yelled to the guard, "I'm here to see Alan P. I'm a classmate of his from DINFOS."

"Alan P.?" the guard said back to him.

"Yes."

"I happen to know Alan, and he's off today. For sure, he's not here. But I'd bet you could catch him over at his billet, the Da Lat Hotel." Then he directed his comments to Stoney the driver. "Do you know where that is?"

"No," Stoney immediately admitted.

"Le Loi Street. Go toward the canal out of the roundabout and two blocks past. Make a right, and it's right there, not far from Tu Do Street."

"Oh yeah, I think I know exactly what you're talking about!" With that, Stoney did a U-turn in the parking lot of Armed Forces Radio and TV Saigon and was waved right back through the out-gate. "This is like two minutes from here," he said with a wide grin on his face, shifting into third gear.

It was just 1500 hours, and the afternoon rush, people coming back from the midday nap, hadn't started yet. In what was only an instant, the jeep came to park in front of the Da Lat Hotel. A fairly substantial old colonial hotel, it was guarded by bunkers on either corner of the parking area right in front of the entrance, which sat back from the broad sidewalk as was the norm in downtown Saigon. At one time, there had been a sidewalk cafe at the Da Lat, but now it was parking and security.

"You might as well go in there and see if he's there while I wait with the jeep." Stoney motioned to the Kid with his hand, then pointed toward the door. "Then, if he's there and we're gonna stay awhile, I'll make arrangements with the guards to watch the jeep, then come on up!"

"Sounds like a plan, Stoney. One way or another, I'll be right back with the recon!" The Kid hopped from the jeep and strode up to the front door of the Da Lat. The guards did not look at the American twice. Into the lobby he went, where he spied a billet room roster.

Let's see, Alan P. Alan P. There he is, in a room with George C. Not George C.? Now he's here too? Room 780.

George C. was another member of the class behind the Kid's at DINFOS. How ironic, the Kid thought, walking over to a bank of three old wrought iron cage-like elevators that served the eight-story hotel.

Riding up, he was all excited to see his friends, but he was tinged with jealousy; they had all made it to Armed Forces Radio, and he, the Kid, the main man from Nashville, the hardest-working man in show business from midnight to six o'clock in the morning, had not! *Boy, I sure wouldn't want to be caught in one of the elevators during a mortar attack or some such bullshit that would knock out the power. Here it is, the seventh floor. Room 780 must be down the hallway to the left. There it is. Hope they're home, because this will be a shock!*

The Kid stood in front of the door and listened. Hearing voices inside, he knocked firmly upon the door and said loudly in a deep voice, "MPs. Open up!"

From inside the room, he heard silence, followed by someone muttering, "What the fuck?"

Then the Kid knocked again and said sharply, "Open up!" The sound of someone shuffling over in flip-flops was a prelude to the door's opening. Then there stood Alan P., with his dog tags hanging around his neck and wearing only a pair of boxer shorts and flip-flops. Once he saw who it was, his jaw hit the floor.

"Oh my God! It's the fucking Kid! The Kid himself!" They embraced and slapped each other on the back. "MPs, my ass! Ha, I thought to myself when I heard you, *That sounds like something the Kid would do!* And here you fucking are!"

"Alan P. to the third degree! You SOB!" They shook hands and exchanged more slaps on the back in a jubilant hug.

"Come on in! Shit, Kid, here ya are in Saigon! George! Look at what the fricking cat's drug in!"

"Hey, Kid!" George C. enthusiastically greeted him. "It's good to see you, man!"

"How long you here for? How'd you swing it? Are you still way out in the boonies down south? How long ya here for?" Alan peppered the Kid with questions.

"Alan, Alan, Alan, didn't you learn anything in journalism class?" The Kid smiled. "You ask one question and get one answer, then you ask another question, not ask the same question twice!"

Alan displayed an expression of mock surprise at being admonished, his hand to his chest with his fingers spread.

"See the shades? All I got left. I've broken one pair and lost one pair down a well, so they had to send me in for new glasses! Yes, I'm still stuck way the fuck out in the butt-fucking Mekong Delta, and as far as I know—I hope to God—I can milk this thing for three or four nights."

"And you grew a mustache! Look at that, Georgie, the Kid grew a mustache!"

"George, you mutha!" The Kid straight-armed the six-foot-tall, almost bald GI, taking him by his left shoulder, which was bare. "When did you get in-country?"

"Well!" He regained his balance. "I've been here for just six weeks! I finished Broadcast Specialist, and we all got stuck there with some order mess-up bullshit. So, I'm long, compared to you fuckers." He pushed his gray glasses up his nose and bent over to pick up a pack of cigarettes from the coffee table.

"You heard about Imbach?" the Kid interjected.

"Oh yeah. Right. We did." Alan was immediately sobered. "The Boy Scout. Did you ever hear how it happened?"

"No. I've written to Waterhouse but haven't heard back yet. Don't know if he's not getting my letter or I'm not getting his. Shit, at Cang Long, the place I'm at, we might go a week without a mail call! And I've been all over hell and back around the Delta; I've probably got mail strung out that I'll never see!"

"Ouch!" Alan barked. "I bet that cuts down on the Flo perfume bombs! Did she send you the Dear John yet?"

The Kid looked a little shocked at the thought. "No! Everything is fine, I think. 'Course, the longer you're over here, the less you really know, is kinda what I'm feeling. Oh shit! I've got a driver waiting downstairs to see if I'm staying or going back to Fourth Group. Shall I go get him? I mean, have you guys got something going, or do you have time to hang, or what? They told me at AFVN, Alan, that it was your day off. And I've got this guy and the jeep for the afternoon, making a huge PX run for a ton of stuff, and then maybe we could just drive around for a while and see some stuff?"

Alan glanced over at George and shrugged his skinny shoulders. "Georgie? You got any plans? Other than lying up here and smoking some of the most outrageous weed in all of Saigon?"

"Uh, let me check my book." He opened his palms like an appointment book and then took one hand and pointed at the other hand. "Nope."

"You know he's cool?" Alan inquired, with his head cocked to the left.

"Yeah, he already lit me up, and his nickname is 'Stoney'!" "Well, hell, go get him!"

574

Upon returning from the street, with Stoney in tow, the Kid was let into the room by George and Alan, who were sitting on their brown couch with one of the most ornate bongs—made of both red and clear glass—the Kid had ever seen.

"OK!" Stoney said, picking an easy chair in which to sit in the room that was nicely furnished with tables, chairs, beds, and dressers. It also had a bathroom with a private shower and everything you'd expect from a real hotel, including furniture that wasn't made out of discarded packing materials.

They had their own little refrigerator!

Alan and George had built an entertainment center from cinder blocks and planks on which they had set up a stunningly modern-looking Awai tape deck, an amplifier, and a turntable—with some really nice speakers, one in each corner of the room. The Kid was as green as his uniform with jealousy. Up on the top shelf was a big-ass transistor radio, and AFVN Saigon was playing low in the background.

As Alan fired up the bong, George went over and turned off the transistor. Then he threaded a tape onto the reel-to-reel. "Anybody up for a little Big Brother and the Holding Company?"

As Janis Joplin wailed about a piece of her heart being taken, the boys passed the bong and kept time to the music. They grinned at seeing each other, having a little fun thing in the midst of war.

"So, Kid!" Alan faced him. "Tell us, have you got any war stories? Seen any action?"

The Kid turned to look at Stoney, who kind of smirked at the same question he'd asked earlier that day. "Oh yeah," the Kid said in a measured voice that portended something seriously heavy. "Just a few days ago, they ambushed the morning bridge and minesweeping patrol using a command-detonated mine, and they killed four guys, including the captain who was our CO. He was fucking blown in half!" Mouths fell open. *Yes, siree, you've got it pretty damned easy here in Saigon, brothers.* "But I wasn't there for that. I was securing the fucking LZ for the medevac. Man, I was shaking in my boots, but the VC chose not to hit us there—or couldn't. I don't know which. You never know out there." He took a drink of the Budweiser that George had set open in front of him.

"Hey! I saw this one guy get shot out of a tree!" "Say what?" Alan refilled the pipe as he listened. "Yeah! We made this assault on ARVN navy junks!" "No! You're bullshitting!" George barked.

"BS? I don't need no fucking BS!" The Kid sounded insulted. "We travel up this branch of the Mekong, the Bassac, and turn up into this canal. I'm fuckin' scared shitless because I feel so exposed out on the water coming up to the bank. But anyway, we get off the boats OK, and the VC let us screw around for a few minutes. Then, when this one ARVN private climbs a tree to get some coconuts—*pow!*" The Kid went loud for effect. "They shoot his ass out of the sky! *Pow!* One shot. He falls out of the tree. Anybody would've sworn he was dead, and then all hell breaks loose and a bunch of other ARVNs get wounded. Well, this lieutenant, the one who is in charge of me, incidentally, calls the guy in as killed in action, but then come to find out, the ARVN landed in a fishpond and lived! So we call back in to the TOC with no KIAs, and they wanna know if we had a combat resurrection!" Laughter abounds.

"Yes, Alan, my boy," the Kid said, imitating the voice of W. C. Fields, "I've seen some heavy shit. Hmm, yes." Returning to his regular voice, he said, "I'm so pissed that I signed up for Armed Forces Radio and I'm out there and ... Get this!" He jumped to his feet. "There ain't no fucking *loudspeakers!* Those lying sacks of shit! Foreign-language announcer, my fucking ass! Ain't no announcin' going on anywhere! I have spent the night in the jungle after fighting all day, then fought all the next day too! A couple of times! Only good thing, even though I'm now a spec. 4 because we're with the ARVNs, is that I fucking get treated just exactly like all the officers! Check this out!"

He stood and smiled slyly as he unbuttoned his fatigue top and, throwing his shirt back, revealed his .38 snub nose, packed discreetly in the fold of his arm in the shoulder holster. "In the field, I get to wear this thing on the outside and nobody gives a shit!" He pulled it out and, flipping open the cylinder, emptied out the five bullets, before flicking it closed with his wrist and tossing it underhanded to a gaping-mouthed Alan P.

"Oh wow!" Alan held it in his hands. "I wish I could carry a pistol here in town!" He hefted it, sighted it on the stereo amplifier, and pulled the trigger, making a *click.*

"Oh, whoa, I wish I was a disc jockey here in town! So, Alan," the Kid said, turning the tables, "you have any close calls yet? Sappers in the latrine at the radio station? Anything like that?"

The thought made him chuckle. Alan thought for a second, head cocked. "No, not really. Me and Georgie heard that a restaurant we ate in a couple of weeks got hit with a terrorist bomb about a half hour after we left , but that's about it. You hear about guys getting popped by snipers on the street every once in a while, but action here in town has been pretty rare since the end of the Tet thing, thank God!"

"All I know is that I want to get out into the field one way or another!" Stoney emphasized his position, saying, "By hook or by crook!" Then he picked up the church key and cracked open another beer that George had just set in front of him, which made the Kid start to keep an eye on him. After all, he was the driver.

"Yes, and I want to get back here by hook or by crookie nookie!" the Kid responded. "I wanna be in Saigon! Alan, I brought my tape. Is there any chance you can introduce me to the powers that be here and I can talk to them?" The Kid's voice was pregnant with anticipation. "I've already had one 1049 refused, and I've got another one in the mail. I'm not going to quit until I succeed. And I think that if only I could talk to the guys who make the decision, I could seal the deal!"

"Well, yeah, that's no problem. I'll introduce you to Master Sergeant Shamus, the program director, and you can probably even meet Colonel Armstrong, the commanding officer. The problem is a position. A slot. A spot, Kid, that's the problem." Alan took a drink, followed by a puff on his Winston. "But hell yeah, I can give you the introduction! The rest would be up to you, considering how far you might want to go," the P-man said with a vibe of mystery.

"What exactly do you mean?" The Kid was immediately in tune.

"You know, Kid, I can tell you right now what they're going to do," Alan replied, leaning back against the brown Naugahyde sofa. "They are going to ask you if you would be willing to extend your tour and serve another year in Vietnam in exchange for the transfer."

"No shit?" The Kid was surprised at the mere fact that there might be any kind of chance to get out of psyops early, if only by a day. "Why do you say that?"

"Because that's their SOP; I've seen them make the offer before." Alan stood and went to a desk, where he opened a drawer and pulled out a huge plastic bag full of what appeared to be some outrageous tops. "Almost everybody at AFVN is here under those circumstances."

"Really?"

"Oh yeah. Me and Georgie, we flat got lucky!" Alan grinned as he set the bag of weed in front of the Kid, who immediately began checking it out.

"Wow! This is some fabulous-lookin' shit!"

"Wait till we smoke it. This is not what we've been smokin'," said George C.

"Let me see." Stoney moved into position to examine the perfectly formed dark green buds of Asian weed.

"Yeah, well, look at this," the Kid said with a haughty air as he stood and pulled his cache from his right front fatigue pocket, which was now down to about two ounces and all smashed to shit. Next to the buds belonging to Alan and George, the Kid's cache looked so pathetic that it got a big laugh. "When I bought this, I figured it was a little over half a pound. I've been moving around so much that I have to keep it in my pocket here, or else I wouldn't know when I'd see it again. So, I've been holding since I got it! What I do is just dip in my pipe and take a hit when I get the chance. I can't imagine what it would be like to be someplace permanent, like this." He made a broad sweeping gesture at the spacious digs of his compadres. "Someplace where there was a shower every night, and movies, and restaurants, and a huge fucking PX. Which reminds me, I gotta make a run. You guys want to go? We've got a jeep!"

"Sure, why not?" George C. said. "I need some cigarettes and a bunch of other shit too."

After smoking another couple of bowls, off they went, Stoney at the wheel, the Kid riding shotgun, with Alan P. and George C. in the back, everybody having a great time.

When they came around the corner and the Kid got his first glimpse of the Saigon main PX, he was blown away. The fucking place was huge, the size of a Montgomery Ward or a JCPenney store with a Safeway tacked on for good measure. There were pillboxes and MP guards all over the place, and over to one side, there were many members of the Vietnamese National Police, the ever-present White Mice, milling about in a shady area of the sidewalk, a congregation that caused to Kid to immediately think of wolves or sharks. They gave off a totally predatory vibe.

"Tons of money to be made here on the black market," Alan P., leaning forward, yelled over the din of traffic into the Kid's ear. "Everybody in Saigon maxes out their ration cards, buying everything they are allowed, and sells the stuff to the gooks. You're entitled to buy one refrigerator, and everybody gets one and sells it because you can quadruple your money."

"Along with the staples of life—perfume, liquor, and of course, cigarettes," George C. added.

As the Kid walked the aisles, shopping for the stuff he needed and the things he promised to get for Sweet, Reyes, and Jonesie, his mind was racing. *I could really get used to living in Saigon. Another year here wouldn't be so bad, living in the Da Lat Hotel, working at bunker-safe AFVN, having all the conveniences of the city and no rice paddies or infantry operations. I would make more money and get out six months early. And best of all, I'd get out of psyops two months early! If tomorrow the brass at AFVN offer me an assignment to Radio Saigon in exchange for an extension, I will sign so fast that I might break my wrist!*

Chapter 56

The cyclo driver wasn't going fast enough to suit the Kid. As the hot breeze generated by the midday Saigon traffic cooled him not, sweat rolled off his neck and down his back. He leaned forward and yelled at the driver in Vietnamese, "Ong. Di di mau beacoup! Cam on!" (Hurry the fuck up! Thank you very much!)

Wearing his shades, the Kid had two pairs of new army eyeglasses tucked neatly into his cargo pants pocket on the opposite side of his body from his cache of grass.

First stop was the Fourth Psyop Group, where he would drop off one pair of glasses and his cache and pick up his tapes before heading directly over to Radio Saigon, where he was to meet Alan P. at 1500 hours. That was when, according to Alan, Master Sergeant Shamus would be free to meet with him and listen to his air check.

And of course, the Kid would work his magic on the sergeant, charming the living shit right out of him.

Outside the gate to the Fourth Psyop Group's compound, the Kid was surprised that he knew enough Vietnamese to ask the driver if he knew the way to AFVN. When it became clear that the driver did know the way, the Kid pressed an MPC dollar into his hand and said, "Dung lai!" (Wait here!)

From the transit hut, where he stowed his stuff and grabbed his tapes, the Kid briskly walked up to the headquarters hut and found Specialist Scarberry, the clerk on duty.

"Hey, I'm going over to visit some friends at AFVN, and they said I could spend the night with them in their air-conditioned room at the Da Lat Hotel. Is that OK? Like, do I need to sign out, or what?"

"It is OK, and yes, you do need to sign out." Scarberry rose and walked over to the desk where the day logbook sat. He opened the page to September 28, 1968. "Sign out to the Da Lat Hotel—that is an official billet—and don't be out after curfew or go home with no frickin' bargirl to her place tonight. That's a good way to get killed."

"Don't worry." The Kid picked up the pen and signed out. "I've got too much to live for!"

Outside the gate, the cyclo driver waited astride his Honda for the Kid to return. As the Kid bounded into the back of the rickshaw-like aluminum gondola, the driver stroked his kick-starter and the motor sputtered to life, making the Kid cough upon inhaling some of the carbon monoxide.

Now it seemed that the only parts of his body sweating were the palms of his hands as the driver skillfully made his way through the light traffic toward the Allied radio station installation. Arriving at the front gate, the Kid paid the driver and told him not to wait. "Toi de lam. I'm going to work," he said. "Ciao, Ong. Cam on u lam" (Goodbye, Ong. Thanks a lot), he added, knowing that he was going to be working harder than he ever had to make something positive happen in his life. *High-stakes poker. Ha! Even if they say I can transfer, I still gotta live long enough to do it. I can't believe I have to go back to Cang Long whatever happens here today. Shit.*

Strolling past the guards, the Kid entered the foyer of Armed Forces Radio Saigon, where a specialist 4 inquired of him, "Can I help you?"

"Yes, I have an appointment with Alan P." As the Kid spoke the words, Alan P. came bursting out from a door behind the specialist 4, where he had apparently been waiting.

"Ah, the Kid! Right on time!" he said. Turning to the receptionist, he informed him, "I'll take it from here." Then he said, "Come on, Kid, let me show you around!" Alan P. was in his element, showing the Kid around AFVN because he worked there and the Kid didn't. What a coup!

The Kid was somewhat giddy as Alan P. led him through the outer door and into the inner working area of Radio Saigon, the holy grail of military radio. *Pinch me. Am I really here with my tapes in my hands?*

"There's the main control room, Kid." Alan P. stopped in front of an extremely large glassed-in room. The console of the control board was in the way, so the Kid couldn't actually see the setup of the broadcast board, only a portion of the close-cropped-haired announcer on duty, from the neck up.

"Wow. Can we go in?"

"Not right now. Only official business in there, hard-and-fast rule." The Kid looked disappointed. "But if Sergeant Shamus says it's OK or even takes you in there himself, then OK. But we can't just pop in. And we are on our way to Shamus's office, and he can't wait to meet you." He grabbed the Kid by the sleeve and dragged him away from the window. "I've been telling him Kid stories all day, not to mention the fact that Shamus was briefly stationed at Fort Campbell and he got into Nashville every chance he got. He is even familiar with WKDA and the ridiculous Good Guys. But from midnight to six o'clock, he said, he listened to some guy named Ralph Emery on WSM."

The Kid was blown away. What a setup! This was meant to be! Nearing the end of the hall, Alan P. made a left turn into an office, the Kid in tow. He stopped and turned sideways as the Kid came in, to find himself standing in front of the desk of the highest-ranking noncommissioned officer in Radio Saigon, one Michael Shamus, an Irishman through and through, of the black-curly-haired variety. With a big smile on his face, Shamus rose as soon as he saw the Kid and extended his hand to shake. Alan P. completed the introduction, saying, "Sergeant, may I introduce my classmate, the Kid himself, Specialist 4 Curt Stocker. Curt, this is

Master Sergeant Michael Shamus, self-professed lover of all things from the twin N's: Notre Dame and Nashville."

"Specialist Stocker! So good to finally meet you! I've heard so much about you— from a couple of different people, really. Don't know how much of it I believe.

Some of it seems pretty tall. But good to meet you!"

The Kid smiled broadly, flashing the pearly whites under his newly well-established blond mustache, and returned to Sergeant Shamus an equally firm, but nonchallenging, handshake. "A pleasure to meet you too, Sergeant Shamus! I've caught you on the country show a couple of times, and I must say I liked it as much as anything I've ever heard Alan P. do."

"At least I'm doin', Kid," Alan shot back with a huge grin, "not pretending to be on the air with the soap in the shower."

Shamus walked out from behind his desk to stand next to the Kid. He was shorter than the Kid by a couple of inches, but it was his trim frame that made him appear to be much smaller than that. His curly hair was long for an army master sergeant; most of them went for the GI flattop look, but not Shamus: he was latent Everly Brothers or Elvis all the way. He looked the Kid square in the eye and said, "I'm a really big Roy Orbison fan, and I play a little guitar. Alan here tells me you actually know him!"

"Yes. Yes, I do. 'Know him' might be a little bit strong, but I did indeed meet him, and I spent more than a couple of hours with him at the Nashville stock car track one night. He's really good friends with my fellow Good Guy Dave Allen, who is a musician. And Roy did say I could call him anytime he was in town and he'd do an interview on my show."

"You got Roy Orbison's phone number?" The sergeant's jaw dropped, betraying his interest.

"Oh, not his home phone, his office number over at the label," the Kid replied, looking right back into Shamus's eyes, letting him feel the power of the truth. "And when I get back on the air at WKDA in Nashville, that is one of the first things I'm going to do, call him. If I live that long." He let the last sentence sink in. "But what the hell, somebody could flip a grenade into your cyclo here in Saigon, so I guess it doesn't much matter where you are in Vietnam if your number's up. But I could sure as hell dig being here." The Kid pointed at the floor. "I have a 1049 in for a transfer—my second one, to tell you the truth. The first one was already turned down. Submitted that in late June; got back the negative reply in mid-August. And the second one, I put in on my birthday for good luck. I don't imagine it's on your desk there, is it?" The Kid ended his statement with lifted eyebrows, tilting his head in the direction of the desk with an air of expectancy.

Shamus said with a deadpan expression, "Let me think." He pulled on his chin while looking at the ceiling. "I haven't seen anything from any soldiers named 'the Kid.'" He shrugged.

"It never arrived?" The Kid quickly exhibited signs of desperation.

"Ah, Stocker! Yes, I do currently have one on my desk from a Specialist 4 Stocker, who apparently is most qualified to work here." The sergeant broke into a grin before slowly adding, "And I hope Specialist Stocker is not too upset when he gets it back, refused, in a couple of weeks. Or you can just take it with you now if you'd like."

The look on the Kid's face went from light and smiling to doom and gloom as if a switch had been thrown. Then Sergeant Shamus turned to Alan P. and asked, "How was that? Was my timing there? Did I give him enough time to picture his folder on my desk before I yanked the rug?"

"Yes, Sergeant, that was great! Excellent 'look on the face' points! He was devastated!" Alan P. chortled.

The Kid realized he'd been had. *Set piece to Alan. That was pretty good, you fucker.* He gave him a small kudos head nod in acknowledgment.

"There simply is not a spot here for you, Specialist Stocker," the sergeant continued in a serious tone. "Not now, anyway." After the slightest pause to let that comment float, he grabbed the Kid by the elbow and moved him toward the door. "Hey, Alan, let's take the Kid on the tour, and then we can end up in the production room and listen to his tapes! That is what you have there, isn't it?" He pointed to the big manila envelope that the Kid held under his left arm.

"Yes, Sergeant, I've got a couple!"

"Well, all right then, let's go!"

The three of them backtracked up the hall to the main control room, where Sergeant Shamus, seeing that the red light was not on, sashayed right in, with Alan and the Kid in tow. The GI working the board was a touch on the big side. He was large in build but not overly fat or muscular. His hands seemed small for his body, and his name tag told the Kid that this was the ultradeep-voiced Gary

W. Gears.

"Gary, this is the Kid from WKDA in Nashville, Curt Stocker. Curt, this is Gary Gears from WCFL in Chicago."

"Gary Gears from WCFL!" echoed the Kid. He stuck out his hand. "One of the all- time famous stations! Pleased to meet you! Almost got killed listening to your show just the other day!"

"Say what?" Gears said, a little surprised.

"Yep, I was just sitting in this jeep listening to this very show, the New Music show, when a sniper opened up on me. It was like during 'Cry like a Baby'!"

"No shit? What happened?"

"I cried like a baby. But he missed. Here I am. What else can I say?" the Kid said matter-of-factly. "Have you seen any combat yet?"

Gears held up his hand, indicating his request for silence as the song was concluding. He prepared to open the mike. "And there it is, 'Lady Willpower,' the monster new hit from Gary Puckett and the Union Gap! Look out for that one!

You're in Gear with Gears. That's Gary W. Gears on the New Music show from Radio Saigon. And now, fellow GIs, we are really gonna get rocking with the newest one from Tommy James and the Shondells, 'Mony, Mony!'"

The Kid eyed the equipment that surrounded the announcer's position as Gary put away a record and took care of business. Two of the latest, high-quality turntables, three shiny new continuous-loop cartridge machines, a reel-to-reel at one's beck and call. *Not quite as nice as WKDA, but better than the clinic at Cang Long, that's for fucking sure!*

"What station did you say you worked for?" Gears turned down the monitor so they could all talk.

"WKDA, home of the Good Guys, number one in Nashville for eleven years!"

"Nashville. That seems like a pretty cool market. Dylan just cut *Nashville Skyline* there, didn't he?"

584

"Him and everybody else cuts there," the Kid smugly replied.

"Come on," said Shamus, "we've got some more tour. We're on our way to the production room to listen to some of Stocker's air checks. Keep it tight." He led the way from the control room.

Walking out one door and heading down two more, the master sergeant led the Kid into the Radio Saigon music library. "This is the library. We've got more than twenty thousand individual titles in here!" It was evident that the sergeant was very proud of the collection.

It was monstrously large. Row upon row of shelves, from the floor to the ceiling, were stacked with long-playing albums, creating narrow corridor after narrow corridor. Upon long-playing vinyl was inscribed the music of the ages: popular, country, big band, jazz, classical, and rock and roll.

"Want to see something interesting?" Alan P. nudged the Kid, who was standing amid a row labeled "Top Pops records." "Lookee right here." He pulled an album out from the rack and pointed to the list of songs on it, one of which was, 'We Gotta Get Out of This Place," by the Animals. Written next to the title, in red ink, was the notation "DO NOT PLAY!" Removing the record from the sleeve, he showed the Kid that the army had someone scratch it with a beer can opener or screwdriver to render it unplayable, should any DJ get a wild hair up his ass or anything and decide to play it.

Every record in the room had been referenced and cleared for play by the military authorities, but every once in a while, an unforbidden song would become "forbidden" because its lyrics accidently took on new meanings.

"So it's true," said the Kid, recalling that it had been a rumor at DINFOS that the song had been eighty-sixed because its lyrics could be interpreted as expressing the desire to get out of Vietnam: "We gotta get out of this place if it's the last thing we ever do."

"Yes indeed, along with 'Sky Pilot,' so that's two for the Animals," Alan said. "The playlist is pretty tight here, but we do get new stuff, by army standards, all the time."

"And down this way," Shamus said, getting their attention, "is the production suite."

Entering the door at the end of the library, the trio found themselves in the presence of a GI who was obviously trying to make some kind of a spot. Of course it wasn't a commercial, because Armed Forces Radio had no commercials, but the station did run all kinds of army promotional stuff, and somebody had to make that stuff.

"Scott," Shamus said. The skinny GI took off his headphones. "This is the Kid, Curt Stocker, from Nashville. Curt, this is Scott Manning, another product of WCFL in Chicago."

"Wow, you and Gary Gears are both from Chicago?"

"Pretty much!" Scott Manning smiled uncomfortably. "Chicago people have connections, you know. Goes back to Al Capone!" he deadpanned.

Shamus picked up the phone that sat on a table next to the control console and dialed a three-number extension. "Hello? ... Yes, sir, we are in the production suite if you want to come down. ... Uh, no. ... Right now? ... OK, sir, right, I understand. It's taken care of." Returning the handpiece to its cradle, he turned his attention back to Manning. "Scott, if you could hold off on what you're working on, we want to take a couple of minutes and give a listen to Stocker's tapes. He wants to transfer in here, so Colonel Armstrong and I want to give his material a listen."

"OK," Scott said, reaching out for the tapes, now being extended to him by the Kid.

"The one on top is an air check. Why don't you thread that one up first?" the Kid suggested.

In a flash, Manning had the tape cued. Just as he sat back to demonstrate he was in the ready position, the door opened and in walked a very young-looking lieutenant colonel who sported a highly distinct raccoon suntan beneath his dark hair that, at first, made the Kid think he was wearing goggles. The Kid's expression must have betrayed his reaction.

"You must be Specialist Stocker. I'm Lieutenant Colonel Bernie Armstrong! Don't bother with the salute." He stuck out his hand, and they shook. "Oh, you're looking at my sunburn! Too much tennis without the suntan lotion or a hat, I suppose!"

"Yes, sir, I was actually looking at the shape your sunglasses made on your face. It's quite eye-catching. It's like the boss man in *Cool Hand Luke*, only with no glasses! You should certainly get somebody to take a picture for you and send it home! They'll love it!" *Flatter the hell out of him!*

"Specialist Stocker here, as you know, is a DINFOS grad and has all the necessary MOS's to work for us. If only we had a slot, that is, sir," Shamus commented to the colonel.

"Isn't that always the rub?" Armstrong said in a philosophical tone, although the very words he'd selected demonstrated to the Kid that it personally made no difference to him. "Being a DINFOS grad myself, in the officers program, I always like to give a fellow alum a chance anyway, slot or no slot. So, Scott, if we're ready?"

Manning's cobra-like hand darted out and hit the button. The tail end of the hit by Ronnie and the Daytonas, "Little GTO," came blaring out of the speakers. It was soon followed by the voice of the Kid. "And there he goes, Ronnie and the Daytonas. Don't forget the Daytonas. I know Ronnie never does, although he told me he had to fire the bass player last week. And for those of you who know that Ronnie sings every part and plays every instrument on that record, you also know how hard it must have been!" He hit the jingle and came out of it with "I Can't Take My Eyes Off of You" by Frankie Vallie and the Four Seasons. "It's five fifteen, a quarter after five in the morning for you purists, and here's the man, Frankie Vallie, with something that David is sending out to Annie as she stocks the shelves with the night crew at Bradyville Pike Kroger: 'You're just too good to be true ...'"

Listening to the air check made the Kid a little homesick. He slipped easily into reveries of WKDA, to one hot July night the previous year. It was his handpicked best one, in the hour from five o'clock to six o'clock in the morning, where he hit all the intros perfectly and had some funny stuff included, as well as a lot of produced drop-ins. The air check was from the Kid's *Happy Sunup Hour,* which he always approached with increased energy every morning, since Dick Buckley, the WKDA program director, usually got up at half past five in the morning and listened to his last half hour and then the first hour of Doc Holliday's show while he got ready to drive in for work.

When the tape ended, Shamus nodded his head in a positive manner. "All right! That was some fun radio! Excellent, Kid!"

He used my nickname. Always a positive sign.

"You've got off some funny stuff in there, Specialist Stocker," the colonel added, seeming to be amused.

"Thank you, sir." The Kid beamed. He could see out of the corner of his eye, however, that Scott Manning did not seem to be overly impressed as he finished rewinding the tape and loading up the second selection.

"Now this next one is the concept intro to a show I'd like to do here. It would be called *The Sergeant Pepper Family Band and Hit Parade Show.* I got drafted right when *Sgt. Pepper* hit, and I had, like, almost a vision when I got accepted to DINFOS. This idea came to me that the army was the perfectly natural place to do a *Sergeant Pepper* show. I wrote this, but the extra fancy production stuff was a gift to me from my friend Bill Berlin, the Wild Child, who produced this as a going-away present."

587

Manning had a truly sarcastic sneer on his face as he had his finger poised above the start button. "So, do all you Nashville guys use juvenile nicknames like 'the Kid' and 'Wild Child'?"

"No. But we do have one other guy there, Bill Craig, who uses 'Baby Bill Craig.' Uh, did you have a nickname at WCFL? Or are you still too new to the business?" the Kid cut back.

Manning did not answer, instead hitting the start button, causing the Kid's *Sgt. Pepper* intro to fill the room. He had lifted a few bars of the opening to the Beatles's *Sgt. Pepper's,* but the fade-overs, rising and falling, rendered it nearly imperceptible. Then over the tune came the voice of Bill "the Wild Child" Berlin: "Ladies and gentlemen, soldiers and sailors in foxholes and forts, and all ships at sea, the United States Army is proud to present, live and in color, strictly for your entertainment, the one and only, but don't call me lonely, real Sergeant Pepper, with his Family Band and Hit Parade Show!" The crowds cheered, jets flew over, cannons went off from the 1812 Overture, and Bill's voice returned: "Stand by now and know that it's the truth. If you've got the ears, Sergeant Pepper's got the juice. And the time has come to turn him loose! And here he is, the man himself, the one and only Sergeant Pepper!" Clapping and cheering made a bridge to the end.

"Ha!" Shamus said. "That's really cool! What do you think, sir?" "Absolutely! That is one of the wildest openings I've ever heard!"

"Yeah, really cool." The patronization in Manning's voice was not lost on the Kid.

"So, what do you think?" The Kid turned to the colonel. "If I got transferred in here, I could do this show?" The Kid brightened as he made his pitch to the colonel and Shamus both. "The show will feature all the hottest stuff. And I know all kinds of people back in Nashville who will send me interviews and greetings to the men, and early cuts of lots of artists' latest sessions so we can get it to the men quicker! Make 'em feel like they aren't six months out of touch! Do a lot of requests from home, have side characters, the whole nine yards!"

The colonel and Shamus exchanged knowing glances as the Kid waited for a response to his idea.

"Well, we can talk about that," Armstrong said slowly. "They're pretty strict here about not playing stuff that isn't officially cleared by the Pentagon. We've all been down that road, but hellfire, you never know! If something came along that was totally unique, it could happen. Tell you what, let's go down to my office and discuss all of this, Kid!"

The commanding officer called me Kid! Fucking pinch my ass! I am dreaming! Out of the corner of his eye, the Kid could see an expression on Alan P.'s face that said, *I told you so.*

Manning handed back the rewound tapes. The Kid thanked him and followed Armstrong and Shamus out the door, then walked back through the library. As they moved among the thousands of songs, Alan, walking behind him, droned low and sarcastically in his ear, "Hear the sirens, brave Kid Ulysses. Come to Radio Saigon. We have a slot. We have a sssslllaaawwwwttt." He modulated his voice. "All you must do is give us one more year of your life. Wrrrrrrk!" He ended with the call of a squawking bird.

As they arrived at Armstrong's office door, Shamus and Alan P. stopped outside. "My desk is in the common area up this way." Alan pointed. "Come pick me up when you're finished talking. I should be done with the stuff I have to get done today, and then we can go grab some chow."

"Roger chow," replied the Kid. He gave Alan a thumbs-up and entered the very large and spacious office behind Armstrong.

"Grab a chair." The colonel pointed as he slipped in behind his desk and lit up a cigarette. "How do you like our facility, Specialist?"

The Kid grinned broadly. "Like it? I love it, sir, and I want to join your staff. I'd do just about anything except blow you to get a slot here."

"When you say anything, soldier, does that include extending?"

The Kid paused. *Cuts right to the chase, doesn't he!* "Well, sir, if I did agree to extend, how exactly would that work?"

"Stocker, I've got your 1049 right here." He lifted a manila folder off his desktop. "Which we are going to have to deny. However, if, when you get back to your unit, you put in another one, with a paragraph stating that you will extend a year here, we will accept it. Now, when is your current DEROS date, and what is your ETS?"

"That would be 21 May 1969 for DEROS, sir," he said, informing the colonel of his estimated date of return from overseas, "and my ETS [estimated time of separation from the military] is 10 September 1970."

"OK." The colonel screwed up his face as he figured the dates in his head. "If you extended in 'Nam for a year to get assigned here, first thing, you'd get a sixty-day drop, so you'd be home in March and get a month's leave before coming back here in April. Do your year and then you'd ETS and be out of the service five months early. How does that sound?"

Hmm, that means I'd only have another six months in psyops and just a year and a half left in the army. I'd see Flo two months early and be back in Nashville at WKDA by April of 1970. "Yes, I think I'd like that, sir. I'll do it!"

"Excellent! I must say, we look forward to having a man with your talent as a member of our staff!" He rose from his chair and extended his hand. The

589

two of them shook to seal the deal. "All right!" The colonel snuffed his butt in the clear glass ashtray sitting atop a stack of papers. "I'll inform Sergeant Shamus that we have an agreement in principle, and when your new 1049 comes in, it will be accepted and we'll be in business!"

"Yes, sir!" The Kid snapped off a smart salute. "Thank you, sir!"

Exiting the office, he made his way up to the common area, where he spied Alan

P. sitting at his desk. Standing in front of him, the Kid was grinning from ear to ear.

"You did it, didn't you?" Alan looked up with a wry expression painted across his Italian face. "You agreed to extend for a year."

"Yes I did!"

"Well, Kid, I hope you're not sorry when you arrive back here for your second year."

"Alan, my boy." The Kid looked him in the eye. "There is nothing in the world sorrier than the place or the situation I am fucking stuck in right now. I can only hope to fuck I live long enough to be sorry about working here!"

Chapter 57

The name of the bar was the Che Thuah. "We refer to it as 'the Shaved Twat,'" Alan said, chuckling, as he pulled open the door of the white-painted and pink- trimmed building about two blocks from the Da Lat Hotel.

"Compared to the shit that goes on at just about any club over on Tu Do Street, this place is basically GI-friendly," George said, removing his baseball hat and wiping the sweat from his forehead as they entered the air-conditioned establishment. "The girls here are really nice, and they only charge you a dollar for a Saigon tea."

Saigon tea, as it was called, was the drink that bargirls had the GIs buy them as the price of conversation. It all began early in the war. When a GI would agree to buy a bargirl a drink, with the goal of getting her a little drunk, the establishment would charge the GI for bourbon but would serve the young woman caramel- colored tea, thereby making a huge profit by selling tea at bourbon prices.

Eventually the GIs found out there was no liquor in the drinks being brought to the bargirls, and thus the name for the drink, "Saigon tea," was coined. After a while, the pretense was dropped and the bargirls would say, "You buy me tea, GI?" with all parties to the transaction knowing there would be no booze involved.

The Che Thuah was contained in a fairly spacious room that measured about forty feet square. To the right of the door, a very ornate wooden bar stretched from one end of the room to the other and was lined with stools, upon which sat a half dozen GIs, each flanked by a young woman, with whom they were engaged in conversation. Behind the bar, a mirror ran the length and reached from the counter to the ceiling, giving the place an appearance of depth and size beyond its limitations. A row of booths lined the pink-painted wall opposite the bar, and in between were two dozen Formica-topped tables, about half of which were occupied by GIs and more bargirls.

The Kid thought he had died and gone to heaven. The young women in the bar— there must have been at least twenty of them—were overall. as a group, quite attractive. Some wore tight, sleeveless minisheaths that accented

591

their very tight, slim asses and stunning legs. Others were dressed in loose-fitting white and pastel-colored slacks with a style of breezy sleeveless top, unbuttoned enough to show hints of their white bras.

It was 1900 hours, and the three GIs had about three hours to kill before the Saigon curfew, ten o'clock at night, would require them to be safely back in their hotel. The place was less than half full, with a mix of black and white GIs spread out among the tables, all of them nursing beers and drinks, and almost all of them talking to bargirls. Naturally, they had toked up big-time before and after dinner, so they were packing major buzzes as they sat down in one of the open booths, Alan P. and George C. facing the Kid.

Almost immediately as they settled into the booth, three young women detached from a cluster of as-yet-unengaged women at the far end of the bar and approached them. The Kid's eyes were drawn to the one on the left; she was stunningly good-looking with a slightly dark-skinned complexion that indicated she might be part Cambodian. She wore white slacks and a pink blouse with the collar turned up, and her facial features, especially her eyes, had a more European than Asian cast to them, revealing the possibility of French blood in her ancestry. *What a face. And oh my God, what a beautiful fucking body!*

With a sultry look, she exuded boredom as she sat down in the booth next to the Kid. *Hot, hot, hot!* "Men yoi, Co dep. An mun Saigon tea?" he said to her.

Her face lit up in a huge smile, showing nearly perfect teeth. "An bic Vietnam con hoa?" She was asking him, "You understand Vietnamese?"

"Bic ti ti. I know only a little," he replied, feeling the heat of her touch as he gazed into her absolutely gorgeous face. "An dep hoa beaucoup!" he said, telling her that she was very beautiful!

At that, she intertwined her arm with his and gave it a squeeze, saying, "Cam on u lam, an menoi ong, an bic Vietnam!" which means, "Why, thank you very much. You're a darling man! And you speak Vietnamese."

"I'm gonna spend the whole night with you!" she said in English, with a gushing feeling of warmth that the Kid could hardly believe. As he looked across the table, he saw Alan P. and George C. sitting there with their jaws on the table.

"Well, look at this!" Alan P. recovered his power of speech. "It looks like Li likes the Kid more than a little bit! Unbelievable! This is the most unobtainable woman in the whole place, Kid!"

"Unobtainable?" The Kid peered sideways at Alan, while looking down at the arm of Li, which was woven around his. Her right leg was now firmly entwined along the length of his left.

"Yes. I'll explain it to you here when we can get a minute." He tapped out a cigarette and lit it. "But we know these ladies, don't we, Georgie?"

"Yep. Hello, Wan. Hello, Su! How are you tonight?" Alan stood and let Wan slip in beside George. As he sat back down, Su brought over a chair and sat down at the end of the table, which was tilted to Alan's side, meaning four on one side of the booth wouldn't have worked.

"An Li?" The Kid turned to what was now apparently his companion for the evening. *I wonder what Alan could possibly have to explain?*

She nodded. "Li, Ten Ong la gi?" she said, asking him his name.

"Curt."

"Cut," she repeated back.

"Close enough." The Kid grinned, reaching into his pocket for a smoke of his own.

Beers and teas arrived at the table. The Kid paid, in appreciation of Alan for what he had done for him at Armed Forces Radio.

"Alan P., the man with the key!" The Kid lifted his can of Budweiser. "Thanks, buddy!"

"I don't know, Kid, do you really want to spend what is going to amount to two years over here?"

"Here? Oh yes, if here is Saigon, shit yeah!" the Kid exclaimed. "The more I think about it, the better it gets!" He lifted his left hand and ticked off the positives on his fingers. "I get out of psyops two months early, see Flo two months sooner, and get a month's leave. I'll be in Saigon where, you yourself pointed out earlier today, I can make a great deal of money on the black market, and I get a five- month drop, almost half a year of my life back! And my brother, Scott, who is getting married in December, will not have to come for another year. And he's going to be a medic! So this will definitely save him some bad shit!"

As the evening unfolded, the Kid was actually amazed at himself for having assimilated so much Vietnamese into his speech in the past four months. He prattled on with Li and was even able to make her laugh. Wan and Su, on the other side of the table, were participating in his and Li's conversation to the point that Alan and George had become spectators.

After the second round of beers, Alan gestured that he needed to visit the men's room. "Slide over there," he drawled to Wan and George. "I gotta see a ma-an about a horse." They stood to let him out of the booth.

"I'll join you," George said, already standing. The pair left the Kid alone with the women at the table.

Li, with a smile painted upon her delicate face, was clearly having a good time with the Kid. And the Kid, having not been laid since July in Sa Dec, was beginning to feel the overwhelming desire to have this beautiful prize before he left to return to the hellhole that was Cang Long. However, the more he felt the urge to find a way to bed Li, the more his conscience reminded him he was engaged. All afternoon, the Kid had already been wrestling with how he was going to break the news to Flo that he was going to volunteer for Radio Saigon and spend another year in 'Nam. True, it was against the mantra he practiced religiously in the army—never volunteer for *anything*—but as his thoughts were once again invaded by the mental picture of Captain Robinson's exposed intestines, he was convinced he was doing the right thing. As for Li, he rationalized that it would be virtually impossible for any real red-blooded man to look at her and not want to possess her in every conceivable way. *Hmm, who is it that she reminds me of? Somebody ...*

"Now it's my turn." The Kid pointed toward the restroom from which Alan and George were emerging. Li immediately stood to let him out. She slapped the Kid's ass as he exited, getting huge laughs from Wan and Su.

She's asking for it! I gotta figure out how to work this, the Kid pondered as he made his way across the barroom to the head. He knew he couldn't go home with Li, so he began wondering if it was kosher to take a woman back to the Da Lat Hotel for the night. *I wonder what she costs? I don't care. She is so smoking hot that I've got to have her! Forgive me, Flo. I'm going back to Cang Long, where people get killed, and I don't want to die with a perpetual hard-on.*

Emerging from the restroom after relieving his bladder, the Kid was slightly surprised to find Alan P. waiting for him right outside the door.

"Uh, Kid," he began in a serious tone of voice, "do you see that throng of black GIs over there?" He gestured with his head to a group of about a dozen soul brothers congregated at the far end of the bar.

"Yeah. So?" The Kid had never had any kind of a problem with the brothers.

"Well, I was just standing over there taking to a guy I know, and I overhead them talking about you. They are planning on taking you outside and beating the living shit out of you because you have monopolized the attentions of Li all night. And it's her they come in here to see, because she looks so much like Diana Ross."

That's who she looks like! Yes! The Kid was startled into silence at the news of his impending beating.

"Let me repeat myself. I suggest we leave right now." Alan was not joking. "Unless all of your combat experience has made you dinky dau to the point that you want to take on a dozen pissed-off black guys. This is what George and I meant when we said Li was unobtainable, because the black GIs love her to death and, like, view her as their property, to the point that no white guy ever even tries to approach her, let alone totally get her attention like you've done here tonight."

"OK." *Rats!* "Let me go say goodbye."

Walking up to the booth, the Kid did not sit back down. "Li?" He leaned over as she cocked her head to hear what he had to say. "Something has come up. We have to go."

"Oh no!" Disappointment swept across her face. "Di sao? Why?"

"Cambod GIs soc mau toi," the Kid said, telling her that the black GIs were going to beat him up.

Li looked past the Kid's shoulder to the group of black GIs and spewed some rapid-fire words to Su, who walked quickly over to the bar and returned with a yellow piece of paper and a pen. After writing something down, Li handed the paper to the Kid.

"This my address. You give to taxi driver and come see me tomorrow at ten. OK? You can do?" She smiled brightly. To the Kid, the sparkle in her eye was hotter than the tip of an arc welder's torch.

He looked down at the piece of paper and then crushed it into his fist. "Can do, menoi!"

With that, he grabbed his hat and turned to join Alan and George, who were waiting for him by the door. As they exited through the window, the Kid could see the entire throng of black GIs moving as a unit toward the booth where Li, Su, and Wan had remained.

Strolling toward the Da Lat in the hot Saigon night, the Kid held up the piece of paper and, with an ear-to-ear grin on his face, declared to Alan and George, "She invited me over to her house tomorrow!"

"The luck of the Kid!" Alan shook his head. "It never ceases to amaze me!"

Chapter 58

Dearest Parnelli,

Finally got my new glasses! They are the ugly Army ones, but my Dad is sending me some John Lennon glasses for my birthday, you know, the gold round ones. Can't wait for them to get here. They might even be waiting for me back in Tra Vinh. I guess it will never hurt to have an extra pair in this place.

I am writing this from Alan's room in the Da Lat hotel in Saigon, where I was their guest last night, sleeping in air-conditioned comfort! What a cush deal they have. They don't even have to use mosquito nets! Can't believe it, while I'm playing grab ass with the ARVNs out in the Boonies, they've got a sound system to rival anything in the states, a refrigerator, incredible chow and a ton of really cool restaurants, movies every night in the hotel lobby and a freaking huge PX! I could get used to this!

This has been a very interesting trip in many respects, and there might be some changes coming down the line. Alan introduc3ed me to the OIC and NCOIC of the radio station yesterday and I got to play them my air check. Bottom line is that they liked it, including the Sgt Pepper idea and they said if I would agree to extend for another year in Vietnam, they could get me here. And that's not all, if I did extend, I would get to come home two months early and get a month leave and when I got back, I'd get totally out of the Army 5 months early! It's called an early out and its part of what they offer to make people extend.

I know this is coming as a surprise to you, the thought of me being here for 2 years, but the advantages are immense: I'll make a ton more money for when we start our married life... We'll get to see each other two months sooner than we expected and I'll have a month's leave. Maybe we could get married then and THEN your Mom and Dad would have to let us be together for R&R in Hawaii during the second tour, so it would only be 6 months at a pop that we were apart and then I'd be done with the Army! Plus it is pretty safe here in Saigon, compared to what I have going on in my life in Cang Long.

Anyway, who knows what is going to happen? I still have to make it for another 6 months before I can ever get out of PSYOPS. All I know for certain is I love you and want to be with you for the rest of my life. Why do you have this effect on me? Whatever it is, don't stop!

My flight back to CAn Tho is set for tomorrow. Today I have a bunch more shopping to do so I will ge going back to the PS and checking out some of the stores downtown, where I can bargain with my Vietnamese!

Thinking about you and looking at your picture a lot: hope I don't wear it out...

Love, Curt

PS: ISYL!

As he dropped the letter into the Da Lat postbox, his hand reached into his pocket and withdrew the yellow slip of paper handed to him by Li the night before. Checking his watch; it was 0930 hours. He had no idea where in Saigon the address was, or how long it would take to get there, but he knew he did not want to be late.

Of course, he was armed with his .38, snuggly tucked into his left armpit, as he hailed a minicab outside the hotel and prepared for his sortie alone into the bowls of the city. He had picked a minicab because he thought it would be safer concealed rather than riding out front on a pedicab, when going into an area he did not know.

The miniscule yellow and blue painted vehicle was half the size of his VW bug back home in the states. It was beat to shit on the outside but as he settled into it, he was surprised how roomy it was. Handing the piece of paper up to the driver, he asked in Vietnamese, if he knew where to go; *An bic?* The driver, a bristly haired man in an odorously stained faded blue t-shirt, nodded to the affirmative and they were off!

As they motored through the city, the Kid attempted to keep track of approximately where they were, in relation to the Da Lat. Soon they were in the thick of traffic on Le Loi Street. Motor scooters swarmed all around them, the majority driven by long haired and very haughty looking young men, who appeared to be of military age, but clearly were not in the army. They were known as "cowboys", and the Kid suspected, if they all were in the army, there would be no need for American troops to be here fighting this war.

"I will not send American boys halfway around the world to do what Asian boys should be doing for themselves..." or words to that effect, the Kid recalled a line from one of Johnson's 1964 campaign speeches.

After a couple more turns, as far as knowing where he was in Saigon, the Kid was toast. Then his conscious thought was struck by one of those moments where he envisioned the poncho blowing off the body of Captain Robinson; since the event, it had been happening quite frequently, where that scene vividly appeared in his mind. He shook it off and reaching into his side pants pocket, he pulled out his pipe and cache and fired up a bowl. Turning sideways on the dirty upholstery of the of the smooth-running little cab's sweat stained back seat, he tried to stretch out and relax. After a couple of hits, he began to examine his relationship with Flo and marveled at how far away, in time and space, that life all seemed to be. It was the strongest thing he'd ever felt, but when Li invited him over to her house, there was no way he could have said no. *There will be plenty of time for monogamy after we're married.*

Soon the cab turned off the mercantile streets and began traveling through neighborhoods that were obviously residential. On one tree-lined lane, where the houses were right up next to each other in long rows, the cabbie pulled to a stop and pointed at a gate. Each dwelling had a patio-like courtyard, visible beyond the chest high masonry wall and above that, each had second floor balconies fronted by intricate wrought iron railings.

Very French, the Kid thought as he reached into his pocket for the money to pay the driver. *"Bon U?"* How much, The Kid asked.

"Nam chop," fifty piasters, the driver told him the amount of the fare, and when the Kid handed him an MPC five dollar bill, which was worth double, and signaled for him to keep the change, the Kid could tell he was pleasantly surprised, by the tone of his *"Cam on u Lam!"*

Checking his watch, he discovered he was about 10 minutes early, but when he looked over the gate, he saw that Li was coming out the door to meet him; *she must have seen the cab arrive!* The same bright smile and sparkling eyes from the night before made it difficult for the Kid to take his eyes off her face. She was clad in faded cutoff jeans and a blue sleeveless top with a Vee neck as she dashed barefooted to open the gate for him.

My God! This is like an Asian Gidget movie! "Men yoi Li!"

"Men yoi, Cut!" Li smiled nervously, stopping short of embracing him on the street in front of whoever might be watching. "Welcome to our house," she gestured toward the entrance with her hand, "I live here with my sister and her husband, who works for the Americans."

They navigated up the walkway and entering the door, stepped into a quite spacious area that was designed to be a combination kitchen and living room. There was a heightened rectangular wooden table that was sided by bar stools, like the ones at Che Thuah, giving the place an entirely un-Vietnamese art deco look. A woman sat drinking a coke from a can at the table and she slid off the

stool to stand for her introduction to Li's American friend.

"Cut, this is my sister, Quan," Li switched to English for the introduction and Quan replied in English as well.

"Pleased to meet you, Cut." Quan extended her hand and the Kid gently shook it as he looked into the smiling face of a short woman, showing the first traces of chubbiness in her cheeks that were framed by black hair parted down the middle and cut to shoulder length. "Li say that you speak very good Vietnamese, but we like to practice our English, too!"

"Please to meet you, then," the Kid adapted, as Quan turned and said something in rapid-fire Vietnamese to her sister, that was far beyond the Kid's weak grasp of the language.

Grinning, Li translated, "My sister says that she would enjoy having an American boyfriend maybe just once, but she love her husband too much!" Li joked, making Quan gasp in surprise that her sis would divulge such intimate information.

"Come upstairs, Cut, I want to show you my room," she took him by the hand and lead him to a louvered door that enclosed a staircase that when they clinmbed it, delivered them into a hallway lit by two skylights. Walking to the second door, Li opened it and bade the Kid enter.

All right!

With her hands in her hip pockets, she observed the Kid survey her room and waited with a shy smile to see his reaction.

The room was quite spacious and the furniture in it; a double bed, a vanity with a round mirror, a chest of drawers and a small, padded chair with a dark red seat and a stand with a small portable record player sitting on it, didn't really fill it up all that much. The walls were painted in a light green and were decorated with several black and white pictures of Li and what must be her family and friends.

"Very nice," nodded the Kid, as he stepped forward and slowly placed his arm behind her back and drew her to him and made a move to kiss her. He was slightly shocked when she turned her head to one side and then brought her arms up to firmly push him back.

"Not here," she said with a serious look, "don't worry, I want you know that we make love today, but no can do here. Quan's husband would be furious if he even thinks I make love to GI here. He *cocky dao* us all! I have a place. But first, we go shopping, I give you money and you buy me perfume, soap and cigarettes from PX. OK? Then I sell on black market later. That way, you help me, OK?"

"Beau coup OK!" the Kid responded to her proposition. *Oh my God... is this like a real date or what?"*

"I need to change clothes; do you want to listen to American record?" Li asked. Moving to the machine and switching it on, she carefully placed the needle arm onto a 33 &1/3 record, already sitting on the turntable. "This is my favorite!"

The Kid sat down on her bed and lit a cigarette, in anticipation of listening to some American music while watching Li change clothes. *What'll it be? The Beatles... The House of the Rising Sun? Hey; something by the Supremes!* But what came out of the minuscule speaker was the vocal stylings of Rosemary Clooney; *'How much is that doggy in the window, the one with the waggling tail..."* He wanted to laugh, but he didn't dare. And as she sang along, she stripped down to a white bra and stylish light pink bikini panties. Turning to face the Kid, she struck a pose with her arms and hands up turned and one leg facing out at an angle. "You like?" she asked, with the sweetest smile.

"Dep hoa!" replied the Kid in pure awe. That was as good as he could do because all the blood was rushing from his brain to another part of his anatomy and the Kid was having a rough time adjusting the diamond-cutter boner that had immediately materialized in his pants, upon seeing Li in her undies.

But, when Rosemary got to the line in the song that said: *"I must take a trip to California..."* the Kid had a major guilt attack. *Ah, Flo, I love you and would give anything to be with you this second... but you said I could and the pressure of possibly being killed on any given day is too much! I need this to keep from going totally fucking crazy!*

Li tapped her underarms and neck with talcum powder before slipping on white silk ao dai slacks and a mostly yellow and green intricately flowered top. Luckily, when she was ready to go and the Kid had to stand up, he was glad his

600

fatigue shirt nicely concealed his raging boner, and he was able to adjust it while her back was turned to pick up her purse and a woven shopping bag.

Downstairs, Li completed her ensemble with the addition of a dark yellow silk scarf, that wrapped around her head and neck, and a pair of sunglasses. She inserted her feet into a pair of flats kept by the door, and she was ready to go. Quan said goodbye to the Kid in English and he answered her in Vietnamese, which made them all laugh.

She lead the Kid out of the courtyard, where he discovered the heat was overwhelming, even in the shade of the trees. At the first cross street they came to, Li was able to quickly wave down a cyclo and she gave the man directions as the Kid settled in. He would have preferred a minicab, but there was no way he was not going to let Li be in charge.

Leaning back in the seat, she tucked her arm into his and proceeded to draw circles on the back of his hand as they rode along, shoulder to shoulder, with the thick mixture of motor scooters, cars, jeeps, cyclos, pedicabs and bicycles bustling all around them. But the Kid only had eyes for Li. This woman had as much stated that they were off to some location where he was going to learn every intimate detail of her anatomy, including what it felt like to be inside her.

But, he had to be cool; knowing there were going to be some stops and shopping to be done before he got to taste the fruits of his dutiful efforts to learn how to speak the native tongue.

How right he was. The first stop was at the great Saigon indoor street market. The building itself took up as much as four normal city blocks; wooden and painted white, its ceiling was easily 20 feet high. There were a number of cavernous openings where one could enter and begin walking among the hundreds of booths, selling everything from toothpaste and radios to pig's ears and tomatoes.

As they made their way up and down the aisles, the Kid spotted a couple of other GIs, who were there shopping with their Vietnamese girlfriends. They exchanged knowing smiles. There were even a few American men who were there in civilian clothes and shopping by themselves... *CIA?*

After Li purchased a pair of white sandals, they found an exit and once back on the street, she again waved down a mode of transportation; this time it was a pedicab. After telling the peddler their destination, she drew the wallet out of her purse and pulled out a wad of MPC and a small hand-written list. She counted out $50 into his hands and gave him the list. "We go to American PX and you buy me this."

601

Taking the money and the list, the Kid tucked it into his top right fatigue shirt pocket, smiling at her, revealing at the fact that he wasn't going to pay her money directly for sex, making the encounter take on an entirely new level of allure.

Looking at his watch he noticed it was high noon when they pulled up to the edge of the ultra large American PX, stopping at the point where a civilian mode of transportation could approach no closer. They got out of the pedicab and the Kid paid the driver. Smiling, he left Li in the shade of the trees on the sidewalk and headed for the entrance. Out of the corner of his eye, he thought he caught one of the White Mice, the Vietnamese national police, pointing at him but he quickly dismissed it as meaningless.

Once inside, he made his rounds, finding the perfume and soap and then, hitting the cigarette display and picking out 4 cartons of Salmes, the favorite American cigarette of most Vietnamese, he quickly headed for the checkout lines.

The Vietnamese clerk smiled knowingly at him as she punched up the purchases for the perfumes and soap on her register, easily determining the Kid had no personal need for the perfume himself. She marked his ration card, quickly placed the items in a paper sack and the Kid was out the door.

Emerging from the PX, he looked for her at the spot where he had left her, but she was not there. Glancing nervously around the grounds, he was shocked to quickly find her involved in what appeared to be a heated conversation with one of the White Mice. Walking over, he was again surprised at the distress etched on her face as he motioned for her to join him. The national policeman, eyes hidden by their nearly uniform love of mirrored aviator sunglasses, did not have a pleasant expression on his face as Li turned to speak to the Kid.

"What's going on?" the Kid asked.

"Oh, Cut, this policeman want me to pay him money because he say he knows you are buying things for me to sell on the black market and if I do not pay him, he will arrest me!" she exclaimed.

"Let's just leave!" the Kid shifted the sack to his left arm and took her by the elbow to lead her off but she pulled it away from him.

"No can do! I must take care of this. Give me the sack and go wait. If I try to leave without paying, they take me, lock me up, take everything and fine me even more money! Please! *You let me handle this!*"

As much as he wanted to whip out his .38 and tell the policeman they WERE leaving, the Kid just handed Li the sack of goods and with an angry look on his face, stepped back about 10 meters and resolutely folded his arms.

Grabbing the sack out of her hands, the policeman sat it on the ground and began to rifle through it as Li talked to him, gesturing emphatically as he lifted up the perfume and then the soap before extracting two cartons of cigarettes from the bag before shoving it back into her possession with his black jack-booted right foot. Placing the two cartons casually under his arm, he wheeled and walked off with his graft, back to where the other White Mice waited their turns to extort whomever might be next.

Picking up her remaining goods, the Kid thought she might start crying as she returned to him. "God damn them!" she swore in English, "I hate them!"

Taking the sack from her, the Kid carried it as they walked over to where a line of pedicabs waited to pick up fares. As they climbed into the back, she was obviously now in a bad mood as the man pedaled them away from the PX, to the destination she had given him.

He put has arm around her shoulder and tried to comfort her by rubbing her neck. "Those bastards!" he frothed, "I could go back and get some more cigarettes!"

"No, Cut, we go now, if we go back to the PX, they will make me pay again!"

The Kid continued to gently rub her neck and shoulders as they made their way to their destination, which was about a fifteen-minute ride from the PX. It was in a neighborhood where there were shops and storefronts that had two and three stories of habitations built on top of them. Paying the cabbie, the Kid carried Li's sack as he followed her into a doorway between two of the shops and up a stairway to the second floor where she knocked on a door to an apartment.

It was opened by a slightly stocky middle-aged woman with a head of graying hair, dressed in white pants and a faded dark blue blouse. She wore a pair of rectangular shaped silver wire framed glasses and smiled broadly when she saw it was Li and opened the door wide for them to enter.

"Chao, Mama San," Li gave the older lady a peck on the cheek and then reached

back and took the sack from the Kid, who stood behind her.

"Chao, Mama San," the Kid made a little bow in her direction.

Mama San's place was just one big room, made distinct by its hardwood floor that lead out onto another one of those ornately iron-railed balconies. From it, there was an excellent view of the intersection below, on streets that he imagined were once just French suburbs of the main city.

Lining the walls were some shelves that contained a great deal of clutter and other than a small wooden table with three chairs, and her Buddhist shrine in one corner, the only real furniture in the entire place was the bed. It was one of the biggest beds the Kid had ever seen. Around it was draped a very thin mosquito netting and clearly visible through the gossamer thin fabric, was a large pile of assorted pillows at the bed's head.

Li sat the sack of PX goods on the table. "You pay her $5, OK," she said, as she unwrapped the scarf from around her head, put it on the table and tossed her sunglasses down on top of it.

Obligingly, the Kid reached in, pulled out his wallet and paid Mama San the $5 MPC. *Cheap at twice the price!* She took it and stuffed it into a small black lacquer box on one of the higher shelves behind her table. As she did it, Mama San conversed with Li, in a typical quick talking Vietnamese conversation that the Kid could barely make out every 10th word.

"Mama San says we can stay long as you like but, Toi de lam sau," she pointed to her lady Seiko; Li had to be to work by 6 o'clock.

That will be plenty of time. "Yes, I must be back by then, too, to get ready to leave tomorrow for Can Tho."

Li pulled back the mosquito net on one side of the bed and bade him to come sit beside her, by tapping his place with her hand on the mattress. The Kid complied and once seated, took off his combat boots, stuff his socks inside and slid them down toward the foot of the bed. As he began unbuttoning his fatigue shirt, Li also began undoing her top.

"What about Mama San?" the Kid glanced at the smiling woman, now seated in her chair at the table, and back to Li, "is she going someplace while we do this?"

"No."

"O.K."

Li stopped undressing and had a quirky little expression on her face, "Oh, she not my real Mama San... she just my friend. If Mama San watch, so what? You want to go to a hotel and pay $20 for short time?"

"Uh, no," the Kid was sure he didn't want to do that and sighing agreeably, he nodded his head in the affirmative, "this is okay, Li." *Like I'm gonna care if Mama San watches!*

Li continued to disrobe down to her bra and panties, at which point she climbed over to the center of the bed, grabbed a yellow pillow for her head and lay down on her back waiting for the Kid to take off his clothes.

Removing his fatigue shirt, Mama San let out a noticeable little gasp as his shoulder holster and .38 came into view. After folding the shirt and placing it on his boots, the Kid removed the black holster from around his back and smiling at Li, who now watched with a slightly higher level of interest, sat the pistol on the top corner of the mattress. While still standing, he dropped his fatigue pants, stepped out of them, and kicked them in the general direction of the pile on his boots.

Clad only in his boxers and the chain that carried the lucky beaver nickel around his neck, the Kid slid over next to Li, with his back to mama San and laying on his left side, propped up on his elbow, looked at her deep brown eyes... *brown like Flo's*... But, as she smiled up at him, the similarities ended. "You really do look a lot like that American singer the black GIs say, Diana Ross. She is very beautiful, and you are incredibly beautiful Li! *Beau coup dep hoa!*"

"Cam on," she thanked him. Then, rising up on one elbow herself, she looked at the Kid's crotch and said with a rye smile, "I can see you are plenty ready to fuck me right now *beau coup,* Cut." And with that, she took her hand and repositioned the Kid's shorts so that the throbbing head of his penis emerged through the front opening.

Yes, he was ready, but the Kid was also in a frame of mind where he wanted to stretch this exquisite experience out for as long as humanly possible. At last, he kissed her, moving his left arm behind her and pulling her to him as they both lay back down on the bed, locked in the embrace. Mama San had an electric fan in one corner, pointed in the general direction of the bed. It made the wispy, transparent mosquito netting bellow like a sail, but there was no way it was ever going to cool the heat that was between their skins.

Li was at first reluctant when he sought the taste of her mouth, but soon her lips parted, and the tips of their tongues engaged in a fencing duel of parrying and penetrating. This made the Kid think there was an outside chance she wanted this as much as he did.

Then, rising to his knees, with a hand on either side of her lingerie, he tugged and Li lifted her hips and allowed them to easily come off. She kicked them with her right foot, down toward the end of the bed. The Kid's eyes followed the flight of the panties and from beyond where they landed, he could see that Mama San was apparently enjoying the show with great relish!

Rolling over onto his back, the Kid removed his own shorts. Oh, he was sporting wood, all right; having not been laid since early July and only twice in the last four months, his boner was so hard it hurt.

There was nothing else on earth in those moments for the Kid, other than feeling his manhood being engulfed over and over again by her hot secret place. No Robinson, no Cang Long, no Wilson, no Viet Cong. And when he felt the shudders roll forth from her pelvis, he couldn't hold back any longer and the two of them thrashed, gasped and roiled in a shared orgasm until at one point, the Kid thought he heard Mama San pass out and hit the floor, but it was only somebody dropping something heavy on the street down below.

Once they had exhausted each other and lay back apart, the Kid saw Mama San rise up from her chair, pick up a fan and fanning herself rapidly as she walked out on to the balcony. Li got up from the bed and from a shelf over the table, brought them a warm coke to share. After a couple of sips, the Kid leaned over the bed and out of his pants, pulled a pack of KOOLs and his Zippo lighter.

Li said something to Mama San and she came in off the balcony to fetch the kid an ashtray as he lit up. The Kid was a spent round. Exhaling in a big sigh, he smiled at Li.

"You give me $25 MPC," she suddenly said, much to the Kid's surprise.

"Give you $25? I just bought you a bunch of stuff at the PX and you are going to make over $100 profit and now you want me to give you $25?"

The look on her face was halfway between anger and a pout but as she spoke, her tone quickly turned to the anger side. "You Americans. Someday soon, you go home to your girlfriend or wife in America. I stay here, You no love me and if you got me pregnant, you not here to support baby. You never support baby and you won't give me $25? You some kind of cheap bastard!" She looked away from his face and bit her lip as she tried to stifle a sob.

Shock was the Kid's reaction at being labeled a cheap bastard. All the thoughts he had about having as Vietnamese woman who was not technically a prostitute and who actually liked him, flew out the window and he could see the mechanics of the situation were actually the same as if he'd gone to Mama San's down by the river in Sa Dec.

Picking up his pants, he pulled out his wallet and looked through it to appraise his financial situation. He had $40 left to his name. Taking out a 20 and a 5, he laid the money on the mattress between them and rose to his feet to get dressed. Li picked up the two bills and wadding them up, threw them at the foot of the bed.

Jeezus! Talk about taking the shine off the apple!

Mama San had watched quietly from her chair as the Kid pulled on his boots, looped his arms through his shoulder holster, buttoned up his uniform shirt and looked around for his regulation Army baseball cap. All the while, Li sat nude on the bed and refused to make eye contact with him.

Once dressed, holding his hat in his hands, he bowed his head in the direction of Mama San, "Cam on u lam," he thanked her. She returned him a slight smile and nodded her appreciation.

Then, picking up the money Li had thrown to the foot of the bed, he unrumpled the bills and laid them again in front of her. "Toi xin loi," he apologized for being a cheap bastard. She still refused to make eye contact with him so he turned and left.

In the cyclo on the way back to the Da Lat Hotel, the comment Li made to him about *what if you get me pregnant,* began to sink in. His mind struggled with the double conundrum; *I could have a son and never know... or he could come knocking on the door of my house with Flo someday. Curt, there is someone here to see you... Are you my daddy? Hmmm, I said I could forgive Flo anything but having another man's baby... would she forgive me that?*

The Kid's official WKDA publicity pic, March '67. When I finished rolling this cigarette, Dave Allen from behind me said in a whisper, "anybody who can roll a cigarette that well has been smoking pot!"

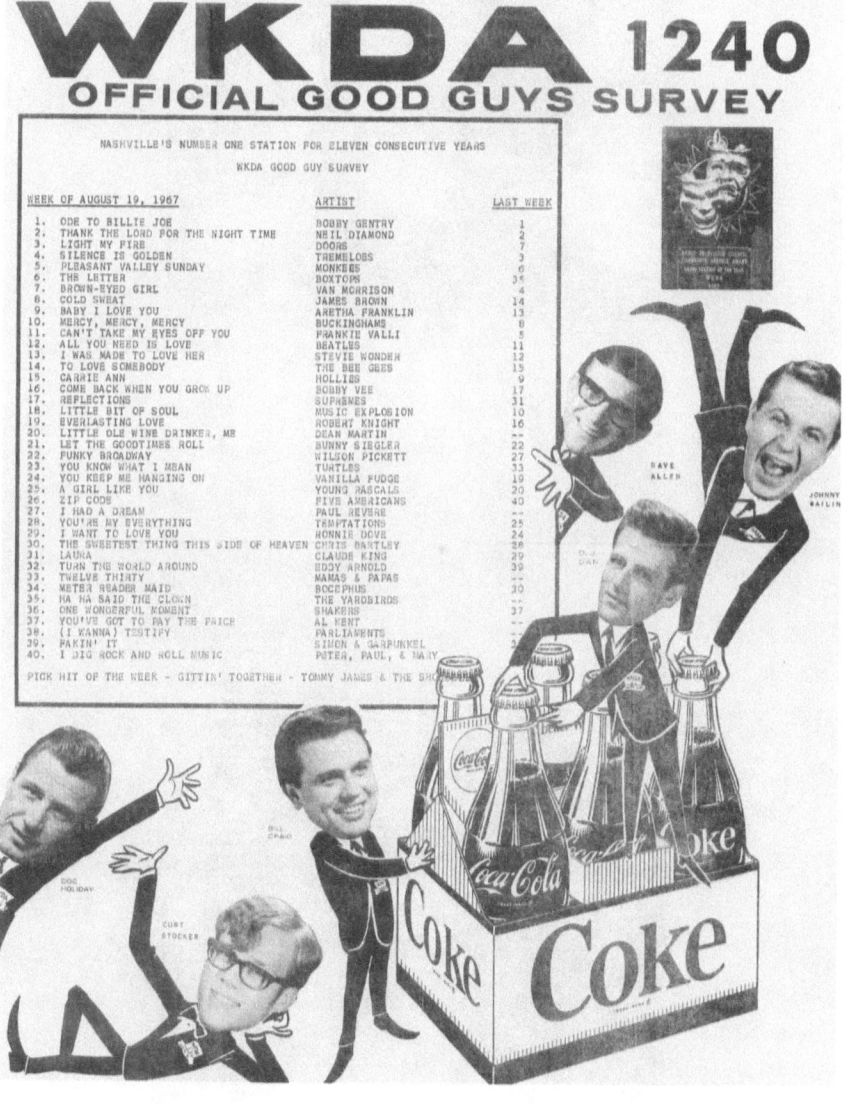

The WKDA am Top 40 Survey, on the counter of every record store in Nashville, every week, for years!

Dave Allen, DJ Dan, and Johnny Wailin. Picture by Pat Bowen, who sent it to me in Basic Training, at Ft. Campbell, KY, Oct. '67.

WKDA's custom designed am control room,
turntables left side.

WKDA control room, 5 cart machines to the right.

Dave Allen, DJ Dan, and Johnny Wailin. Picture by Pat Bowen, who sent
it to me in Basic Training,
at Ft. Campbell, KY, Oct. '67.

The Bowen Sisters, my most loyal fans to this day; 57 years and counting!
Teresa Bowen, left, with unknown fan, right, at the celebrity softball game:
The WKDA Good Guys vs. The Marty Robbins' Maids of Music.
(they creamed us)!
Photo by Pat Bowen.

Pat Bowen, with Ronnie Dove.
She was president of his official fan club and is to this day,
the *"Official President of the Un-official 'The Kid' Fan Club."*

Floretta K. Stuckey, aka Flo. Senior picture, Vista, California, 1969.

First Lieutenant Herschel Ross Wilson.

Corporal Ba, our 19-year-old interpreter, from Saigon.
We were his first assignment.

John Bujold, clowning around at the New Villa, Can Tho,
Dec. 1967, dressing up for a picture home.
Photo by Tom Roberts

Saigon Headquarters, 4th PSYOP Group, Republic of Vietnam.

Lucky 9 Lounge, ARVN 9th Division HQ, Sa Dec, Vietnam. There were too few Americans to have separate Officers and Enlisted men's clubs, so we had to fraternize!

Tra Vinh Compound, combination officers and enlisted men's mess hall and club. This was the servant's quarters when the French ran the roost from the Big House.

ARVN 14th Regiment HQ. The old French mansion was where the officers bunked.

The Cang Long Municipal Building.
Half the Mayor's office, half officer's billet.

Jim Sweet, with the Mayor of Cang Long,
his two daughters and their dog.
We joked that their dog was too skinny to eat!

Air America STOL-craft (short takeoff and landing)
from which we flew pinpoint leaflet drops,
frequently in Cambodia.

The Cang Long Monks from their balcony.

The Kid, on the balcony of the New Villa, April '68.
Photo by Tom Boyett

The White Mice.

www.ingramcontent.com/pod-product-compliance
Lightning Source LLC
Chambersburg PA
CBHW020914140626
46545CB00015B/9